the **BERKELEY** guides

CRITICAL ACCL[...]IDES

"Planet-wise instruc[...]r the price, the time of you[...]
[...]etails

"[The Berkeley Guide[...]information for the low-budget traveler—material delivered in a fresh, funny, and often irreverent way."
—The Philadelphia Inquirer

"The [Berkeley Guides] are deservedly popular because of their extensive coverage, entertaining style of writing, and heavy emphasis on budget travel . . . If you are looking for tips on hostels, vegetarian food, and hitchhiking, there are no books finer."
—San Diego Union-Tribune

"[The Berkeley Guides] offer straight dirt on everything from hostels to look for and beaches to avoid to museums least likely to attract your parents . . . they're fresher than Harvard's Let's Go series."
—Seventeen

"The [Berkeley Guides] give a rare glimpse into the real cultures of Europe, Canada, Mexico, and the United States . . . with in-depth historical backgrounds on each place and a creative, often poetical style of prose."
—Eugene Weekly

"The new On the Loose guides are more comprehensive, informative and witty than Let's Go."
—Glamour

"The Berkeley Guides have more and better maps, and on average, the nuts and bolts descriptions of such things as hotels and restaurants tend to be more illuminating than the often terse and sometimes vague entries in the 'Let's Go' guides."
— San José Mercury News

"The well-organized guides list can't miss sights, offbeat attractions and cheap thrills, such as festivals and walks. And they're fun to read."
— New York Newsday

"Reading (these guides) is a lot like listening to a first-hand report from a friend...They're also just plain fun to read."
— Greensboro News & Record

"Written for the young and young at heart...you'll find this thick, fact-filled guide makes entertaining reading."
— St. Louis Dispatch

"...bright articulate guidebooks. The irreverent yet straightforward prose is easy to read and offers a sense of the adventures awaiting travelers off the beaten path."
— Portland Oregonian

THE BERKELEY GUIDES are printed using soy-based ink on 100% recycled paper, including 50% post-consumer fiber and 100% de-inked newspapers, magazines and catalogs. What's the use of traveling if there's nothing left to see?

THE BERKELEY GUIDES

California 1996
Central America (2nd Edition)
Eastern Europe (3rd Edition)
Europe 1996
France 1996
Germany & Austria 1996
Great Britain & Ireland 1996
Italy 1996
London 1996
Mexico 1996
Pacific Northwest & Alaska
(2nd Edition)
Paris 1996
San Francisco 1996

the BERKELEY guides

san francisco '96

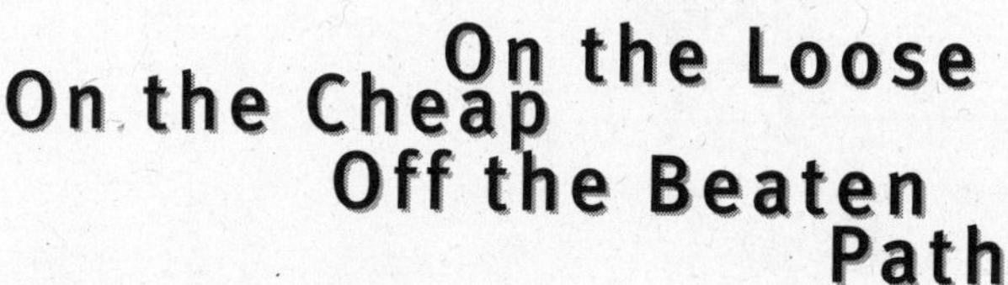

WRITTEN BY BERKELEY STUDENTS IN COOPERATION WITH THE ASSOCIATED STUDENTS OF THE UNIVERSITY OF CALIFORNIA

ISBN 0-679-02989-3

SAN FRANCISCO

Editor: Jennifer Wedel
Managing Editors: Nicole Harb, Kristina Malsberger, Sharron Wood
Executive Editor: Scott McNeely
Cartographer: David Lindroth, Inc.; Eureka Cartography
Text Design: Tigist Getachew
Cover Design: Fabrizio La Rocca
Cover Art: Poul Lange (3-D art), © Robert Holmes (photo in frame), Paul D'Innocenzo (still life)

SPECIAL SALES

The Berkeley Guides and all Fodor's Travel Publications are available at special discounts for bulk purchases for sales promotions or premiums. Special editions, including personalized covers, excerpts of existing guides, and corporate imprints, can be created in large quantities for special needs. For more information, contact your local bookseller or write to Special Markets, Fodor's Travel Publications, 201 East 50th Street, New York, NY 10022. Inquiries from Canada should be directed to your local Canadian bookseller or sent to Random House of Canada, Ltd., Marketing Department, 1265 Aerowood Drive, Mississauga, Ontario L4W 1B9. Inquiries from the United Kingdom should be sent to Fodor's Travel Publications, 20 Vauxhall Bridge Road, London SW1V 2SA, England.

PRINTED IN THE UNITED STATES OF AMERICA

10 9 8 7 6 5 4 3 2 1

Contents

Thanks to You

Lots of people helped us put together the *Berkeley Guide to San Francisco.* Some are listed below, but many others, whom our writers met briefly on buses, in cafés, and in clubs, also helped out. We would like you to help us update this book and give us feedback. Drop us a line—a postcard, a scrawled note on some toilet paper, whatever—and we'll be happy to acknowledge your contribution below. Our address is 515 Eshleman Hall, University of California, Berkeley, CA 94720.

Special thanks go to Katherine "Petunia" Audley and Eric Gilmore (Mill Valley); Chris Baty (Berkeley); John Blacker (Berkeley); Steph Bornstien (San Francisco); co-editor in spirit, Jen Brewer (San Francisco); Robert Hoyle Brown (Danville); Bryan from *Cups: A Café Journal* (San Francisco); Joe Catalano (Berkeley); Nicki Corfanta (Fresno, CA); Stephen Dunifer (Berkeley); Laurien Eck; David Glickman (Oakland); Helga Goertz (Napa); Jennifer Griesback; Tania Gutierrez (Arlington, TX); Mishy Harman (Jerusalem, Israel); Frank Jakubka (Kenwood); Mara Katz (San Francisco); Ronald Loshin (Kensington); Jen Lutz (Sebastopol); Bonnie and Dale Malsberger (Napa); Michael Moore (Tucson, AZ); Patricia and the staff at Peet's Coffee & Tea on Vine Street (Berkeley); the staff at Point Montara Lighthouse AYH-Hostel (Montara); Mary Reisch (San Francisco); Michael Richards (Oakland); Royal Robbins (Yosemite National Park, CA); David Rosnow (San Francisco); Lisa Roth (San Francisco); Carole and Stuart Sellars (Minnesota); Jeremy Silverstein; Rick Sine (Mill Valley); Dick and Joy Smith (Napa); Erik Smith (San Francisco); the people who push-started Kristina Malsberger's car (Sonoma); Jane Sperling (San Francisco); the staff of Spinelli's Coffee in Noe Valley (San Francisco); Wayne Stedman (Walnut Creek); Maria Stienman (Berkeley); Sarah Tabacco (Berkeley); Edith Towler (San Rafael); Steve Von Pohl (Oakland); Armen Yampolsky (Boston, MA); Hannah Yampolsky (San Francisco); Evan Yeh (Berkeley).

Berkeley Bios

Behind every restaurant blurb, lodging review, and introduction in this book lurks a student writer. After years of living in San Francisco and the East Bay, the writers had plenty of ideas about how to have a great time here for next to nothing. They spent the spring and summer sizing up all their favorite places and dozens of unknown, out-of-the-way joints to bring you the very best ways to live in and explore the Bay Area on a budget (though they may have kept one or two secrets to themselves).

The Writers

After writing for the Great Britain & Ireland book last year, **Alice Chang** decided to stay close to home (summer school) and subject herself to another stint at the Berkeley Guides. She squeezed meals in between classes in the name of the East Bay Food section and frolicked with elephant seals at Año Nuevo while exploring the South Bay. But her moment of epiphany came while updating Café Culture: Alice suddenly realized (after getting lost in the Mission and locking her keys in her car) that there's a fine line between a caffeine high (temporarily elevated IQ) and espresso overkill (attention deficit disorder). Last time we saw her, she was slowly sipping coffee from a bowl at a swank North Beach café.

Despite the difficulties of getting stuck in an unseasonable May blizzard, **Kelly Green** found that the poor weather conditions actually made her stay in Lake Tahoe more pleasant—no crowds, cheap lodging, and most important, plenty of space at the $2 blackjack tables. After a brief respite covering the restaurant scene in San Francisco, Kelly hit the road again. This time it was off to Santa Cruz, where the 90° temperatures were a welcome change from her regular 9-to-5 job as an editor (don't tell her boss she's moonlighting). She longs to breathe that sweet, unrecirculated air again someday. . . .

Danna Harman, from Jerusalem, Israel (via lots of other places and en route to graduate school in England), updated the highly coveted Where to Sleep and Basics chapters. As other writers set off on mountain bikes or downed martinis, Danna was holding for a SamTrans operator (Bus 58B does have weekend service, in case you wanted to know) and comparing parking lot prices throughout the Bay Area. She tracked down things you might not find if you let your fingers do the walking, including lesbian direct-action groups, pirate radio stations, the manager of the San Jose Sharks, and a leather-and-Levi's bed-and-breakfast in the Castro. She would especially like to thank the guys at Berkeley Fire Station #3 and her roommates, for taking down 45-minute-long messages from tour operators in Chinatown.

Emily Hastings, a recent U.C. Berkeley graduate with a degree in Media Arts, has been a marketing researcher, a legal assistant, a political campaign assistant, and an exhibited photographer. After traveling in Europe and North Africa, she now resides in San Francisco where she spends her days regaling her plants with tales of the good times she had updating Outdoor Activities.

Ray Klinke roamed the streets of San Francisco in pursuit of the swankiest place to have a cocktail, the grungiest venue to hear new bands, and the sweatiest club for dancing the night away. A long-time resident of San Francisco, Ray embarked on his adventure confident in his knowledge of the city's nocturnal activities. However he soon realized that he had no idea where to find a free drag show or a Bloody Mary at 6 AM. Many happy hours later, Ray can confidently answer those questions; he is still trying to figure out how many drinks he had and which S&M clubs now have him on their mailing lists. He looks forward to returning to the comfort of his neighborhood bar.

After three years of Eurocentric work for the Berkeley Guides, music major **Baty Landis** settled down for a few months of local focus, covering the Bay Area's performing and visual arts. Her biggest challenge was in combing the streets of SoMa and the Mission, where each time she went back, she would find newer, funkier galleries and performance spaces.

Although a native of the strip-mall hell known as the South Bay, **Cynthia Leung** could never quite embrace it. Her need for late-night apple pie à la mode and a love for all things polyester have both been nurtured in the chaos that is Berkeley. She survived updating the Shopping chapter and now firmly holds that shopping is a vicious, consumer-culture activity aggravated by the capitalist, corporate powers-that-be. But you might still find her at the Salvation Army.

Ever since her freshman year at Berkeley, **Kristina Malsberger** has been haunted by the words "You're from Napa; you pick out the wine." Loath to admit that a Napa Valley native had never set foot in a winery, Kristina resigned herself to a college career spent recommending the perfect compliment to Top Ramen. Needless to say, she jumped at the chance to receive a proper viticultural education while writing the Wine Country section. Somewhere between her 53rd and 54th glass, Kristina decided to relocate to the Burgundy countryside, change her name to "Chardonnay," and spend the rest of her natural life becoming rich and mellow with age.

Alan Phulps, a California native, has gone through at least 20 jobs—from dish-washing to bicycle messengering—to afford the luxuries of travel and rock climbing. He spent years traveling through North America and Asia looking for *something* before he realized it was right here in the Sierra Nevada. After updating Yosemite National Park, Alan ventured onward in his precarious '71 Fukengrüven van to update the Sierra Nevada and Cascades chapters for the *Berkeley Guide to California.* He may still be out there; if you see him, say "Hi."

A resident of San Francisco's Mission district, **David Walter** has been working for several years on a revolutionary invention designed to short circuit car alarms and blow up car radios from a remote second-story location. He has found time between prototypes and patent suits to travel extensively in Latin America, edit a financial newsletter, and attend Berkeley's prestigious comparative literature program. How does he do it all? Gotta do *something* while waiting for the police to arrive.

After writing for the San Francisco book three years running while working full-time as the Berkeley Guides editorial coordinator, an overworked **Sharron Wood** says "No more!". Of course, she doesn't really mean it. Writer of the Marin County, Berkeley, and Oakland sections, Sharron has spent the last five years living in Berkeley and Oakland, championing the cause of the much-maligned East Bay. (Only in Berkeley, she argued, could you go hiking in Tilden Regional Park, see a 16th-century altar panel at the University Art Museum, and discuss your path to salvation with a Jew for Jesus all in one day.) Recently, however, she set up house in San Francisco within a five-block radius of all her favorite bars, restaurants, and co-workers. By next year she expects to have completed her transformation into a San Franciscan and will probably be clamoring for writing assignments closer to her new home.

The Editor

Just looking at that singular noun, editor, makes **Jennifer Wedel** (pronounced like ladle or cradle, *not* like needle or beetle or pedal or mettle) shake with both fear and joy. Taking sick pleasure in the fact that she is one of few *non*-native Californians in the office, Jennifer escaped mentally to Lake Josephine, Minnesota, when the task of editing the San Francisco book overwhelmed her sometimes-fragile sensibilities. Having survived this baptism by fire, Jennifer will soon endure another, more literal one when she moves to Tucson, AZ, deep in the hellish heart of the Sonoran Desert. "The things you do for love," she has been heard muttering to her computer screen.

We'd also like to thank the Random House folks who helped us with cartography, page design, and production: Steven Amsterdam, Bob Blake, Fionn Davenport, Denise DeGennaro, Tigist Getachew, Laura Kidder, Fabrizio La Rocca, and Linda Schmidt.

The Bay Area

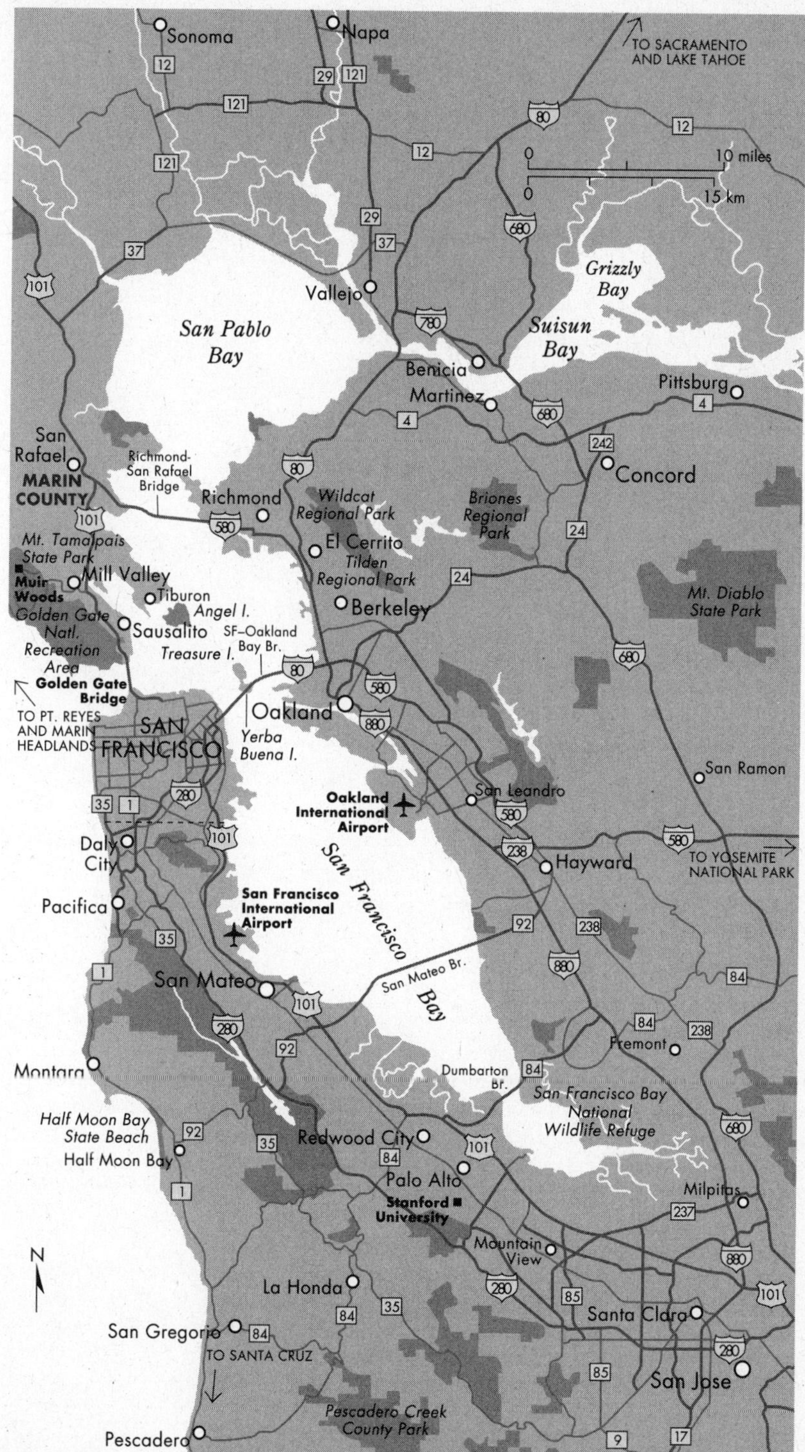

Sonoma
Napa
TO SACRAMENTO AND LAKE TAHOE
0 10 miles
0 15 km
Grizzly Bay
Suisun Bay
San Pablo Bay
Vallejo
Benicia
Martinez
Pittsburg
Concord
San Rafael
MARIN COUNTY
Richmond-San Rafael Bridge
Richmond
Wildcat Regional Park
Briones Regional Park
El Cerrito
Tilden Regional Park
Mt. Tamalpais State Park
Muir Woods
Mill Valley
Tiburon
Angel I.
Berkeley
Mt. Diablo State Park
Golden Gate Natl. Recreation Area
Sausalito
SF–Oakland Bay Br.
Treasure I.
Golden Gate Bridge
TO PT. REYES AND MARIN HEADLANDS
SAN FRANCISCO
Oakland
Yerba Buena I.
San Ramon
Oakland International Airport
San Leandro
Daly City
San Francisco Bay
Hayward
TO YOSEMITE NATIONAL PARK
Pacifica
San Francisco International Airport
San Mateo
San Mateo Br.
Fremont
Montara
Dumbarton Br.
San Francisco Bay National Wildlife Refuge
Half Moon Bay State Beach
Half Moon Bay
Redwood City
Palo Alto
Stanford University
Milpitas
Mountain View
La Honda
Santa Clara
San Gregorio
TO SANTA CRUZ
San Jose
Pescadero Creek County Park
Pescadero
N

BASICS 1

By Danna Harman

Sometimes it's wonderful to drift through the city without thinking, letting Zen adventures come your way. But there are other times when you need to have a clue about things, whether it's how to get from San Francisco's Sunset district to downtown Oakland, where to look for this weekend's live music line-up, when next year's San Francisco Book Festival will take place, or what organizations exist to help women in trouble. Below are some basic facts to help you survive and keep your sanity in the Bay Area. For more comprehensive listings, let your fingers do the walking through the Pacific Bell Yellow Pages; the Local Access pages, in the front of the book, can help you with everything from choosing seats for a concert to finding the nearest park with a swimming pool.

Getting In, Out, and Around

San Francisco has one of the most comprehensive public transportation systems of any U.S. city, making it easy for commuters and travelers to get around without contributing to traffic jams. Enviro-friendly public transportation is almost hip here, and cycling, the ultimate in green commuting, also has an avid following. Although many Bay Area cities, and San Francisco in particular, are seriously lacking in bike lanes, BART and CalTrain (*see below*) let you bring your bike along for the long haul. For the lowdown on public transit, get your hands on the *Regional Transit Guide* ($4.95), an excellent resource listing transportation agencies, lines, and frequency. Pick one up at the Berkeley TRiP store (*see* AC Transit, *below*), or send a check for $5.30 to MTC/Regional Transit Guide, 101 8th St., Oakland 94607.

BY CAR

No, it's not Los Angeles, but no one's going to mistake Bay Area driving for a relaxing spin down a country road. Common frustrations include high tolls on the Golden Gate Bridge, traffic jams at any time of the day or night, and a notable lack of places to leave the damn car once you've arrived at your destination. For degree-of-difficulty bonus points, go straight to San Francisco: If you learned to drive just about anywhere else, the combination of hills and traffic should present a formidable challenge to your driving skills—not to mention your car's brakes and transmission.

North of the Golden Gate Bridge lie Marin County and the Wine Country; to the south are San Francisco and the South Bay Peninsula (including Palo Alto and the San Mateo County Coast); and on the east side of the bay lie Berkeley and Oakland. A network of freeways helps you move your vehicle from one town to another. The most beautiful of these roads, **Highway 1** (a.k.a. the Pacific Coast Highway), runs north–south along the coast, right over the Golden Gate Bridge. Renowned for stunning views and treacherous curves, Highway 1 provides an excellent opportunity to gaze into the great, pounding nothingness of the Pacific and ponder your insignificance. Although it extends almost the entire length of California, Highway 1 is so narrow and winding that you shouldn't drive it if you're in a hurry. As the highway enters San Francisco from the south, it becomes 19th Avenue, then Park Presidio Boulevard, and then the Golden Gate Bridge. On the bridge, it merges with the north–south U.S. 101, eventually splitting from that road and heading back toward the coast at the Stinson Beach/Highway 1 exit in Marin County.

Running parallel to Highway 1, but a ways inland, **U.S. 101** will whisk you from the South Bay through the city and over the Golden Gate Bridge into Marin County. Avoid the leg of the highway that runs along the Peninsula between San Francisco and the South Bay (Palo Alto and San Jose), unless you're a traffic fetishist. Instead, take the meandering **I–280,** fairly accurately called "The World's Most Beautiful Freeway." This route is a bit longer mile-wise, but at least your car will be moving the entire time. You'll pass verdant hills, a sparkling reservoir, and exquisite vista points. On U.S. 101 the trip from San Francisco to Palo Alto takes about 45 minutes in good conditions, up to an hour and 15 minutes in traffic. On I–280, count on 50 minutes to an hour at any time of day.

You wouldn't be the first to shudder as you sit at a stoplight on a steep San Francisco hill in a temperamental stick shift, staring in the rearview mirror at the car you expect to cream as soon as you lift your foot off the brake.

In the East Bay, all the freeways are miserable. From San Francisco, **I–80** carries you east across the **Bay Bridge** to Berkeley and Oakland, continuing northeast toward Sacramento and Lake Tahoe. It could use a few more lanes for optimal traffic flow, but there's no avoiding it if you're heading east. The trip from downtown San Francisco to Berkeley takes about 20 minutes in optimal conditions, closer to 45 minutes or an hour during rush hour. For a truly bleak driving experience, at the eastern end of the Bay Bridge head straight toward Oakland and follow the signs to **I–880** south. It brings new meaning to the term industrial blight, but it's *the* East Bay corridor, taking you to such thrilling suburban destinations as Hayward, Fremont, and eventually San Jose. It also runs to the Bay Area's two southern bridges, the **San Mateo Bridge,** connecting Hayward and San Mateo, and the **Dumbarton Bridge** farther south, which links Fremont and Palo Alto. Running parallel to I–880 between Oakland and Hayward (at which point it veers off to the east, eventually hooking up with I–5), **I–580** has a small but avid cult following. The rolling hills, the green bushes, and the rows of windmills just past Livermore all seem to inspire affection.

RENTAL CARS Because of the dearth of parking, the excellent public transportation, and the high insurance rates in much of the Bay Area, many residents choose to forgo car ownership entirely. But for those times when you're seized by the urge to meander up the coast, a rental car can be a great convenience.

Your best bet is always to rent at one of the region's airports. Although the cheapest rates are available only to those who can present a plane ticket, even residents can save as much as $15 a day over the rates at downtown rental franchises. If you absolutely can't make it to the airport, almost all rental car agencies have pick-up and drop-off spots in downtown San Francisco within 5 or 6 blocks of Union Square. The cheapest rates vary quite a bit, depending on who's running a special deal. No matter where you pick up your car, you'll always pay a heavy surcharge (starting at about $25) if you don't return it to the same spot.

Small, independent agencies generally have cheaper daily rates than the national chains but usually impose mileage charges. A typical weekday price for a subcompact at an independent company is $18–$30, with a limit of 50–100 miles a day. **Flat Rate Rent-A-Car** (830 Huntington Ave., San Bruno, tel. 415/583–9232), located near San Francisco International Airport, rents cars for a rock-bottom $16 a day with 75 free miles, but restrictions against taking the car more than 100 miles from the city could cramp your style. The national companies (Avis, Hertz, Budget, etc.) usually offer unlimited mileage, so if you're planning on going far, they may end up being cheaper. If you call around, you should be able to find a subcompact car for about $30 a day on weekdays, $25 on weekends. At press time, **National Car Rental** (tel. 800/CAR–RENT) at

Oakland International Airport offered the cheapest rates of any big company in the Bay Area. They, along with many other companies, won't rent to you if you're under 25. The 21-to-24 set does best at **Enterprise** (tel. 800/325–8007), which charges only $8 extra a day.

Unfortunately, all Bay Area companies require a credit card for deposit purposes. The upside to this restriction is that some cards—American Express, for example—provide liability and damage insurance as a service for card members. Make sure to check with your credit card company before paying for the rental agency's insurance policy. Some final notes: As with airline tickets, you'll usually pay less if you reserve in advance. Also, always ask about specials and discounts before accepting the base rental rate—some rental agencies, for example, offer 10%–20% discounts if you have AAA or frequent-flier miles on certain airlines.

PARKING Welcome to the Bay Area—hope you left your car behind. If you do find a parking space, it may be on the side of a sheer precipice. Should you succeed in the hideous task of parallel parking on a slope that looks like the north face of Everest, remember: Curb the wheels so they point toward the curb, set the emergency brake, and, if you're in a stick shift, leave the car in gear.

Circled Union Square for half an hour? Ready to dump your car any place it fits? Think again. The city issues 2.4 million parking tickets a year—and the number is only expected to increase.

If all this seems too much for you, there are plenty of parking lots and garages that offer parking by the hour or by the day. Pay close attention to rates—they can get quite steep, especially around prime tourist country like San Francisco's Fisherman's Wharf. In the Union Square area, the large **Sutter-Stockton Garage** (444 Stockton St., tel. 415/982–7275) charges a graduated rate—$3 for three hours, $8 for five hours, and $18 for 24 hours. The cheapest lot near Fisherman's Wharf ($2 an hour) is the **Wharf Garage** (350 Beach St., btw Taylor and Mason Sts.). Parking in the East Bay is less difficult, though finding places near the U.C. Berkeley campus isn't exactly fun. At **Sather Gate Garage** (2450 Durant Ave., just west of Telegraph Ave.), the rate is $1 an hour for the first two hours, $1.50 for each hour thereafter. The daily rate is $10. The garage is open weekdays 7 AM–1 AM, Saturday 7 AM–2AM, and Sunday 8 AM–10 PM. For all-day parking, the lot next to **Berkeley Arts** (2590 Durant Ave.) is a better deal; $6 lets you park from 8 AM to 7 PM.

BRIDGE TOLLS Toll on the **Golden Gate Bridge** (tel. 415/921–5858) is $3, collected only when you travel south into San Francisco. Discount ticket books are available at the bridge, Westamerica banks, Safeway stores, and some gas stations. For $16 you get six crossings, or 15 crossings for $40. There is no toll 5–9 AM and 4–6 PM weekdays for cars carrying at least three passengers.

All the state bridges, including the **Bay Bridge, San Mateo Bridge, Dumbarton Bridge,** and **Richmond/San Rafael Bridge,** have the same toll ($1), collected in the westbound direction. A discount book, good for four months from purchase, is available at Safeway and Lucky stores as well as at the bridges. For $34 you get 40 crossings. Carpoolers (three or more people in a car) cross free 5–10 AM and 3–6 PM weekdays.

Since carpoolers don't pay tolls and often get to ride in special lanes on Bay Area bridges, commuters are often grateful for the chance to pick up a couple of passengers for the drive over the bridge. Wily types who lack cars can head to **Park and Ride** locations—or to the Emeryville bus nexus (cnr Yerba Buena and San Pablo Aves.) or the North Berkeley BART station in the East Bay—and hitch a ride into the city. For more info on sharing a ride, call **Rides for Bay Area Commuters** (tel. 800/755–POOL), **Berkeley TRiP** (tel. 510/644–POOL), or **Solano Commuter Information** (tel. 800/53–KMUTE). Tell them your commute information, and within a few days you'll get a list of commuters who live and work near you and want to share a ride.

BY BUS

Despite all the griping about graffiti and rising fares, Bay Area bus systems do provide excellent coverage of most towns. If you'll be using both BART and buses on a regular basis, look into **BART Plus** passes, good for a fixed amount of BART travel and unlimited rides on AC Transit, MUNI, and SamTrans, among others (*see* By BART, *below*). The bus companies listed below all have wheelchair-accessible buses for most routes; call for specifics.

MUNI San Francisco's main bus and streetcar service covers the city with 91 lines. Buses run as often as every five minutes in certain well-traveled parts of town, though frequent breakdowns and delays gum up the works considerably. Between 1 AM and 5 AM, the Owl service offers just 9 lines that run every 30 minutes. Should you be stranded someplace within the city, anxious to get elsewhere but unsure how, call 415/673–MUNI weekdays 7–5 or weekends 9–5 and an operator will tell you exactly which bus(es) to use. If you lose something on board, call 415/923–6168.

The adult fare is $1; the youth, senior, and disabled fare 35¢. Your fare gets you a free transfer good for at least an hour. **Passport** passes allow unlimited access to MUNI (including cable cars) for one day ($6), three days ($10), or one week ($15). You can buy a one-day pass from the driver when you board; three-day and one-week passes are available from a number of locations, including the visitor information booth at the Powell and Market cable car turnaround and **TIX Bay Area** (251 Stockton St., btw Post and Geary Sts., tel. 415/433–7827) on Union Square. But if you're going to be using the system regularly, you're better off getting a **Fast Pass,** which allows unlimited travel on MUNI buses, light-rail vehicles, and cable cars, as well as on BART within San Francisco. The $35 adult pass, good for one calendar month, is available from any Safeway grocery store in San Francisco, as well as many liquor stores and check-cashing places. The $8 youth, senior, and disabled pass can be purchased at City Hall. Bikes are not allowed on MUNI buses.

An estimated 95% of San Francisco's addresses lie within 3 blocks of a MUNI stop.

➢ **CABLE CARS** • San Francisco's cable cars were the world's first large-scale mechanized street transportation. Developer Andrew Hallidie drove the first run on August 2, 1873. In 1964, the cable cars were declared a National Historic Landmark, the first moving entity to receive that honor (also *see* Nob Hill and Russian Hill, in Chapter 2). If you can handle throngs of tourists, the cable cars are actually pretty groovy; you should take the ride at least once, if only to feel like you're in a Rice-A-Roni commercial. They run at a pace straight out of the early 1900s (the cables that propel the cars move at 9½ mph), so if you're Type A, take the bus. Fare is $2, though many discount passes (*see above*) allow you to ride for free. For great views, take the Hyde and Powell line, which travels from Fisherman's Wharf to Powell and Market streets downtown. Along the way, you'll get a gander at Alcatraz and pass right by Lombard Street, the crookedest street in the world. Unfortunately, the wait to get on at the Hyde Street turnaround can be more than an hour.

In Maya Angelou's autobiography, "I Know Why the Caged Bird Sings," she professes to be the first African American hired as a conductor on a San Francisco streetcar.

AC TRANSIT With more than 100 lines, AC Transit (tel. 510/839–2882) covers the East Bay from north of Richmond to south of Fremont. For personalized trip planning and the hours of various lines, call 800/559–INFO weekdays 7–6 or weekends 9–5. Stop by the **Berkeley TRiP Commute Store** (2033 Center St., tel. 510/644–7665) or the **AC Transit office** (1600 Franklin St., Oakland) for schedules and a map of the whole system. Maps are also sporadically available on the buses. The adult and youth fare is $1.25; seniors and disabled 60¢. Transfers (25¢) are good for 90 minutes. Monthly passes run $45 for adults, $25 for youth, and $11 for seniors and the disabled. Books of 10 tickets cost $10 for adults (blue) and $5 for youth, seniors, and the disabled (yellow).

AC Transit lines designated by letters rather than numbers cross the Bay Bridge to San Francisco's **Transbay Terminal** (1st and Mission Sts.). Most run from dawn to dusk, but the F and T lines operate until 2 AM and the N runs 24 hours. Fare to San Francisco is $2.20 for adults ($1.10 youth, seniors, and disabled). Monthly transbay passes cost $75. AC Transit allows bikes only during the summer on lines 65 and 67 to Tilden Park.

GOLDEN GATE TRANSIT Golden Gate Transit (tel. 415/455–2000 in Marin County, 415/923–2000 in S.F., 707/541–2000 in Sonoma County) provides excellent service almost everywhere in the North Bay. Buses connect San Francisco with Sausalito, Mill Valley, Tiburon, San Rafael, Novato, Rohnert Park, and Santa Rosa every half hour during the week. Many buses run weekdays only, from dawn to dusk, but some routes (including the 20 and 50) run on weekends and go as late as 4 AM. Unfortunately, no buses travel from San Francisco directly up Highway 1 to coastal destinations like Stinson Beach and Point Reyes. To reach Stinson on weekends, you can take Bus 80 (which is the most direct) or Bus 50 from San Francisco to San Rafael, then transfer to Bus 65, which stops in Inverness, Point Reyes, Olema, and Stinson Beach. Bus 20 will take you to Marin City where you can catch Bus 63 directly to Stinson Beach. Within San Francisco, buses leave from the **Transbay Terminal** (1st and Mission Sts.), and make stops throughout the city. Rates range from $2 to $4.50 depending on how far you're going. Books of 20 tickets at a 25% discount can be purchased at the **San Rafael Transit Center** (Hetherton and 3rd Sts., San Rafael); at the **Larkspur Ferry Terminal** (101 E. Sir Francis Drake Blvd., Larkspur); and at many bookstores, gas stations, and grocery stores. During non-commute hours, bikes are allowed on Bus 40 (El Cerrito del Norte BART–San Rafael) and Bus 80 to Stinson Beach.

SAMTRANS South of the city, SamTrans (tel. 800/660–4BUS) runs buses regularly throughout San Mateo County. They leave from the Daly City BART station, downtown San Francisco, and San Francisco International Airport (*see* By Plane, *below*), and go as far as Año Nuevo State Reserve at the southern end of the county (*see* South Bay, in Chapter 2). Bus 1L travels from Daly City BART along the coast to Half Moon Bay ($1) about five times daily on weekends. Most other buses run weekdays only, though some heavily trafficked routes are covered all week; call SamTrans for help planning your trip. Fares are $1–$2 for adults, 50¢–$1 for youth, and 35¢–$2 for seniors and the disabled. No transfers are issued. Monthly passes cost $36 for adults ($72 for an express route pass), $18 for youth, and $13 for seniors and the disabled. Bikes are allowed on SamTrans buses at the driver's discretion.

GREYHOUND Greyhound (tel. 800/231–2222) travels to and from Bay Area cities all day, every day, but it's more useful for long distances than for local jaunts. They're the folks to call if you're *sans* auto and need to get to Tahoe (5–6 hrs, $20 one way), Santa Cruz (2–4 hrs, $14 one way), L.A. (11–12 hrs, $35 one way), or Seattle (20–26 hrs, $62 one way). In San Francisco, Greyhound operates out of the **Transbay Terminal** (1st and Mission Sts., tel. 415/495–1569), where many MUNI lines (*see above*) begin. The terminal is not the safest place, so you may want to plan your arrival for daytime. You'll find Greyhound on the terminal's third floor. In the East Bay, the Greyhound office is in **Oakland** (2103 San Pablo Ave., at 20th St., tel. 510/834–3213); in the South Bay in **San Jose** (70 Almaden Ave., at Santa Clara St., tel. 408/295–4151); and in Marin County the station is in downtown **San Rafael** (850 Tamalpais St., at 3rd St., tel. 415/453–0795).

GREEN TORTOISE Green Tortoise Travel (494 Broadway, San Francisco 94133, tel. 415/285–2441) is *the* cheap, fun alternative to humdrum bus travel. Only on Green Tortoise does your journey to Seattle (24 hrs, $49 one-way) feature a cookout ($3) and skinny-dipping. Buses come equipped with sleeping pads, kitchens, and stereos to make the ride enjoyable. Regularly scheduled runs also go from the Bay Area to L.A. (12 hrs, $30), Eugene (17 hrs, $39), and Portland (20 hrs, $39). Plus—get this—they'll stop almost anywhere else on I–5 for an additional $10. All fares are for one-way travel and must be paid in cash, traveler's checks, or money orders. Make reservations before you show up at their pick-up point in San Francisco (1st and Natoma Sts.) or Berkeley (Berkeley Marina, across from the bait shop).

BY BART

Relatively clean and quiet, **Bay Area Rapid Transit** (tel. 415/992–2278 or 510/465–BART; lost and found 510/464–7090) is a smooth subway system that's better at moving you from one town to another than getting you around town. Its four lines serve San Francisco, Daly City, and the East Bay from Richmond to Fremont and out to Concord. An extension to Colma, southwest of Daly City, should be completed by late 1995. A BART extension to San Francisco International Airport is also being planned, but the project has yet to get off the ground. All BART stations and trains are wheelchair accessible.

BART trains begin their last run around midnight; you may be able to catch trains from some stations as late as 1 AM, but don't bank on it. Service starts up again at 4 AM weekdays, 6 AM Saturdays, and 8 AM Sundays. Expect trains every 15–20 minutes; schedules are available at the stations, or you can call ahead to plan your journey. A special Sunday route—"Sunday Double-Header Express"—runs from around noon to 5 PM and stops only at MacArthur, 12th Street, Embarcadero, Powell Street, Civic Center, 24th Street, and Daly City stations.

➢ **FARES AND DISCOUNTS** • The cost of a BART ticket ranges from 90¢ to $3.45, depending on the length of the journey. For example, a 15-minute ride from San Francisco's Embarcadero Station to Oakland's MacArthur Station costs $1.85; a ride from Concord to the Oakland Coliseum takes 52 minutes and costs $2.30; from downtown San Francisco to Berkeley (20–25 min) you'll pay $2.10.

BART is seriously lacking in discount fares. Adults can purchase a "discount" ticket that gets them $32 worth of rides for $30—big whoop. Seniors, children under 12, and the disabled get a much better deal: a $16 ticket for $4, available at most Safeway and Lucky stores. You can pick up discounted BART-to-MUNI transfers ($1, good for use within three days to and from a BART station only) and BART-to-AC Transit transfers (60¢) from the white machines near the exit gates. The **BART Plus** ticket, though it doesn't save money on BART tickets, gives a discount on local bus systems. A $24–$57 ticket entitles you to $15–$50 worth of BART rides plus unlimited rides on MUNI, AC Transit, SamTrans, BART Express, the County Connection, Dumbarton local service, Martinez Link, Santa Clara County Transit local service, and Union City Transit. Call 510/466–7106 for more information.

➢ **BIKES ON BART** • Bearers of BART bicycle permits ($3 for three years) can bring their bikes onto trains. Bikes are allowed only in the last car, and generally during non-commute hours only (though sometimes in the non-commute direction during rush hour). Call 415/464–7133 for more info, or 415/456–7135 for a permit application. A free, three-week permit, available once only, can be obtained on the spot at BART stations when you show ID. Most stations have bike lockers; call 415/464–7136 for details.

BY TRAIN

CALTRAIN CalTrain (tel. 800/660–4BUS) offers regular service from San Francisco (4th and Townsend Sts.) to downtown San Jose (65 Cahill St.). A one-way trip costs $4.50 and takes 1½ hours; trains leave hourly between 5 AM and 10 PM, more frequently during commute times. Along the way, the trains stop at a number of Peninsula cities, including Burlingame, Palo Alto, Mountain View, and Santa Clara. Bikes are allowed on the trains.

AMTRAK Several Amtrak (tel. 800/USA–RAIL) lines, including the *Zephyr* from Chicago via Denver, the *Coast Starlight* from San Diego or Seattle, and the *Capitol* from Sacramento and the San Joaquin Valley, stop at the four East Bay stations: **Richmond** (16th St. and MacDonald Ave., adjoining Richmond BART), **Berkeley** (3rd St. and University Ave.; you can board, but you can't buy tickets), **Oakland** (245 2nd St., at Jack London Square), and **Emeryville** (5885 Landregan St.). From the Emeryville station, you can catch a connecting Amtrak bus that will drop you off at the CalTrain station (4th and Townsend Sts.) in San Francisco. Fares vary according to the time of year and other factors; a Bay Area–Seattle round-trip (24 hrs each way) runs $88–$176, while Bay Area–Los Angeles round-trips (12 hrs each way) are $78–$146.

BY TAXI

You can usually hail a cab in San Francisco, but sometimes they are inexplicably scarce. Most residents phone. All taxis are metered, but you may be able to negotiate a flat rate to the airport. Both **Veteran's Cab** (tel. 415/552–1300) and **Yellow Cab** (tel. 415/626–2345) in San Francisco charge a base fee of $1.70, 30¢ every sixth-mile, and 30¢ for every minute of waiting time or traffic delay. In the East Bay, both **Friendly Cab** (tel. 510/536–3000) and **Yellow Cab** (tel. 510/841–8294) offer competitively priced service ($2 base fee, $2 a mile). Fares to San Francisco are $25–$30. Don't forget to tip the driver (15% is typical).

BY FERRY

If you're sick of Bay Area traffic or in the mood for a change of pace, pack a thermos of coffee and a warm jacket and hop on one of the Bay Area's commuter ferries. The ferries are comparable to other forms of transport in speed (though not in price), and you can drink your morning java in peace while taking in a lovely view.

GOLDEN GATE FERRY Golden Gate Ferry (tel. 415/332–6600) crosses the bay between Marin County and the **San Francisco Ferry Building** (on the Embarcadero, at the bottom of Market St.). Ferries run from about 7 AM to 8 PM. The 30-minute journey to the **Sausalito Ferry Dock** (south end of Bridgeway) costs $4.25; the 50-minute trip to the **Larkspur Ferry Terminal** (101 E. Sir Francis Drake Blvd.) is $2.50 one way, $4.25 weekends. Tickets include free transfers for Golden Gate Transit buses (*see* By Bus, *above*).

RED AND WHITE FLEET The fleet (tel. 415/546–BOAT or 800/229–2784) leaves from **Pier 43½** at Fisherman's Wharf for the **Sausalito Ferry Dock** (south end of Bridgeway). Fare is $5.50 ($2.75 children), and the trip takes 20–30 minutes. The fleet also runs commuter services to **Tiburon** ($5.50), and excursion trips to **Angel Island** ($9) and **Alcatraz** ($5.75). A number of these ferries leave from **Pier 41;** call for details.

BLUE AND GOLD FLEET The Oakland/Alameda Ferry (tel. 510/522–3300) leaves from **Jack London Square** (Embarcadero and Broadway) in Oakland or the **Alameda Ferry Dock** (2990 Main St., Alameda) and arrives at the **San Francisco Ferry Building** (foot of Market St., at the Embarcadero) 30 minutes later; the ferry then continues to **Pier 39** at Fisherman's Wharf. Ferries begin running from the East Bay at 6 AM on weekdays, 10 AM on weekends and holidays, and leave on their last run at 7:55 PM. One-way adult fare is $3.75; buy tickets on board the ferry. Parking at the Alameda and Oakland terminals is free, and ferry stubs serve as transfers to MUNI and AC Transit.

The Blue and Gold Fleet's **Vallejo Ferry** (tel. 415/705–5444) has a commuter run ($7.50) and an excursion fare to **Marine World/Africa U.S.A.** ($36 round trip; includes park admission). The ferries leave from the Ferry Building and Pier 39 in San Francisco.

BY PLANE

SAN FRANCISCO INTERNATIONAL AIRPORT San Francisco International (tel. 415/876–7809), the big cheese of Northern California airports, lies about 10 miles south of San Francisco on U.S. 101 (take the San Francisco International exit, *not* the Airport Road exit). All major domestic airlines and many international ones fly to SFO, as it's called; contact individual carriers for specific information. The airport has two **currency exchange** offices, both in the International Terminal. Here you'll also find **baggage storage** (near the Air France ticket desk, tel. 415/877–0422), open 7 AM–11 PM. Charges are based on luggage size; an average bag runs $3.50 per day. There are also medium-sized lockers available that cost $1 for 24 hours, $2 for every day after that.

➢ **AIRPORT TRANSIT AND PARKING** • Until BART finally extends its service to the airport (sometime around 2002), the cheapest public transit to SFO is **SamTrans Buses 7B** and **7F** (*see* By Bus, *above*). Both lines travel between the airport and San Francisco's Transbay Terminal (board in front at Mission and Fremont Sts.) and can also drop you along Mission Street, within 2 blocks of any of the downtown BART/MUNI stations. The buses run every half hour from about 4:45 AM to 12:45 AM. Express Bus 7F costs $2 and takes 35 minutes; you're restricted to one small carry-on bag. Bus 7B costs $1, takes 55 minutes, and has no luggage restrictions. Bus 7F will also tote you from Palo Alto, near the Stanford Shopping Center, to the airport. Another option is to take a private shuttle (*see box, below*). If you can't bear to relinquish your car, parking (tel. 415/877–0227) is $2 the first hour, $4 for two hours, and $20 for the day in the short-term lot. Long-term parking is $10 a day, but this lot tends to fill up during peak travel times, especially three-day weekends. Call the above number and listen to their recording on availability before you set out, and plan for extra time to take the shuttle from the lot to the terminal.

OAKLAND INTERNATIONAL AIRPORT Oakland International (1 Airport Dr., off Hegenberger Rd., tel. 510/577–4000), located off I–880, is a smallish airport, easily accessible by public transportation from points throughout the Bay Area, and less hectic and crowded than SFO. It's often much cheaper to arrive here, particularly on **Southwest** (tel. 800/435–9792), which has more than 80 flights in and out of Oakland, many of which go to Los Angeles. With Southwest's Friends Fly Free program, two people can fly round-trip to Los Angeles for a total of $144 on selected flights; reservations for these fares should be made well in advance.

➢ **AIRPORT TRANSIT AND PARKING** • Short-term parking (tel. 510/633–2571) is 85¢ for a half hour, or $17 per day; long-term parking runs $1.65 an hour, $8.25 daily; "economy" rates (in lots farther away) are $1.65 an hour, $6.60 daily. Or, for $2 (in exact change), the **Air-Bart Shuttle** (tel. 510/562–7700) runs every 15 minutes (Mon.–Sat. 6 AM–midnight, Sun. 8:30 AM–midnight) between the airport and the Coliseum BART station in Oakland, allowing you to connect to all destinations served by BART. AC Transit **Bus 58** also runs between the airport and Jack London Square, stopping at Lake Merritt and near the Coliseum BART station until around 1 AM daily. Another option is an airport shuttle (*see box, below*). A taxi to downtown Berkeley from Oakland International costs about $30–$35.

SAN JOSE INTERNATIONAL AIRPORT Fourteen carriers, most notably **American Airlines** (tel. 800/433–7300), fly into San Jose International Airport (1661 Airport Blvd., off I–880 near U.S. 101, tel. 408/277–4759). The airport is served by San Jose Light Rail, Santa Clara County Transit, and various private shuttles (*see box, below*). Short-term parking runs 75¢ per half hour and $15 per day; long-term is $8 per day.

Bay Area Directory

LOW-COST MEDICAL AID

The post-college years can be tough on your health in any number of ways, but one of the biggest threats is lack of insurance. You've graduated from Mom and Dad's coverage, you no longer get to use the university health services, and chances are you don't have a full-time job with benefits to take up the slack. Suddenly the new contact lenses and the checkup at the dentist become a real problem. That's when you turn to the clinic. The health clinics listed below are all either free or low-cost. Many use a "sliding scale": The higher your income, the higher your fees. If your income is low enough, services are sometimes free. Many clinics also accept Medi-Cal and Medicare.

Whether publicly funded or privately supported, all clinics are in constant financial straits because of the limited amount of money our country puts toward affordable health care. Sadly, they often have to cut back on services and staff—or close altogether—when funds dry up. Always call first to make sure the clinic is still there, and to see if you should make an appointment. All provide quality care and try to operate as efficiently as possible, but long waits are not uncommon. Bring a book and try to be thankful that the clinic exists at all.

Clinics don't always make you prove how much money you make, which helps when you're truly strapped for cash; but try to be a good socialist and give according to your ability.

For medical information 24 hours a day, you can call Alta Bates Medical Center's **Audio Health Library** (tel. 800/606–2582), where you'll have access to information on more than 400 health-related topics. The audio library is designed to help you make informed decisions about your health. The service can also refer you to a private practitioner or clinic in your area, should you need one. When you need any advice, testing, or treatment having to do with AIDS, let your first call be to the **San Francisco AIDS Hotline** (tel. 415/863–AIDS). They have the most up-to-date information on programs to help those who are infected, as well as comprehensive listings of free or low-cost HIV testing sites in every city. For affordable family planning services, **Planned Parenthood** has many locations around the Bay Area that administer pregnancy tests and gynecological exams; prescribe birth control; perform abortions; treat sexually transmitted diseases (STDs); and offer free, anonymous AIDS tests. Look in the Yellow Pages under "Family Planning" or the white pages under "Planned Parenthood."

The following codes are used below to indicate services provided: DEN—dentistry; EYE—optometry; GM—general medicine; GYN—gynecology and family planning; OB—perinatal care; PED—pediatrics; STD—sexually transmitted disease treatment.

SAN FRANCISCO The **San Francisco Department of Public Health** has eight sliding-scale health centers throughout the city; services include GM, GYN, PED, STD, and HIV testing and referrals. Call the Health Department's main office (tel. 415/554–2500) for the one nearest you.

Buena Vista Women's Services. Cost: sliding. Services: GYN, STD. *1801 Bush St., at Octavia St., tel. 415/771–5000.*

Haight-Ashbury Free Medical Clinic. Cost: free, donations requested. Services: GM, GYN, STD; HIV programs. *558 Clayton St., at Haight St., tel. 415/487–5632.*

Mission Neighborhood Health Center. Cost: sliding. Services: DEN, GM, GYN, PED. *240 Shotwell St., at 16th St., tel. 415/552–3870.*

Native American Health Center. Cost: free. Services: DEN, GM, GYN, PED, STD. *56 Julian St., btw 14th and 15th Sts., tel. 415/621–8051.*

North East Medical Services. Cost: sliding. Services: DEN, EYE, GM, GYN, PED, STD. *1520 Stockton St., btw Green and Union Sts., tel. 415/391–9686.*

San Francisco City Clinic. Cost: sliding. Services: GYN, STD. *356 7th St., btw Folsom and Harrison Sts., tel. 415/487–5500.*

South of Market Health Center. Cost: sliding. Services: DEN, GM, GYN, OB, PED, STD. *551 Minna St., btw 6th and 7th Sts., tel. 415/626–2951.*

Man, I Need a Van

Can't find a friend to take you to the airport for that 5 AM flight? No worry—just call an airport shuttle, one of the Bay Area's favorite ways to ride (and the biggest thing to happen to vans since the 1970s). If you call about a day in advance, shuttles will pick you up at your doorstep at any time, day or night, and whisk you to the airport. Fare from San Francisco to SFO runs a mere $10–$11; expect to pay roughly $20 from Oakland to SFO, and about the same from downtown San Francisco to the Oakland airport. There's often a reduced rate for pickup of two or more people. You can save a couple bucks (up to $10) by getting on the shuttle at a major hotel, rather than at your home.

The king of airport service is Super Shuttle (tel. 415/558–8500), serving SFO from San Francisco and the Peninsula. You can hardly take a drive on U.S. 101 without seeing one of their blue vans speeding anxious vacationers to their flight. If big companies turn you off, try reliable, employee-owned Quake City (tel. 415/255–4899): It costs a dollar less than Super Shuttle and its friendly drivers can be counted on for pleasant chitchat during the trip.

In addition, Yellow Shuttle Service (tel. 415/282–7433) and Airport Connection (tel. 510/841–0150) run from most Bay Area cities to SFO, Oakland International, and San Jose International. The BayPorter Express (tel. 415/467–1800) runs from the East Bay and South Bay to SFO, Oakland, and San Jose; and from San Francisco to Oakland. The Marin Airporter (tel. 415/461–4222) will take you from Marin County to SFO.

UCSF Eye Clinic. Cost: sliding. Services: EYE. *400 Parnassus Ave., near 3rd Ave., tel. 415/476–3700.*

EAST BAY

➢ **BERKELEY • City of Berkeley Health Clinic.** Cost: sliding. Services: GYN, STD; free, anonymous HIV testing. *830 University Ave., at 6th St., tel. 510/644–8571.*

Berkeley Free Clinic. Cost: free. Services: DEN, GM, GYN, STD; free, anonymous HIV testing. *2339 Durant Ave., at Dana St., tel. 510/548–2570.*

Berkeley Women's Health Center. Cost: sliding. Services: GM, GYN, OB, STD. *2908 Ellsworth St., tel. 510/843–6194. 1 block from Ashby Ave. near Howe St.*

➢ **OAKLAND • Asian Health Services.** Cost: sliding. Services: GM, GYN, PED, STD; HIV services. *310 8th St. #200, at Harrison St., tel. 510/763–4411.*

Central Health Center. Cost: sliding. Services: GM, GYN, PED, STD. *470 27th St., near Telegraph Ave., tel. 510/271–4263.*

East Oakland Health Center. Cost: sliding. Services: DEN, EYE, GM, GYN, PED, STD. *7450 E. 14th St., at 74th Ave., tel. 510/430–9401.*

La Clinica de la Raza. Cost: free with $25 annual family membership. Services: DEN, EYE, GM, GYN, OB, PED, STD; there's a special "teen clinic," too. *1515 Fruitvale Ave., at E. 14th St., tel. 510/535–4000.*

Native American Health Center. Cost: sliding. Services: GM, GYN, OB, PED, STD; HIV services. *3124 E. 14th St., near Fruitvale Ave., tel. 510/261–1962.*

West Oakland Health Center. Cost: sliding. Services: DEN, EYE, GM, GYN, OB, PED, STD. *700 Adeline St., btw 7th and 8th Sts., tel. 510/835–9610.*

Women's Choice Clinic. Cost: sliding. Services: GYN, STD. The clinic also gives referrals for Chinese medicine and acupuncture. *2930 McClure Ave., btw 29th and 30th Sts., tel. 510/444–5676.*

MARIN COUNTY **Marin Community Clinic.** Cost: sliding. Services: GM, GYN, PED. *250 Bon Air Rd., on the grounds of Marin General Hospital in Greenbrae, tel. 415/461–7400.*

Marin County STD Clinic. Cost: $20 for adults, free for those under 18. Services: STD. *920 Grand Ave., San Rafael, tel. 415/499–6944.*

SOUTH BAY **Drew Health Foundation Community Medical Clinic.** Cost: sliding. Services: DEN, EYE, GM, GYN, PED, STD. *2111 University Ave., East Palo Alto, tel. 415/328–5060.*

Seton Medical Center Family Health Care Program. Cost: free. Services: GM, GYN, PED, STD. *1900 Sullivan Ave., Daly City, tel. 415/992–4000.*

PHONES AND MAIL

The area code for Oakland, Berkeley, and the East Bay is **510;** for San Francisco, Marin County, Palo Alto, and San Mateo County, it's **415;** and for San Jose and Santa Cruz, it's **408.** The **Postal Answer Line** (tel. 415/695–8760) is a 24-hour automated service that provides info on post office hours, postal rates, and more. A good all-purpose source of information is the front section of the San Francisco or Oakland Yellow Pages, which lists community organizations, public transit information, maps, descriptions of tourist attractions and community parks, seating plans for Bay Area theaters, and much more.

MEDIA

DAILY PAPERS The Bay Area's two big dailies, the ***San Francisco Chronicle*** (morning) and the ***San Francisco Examiner*** (afternoon), are equally unremarkable. The "Chron" does have some great columns, and it has strangely endeared itself to local readers despite its lightweight coverage. The combined *Chronicle-Examiner* Sunday paper comes with the "Pink Section," useful for its extensive movie reviews and listings of all sorts of upcoming events.

The ***Oakland Tribune,*** formerly one of the country's premier African-American–owned dailies, was recently bought by a large newspaper chain. The paper is stronger on community happenings than politics. Many Berkeleyans read the student-produced ***Daily Californian,*** which has recently come out only two–three times a week due to financial problems. At press time, the paper had announced a return to publication Monday through Friday in fall 1995. The ***Marin Independent Journal*** focuses mostly on Marin County, but also tackles some more general issues. The big surprise in Bay Area dailies is the ***San Jose Mercury News,*** a paper that's well-read throughout the area and highly respected in the journalism community. It's stronger on national and international news than most Bay Area papers.

WEEKLY PAPERS San Francisco sustains two free alternative weeklies, the ***San Francisco Bay Guardian*** and the ***SF Weekly.*** The *Guardian* has full listings of San Francisco's cultural events, and is especially strong on local politics. Around election time, the *Guardian* offers extensive analyses of local and state candidates along with their recommended slate. Their "Cost of Living" column tells you how to manage life in the city on a budget, with tips on dealing with landlords, the phone company, etc. Best of all, the paper carries the entertaining and educational sex question-and-answer column "Ask Isadora." Look for the *Guardian*'s "Best of the Bay Area" special every August. The *Weekly,* recently bought by a national corporation, tries to give the Guardian a run for its money, but, especially after the buy-out, most San Franciscans pass it by, stopping long enough only to laugh at the quality of its graphic design. The *Weekly* can be strong on coverage of cultural events, though.

The SF Weekly sex-advice column "Savage Love" is fun and informative (if you need advice on having your nipples tattooed, that is), but "Ask Isadora" Alman has described her competitor's column as "monumentally offensive."

The ***East Bay Express*** comes in two parts: The front section includes articles, and "Billboard" has the best events listings in the East Bay as well as a huge classified section. While folks sometimes make fun of the idiosyncratic *Express* for its marathon front-page articles, it's one of the few papers willing to publish thorough pieces in an age of sound bites and MTV.

Other Bay Area weeklies include Marin County's ***Pacific Sun,*** which has an events calendar but dubious politics and a cheesy tone, and the much better Santa Clara ***Metro,*** which covers the whole South Bay with high-quality feature articles and events listings.

Who to Call When Nobody Else Is Home

No need to spend money on a 900 line just because you're sitting by the phone feeling bored. The Bay Area offers plenty of information lines to amuse you at any hour of the day or night. For starters, try the Public Library's Dial-a-Story (tel. 415/626–6516), where the tale changes once a week. Then move on to the U.C. Berkeley Seismographic Station (tel. 510/642–2160) for the latest on any recent earthquakes. Call the Audubon Society's Rare Bird Summary (tel. 415/738–1499) for a rhapsodic account of local sightings of unusual birds. The Morrison Planetarium Information Line (tel. 415/750–7141) tells you all you need to know about sky watching. The Hearing Society Dial-a-Test (tel. 415/834–1620) lets you know if the old eardrums are still in working order.

MONTHLY PUBLICATIONS ***San Francisco Focus,*** published by KQED, has an arts focus, with theater and opera listings and profiles of local artists. It's geared toward a rich-white-liberal audience. (Witness the personal ads, which cost $5 a word and often run to 50-plus-word descriptions of lonely doctors and lawyers who "love fine wine, ocean breezes, and gourmet cooking" and seek "professionally established, classy partner with great warmth and panache, who understands investments.") But this monthly magazine sometimes surprises readers with high-quality articles on controversial local and national issues. KQED members get it free; for the rest of us, a subscription costs $19 a year. Call 415/553–2800 to sign up. You can also find *Focus* at some newsstands for $1.95. In the East Bay, ***The Monthly,*** heavy on local ads and light on journalism, presents *Focus* with little competition, but at least it's free.

GAY AND LESBIAN PUBLICATIONS The ***Bay Times*** comes out every two weeks and has a pronounced left-of-center bent. This was the paper responsible for the downfall of police chief Richard Hongisto in 1992; he was buried in negative publicity when he tried to pull a controversial *Bay Times* issue from the racks. Along with thoughtful articles on local and national news, it serves as an information network, listing clubs, political organizations, AIDS groups, information hot lines, and much more.

San Francisco's other major gay paper, the free ***Bay Area Reporter,*** appears every Thursday and offers excellent political and social commentary, personals, an arts and style section, and several great contributing writers. The *Reporter* is also stronger on lesbian issues than the other gay papers. For a more conservative gay perspective, pick up ***The Sentinel,*** which emphasizes national gay news and has an interesting column called "This Week in Leather." The section "168 Hours" is an excellent listing of arts, films, literary events, and social goings-on. In the South Bay, the biweekly ***Out Now!*** is a San Jose–based forum for local gay and lesbian news and community happenings.

On Our Backs and ***Deneuve*** are two popular lesbian pseudo-porn mags, both based in San Francisco. Pick them up at **A Different Light** (489 Castro St., tel. 415/431–0891), the Bay Area's best gay bookstore. Among the store's wide selection of queerzines, published by special-interest groups that sometimes consist of as few as one member, are ***Bear,*** the magazine for big, hairy, husky men, and the men who love them; ***Girljock,*** the tongue-in-cheek magazine for girls who like sports; ***Girlfriend,*** aimed at drag queens; and ***Raw Vulva,*** for the bike-riding dyke.

Desperately Seeking . . .

If you read enough Bay Area papers you'll soon realize that all classified sections are not created equal. The free weeklies are short on nuts-and-bolts info, but make up for this in entertainment value. Take a gander at the Bay Guardian's relationships department, where ads promise everything from fairy-tale romance to "oral worship." The SF Weekly's personals are even more experimental (requests for hermaphrodites are not uncommon). The East Bay Express is less dominated by personal ads; look here for massage therapy, counseling, and housing in Oakland and Berkeley. Daily papers like the Chronicle and the Examiner are stronger on employment and housing opportunities than any of the free weeklies. The Oakland Tribune lists tons of rentals all over Alameda County, and the San Jose Mercury News is full of job listings and cars for sale. The gay and lesbian Bay Times has an extensive resource guide, pointing you to hundreds of organizations that deal with issues like addiction and recovery, parenting, and AIDS. The classified section of the Bay Area Reporter is dedicated solely to personals, and is chock-full of pictures of mostly nude males with captions like "Ex football player rubs you the right way."

RADIO STATIONS The Bay Area radio scene isn't as bleak as you might think after hearing all those Top 40, classic rock, and soft-rock mega-stations as you twirl the dial. Browse the left end of the FM range to find some less conventional programming. U.C. Berkeley's **KALX** (90.7 FM), a typically cool, alternative college station run by an all-volunteer staff 24 hours a day, can be counted on for the eclectic, the avant-garde, and the noisy. They have some excellent regular programs: "Women Hold Up Half the Sky" (Sat. 11–noon) features interviews with fierce and fabulous women from around the country; and "Straightjackets" (Mon. noon–12:30) deals with issues of gender and (homo)sexuality. Unfortunately, you can rarely pick up KALX's signal from San Francisco. **KUSF** (90.3 FM) comes out of the University of San Francisco, playing new music, ethnic music, and specialty shows.

Much-loved, listener-sponsored **KPFA** (94.1 FM) broadcasts all over central and Northern California. You can listen to classical, reggae, rap, soul, folk, blues, and national news all in one place. Also look for interviews with artists and members of special-interest groups you didn't know even existed. **KFJC** (89.7 FM) operates from Foothill College in Los Altos Hills in the South Bay. They play every kind of music you can think of, but are best known for their outstanding specialty shows, including the award-winning "Norman Bates Memorial Soundtrack Hour," playing your favorite TV and movie themes Saturday 9–noon; "Phil's Garage," featuring grungy garage-band music Saturday 7–10 PM; and the news show "One Step Beyond" on Sunday 7–11 PM. Again, listeners in San Francisco are subject to the whims of atmospheric conditions when tuning in.

News junkies have a few different options. On the AM dial, **KCBS** (740 AM) has rapid-fire news bites around the clock. They may not have the most in-depth coverage, but they certainly have the quickest. For higher-quality reportage, try **KQED** (88.5 FM), which broadcasts a lot of National Public Radio programming. "All Things Considered" starts at 2 PM and is repeated at 4:30 PM. The BBC News Hour airs at 9 PM and is repeated at 1 AM. **KALW** (91.7 FM) also plays NPR and BBC throughout the day.

RESOURCES FOR GAYS AND LESBIANS

Even if you're not looking for them, resources for the lesbian and gay communities will jump out at you. Publications focusing on gay issues can be found in most San Francisco cafés and in gay-oriented bookstores and cafés in other parts of the Bay Area. San Francisco has the *Bay Times*, the *Bay Area Reporter*, and *The Sentinel;* and the South Bay has *Out Now!* (for more information, *see* Gay and Lesbian Publications, *above*). The San Francisco gay community, particularly in the Castro district, is extremely supportive and close-knit. If you're trying to find your niche (be it a support group or a political organization), some friendly asking around at one of the Castro cafés or diners should get you helpful advice, if not a pal. **Café Flore** (*see* Chapter 5), despite all the winking and butt-wagging going on, is actually a great spot to start getting down to business with those in the know. If you don't find the resources you're looking for in the gay papers or by poking around the Castro, get a copy of the 200-page ***Gaybook*** ($9.95), published by Rainbow Ventures Publishing (584 Castro St., Suite 632, tel. 415/928–1859). Each biannual edition contains a resource guide listing organizations that cater to gays and lesbians, as well as a classified advertising section. If you're traveling, pick up ***Bob Damron's Address Book*** ($13.95 plus $5 shipping), which lists services and entertainment options for gay men, or ***The Women's Traveler*** ($10.95 plus $5 shipping), with resources for lesbians and women in general. Both are available through the **Damron Company** (tel. 415/255–0404).

In Berkeley, the **Pacific Center for Human Growth** (2712 Telegraph Ave., at Derby St., tel. 510/548–8283) is a well-known gay and lesbian gathering place. The organization offers counseling, social gatherings, rap sessions, and support groups (covering stuff like coming out, jealousy in relationships, parents, etc.). Also check out the bulletin boards, littered with tidbits that run the gamut from apartment rentals to invitations to socials. You can drop in weekdays 10–10, Saturday noon–4 and 6–10, or Sunday 6 PM–10 PM to see what's going on and to use any services. The **Pacific Center's Gay, Lesbian, and Bisexual Switchboard** (tel. 510/841–6224) doles out information and referrals.

In San Francisco, the **Lavender Youth Recreation and Information Center** (127 Collingwood St., at 18th St., tel. 415/703–6150, hotline 415/863–3636 or 800/246–7743) is a social and support organization for gays, lesbians, and transgenders 23 years old and younger. If you call the hotline Monday–Wednesday 4–9 PM or Thursday–Sunday 6:30–9 PM, you can talk to other young gays and lesbians, or a counselor (at off hours, you get recorded info). **Communities United Against Violence** (973 Market St., Suite 500, tel. 415/777–5500, 24-hour emergency hotline 415/333–HELP) provides crisis counseling and referrals for gays and lesbians who are victims of anti-gay violence.

In Palo Alto, the **Stanford Lesbian/Gay/Bisexual Community Center** (Fire Truck House, Stanford Campus, tel. 415/725–4222 or 415/723–1488 for event information) knows all about gay and lesbian happenings around campus and can refer you to a vast number of support groups and resources. During the school year, the center is generally open weekdays noon–5; during summer, hours vary. The place is staffed by volunteers (who have other lives), so it's best to call ahead to see if anyone will be there.

One of the few positive things to emerge from the AIDS epidemic is the gay community's creation of a tremendous flood of support groups, political organizations, and other AIDS-related services. If you or a loved one has AIDS, or you just want to learn more about it, head to the **San Francisco AIDS Foundation** (25 Van Ness Ave., at Market St., tel. 415/864–5855), an umbrella organization that can direct people to whichever AIDS-related group best suits them. **Shanti Project** (1546 Market St., at Van Ness Ave., tel. 415/864–2273) provides emotional support and has housing and activities programs for people living with AIDS. For late-night counseling or information, call the **AIDS/HIV Nightline** (tel. 415/434–AIDS, 800/273–AIDS in Northern California) 5 PM–5 AM seven nights a week. If you're pissed about the AIDS crisis and want to do something about it, call **ACT-UP SF** (tel. 415/252–9200). Making headlines with its confrontational tactics, ACT-UP rallies for increased AIDS research and an end to discrimination against those living with AIDS. You can attend a meeting every Tuesday at 7:30 PM at 592 Castro St., Suite B. **ACT-UP East Bay** (tel. 510/568–1680) meets monthly at different locations; call for specifics.

Pump Up the Volume

Pirate radio operators are busting out all over the Bay Area, whiling away the hours with political back-and-forths, eclectic music playlists, and chitchat. These micropower free-speechers say that commercial radio is as worthless as static to their communities, and have taken matters into their own hands for the low, low price of $600 in start-up fees. (Compare this to the $3,000 cost of a Federal Communications Commission license.) They broadcast from undisclosed (sometimes mobile) locations, seize unoccupied frequencies, and have even started their own network, the Free Communications Coalition–the People's FCC (tel. 510/464–3041). The real FCC, needless to say, is furious. Complaining that the "guerrilla stations" (ooh, scary) create chaos by interfering with legit frequencies, the FCC has counter-attacked by seizing equipment and imposing $10,000 fines. However, in a historic ruling in January, 1994, the Oakland Federal District Court denied the FCC's request for an injunction to silence Free Radio Berkeley and its operator, Stephen Dunifer.

Due to low frequencies, you need to be nearby to pick up the following stations' broadcasts. Radio Libre (103.3 FM) is heard in the Mission, parts of Noe Valley, and in the South of Market area; San Francisco Liberation Radio (93.7 FM) can be picked up in the Richmond and Sunset districts; North Beach Radio (88.1 FM) transmits in the area between Columbus Avenue and Pier 39 in San Francisco; and Free Radio Berkeley (104.1 FM) can be heard in parts of Alameda County, mainly on Sunday nights.

Generally, lesbian resources are much harder to ferret out. The Castro is definitely slanted toward gay men; women should head to Valencia Street in San Francisco's Mission district, home to several women's bookstores and organizations. **Old Wives' Tales** (1009 Valencia St., at 21st St., tel. 415/821–4675) sells feminist and lesbian books of every stripe and sponsors readings and lectures. Berkeley is another good spot for lesbian resources and hangouts. In particular, the bookstore and coffeehouse **Mama Bears** (6536 Telegraph Ave., Oakland, tel. 510/428–9684) offers readings and social events in a warm, supportive environment. The lesbian-owned and -operated café **Ann Kong's Bleach Bottle Pig Farm** (2072 San Pablo Ave., Berkeley, tel. 510/848–7376) is another happening spot—look in the papers for readings and other evening activities. For action of a more direct nature, check out the **Lesbian Avengers,** a group of lesbian, bisexual, and transgendered women. Call 415/267–6195 for the lowdown on meetings and events.

RESOURCES FOR PEOPLE OF COLOR

Northern California has a rich mix of ethnicities, but the melting pot is more often like a tossed salad, with everyone maintaining strong individual cultural identities. A wealth of resources support, educate, celebrate, and bring together people of color in the Bay Area. In addition to community organizations, look into student services and groups at the universities.

AFRICAN-AMERICAN RESOURCES Oakland's **Black Women's Resource Center** (518 17th St., Suite 202, tel. 510/763–9501) works to establish, improve, and maintain support systems that empower African-American women, especially those with low incomes. They offer information and referrals and publish a newsletter for women in the community. The **Northern California Center for African-American History and Life** (5606 San Pablo Ave., Oakland, tel. 510/658–3158) is an extensive museum, archive, and research center. The preeminent local African-American bookstore is **Marcus Books,** with a location in Oakland (3900 Martin Luther King Jr. Way, tel. 510/652–2344) and in San Francisco (1712 Fillmore St., btw Post and Sutter Sts., tel. 415/346–4222).

Check out "Historic Black Landmarks: A Traveler's Guide" (Gale Research Inc.; $18), or "African American Historic Places" (National Park Service, Preservation Press; $26), two solid travel books that include information on African-American landmarks in California.

The **Center for African and African-American Art and Culture** (762 Fulton St., San Francisco, tel. 415/928–8546) provides a home for six different African-American groups that sponsor poetry readings, speakers, and storytelling in the African tradition. The center also has research materials and will refer you to other Bay Area African-American events and organizations. The **Oakland History Room** (tel. 510/238–3222) in the main branch of the Oakland Public Library (125 14th St., btw Oak and Madison Sts.) has an extensive archive of past African-American life in Oakland. Bill Sturm, who runs the room, is reputed to know everything.

ASIAN-PACIFIC RESOURCES In Oakland, **Asian Immigrant Women Advocates** (310 8th St., Suite 301, tel. 510/268–0192) works to empower immigrant Asian women through leadership development and education. The **East Bay Vietnamese Association** (1218 Miller Ave., Oakland, tel. 510/533–4219) provides employment services and other assistance for the Vietnamese community. In San Jose, **Korean American Community Services** (2750 Westfield Ave., tel. 408/248–5227) helps recently arrived Koreans with English skills and other issues. Oakland's **Filipinos for Affirmative Action** (310 8th St., Suite 308, tel. 510/465–9876), a nonprofit social agency, works with the community on employment issues, AIDS and substance abuse education, and activism. Also in Oakland, the **Japan Pacific Resource Network** (310 8th St., Suite 305B, tel. 510/891–9045) can point you to all sorts of resources for the Japanese community in the Bay Area. In San Francisco, the **Chinese Cultural Center** (750 Kearny St., 3rd Floor, tel. 415/986–1822) is dedicated to the preservation of Chinese culture and community. Stop by and talk to the helpful staff for information on Chinese community events.

CHICANO/LATINO RESOURCES San Francisco's entire Mission district is a resource for Chicanos and Latinos, with theater groups, cultural centers, and zillions of Latino-owned restaurants and bookstores. One important meeting place is the **Mission Cultural Center** (2868 Mission St., btw 24th and 25th Sts., tel. 415/821–1155), site of an art gallery and dance, music, and theater classes. In the East Bay, **La Peña Cultural Center** (3105 Shattuck Ave., Berkeley, tel. 510/849–2568) has concerts and dances, workshops, a store with Latino books and music, and a café. In the South Bay, the **Centro Cultural Latino** (tel. 415/343–7476) has after-school and summer programs for Latino youth and sponsors cultural activities.

NATIVE AMERICAN RESOURCES The **International Indian Treaty Council** (54 Mint St., Suite 400, San Francisco, tel. 415/512–1501) is an information center that works with indigenous people both locally and around the world, promoting sovereignty, human rights, and indigenous prisoners' rights. They work as a consultant to the United Nations. The **American Indian Center of Santa Clara Valley, Inc.** (919 Alameda, San Jose, tel. 408/971–9622) has a spectrum of support services and a reference library (tel. 408/971–0772). For medical help, the **Native American Health Center** has two free clinics in the Bay Area (*see* Low-Cost Medical Aid, *above*).

RESOURCES FOR WOMEN

The most comprehensive resource center in the Bay Area is the **Women's Building** (3543 18th St., San Francisco, tel. 415/431–1180), which provides a wealth of information for women. The building houses nine women's organizations, including the **National Organization for Women (NOW), San Francisco Women Against Rape (SF WAR),** and **Mujeres Unidas y Activas.** The Women's Building staff can also help you find housing, health care, employment, or just about anything else. Regular meetings at the Women's Building include **NOW** (third Tuesday of the month at 7 PM) and **Women Embracing Life** (Mondays 6 PM–9 PM), a support group for women living with HIV. Also in the Mission district, the **Women's Action Coalition** (1360 Mission St., btw 9th and 10th Sts., Suite 200, tel. 415/255–6352) is an open alliance of women committed to direct-action support of women's rights. Bimonthly meetings are held in the Mission Street office; free child care is provided. The **Young Women's Christian Association (YWCA)** (620 Sutter St., San Francisco, tel. 415/775–6502) offers social-service programs and lodging referrals for women. The San Francisco office can refer you to the six other YWCAs in Marin and the East Bay.

In the East Bay, one of the best resources is the **Women's Resource Center** (250 Golden Bear Center, U.C. Berkeley, tel. 510/642–4786). Come here to get referrals for other organizations. Only U.C. students and staff can borrow materials from the book and audiovisual collections, but anyone can dig through the community resources files, which have info on support groups, internships, grant opportunities, and more.

An important women's health resource is **Planned Parenthood,** a pro-choice family-planning clinic (*see* Low-Cost Medical Aid, *above*). The **Women's Needs Center** (1825 Haight St., San Francisco, tel. 415/487–5607) also offers pro-choice gynecological services for low-income women and anonymous HIV testing for men and women. San Francisco Women Against Rape (*see above*) runs a 24-hour crisis hotline (tel. 415/647–7273 or 510/845–RAPE). Female victims of domestic violence can call **A Safe Place** (tel. 510/536–7233), a shelter for battered women, 24 hours a day.

Mama Bears (6536 Telegraph Ave., Oakland, tel. 510/428–9684) stocks female-oriented literature, sponsors readings, and can refer you to other bookstores around California if they don't have what you want. The **Women of Color Resource Center** (2288 Fulton St. Suite 103, Berkeley, tel. 510/848–9272) publishes the excellent book *Women of Color, Organizations and Projects: A National Directory* ($8.95 plus shipping), which points you to hundreds of organizations dedicated to women of almost every ethnicity.

RESOURCES FOR THE DISABLED

The Bay Area is an important national center for disabled resources, thanks mostly to Berkeley's **Center for Independent Living,** started in the early '70s by a group of disabled people who fought for their right to be accepted at U.C. Berkeley. There are now more than 300 independent living centers nationwide, working for rights for the disabled, helping disabled people discover their potential, and giving referrals. You'll find several in the Bay Area: in Berkeley (2539 Telegraph Ave., tel. 510/841–4776); in Hayward (439 A St., tel. 510/881–5743); in San Rafael (710 4th St., tel. 415/459–6245); in Santa Clara (1601 Civic Dr., Suite 100, tel. 408/985–1243); and in San Francisco (70 10th St., tel. 415/863–0581). The San Francisco office is especially helpful. Ask for Tricia Leetz, who knows Bay Area resources like the back of her hand.

Transit organizations in the Bay Area have joined ranks to create an ID card that gives disabled people discounts on travel throughout nine Bay Area counties; each transit company decides what kind of a discount to give (*see* Getting In, Out, and Around, *above*). You can get the pass at any transit office by filling out a form and getting proof from your doctor. The **BART Customer Service Office** (800 Madison St., at the Lake Merritt BART Station, tel. 510/464–7136) can tell you where to buy a $16 ticket for a mere $4. All BART stations have elevators. Contact San Francisco MUNI's **Elderly and Handicapped Discount ID Office** (tel. 415/923–6070) for discount pass and access information for that system. Most buses are wheelchair accessible and you'll pay 35¢ instead of $1. Monthly passes for the disabled are $8. **AC Transit** (tel. 510/891–4777) issues a disabled ID card allowing the bearer to pay 60¢ instead of $1.25 to ride the bus. To find out which bus routes are wheelchair accessible, contact their bus information line (tel. 510/839–2882). All **Golden Gate Transit** (tel. 415/332–6600) buses are wheelchair accessible and you get 50% off the bus fare.

Some major car-rental companies are able to supply hand-controlled vehicles with a minimum of 24 hours advance notice. **Avis** (tel. 800/331–1212) will install hand-control mechanisms at no extra charge if given a day's notice. **Hertz** (tel. 800/654–3131, TDD 800/654–2280) asks for 48-hour notice (except at San Francisco International Airport, where a day will suffice). Rental companies often can't install hand controls on economy cars.

In the East Bay, **Grand Mar** (1311 63rd St., at Doyle St., Emeryville, tel. 510/428–0441) rents and repairs wheelchairs. Manual wheelchairs rent for $10 the first day, $5 each subsequent day, or $45–$97 a month; power wheelchairs are $20 a day, $348–$500 a month. **Abbey Home and Healthcare** (390 9th St., San Francisco, tel. 415/864–6999) rents manual wheelchairs for $56 a month.

American Foundation for the Blind (111 Pine St. #725, San Francisco, tel. 415/392–4845) has brochures and catalogues to help people access resources. **Lighthouse for the Blind and Visually Disabled** (214 Van Ness Ave., at Grove St., San Francisco, tel. 415/431–1481) has assistant devices (canes, talking watches) and can direct people to support groups. **Lion's Blind Center** in Oakland (3834 Opal St., at 38th St., tel. 510/450–1580) or San Jose (101 North Bascon Ave., tel. 408/295–4016) also has resources for blind people. **Peninsula Center for the Blind** (2470 El Camino Real, Suite 107, Palo Alto, tel. 415/858–0202) has orientation and mobility specialists, social workers, and short-term counseling. For the hearing-impaired, **Hearing Society for the Bay Area** (870 Market St., Suite 330, tel. 415/693–5870, TDD 415/834–1005) provides social services, interpreting, vocational rehab, and referrals.

ACCESS/ABILITIES (Box 458, Mill Valley 94942, tel. 415/388–3250) is a small travel center that provides travel opportunities for the disabled. They've got info on accessible tours and they customize itineraries for both the Bay Area and other places in the country. In San Francisco, the non-profit **Environmental Traveling Companions** (Fort Mason Center, Bldg. C, tel. 415/474–7662) organizes cross-country skiing, kayaking, and rafting trips for the physically disabled and other people with special needs—cancer survivors, the developmentally disabled, etc.—as well as the population at large. Their prices are very reasonable (one-day trips start at about $38 per person), and they're willing to negotiate if you're truly unable to pay. In the East Bay, **Bay Area Outreach and Recreation Program** (tel. 510/849–4663) organizes sports events and outdoor activities for the disabled, with programs for youth, adults, and seniors.

SPECTATOR SPORTS

The Bay Area is fertile ground for armchair athletes, with two pro baseball teams, a championship football team (and quite likely a second), an NBA franchise, enthusiastic college sports rivalries, and thousands of loyal fans. The city's major sports venue is the unfortunately located

Candlestick Park (south of S.F. in Daly City), where the San Francisco Giants play baseball and the San Francisco '49ers play football. The park's management recently sunk $5 million into renovation, adding 130,000 square feet of Kentucky Blue Grass and 1,600 new seats, but that doesn't alter the fact that, thanks to wind and fog, the 'Stick is butt-cold most days and almost every night. To get to Candlestick Park, take U.S. 101 south to the Candlestick exit, or catch the MUNI 9X "Ballpark Express" at the Sutter Street exit of the Montgomery BART Station. Round-trip costs $5 ($2 for those with a MUNI pass), and buses leave every 10 minutes, starting 90 minutes before the game on weekdays or three hours before on weekends. SamTrans also has buses from the Palo Alto Transit Center for $3 round-trip. Call 800/660–4BUS for departure times, which vary according to game time.

If you can't bring yourself to watch baseball with your mittens on, go see the Oakland Athletics play at the **Oakland Coliseum** (tel. 510/639–7700); the Golden State Warriors play basketball in the Coliseum's indoor stadium next door. You can reach either stadium by taking I–880 to the Hegenberger Road exit; or, if you want to avoid parking fees and traffic, take BART to the Coliseum Station.

BASEBALL The baseball rivalry between San Francisco and the East Bay came to a dramatic head in the 1989 "Bay Bridge Series," when the American League's **Oakland A's** and the National League's **San Francisco Giants** duked it out for the championship, and God intervened to sever the bridge between east and west with a major earthquake. But usually the competition between the two teams is less heated, and many fans are perfectly happy to alternate between cheering the A's on at the Oakland Coliseum (*see above*) and rooting for the Giants at Candlestick Park (*see above*).

It's easy for Giants fans to show their loyalty: Just sitting through a game at the freezing 'Stick is enough to test the most ardent fan's dedication.

Unfortunately, the A's haven't been playing up to par in recent years, and even the Giants have been struggling. Now that the 1994 baseball strike is over, both teams are struggling to regain popularity, offering special promotions and even cheaper seats than usual, making this the most accessible professional sport in the Bay Area. You can enjoy a bleacher seat for just $4.75 at the 'Stick or $4.50 at the Coliseum. Especially at Candlestick, the bleachers are a great deal: They command a better view than many of the $7 seats, and they're a good place to get a good look at Barry Bonds. At the Coliseum, those who don't want to slum it with the bleacher bums can get half-price tickets to the plaza level (normally $13) or upper-deck (normally $7) seats with a student ID. For a printed pocket schedule of games and information about A's tickets, call 510/638–0500 Monday–Saturday 9–5. For Giants information and schedules, call 415/467–8000 weekdays 8:30–5:30. To charge tickets for either team, call BASS (tel. 415/776–1999 or 510/762–BASS), but expect to pay an extra $3–$4 per ticket in service charges. Unless you think the game will be a sellout, get your tickets at the stadium box office.

FOOTBALL Thanks to their 1995 Super Bowl victory, the **San Francisco '49ers** now hold the NFL record for the most Bowls won. Because of their consistent success, the '49ers have built up a huge fan base from all over Northern California, and tickets for home games at Candlestick Park (the season runs Sept.–Jan.) are nearly impossible to get. Season-ticket holders have a lock on most seats, and when the rest go on sale in July, they usually sell out within the hour, despite the $40 price tag. Call the ticket office (tel. 415/468–2249) to find out what day tickets go on sale (usually in mid-July). Then all you can do is call BASS (tel. 415/776–1999 or 510/762–BASS) at 9 AM that day and hope you get through before someone else snatches the last ticket.

The big news, though, is the return of the **Los Angeles Raiders** to Oakland, a move that is bringing Raiders fans out of closets all over the Bay Area. The city of Oakland is also thrilled, no doubt by the revenue and publicity that the popular team, who left Oakland for L.A. in 1982, will rake in. Although at press time the NFL had not yet approved the move, word around town was "Welcome Home Raiders!"

BASKETBALL Having secured first pick in the 1995 NBA draft, many people feel that the **Golden State Warriors** are now a team worth watching. With new blood to fill the void left by Chris Webber's tumultuous departure—and if Tim Hardaway's injured knee holds up—they just might go all the way to a championship. Tickets ($17.50–$28; no student discounts) go on sale in late September or early October, and are available through BASS (tel. 415/776–1999 or 510/762–BASS). They sell out fast.

HOCKEY The **San Jose Sharks** repeated their miraculous '94 playoffs performance in '95, beating the Calgary Flames in a seventh game double-overtime victory to win the first round of the Stanley Cup Games. They eventually lost in the second round to New Jersey. Sharks aficionados continue to be one of hockey's most enthused group of fans, and tickets to games in the new San Jose Arena ($15–$71) sell quickly; call 408/287–4275 for information. The season runs October–April. From San Francisco, CalTrain (*see* Getting In, Out, and Around by Train, *above*) will get you to the San Jose Arena and back to S.F. after the game. There's also a shuttle to and from parking lots in downtown San Jose.

COLLEGE SPORTS Most college sports in the Bay Area take place at either U.C. Berkeley (called "Cal") or Stanford University in Palo Alto. Both schools are supported by huge alumni bases that love to recapture their youth by getting sloshed and cheering like banshees at school events. The **Cal Bears** football team, which plays in Memorial Stadium on the east side of campus, has improved a bit in recent years. But whether or not it's a winning season, even the most blasé Berkeley bohemian may work up an ashamed sweat over the cut-throat "Big Game" between Cal and Stanford.

Cal men's basketball has been weakening since hoops star Jason Kidd announced his decision to enter the NBA draft in 1994. A young team, they finished the '94–'95 season with 13 wins and 14 losses, though they did manage to beat UCLA—the eventual national champs. In '95–'96, with top freshman recruit Sharef Abdul-Rahim and the talented Pac-10 player Tremaine Fowlkes, coach Todd Bozeman hopes to return the team to the top 20 and make another trip to the NCAA. Thousands of enthusiastic fans wait anxiously. At press time, tickets for the '95–'96 season, played on campus at Harmon Gym, were still available but going fast. Luckily, it's much easier to get tickets to the few games each season (six in '95–'96) that are played at the Oakland Coliseum.

The **Cal women's basketball** team did not fare much better than the men last season, but 17-season veteran coach Gooch Foster, along with loyal fans, is hoping for a better '95–'96. The team has a number of excellent players, including point guard Eliza Sokolowska.

To buy tickets for Cal sports, call 800/GO–BEARS. Football tickets cost $12 for general admission, $20 for reserved seating. Basketball tickets for games at the Coliseum cost about $16. Baseball, played at Evans Diamond on the corner of Bancroft Way and Oxford Street, costs $5 for adults, $3 for Cal students and minors. Women's basketball is played at Harmon Gym and tickets are $5, or $3 for Cal students and youth.

Stanford's spectator sports revolve mainly around the university's football team, **The Cardinal** (named for the color, not the bird), which plays at Stanford Stadium. The other strong team on campus is women's basketball, a consistent NCAA championship contender that made the Final Four in '95. Palo Alto may seem a little out of the way to some people, but Stanford fans are gung-ho. The school is also notorious for its goofy band. For information on tickets for all Stanford sports, call 800/BEAT–CAL weekdays 9–4. Football tickets cost $9 general admission ($7 for youth), $22 reserved, and $35 for the "Big Game," and they go on sale at the beginning of June. Tickets to basketball games, played at Maples Pavilion, go on sale in September and cost $5 general admission ($3 for youth), $11 reserved.

FESTIVALS

JANUARY In addition to the kick-off of the ballet and chamber orchestra seasons, January is a big month in the California **whale-watching** season, which runs through April. Patient watchers bundle up and pull out their binoculars at Point Reyes (*see* Chapter 8). The rangers at the Point Reyes lighthouse (tel. 415/669–1534) can tell you how many beasties have swum past in the past few days.

Tet Festival. This one-day street fair is held on the Saturday nearest the Vietnamese New Year (the first new moon after January 20). The streets around Civic Center come alive with performances by Vietnamese, Cambodian, and Laotian singers and dancers, and numerous booths sell Southeast Asian delicacies. The festival is not just a celebration of the New Year, but also of the diverse neighborhood in which it takes place. *Tel. 415/885–2743.*

FEBRUARY **Chinese New Year and Golden Dragon Parade.** Celebrate the dawn of the Year of the Rat (year 4694 on the lunar calendar) with North America's largest Chinese community. The Chinatown Chamber of Commerce (730 Sacramento St., San Francisco, tel. 415/982–3000) has the lowdown on cultural events, which take place during the last two weeks of February. The justly famous Golden Dragon Parade—March 2 at 6 PM—explodes with fireworks and a riot of colorful costumes.

MARCH During **Tulipmania** (March 4–18), more than 35,000 tulips bloom around Pier 39 at Fisherman's Wharf. You can walk around on your own, or show up at the Entrance Plaza any morning at 10 for a free guided tour. *Tel. 415/705–5512.*

St. Patrick's Day Parade. Boasting shamrocks, Guinness stout, and enough green to make even Mother Nature envious, this parade is a party in motion. The United Irish Cultural Center sponsors the parade, which winds through San Francisco to City Hall on March 17 at 12:30. Despite the recent politicization of the parade, with "Gaylic Pride" and "IRA All the Way" banners popping up, the emphasis for San Francisco's rowdy Irish community is still firmly on green beer and folk tunes. *Tel. 415/661–2700.*

APRIL **Cherry Blossom Festival.** This cultural festival in Japantown features such traditions as ancient tea ceremonies and martial arts and cooking demonstrations. Nearly 400 Japanese performers come to dance, and there are numerous exhibits of Japanese art. Perhaps the most popular attraction is the taiko drum performance on Saturday night. For a schedule of events, send a self-addressed, stamped envelope to Cherry Blossom Festival, Box 15147, San Francisco 94115. The festivities conclude with a 2½-hour parade. Most events are free. 1996's festival will take place April 12–14 and 19–21. *Tel. 415/563–2313.*

San Francisco International Film Festival. Taking place at the end of the month, the oldest film festival in the United States features two full weeks of movies and seminars and many opportunities to mingle with the creative minds behind them. Films range from the almost-mainstream (Pedro Almódovar, Wayne Wang) to the truly obscure. Screenings take place at the Kabuki 8 and the Castro Theatre in San Francisco, the Pacific Film Archive in Berkeley, and other locations in the South Bay and Marin. *Tel. 415/929–5000. Admission: $7.50 per program, $5.50 students, seniors, and the disabled.*

Whole Life Expo. If your energy needs to be rechanneled, come to this New Age fest, held at San Francisco's Fashion Design Center (8th and Brannan Sts., next to the Concourse Exhibition Center). During the last weekend in April, more than 250 booths display energy pyramids, massage tools, and sprout-growing paraphernalia. The biannual festival also happens the third week in October, when the emphasis is on food and health. *Tel. 415/721–2484. Admission: $7 Fri., $12 Sat. or Sun.*

MAY **Cinco de Mayo.** Vibrant mariachi bands and colorful Mexican folklórico dancers congregate in the Mission district the weekend nearest May 5 to celebrate the anniversary of Mexico's independence from France. On Sunday, floats, bands, and salsa dancers wearing little more than feathers parade through the Mission, starting at 24th and Bryant streets and ending at 8th and Market streets. *Tel. 415/647–8622.*

Festival of Greece. On May 19–21, the emphasis is on food—moussaka, dolmas, baklava—and wine, though music and Greek crafts also make an appearance. Costume-clad dancers perform for the crowds, but when the bands pull out their bouzoukis, everyone gets in on the action. Each year a few celebrities make an appearance: In years past Jeff Smith (the Frugal Gourmet) has given a demonstration, and George Stephanopoulos has showed up to cook some dolmas. The festival takes place at the Greek Orthodox Cathedral of the Ascension (4700 Lincoln Ave., at Hwy. 13 in Oakland, tel. 510/531–3400) from approximately 11 to 11 Friday and Saturday and noon to 9 on Sunday. *Tel. 510/531–3710. Admission: about $5.*

Bay to Breakers. Listed in the *Guinness Book of World Records* as the world's largest foot race, this zany 7½-mile race pits world-class runners against costumed human centipedes and huge safe-sex condom caravans. The half-comical, half-serious event attracts more than 100,000 people, who get a charge out of running (or walking, or drinking) from the Financial District across San Francisco, through Golden Gate Park, and out to Ocean Beach. The race takes place the third Sunday of every May (May 19 in 1996). Entry forms start appearing in the *San Francisco Examiner* (*see* Media, *above*) March 1. If you like crowds and silly fun, this is the event for you, but be warned that you could spend 45 minutes just jostling your way across the starting line. *Tel. 415/777–7770.*

Carnaval. On Memorial Day Weekend, long after Carnaval celebrations in New Orleans and Rio are over, the Mission district revives the party. Dozens of South American musical groups and the Aztec group Xiuhcoatc Danza Azteka are just a few of the people likely to participate. The parade along Mission and 24th streets generally starts at 11 AM on Sunday. The fair on Harrison Street (btw 16th and 22nd Sts.) features food, craft booths, and live dance and music performances. Escola Nova de Samba and Caribbean All-Stars are popular performers here. *Tel. 415/826–1401.*

JUNE Summer brings out all the neighborhood celebrations, including the **Haight Street Fair** (tel. 415/661–8025), the **Polk Street Fair** (tel. 415/346–4561), the **North Beach Festival** (tel. 415/403–0666), and the **Union Street Spring Festival** (tel. 415/346–4561), all of which feature craft booths, music, and food.

Free Folk Festival. It's surprising that more Bay Area residents haven't been turned on to the free, feel-good festival that takes place for two days every June at the John Adams Campus of City College (1860 Hayes St., at Masonic Ave. in San Francisco). Bring your guitar, harmonica, or whatever you can carry a tune on to the workshops and impromptu jam sessions that spring up between concerts of folk, blues, and international music. It's a very loosely organized event, and participants change yearly, but if you check entertainment listings in the newspapers you should be able to track it down.

Festival at the Lake. After a 1994 clash between police and young festival-goers, Oakland's Festival at the Lake, held along the shores of Lake Merritt, was back on a more peaceful track in 1995. The East Bay's largest urban fair features crafts, international food, storytelling, and world music. The festival happens the first weekend in June. *Tel. 510/286–1061. Admission: $2–$7.*

Juneteenth. The day Lincoln's Emancipation Proclamation was read in Texas is celebrated in nearly every city in the Bay Area, mostly by a scattered series of community events; keep your eye on local papers for information as June 19th approaches. One of the larger events is the **Oakland Juneteenth Celebration,** held at Lakeside Park at Lake Merritt. Organizers emphasize cultural enrichment and the history of the African-American community. Show up at the park June 16 noon–6 for big-name blues and R&B acts, ethnic food booths, arts and crafts, and lots of activities for the kids (face painting, clowns, and an interactive play area). *Tel. 510/238–3866.*

San Francisco Lesbian, Gay, Bisexual, Transgender Pride Celebration. Known as San Francisco Pride for short (and formerly known as the Gay and Lesbian Freedom Day Parade), this is San Francisco at its queer best. The parade traditionally attracts huge names in the gay community; one of 1995's grand marshals was Candice Gingrich, Newt's out half-sister. The 1996 parade and street festival will take place June 30; check local newspapers or call for location. June also brings the much-loved and internationally famous **Lesbian and Gay Film Festival** (*see* Movie Houses, in Chapter 6). *Tel. 415/864–3733.*

JULY **Fourth of July Waterfront Festival.** The biggest Independence Day celebration in the Bay Area takes place along the waterfront between Aquatic Park and Pier 39. Fireworks explode from several locations; stake out a place on the grass early to ensure a good view. Festivities start in the afternoon, when Bay Area musicians play at stages along the waterfront. The fireworks display is always impressive, even when the waterfront is fogged in. *Tel. 415/777–8498.*

Jazz and All That Art on Fillmore. In the 1940s, '50s, and '60s, the Fillmore area was locally famous for its happening jazz and blues clubs. The clubs were erased by gentrification in the '70s, but performers revive the tradition the first weekend of every July on Fillmore Street between Post and Jackson streets. Musicians, such as 72-year-old S.F. native Charles Brown, play every day from 10 to 6, while crowds wander among booths laden with arts and crafts.

And, of course, there's the requisite number of outdoor cafés serving everything from barbecue ribs to knishes. Admission to all shows is free. *Tel. 415/346–4446.*

KQED International Beer and Food Festival. If you're looking to acquire a beer belly, join 5,000 San Franciscans at the Concourse Exhibition Center (Brannan and 8th Sts.) in early July to sample 250 different beers. It's the largest international beer festival in the nation, featuring beers from around the world as well as domestic microbrews. There's live music on two stages, and food booths hand out everything from Thai cuisine to pizza. Free cable car shuttles run from Civic Center BART Station. KQED suggests that you get tickets in advance by calling the number below; members get a 15% discount on advance tickets. *Tel. 415/553–2200. Admission: about $35.*

Jewish Film Festival. Taking place during the last two weeks of July, the festival is the largest of its kind in the world. Films are shown at theaters in Berkeley and San Francisco. Call for admission prices. *Tel. 510/ 548–0556.*

Intertribal Powwow. The Oakland Zoo has teamed up with the Intertribal Friendship House to put on this one-day event, where Native American dancers and drummers get a chance to show their stuff, while vendors sell Native American crafts. The event generally takes place in late July in the Zoo Meadow, but call the number below for the latest information. *Tel. 510/632–9525.*

AUGUST The **Festival of the Sea** will appeal to people trying to get in touch with their past nautical lives. Festivities include sailmaking and rope making demonstrations, sea-faring music, and a parade of tall ships and yachts along the San Francisco waterfront. The free festival takes place at San Francisco's Hyde Street Pier, usually late in the month. *Tel. 415/929–0202.*

SEPTEMBER **San Francisco Shakespeare Festival.** Free outdoor performances of a selected Shakespeare play begin Labor Day weekend in San Francisco's Golden Gate Park. In 1996, the play will also be staged at San Jose's St. James' Park, Oakland's Duck Pond Meadow, and San Ramon's Central Park. *Tel. 415/666–2221.*

Opera in the Park. To kick off the opera season, the San Francisco Opera presents a free concert in Golden Gate Park's Sharon Meadow the Sunday after the first performance of the season, usually the week after Labor Day. The program isn't announced until the day of the show, but it usually features a few high-powered singers appearing as guest performers with the opera. *Tel. 415/861–4008.*

Festival de las Americas. This Mission district festival, celebrating the independence of Mexico and seven other Latin American countries, attracts more than 80,000 people to 24th Street between Mission and Hampshire streets. The socially responsible, alcohol-free, family-oriented event promotes pride in the Latino community. Latino musicians, ethnic food, and booths selling original crafts will crowd the streets Sunday, September 17, from 11 to 6. *Tel. 415/826–1401.*

San Francisco Blues Festival. You get big-name performers for big bucks at the country's oldest blues festival, which takes place at Fort Mason's scenic Great Meadow (cnr Marina Blvd. and Laguna St.). The lineup for the 1996 festival, September 22–23, had yet to be set at press time, but past performers have included B.B. King and Robert Cray. One-day tickets are $16.50 in advance, $20 at the door; two-day tickets are $28, advance purchase only. Performances take place 11–5:30 each day, and all seating is on the lawn. A free kick-off concert happens at the Justin Herman Plaza on September 21. *Tel. 415/826–6837 or 415/979–5588 for recorded info.*

OCTOBER **Castro Street Fair.** On the first Sunday of the month, the Castro Street Fair brings out crafts vendors; booths run by community, health, and social organizations; and musical entertainment. *Tel. 415/467–3354.*

Halloween. Traditionally, this huge, raucous, queers-only party has taken place on the closed-off streets of the Castro district, but at press time, a change of venue was being considered due to overcrowding and the recent influx of gawking "breeders." Check local papers near Halloween or ask around as the holiday approaches. And if you aren't dressed to the nines, don't even bother.

Great Halloween Pumpkin Festival. Though it takes place in San Francisco, this free festival features all the rural traditions—hayrides, pie-eating contests, a pumpkin weigh-off, and a costume parade. Bring the kids for trick-or-treating or pumpkin carving. The two-day event traditionally takes place on Polk Street (btw Broadway and Filbert St.) one or two weekends before Halloween, but call for the latest. *Tel. 415/346–4446.*

NOVEMBER **San Francisco Book Festival.** Bibliophiles eagerly await this big festival—held at the beginning of the month—at the Concourse Exhibition Center. Over 300 booths representing big publishers and small alternative presses show off their books, often selling them at a discount. About 250 authors show up to read and sign their books; Isabel Allende, Tony Hillerman, and June Jordan are just a few who have appeared in recent years. *Tel. 415/861–BOOK. Admission: $2.*

Show up late on the last day of the San Francisco Book Festival to get the best discount deals on all sorts of new books.

The day before Thanksgiving, there's a **Christmas Tree Lighting Ceremony** at Pier 39 on Fisherman's Wharf (tel. 415/981–8030). Also look for the traditional Mexican celebration of **Día de los Muertos** (Day of the Dead) on November 2 in San Francisco. Derived from Aztec rituals and the Catholic All Souls' Day, the holiday is commemorated in the Mission with art exhibitions and a parade starting from the Mission Cultural Center (2868 Mission St., tel. 415/821–1155).

Run to the Far Side with Gary Larson. More than 13,000 people dress like their favorite Gary Larson characters to compete in a 5-kilometer walk and a 10-kilometer run through Golden Gate Park on the Sunday after Thanksgiving. The cost is about $18 if you pre-register, $22 on the day of the race; the event benefits the California Academy of Sciences' environmental education programs. *Tel. 415/221–5100.*

DECEMBER In celebration of the season, the San Francisco Ballet (tel. 415/865–2000) presents ***The Nutcracker*** every year. In Oakland, the Mormon Temple (4766 Lincoln Ave., tel. 510/531–0704) holds a **tree-lighting ceremony** early in the month and offers musical entertainment during the evenings until Christmas Eve.

Celebration of Craftswomen. This fair, held during the first two weekends of December at Fort Mason, features leather work, wearable art, and glasswork along with gourmet food and live entertainment. Admission is $6 ($4 for seniors). *Tel. 415/821–6480.*

Yacht Parade. After a day of magic shows and other fun for the kids at Oakland's Jack London Square, people of all ages will get a bang out of the festively lit yachts that parade up the estuary. Call for further info and dates. *Tel. 510/814–6000.*

CLIMATE

The Bay Area is home to something called "micro-climates." In lay terms, this means that while you're burning furniture to stay warm in San Francisco's Sunset district, your friend is talking to you cordless and poolside in 80° Palo Alto, a mere 45 miles away. And when you call the **National Weather Service** (tel. 415/364–7974) to figure out what to wear, they tell you something helpful about "highs from the upper 50s to the low 90s." At least if you call between 10 and 6 you can talk to a live meteorologist, who might be able to narrow things down. For ski conditions in Northern California, Tahoe, or the Sierras, call the **California State Automobile Association's Ski Report** (tel. 415/864–6440).

SAN FRANCISCO A local writer in the *East Bay Express* put it best: When it comes to San Francisco weather, "summer is winter, winter is spring, and fall is summer." In sum, it never snows here, but it's cold and windy a lot of the time—except in September and October, the Indian summer months. Late fall gets real cold, it rains pretty often in winter, and June is notoriously blustery and foggy. The average high temperature is 69°, the average low 46°.

EAST BAY The East Bay tends to be a few degrees warmer than San Francisco. Summer is mild, fall hot, winter unpredictable but usually rainy, and spring mild again. Overall, the climate here is pretty fabulous, especially if you enjoy mellow, overcast days or cool but sunny afternoons. It's smart to layer your clothing, because there's no guarantee that the morning's foggy turtleneck weather won't betray you and become an afternoon tank-top heat wave. Highs average 72°, lows 43°.

MARIN COUNTY In a region of micro-climates, Marin goes one better: Even within the county, the weather differs from town to town. The coast is usually fogged in, the bayside towns of Tiburon and Sausalito get a cool breeze, and San Rafael checks in at a solid few degrees warmer than most of the Bay Area (with an average summer high of 82°).

SOUTH BAY Don't move to the South Bay if you thrive on unpredictability. Spring and fall are sunny and warm, and summer is sunny and hot (average summer highs, both on the coast and inland, hover in the 80s). In the winter, things cool down to a medium-rare, with lows dipping to 40°.

VISITOR INFORMATION

SAN FRANCISCO If you're into pre-trip planning, write or call the **San Francisco Convention and Visitors Bureau** for free info about hotels, restaurants, festivals, and shopping. *201 3rd St., Suite 900, 94103, tel. 415/974–6900. 3 blocks from Montgomery St. BART. Open weekdays 8:30–5.*

Visitors can stop in for maps and brochures at the city's **Visitor Information Center** in the lower level of Hallidie Plaza, next to the Powell Street BART station. Their phone number also connects you to an events hotline. *Tel. 415/391–2000. Open weekdays 9–5:30, Sat. 9–3, Sun. 10–2.*

EAST BAY Stop by the straight-laced **Berkeley Convention and Visitors Bureau** for a decent selection of pamphlets and listings of Berkeley events. *1834 University Ave., at Martin Luther King Jr. Way, tel. 510/549–7040 or 510/549–8710 for recorded info. Open weekdays 9–5.*

The **East Bay Regional Parks District** has maps and information about the 46 parks and 13 regional trails in the Oakland hills. *2950 Peralta Oaks Ct., at 106th St. in Oakland, tel. 510/635–0135. Open weekdays 8:30–5.*

Walk This Way

Have a laugh at all the bus-riding, pastel-clad, camera-toting tourists that infiltrate Fisherman's Wharf if you like, but don't let them turn you off tours entirely. Even longtime residents can learn something from the enthusiastic guides, who know the city's neighborhoods inside out. Wok Wiz Chinatown Tours and Cooking Company (tel. 415/981–5588) leads the popular I Can't Believe I Ate My Way Through Chinatown tour ($50). Though the name is pure fromage, this is a great way to single out the neighborhood's best restaurants and learn a lot about Chinese cuisine from cookbook author Shirley Fong-Torres. Tours usually start on Saturday mornings at 10 and end, according to Shirley, "when the first person explodes." Trevor Hailey (375 Lexington St., tel. 415/550–8110), a prominent member of the San Francisco lesbian community, leads a highly recommended tour of the city's famous gay neighborhood called Cruisin' the Castro ($30). The 3½-hour tour, which includes brunch, leaves about four times a week; call for reservations. Finally, to be led around San Francisco for free, call City Guides (tel. 415/557–4266), whose frequent guided walks are sponsored by the San Francisco Public Library. Tours, which cover almost every corner of town, include Roof Gardens and Open Spaces, the Telegraph Hill Hike, Art-Deco Marina, and the Mission Murals. Quality varies according to the skills of the library volunteer, but it's hard to beat being shown around the city for free by an enthusiastic local.

The **Oakland Convention and Visitors Bureau** is geared toward convention-goers, but the staff is happy to answer all inquiries. Pick up a copy of their small pamphlet, "The Official Visitors Guide," which lists dozens of museums, historical attractions, and community events. *1000 Broadway, Suite 200, tel. 510/839–9000. From 12th St. BART, walk down Broadway to 11th Street. Open weekdays 8:30–5.*

MARIN COUNTY The **Marin County Convention and Visitors Bureau** distributes the free *Weekender Magazine,* which lists live music and cultural events in the area. *Marin Center, on Avenue of the Flags in San Rafael, tel. 415/472–7470. Open weekdays 8:30–5.*

Point Reyes National Seashore's **Bear Valley Visitors Center** has exhibits on park wildlife, topographical and hiking maps, and loads of information on exploring the area. Look for the sign marking the turnoff for the center a quarter-mile past Olema on Bear Valley Road. *Tel. 415/663–1092. Open weekdays 9–5, weekends 8–5.*

For recorded info on music, theater, sports, and all sorts of entertainment in Oakland, call the city's 24-hour cultural arts hotline (tel. 510/835–2787).

Muir Woods Visitor Center. *Tel. 415/388–2596 or 415/388–2595 for recorded information. Take U.S. 101 north to the Stinson Beach/Hwy. 1 exit and follow the signs to Muir Woods. Open daily 8–6.*

The **West Marin Chamber of Commerce** (Box 1045, Point Reyes Station 94956, tel. 415/663–9232) has a free pamphlet, "The Coastal Traveler," with great information on out-of-the-way beaches, bike rides, and backpacking trips. You can also visit the **West Marin Network** to get information on activities in the region. *Center Mesa Rd., 3 mi north of Olema on Hwy. 1, tel. 415/663–9543. Open Mon.–Sat. 9–6.*

SOUTH BAY The **Palo Alto Chamber of Commerce** (325 Forest Ave., Palo Alto, tel. 415/324–3121) has maps of the city, as well as limited information on sights, restaurants, and lodging.

The **San Jose Convention and Visitors Bureau** (150 W. San Carlos St., San Jose, tel. 408/283–8833) is open weekdays 8–5:30, weekends 11–5. You can call the **San Jose Events Hotline** (tel. 408/295–2265) anytime for listings of community events and after-dark diversions.

The **Pacifica Chamber of Commerce** has info on Pacifica and Montara as well as limited materials about Half Moon Bay and points south. *450 Dondee Way #2, Pacifica, tel. 415/355–4122. Near Rockaway Beach. Open weekdays 9–noon and 1–5, weekends 10–4:30.*

The friendly staff at the **Half Moon Bay Chamber of Commerce** will give you more info than you ever wanted on Half Moon Bay and the immediately surrounding area, as well as a smattering of maps and brochures for the entire San Mateo County Coast. *520 Kelly Ave., Half Moon Bay, tel. 415/726–8380. Open weekdays 10–4.*

At the **Half Moon Bay State Parks District Office** you'll find limited information on state parks and beaches from Montara to Año Nuevo. *95 Kelly Ave., Half Moon Bay, tel. 415/726–8800. Open weekdays 8–5.*

EXPLORING THE BAY AREA 2

By Alice Chang, Baty Landis, David Walter, and Sharron Wood

You'll never run out of opportunities for adventure in the Bay Area, no matter how long you stay. San Francisco is a cosmopolitan city with a European ambience. The best way to explore is by walking its dozen distinct neighborhoods; along the way, you'll encounter shops, parks, and cafés that invite you to stop and soak up the atmosphere. On days when you feel more rugged, head for Marin County's stunning cliffs, forests, and beaches—an impressive backdrop to the multimillion-dollar homes that dot the landscape. The East Bay offers acres of hilly parks with incredible views of the city and the bay beyond. The East Bay's two major cities are Berkeley, known for its university, its radical politics, and its wacky street people; and Oakland, a sprawling, unpretentious city with a strong African American identity. If you miss the bland suburban flavor that pervades much of the rest of the United States, check out the South Bay. Hidden in the 70 or so miles of sprawl is one of the better-kept of the Bay Area's myriad secrets: the striking, wind-swept San Mateo County Coast.

San Francisco

No matter how well you think you know San Francisco, the dense, eclectic city will surprise you. Whatever's hit the streets, from the drinking and whoring of the gold prospectors to the living and loving of the country's largest lesbian and gay population, has left reminders of its presence in nooks and crannies all over this eminently explorable city. And damn, it all changes so quickly. One minute you're marveling at the frenetic pace of Financial District workers and the next you're strolling through Chinese herb shops and produce markets. You down a cappuccino and biscotti at a noisy Italian café, and 10 minutes later you're gazing at the Golden Gate Bridge from the water's edge. Bored? You should be ashamed of yourself.

You can spend endless days—and no money at all—just kicking around the hilly streets. Expound upon the latest artistic trend as you gallery-hop South of Market; get your exercise climbing through other people's backyards on hidden stairway streets; gawk at the mansions that dominate the peaks of Pacific Heights and the Presidio; or get lost for a day in Golden Gate Park. When your dogs get tired, as they inevitably will on the dizzying hills in some parts of the city, hop a bus for a higher-speed version of the San Francisco scene. You can get a MUNI transportation map at most liquor and grocery stores for $2; carry it with you, and when you're all tuckered out you should be able to find a bus to take you someplace interesting.

Golden Gate Bridge
Fort Point National Historic Site
101
Golden Gate National Recreation Area
PACIFIC OCEAN
1
The Presidio
Baker Beach
Phelan Beach
W. Pacific Ave.
Presidio Ave.
Lands End
Lincoln Park
Palace of the Legion of Honor
SEACLIFF
Lake St.
Clement St.
8th Ave.
Arguello Blvd.
Park Presidio Blvd.
Point Lobos
Cliff House
43rd Ave.
34th Ave.
Geary Blvd.
25th Ave.
19th Ave.
Balboa St.
Turk
Masonic Ave.
RICHMOND
Fulton St.
Golden Gate Park
Kennedy Dr.
Middle Dr.
Martin Luther King Jr. Dr.
Stanyan St.
Clayton St.
COLE VALLEY
Lincoln Way
Judah St.
Funston Ave.
7th Ave.
28th Ave.
Lawton St.
Ocean Beach
Great Highway
Noriega St.
Ortega St.
19th Ave.
Clarendon Ave.
SUNSET
41st Ave.
Sunset Blvd.
Quintara St.
McCoppin Square
14th Ave.
Dewey Blvd.
Taraval St.
Larsen Park
Vicente St.
Mt. Davidson
Portola Dr.
Yerba Buena Ave.
Stern Grove
San Francisco Zoo
Sloat Blvd
STONESTOWN
Monterey Blvd.
Ocean Ave.
Miramar Ave.
Junipero Serra Blvd.
Harding Park
Lake Merced
Skyline Blvd.
Lake Merced Blvd.
San Francisco State Univ.
Font Blvd.
Holloway Ave.
Garfield St.
Fort Funston
Brotherhood Way
Plymouth Ave.
280
35
N
0
1 mile
0
1 km

San Francisco

Major Sights

With the exception of Fisherman's Wharf, which bludgeons visitors with its banality, San Francisco's major sights are considered major for a reason. Even the most jaded natives can't help but inhale a reverent breath at the sight of the Golden Gate Bridge looming overhead. The Alcatraz tour explores such a fascinating place—on such a genuinely stark, scary island—that, for all the hype, it is utterly compelling. This is the city's true appeal: Despite the best efforts of merchants selling tourist schlock, the spirit of San Francisco refuses to yield, and the real city pulses through the neon surface.

GOLDEN GATE BRIDGE

The bridge to end all bridges has come to symbolize San Francisco more than any other monument. This masterpiece of design and engineering, which links San Francisco to its wealthy neighbor, Marin County, has endured winds, fogs, the ignominy of over 1,000 suicides, and the weight of more than 200,000 people who showed up to celebrate its 50th birthday in 1987. More than a mile long, the bridge is painted International Orange for visibility in fog (so the seagulls don't crash into it). Engineer Joseph Strauss designed the bridge to withstand winds of more than 100 miles per hour and to swing nearly 27 feet in its center. The cables that support it are more than 3 feet in diameter, and the combined lengths of the individual strands would wrap around the earth three times.

In order to catch a glimpse of the bridge, you'll have to scale a hill or two or head to the waterfront near Fisherman's Wharf. Bus 28 will drop you at the toll plaza, located at the northern tip of the Presidio (*see* Neighborhoods, *below*), from which point you can hoof it or hitch. And of course, you'll want to cross the bridge. To walk across and back takes about an hour and the wind can be freezing. Bicycling across the bridge is a thrill; Lincoln Boulevard in the Presidio is a gorgeous way to get there. (To reach Lincoln, take a gentle ride west down Lombard Street, or go for the screaming downhill adventure by approaching from the south on Presidio Boulevard.) The pedestrian walkway and the bicycle path are both open 5 AM–9 PM.

Four Great Views of Golden Gate Bridge

- ***Up close, from Municipal Pier in front of the Maritime Museum, just west of Fisherman's Wharf. Walk all the way out until you feel almost surrounded by water and you'll see the bridge, picture perfect, in one direction and the city in miniature in the other.***
- ***From Fort Point, a brick and granite fortification that defended the bridge from 1861 until 1943, when the army transferred it to the National Park Service. Brave the rough winds and climb up to the roof for superlative views of the Golden Gate directly overhead. A trail connects the fort to the bridge's toll plaza. Fort Point is open daily 10–5 and admission is free.***
- ***From Baker Beach. The bridge looms above to your right, the ocean extends endlessly to your left, and the craggy, green Marin Headlands lie right in front of you. It's one of the most beautiful views in the city.***
- ***From Grizzly Peak Boulevard in the Berkeley Hills, one of the few spots where you can see the entire span backlit as the sun sinks into the Pacific.***

ALCATRAZ ISLAND

Known as the Rock, Alcatraz Island served for 60 years as the nation's most notorious federal penitentiary, holding high-risk prisoners in its isolated maw. Al Capone, Robert "The Birdman" Stroud, and Machine Gun Kelly were among the more famous bad guys who got "Rock fever" gazing out day after day at the bittersweet sight of San Francisco.

Of course, ever since the prison closed in 1963, people have been trying to get onto Alcatraz Island rather than off it. In 1969, a group of Native Americans attempted to reclaim the land, saying that an 1868 federal treaty allowed Native Americans to use all federal territory that the government wasn't actively using. After almost two years of occupation, the United States government forced them off, none too gently. The bloody incident is recounted in the island's small museum, and graffiti still reminds visitors that "This is Native American Land."

Today the island is part of the national park system, and tourists visit the grounds in hordes—though even heavy weekend crowds don't affect the lonely, somber, abandoned feel of the place. Rangers on Alcatraz offer a variety of free talks—subjects include the island's history as a 19th-century military fort, the Native American occupation, and Alcatraz's unique properties as part of an island chain in San Francisco Bay. Check for schedules at the ranger station at the ferry landing when you arrive or call the dock office at 415/705–1042.

The **Red and White Fleet** (tel. 415/546–2896 for info or 415/546–2700 for tickets) ferries you to the island from San Francisco's Pier 41. The price ($9) includes the ferry ride and an audiocassette tour of the prison itself; tapes are available in several languages, and the average tour takes about 2½ hours. You can skip the cassette tour and pay only $5.75, but the tape, which features former inmates and guards talking about their experiences on Alcatraz, is one of the best parts of the experience. Ferries leave Pier 41 9:30 AM–2:15 PM year-round and until 4:15 PM June–August. You'll need a Visa, American Express, or MasterCard to reserve tickets by phone and you'll pay a $2 service charge. If you're buying tickets in person, go to the ferry ticket office (open 8:30–5) at Pier 41. You should reserve or purchase tickets *several* days in advance. During the summer months, ferries may be booked three or four days ahead of time. Bus 32 will get you to Pier 41 from the Ferry Building downtown. All tours are wheelchair accessible.

FISHERMAN'S WHARF

Once the domain of Italian fishermen, the wharf is now San Francisco's prize tourist trap, whose sole purpose is to get you to spend money. You won't get to see many fishermen here unless you arrive in the misty early morning hours (around 5 AM) to watch the fishing boats unload. Otherwise, it's schlock city. Jefferson Street, the wharf's main drag, is now packed with expensive seafood restaurants, tacky souvenir shops, and rip-off "museums" like the **Wax Museum, Ripley's Believe It or Not!,** the **Guinness Museum of World Records, The Haunted Gold Mine,** and the **Medieval Dungeon** (featuring graphic re-creations of torture devices from the Middle Ages). Each can be yours for the low admission price of $6–$9. The only thing that remains fairly authentic (albeit rather pricey) is the array of seafood stands along Jefferson Street. Buy clam chowder ($3–$4) or a half-pound of shrimp ($6) from one of the sidewalk vendors and a loaf of sourdough bread ($2.50–$3) from **Boudin Bakery** (156 Jefferson St., tel. 415/928–1849), and eat on one of the piers, watching cruise ships and fishing boats glide in and out of the harbor. Then hightail it out of there to catch a ferry to Alcatraz (*see above*) or Angel Island (*see* Tiburon and Angel Island, in Marin County, *below*) or walk over to Fort Mason to check out the museums.

Comedian Jonathan Winters was once briefly institutionalized after he climbed the mast of the Balclutha and hung from it, shouting "I am the man in the moon!"

If you must stick around the wharf, check out the **Maritime Museum** (Beach St., at foot of Polk St., tel. 415/929–0202), housed in an art-deco building that features all sorts of artifacts from the maritime history of San Francisco. The museum is free, but if you have $2 to spare, you might have more fun walking around on one of the old ships at Hyde Street Pier, between the

Cannery and Ghirardelli Square. Among the ships docked there are the ***Balclutha,*** a 100-year-old square-rigged ship, and the ***Eureka,*** an old ferry that now holds a classic car collection.

Three shopping complexes girdle the wharf: **Pier 39,** the **Cannery,** and **Ghirardelli Square.** Owned by the billionaire Bass brothers of Texas, Pier 39 is a bland imitation of a turn-of-the-century New England seaport village—the shopping mall of your worst nightmares. Pier 39's one redeeming quality is the swarm of sea lions that took over several of the marina docks next to the development a few years ago and have refused to leave. The owners wanted them removed, (killed if necessary) until they realized the barking sea mammals were attracting more tourists. To shake the "I'm-being-ripped-off" feeling that accompanies any visit to Pier 39, eat at the Eagle Café (*see* Chapter 4); take a moment to read the yellowed news clippings describing how the establishment was lifted whole from its former location in 1978 and plunked down on the upper level of the pier.

A former Del Monte peach-canning factory, the **Cannery** (Jefferson, Leavenworth, Beach, and Hyde Sts., tel. 415/771–3112) is now a gallery of chic boutiques. Chocolate is no longer made on-site at **Ghirardelli Square** (900 North Point St., tel. 415/775–5500), but you can buy it here in bars or atop a huge, tasty ice cream sundae ($5.50). To reach Fisherman's Wharf, take MUNI Bus 32 from the Ferry Building downtown. Or fulfill your other tourist obligation by taking a cable car from Powell Street (*see* Getting In, Out, and Around, in Chapter 1) to the end of the line (a nice metaphor for Fisherman's Wharf).

COIT TOWER

Built to memorialize San Francisco's volunteer firefighters, the 210-foot concrete observation tower atop Telegraph Hill is named for the colorful woman who left the funds to build it, Lillie Hitchcock Coit (1843–1929). Heiress Coit was a cross-dresser (in men's clothes she could gain access to the most interesting realms of San Francisco) who literally chased fire engines around town. Most people agree the building looks like a fire nozzle, though, supposedly, that was not intentional.

The walls inside the lobby are covered with Depression-era murals in the style of Diego Rivera, painted by local artists on the government dole. **City Guides** (tel. 415/557–4266) offers free descriptive tours of the murals every Saturday at 11 AM, including the second-floor works normally closed to the public. For $3, the elevator inside the tower will take you to the top for a drop-dead, 360° view of Golden Gate Bridge, the Bay Bridge, and Alcatraz Island. One warning: If you have a car, you will get a headache trying to park near Coit Tower on weekends. *Tel. 415/362–0808. From Market and 3rd Sts. downtown, Bus 30 or 45 to Washington Sq.; walk 2 blocks east on Union St., left on Kearny St. Or Bus 39 from Fisherman's Wharf to top of Telegraph Hill. Tower open daily 10–6:30.*

GOLDEN GATE PARK

The western keyhole to San Francisco is Golden Gate Park—1,000 acres of plant life, museums, Dutch windmills, sporting events, open-air performances, and even a herd of bison. Packed into an area that is 4 miles long and less than a mile wide are zillions of varieties of vegetation, wooded areas, wide swaths of grass, and tiny gardens. And, as a bonus, if you make it all the way to the western end of the park, you'll hit blustery Ocean Beach and the Pacific Ocean. Bordered on its east side by Haight Street, the park has always been a natural hangout for the countercultural denizens of that neighborhood: Hippie historians should note that Ken Kesey and friends celebrated the first **Human Be-In** here on January 14, 1966. The park has also hosted rock concerts ranging from the Grateful Dead and the Jefferson Airplane to Peter Gabriel's WOMAD (World of Music and Dance) and Pearl Jam.

Once a collection of sand dunes, Golden Gate Park was designed in 1868 by William Hammond Hall, a 24-year-old civil engineer with no prior experience (his bid was lowest), and landscaped by John MacLaren. The park is the largest of its kind and is much prettier than New York's Central Park, debunking the claim of that park's designer, Frederick Law Olmsted (who also designed the Stanford University campus), that "beautiful trees could not be made to grow

Golden Gate Park

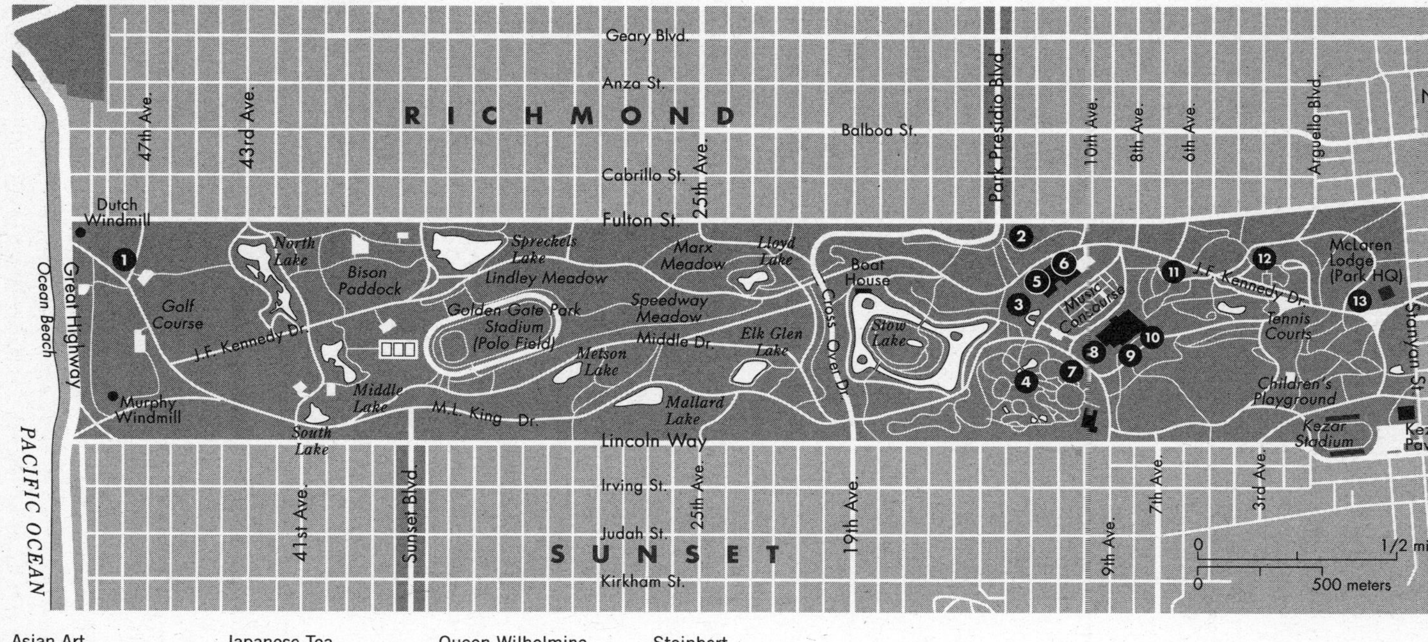

Asian Art Museum, **5**

California Academy of Sciences, **8**

Conservatory, **12**

Fuchsia Garden, **13**

Japanese Tea Garden, **3**

M.H. de Young Memorial Museum, **6**

Morrison Planetarium, **10**

Queen Wilhelmina Tulip Garden, **1**

Rhododendron Dell, **11**

Rose Garden, **2**

Shakespeare Garden, **7**

Steinhart Aquarium, **9**

Strybing Arboretum, **4**

in San Francisco." Today, blue gum eucalyptus, Monterey pine, and Monterey cypress, not to mention one of the world's foremost horticultural displays, are peppered throughout the park.

The park's first building was the delicate **Victorian Conservatory** (off John F. Kennedy Dr., near east entrance, tel. 415/752–8080), a knockoff of London's Kew Gardens that features a tropical garden and exotic orchids. Admission is $1.50. **Strybing Arboretum and Botanical Gardens** (tel. 415/661–1316), off Martin Luther King Dr. near the museum complex, has a more dazzling display of 70 acres of plants, featuring some 5,000 specimens arranged by country of origin, genus, and fragrance. Admission is free. One of the park's star attractions is the **Japanese Tea Garden,** (tel. 415/752–4227) originally built for the 1894 Mid-Winter Fair, San Francisco's first world's fair. During the week or on a rainy day, the garden is well worth the $2 admission (free before 9:30 AM); at other times, crowds spoil any chance at contemplative serenity. The meticulously designed garden, open daily 9–6:30, features an exquisite 18th-century Buddha and a scanty number of koi in the fish ponds—survivors of raids by local raccoons and hawks. The Hagiwara family took care of the garden until World War II when they, along with other Japanese Americans, were removed to internment camps. In 1994, on the garden's 100th-year anniversary, a cherry blossom tree was planted in their memory.

The park's many free gardens include the **Shakespeare Garden,** which features all the types of plants that are mentioned in Shakespeare's works—don't eat the nightshade. With its comfortable benches and the opportunity to muse over quotations engraved in bronze, it's perfect for a contemplative moment; the **Rose Garden,** especially in early June, is too noisy to be at all contemplative. There's also **Rhododendron Dell, Fuchsia Garden,** and the **Queen Wilhelmina Tulip Garden,** with its two nearby Dutch windmills. A herd of bison lives near the park's northwest end, though it usually takes some effort to see them in the large paddock.

On Sundays, John F. Kennedy Drive, the park's main thoroughfare, is closed to car traffic between Stanyan Street and 19th Avenue, when flocks of bicyclists, in-line skaters, and skateboarders take over. Hang out by the Conservatory and watch some expert bladers do their thing.

The park's fixtures also include three world-class museums: the **Asian Art Museum;** the **M. H. de Young Memorial Museum,** notable for its collection of American art; and the **California Academy of Sciences** (*see* Museums, *below*). Or head to the **Laserium** (in the California Academy of Sciences, tel. 415/750–7138), where *Dark Side of the Moon, Lollapalaser,* and other high-tech music and light shows are projected onto the planetarium's dome. Shows are held three or four times daily Thursday–Sunday, and admission is $7 (matinee $6).

Golden Gate Park is bordered by Stanyan Street, the Great Highway, Lincoln Way, and Fulton Street. Several places near the park rent bikes and in-line skates. **Park Cyclery** (1749 Waller St., at Stanyan St., tel. 415/752–8383) rents mountain bikes for $5 an hour or $30 a day. **Skate Pro Sports** (27th Ave., at Irving St., tel. 415/752–8776), near a less traveled part of the park, offers a good deal on blades: $20 a day, including pads and helmet. To reach the park from downtown or Civic Center, take Bus 5, 71, or 73.

Neighborhoods

Though the city of San Francisco is only 49 square miles, its neighborhoods often seem worlds apart. Each district is a distinct entity culturally, socially, and often politically, and they are all fascinating grounds for urban exploration. The best way to experience the city's neighborhoods is to plunk yourself down in one and walk until you drop, preferably into a chair on some café patio. You can use a map to plan your walks, or just start off in an interesting spot and surrender to the whims of the streets. Certain parts of the city lend themselves especially well to the second type of exploration. One such area is the Mission–Noe Valley–Castro region. Get off BART at 16th and Mission streets, and head west on 16th or south on Mission or Valencia, or do a little bit of both. In either direction, you'll find a real neighborhood: funky shops, galleries, cafés, and restaurants aplenty when it's time to refuel.

DOWNTOWN

For better or worse, downtown is grand old San Francisco, the San Francisco of tea dances and cocktail hours and piano bars and fedoras and big winter overcoats: Looking up at the beautiful architectural details, you can forget what decade it is. Noteworthy architectural stops include the 1929 art deco **Shell Building** (100 Bush St., btw Battery and Sansome Sts.) and the 1926 chateauesque-and Romanesque-style **Hunter-Dulin Building** (111 Sutter St., btw Montgomery and Kearny Sts.). The modern face of downtown is still big, though maybe not so grand—big consumerism, big banking, big cafeterias, and waitresses with big hair. But look a little lower and you'll descry dozens of low-rent electronics stores and hundreds of nomadic homeless people. It's typical cosmopolitan walking territory, with all of the fascinating and horrifying elements of urban American life.

UNION SQUARE Union Square is the physical heart—though not the soul—of the city, especially for tourists who come to shop, browse the galleries, attend the theater, and then sleep in the finer hotels. The square, bordered by Powell, Post, Stockton, and Geary streets, was named in honor of rallies held prior to the Civil War in support of the Union. Some San Franciscans will tell you the name more appropriately refers to the huge demonstrations held here in the 1930s by labor organizations, which at one point effectively shut down the city for a week.

Today, Union Square consists of a park (graced with a few palm trees to remind you that you're still in California) encircled by a ring—make that a solid gold band—of the city's ritziest stores and boutiques, including Neiman-Marcus, Saks, Chanel, Tiffany, Cartier, Hermès, and Gump's. The park can be a relaxing place to rest your weary feet after a hard day's window-shopping, if you don't mind pigeons and homeless folks for company. At Christmas time, merchants haul in some snow and dump it in the park to satisfy all those who have dreamed in vain for a "White Christmas" in California. By nightfall it starts to get a little seedy, so it may be time to hop a bus out of here.

Heading south on Powell Street from Union Square, you'll come to the intersection of Market and Powell streets. Everyone passes through here: proselytizers, street musicians, artists, punks,

Two Mind-Blowing San Francisco Tours

- ***When city-style craziness has just about done you in, head out of the concrete canyons of downtown and surrender yourself to Golden Gate Park (see Major Sights, above). Romp among the rhododendrons and spend a meditative moment among fragrant eucalyptus trees. To induce a rapture that will last for days, head farther west to Ocean Beach and the Pacific Ocean, then north to Lands End, a quiet, green, almost wild chunk of land where the ocean and bay meet. The views of the water, the Golden Gate Bridge, and the Marin Headlands are not of this world, which is entirely the point.***

- ***For a quick tour of some of the city's most varied neighborhoods that only costs a buck, hop on MUNI's 30 Stockton Bus. From the Montgomery Street BART Station, the bus transports you through the thick of downtown up to Broadway, then west on Columbus Avenue past North Beach. Skirting the Victorian homes of San Francisco's upper crust on Russian Hill, the bus continues along Chestnut Street to the Palace of Fine Arts, the Exploratorium, and reaches the eastern edge of the Presidio at the end of the line. The route then returns through the picturesque Marina and touristy Ghirardelli Square, back up Columbus, and then plows through the heart of Chinatown on Stockton Street before depositing you back on Market Street at the Powell Street BART Station.***

San Francisco

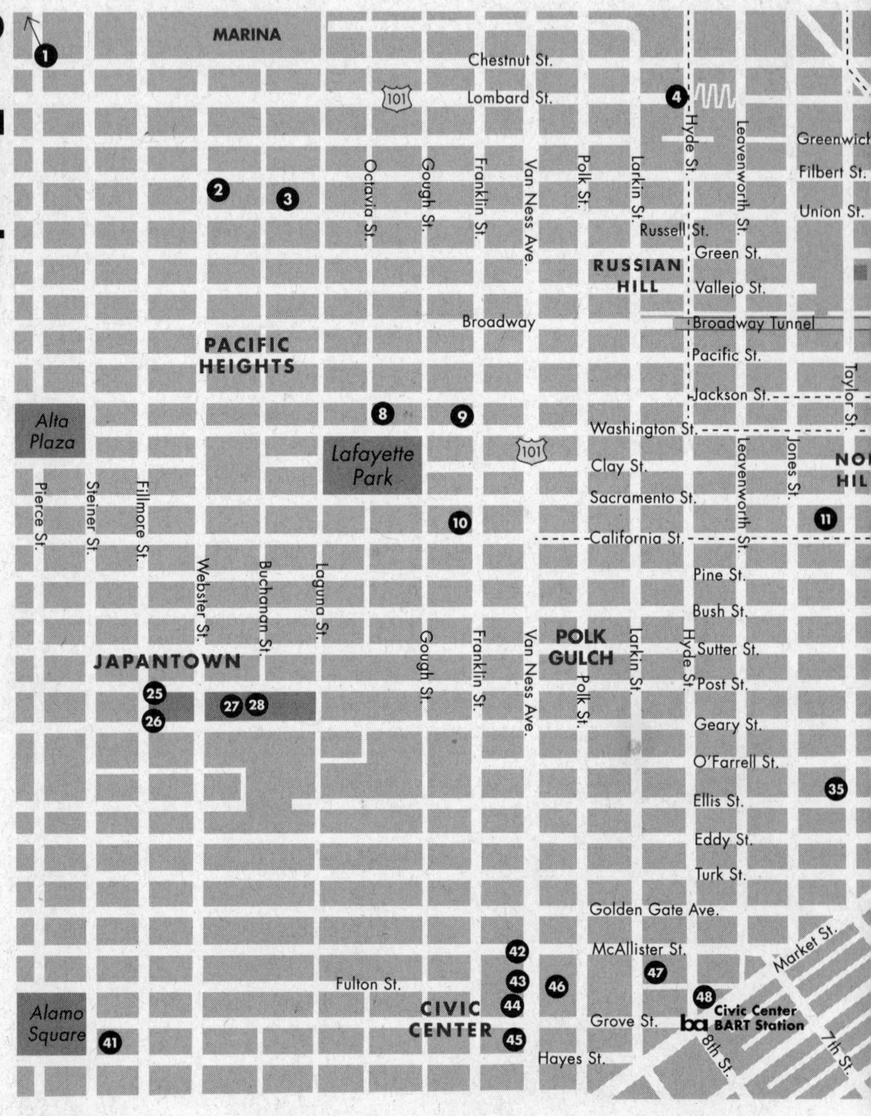

Ansel Adams Center, **54**

Bank of America World Headquarters, **30**

Cable Car Museum, **12**

Capp Street Project, **56**

Cartoon Art Museum, **50**

Center for the Arts, **52**

Chinatown Gate, **29**

Chinese Historical Society of America, **20**

Chinese Telephone Exchange, **16**

Circle Gallery, **36**

City Hall, **46**

City Lights Bookstore, **13**

Coit Tower, **7**

Coleman House, **10**

Crocker Plaza, **37**

Embarcadero Center, **22**

Ferry Building, **24**

Glide Memorial Methodist Church, **35**

Golden Gate Fortune Cookie Factory, **14**

Grace Cathedral, **11**

Haas-Lilienthal House, **9**

Hallidie Building, **38**

Herbst Theatre, **43**

Hunter-Dulin Building, **39**

Jackson Square, **18**

Japan Center, **28**

Jewish Community Museum, **34**

Justin Herman Plaza, **23**

Kabuki Hot Springs, **26**

Kabuki 8 Theatres, **25**

Lombard Street, **4**

Louise M. Davies Symphony Hall, **45**

Main Library, **47**

North Beach Museum, **6**

Old Temple, **2**

Pacific Stock Exchange, **31**

Painted Ladies, **41**

Palace of Fine Arts, **1**

Peace Plaza, **27**

Portsmouth Square, **17**

Rincon Center, **33**

San Francisco Centre, **49**

San Francisco Museum of Modern Art, **53**

Shell Building, **32**

South Park, **55**

Spreckels Mansion, **8**

Tin Hou Temple, **15**

Transamerica Pyramid, **19**

Transbay Terminal, **40**

United Nations Plaza, **48**

Veterans Building, **42**

War Memorial Opera House, **44**

Washington Square, **5**

Wedding Houses, **3**

Wells Fargo History Museum, **21**

Yerba Buena Gardens, **51**

young professionals, vendors, protesters, dogs, pigeons, and tourists in matching jogging suits. All converge around the cable-car turnaround, the Powell Street BART Station, and the **San Francisco Visitor Information Center** (900 Market St., tel. 415/391–2000), tucked below the street in the underground Hallidie Plaza.

The stretch of **Market Street** near Union Square is home to a string of cheap fast-food joints and, adjoining the Emporium department store, San Francisco's latest monument to shopping, the **San Francisco Shopping Centre** (865 Market St., at 5th St., tel. 415/495–5656). Ride the seven-story-high vertiginous spiral of escalators that surrounds the open interior of the building, leading up to Nordstrom, an expensive department store.

➢ **MAIDEN LANE** • This short alley off the east side of Union Square was once the lair of the "cribs" (brothels) that formed the center of a notorious and extremely violent red-light district. Now it's a shopping arcade for the thick-walleted and the site of San Francisco's only Frank Lloyd Wright building, the **Circle Gallery** (140 Maiden Ln., tel. 415/989–2100), which served as the prototype for the Guggenheim Museum in New York. Wright also designed the gallery's gorgeous Philippine mahogany cabinets and chairs. The gallery sells paintings by artists as incongruous as *Love To Love You Baby* diva Donna Summer, Yaacov Agam, and fashion illustrator René Gruau.

FINANCIAL DISTRICT San Francisco is the financial capital of the West Coast; the center of San Francisco's Financial District is **Montgomery Street,** the "Wall Street of the West," where the towers of wealth block out the sun at street level. This part of town is built on landfill comprised of the remains of hundreds of abandoned ships and docks. Nowadays, it's a monument to the Type A personality, where traffic lights stop vehicles in all four directions to allow harried office workers to cross diagonally and bicycle messengers to cheat death.

Since you're in the Financial District, you may as well see what those monstrously large California banks are doing with your savings. You'll find the glowering **Bank of America World Headquarters** at the corner of California and Kearny streets. Its north plaza is graced with a black granite shard of public art officially called *Transcendence,* but popularly known as "The Banker's Heart." Up on the 52nd story in the elegant **Carnelian Room** (tel. 415/433–7500), you can nurse a $6.50 cocktail and gaze in wonder at the city below. Bank of America's archrival, Wells Fargo Bank, lures you in with the free **Wells Fargo History Museum** (420 Mont-

Welcome All Ye Sinners

Ever been to church and come away humming, tapping your toes, and with the phone number of the stranger you sat next to? Enjoy all of the religion, and none of the guilt, at Glide Memorial United Methodist Church. You may not see a single religious icon at the Sunday morning "celebration" presided over by a beaming Reverend Cecil Williams in his colorful robe. Instead of organ music, a funky band and choir give parishioners reason to stand up and groove with the music when the spirit moves them. Celebrations at Glide attract all ethnicities, classes, and sexual orientations. Bobby McFerrin often comes to Glide; Bill Clinton and Maya Angelou stopped in when they were in town. The Rev. Williams is also a famous community activist in San Francisco; among the many community programs offered at Glide are a daily free meal program, an HIV/AIDS project, a families in crisis center, recovery programs for men and women, and women's health services. Celebrations occur every Sunday morning at 9 and 11. It gets crowded and hot in here, so try to arrive a few minutes early. 330 Ellis St., at Taylor St., tel. 415/ 771–6300. From Powell St. BART/MUNI, walk 1 block on Powell St., left on Ellis St.

gomery St., tel. 415/396–2619), detailing the history of California's oldest bank and interminably celebrating the short-lived but picturesque Pony Express. Nearby, two giant sculptures, *Earth's Fruitfulness* and *Man's Inventive Genius,* attempt to inject some life and soul into one of the least fruitful, least inventive places in the city: the **Pacific Stock Exchange,** on the south side of Pine Street at Sansome Street. It's closed to the public.

➢ **TRANSAMERICA PYRAMID** • A high concentration of San Francisco's architectural landmarks are in the Financial District, including the Transamerica Pyramid (600 Montgomery St., btw Clay and Washington Sts.), *the* distinguishing feature of the San Francisco skyline, whose perky peak sophisticated locals at first studiously ignored. You can ride the elevator to the 27th-floor observation area for a bird's eye view of Coit Tower and down Columbus Avenue, but the building itself seems much less impressive once you're in it. Adjacent to the Pyramid, a little redwood park, complete with fountain, provides a peaceful retreat from the frenzied commercial pace—the perfect setting for an urban picnic. The park is open weekdays 8–6. A block north, **Jackson Square,** lined with expensive antique shops and upholstery stores, has some of the few buildings that survive from the days when this area was overrun with brothels and saloons, not stockbrokers. The atmosphere of gentility and calm here contrasts markedly with the frenzied and rapacious feel of the rest of the Financial District.

➢ **CROCKER PLAZA** • When you're ready for a respite from the crowded downtown streets, retreat to one of two rooftop gardens on top of Crocker Galleria (50 Post St., near Montgomery St.). The one on top of the Wells Fargo Bank has the better view, but both are beautiful places to eat lunch and look down at the bewildered tourists and bustling corporate tools. Two blocks northeast, the 1917 **Hallidie Building** (130 Sutter St., btw Kearny and Montgomery Sts.), dedicated to the inventor of the cable car (*see box, below*), has the dubious distinction of being the first glass curtain office structure.

EMBARCADERO The Embarcadero, Spanish for "wharf," looks more like a string of office buildings than anything vaguely maritime. One exception is the **Ferry Building** at the end of Market Street. The 230-foot clock tower is an attractive landmark that can be seen along much of Market Street. Ferries still depart from here for Sausalito or Larkspur (*see* Getting In, Out, and Around, in Chapter 1).

Dominating the Embarcadero is the concrete Embarcadero Center, on Sacramento Street between Battery and Drumm streets. The center is a conglomeration of four nearly identical office towers connected to each other by bridges, with shops, restaurants, and a movie theater below that cater to a corporate crowd. From a distance they look like rectangular pancakes planted in an unnaturally tidy row; during the holidays they're festively lit to encourage that Christmas (consumerism) spirit. The fifth tower you'll see is the **Hyatt Regency Hotel,** which offers occasional tea dances (finally, a place to wear your Easter hat and little white gloves!) and an elevated, revolving bar with an incredible view of the city and the bay. Unless you're going through Benetton withdrawal, save your shopping expeditions for other areas of town.

If you've sold out to corporate America but still have a rebellious bone or two left in your body, leave your cubicle at 5:30 PM the last Friday of the month and head to Justin Herman Plaza to join Critical Mass, a semi-underground event in which hundreds of environment-friendly downtowners and cycle-rights activists bike home from work, blocking most automobile traffic in the process.

➢ **JUSTIN HERMAN PLAZA** • Between the Embarcadero Center and the Ferry Building stretches Justin Herman Plaza, a favorite haunt of the office bag-lunch crowd and young skateboarders who favor long expanses of brick and concrete. Here, Jean Dubuffet's mammoth stainless-steel sculpture *La Chiffonière* poses like a Napoleonic Pillsbury doughboy. Nearby, Armand Vaillancourt's huge building-block fountain looks a little too much like prehistoric plumbing, but you can gambol among its girders even when the water is streaming through. The plaza hosts sporadic free concerts and shows, usually Wednesdays or Fridays at noon when the weather is nice. During a free, unannounced concert by the band U2 in the plaza in 1988, Bono spray-painted the fountain, earning the ire of city officials, who were waging a war against graffiti at the time. (Bono later apologized.) The "anarchist" gesture is recorded for posterity in the concert movie *Rattle and Hum.*

➢ **RINCON CENTER** • Another water adventure awaits nearby at the stately, restored Rincon Center, formerly the city's main post office. The outside of the building is unassuming—you'll recognize it by the raised blue dolphins on its sides—but inside there's a recently restored 1940s lobby and a stately atrium into which a tall, shimmering column of water descends. The social realist murals in the lobby depict the history of California, including the oppression of Native Americans and the exploitation of workers by capitalist overlords similar to those who own the building, which now houses shops, offices, and apartments. *101 Spear St., at Mission St., tel. 415/543–8600.*

CIVIC CENTER

The Civic Center is the locus of San Francisco government and home of many of the city's cultural events, including dance, opera, and big-name theater. It's also where a good percentage of San Francisco's homeless have camped out since the 1940s. To reach the area, take BART to the Civic Center station, or catch any of a thousand buses down Market Street.

CITY HALL The offices of San Francisco's mayor and board of supervisors are located in this building, built in classic beaux arts style with a prominent bronze rotunda that can be seen blocks away. City Hall has a fascinating history. In 1960, civil rights and freedom of speech protesters were washed down City Hall's central stairway with giant fire hoses, while the hearings of the House Un-American Activities Committee went on inside—all of which is depicted in the amusing government propaganda effort (now a cult film) *Operation Abolition.* Joe DiMaggio and Marilyn Monroe got married here on January 15, 1954. Mayor George Moscone and Supervisor Harvey Milk were murdered here on November 27, 1978. On February 14, 1991, scores of gay couples lined up to get "married" in celebration of the passage of San Francisco's Domestic Partners Act the previous November. Has this building seen some crazy times or what? *Btw Van Ness Ave. and Grove, McAllister, and Polk Sts.*

Surrounding City Hall are many of the city's cultural mainstays. On Van Ness Avenue the **Louise M. Davies Symphony Hall,** with its glass-enclosed lobbies and wafer-shaped balconies, and the more stately **War Memorial Opera House** offer San Franciscans their fill of high culture (*see* Classical Music, in Chapter 6). You can catch a variety of cultural events, including concerts, readings, and lectures at the **Herbst Theatre,** located just north of the Opera House. In 1996, the Opera House will be closed for renovations, but volunteers conduct 75-minute tours of the other two buildings every Monday on the hour and half hour from 10 to 2, leaving from the Grove Street entrance of Davies Symphony Hall. Tickets are $3. Call 415/552–8338 for more info. The **San Francisco Main Library** (Larkin St., at McAllister St., tel. 415/557–4400), which will move around the corner in the spring of 1996, has a fine collection of books, records, CDs, and San Francisco memorabilia. Stop by the library's Gay and Lesbian Archive Center, the first in the nation. If you're walking around the area, head to **Hayes Street** between Franklin and Webster streets; it's loaded with specialty shops, art galleries, cafés, and restaurants.

Across from City Hall on the south side is the large plaza where protest marches usually culminate in rallies (including a few 200,000-people-plus ones during the Persian Gulf War) and an occasional riot. Leading away from City Hall toward Market Street is the **United Nations Plaza,** commemorating the founding of the U.N. in San Francisco in 1945. The plaza is presided over by a dramatic statue of Simón Bolivar. The widest street in the city, **Van Ness Avenue,** provides a drab and themeless hodgepodge of businesses grouped in unintelligible multiples—steak houses, electronics stores, bakeries, movie theaters, and car dealerships—north from Market Street to the Golden Gate Bridge.

POLK GULCH Once the gay heart of San Francisco, Polk Gulch is now the city's second most prominent gay area after the Castro. Polk Gulch is part yuppie neighborhood, part urban blight. In other words, it's is a good place to buy roasted coffee for yourself and leather and Spandex for cousin Bob back east. For the coffee purchase, try one of two **Royal Ground** locations (2216 Polk St., near Vallejo St., tel. 415/474–5957; 1605 Polk St., at Sacramento St., tel. 415/749–1731). Two of Polk's big growth industries are drug sales and prostitution. Rumor has it that the call boys get more expensive by the block—the most expensive block is the stretch from Bush to Pine streets. The bargain basement is around Geary Street.

Once you get past the sleaze, Polk Street makes a nice 15-minute walk to Aquatic Park and Fisherman's Wharf. The street is lined with small businesses and cafés, including **Les Croissants** (1406 Polk St., btw Pine and California Sts., tel. 415/922–3286), a popular place to drink coffee, eat sandwiches, and loiter. Satisfy your carnivorous cravings at **Hot 'n' Hunky** (*see* Chapter 4) with a burger and a Ménage à Trois (fried mozzarella, mushrooms, and zucchini) on the side. Bus 19 from Civic Center BART runs up Polk Street on its way to Ghirardelli Square at Fisherman's Wharf.

CHINATOWN

The best way to experience San Francisco's Chinatown—possibly the most famous immigrant community in the world—is to go in hungry and energetic, with open eyes and ears. The shops are nice, but the real appeal of Chinatown is its street life. In fact, no matter how tourist-oriented some of the shops are, Chinatown steadfastly remains a residential area, where the largest Chinese community outside Asia has made its home for 140 years. The original immigrants were refugees from the Opium Wars who came to San Francisco to seek their fortune during the Gold Rush; most ended up working on the railroad, not what they'd expected, perhaps. To learn more about the history of Chinese immigration to San Francisco and the development of Chinatown, visit the **Chinese Historical Society of America** (*see* Museums, *below*).

To reach Chinatown, take Bus 45 from Market and 3rd streets downtown. You'll know you're in the 16-block neighborhood when you see street signs in Chinese. The best way to enter is through the dragon-crowned **Chinatown Gate** on Grant Avenue at Bush Street. Or enter through **Portsmouth Square** (Washington St., at Kearny St.), where dozens of old Chinese men gather in groups, gambling or shooting the breeze.

Don't miss the huge, week-long Chinese New Year's festival held during the first new moon in February. Come early to get a spot for the final parade—a riotous celebration of Asian culture, featuring firecrackers, lion dancers, and painted dragons.

GRANT AVENUE This is the main tourist thoroughfare in Chinatown, crowded with souvenir shops; Chinese restaurants; intricate red, green, and gold lampposts; and flocks of wide-eyed visitors clutching $1.50 bamboo back-scratchers. The real Chinatown can be better found by exploring the numerous small alleys that branch off of Washington, Clay, and Sacramento streets, where you're more likely to see locals shopping for groceries and carrying grandchildren down the street on their backs. The old **Chinese Telephone Exchange** building, now the Bank of Canton, stands at 743 Washington Street, at Grant Avenue. It's both architecturally and historically interesting: Operators here had to memorize the names of all their customers and speak English and five Chinese dialects.

WAVERLY PLACE One of the most colorful streets is Waverly Place, off California and Clay streets, between Grant and Stockton streets. You may recognize the name from Amy Tan's *The Joy Luck Club;* it's also known as the "street of painted balconies." There are a number of Chinese temples along Waverly Place, including the **Tin Hou Temple** (125 Waverly Pl., top floor), purportedly the oldest in the city. Don't miss nearby **Ross Alley,** between Grant and Stockton and Jackson and Washington streets, the home of the **Golden Gate Fortune Cookie Factory** (56 Ross Alley), where you can watch old women fold cookies and also pick up risqué fortunes. Fun at parties. At the end of Ross Alley is **Jackson Street,** where you'll find several Chinese herbal medicine shops with drawers that contain the therapeutic plants lined along the walls.

NORTH BEACH

Walk north on Columbus Avenue from the Columbus and Broadway intersection (long the site of one of San Francisco's best-known red-light districts) and you'll find yourself in the heart of the legendary Italian district where the Beat movement was born. Nowadays North Beach offers an incredible selection of restaurants, delis, and cafés. Poets and writers that included Jack Kerouac, Lawrence Ferlinghetti, and Allen Ginsberg came to North Beach around 1953 to write, play music, and generally promote a lifestyle that emphasized Eastern religions, free love, drugs, and crazy new means of artistic expression. Ferlinghetti's **City Lights Bookstore** (261 Columbus Ave., tel. 415/362– 8193) continues to publish and sell works by little-known, alternative authors, as well as stuff by the Beats, who have been anthologized to high heaven and hardly qualify as alternative anymore. In the late 1980s Ferlinghetti led a movement to rename a number of small San Francisco streets after authors who had lived here; the recently renamed **Jack Kerouac Lane** is right next to the store. In 1994, Ferlinghetti received the same honor: An alley off Union Street near Stockton Street was renamed **Via Ferlinghetti,** though the short, dead-end street is barely longer than its new name.

Although the Beats reached their peak back in the late 1950s, and the number of Italian Americans living in North Beach is diminishing, the neighborhood remains one of San Francisco's most interesting. Some of the shops and watering holes here have been catering to the same clientele since North Beach's bohemian heyday. Those looking to immerse themselves in Beat history can poke around **Vesuvio** (255 Columbus Ave., tel. 415/362–3370), a bar just across the alley from City Lights, where the boys undoubtedly consumed more than one glass of red. **Caffè Trieste** (601 Vallejo St., at Grant Ave., tel. 415/392–6739) fueled the Beats with their favorite legal amphetamine, espresso; the clientele, some 35 years later, still looks pretty beat.

Park yourself in a North Beach café and spend the afternoon watching the twentysomething crowd try to capture the spirit of their famous Beat predecessors, whom James Baldwin called "uptight, middle-class white people, imitating poverty, trying to get down, to get with it . . . doing their despairing best to be funky."

Continue the pilgrimage by leaving a poem or a stick of incense in front of **29 Russell Street,** a hefty walk away on Russian Hill (btw Larkin and Hyde Sts. and Union and Green Sts.), where Kerouac crashed with Neal and Carolyn Cassady for a time in the early '50s. (His relationship with Neal is immortalized in his popular tome *On the Road,* though *The Subterraneans* better evokes Kerouac's North Beach days.) The **North Beach Museum,** on the mezzanine level of Eureka Federal Savings (1435 Stockton St., at Columbus Ave., tel. 415/391–6210), contains a handwritten manuscript of Ferlinghetti's "The Old Italians Dying," a poem about the old men of North Beach.

Some people choose to live in North Beach—and subject themselves to dealing with tourists on a daily basis—just for the food. Stop in at **Liguria Bakery** (1700 Stockton St., at Filbert St.,

The Root of the Problem

Purchasing Chinese herbs for medicinal purposes is a tricky business. Unlike Western medications, which mainly treat generic symptoms of an ailment, like a stuffy nose or depression, herbs need to be chosen and combined with the individual in mind. Some ingredients, like ginger and ginseng, are widely used in teas; you can pick these up in one of the many stores along Stockton or Washington streets. Besides tasting good, ginger prevents motion sickness and may also help prevent blood clots that cause heart attacks. Ginseng stimulates the immune system, helps defend the liver against toxins, and acts as a stimulant. Some people believe it also increases sexual potency. If you're looking for teas, your first stop should be Tea Ren Tea Co. (949 Grant Ave., tel. 415/362–0656), which stocks a variety of teas for both enjoyment and medicinal purposes.

tel. 415/421–3786) for focaccia right out of the oven. **Molinari Delicatessen** (373 Columbus Ave., at Vallejo St., tel. 415/421–2337) has an insane selection of salami, olive oils, cheeses, pastas, wines, chocolate, and bread to sate your need for a coma-inducing picnic at **Washington Square Park** (*see* Parks, *below*).

In addition to having some of the city's best restaurants, the area has plenty of specialty shops for all you grazers. Among the most authentic old-time businesses are **Figoni Hardware** (1351 Grant Ave., tel. 415/392–4765), a musty, dark repository for tools and other useful knick-knacks, and the **Shlock Shop** (1418 Grant Ave., tel. 415/781–5335), an even darker, mustier place that specializes in, well, schlock. And, yes, they meant to spell it that way. Look here first for that used porkpie hat or Las Vegas snow globe you've been dying for. You can even buy an "authentic" Beat beret here, available in basic black or a variety of colors. Buses 30 or 45 will get you to North Beach from Market and 3rd streets.

NOB HILL AND RUSSIAN HILL

The most classically elitist of San Francisco's many elitist districts is **Nob Hill,** the locus of San Francisco high society for more than a century. The hill has great views that even the downtrodden will enjoy, assuming they aren't too out of breath from the strenuous walk up the hill. North of Nob Hill lies **Russian Hill,** originally the burial ground for Russian seal hunters and traders, which today houses a combination of old Victorian homes, new high-rises, and even more of San Francisco's upper crust.

A steep walk (or an expensive cable-car ride) north up Powell Street from Union Square brings you to what once were the hilltop estates of some of the city's biggest robber barons, er, entrepreneurs; now the city's poshest hotels are located here. Ignore the doormen's suspicious looks as you nose around the lobbies of the **Fairmont Hotel,** at California and Mason streets; the **Mark Hopkins,** across California Street from the Fairmont; and the **Stanford Court Hotel,** at California and Powell streets. See how many times you can ride up and down the glass elevator at the Fairmont before the management ever-so-politely suggests that you scram.

If you're anywhere near the Fairmont Hotel, have a drink in its South Pacific-themed Tonga Room, with cocktails in coconuts, a $2 happy-hour buffet (weekdays 5–7), and a lashing monsoon every half hour.

CABLE CAR MUSEUM On your way from Nob Hill to Russian Hill, check out this small museum, which has photographs, scale models, vintage cars, and other memorabilia from the cable car's 121-year history. From the adjacent overlook you can gander at the brawny cables that haul the cars up and down the city's hills, or watch the cables turn from an underground viewing room. *1201 Mason St., at Washington St., tel. 415/474–1887. Admission free. Open daily 10–5.*

GRACE CATHEDRAL Come to Grace Cathedral and repent for all the trouble you've caused the employees at Nob Hill's fancy hotels. The cathedral is a nouveau Gothic structure that took 53 years to build; it's essentially a poured-concrete replica of an old European-style cathedral. The gilded bronze doors at the east entrance were taken from casts of Ghiberti's *Gates of Paradise* on the Baptistery in Florence. For a truly sublime experience, come for the singing of **vespers** every Thursday at 5:15 PM; an all-male choir will lift you out of the muck of your petty little world and leave you feeling almost sanctified. Guided tours of the cathedral are free, but donations are accepted. *1051 Taylor St., at California St., tel. 415/776–6611. From Embarcadero BART/MUNI, Bus 1 west to cnr Sacramento and Jones Sts. Admission free.*

LOMBARD STREET AND ENVIRONS Since you've made it all the way up here, don't miss the chance to do some strenuous walking around Russian Hill's well-maintained streets. The most famous is undoubtedly **Lombard Street,** the block-long "crookedest street in the world." It descends the east side of Russian Hill in eight switchbacks between Hyde and Leavenworth streets. Most recently, this street was the site of the hipster house on MTV's *Real World.*

The insanely steep Russian Hill has a number of funky little stairway streets that wind through the trees or lead up to miniature parks. Try the steps at Lombard and Larkin streets; you'll eventually reach a small rest spot with benches, plants, and an incredible view of the Golden Gate to help you recover from the climb. The stairs at Taylor and Vallejo streets lead up small alleys to two beautiful old houses, **Russian Hill Place** and **Florence Place.** Vallejo Street at Mason Street turns into a set of steps that will transport you to **Ina Coolbrith Park,** a hilly spot with outrageous views of the bay and Alcatraz; on Taylor Street between Green and Union, a wooden staircase leads up to **Macondray Lane,** a tiny, cobblestone alley lined with houses on one side and foliage on the other. This was the thinly veiled setting of Armistead Maupin's *Tales of the City.* Also look for the dark, wood-shingled houses designed by Willis Polk that date from before the 1906 earthquake. One lies on the **1000 block of Green Street,** which also contains one of the city's two remaining eight-sided houses, built in the 1850s, as well as a firehouse dating from 1907.

THE PRESIDIO AND MARINA

Stretching over a gorgeous strip of waterfront between Fort Mason and the Presidio and bordered to the south by **Union Street,** the Marina provides a home—actually a series of pricey, Mediterranean-style homes—for San Francisco's yuppies. Business suits and athletic wear (depending on whether one is in "work" or "leisure" mode) are the uniforms of choice, and the mostly characterless specialty shops, cafés, and restaurants in the neighborhood reflect the lifestyle of its inhabitants. This is the kind of neighborhood where they still use the word "lifestyle." Aspiring yupsters come to the Marina's main drag, **Chestnut Street,** from all over the city to chow down and drink up at innumerable restaurants and bars and engage in yuppie mating rituals at singles bars.

Hallidie's Folly

On a rainy evening in 1873, young engineer Andrew Hallidie witnessed a horrible sight: One of four horses drawing a streetcar slipped; when the car driver applied the brake, the brake chain broke and the streetcar went barreling down one of San Francisco's hills, dragging the helpless horses behind it. This tragic incident, it is said, inspired Hallidie to devise the era's most complex and industrious transportation system: the cable car.

The cars have no engine; instead, they are pulled uphill by a single underground cable that is looped like a bicycle chain around several pulleys and threaded beneath city streets. The cables run at a constant speed of 9.5 miles per hour and are powered by gigantic turning wheels, which are hidden away in the appropriately named cable car barn at the top of Nob Hill (see above). Instead of drivers, cable cars have a gripman who operates a heavy lever that sinks into the continuous groove in the street and grabs the moving cable, thereby pulling the car. Here's the tricky part: Large underground pulleys angle the cable around curves; as the car approaches a turn, the gripman must release the lever so the car can coast around the curve without hitting the pulleys, after which he "takes up" the cable again. Each car also comes complete with a brakeman, whose job is to keep the cable cars from running away, an equally difficult test of skill and coordination when the six-ton cars descend steep hills toward throngs of impatient tourists.

Even if it's not your scene, you'll probably find yourself wandering Chestnut Street at some point. It's the most convenient place to come for a bite to eat or a drink after visiting Fort Mason. A well-stocked **Safeway** (15 Marina Blvd., btw Laguna and Buchanan Sts.), right across the street from Fort Mason, provides cheap food for guests of the **San Francisco International Youth Hostel** (*see* Hostels, in Chapter 7) or victims of Fisherman's Wharf tourist shock. If you're in a picnicking kind of mood, **Marina Green,** directly west of Fort Mason, provides the necessary lawn as well as stunning views of the bay and the Marin Headlands.

FORT MASON Fort Mason, a series of warehouses built on piers, forms the Marina's eastern border. Once an army command post, Fort Mason is now a nexus of artistic, cultural, and environmental organizations (also *see* Museums, *below*). Although it's fairly quiet most days (except for a trickle of people taking advantage of classes, lectures, and museums), Fort Mason is well worth a trip or two. While you're here, read through their newsletter to find out what's going on this month (you can pick one up at the museums).

But let's face it: You're probably coming here not to fill your mind with all this great culture but to fill your belly at the renowned vegetarian restaurant **Greens** (*see* Chapter 4), also tucked into one of the warehouses. If you're too immobilized after the meal to even think about a museum tour, relax at the **Book Bay Bookstore** (Fort Mason Center, Bldg. C, tel. 415/771–1076), run by the Friends of the San Francisco Public Library, where you can still get a book for 25¢. From Fisherman's Wharf, it's about a ten-minute walk west to Fort Mason: go down Beach Street past the Municipal Pier, climb the forested hill past the hostel; as you descend on the other side, you'll see it spread out on the waterfront. *Fort Mason general info: tel. 415/979–3010. Buses 22, 28, 30, 42, 47, and 49.*

PALACE OF FINE ARTS At the far western edge of the Marina is the Palace of Fine Arts, which looks like a classic Roman temple, complete with columns and a pond in front. A bunch of similar structures were built for the 1915 Panama Pacific Expo, but this is the only one that remains. Inside, you'll find the **Exploratorium** (*see* Museums, *below*), a hands-on museum devoted to making science interesting for common folk. If you're visiting on Sunday, MUNI Bus 76 north from Montgomery Street BART/MUNI station takes you within a few blocks of Fort Mason, skirts the southern edge of the Marina, passes the Palace of Fine Arts, and goes all the way to Golden Gate Bridge. Otherwise, pick up Bus 30 from Montgomery Street BART/MUNI, which follows a similar route, but stops short of the Presidio. *Baker and Beach Sts., tel. 415/563–6504.*

THE PRESIDIO The Presidio, a huge chunk of prime waterfront land stretching from the western end of the Marina all the way over to the Golden Gate Bridge, was one of the oldest military installations in the United States. The land was officially turned over to the National Park Service on October 1, 1994, but the army will remain here for a while in a reduced capacity. Since it's some of the most desirable real estate in the city, profit-hungry developers are fighting with conservationists over its future.

While the original plan for the park was to include office space for nonprofit organizations, big businesses like Pacific Gas & Electric Co. threaten to take control of the park's facilities. It is yet to be determined how much of the park will remain open space and how much will be developed. Enjoy the park while you can: rolling hills crossed by plenty of trails and paths through cypress and eucalyptus forests (for specifics on hiking, *see* Chapter 8); historic military buildings; and terrific views of the bay. Check out the **Officer's Club** (Moraga Ave.) which contains one adobe wall reputed to date from 1776, the year the base was founded. Find out more about the Presidio's history at the **Presidio Army Museum** (Funston Ave., at Lincoln Blvd., tel. 415/921–8193).

The easiest way to get to the Presidio is to drive north toward the bay on Van Ness Avenue, turn left on Lombard Street, and then follow the signs. Otherwise, take Bus 38 from Montgomery Street BART/MUNI Station to Geary Boulevard and Presidio Avenue, then switch to Bus 43, which travels into the Presidio.

UNION STREET If you've come to San Francisco to shop and lounge about without such nasty distractions as homeless people or street life, Union Street is for you. Its rows of sparkling, refurbished Victorian houses are undoubtedly beautiful, but the area clobbers you on the cranium with quaintness; dozens of restaurants, cafés, boutiques, and galleries (all housed in spruced-up Victorians) vie for your attention and money.

If you do elect to come for some window shopping or a latte, stop in at **Carol Doda's Champagne and Lace Lingerie Boutique** (1850 Union St. No. 1, tel. 415/776–6900), owned by the woman who led the vanguard to legalize topless dancing in the 1960s, when she became the first woman to bare her breasts as part of a nightclub show. She never waitressed again. If you get lucky, Carol herself will be on hand to advise you on all of your intimate apparel needs.

Other neighborhood landmarks include the **Wedding Houses** (1980 Union St., near Buchanan St.), two identical houses built side by side by as wedding presents for two daughters who got married at the same time. The father's bride had the houses stationed next to each other so he could keep an eye on them. These days, all he'd see are two stunning Victorians filled with upscale shops. The Vedanta Society of Northern California's **Old Temple** (2963 Webster St., at Filbert St., tel. 415/922–2323), a Hindu Temple built in 1905 (closed to tourists), combines all the best elements of Victorian architecture and the Taj Mahal. No joke. Bus 41 from Embarcadero BART/MUNI Station runs down Union Street.

PACIFIC HEIGHTS

Rising above the Marina and the Western Addition, Pacific Heights is the posh neighborhood of Victorian mansions that stretches up from Van Ness and over to the Presidio, between California and Union streets. The mostly residential area is bisected by Fillmore Street, separating the eastern and western halves with its upscale boutiques and trendy restaurants. If you like that sort of thing, the stretch of Fillmore from Bush Street to Jackson Street—known as **Upper Fillmore**—is a "cute" area in which to stroll, browse, and have a cup of espresso. Pacific Heights's defining characteristics, however, are the Victorian mansions, spared from the 1906 fire that ravaged the rest of the city east of Van Ness Avenue (houses along Van Ness were dynamited in order to create a firebreak).

HAAS-LILIENTHAL HOUSE A good place to start your tour of Victorian Pacific Heights is at the Haas-Lilienthal House, the only one that's open to the public. Modest in comparison to the mansions that once stood along Van Ness, the 1886 Queen Anne-style house is now the property of **The Foundation for San Francisco's Architectural Heritage,** headquartered here. The trick is, in order to step inside and see the original furnishings, you must spend $5 to join an hour-long, docent-led tour. These leave Wednesdays noon–3:15 and Sundays 11–4, whenever a small group is gathered. Meet here at 12:30 PM on Sundays for a $5 walking tour covering the surrounding blocks of Victorians and Edwardians—and learn once and for all that these terms refer to periods (1837–1901 and 1901–1911, respectively), not architectural styles. *2007 Franklin St., near Washington St., tel. 415/441–3000.*

LAFAYETTE PARK From the Haas-Lilienthal House, walk 1 block south to the corner of California Street, the location of the **Coleman House** (1701 Franklin St.), which is now filled with law offices and closed to the non-litigious public. This a Queen Anne tower house—you'll see the aforementioned tower prominently displayed on the corner. Turn right on California Street and right again on Octavia Street to reach **Lafayette Park.** Visited by dog walkers, picnickers, and sun bathers, the park's expansive lawns slope to a wooded crest, just as a well-behaved, English-style garden should. On the north side of the park, behold the **Spreckels Mansion** (2080 Washington St.), an imposing 1913 French baroque structure now owned by author Danielle Steele and her husband. You can see the effects of San Francisco's moist and salty air on the ill-chosen Utah limestone, which has noticeably eroded. Blame architect George Applegarth (who also designed the California Palace of the Legion of Honor).

JAPANTOWN

Modern Japantown, which spans the area north of Geary Street between Fillmore and Laguna streets, unfortunately consists mostly of the massive, somewhat depressing shopping complex called Nihonmachi, better known as the **Japan Center.** The community was once much larger, until it was dispersed during World War II when California made a practice of "relocating" Japanese-Americans to concentration camps. Today, there are several shops selling Japanese wares in the area, as well as a number of good restaurants (*see* Chapter 4).

Chilling by the Ocean

Step off the bus at Ocean Beach in your bikini top and flip-flops, all sunscreened and ready to catch some rays, and you may be in for a big shock. San Francisco's beaches, though numerous and lovely, rarely greet you with the kind of radiant heat and sun that'll make you crave a swim in the ocean. Residents quickly learn to use the city's beaches (listed below) for things other than swimming—which can be quite dangerous—like meditating, kite flying, exercising their dogs, or walking (try the 7-mile trek from Fort Funston to the Cliff House at Ocean Beach).

- ***Fort Funston. San Francisco's southernmost beach is nice for a visit before or after going to the zoo. Wildflowers grow out of the cliff's face, and you'll see hang gliders soaring overhead. From Balboa Park BART, MUNI Bus 88 west.***

- ***Ocean Beach. The surfers' beach, the tourists' beach, the family beach, the walkers' beach. It's all-purpose. Have a drink at the Cliff House, a restaurant and historic San Francisco landmark perched on the cliffs, or pick up information on the Golden Gate National Recreation Area at the National Park Service office underneath the restaurant. Across the plaza from the park service office is the offbeat Musée Méchanique (see Museums and Galleries, below). Just west of the Cliff House lie the ruins of the Sutro Baths, a huge complex of fresh and saltwater pools modeled after ancient Roman baths. They were torn down in 1966. People still climb around on the foundation of the baths, trying to get a look at some sea lions or crustaceans. Remember the scene from the movie Harold and Maude that was shot here? To reach Ocean Beach, take the N Judah streetcar from any downtown underground MUNI station.***

- ***Lands End. A nude beach that's no longer exclusively gay, it's rocky and unsafe for swimming, but you'll find some sand, as well as a respite from the wind in the small walled-off areas that people have built. To get here from downtown, go west on Geary Street and turn right on El Camino del Mar, or take Bus 38 west from Union Square. From the parking lot at the end of the road, take the steps down by the flag and head east on the trail. When it branches, head down to the beach.***

- ***China Beach. Stroll through Seacliff, with its million-dollar homes tucked between Lands End and the Presidio, to reach this small beach with views of the Golden Gate, or take Bus 1 from Clay and Drumm streets near the Embarcadero.***

- ***Baker Beach. Beautiful views of the Marin Headlands, the Golden Gate Bridge, and the bay: One end sees families, tourists, anglers, and wealthy homeowners walking their dogs; the other end is a nude beach. Take Bus 1 from Clay and Drumm streets near the Embarcadero, and transfer to Bus 29 heading into the Presidio.***

The **Peace Plaza** and five-story **Pagoda** in the Japan Center were designed by architect Yoshiro Taniguchi as a gesture of goodwill from the people of Japan. The plaza is landscaped with traditional Japanese-style gardens and reflecting pools, and is the site of many traditional festivals throughout the year (*see* Festivals, in Chapter 1). The **Nihonmachi Street Fair** (tel. 415/771–9861), held in early August, is a two-day festival celebrating the contributions of Asian Americans in the United States. The popular **Cherry Blossom Festival** (415/563–2313), held in late April, features taiko drumming, martial arts, food, music, dance, and a parade.

To relax after a tough day, try a Japanese steam bath at the **Kabuki Hot Springs** (1750 Geary Blvd., tel. 415/922–6000 for appointments), where you can use the steam room, sauna, and hot and cold baths (all sex-segregated) for $10, or get a 25-minute shiatsu massage and unlimited bath use for $35. The bath is reserved for women on Sunday, Wednesday, and Friday; men get to use it the rest of the week. Also in the Japan Center, the **Kabuki 8 Theaters** (1881 Post St., tel. 415/931–9800) shows first-run films in a high-tech complex. Moviegoers should take advantage of the Kabuki's validated parking in the Japan Center; your parking choices outside are pretty seedy. On public transportation, Buses 2, 3, 4, and 38 will deposit you in Japantown from the Montgomery Street BART/MUNI Station.

RICHMOND DISTRICT

The Richmond District, a sprawling, unassuming area north of Golden Gate Park, is full of quiet streets and rows of bland town houses that have attracted a lot of Southeast Asian and Chinese families who have moved away from the cramped conditions of Chinatown. The main shopping blocks on **Clement Street,** between Arguello Boulevard and 8th Avenue, contain a dizzying array of produce markets, Chinese herb shops, and Asian restaurants, as well as a smattering of Irish pubs and a couple of good used bookstores. Bus 2 from Montgomery Street BART/MUNI Station downtown will get you here.

Clement Street can be a comforting place to hang out—show up here after a day in Golden Gate Park or at the beach for a stroll and some tasty, cheap food. **Haig's Delicacies** (642 Clement St., tel. 415/752–6283), a one-of-a-kind market and delicatessen, imports interesting food items from the Middle East, India, and Europe and is a great place to stock up on picnic goods. **New May Wah Supermarket** (547 Clement St., no phone) offers a huge number of special ingredients (sauces, tea, noodles, and much, much more) for Chinese, Vietnamese, Thai, or Japanese food. Also don't miss **Green Apple Books** (506 Clement St., tel. 415/387–2272; also *see* Chapter 3) for a huge selection of new and used books—you could lose yourself in this store for days.

THE HAIGHT

East of Golden Gate Park sits the Haight-Ashbury district, the name of which still strikes fear in the hearts of suburban parents everywhere. The Haight began its career as a center for the counterculture in the late 1950s and early '60s, when some of the Beat writers, several more or less illustrious fathers of the drug culture, and bands like the Grateful Dead and Jefferson Airplane moved in. There went the neighborhood. Attracted by the experimental, liberal atmosphere, several hundred thousand blissed-out teenagers soon converged on the Haight to drop their body weight in acid, play music, sing renditions of "Uncle John's Band" for days at a time, and do things that they would still be reminiscing about with utopian exaggeration 20 years later. But like the '60s themselves, the Haight's atmosphere of excitement and idealism was pretty much washed up by the mid-1970s. Nowadays, the Haight is a punky hangout where '90s kids do things that frighten their formerly hippie parents.

Since the 1970s, the stretch of Haight Street between Divisadero and Stanyan streets—often called the upper Haight to distinguish it from the lower Haight (*see below*)— has gone through various stages of increasing and decreasing seediness and gentrification. With no little irony, its countercultural spirit survives largely in terms of the goods you can buy—like bongs, leather harnesses, and rave wear. Neo-hippies still play guitar on the street corner, but the revolution is nowhere in sight. The youthful slackers who live here now wear black, ride motorcycles, pierce body parts, and listen to dissonant music at bars like **The Thirsty Swede** or to live jazz and swing at **Club Deluxe** (*see* Bars, in Chapter 6). The attraction is probably less the neighborhood's historical legacy than its cheap apartments and its bars, cafés, and breakfast joints, like the **Pork Store Café** (*see* Chapter 4). You can still buy drugs at the intersection of Haight Street and Golden Gate Park; in fact, it's pretty rare to walk through the Haight *without* being offered 'shrooms, green kind buds, or doses.

The upper Haight doesn't have many real sights or attractions. It's more a place where people come to hang out or to shop the jewelry and clothing stores lining the blocks between Masonic and Clayton streets. It's also a great place to people-watch, though the arrogance of panhandlers in advanced stages of inebriation can get old. In addition to the used-clothing standbys **Wasteland** and **Buffalo Exchange** (*see* Secondhand Clothing, in Chapter 3), you'll find T-shirts on the Haight that you just can't get anywhere else. The Grateful Dead, Speed Racer, Alfred E. Newman, Bob Marley, and more of the Grateful Dead are all represented on the walls of **Haight-Ashbury T-Shirts** (1500 Haight St., at Ashbury St., tel. 415/863–4639). Down the street, the **Haight-Ashbury Free Medical Clinic** (558 Clayton St., at Haight St., tel. 415/487–5632) is one of the last vestiges of hippie idealism on the street—it's been offering free medical care ever since the '60s. Just east of Masonic Street, strategically located **Pipe Dreams** (1376 Haight St., tel. 415/431–3553) is a well-stocked head shop adjacent to a tattoo parlor. When the weather is warm, head down the street to **Buena Vista Park** (*see* Parks, *below*), which has become a hangout/meeting spot/home for skaters. Buses 6, 7, 66, 71, and 73 will get you to the Haight from downtown Market Street.

HOME SWEET HOME:

- *Janis Joplin: 112 Lyon St., btw Page and Oak Sts.*
- *The Grateful Dead: 710 Ashbury St., at Waller St.*
- *The Manson Family: 636 Cole St., at Haight St.*
- *Jefferson Airplane: 2400 Fulton St., at Willard St.*
- *Sid Vicious: 26 Delmar St., at Frederick St.*

LOWER HAIGHT AND THE WESTERN ADDITION

Despite everything you've heard, the hip, alternative Haight of the '60s isn't dead, it's just relocated. You'll find the sleazy-yet-hip new digs of young urban nihilists in the lower Haight—between Fillmore and Steiner streets. Like the upper Haight, consumerism and counterculture go hand-in-hand here; the street is full of head shops, record stores, underground cafés, and nightclubs. This colorful haven of new subcultures is itself subverted, however, by the very real poverty of its neighboring district to the north, the Western Addition.

LOWER HAIGHT Full of disaffected youths and bedraggled Victorian houses, the lower Haight is a new breeding ground for a community of angry youth, eccentrics of all ages, mental cases, and—perhaps an amalgam of all three—aspiring artists and writers. Take a stroll down the dirty sidewalks and you're bound to see an American flag hanging upside down from an iron window grate and folks hawking a variety of stolen goods at low, low prices. At night, the street is loud with the din of '70s funk or '90s hip-hop blaring from the doorway of **Nickie's BBQ** (460 Haight St., tel. 415/621–6508), which overflows with sweaty, dancing youth of all races. If you're looking for a more laid-back scene, skirt the ornery drunks and drug dealers and head for **Tornado** or **Mad Dog in the Fog,** an English-style pub (*see* Bars, in Chapter 6). During daylight, the **Horse Shoe Coffee House** (*see* Chapter 5) is a meeting place for neo-psychedelic artists and trust-fund poets, while **Café International** (508 Haight St., near Fillmore St., tel. 415/552–7390) plays those old Donovan songs you thought you'd finally escaped. Join the neo-beatniks and punks for brunch at **Spaghetti Western** (*see* Chapter 4), or head to **Naked Eye News and Video** (533 Haight St., tel. 415/864–2985) for underground magazines and avant-garde videos.

WESTERN ADDITION Though best explored during daylight hours, the Western Addition is worth checking out as a friendly community struggling with a legacy of poverty and discrimination. During World War II, African Americans migrated here in droves to fill vacated factory jobs; after the war, most lost their jobs to returning whites and the neighborhood became a nest of brothels and gambling joints. Later, many of the older buildings were torn down as part of the "urban renewal" program in the 1960s. The main commercial drag is Fillmore Street between Oak Street and Geary Boulevard. If you're interested in African American literature or history, make a beeline for the outstandingly comprehensive **Marcus Books** (1712 Fillmore St., btw Post and Sutter Sts., tel. 415/346–4222). Nearby, at the corner of Octavia and Bush streets, a half-dozen eucalyptus trees and a memorial plaque mark the former residence of Mary Ellen Pleasant (1816–1904), the heroine of the Western Addition. Rumored to be a madam, a murderer, a witch, or some combination thereof, Pleasant was most renowned for her business savvy, profits from which financed the western leg of the Underground Railroad.

➢ **PAINTED LADIES** • The most famous row of houses in San Francisco is situated across from Alamo Square, a block west of Fillmore Street. Featured on hundreds of postcards and the opening credits of several TV shows set in San Francisco, The Painted Ladies—six beautifully restored, brightly painted Victorians—sit side by side on a steep street with the downtown skyline looming majestically behind. To snap the obligatory picture, take Bus 6, 7, 66, or 71 from downtown to Haight and Steiner streets, and walk north on Steiner to Hayes Street.

CASTRO DISTRICT

To get to the Castro, just follow the trail of rainbow flags adorning businesses and homes and the pink triangle bumper stickers on the back of many of the cars. Since the early 1970s, the

Gay and Lesbian San Francisco

San Francisco promotes the fact that it is a gay city, the gayest in the world, even. Some neighborhood populations are as much as 95% gay, and it is feasible here for lesbian women and gay men to go about their lives dealing almost exclusively with other gays and lesbians, both in business and in pleasure. And while "gay-bashing" is still a reality, at least here many such cases are fully prosecuted.

San Francisco's most concentrated gay neighborhood is the Castro district, followed closely by Polk Gulch. Although there isn't a lesbian neighborhood per se, many young lesbians gravitate to the Mission. Bernal Heights seems to attract slightly older women-loving women, while the more upwardly mobile lesbian set heads to Noe Valley. Valencia Street in the Mission is home to the greatest concentration of women-oriented shops, though it is not nearly the "dyke enclave" it was in the 1980s.

Until the late 1960s, the Castro was a neighborhood of middle-class heterosexual families. But when the countercultural fervor in nearby Haight-Ashbury came too close for comfort, whole blocks of families fled for more suburban digs. Houses stood vacant, rents plummeted, and young single men moved in. By 1967, the first gay bars opened on Castro Street and in the '70s the scene exploded. Lured by national publicity, gay men and lesbian women from all over the country migrated to the Castro and Polk Street and the community became a real political force in the city. Gays and lesbians are the city's most prominent special-interest group and many hold public office, ranging from the Board of Supervisors to the Police Commission to the judges on the Municipal Court.

area around Castro Street has been attracting gay men and women from around the world. Before the AIDS epidemic, it was known as a spot for open revelry, with disco music pumping 24 hours a day. Today, the community is less carefree than since the first days of open gay pride, but, especially on weekends, it still bustles with people on the streets, in the bars, and at the gyms, socializing and checking one another out.

The heart of the district is **Castro Street,** between Market and 19th streets. At the southwest corner of Market and Castro, where the K, L, and M MUNI streetcar lines stop, is **Harvey Milk Plaza,** named in honor of California's first openly gay elected official. On November 27, 1978, Milk and then-Mayor George Moscone were assassinated by Dan White, a disgruntled former supervisor. That night, 40,000 San Franciscans gathered at the plaza and proceeded to City Hall, where the murder took place, in a candlelight march. The procession is repeated every year on the anniversary of the event.

One block away, 18th and Castro streets meet at the gayest four corners in the world. On weekends, people hand out advertisements and discounts for clubs and upcoming queer events and canvas for political causes. The 24-hour Walgreen Drug Store at 18th and Castro is one of the biggest distributors of AZT, the drug prescribed to minimize the effects of AIDS—something to think about as you're buying your bubble gum or saline solution. The photo shop on the northeast corner displays pictures of happy couples from the latest gay festival or event.

All of the shops, bars, and cafés in the neighborhood cater to the gay community. Travel agencies bill themselves as gay and lesbian vacation experts and card shops have names such as **Does Your Mother Know . . .** (4079 18th St., tel. 415/864–3160). The **Castro Theater** (*see* Movie Houses, in Chapter 6) is an impressive, art deco repertory house that hosts the much-loved International Lesbian and Gay Film Festival each summer. The Castro is also a good area to pick up information on gay and, to a lesser extent, lesbian resources—try **A Different Light Bookstore** (*see* Books, in Chapter 3), with its extensive collection of lesbian and gay literature. Look for special interest listings, abundant free publications, and advertisements for clubs or events in neighborhood shop windows.

The Castro is filled with unique gift shops and boutiques, especially those selling men's clothing. At **Man Line** (516 Castro St., tel. 415/863–7811), you can buy Keith Haring earrings and a rainbow-striped robe for yourself, and a decorative wine bottle holder and an American flag in a red, white, and Roy G. Biv rainbow motif for your home. **Under One Roof** (2362 Market St., tel. 415/252–9430), adjacent to the NAMES Project Foundation (*see below*), gives 100% of its profits to AIDS organizations. The shop carries license plate holders bearing pink triangles, red ribbon pins, and a good selection of soaps, lotions, books, cards, and wind chimes. Don't step into **Jaguar** (4057 18th St., tel. 415/863–4777) unless you're prepared to be confronted with a foot-long silicon fist and other "objects of art" and books on how to use them. Not for the faint of heart. Visit **Gauntlet** (2377 Market St., at Castro St., tel. 415/431–3133), the friendly neighborhood piercing studio, to see photos of piercing possibilities and to chat with the knowledgeable staff.

Don't leave the Castro without catching a film at the art deco Castro Theater, complete with a live organist and trippy ceiling decorations.

The social hub of the neighborhood is east of Harvey Milk Plaza at **Café Flore** (*see* Chapter 5), where the eyes turn and the gossip mills churn. Closer to Castro Street, **The Café** (*see* Bars, in Chapter 6), is the only bar in the area where women represent a majority of the clientele. At the intersection of Castro and Market streets, **Twin Peaks** (401 Castro St., tel. 415/864–9470) has the distinction of being the first gay bar in the city with clear glass windows, a celebration of the fact that gay bars no longer feared arbitrary and frequent police raids. Note that Castro area bars get going in the afternoon. Why waste any time?

If you're in the city around the end of June, come to the Castro to witness one of San Francisco's craziest parties—the **San Francisco Lesbian, Gay, Bisexual, Transgender Pride Celebration** (tel. 415/864–3733), which attracts tens of thousands of participants. The Castro is also the traditional home of the city's other big bash—Halloween. At press time, however, a change of venue was being considered due to overcrowding and the recent influx of gawking "breeders" (*also see* Festivals, in Chapter 1).

NAMES PROJECT FOUNDATION For a sobering reminder of the continuing crisis facing the gay community, drop by the NAMES Project Foundation's **Visitor Center and Panelmaking Workshop,** where panels from the now famous NAMES Quilt—a tribute to those who have died of AIDS—are displayed. The project started in 1987 when gay rights activist Cleve Jones organized a meeting with several others who had lost friends or lovers to AIDS, in hopes that they could create a memorial. They decided on a quilt, each panel to be created by loved ones of individuals who have succumbed to the disease. The idea caught on big and people from all over the country sent in quilt panels. To date, the entire quilt (more than 30,000 panels) has been displayed in front of the White House four times. There are always some panels on display in the San Francisco office, as well as in other offices all over the world. For those who are interested in creating a panel, the foundation provides sewing machines, fabric, company, and support, as well as a weekly "quilting bee" (Wednesdays 7–10 PM), if you need to brush up on your sewing skills. *2362A Market St., tel. 415/863–1966. Visitor center open daily 12–5.*

TWIN PEAKS Looming high above the Castro, Twin Peaks is one of the few places in the city where you can see both the bay and the ocean, and everything in between. Naturally, it's one of the prime make-out spots in San Francisco. If you surface long enough to look at the view, you'll have to admit it's truly spectacular—definitely worth the hassle of getting here on public transportation. Bring a picnic, and budget at least 30 minutes to walk up and around this twin-peaked mountain. When the Spanish came to this area in the 18th century, they named the peaks *Los Pechos de la Choca* (the Breasts of the Indian Maiden). Just another example of missionaries hard at work converting the heathens. To reach Twin Peaks, take Bus 37 west from Castro and Market streets.

NOE VALLEY

Lying one major hill away from the hectic Mission and Castro districts, Noe Valley seems like their sedate older sister—you know the type, the one who traded the glitz and glamour and hard edges of city life for a more settled arrangement. Home to large numbers of babies and dogs and those who love them, Noe Valley provides a sunny, neighborly venue for the eco-conscious set to convene and exchange child-care advice.

Noe Valley's main drag, **24th Street** beginning at Church Street and heading several blocks west, has plenty of solid, old-timey restaurants, pubs, and clothing stores, as well as a few trendy upstarts. **Global Exchange** (3900 24th St., near Sanchez St., tel. 415/648–8068) satisfies the neighborhood's social conscience: It's an international organization that promotes

Great San Francisco Views

- ***Treasure Island.** A slightly different angle reinvigorates the familiar San Francisco skyline. The Bay Bridge, dramatically draped in lights, frames the panorama. By car, take the Treasure Island exit from the Bay Bridge and park at the water's edge.*
- ***Upper Market Street.** Where Portola Street ends and Market Street begins, near Twin Peaks, you'll find a gorgeous view of the city and the East Bay.*
- ***Tank Hill.** Take Stanyan Street south and go left on Belgrave Avenue until it deadends. Follow the footpath to the high, craggy outlook and gaze to your heart's content. This is one of the finest views of San Francisco.*
- ***Top of the Mark.** The lookout point at the top of the Mark Hopkins Hotel, on Nob Hill at the corner of California and Mason streets, is accessible only to those in proper attire who are willing to pay dearly for a drink.*

exchange between the United States and developing countries. In their Noe Valley store, they sell crafts their representatives have brought from all over the world and distribute information on exchange programs and dire situations worldwide. Gift shops that smell nice and invariably carry some combination of ethnic crafts, wind chimes, crystals, stationery, candles, lotions, oils, and fancy cookie cutters pop up at least once a block in this neighborhood. Doesn't sound tempting? Grab a cup of espresso at **Spinelli** (3966 24th St., near Noe St., tel. 415/550–7416), kick it on one of the benches outside, and contemplate which brie you're going to bring home from the **24th St. Cheese Co.** (3893 24th St., tel. 415/821–6658). For the melodically inclined, the **Noe Valley Ministry Presbyterian Church USA** (*see* Live Music, in Chapter 6) features an eclectic assortment of performances, including traditional Scottish and Celtic music, modern jazz, and Indian music. Call for listings of daytime performances.

Noe Valley was once an enclave of Irish and German immigrants. These days, you can still find grandmotherly types gabbing in German on Sunday morning ambles. Pick up a bottle of bitters, some Bavarian tunes, and a packet of Gummi bears at **Lehr's German Specialties** (1581 Church St. at Duncan St., tel. 415/282–6803). What goes best with Gummi bears? How about a sit-in-your-gut wurst and yummy goulash soup across the street at **Speckmann's** (1550 Church St., tel. 415/282–6850), which also has a deli stocked with your favorite German specialties (nothin' like bloodwurst for breakfast).

MISSION DISTRICT

Unplagued by fog, the sunny Mission District—named after the Mission Dolores (*see below*) and stretching from the South of Market area to César Chavez (Army) Street—was once San Francisco's prime real estate, first for Ohlone Native Americans and then for Spanish missionaries. Over the years, various populations, primarily European, have given way to immigrants from Central and South America, though the neighborhood also includes a significant contingent of artists and radicals of all ethnicities. The Mission is colorful, friendly, and a great place to hang out, but it can also be dangerous. Most women won't feel comfortable walking alone here at night, and while you can actually find a parking space, you might think twice about leaving your car. Luckily, public transportation is a snap: Two BART stations (one at Mission and 16th streets, the other at Mission and 24th streets) put you right in the heart of things.

The Mission provides a bounty of cheap food, especially in the form of huge burritos and succulent tacos made up fresh in the numerous storefront taquerías. The area also abounds with specialty bookstores, inexpensive alternative theater companies, and an increasing variety of bars, some of which offer live music, poetry readings, and dance spaces. For a listing of cultural hubs in the Mission, pick up a free copy of *A Booklover's Guide to the Mission,* a foldout map that is available at most bookstores in the area.

Much of the artsy scene is concentrated in the northern half of the Mission, while the southern half is densely Mexican and Latin American, especially on **24th Street,** between Mission and Potrero. A lively, sometimes hectic area, the strip is filled with people shopping at the many cheap produce stands, markets, and *panaderías* (bakeries). In case you need to chase down your burrito with something sweet, head down to 24th and York streets, where you can have homemade ice cream at the **St. Francis Soda Fountain and Candy Store** (2801 24th St., tel. 415/826–4200), or grab a pair of tongs and pick out a pastry or three at **La Mexicana Bakery** (2804 24th St., tel. 415/648–2633)—it'll still cost less than a scone from your favorite North Beach café.

VALENCIA STREET A good place to discover the offbeat side of the Mission is on Valencia Street (a block west of Mission St.) between 16th and 24th streets. This low-key strip is lined with cafés, secondhand furniture and clothing stores, galleries, garages, **Epicenter** (*see* Records, Tapes, and CDs, in Chapter 3), and a variety of bars. Around the corner is the **Women's Building** (3543 18th St., tel. 415/431–1180), a meeting place for progressive and radical political groups. Note the recently completed mural *Women's Wisdom Through Time* (*see box, below*). Nearby, the **New College of California** (50 Fell St., off Van Ness Ave., tel. 415/241–1300), a center for alternative education, offers a renowned degree in poetics, innovative programs like *Art and Activism,* and an excellent women's resource center.

The Haight, Castro, and Mission Districts

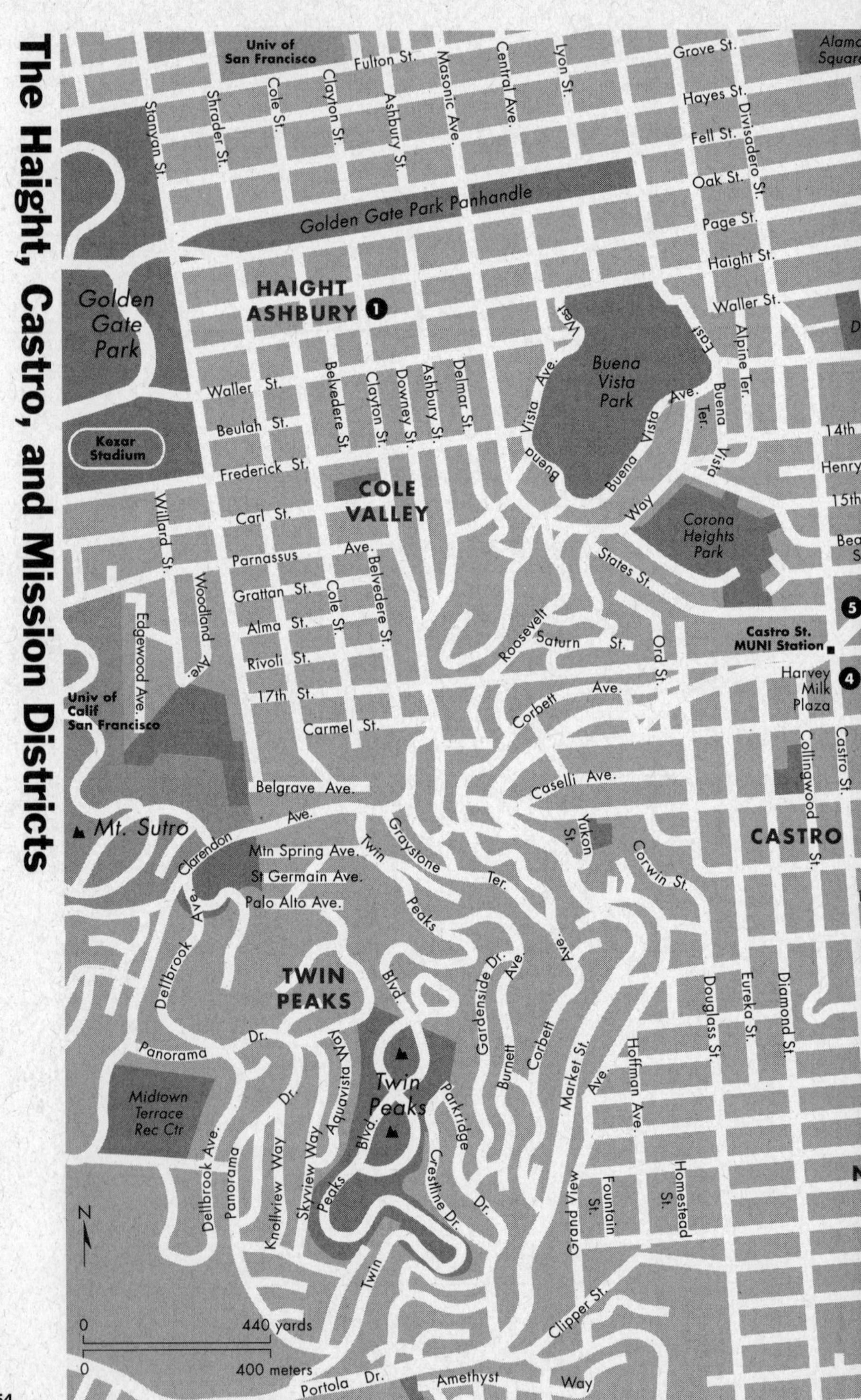

The Haight, Castro, and Mission Districts

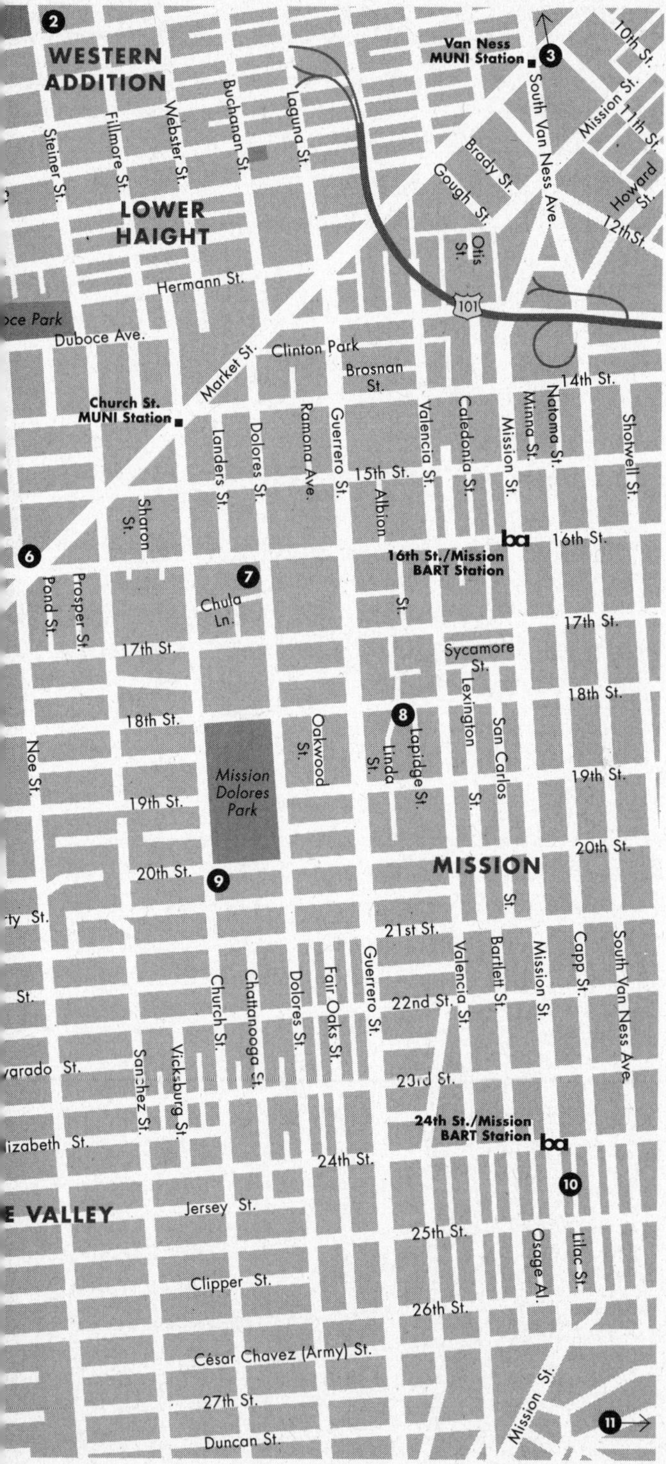

Café Flore, **6**
Castro Theatre, **4**
Gold Fire Hydrant, **9**
Haight-Ashbury Free Medical Clinic, **1**
Mission Cultural Center, **10**
Mission Dolores, **7**
NAMES Project, **5**
New College of California, **3**
Painted Ladies, **2**
Precita Eyes Mural Arts Center, **11**
Women's Building, **8**

Back on Valencia, **Yahoo Herb'an Ecology** (968 Valencia St., tel. 415/282–WORM) specializes in worm boxes for composting. They also sell herbal teas, organic seeds, and products made of hemp fiber. At **Botanica Yoruba** (998 Valencia St., at 21st St., tel. 415/826–4967), you can pick up incense, candles, herbs, and oils—or make an appointment for a *limpieza* (spiritual cleansing), one of the rituals of the Santeria religion. Valencia Street is also the site of several good used and new bookstores, including the leftist **Modern Times** (888 Valencia St., tel. 415/282–9246) and the feminist **Old Wives' Tales** (1009 Valencia St., tel. 415/821–4675). Also check out **Good Vibrations** (*see* Specialty Items, in Chapter 3), a user-friendly vibrator and sex-toy store that's so respectful of the sacred act you could bring your mom here.

Murals with a Mission

For a little more than 20 years, artists in San Francisco have actively explored the tradition of mural painting originated by Mexican muralists like Diego Rivera by creating huge, vibrant works on walls all over the city. Approximately 60 murals are within an area of about eight blocks in the southeast part of the Mission District. The Precita Eyes Mural Arts Center (348 Precita Ave., near Folsom St., tel. 415/285–2287) offers an excellent two-hour tour of said murals, led by one of its muralists-in-residence, along with an introductory slide show. Tours cost $4 and leave from the center every Saturday at 1:30 PM. Otherwise, stop by any weekday between 1 and 4 and pick up a copy of their handy "Mission Mural Walk" map for a $1 donation. To get to the center, take MUNI Bus 27 from 5th and Market streets downtown and get off at 27th and Harrison streets; the center is across the park.

A do-it-yourself tour could start at the Arts Center and go north down Harrison Street (drug-selling activity makes it best to do this stretch in the daytime). Make sure to duck into Balmy Alley (btw Harrison St. and Treat Ave., and 24th and 25th Sts.), an entire alley of garage and fence murals begun in 1971, mostly depicting scenes of Central American life and politics. The stretch of 24th Street from Mission to Potrero streets teems with murals in every corner. A little farther north, between 22nd and 23rd streets and Folsom and Shotwell streets, César Chavez School is bedecked with an incredible array of murals by children and adults. The small panels along the top depict each letter of the alphabet in English, Spanish, and American Sign Language. Another heavy concentration of murals lies along Mission Street between 20th and 26th streets, including one right by the 24th Street/Mission BART Station that seems to depict BART being built on the backs of the people. "Inspire to Aspire," a huge tribute to local idol Carlos Santana, decorates three buildings at South Van Ness Avenue and 22nd Street. Begun in 1993, the Clarion Alley Mural Project (between 16th, 17th, Mission, and Valencia streets) is a site for emerging artists; look for it right near the Elbo Room (see Bars, in Chapter 6). Finally, there is the truly spectacular Women's Building mural (18th St., btw Valencia and Guerrero Sts.). Completed in 1995, more than 500 artists helped work on this mural honoring women from every culture. Look for Audre Lorde, Georgia O'Keeffe, and Rigoberta Menchú, among many other women's names woven into the fabric of the mural.

16TH STREET A busier and denser offshoot of Valencia Street, 16th Street, between Mission and Guerrero, has its own share of hip cafés, bars, cheap restaurants, unusual shops, and an independent movie theater, **The Roxie Cinema** (*see* Movie Houses, in Chapter 6). Two blocks north of Valencia, the **Pink Paraffin** (3234 16th St., tel. 415/621–7116) is noteworthy for its collection of secondhand religious items, cement gargoyles, and brand-new Virgin Mary night lights. Just north of here, **Red Dora's Bearded Lady** (*see* Chapter 5), a lesbian-owned café, is the only full-time dyke space around.

DOLORES STREET AND MISSION DOLORES West of the busy, sometimes dangerous, thoroughfares of Mission and Valencia streets, the scene becomes green, hilly, and residential. Dolores Street, bisected by a row of palm trees, marks the edge of the district. While the Castro, just west of here, is where many gay men call home, Dolores Street and the surrounding residential area is quietly, though not exclusively, lesbian. San Franciscans converge upon the expansive **Mission Dolores Park** (*see* Parks, *below*) to stretch their limbs, while tour buses make the obligatory stop at the old mission, 2 blocks away.

Though it's made of humble adobe, **Mission Dolores,** the oldest building in San Francisco, has survived some powerful earthquakes and fires. It was commissioned by Junípero Serra to honor San Francisco de Asis (St. Francis of Assisi) and completed in 1791. The Spanish nicknamed it Dolores after a nearby stream, *Arroyo de Nuestra Señora de los Dolores* (Stream of Our Lady of the Sorrows), and the name stuck (though the river is gone). Mission Dolores is both the simplest architecturally and the least restored of all the California missions, with a bright ceiling in a traditional Native American design painted by local Costanoan Indians. The mission bells still ring on holy days and the cemetery next door is the permanent home of a few early *rancheros,* including San Francisco's first mayor, Don Francisco de Haro. For the $1 admission fee, you get access to a small museum with old artifacts, plus as much time as you'd like in the fascinating old cemetery and the mission itself. *16th and Dolores Sts., tel. 415/621–8203. Admission: $1. Open daily 9–4.*

The gold fire hydrant on the corner of 20th and Church streets kept pumping water when others went dry during the firestorm that followed the 1906 earthquake.

SOUTH OF MARKET

Until recently, SoMa—the area bordered by Mission Street, Townsend Street, the Embarcadero, and 12th Street—was merely a nondescript stretch of abandoned factories. Now, thanks to two factors—a resurgent art and theater scene, and a happening nightlife—the region is coming alive. The South of Market nightlife scene centers around **Folsom Street,** where the city's predilection for loud music combines nicely with cheap warehouse space and a lack of neighbors to disturb, creating a heathen's haven of dance clubs (*see* Chapter 6). While hot spots change almost daily, such perennially fashionable discos as **Club Townsend** and **1015 Club** are here for the duration.

Folsom Street is the center of the hyper-macho leather-oriented gay circuit. At no time is this more obvious than during September's Folsom Street Fair (tel. 415/861–3247), when a multitude of studded bikers, cowboys, and construction workers choke the strip.

The brand-new Yerba Buena Gardens and the San Francisco Museum of Modern Art (*see below*) are the stars of the SoMa arts scene, both figuratively and literally. Smaller, hipper galleries are relocating to the neighborhood as fast as they can, using light from the big names to draw attention to themselves. To test this theory, wander *behind* the SFMOMA and try to count the warehouse-cum-gallery spaces within a three-block radius. In particular, check out the **Capp Street Project** (525 2nd St., btw Bryant and Brannan Sts., tel. 415/495–7101) and the two controversial murals they sponsor South of Market: The first, at 6th and Brannan streets, focuses on low-income housing; the second, at 10th and Brannan streets, points to the dearth of natural features in the city.

South of Market is home to the city's outlet stores and bargain warehouses (*see* Chapter 3). At **660 Center** (660 3rd St., btw Brannan and Townsend Sts., tel. 415/227–0464), you'll find the ultimate bargain basement—a conglomeration of 22 outlet stores under one roof. Toward the water, the downtown suits-and-heels crowd has infiltrated the South of Market area, but you'll still find several sorta-hip, sorta-yuppie cafés and restaurants around the surprisingly green **South Park** (*see* Parks, *below*).

YERBA BUENA GARDENS This 8.3-acre arts and performance space finally opened in October 1993, after more than 30 years of planning and bureaucratic disputes. On the east side of the garden complex, the **Center for the Arts** houses galleries (*see* Museums, *below*) and a theater (*see* Multimedia, in Chapter 6) meant to celebrate the multicultural nature of the Bay Area. Critics point out that the multicultural emphasis may be to the exclusion of mainstream arts. Others smirk at the money spent building the center: a whopping $41 million. *701 Mission St., tel. 415/978–2787.*

Aside from the performing and visual arts, Yerba Buena Gardens offers a welcome respite from the frenzy of downtown—yet it's just a couple of blocks southeast of the Montgomery Street BART station. Take a walk along the paths of the grassy, spacious esplanade to the Martin Luther King, Jr. Memorial: 12 glass panels, all behind a shimmering waterfall, engraved with quotes from Dr. King in English and in the languages of each of San Francisco's sister cities.

A number of the city's most hoity-toity museums and galleries are a part of the SoMa landscape. But then there's the Cartoon Art Museum (814 Mission St., at 4th St., tel. 415/546–3922), which will teach you all you ever wanted to know about the history of the cartoon, comics, and underground comix for an admission price of $3.50 ($2.50 students).

Across the street from the Center for the Arts, 1995 also saw the opening of the new location of the **San Francisco Museum of Modern Art** (*see* Museums, *below*), and the relocation of the **California Historical Society** (678 Mission St., at 3rd St., tel. 415/567–1848). A Children's Center should open in 1996, and the Mexican Museum, now in cramped quarters at Fort Mason, will make its new home here around 1998.

Parks

Along with Golden Gate Park (*see* Major Sights, *above*), the city has an abundance of smaller strips of greenery where you can cavort like a hyperactive kid when your energy overflows or rest when your feet have become a little too accustomed to the feel of pavement. In several of these, the sheer horticultural magnificence and diversity will amaze you as you laze beneath cypress or gaze at palms and say: "I *am* in California! So why is it so damn cold?"

BUENA VISTA It ain't called Buena Vista (good view) for nothing. Set on a steep hill covered with cypress and eucalyptus and tumbling down toward Haight Street at about 100 miles per hour, Buena Vista offers potheads, dog walkers, skateboarders, and lovers some serious inspiration to do their thing. The park has a reputation for being dangerous at night, but in the daytime it's a largely undiscovered escape from the Haight's asphalt chaos. From the summit, the views of the Golden Gate, the ocean, the Bay Bridge, and downtown create a mystical backdrop for whatever activity you choose to indulge in. Here's a great place to check out the hilly, water-locked stretch of land the city is built on, to imagine the time when it was just a big sand dune, and to contemplate the kind of damage an 8.0 earthquake could do. The park fronts Haight Street at the intersection of Haight and Lyon streets; from Market Street downtown, take Bus 6, 7, 66, or 71.

DUBOCE PARK Twenty-year-olds with assorted dogs, tattoos, drug habits, and musical instruments seem especially drawn to this tiny park, which is crammed in between the lower Haight and the Castro and offers no view beyond that of streetcars trundling by. (It's on the N Judah line, which runs from Market Street out to Ocean Beach.) Despite its utter mediocrity compared to such jewels as nearby Buena Vista or Alamo Square (*see* Lower Haight and Western Addition, *above*), it's a grassy enough place to enjoy the cup of coffee or a piece of pizza you just bought on Haight Street; unlike the other two, it requires barely any energy to reach.

GLEN CANYON Hidden in a part of the city that isn't crawling with visitors, a visit to Glen Canyon Park might just revitalize you after an overdose of city life. Eucalyptus trees loom above you and scent the air, zillions of birds sing to you and only you, and grass-covered slopes lead down to a shady path, equal parts poison oak and soothing stream. There are even rocks to climb on. Take BART to Glen Park, walk uphill on Bosworth Street to the end, and go hiking. Don't tell anybody.

MISSION DOLORES PARK In a sunny residential area between the Mission and the Castro, beautiful Dolores Park attracts picnickers, families with children, dogs and their owners, and men in Speedos if the weather is right. Set on a gently sloping hill, the park contains tennis courts, a basketball court, a playground, local kids playing soccer, palm trees, and wide expanses of grass where you can catch some of the city's hard-to-find rays. Head toward the west and southwest edges of the park known, with tongue in cheek, as Castro Beach (where the serious sun-worshipers hang out) for spectacular views of the city and the Bay Bridge. While the open areas feel quite friendly and safe, the thoroughfare down the middle of the park is where drug dealers and other sketchy-looking types transact business. Avoid this area at night. On July 4 and Labor Day, the San Francisco Mime Troupe (*see* Theater, in Chapter 6) performs for free in the park. *Btw Dolores, Church, 18th and 20th Sts. From downtown, J Church streetcar to 18th or 19th St.*

SOUTH PARK Set in the middle of the warehouse-laden and utterly ungreen SoMa district is a welcome surprise: South Park, a tree-filled square that looks like it just dropped in from Paris to say hi. With a playground, several cafés and restaurants, inviting benches, and a bit of quiet, it's a perfect old-fashioned antidote for those postmodern moments when you feel like you've spent the whole day on the set of *Mad Max.* During the week, graphic artists, writers, architects, and attorneys pass through here sipping lattes. Sundays, when the surrounding cafés, offices, and galleries are closed, are quietest. *South Park Ave., off 2nd and 3rd Sts., btw Bryant and Brannan Sts.*

SUTRO FOREST Sometimes you'll be walking around the city and off in the distance you'll see a big patch of trees. You know it's not Golden Gate Park, but it looks awfully tempting anyway. This wild, densely forested place is Sutro Forest, off Stanyan Street behind the UCSF Medical Center. Just when you think it might be possible to get lost along one of its deserted, overgrown trails, among the ferns and ivy-covered eucalyptus trees, you stumble upon UCSF residence halls. The least strenuous way to get here is to take the N Judah streetcar to Willard Street, head south on Willard, right on Belmont Avenue, and left on Edgewood Avenue until it dead ends. There's your hiking trail.

WASHINGTON SQUARE This park between Filbert, Union, Powell, and Stockton streets embodies the blending of cultures that makes San Francisco unique. Old Italian men chew on long-dead cigars as the bells of a Romanesque church ring on the hour. In the early morning, Chinese women engage in the graceful movements of tai chi, surrounded by lingering wisps of fog. An Italian-style picnic grabbed from any of North Beach's numerous delicatessens, a bottle of Chianti hidden discreetly in a brown paper bag, and someone you feel like relaxing with will only heighten the good vibes. Make the hike to **Coit Tower** (*see* Major Sights, *above*), a few steep blocks east of the park, to work off those calories. From Market Street downtown, Bus 15 or 30 will bring you to the square.

Museums

Although San Francisco has been trying to build a name for itself as a city of big, impressive institutions of art—note the newly relocated Museum of Modern Art and the renovated California Palace of the Legion of Honor—the increasing attention is also a boon to the smaller, funky spaces that fit more naturally into the city's eclectic cultural landscape. The city's fine arts collection is divided between the M.H. de Young Museum, which showcases the art of Africa, the Americas, and Oceania; and the California Palace of the Legion of Honor, which hangs the works of dead European males.

AFRICAN AMERICAN MUSEUM This African American cultural center offers a contemporary art gallery featuring works by African and African American artists, an intriguing gift shop that sells jewelry and artifacts, and a historical archive and research library. In addition, the museum has performing arts classes and lecture series. *Fort Mason Center, Bldg. C, tel. 415/441–0640. Donation requested. Open Wed.–Sun. noon–5.*

ANSEL ADAMS CENTER If you're even remotely interested in serious photography, come here. The largest repository of art photography on the West Coast, the center has five rotating exhibits, one of which is devoted to Adams's work; the other exhibits range from traditional portraiture to computer-altered images. Born of the Friends of Photography, a national group founded by Adams, the center serves photographers with publications, awards, an educational series taught by famous shutterbugs, and an incredible bookstore. The center's 1993 Annie Leibovitz retrospective put it on the pop-culture map. *250 4th St., btw Howard and Folsom Sts., tel. 415/495–7000. Admission: $4, $3 students. Open Tues.–Sun. 11–5 (until 8 first Thurs. of month).*

ASIAN ART MUSEUM Housed in the same building as the M. H. de Young (*see below*), this is the West Coast's largest Asian museum. The first floor is devoted to Chinese and Korean art; the second floor holds treasures from Southeast Asia, India and the Himalayas, Japan, and Persia. The collection of more than 12,000 pieces from major periods of Asian art is rotated periodically, so everything comes out of storage once in awhile. Highlights of the permanent collection include the oldest known Buddha image (AD 338) and superb collections of jade and ancient Chinese ceramics. *John F. Kennedy and Tea Garden Drs., Golden Gate Park, tel. 415/668–8921. Admission: $5, $3 students; free first Wed. of month, first Sat. of month until noon. Open Wed.–Sun. 10–5 (until 8:45 first Wed. of month).*

CALIFORNIA ACADEMY OF SCIENCES This huge natural history complex houses one of the country's best natural history museums, subdivided into blockbuster sights that include the **Steinhart Aquarium** and **Morrison Planetarium** (*see* Golden Gate Park, in Major Sights, *above*). One big draw is the aquarium's **Fish Roundabout,** which places you in an underwater world of 14,500 different creatures. The living coral reef, with its fish, giant clams, and tropical sharks, is super cool. Go mid-morning so you can watch the penguins and dolphins at feeding time. If earthquakes are inextricably linked with San Francisco in your imagination, try the trembling earthquake floor in the Space and Earth Hall. Also worth checking out are the Life through Time Hall, which chronicles evolution from the dinosaurs through early mammals, and the Birds of a Feather exhibit, which explores the languages, songs, physical features, and learning of birds. Temporary exhibits often examine environmental issues. *Btw John F. Kennedy and Martin Luther King, Jr. Drs., Golden Gate Park, tel. 415/750–7000; laser shows at planetarium, tel. 415/ 750–7138. Admission to museum and aquarium: $7, $4 students; free first Wed. of month. Admission to planetarium $2.50, to laser shows $7. Open daily 10–5.*

CENTER FOR THE ARTS The visual arts building at the Center for the Arts at Yerba Buena Gardens houses three spacious galleries exhibiting contemporary works, usually of emerging local and regional artists; a media screening room for video and film; and a multi-use forum. The idea of the center is to reflect San Francisco's multicultural community in a space that is welcoming, unpretentious, and appealing to as large a community as possible. *701 Mission St., at 3rd St., tel. 415/978–2700 or 415/978–2787. Admission: $4, $2 students; free first Thurs. of month 6 PM–8 PM. Open Tues.–Sun. 11–6 (until 8 first Thurs. of month).*

CHINESE HISTORICAL SOCIETY OF AMERICA This nonprofit organization houses a modest museum in its basement headquarters. Historical photos and graphics, accompanied by often moving explanations, trace the experiences of Chinese Americans from the 1850s to the present. Among other artifacts, the small museum contains opium pipes, a *queu* (the long braid men wore as a symbol of allegiance to the Manchu emperor of China before the 1911 Revolution), an altar built in the 1880s, and a parade dragon head from 1909, one of the first to use lights. *650 Commercial St., btw Kearny and Montgomery Sts., tel. 415/391–1188. Admission free, donations accepted. Open Tues.–Sat. noon–4. Closed major holidays.*

EXPLORATORIUM Come here for the ultimate fourth-grade field trip you never took—it's a great place for children and grown-ups to learn about science and technology in a big, drafty warehouse. In the more than 650 exhibits, many of them computer-assisted, a strong emphasis is placed on interaction with the senses, making it especially popular with people on hallucinogenic drugs. Advance reservations are required for the excellent crawl-through Tactile Dome, where you slither through several differently textured small rooms in complete darkness. *3601 Lyon St., btw Marina Blvd. and Lombard St., tel. 415/561–0360. Admission: $8.50, $6.50 students, $4.50 disabled; free first Wed. of month. Open Tues.–Sun., winter 10–5 (Wed. until 9:30); Memorial Day and Labor Day 10–6.*

JEWISH MUSEUM This handsome, small museum features revolving exhibits that trace important moments in Jewish history and the works of Jewish artists—contemporary, as well as old masters. In early 1996, the museum will feature an exhibit of Hebraic treasures from the Library of Congress. *121 Steuart St., btw Mission and Howard Sts., tel. 415/543–2090 or 415/543–8880 for recorded info. Admission: $3, $1.50 students. Open Sun. 11–6, Mon.–Wed. noon–6, Thurs. noon–8. Closed Jewish holidays.*

LEGION OF HONOR San Francisco's European fine arts are on display, once again, in the newly reopened, seismically sound California Palace of the Legion of Honor. What was once a basement has become an underground complex of extra gallery space; what was once a café is now a full-service restaurant overlooking the Pacific Ocean. The collection is not exactly stunning, but it does include some fine pieces from the late 19th century, among them one of Monet's *Water Lilies* and several Rodin sculptures, including a cast of *The Thinker. In Lincoln Park, enter at 34th Ave. and Clement St., tel. 415/750–3600. Admission: $6. Open Tues.–Sun. 10–5 (until 8:45 first Sat. of month).*

M. H. DE YOUNG MEMORIAL MUSEUM While home to art from Africa, Oceania, and the Americas, the de Young is best known for its substantial survey collection of United States art, from paintings and sculpture to decorative arts, textiles, and furniture. Some pieces date from as far back as 1670; the artists represented include Sargent, Whistler, Church, and Wood—among the highlights are George Caleb Bingham's *Boatmen on the Missouri* and Georgia O'Keeffe's *Petunias.* Docent-led tours are offered on the hour. Call the recorded message to find out about special lectures and events. If you're a student, you can get a $35 membership that includes free admission for an entire year. *Golden Gate Park, btw John F. Kennedy Dr. and 8th Ave., tel. 415/750–3600 or 415/863–3330. Admission: $5, free first Wed. of month. Open Wed.–Sun. 10–4:45 (Wed. until 8:45), additional open hours during special exhibitions.*

MEXICAN MUSEUM It is the bittersweet curse of the Mexican Museum to have an enormous permanent collection (including works by Rodolfo Morales and Diego Rivera), a strong reputation as a national center for Mexican and Chicano culture, and only a few tiny rooms to move around in. The museum is trying to break out into new quarters at the Center for the Arts in Yerba Buena Gardens—they even have the building designed—but it'll be a few years yet. Meanwhile, come and enjoy the few pieces they can exhibit, usually focusing on 20th-century artists. A temporary exhibit through March 10, 1996 will showcase narrative photography of the American West by Latino photographers. *Fort Mason Center, Bldg. D, tel. 415/441–0404. Admission: $3, $2 students; free first Wed. of month. Open Wed.–Sun. noon–5 (until 8 first Wed. of month).*

MUSEE MECHANIQUE This quirky museum lurks near the Cliff House at the end of Geary Boulevard. As museums go, the Méchanique is tops, stuffed with antique carnival attractions that include player pianos, marionette shows, fortune tellers, and a truly frightening mechanical laughing lady. Admission is free, but you'll want to spend handfuls of quarters playing with all of the gadgets. Don't miss the miniature amusement park—complete with a Ferris wheel—built out of toothpicks by inmates at San Quentin. *1090 Point Lobos Ave., tel. 415/386–1170. Admission free. Open weekdays 11–7, weekends 10–8.*

MUSEO ITALOAMERICANO If this little collection of 20th-century Italian and Italian American art seems oddly out of place, consider that it actually was founded two decades ago in North Beach. Though throngs of Italian Americans do not seem to be pouring in, the museum has stuck to its mission to research, collect, and display new works by Italians and Italian Americans, in an effort to restore appreciation of contemporary Italian art and culture. The one important work of the rotating permanent collection is Arnaldo Pomodoro's bronze sculpture *Tavola della Memoria* (1961). *Fort Mason Center, Bldg. C, tel. 415/673–2200. Admission: $2, $1 students; free first Wed. of month. Open Wed.–Sun. noon–5 (until 8 first Wed. of month).*

SAN FRANCISCO MUSEUM OF MODERN ART Designed by Swiss architect Mario Botta, the new brick and stone home of the SFMOMA is dominated by a huge, cylindrical skylight trimmed with black-and-white stripes of stone. The interior is just as impressive: the spacious, attractive hall and galleries provide a sleek setting for the museum's sprawling exhibits. The space doubles that of the museum's prior home at the War Memorial Veterans Building, where it opened in 1935 as the West Coast's first museum devoted to 20th-century art. The excellent permanent collection includes works by Jackson Pollock, Jasper Johns, Frida Kahlo, Henri Matisse, and Frank Stella, as well as a healthy representation of contemporary photography. You could easily spend several hours here, in which case **Caffè Museo** (tel. 415/357–4500), where a cappuccino costs $2.50, probably becomes an integral part of your SFMOMA experience. *151 3rd St., tel. 415/357–4000. Admission: $7, $3.50 students; free first Tues. of month, half-price Thurs. 6–9. Open Tues.–Sun. 11–6 (Thurs. until 9). Closed major holidays.*

Galleries

For those in higher tax brackets, galleries are stores where one might actually purchase a "little something" for the living room wall. For the rest of us, art galleries are mini-museums where the "look, but don't touch" rule holds firm. Except for the postcards, of course. The best time to wade into the gallery world is the first Thursday evening of each month, when most host receptions with free drinks, sometimes snacks, and occasionally some interesting new art. It's a great, and fairly casual, scene. For current happenings, keep an eye on publications like the *San Francisco Arts Monthly* and *San Francisco Gallery Guide,* both available at galleries throughout town.

DOWNTOWN No fewer than 30 galleries, most relatively mainstream and high-end, are located in this area, a stone's throw from ritzy Union Square. The thickest concentrations are along the first three blocks of Grant Street, the 100 block of Geary, the 100 and 200 blocks of Post, and the 200 block of Sutter. For the most gallery per hour, head to **49 Geary Street,** where each of the second through fifth floors claims a separate swank gallery. On the fifth floor, **Robert Koch** gallery (tel. 415/421–0122) explores traditional and experimental photography. Other floors focus on painting or multimedia art. All four galleries are open at least Tuesday–Saturday 11–5.

Keane Eyes Gallery. This entire gallery is devoted to that cornerstone of American kitsch, the Keane painting. Back in the 1960s Walter Keane became famous for painting poor little waifs with enormous vacuous eyes—you know the ones. America loved them, America hated them. When his marriage was breaking up, Walter's wife, Margaret, revealed that she had actually created all of the paintings he had taken credit for. Her "masterpieces" now sell for thousands of dollars, but you can buy a T-shirt for considerably less. *651 Market St., tel. 415/495–3263. Open weekdays 10–6, Sat. 10–4.*

Monthly Museum Free Days

Asian Art Museum: first Wednesday 10–8:45 and first Saturday 10–noon. California Academy of Sciences: first Wednesday 10–5. Center for the Arts: first Thursday 6–8. Exploratorium: first Wednesday 10–9:30. M. H. de Young Museum: first Wednesday 10–8:45. Mexican Museum: first Wednesday noon–8. Museo Italoamericano: first Wednesday noon–8. San Francisco Museum of Modern Art: first Tuesday 10–6, half-price Thursdays 5–9.

MISSION DISTRICT This neighborhood is the undisputed center of the city's Latino arts scene. **Galeria de la Raza** (2857 24th St., tel. 415/826–8009), founded in 1970 by members of the Chicano Arts movement, was the first Mexican museum in the United States; it remains an influential cultural resource with its exhibits of local Latin American art and community arts programs. Many galleries in the Mission also host occasional exhibits of women artists, for which you can thank the **Women's Building** (3543 18th St., tel. 415/431–1180), which itself sometimes hosts visual arts installments. **EYE Gallery** (1151 Mission St., tel. 415/431–6911) is a reliable alternative space that usually exhibits paintings.

Mission Cultural Center. This Mission District landmark has not only gallery space but also classrooms, dance spaces, painting studios, and a theater, all devoted to promoting the Latino arts community. Current budget woes are keeping performance arts to a minimum, but visual arts exhibits continue, often featuring neighborhood artists, and the center is a great place to find out what's going on in the neighborhood. Call or stop by for a complete rundown of events, including exhibits, performances, lectures, and classes. *2868 Mission St., btw 24th and 25th Sts., tel. 415/821–1155. Donation requested. Open Tues.–Fri. 10–6, Sat. 11–4.*

SOUTH OF MARKET This is downtown's younger, more intriguing counterpart. In SoMa, plain old paintings won't draw a crowd anymore; everyone who's anyone is jumping on the mixed-media and multimedia bandwagons. Two galleries that are old hands at the multimedia game are **SOMAR** (934 Brannan St., tel. 415/552–1770), which does theater better than visual arts, and **New Langton Arts** (1246 Folsom St., btw 8th and 9th Sts., tel. 415/626–5416), the granddaddy of the city's mixed-media centers, which does it all well.

Also check out the endearingly awkward **Gallery 111** (111 Minna St., btw Mission and Howard Sts., tel. 415/974–1719), where you can catch installations by contemporary California artists and get a $1 cappuccino or similarly cheap glass of wine until 2 AM or so. Evenings often include music or other performances. **ACME** (667 Howard St., near 3rd St., tel. 415/512–7572) is another good, tiny space to see a strange creation or two.

If photography is your thing, try **Vision Gallery** (1155 Mission St., tel. 415/621–2107), a slightly upscale spot with consistently good exhibits. **SF Camera Work** (70 12th St., tel. 415/621–1001) is another good photography gallery with strong alternative shows in an airy warehouse space.

Cheap Thrills

San Francisco is a paradox. It's an expensive city that is also proud of its healthy contingent of bohemians and starving artists. In addition to the thrills listed below, consider some of the cheap forms of entertainment discussed in other sections, such as author readings, open mike nights at bars and cafés, museum free days, gallery hopping, Sunday morning celebrations at Glide Church (*see box above*), and the many annual festivals and street fairs, especially in summer (*see* Festivals, in Chapter 1).

Golden Gate Ferries (*see* Getting In, Out, and Around, in Chapter 1), the commuter ferry between San Francisco, Sausalito, and Larkspur, offers the cheapest way to experience the bay in a boat ($3–$5). They have all the features you've come to associate with fine ferry travel: outdoor decks, food for sale, a complete wet bar, and no irritating commentary. Bring stale bread to throw to (or at) the seagulls.

The **Anchor Brewing Company,** on Potrero Hill east of the Mission District, offers free brewery tours; these include a history of the brewery, a step-by-step explanation of the brewing process, and, yep, free samples at the end. Tours run twice a day June–August, and once a day the rest of the year. You *must* make reservations three to four weeks in advance. *1705 Mariposa St., at De Haro St., tel. 415/863–8350.*

You may already be a member of the **Cacophony Society,** "a randomly gathered network of free spirits united in the pursuit of experiences beyond the pale of mainstream society . . . the canaries that swallow whole the paper tigers of authority." In other words, upsetting the mundane flow of life as often as you can. Join in events like the Urban Iditarod, a re-creation of the

Alaskan dog sled race that substitutes barking humans for dogs, shopping carts for sleds, and the streets of San Francisco for the Alaskan tundra. More laid-back free spirits may prefer Dorothy Parker's Perpetual Perambulating Pedagogic Paperback Pow Wow. Call 415/665–0351 for information on these and other events, usually free, that surface randomly and irrationally throughout the year.

An especially discombobulating and/or morbidly fascinating diversion awaits you in the Richmond District at the **Neptune Society Columbarium,** a four-story beaux arts structure displaying urns that contain the cremated remains of San Francisco's dearly departed. The domed structure alone can make you kind of dizzy: a perfect circle with niches carved throughout and doors leading to rooms with elaborate display cases and 19th-century stained glass. Get the greenskeeper going and he'll tell you all sorts of interesting stories. *1 Lorraine Ct., tel. 415/221–1838. Off Anza St. btw Stanyan and Arguello Sts. Admission free. Open daily 10–1.*

For entertainment of an entirely different kind, borrow the kid next door (for appearances' sake), and head to the **Basic Brown Bear Factory and Store,** where you can tour—for free—one of the few remaining teddy bear factories in the United States. Tours happen Saturdays at 11 and 2. *444 DeHaro St., at Mariposa St., tel. 415/626–0781.*

Wise Fool Puppet Intervention is a theater-arts project that brings giant puppets and stilt characters to the city's streets and public parks. The puppets and masks are handmade with recycled materials. The processions and performances are moving, magical, and just might inspire you to sign up for a volunteer program in your own community. They also hold open workshops, where you can help build a puppet or make a mask and then join one of the processions (you pay only for materials). For more info call 415/905–5958.

East Bay

So you've had a burrito at every taquería in the Mission. You've worn a groove in your seat at your favorite San Francisco café, and you know where each book at City Lights is shelved. You've had more than your share of great times in the city by the bay, but at the moment you're asking yourself somewhat anxiously: What next? Luckily, the funk and soul of San Francisco extend beyond the city limits. Only a bridge away lie Berkeley and Oakland, each with its own character and some attractions the city can't match—from the hiphop Oaktown beat to the hippie parade in Berkeley. Whether you're looking for a New Age healing session or a grungy blues band, odds are good that you'll find it somewhere in the East Bay.

Berkeley

Berkeley and University of California may not be synonymous, but they're so interdependent that it's difficult to tell where one stops and the other begins. You won't find many backpack-toting students in the upscale neighborhoods that buffer the north and east sides of campus, but for the most part Berkeley is a student town, dominated by the massive U.C. campus and its 30,000 enrollees. Because of its offbeat, countercultural reputation, the university attracts every sort of person imaginable—from artists, anarchists, and hypergenius intellectuals to superjocks, sorority girls, and fashion slaves, not to mention the stubbornly apathetic and the piously ideological. Most recently, the city received national publicity due to the presence of The Naked Guy, a Cal student who was expelled for attending classes in the nude. But anyone who has watched the documentary *Berkeley in the Sixties* might be surprised to find out that the city ain't what it used to be. Berkeley *is* still a breeding ground for alternative social trends both important and inane, for posters and protesters that urge onlookers to "Resist Proposition 187" (the anti-illegal immigration initiative), "Fuck the Police," or "Legalize Marijuana." But with the 1994 election of a more conservative mayor, Shirley Dean, there seems to be a reaction by some Berkeley residents against the city's free-for-all reputation.

Perhaps the most poignant symbol of the conflict between '60s and '90s Berkeley is the continuing struggle over People's Park (*see* Exploring, *below*). Activists consider the place a symbol of the people-power spirit of the 1960s, and want to keep the park pure open space. The

Berkeley

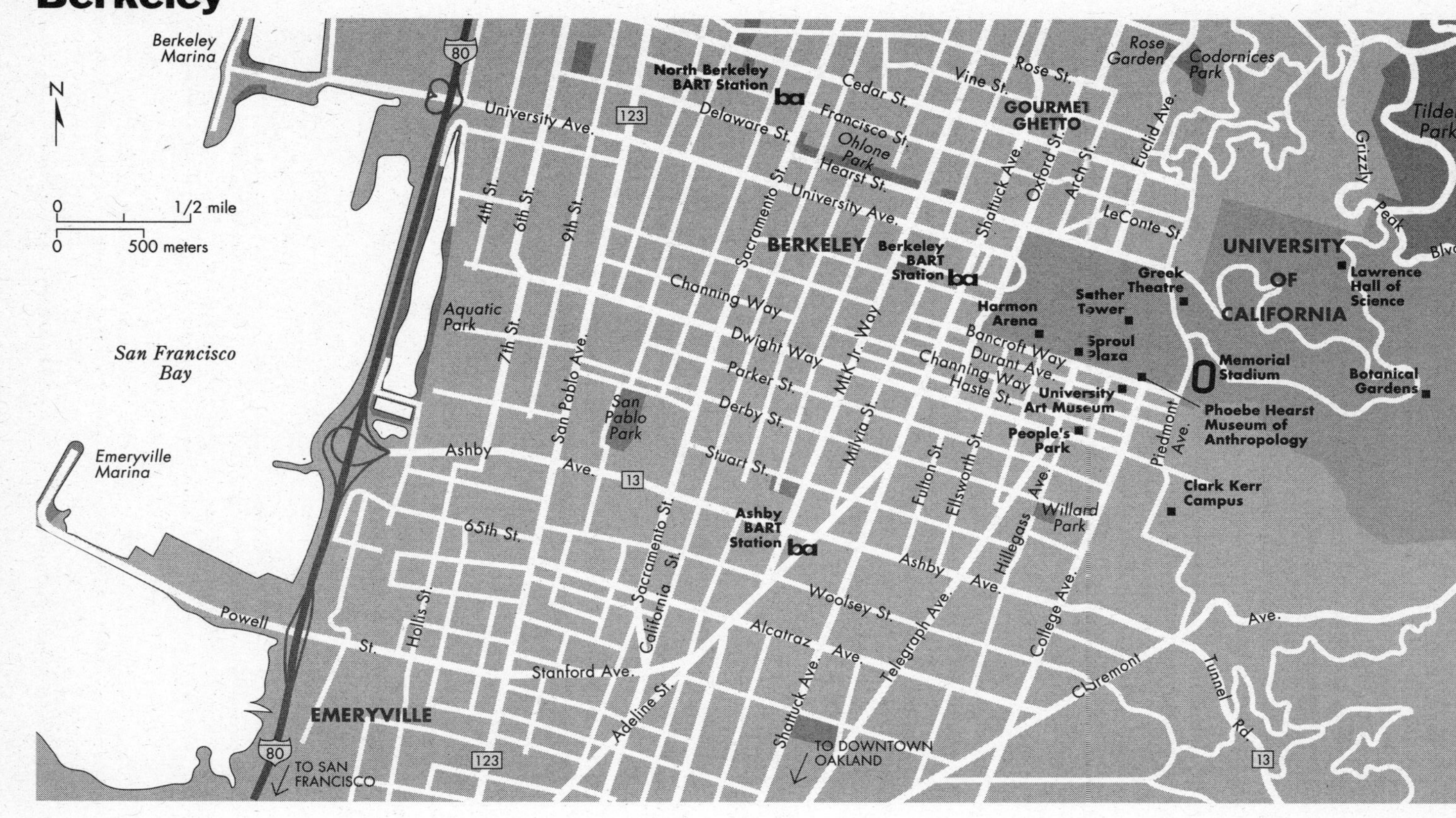

Berkeley Marina
N
0 1/2 mile
0 500 meters
San Francisco Bay
Emeryville Marina
Aquatic Park
80
123
13
North Berkeley BART Station
University Ave.
Delaware St.
Cedar St.
Vine St.
Rose St.
Rose Garden
Codornices Park
Tilden Park
Francisco St.
Ohlone Park
Hearst St.
GOURMET GHETTO
Shattuck Ave.
Oxford St.
Arch St.
Euclid Ave.
Grizzly
Peak
Blvd.
LeConte St.
4th St.
6th St.
9th St.
7th St.
San Pablo Ave.
Sacramento St.
BERKELEY
Berkeley BART Station
UNIVERSITY OF CALIFORNIA
Lawrence Hall of Science
Greek Theatre
Sather Tower
Harmon Arena
Sproul Plaza
Memorial Stadium
Botanical Gardens
Channing Way
Dwight Way
MLK Jr. Way
Bancroft Way
Durant Ave.
Haste St.
University Art Museum
Phoebe Hearst Museum of Anthropology
Parker St.
Derby St.
Milvia St.
People's Park
Piedmont Ave.
San Pablo Park
Ashby Ave.
Stuart St.
Fulton St.
Ellsworth St.
Hillegass Ave.
Willard Park
Clark Kerr Campus
65th St.
Ashby BART Station
California St.
Woolsey St.
Telegraph Ave.
College Ave.
Powell St.
Hollis St.
Alcatraz Ave.
Stanford Ave.
Adeline St.
Claremont Ave.
Tunnel Rd.
EMERYVILLE
TO SAN FRANCISCO
TO DOWNTOWN OAKLAND

university, however, has seen fit to install basketball and volleyball courts in the 2.8-acre park, and the Berkeley City Council has stated its commitment to curbing drug dealing and crime to make it more popular with students and other city residents. Those who continue their love affair with the '60s still influence the city, but others seem to want to drag them, kicking and screaming, into the '90s.

Berkeley's University of California **campus** is surprisingly beautiful, with walking paths, a creek, and eucalyptus and redwood groves. Southside, or the area south of campus, is ruled by chaotic **Telegraph Avenue,** while North Berkeley, the more sedate and residential area north (surprise) of campus, is where you'll find the **Gourmet Ghetto,** home of the famed restaurant Chez Panisse and a number of excellent organic food markets. The Berkeley Hills, rising north and east of campus, offer the huge **Tilden Regional Park** and acres of densely forested slopes. Further west, around **University and San Pablo avenues,** you'll find working-class Berkeley, a gritty neighborhood that is also among the city's most ethnically diverse.

To visitors, it may seem as if Berkeleyans exude a bit of moral superiority—nowhere else does the cashier at the store make the question "Paper or plastic?" sound like a political interrogation.

Don't be afraid to make the easy journey from San Francisco to load up on espresso, organic produce, and alternative literature. No matter what part of town you're in, you're never far from movie houses and bookstores geared toward the young and ideological, used-clothing stores, cafés, and restaurants that cater to student budgets.

MAJOR SIGHTS

TELEGRAPH AVENUE When most people think of Berkeley, they think of Telegraph Avenue, which begins at the campus and runs south into Oakland. Whether you love it or hate it, the first five blocks of this congested and colorful avenue form the spiritual heart of Berkeley—a jumble of cafés, bookstores, art shops, harried students, long-haired hippies, homeless buskers, metaphysical warriors, and wide-eyed tourists. Every day—rain or shine—street vendors line the avenue's sidewalks, selling everything from handmade jewelry and crafts to crystals, incense, and tie-dyed T-shirts. New Age prophets offer tarot and numerology readings to passersby while baggy-jeaned hip-hop fans skateboard down the sidewalks. Telegraph today is a unique fusion of '60s and '90s counterculture, and the two elements blend nicely. This is especially evident on Sundays between 11 and 3, when students, hippies, former hippies, and yuppies with a penchant for organic produce gather on Telegraph around Haste Street for the weekly farmers' market.

Shops along Telegraph (*see* Chapter 3) come and go, but neighborhood landmarks include **Rasputin's Records** and **Leopold Records**; both feature vinyl. Book lovers should check out **Cody's Books** (at Haste St.) and **Moe's** (btw Haste St. and Dwight Way). Cody's hosts regular readings and has probably the largest selection of new books in the area, while Moe's specializes in used and rare books. For candles, incense, black-light posters, and, um, any other *recreational* needs, stop by Southside's corner head shop, **Annapurna** (2416 Telegraph Ave., at Channing Way, tel. 510/841–6187). One more block south, **Caffè Mediterraneum** (btw Haste St. and Dwight Way, tel. 510/841–5634), opened in 1957, is more popular with long-time Berkeley residents than with students, who prefer to study in the cafés along Bancroft Way. The alleged workplace of Beat poet Allen Ginsberg, the Med was immortalized by an anxious Dustin Hoffman in the film *The Graduate.*

Telegraph Avenue is a haven for street musicians. In particular, look for the **Spirit of '29,** a local Dixieland blues and jazz ensemble distinguished by what so many of the other players lack—harmony. They're not very punctual, but about once a week they set up on the corner of Telegraph and Bancroft avenues and let it loose (try calling 510/883–0650 for more info on where to find them). As always, a small donation is encouraged.

PEOPLE'S PARK Just east of Telegraph, between Haste Street and Dwight Way, is a small park that has been the site of 25 years of conflict. People's Park was originally created by students in 1969 from a fenced-off and abandoned asphalt lot. Shortly thereafter, the university tried to replace the park with a dormitory. Within a few days, thousands of students and locals converged here and refused to leave. The university reacted by erecting a chain-link fence around the park; ensuing protests ended in the death of one protester, the dropping of tear gas on Sproul Plaza, and the 17-day occupation of Berkeley by the National Guard. Over the years, the park decayed while activists and university and city officials argued. There isn't that much to do here; you can play basketball or volleyball on the much disputed courts. The homeless and activists are still here; check out the elaborately graffitied bathrooms covered with murals, poetry, anti-government statements, and witty slogans like "Kill the Narks in People's Park."

UNIVERSITY OF CALIFORNIA CAMPUS Established in 1868 as the first branch of the statewide University of California system, the U.C. Berkeley campus retains some of the beauty and gentility of its early years (especially in the old brick and stone buildings scattered about campus), some of the fire of the revolutionary 1960s (check out Sproul Plaza at noon), and some of the apathy and complacency of the 1980s (also visible on Sproul Plaza at noon). On a walk through campus you'll find peaceful glades, imposing academic buildings in the architectural style known as brutalism, as well as battalions of musicians, random dogs, zealots, and students "on their way to class" (i.e., napping in the sun). For a map, stop by the **Student Union Building** on the west side of Sproul Plaza (*see below*). Inside the lobby there's a small visitor center (tel. 510/642–3361) staffed by students. Free student-led tours of campus, held on Monday, Wednesday, and Friday at 10 AM and 1 PM, start from a second visitor center (101 University Hall, tel. 510/642–5215), at the corner of University Avenue and Oxford Street on the west side of campus.

➢ **SPROUL PLAZA** • Just north of the Telegraph and Bancroft intersection, Sproul Plaza is widely known as the spot where the Free Speech Movement began in 1964. Look inside **Sproul Hall** (the nearby white, imposing administration building) for a display of photographs from this first demonstration, in which 3,000 students surrounded a police car that was holding Jack Weinberg, a U.C. Berkeley student arrested for distributing political flyers on Sproul Plaza. (This activity will no longer get you arrested, as five minutes spent on the plaza will attest). Both the man and car were released after 32 hours, but the students, led by Mario Savio, continued to battle university head Clark Kerr. Today, Sproul Plaza is a source of endless entertainment for locals and tourists alike, where some of Berkeley's most famous loonies get a chance to match wits. Here's your chance to see a man in a bra and high heels heckle an evangelist who's preaching damnation and hellfire to fornicators and sodomites, or engage in a debate on foreign policy or the existence of God with street philosophers of all stripes, or listen to an endless stream of bad show tunes sung by the intensely annoying Rick Starr, who apparently believes his unplugged Mr. Microphone will bring him international acclaim. **Lower Sproul Plaza,** just west of Sproul Plaza, is the site of sporadic free noon concerts, threatened with extinction at press time, as some university employees have complained about the music's disruptive force on their workday. Nearby **Zellerbach Hall** (*see* Theater, in Chapter 6) hosts professional (as opposed to street) theater and concerts; check the box office for upcoming events.

If you're lucky you may cross paths with the Bubble Lady (poet and bubble maker Julia Vinograd), Rare (lunatic and sports-trivia fiend), the Hate Man (high heels, lipstick, and a professed hatred for everything and everybody), or any of the other wacked-out denizens who give Berkeley its odd appeal.

➢ **SATHER GATE AND DOE LIBRARY** • North of Sproul Plaza, pass through Sather Gate, the main entrance to campus until expansion in the 1960s. The second building on your right, Doe Library, is worth a look for its cavernous and beautiful reference room and the cozy **Morrison Reading Room** (open weekdays 10:30–5). Stop in the latter if you want to curl up somewhere and recuperate from the incessant clamor of people outside. The subdued brass lamps, oak paneling, and ornate tapestries inspire calm; anyone is welcome to peruse the international newspapers and magazines, listen to the collection of compact discs and records with headphones, or just plant themselves in a cushy leather easy chair.

The Doe Library building also contains the **Bancroft Library,** accessible from the east side of the building, which houses a vast collection of historical documents, rare books, and old photographs. Anyone with a photo ID can get access to the huge, non-circulating collection. On permanent display in the administrative office is a gold nugget purported to have started the California Gold Rush when it was discovered on January 24, 1848 at Sutter's Mill.

➢ **CAMPANILE AND AROUND** • Directly east of Bancroft Library is **Sather Tower** (more commonly known as the Campanile), a 307-foot clock tower modeled after the one in Venice's Piazza San Marco. The carillon is played daily, weekdays at 7:50 AM, noon, and 6 PM; Saturdays at noon and 6; and Sundays at 2 for an extended 45 minutes. You can watch the noon performances from the approximately 200-foot observation deck, open Monday–Saturday 10–3:30, Sunday 10–1:45. You reach the deck via an elevator (50¢). Even if you miss the carillon show, the views from the observation deck are stunning. Take note that the bell concerts are suspended during the final exam period. Southwest of the Campanile, the red-brick South Hall is the only one of the original university buildings still standing. Or walk northeast from the clock tower to check out the **Hearst Mining Building,** a masterpiece of beaux arts architecture designed by John Galen Howard.

If you're feeling studious (or want to remember what it's like to feel studious), slip into one of campus's cavernous lecture halls, like Wheeler Auditorium, Rooms 145 and 155 of Dwinelle Hall, or the Physical Sciences Lecture Hall, and imbibe some wisdom.

NEIGHBORHOODS

If you did nothing but visit the U.C. campus and Telegraph Avenue, you would only see Berkeley through student eyes. Once you've checked out the student haunts, expand your exploration to working-class West Berkeley (along University Ave.) or moneyed North Berkeley, for a look at the town from some other points of view.

UNIVERSITY AVENUE University Avenue stretches all the way from I–80 and the bay to the U.C. campus, providing easy access to (or a quick escape from) downtown Berkeley and the university. It's not as walker-friendly or trendy as some of Berkeley's other neighborhoods, and you won't find as many people wandering around, but it teems with budget ethnic restaurants, cafés, and foreign clothing stores, as well as car repair shops, futon shops, and gas stations. In case you missed the first run of *Brazil* or this year's Festival of Animation, the **U.C. Theater** (*see* Movie Houses, in Chapter 6) shows a diverse range of classics, along with Saturday midnight performances of *The Rocky Horror Picture Show.*

A few miles west of the university, **San Pablo Avenue** crosses University at a perpetually gridlocked intersection. San Pablo is a largely uninteresting thoroughfare full of thrift stores and fast-food joints. Recently, however, it has been attracting a more youthful crowd with a smattering of funky shops and bars, including a recently-opened branch of the San Francisco-based feminist sex shop **Good Vibrations** (*see* Chapter 3); the lesbian-owned café **Anne Kong's World-Famous Bleach Bottle Pig Farm** (2072 San Pablo Ave., tel. 510/848–7376); the ultra-casual pub **The Albatross;** folk music club Freight and Salvage; and world-music emporium **Ashkenaz** (for more on Berkeley nightlife, *see* Chapter 6). That said, the area can be seedy at night and these gems are too few and far between for San Pablo to be conducive to exploration on foot.

Yuppie types drive straight past San Pablo Avenue another ½ mile west on University to the upscale shops on **4th Street** roughly between University Avenue and Virginia Street. Stores here tend to sell overpriced goodies to those who pay blind obedience to the gospel of Martha Stewart—home accoutrements such as sleigh beds, hummingbird feeders, handmade wooden pull toys, organic cotton waffle-weave bathrobes—you get the idea. The only real bargains you'll find are at the Crate and Barrel outlet (*see* Household Furnishings, in Chapter 3). The street is still a fine place to browse, have brunch, indulge in some little geegaw like a wrought-iron picture frame, or laugh at how much people will pay for a garlic smashing stone, complete with instructions. Once you've reached 4th Street, it would be a shame not to continue down University to the **Berkeley Marina** (*see* Parks and Gardens, *below*), less than a mile away.

NORTH BERKELEY Grad students, professors, and over-thirty folks with steady jobs frequent Northside, lending it a calmer atmosphere than you'll find on the frenzied Southside. The hilly neighborhoods here are architecturally diverse, with many homes dating from the 1920s, and some streets are worth exploring on foot. Cafés and restaurants line a block-long section of **Euclid Street,** where it dead-ends at the campus. A less student-filled, and pricier, area is the **Gourmet Ghetto,** around Shattuck Avenue and Vine Street. Here you'll find specialty stores, bookshops, and hordes of restaurants. Look for that obscure treatise on Nietzsche at **Black Oak Books** (*see* Chapter 3) or just grab a cuppa joe at **Peet's Coffee & Tea** (2124 Vine St., 1 block east of Shattuck Ave., tel. 510/841–0564) and kick back with the locals.

You'll find more stores on **Solano Avenue** (Shattuck turns into Solano about two miles north of University), including the always-packed **Zachary's Pizza** (1853 Solano Ave., one block west of The Alameda, tel. 510/525–5950) with their delicious Chicago-style pies running about $13. **The Bone Room** offers live tarantulas, dinosaur bones, and any other living or fossilized paleontological necessities (1569 Solano Ave., at Peralta Ave., tel. 510/526–5252).

PARKS AND GARDENS

TILDEN REGIONAL PARK The only regional nature area accessible by public transportation, Tilden Park offers more than 2,000 acres of forests and grasslands. Some days, simply driving through the park's winding roads is escape enough from the urban congestion of the lowlands. Follow the signs to **Inspiration Point** for an uncluttered view of two reservoirs and rolling hills where lazy cows graze. If you feel inclined to stay a while, Tilden offers picnic spots (call 510/636–1684 to reserve a group picnic area) and miles of hiking and biking trails (*see* Chapter 8).

Tilden Nature Area Environmental Education Center (EEC) (tel. 510/525–2233; open Tues.–Sun. 10–5), at the north end of the park, has recently been renovated and now has a new exhibit on the Wildcat Canyon Watershed. EEC sponsors a number of naturalist-led programs; pick up a copy of the *Regional in Nature* quarterly at the center for more info. Independent types can borrow or buy a self-guided trail booklet ($2) at the center. For a nice, easy walk (about a mile), take the **Jewel Lake Trail** loop from the EEC office and look out for the salamanders. To make friends with furry or feathered animals, bring green, leafy vegetables to the nearby **Little Farm.**

Want to escape the heat of the dry hillside? If you don't mind sharing a small lakeside beach with toddlers in Mickey Mouse swimsuits, Tilden's **Lake Anza** (tel. 510/848–3028) makes a good swimming hole. The water is clean and the beaches sandy, but you may have to compete with a Girl Scout troop or two for precious towel space on hot summer days. A changing facil-

In for the Long Haul

Want to raise some hell about the latest exploits of the Republican-dominated Congress but don't know where to begin? Looking for an environmental organization to join but haven't found the right one? If you haven't completely succumbed to cynicism and apathy, go to the Long Haul, whose motto is "Information, Organization, Liberation." Groups like Food Not Bombs and the Immigrants' Rights Action Pledge use the meeting space, while volunteers staff the "info shop," stocked with local and national progressive 'zines and pamphlets. Call or stop by for a schedule of events (held about five nights a week), including lectures, musical events, and potluck dinners. 3124 Shattuck Ave., at Woolsey St., tel. 510/540–0751. Info shop open Mon. 4 PM–8 PM for "wimmin only," Tues. and Thurs. 3–9, weekends 3–6.

ity is open when the lifeguards are on duty, mid-May to mid-October, daily 11–6. While the lifeguards are around, adults pay $2. At all other times you swim for free and at your own risk.

Other park activities include pony rides ($2), a vintage carousel ($1), a botanical garden of California plants (free), the 18-hole **Tilden Golf Course** (tel. 510/848–7373 for reservations), and a miniature steam train ($1.50) that takes passengers on a 12-minute ride around the south end of the park. Rides operate on weekends and holidays when school is in session and daily during spring and summer vacations.

To reach the park on weekends, take Bus 67 from Berkeley BART to the end of the line. On weekdays, Bus 65 takes you from BART to the edge of the park. If you're driving, take University Avenue east from I–80 to Oxford Street, go left on Oxford, right on Rose, and left on Spruce to the top of the hill, cross Grizzly Peak Boulevard, make an immediate left on Canon Drive, and follow the signs. The park is open 5 AM–10 PM.

Rumor has it that Lake Anza is a popular spot for skinny-dipping under a full moon.

BERKELEY MARINA Warm days were meant to be spent at the Berkeley Marina, at the end of University Avenue a half-mile west of I-80. First-time visitors head straight to the ¾-mile-long pier jutting out into the bay to enjoy the unbeatable views of the Golden Gate Bridge and Alcatraz Island. Bundle up (or snag one of the high-backed concrete benches) for protection against the cold wind that invariably whips up at the end of the pier. Long-time residents, however, are more likely to be found at the recently renamed **César E. Chavez Park** (formerly North Waterfront Park), a 92-acre expanse of grassy hills overlooking San Francisco Bay. The park is the only Berkeley open space with no leash law for dogs and is also one of the most popular kite-flying areas in the Bay Area.

For a map of the area, stop by the marina's **Nature Center** (160 University Ave., tel. 510/644–8623), which runs all sorts of educational and environmental program for the kiddies (and occasionally for grown-ups, too). For information on renting boats or hooking up with one of the sailing clubs stationed at the marina, stop by the **Marina Office** (201 University Ave., tel. 510/644–6376).

To get to the marina, drive west on University Avenue across I-80 or take Bus 51M west from Berkeley BART. On your way in, stop for picnic goods at the **Seabreeze Market** (598 University Ave., at West Frontage Rd., tel. 510/486–8119); you'll find fresh produce, baked goods, and great hot seafood (clam chowder $3, fish and chips $5.50).

BERKELEY ROSE GARDEN/CODORNICES PARK Built during the Depression, the rose garden is an attractive spot for a picnic or a moment of solitude. There's the multilevel rose garden, an amphitheater with roses, benches aplenty, more roses, and a panoramic view of the bay. It's located north of campus on Euclid Avenue, between Bayview Place and Eunice Street. If you're looking for the more traditional park accoutrements, head across the street to Codornices Park, where you'll find basketball courts, a baseball diamond, swings, grass and sand, and picnic areas—the star attraction is the long concrete slide. At the back of the park, hiking paths lead up the hill along Codornices Creek. To reach the rose garden and the park, walk north from campus on Euclid Street for 20 minutes, or take Bus 65 from Berkeley BART.

U. C. BOTANICAL GARDEN The garden, which is used for both horticultural research and education, is notable for the diversity of its collection—10,000 species of plants, all neatly labeled, from around the world. Located in sloping Strawberry Canyon, the garden is divided into regional areas—with habitats ranging from South African deserts to Himalayan forests. It features three indoor exhibits and a slew of paths to explore. If you need a quick breather, sit on a rock along Strawberry Creek in the cool and shady **Asian Garden,** choose a bench near the sunny **cactus garden,** or lie out on the grass. If you make it to the top of the garden, you'll be rewarded with a view of the bay framed by green. The garden is especially colorful in spring, when the extensive rhododendron collection is in full bloom. Check the visitor center for bulletins on various plant seminars or upcoming public education programs, then take home some outdoor plants, for sale at bargain prices. The garden is quiet and sees primarily older tourists, but that shouldn't deter you from visiting it. *Centennial Dr., tel. 510/642–3343. From Berkeley BART,*

Bus 65; or Hill Service Shuttle (50¢) from Hearst Mining Circle on campus; or walk 15 min. uphill from Memorial Stadium. Admission free. Open daily 9–4:45. Tours weekends at 1:30.

INDIAN ROCK PARK As you head north, Shattuck Avenue dead-ends at Indian Rock Avenue, where you'll see enormous volcanic rock jutting from the hillside. Luckily, there was no way for developers to sandblast the stone; the city eventually set it aside as a park. The view of Solano Avenue far below, Albany Hill in the distance, and the Marin Headlands is humbling. Rock climbers can practice their sport on the north side of the boulder, though steps are available for the elevationally challenged. The park is open from dawn to dusk.

MUSEUMS

LAWRENCE HALL OF SCIENCE Perched on a cliff overlooking the East Bay, the museum is a memorial to Ernest O. Lawrence, the university's first Nobel laureate, who helped design the atomic bomb. The exhibits here are mostly hands-on and geared toward children, with an emphasis on the life sciences. On weekends, and daily during summer, you can catch films, lectures, laboratory demonstrations, and planetarium shows. On the hillside outside the museum's rear patio, look for the long, slender pipes sticking out of the ground. The 36 harmonized aluminum pipes are part of a wind organ. If you walk among them when the wind is blowing, you'll hear their music; you can play with the tones by turning one of the six moveable pipes. *Centennial Dr., near Grizzly Peak Blvd., tel. 510/642–5132. Drive east on Hearst St., which borders campus on the north, and follow the signs; or Bus 8 or 65 from Berkeley BART to end (ask driver for a transfer (25¢), redeemable for $1 off museum admission); or Hill Service Shuttle (50¢) from Hearst Mining Circle on campus. Admission: $6, $4 students and seniors; planetarium shows $1.50 more. Open daily 10–5.*

PHOEBE HEARST MUSEUM OF ANTHROPOLOGY This is one of Berkeley's best museums, with rotating exhibits that cover everything from ancient America to Neolithic China. Also on display are artifacts used by Ishi, the lone survivor of California's Yahi tribe, who was brought to live at the U.C. campus in 1911 after gold miners slaughtered the rest of his tribe. Frequent talks by artists, anthropologists, and other scholars shed light on the artifacts on display—call or look in the *Daily Californian* to find out what's on tap. Keep your eyes open for the modern sculpture and painting in student art displays lining the halls to the museum entrance. *Kroeber Hall, U.C. Berkeley campus, tel. 510/642–3681. Admission: $2, free for U.C. students. Open Wed.–Sun. 10–4:30 (Thurs. until 9).*

UNIVERSITY ART MUSEUM The low concrete building housing the University Art Museum may not look like much from the street, but from the interior or from the whimsical sculpture garden in the rear, you can appreciate the artful arrangement of jutting concrete balconies that render the building both solid and surprisingly airy. The UAM houses the largest university-owned collection in the country. The works displayed are confoundingly diverse and may include anything from a 16th-century altar panel to a passel of sugar candy pastel Bibles made by a Berkeley MFA candidate. One of the museum's most impressive collections is a room full of violently colorful paintings by the abstract expressionist Hans Hofmann. Tables in many of galleries contain a smattering of books related to the gallery's exhibits, giving you a chance to rest your feet and figure out what you're looking at. The UAM is also home to the Pacific Film Archive, on the ground floor—pick up a schedule of upcoming flicks at the museum entrance. *2626 Bancroft Way, tel. 510/642–0808. Admission: $6, $4 students and seniors, free Thurs. 11–noon and 5–9. Open Wed.–Sun. 11–5, Thurs. 11–9.*

CHEAP THRILLS

For bay views from sea level, hook up with the **Cal Sailing Club** (west end of University Ave., tel. 510/287–5905) on the first full weekend of each month from 1 to 4 PM, when the club offers free spins around the bay to all comers. Wear warm, waterproof clothing and be prepared to get wet.

Get your karma healed at the **Berkeley Psychic Institute** (2436 Haste St., tel. 510/548–8020), popular with all sorts of New Agers and alternative enthusiasts. For more info, pick up their free tabloid newspaper, *The Psychic Reader,* which has listings for events, workshops, and classes, as well as photos of paranormal sightings. They offer a free weekly healing clinic Monday evenings at 7:30 and 10; psychic readings, by appointment only, are $20.

Those with musical leanings can hang out with the ragtag group of **bongo drummers** that has congregated on Lower Sproul Plaza most weekends for the past 30 years, usually thumping away from early afternoon until late in the evening. Since the Berkeley Guides office overlooks Lower Sproul, we hesitate to endorse this activity—you try editing when you can't hear yourself *think*—but you might as well bring your own drum or pot (kitchen variety, of course) and join in. On second thought, why don't you just join the dreadlocked, barefooted, wispy-skirted folks who dance around in a trance to the rhythm of the drums? At least they're relatively *quiet.*

The Berkeley Hills may not be the best place for stargazing, what with all the lights of San Francisco gleaming across the bay, but the free **Saturday Night Stargazing** at the Lawrence Hall of Science Plaza (*see* Museums, *above*) is still a lot of fun. Employees and local amateur astronomers break out their telescopes every clear Saturday night, half an hour after sunset, to show any and all comers the moon, planets, star clusters, galaxies, and whatever else the universe has on show that night. Call the info number (tel. 510/642–5132) for specifics.

Thought you had to head to Napa Valley to sample free wine? Not if you go to **Takara Sake** (708 Addison St., at 4th St., tel. 510/540–8250), one of only three makers of *sake* (Japanese rice wine) in the United States. Enthusiastic employees offer a slide show and free samples of their product in a minimally decorated room that seems out of place in this warehouse near the freeway.

Oakland

If you expect Oakland to dazzle you like San Francisco, save the $2 BART fare for a cup of coffee. Oakland isn't glitzy or chic; it's a predominantly working-class city that claims to be the most ethnically diverse in the nation. It's a city with a vibrant African American majority where people go about their business and have a hell of a good time on Saturday night. It's the home of the West Coast blues and, more recently, the Oaktown school of rap and funk, whose practitioners include local artists MC Hammer, Digital Underground, Too Short, Tony! Toni! Tone!, Oaktown 3-5-7, and Tupac Shakur. The city is full of seedy clubs—and folks getting down. Okay, so it's a bit dirty, ugly, and slummy, but in an odd way, that's the root of Oakland's appeal.

If you think Oakland's African American–dominated hip-hop and rap clubs are a new phenomenon, think again. In the 1940s, West 7th Street was home to some of the most famous nightclubs on the West Coast, where Earl "Fatha" Hines and Dinah Washington played to packed crowds.

Oakland is one of the main shipping ports in the United States and a major West Coast rail terminus. On the down side, the city has had economic hardships, and for years has been notorious for its high murder rate. Though the downtown area has been bombarded with a slew of urban renewal projects, it remains spotted with empty storefronts and failed developments. In many parts of Oakland, the streets are very dangerous at night.

But there's a lot to discover in Oakland. Wander through the untouristy **Chinatown** (downtown between 7th, 10th, Broadway, and Alice streets), with its lively restaurants and pungent spices spilling out from the many markets, and afterwards grab a coffee in the trendier areas around Grand, College, or Piedmont avenues. If the city is fraying your nerves, head for the hills to the east. While many of the multimillion-dollar homes here were destroyed in an October 1991 fire, the area manages to retain the look and feel of the 1930s, when Oakland was mostly a cluster of ranches, farms, and lavish summer estates. The parks here (*see* Chapter 8) are rugged and undeveloped, and give an idea of what the topography was like when the Ohlone Native Americans first lived here 2,000 years ago. You'll need a car to explore the hills, but most everything else is within reach of a BART station.

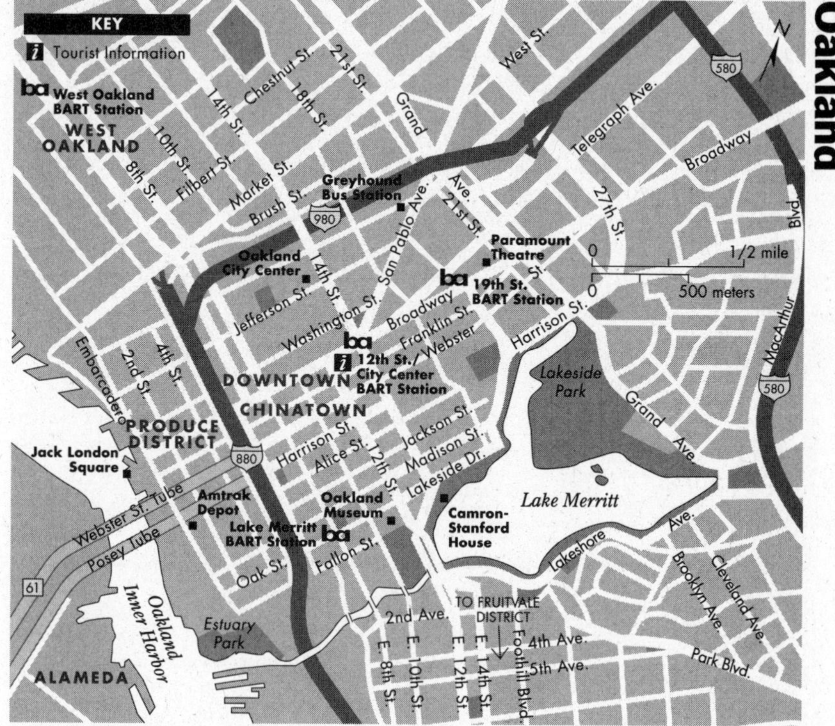

Free walking tours are available early May through October from the **City of Oakland Walking Tours** (tel. 510/238–3234) promptly at 10 AM; call for current itineraries. For those interested in a historical and architectural perspective, **Oakland Heritage Alliance** (tel. 510/763–9218) offers $6 tours on weekends in July and August. The **Port of Oakland** (tel. 510/272–1200) offers free, 90-minute boat jaunts on Oakland Harbor every month; call ahead to make reservations.

WORTH SEEING

DOWNTOWN Downtown Oakland, spreading along Broadway roughly between 10th and 20th streets, is an odd conglomeration of shiny office complexes; art deco, beaux art, and Victorian buildings in various states of repair; and grimy concrete facades of long-abandoned businesses. Though it's not a place you should visit alone at night, it's definitely worth a trip during the day to see some surprisingly impressive late 19th- and early 20th-century architecture. One of the most impressive art deco buildings in the Bay Area is the 1931 **Paramount Theater** (2025 Broadway, at 21st St., tel. 510/465–6400), decorated with an 80-foot mosaic outside and black marble and gilded plaster inside. Call the box office for information on dance, music, and film events held here, or come at 10 AM on the first or third Saturday of the month for a two-hour tour of the building ($1). Next to the Paramount is the emerald green art deco I. Magnin Building; as if symbolizing downtown's problems, it now stands empty.

Farther south, the new federal building at **Oakland City Center** (btw Clay, Jefferson, 12th, and 14th Sts.) is a study in contrast, with funky modern sculptures in the courtyard and a 70-foot-high glass rotunda that rises above a mosaic floor. During business hours, you can enter the building and go up to the two-tiered glass-enclosed walkway that connects the building's two towers. Unfortunately, security is pretty tight in the wake of the 1995 Oklahoma City bombing because the building houses the IRS and the Bureau of Alcohol, Tobacco, and Firearms (as well as other government agencies). You will need picture ID to get in, and some entrances may be closed altogether.

➢ **PRESERVATION PARK** • Located behind Oakland City Center, Preservation Park (cnr Martin Luther King Dr. and 13th St.) is an idyllic cul-de-sac lined with 14 restored Victorian buildings, including Queen Anne cottages and colonial revival homes. Sitting near the fountain, you could almost believe that it truly is the turn of the century—except for I–980 traffic noise from just over the hedges, that is. Most of the buildings are private office spaces and are off-limits to the public (unless, oops, you accidentally went into the wrong one), but one houses the **White House Café** (1233 Preservation Parkway, tel. 510/832–6000), with outdoor seating. The café is open 8–4 weekdays only. You'll find more renovated buildings in **Old Oakland** along 9th Street just west of Broadway. Here bright red-brick facades usually conceal empty buildings, though businesses are slowly moving into the historic structures. On the same street is the **Pro Arts Gallery** (461 9th St., tel. 510/763–4361), which displays local artists' work. Stop in for information about East Bay Open Studios, in which artists' work spaces are opened to the public for two weekends in June.

As a busy transportation hub and the last stop for the Transcontinental Railroad, Oakland boomed in the 1880s; those years saw the construction of some of the finest Victorian homes on the West Coast.

LAKE MERRITT Lake Merritt, a 155-acre oasis in the middle of urban Oakland, is filled with shady trees, meandering paths, and old men feeding the ducks. During the day sun seekers, power walkers, and stroller pushers circle the lake and lounge on the lawns, but in the evening the crowds get a little rougher—those who live nearby have recently raised a ruckus about unruly teenagers who cruise around the lake after dark. **Lakeside Park** (tel. 510/238–3091), on the north shore, has picnic facilities, Japanese and herb gardens, the oldest urban bird sanctuary in the United States (1879), frequent music events, and boat rentals at the **Sailboat House** (568 Bellevue St., tel. 510/444–3807). For $6–$8 an hour (plus a $10 deposit) you can paddle a canoe on the lake; sailboats are $6–$12 an hour (plus $20 deposit). Otherwise, take a tour of the lake aboard the *Merritt Queen,* a miniature replica of a Mississippi River steamboat ($1.50). If you prefer to remain on shore, a 3½-mile paved walking path encircles the lake. **Grand Avenue,** which runs into the north tip of the lake, is also a good place for a stroll, with a number of reasonably good ethnic restaurants and cafés, including **The Coffee Mill** (3363 Grand Ave., tel. 510/465–4224), which claims to be Oakland's oldest coffeehouse and hosts readings and concerts. On your way back to the lake, peek inside the **Grand Lake Theater** (3200 Grand Ave., at Lake Park Ave., tel. 510/452–3556), an art deco movie palace where an enormous chandelier and grand staircase remain from the 1920s. The theater now shows first-run movies on four screens. Near the southwest edge of the lake, you can tour the **Camron-Stanford House** (1418 Lakeside Dr., near 14th St., tel. 510/836–1976), the only remaining Victorian building in this formerly bourgeois neighborhood. Built in 1876, the house

Marching to a Different Beat

Like San Francisco and Berkeley, Oakland has a reputation for being a center of alternative culture and revolutionary politics. In the 1960s, the militant and still widely debated Black Panther Party began here. In the 1970s, the city was headquarters for the Symbionese Liberation Army, who kidnapped Patty Hearst and demanded as part of her ransom that food be distributed to Oakland's poor. Even the city's most famous literary figure, Jack London, was steeped in controversy—an ardent socialist and debauched troublemaker, he wanted California to form its own country (although that's hard to detect in those two novels about dogs).

is meticulously decorated in the style of the 1880s. Tours ($2; free first Sunday of month) are offered Wednesday 11–4 and Sunday 1–5. For information on the **Festival at the Lake** and the **Juneteenth Festival** that take place here every summer, *see* Festivals, in Chapter 1. To get here, walk one-half mile southeast from the 12th Street BART Station downtown, or take BART directly to Lake Merritt station.

JACK LONDON SQUARE Although born in San Francisco, Jack London spent his early years in Oakland before shipping out on the adventures that inspired *The Call of the Wild, The Sea Wolf,* and *The Cruise of the Snark.* In an effort to make a buck and draw a Fisherman's Wharf-type crowd, Oakland created Jack London Square, a mostly upscale collection of waterfront boutiques and restaurants on the Embarcadero, at the end of Broadway west of downtown. Unless you're in the market for an overpriced gift or have an unusual obsession with Jack London, you can skip this part of town with no regrets. If you do stop by, though, look for **Heinold's First and Last Chance Saloon** (56 Jack London Sq., tel. 510/839–6761), the former hangout of Jack London, as well as Robert Louis Stevenson and Joaquin Miller. The proprietors will proudly tell you about the memorabilia on the walls and the crazily sloping floor (the result of the earthquake of 1906)—but if they were shooting for authenticity, they probably should have left off the neon JACK LONDON RENDEZVOUS sign outside. Next door is a reassembled Klondike cabin that Jack once spent a winter in—when it was in Alaska. Near the saloon in a shopping complex called Jack London Village is the small **Jack London Museum** (Suite 104, tel. 510/451–8218), displaying a small collection of Jack-related artifacts ($1 donation requested). But if you're really so interested in Jack's literary pursuits, you'll better enjoy the collection of letters, manuscripts, and photographs in the public library's **Oakland History Room** (125 14th St., tel. 510/238–3222).

MORMON TEMPLE The Mormons have received a lot of flak for believing the Garden of Eden may be in Mississippi, for building their temples near major freeways to attract distraught souls, for barring women from many church services, and for spending millions of dollars on elaborate, marble-covered temples. Well, come see for yourself. Free tours of the outside only are given daily 9–9. Pick up a souvenir in the visitor center, or watch their 15-minute video about Joseph Smith and the gang. If you get lost on your way up here, try coming after dark—the spotlights aimed at the building could illuminate at least three airport runways. *4766 Lincoln Ave., tel. 510/531–1475. From Hwy. 13 (Warren Fwy.), Lincoln Ave. exit, or Bus 46 from Oakland Coliseum BART.*

MUSEUMS

Oakland has a number of excellent museums. In particular, stop by the **Ebony Museum of Art** (30 Jack London Sq., Suite 208–209, tel. 510/763–0745), which features work by African and African American artists. It's open Tuesday–Saturday 11–6, Sunday noon–6, and admission is free. Also free is the **Creative Growth Art Center** (355 24th St., tel. 510/836–2340), which displays arts and crafts by disabled artists. It's open weekdays 10–4, but closes one week out of every five, so call ahead.

AFRICAN AMERICAN MUSEUM The center's Northern California branch focuses on the history of people of African descent in North America, with a special emphasis on Oakland and the Bay Area. Check out the library and the displays of personal mementos from Bay Area residents. *5606 San Pablo Ave., at 56th St., tel. 510/658–3158. Open Tues. 11:30–7, Wed., Thurs., and Sat. 10–5:30, Fri. noon–5:30. From downtown, Bus 72 north on Broadway.*

OAKLAND MUSEUM The three permanent collections at the Oakland Museum cover California's art, history, and ecology. The Cowell Hall of California History puts today's multicultural population into context. Its extensive mixed-media exhibits document the rise and fall of the Ohlone Native American people (the region's first inhabitants), and tackle the issues of urban violence and Oakland's subsequent deterioration. Other exhibits include Spanish-era artifacts, a fire truck that battled San Francisco's 1906 fire, and some hokey relics from the 1967 "Summer of Love." The Gallery of Natural Sciences offers a simulated walk through the state's eight biotic zones and a view of the plants and animals of each. The Gallery of California Art showcases works by everyone from early settlers to painters who probably just got out of art school yesterday. Be sure to visit the museum's terraced gardens and nearby **Estuary Park,** a 22-acre sculpture garden. *1000 Oak St., at 10th St., tel. 510/238–3401. 1 block east of Lake Merritt BART. Admission: $4, $2 students. Open Wed.–Sat. 10–5, Sun. noon–7. Wheelchair access.*

CHEAP THRILLS

No one ever said Oakland had the most picturesque downtown area, so if you need to get away from the bus exhaust fumes, stop by the **Oakland Rose Garden,** (tel. 510/597–5039) off Monte Vista Avenue about a mile northeast of Lake Merritt. The steeply terraced garden may not be as densely planted as the riotous Berkeley Rose Garden (*see above*), but it's still a sublimely mellow place for a picnic or a nap.

Locals get a kick out of wandering around at 3 AM in the **Produce District** downtown (btw Broadway, Webster, 2nd, and 3rd streets) to watch the vendors setting up shop. It's reassuring to see all this excitement in the wee hours of the morning, when most of Oakland looks like a ghost town. After you've had your fill, walk down to the 24-hour, but otherwise undistinguishable, **Jack London Inn Coffeeshop** (cnr Embarcadero and Broadway) for some pancakes.

Dying for a day at the beach but can't stand the thought of fighting the crowds in Marin County? Zip on over to **Robert Crown Memorial State Beach,** a long, thin slice of sand bordered by a swath of grassy picnic areas. The beach is located in Alameda, a naval town that seems to be in a '50s timewarp. Located across the estuary from Oakland, Alameda is in shock due to the imminent closing of its naval base. The beach is in better shape than the local economy—though just barely. So the sand is a bit mucky in spots and you get a view of South San Francisco instead of the pounding Pacific, but it's only a 10-minute drive from downtown Oakland and it's also one of the few places where you can safely swim in the bay. Parking is $3, but you can park for free anywhere along Shoreline Drive, which parallels the beach. To get here from downtown, drive south on Broadway, go through the Webster Street tube to Alameda, continue on Highway 61, turn right on 8th Street, and look for the sign. Or take Bus 51 south on Broadway from downtown to the Webster and Santa Clara streets, then walk a ¼-mile west to the water.

Marin County

Just across the Golden Gate Bridge, Marin is the state's richest county, an upscale playground for children old enough to remember Woodstock. Everywhere you turn you'll see an odd combination of hippie ideals and yuppie wealth. Expensive estates are buffered by ragged log cabins and Porsches and BMWs park next to aging Volvo station wagons and VW vans.

The reason so many '60s-refugees-turned-'80s-success-stories want to live here—and the reason you'll want to visit despite the price tag—is Marin's incredible natural beauty. The stunning ocean views of western Marin give way to thick redwood forests along Mount Tamalpais. On the steep eastern side of the mountain are perched small, woodsy towns, including Mill Valley. You could spend a lifetime describing the pleasures of hiking in Muir Woods and the Point Reyes National Seashore, and it's hard to act blasé about the view from **Highway 1,** no matter how many times you've driven the road.

Filmmaker George Lucas, and out-there musician Todd Rundgren are a few of the cultural heroes who live in Marin County.

Marin's upscale, touristed bayside towns, like Tiburon and Sausalito, are tougher for the budget-conscious visitor to love. You'll have to pick your way through an ostentatious show of wealth to find a cheap organic grocery store where you can stock up on supplies for your hike; an isolated, sunny field hospitable to hackysack players; or an unpretentious restaurant that serves reasonably priced seafood. But these things do exist. Another aspect that keeps both locals and international tourists coming back is that even the most bucolic corners of Marin are little more than two

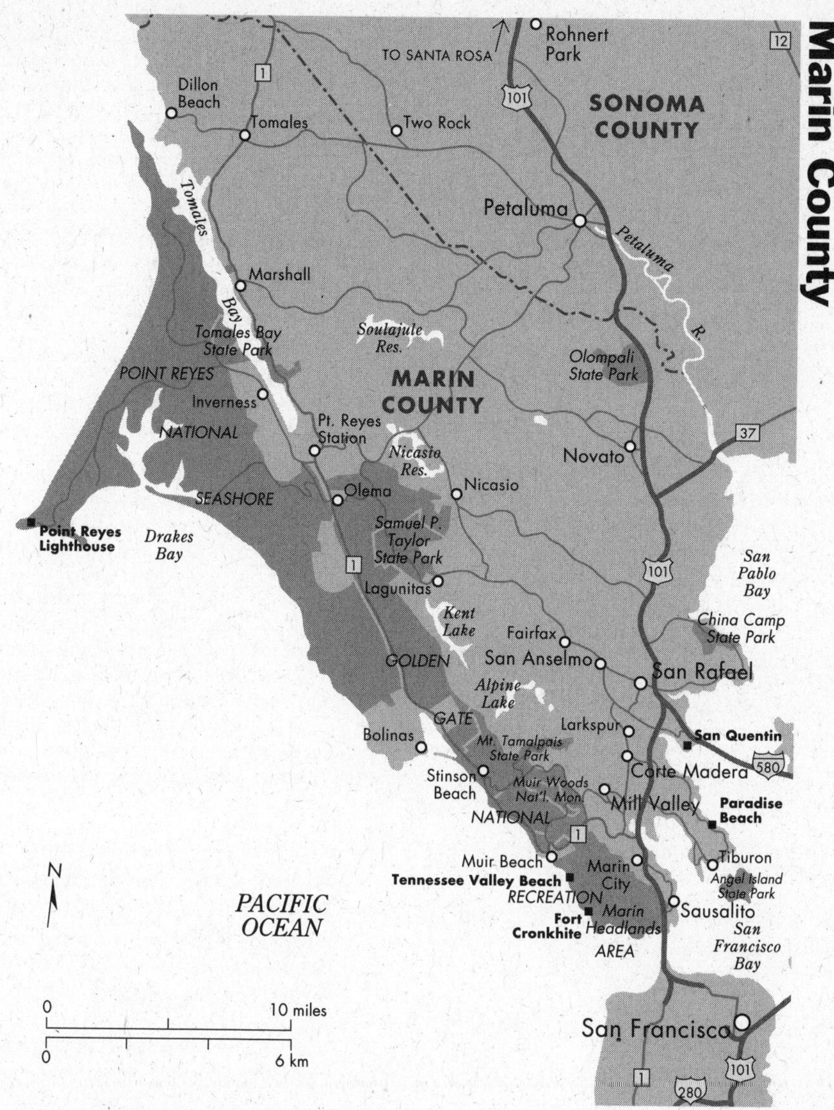

hours from San Francisco (except during rush hour, when it can take nearly an hour just to cross the bridge). However, getting around Marin by public transportation is challenging and often frustrating.

Marin Headlands

For a quick taste of what Marin County has to offer nature freaks, cross the Golden Gate Bridge, exit at Alexander Avenue, and drive up Conzelman Road to the Marin Headlands. Consisting of several small but steep bluffs overlooking San Francisco Bay and the Pacific Ocean, the undeveloped, 1,000-acre headlands are a great place to snap a few photos or while away an afternoon. Thick fog often whips across the headlands, obscuring everything but the top of the towers of the Golden Gate Bridge but, on a sunny day, the views of downtown San Francisco, the East Bay, and Point Reyes to the north are stunning. Hundreds of hiking and biking trails meander along the wind-beaten hills and cliffs (*see* Chapter 8).

The headlands were used as a military camp in the late 19th century, and during World War II emplacements were dug for huge naval guns to protect the approaches to the bay. The guns are long gone, but several overgrown concrete batteries still stand watch along the coast. One of the most impressive, **Battery Wallace,** is off of Conzelman Road just before you reach the Point Bonita Lighthouse. The two forbidding concrete structures you see today, once the site of twelve-inch guns aimed 17 miles out to sea, are only part of the structure: they are connected by an inaccessible series of underground rooms used to hold troops and supplies. Call or stop by the **Marin Headlands Visitor's Center** (Field and Bunker Rds., tel. 415/331–1540) and pick up the free "Park Events" brochure or the almost indispensable map and guide to historic sites and wildlife ($1.60). Note that some trails may be closed due to fires in fall 1995; call for details.

About a mile past the visitor information center (follow signs from Bunker Rd.) is the **Marine Mammal Center.** Docents will happily discuss this elephant seal's skin disease or that harbor seal pup's malnourishment while you watch the noisy critters flop around their pens. A tiny gift shop sells books and wildlife-related knickknacks. *Tel. 415/289–7325. Suggested donation: $1.*

Sausalito

Only a few miles north of San Francisco, Sausalito flourished during the 1880s and '90s as a small whaling town, infamous for its saloons, gambling dens, and bordellos. It had a tough reputation as the sort of place where sailors and riffraff could get drunk and cause trouble on the docks. Even after it became suburbanized in the 1940s, the town continued to attract an offbeat and raffish element, becoming a well-known artists' colony. Over the years, however, Sausalito's wharf rats have been replaced by a new sort of rat—lawyers and investment bankers—and this is now a bland, wealthy resort town, popular with yachters and San Francisco's upwardly mobile crowd. If you have unlimited time to explore the Bay Area, Sausalito is worth a gander, but don't go out of your way. Parking is next to impossible, shops and restaurants are shockingly expensive, and you have to dodge camera-toting tourists who fill the sidewalks and streets.

Still, if privacy is not top priority, Sausalito makes a reasonably good place to while away an afternoon (preferably a weekday) eating a picnic lunch while you watch the yachts drift by. **Stuffed Croissant** (43 Caledonia St., one block inland from Bridgeway, tel. 415/332–7103) sells mammoth scones ($1.75), sandwiches (about $5), and other items you can eat in or take down to the waterfront. Health-conscious do-it-yourselfers should stop at the excellent **Real Food Store** (200 Caledonia St., tel. 415/332–9640). If you're looking for a cheap meal with a view, head to the four-story **Village Fair** (777 Bridgeway), one of the more attractive shopping malls around, complete with a little waterfall. On the top floor is **Café Sausalito** (tel. 415/332-6579), where you'll find affordable fare (coffee $1, sandwiches about $5) and a phenomenal view of San Francisco and Angel Island.

During the Great Depression, a local grocer graciously honored his customers' credit, preventing countless Sausalito residents from going hungry. Today, Yee Tock Chee Park stands as a monument to him, where Bridgeway meets the San Francisco Bay (201 Bridgeway, tel. 415/332–0804).

Bridgeway is Sausalito's main thoroughfare, bordered on one side by waterfront restaurants and the bay, on the other by shops hawking pricey antiques or tacky pelican paperweights. At the south end of Bridgeway is the Sausalito Ferry Terminal, where the commuter ferry from San Francisco docks (*see* Getting In, Out, and Around, in Chapter 1). Farther south—near the end of Bridgeway at Richardson Street—is Sausalito's oldest restaurant, originally known as **Valhalla.** Built in 1893, it was used as a backdrop in the classic Orson Welles film *The Lady from Shanghai.* Today it's just a Chart House restaurant with fantastic views and expensive (about $25) meals.

About a mile north on Bridgeway, look for the **Bay Model,** an enormous working model of San Francisco Bay and the Sacramento–San Joaquin Delta. Don't expect a cute replica of Coit

Tower—this is strictly a scientific tool, used by the U.S. Army Corps of Engineers to study the tides and other forces affecting the bay. The detail of the model is amazing, right down to ebbing tides, actual South Bay mud flats, and rivers that flow at one-tenth of their actual velocity. *2100 Bridgeway, tel. 415/332–3871. Admission free. Open summer, Tues.–Fri. 9–4, weekends 10–6; fall–spring, Tues.–Sat. 9–4.*

After dark, a rowdy over-thirty crowd congregates at Sausalito's No Name Bar (757 Bridgeway, tel. 415/332-1392) to enjoy free live jazz, blues, or Dixieland music Wednesday–Sunday.

Tiburon and Angel Island

Some young urbanites come to Tiburon, a peninsula jutting into the bay just north of Sausalito, with picnic baskets in hand and set out their spread on the harbor-front lawns at the tip of the peninsula. Others dock their boats at the harbor and head to one of the many waterside cafés and restaurants. Do both these things and you'll have just about exhausted the possibilities here. The atmosphere is relaxed and the views of Angel Island and San Francisco are great, but the small cluster of gift shops and pricey boutiques housed in wooden shingle buildings along the waterfront will soon seem cloying. To rise above the strip of tourist shops on Main Street (both literally and figuratively), head up the hill to **Old St. Hilary's Historic Preserve,** which stands in a field of wildflowers on a lonely perch above town. The white, wooden carpenter Gothic church is run by the Landmarks Society as a historical and botanical museum. Come in May or June to see the rare black jewel wildflowers in bloom. *Esperanza and Alemany Sts., tel. 415/435–1853. Admission free. Open April–Oct., Wed. and Sun. 1–4.*

To get to Tiburon, exit U.S. 101 at Tiburon Boulevard and drive 3 miles to the tip of the peninsula, where Main Street curves to the right. Most of the restaurants and boutiques are here or on tree-lined Ark Row, which veers westish at the end of Main Street. For less expensive delis and grocery stores, look on Tiburon Boulevard a few blocks from the waterfront. If you can't afford any wine to pack in your picnic basket, make a pre-picnic stop at **Windsor Vineyards** (72 Main St., tel. 415/435–3113), where you can sample up to six wines for free, all made at their winery in the Russian River Valley. Some bottles sell for as little as $7.

If Tiburon is about to quaint you to death, take a 15-minute ferry ride to **Angel Island.** Here you can explore sandy beaches, eucalyptus groves, and old military installations (across Raccoon Straits), all crammed into a 750-acre state park within spitting distance of the Golden Gate Bridge. **Ayala Cove,** the area around the ferry landing, is congested with picnickers taking advantage of tables and barbecue grills. The 5-mile perimeter road that rings the island, offering access to plenty of scenic and historic sites, is also heavily traveled (for more info, *see* Hiking, in Chapter 8). But it's easy to escape the crowds: For the ultimate isolated picnic, schlep your stuff about a mile from Ayala Cove to **Camp Reynolds,** which functioned as an army camp from the Civil War to World War II. Plenty of people linger at the Commanding Officer's House along the road, but about a ¼-mile past the old army barracks at the water's edge, you'll find some isolated picnic tables and an outstanding close-up view of the Golden Gate Bridge.

On the other side of the island is **Immigration Station,** once known as "The Ellis Island of the west," where immigrants (mostly Asian) were detained when trying to enter the United States between 1910 and 1940. A few poems written by despairing detainees are still etched into the walls. A **visitor information center** at Ayala Cove (tel. 415/435–1915) distributes a brochure with a history of the island and a map for $1.

Ferries (415/435–2131) leave for Angel Island from Tiburon's Main Street Pier (21 Main St.) at 10 and 11 AM and 1 and 3 PM on spring and summer weekdays, and every hour from 10 to 5 on spring and summer weekends. Boats depart from Angel Island 20 minutes after they dock. Round-trip fares are $5, plus $1 for bicycles (no cars). Schedules are subject to change, so call ahead for the latest. Ferries also leave from Fisherman's Wharf in San Francisco in summer. Bicycles are available for rent at Ayala Cove for an atrociously expensive $25 a day or $12 an hour. Those with their own aquatic transportation can dock at the island's boat slips for $5 a day, $9 overnight, $7 off-season.

Mill Valley

Mill Valley, accessible via the East Blithedale exit from U.S. 101, is a community of millionaires and mountain-bikers set amid the California redwoods on the eastern slope of Mt. Tamalpais. It's a mellow town where people have paid enormous sums of money for their solitude and want to keep it that way. It's true that the boutiques in the small, pedestrian-friendly downtown area are too pricey to actually shop in but, unlike Sausalito and Tiburon, the people you'll see actually live here, and haven't just flocked over on the ferry from Fisherman's Wharf.

On weekends all the action is on the plaza at the corner of Miller Street and Throckmorton Avenue, where people play hackysack and drink coffee bought at one of the three nearby coffeehouses. The best of the bunch is the **Depot Bookstore & Café** (87 Throckmorton Ave., at Miller St., tel. 415/383–2665), a favorite of mountain bikers after a run down Mt. Tam. After you've been properly caffeinated, walk less than a block to **Village Music** (9 E. Blithedale Ave., at Throckmorton Ave., tel. 415/388–7400). John Goddard has run the record shop, which stocks almost exclusively vinyl, for more than 25 years. The store has become a landmark on the international music map, attracting many big-name customers. A local waiter boasts of having run into Mick Jagger outside Village Music one day. No guarantees of similar brushes with greatness, but the store's well worth a visit, if only to look at the memorabilia papering the walls. Consider sticking around Mill Valley after sunset to pay a visit to **Sweetwater** (153 Throckmorton Ave., at Miller Ave., tel. 415/388–2820), a tiny club that attracts some of the finest jazz and R&B talents in the country. On any given night local resident Huey Lewis or bluesman Roy Rogers might show up to jam. Covers range from about $5 to $25.

If you've come to enjoy more pastoral pursuits, take a "walk around the block," Mill Valley–style: The short **Three Wells** and **Cascade Falls** walks follow a gentle uphill route through the redwoods, along a creek, past more than one righteous and frigid swimming hole, to a small waterfall. To get here, walk or drive up Throckmorton and turn left on Cascade Drive until you see the THREE WELLS sign nailed to a tree. Follow the path starting at the sign for about ¼-mile, cross the street, and continue uphill at the CASCADES FALLS sign.

San Rafael

Unassuming San Rafael, set between the foot of Mt. Tamalpais and San Rafael Hill, would perhaps attract more day-trippers from foggy San Francisco if people realized it's almost always a few degrees warmer here than anywhere else in the Bay Area. In fact, that's exactly why the town was founded in the first place. In 1817, when Native Americans at San Francisco's Mission Dolores started dying at an alarming rate, missionaries built a hospital here so the sick could receive care in a more hospitable climate. The original buildings of the Mission San Rafael Archangel were torn down in the 1870s, but a replica of the **chapel** (cnr 5th and A Sts.), built of stuccoed concrete instead of the original adobe, now sits next to a gift shop selling Catholic kitsch. If you drive up San Rafael Hill from the chapel on **Robert Dollar Scenic Drive,** you'll see some of Marin County's ubiquitous million-dollar homes. A block away from the chapel, **4th Street** is the town's main drag, lined with used bookstores, a large contingent of department stores, and some good cafés. The best of the latter is **Jazzed** (816 4th St., at Lincoln Ave., tel. 415/455-8077), a smoke- and alcohol-free club modeled after the bohemian cafés of the '60s. Enjoy a light meal ($5–$7) or creative coffee concoction (about $2) while listening to the free live jazz performances, happening every night but Monday, when the café is closed. The best time to pay a visit to San Rafael is on summer Thursdays evenings, when the **San Rafael Farmers' Market** (tel. 415/457–2266) fills 4th Street around B Street. The market is more like a weekly block party than a simple produce sale; locals come in droves to buy handicrafts, listen to live music, and let the kids take pony rides.

Fourth Street is so quintessentially American that George Lucas used it as a backdrop for some scenes in his film "American Graffiti," based on his teenage years in Modesto. Just off 4th Street is Lucas Road, where the director's Industrial Light and Magic studio is located.

North of downtown—take North San Pedro Road exit off U.S. 101—the enormous pink and blue **Marin Civic Center** (3501 Civic Center Dr., tel. 415/499–7407) offers guided tours of its impressive complex, designed by architect Frank Lloyd Wright. Concerned with preserving the natural contours of the site, Wright integrated the buildings into the surrounding landscape, setting them around, in, and under three principal hillocks. The complex looks a lot like a bloated whale from the outside, but the inside has been heralded as one of the most functional and offbeat office spaces ever conceived. Tours are available by reservation, and there's a well-stocked information kiosk in the lobby (open weekdays 8–6) for walk-in visitors. For information on dance and drama performances in the adjoining theater, call 415/472–3500.

When concrete gets tiring, drive 4 miles east on North San Pedro Road to **China Camp State Park,** a beautiful 1,600-acre wilderness area on the fringe of civilization. Luckily, somehow this pristine slice of nature has remained undeveloped and unpublicized. Remnants of an old Chinese fishing village are still visible, and the oak knolls and saltwater marshes are great for hiking (*see* Chapter 8) and camping (*see* Chapter 7). Parking at China Camp Point begins a 5-mile hike along the well-marked **Shoreline Trail.** The **Bay View Trail,** a steeper schlep but wonderfully uncrowded, is a favorite of park rangers. Pick up a trail map from the **ranger station** (tel. 415/456–0766) about a mile from the park entrance on North San Pedro Road. You'll pay $3 to park your car most places in the park.

Muir Woods and Mt. Tamalpais

MUIR WOODS NATIONAL MONUMENT Judging from the crowded parking lot and tacky gift shop, the Muir Woods National Monument looks like just another overtouristed attraction to be avoided. This 550-acre park, however, contains one of the most impressive groves of coastal redwoods in the world, some more than 250 feet tall and over 800 years old. It's crowded, to be sure, and a favorite destination of the older set, but you can find rugged, unpopulated trails that meander along cool, fern-filled ridges high above the clogged canyon. The **Ocean View Trail,** one of the best for beating the crowds, ascends for 1.3 miles before connecting with the **Lost Trail,** which descends through forests of Douglas fir back into the redwoods. Lost Trail hooks up with **Fern Creek Trail,** taking you back to the parking lot. The moderate hike is 3 miles round-trip and passes some of the park's most impressive stands of redwoods and many little streams. (For more trail tips, *see* Hiking, in Chapter 8). To really avoid

John Muir Demurs

It is somewhat ironic that Muir Woods—admittedly beautiful but annoyingly paved and crowded with screaming toddlers—should be named for John Muir (1838–1914). It's true enough that this naturalist and conservationist is largely responsible for the existence of his namesake national monument—he had a talent for gaining the favor of rich and powerful men who had the pull to preserve old-growth forests. But somehow you get the idea that Muir wouldn't be entirely happy about this slice of nature packaged neatly for your viewing pleasure. After all, Muir was a mountain man. He was so entranced with the awesome power of nature that, during the middle of a fierce storm in the Sierra Nevada, he climbed to the top of a wildly swaying Douglas Spruce to get his "ear close to the Æolian music of its topmost needles." What, then, would Muir, a tree hugger in the most literal sense of the word, think of the national monument's Cathedral Grove, where railings keep you from touching the trees and signs politely request that you not stray from the paths? Namesake or no, he would probably split for Mt. Tam.

the camera-toting throngs, try to visit on a weekday morning, or even a rainy day—the forest canopy is dense enough in places to keep you dry.

Neither picnicking nor camping is allowed in the park, but snacks are available at the gift shop, along with every type of redwood souvenir imaginable. The **visitor center** (tel. 415/388–2595) organizes free nature walks through the woods; call for current schedules. The floor of the redwood forest is shady, chilly, and often damp, so dress warmly. From U.S. 101, take the Stinson Beach/Highway 1 exit and follow signs. The monument is open daily 8 AM–sunset, and parking is free, though on sunny weekends, Muir Woods is so crowded you may have to park a mile or more from the lot.

MUIR BEACH If you stick to Highway 1 instead of following the turnoff to Muir Woods, you come to **Muir Beach,** a quiet strip of sand cluttered with oddly shaped pieces of driftwood and hundreds of tidal pools. The strikingly scenic beach, the site of the first coastal settlement north of San Francisco, attracts folks looking to relax—not the Budweiser and volleyball crowd you'll find at Stinson Beach, 6 miles farther north.

If you really want to get a feel for Marin's landscape, park your car at Muir Beach and hike the **Coastal Trail** (*see* Hiking, in Chapter 8), which leads up a steep hill overlooking the ocean and crawls around a series of deserted coves and valleys. Return the same way and reward yourself with a pint of Guinness in front of the fire at the **Pelican Inn** (Hwy. 1 at Muir Beach, tel. 415/383–6000 or 415/383–6005). You can eat lunch here for under $10—the cottage pie ($6.50) is excellent—but dinners run about $20 (prime rib is $16.25). The dining room closes between 3 PM–6 PM, but the adjoining pub, serving a healthy sampling of British ales and bitters, is open 11–11 every day but Monday, when both the pub and the restaurant are closed. There's a stone fireplace in the wood-paneled dining room and a dart board in the pub. Upstairs are seven Tudor-style rooms ($143–$165 a night), filled with antiques and canopied beds—about as atmospheric and romantic as they come. Ask the innkeeper about renting horses from the nearby stables: You can arrange moonlit gallops along the beach.

Less than a mile south of Stinson Beach, the **Green Gulch Farm Zen Center** (1601 Shoreline Hwy., tel. 415/383–3134) is worth a short visit, or, depending on your location on the path to spiritual enlightenment, a seven-week stay for intensive Zen training. The center offers classes and meditation sessions in everything from walking meditation to Japanese tea ceremonies to gardening. (Green Gulch supplies organic produce to the famous vegetarian restaurant Greens, among other places). One of the most popular activities here is the weekly Sunday program: instruction, meditation, a lecture, tea, a discussion period, and lunch ($5 donation). Even if you're not seeking instruction, you're welcome to wander the idyllic grounds and gardens. On Sundays between 8:45 AM and 10:30 AM, expect to pay a $5 parking fee unless you have three or more people in your car; another option is to carpool, as many people do, from the Manzanita Commuter Parking Lot underneath the Stinson Beach/Highway 1 exit off U.S. 101 (look for someone holding a GREEN GULCH CARPOOLING sign).

MT. TAMALPAIS STATE PARK Home to the Coastal Miwok Native Americans for thousands of years before the first European explorers arrived, Mt. Tamalpais is now home to explorers of a different sort, hiking and biking around the forested canyons and up to the 2,571-ft. summit. More than 50 miles of trails crisscross the park, which contains more than 750 species of plant life, from the hardy coastal redwood to the persnickety Calypso orchid.

There are several theories about the origin of the name Tamalpais, but the most commonly accepted one is that it is a combination of the Coastal Miwok words "tammal" (bay country) and "plis" (mountain). A good starting point for your exploration is the **Pantoll Ranger Station** (tel. 415/388–2070), where you can buy a $1 topographic map of Mt. Tam with all the trails and roads clearly shown. Mountain biking is big here (*see* Chapter 8), and the map distinguishes the fire trails (where biking is allowed) from the walking trails (where biking nets you a fat $100-plus fine). One beautiful, strenuous, and popular hike, the 2-mile **Steep Ravine Trail** (*see* Hiking, in Chapter 8), starts from the Pantoll station and takes you down a series of ladders to the Steep Ravine cabins. Parking is $5 in the Pantoll parking lot, but you can park for free anywhere along the road—just make sure you're completely outside the white sideline. The place is packed on weekends, so you'll have trouble parking if you're not there before noon.

The **summit** of Mt. Tam can be reached by car (look for the turnoff opposite Pantoll station), and the gates are open dawn to dusk. Unfortunately, the military owned the summit until recently and left the kind of squat buildings and strange towers that only the military seems to build. According to one park aide, there are several full-size bowling alleys in one of the buildings (and no, you can't have a game). Also near the summit is the open-air **Mountain Theater** where, every summer for six consecutive Sundays, a play or musical is produced. It's a landmark of the local scene and worth a look if you're around. Ask at the Pantoll station for performance and ticket information, or call 415/383–1100.

Stinson Beach

Six treacherous miles north of Muir Beach on Highway 1 lies Stinson Beach, one of the most popular coastal towns in Northern California. It's loaded with rickety wooden houses and friendly general stores, and its 3-mile-long beach—the longest in Marin County—has a beach-bum and barbecue appeal that's hard to find north of Santa Cruz. Despite Stinson's isolated location, the chilly water temperatures, and the threat of sharks lurking offshore, hordes of surfers and sun worshipers descend every weekend upon this town of 1,200. Even if you're not planning to surf or swim, the 20-minute (10-mile) drive from Muir Woods to Stinson, past towering cliffs and jagged granite peaks, is incredible. Traffic can be a problem on summer weekends, but there are plenty of scenic overlooks along the way to cushion the blow of bumper-to-bumper traffic.

The **Livewater Surf Shop** (3450 Hwy. 1, tel. 415/868–0333) rents body boards ($8 a day), wet suits ($10 a day), and surfboards ($25 a day) year-round; just look for the building with a surfboard on the roof. If you're hungry, stop off at the **Parkside Café** (43 Arenal St., tel. 415/868–1272), with good burgers at the cheapest prices in Stinson ($5–$7), though it turns into a pricier Italian restaurant at dinnertime. Turn west at the stop sign on Highway 1 and you'll can't miss it. If hanging out at the park is higher on your agenda than a sit-down meal, the Parkside Snack Bar next door is even cheaper. For groceries, stop by the **Beckers' By the Beach** (101 Calle del Mar, tel. 415/868–1923), next to the stop sign on Highway 1.

Along Bolinas Lagoon, just north of Stinson on Highway 1, you'll find the **Audubon Canyon Ranch** (tel. 415/868–9244). On weekends and holidays between mid-March and mid-July, this 1,000-acre bird sanctuary and ranch (and its 10 or so hiking trails) are open to the public from 10 to 4, offering bird lovers a chance to get up close and personal with blue herons and egrets. There's a small museum ($5 donation suggested) with geological and natural-history displays, a bookstore, gift shop, and a picnic area.

For a different slice of nature, walk down to **Red Rocks Beach** where, during extremely low tides, caves containing hot springs are revealed. Be aware—the locals are likely to be protective of their turf and entirely naked. Even when the caves are concealed by water, the beach is peopled by nudists. Leave your inhibitions in the car. To get here, drive ¾ mile south of Stinson Beach and park in the big gravel lot you'll see on the right (it's often full on sunny weekends). A path leads from there down to the beach.

Bolinas

A few miles north of the Audubon Canyon Ranch (*see above*), lies Bolinas, a town dedicated to discouraging tourism. Need proof? Locals are so tenacious about taking down the sign marking the Bolinas/Olema Road (it's the first left after you curve around the lagoon to your left), it's become a local legend. If you breeze into town to wander Main Street and do some shopping, you'll feel tolerated at best—rarely, if ever, welcome by locals who loathe the idea of tacky Sausalito-style development. You might brave the cold stares to witness the town's **Fourth of July** festivities, which have included outrageous parades and a tug-of-war with Stinson Beach (the loser ended up in the muddy mouth of the estuary between the two towns). One local described Bolinas as the "Zen-purity, earth-magnet, long-hair, free-to-do-what-you-want place to be, man," but a walk past the town's million-dollar homes makes you wonder how much residents really champion the ideals of the '60s.

Despite the elitism, you'll still find a few VW buses and bearded hippies strumming their guitars on street corners. The **Bolinas People's Store** (14 Wharf Rd., at Brighton Ave., tel. 415/868–1433) is famous for its fresh, high-quality local produce, grown by the same sweaty hippies who once gave Bolinas so much of its character. The only nightlife in town is **Smiley's Schooner Saloon** (41 Wharf Rd., at Brighton Ave., tel. 415/868–1311), ostensibly the oldest continually operated saloon in California. Huddled around the pool table and jukebox are an odd combination of suit-and-tie professionals and tie-dyed alternative fringies. For a bite to eat, go next door to the **Bolinas Bay Bakery and Café** (20 Wharf Rd., tel. 415/868–0211), which offers fresh baked goods, pasta salads, and pizzas. Many items feature locally grown organic ingredients.

If the smell of patchouli is fraying your nerves, take Mesa Road 4½ miles north from the second stop sign on Bolinas/Olema Road to the **Point Reyes Bird Observatory** (tel. 415/868–0655), which harbors 225 species of birds. It's open year-round and admission is free. On your way, make the mile-long detour to **Duxberry Reef,** a peaceful breaker that's dotted with hundreds of tidal pools. To get there, go left on Overlook Drive from Mesa Road and right on Ocean Park Way. (For hikes in this area, *see* Chapter 8.)

Point Reyes National Seashore

Exploring the Point Reyes National Seashore—a 66,500-acre mosaic of marshes, ferocious cliffs, and undisturbed beaches—you'll feel a lot farther than 30 miles away from San Francisco, and for good reason. Point Reyes is on the Pacific tectonic plate, while most of the rest of California is on the North American Plate—as a result, its bedrock, plants, and the terrain are all very different from the rest of the Bay Area. Even though it's isolated, Point Reyes is a manageable day trip from San Francisco, a drive of about 90 minutes each way. There are hundreds of hiking trails on the peninsula (*see* Chapter 8) and, if you want to spend the night, four backpackers-only campgrounds and an excellent hostel (*see* Chapter 7).

With its lush grazing land and rambling farms, Point Reyes—a hammerhead-shaped peninsula that sticks 10 miles out into the ocean—could easily pass for western Ireland, minus the pubs.

Twelve miles north of Bolinas on Highway 1, past the block-long town of Olema, look for a sign marking the turnoff for Point Reyes at the end of the block of stores and head for the **Point Reyes Visitor Information Center** (tel. 415/663–1092) off Bear Valley Road. This is the best place to begin your exploration; you can sign up for ranger-led interpretive hikes or get trail maps and camping permits. A short walk away, look for the replica of a typical Coastal Miwok Native American village, built on the ruins of a 400-year-old Miwok farming settlement. Also nearby is the **Bear Valley Trail,** a lightly traveled four-mile hike that wanders through the woods and down to a secluded beach. If you can't make it to Point Reyes Lighthouse (*see below*), the Bear Valley Trail offers a good overview of the peninsula.

Two miles farther down Bear Valley Road (which turns into Sir Francis Drake Boulevard), you'll pass through the quiet town of **Inverness.** Coming across this town's Czech restaurants and architecture—full of oddly colored, intricately carved wooden houses—can be disorienting after miles of uncluttered coast, but the town's Eastern European flavor is definitely real. In 1935, after a freighter ran aground in San Francisco Bay, a number of its Czech deckhands jumped ship and settled here. Since then, dozens of Czech families have settled in Inverness, bringing both their culture and their cuisine. For some of the best dumplings this side of Prague, head to **Vladimir's** (12785 Sir Francis Drake Blvd., Inverness, tel. 415/669–1021). A meal costs around $15; the restaurant's open Tuesday–Sunday.

West of Inverness, at the end of Drake's Beach Road, which intersects Sir Francis Drake Boulevard, lies a massive stretch of white sand known as **Drake's Beach.** It's often windy here and too rough for swimming (oh, by the way, great white sharks swim offshore), but the beach is great for a relaxing day in the sun. Supposedly, Sir Francis himself landed here on his world tour; hence the name. Check with the visitor center for current regulations; if they give the okay, there's plenty of driftwood on the beach for an early evening campfire.

A quarter mile north of Drake's Beach, a sign directs you to the **Point Reyes Lighthouse** (tel. 415/669–1534) 6 miles to the west. It's open Thursday–Monday 10–4:30, though closed during particularly windy weather, and admission is free. From the parking lot, a steep trail leads down to the lighthouse, and a dozen or so trails are etched into the surrounding cliffs. The ¾-mile hike to **Chimney Rock** is one of the most scenic; look for the trailhead in the parking lot. If it's really clear you should be able to see San Francisco, but usually the thick fog provides little visibility. From mid-December to April, and especially in January and March, this is a great place to look for the gray whales on their 12,000–mile round-trip migration along the Pacific coast.

To reach Point Reyes from San Francisco, cross the Golden Gate Bridge on U.S. 101. If speed is more important than scenery, exit at Sir Francis Drake Boulevard and follow it west for 21 miles to the coast. Eventually, you'll end up 2 miles north of Olema on Highway 1. Otherwise, take the Stinson Beach/Highway 1 exit and enjoy the curvy, 30-mile scenic drive along the coast. On weekends, Golden Gate Transit can take you here by bus, but it's a complicated affair (*see* Getting In, Out, and Around, in Chapter 1).

There aren't too many places to eat in Point Reyes, so stock up in San Francisco or at the **Bovine Bakery** (11315 Hwy. 1, 2 mi. north of Olema, tel. 415/663–9420). They have excellent, reasonably priced sandwiches, pastries, and breads—the perfect makings for a picnic. The most popular stop, however, is Inverness's **Perry's Delicatessen** (12301 Sir Francis Drake Blvd., near Vallejo Ave., tel. 415/663–1491). For under $6, you can brown-bag one of their shrimp or crab sandwiches and a freshly made garden salad. Also in Inverness is the **Gray Whale Inn** (12781 Sir Francis Drake Blvd., tel. 415/669–1244), a good pit stop for home-style pizzas, pastries, sandwiches, coffee, and beer. It's more expensive than Perry's, but the sunny patio is a good place to watch day fade into night.

South Bay

A wanna-be philosopher once said that middle America begins but a few miles away from San Francisco. Indeed, just south of the San Francisco International Airport, you'll notice a subtle change in scenery and ambience. As you travel south along U.S. 101, you begin to see a rapid proliferation of shopping malls, industrial parks, tract homes, and brightly lit clusters of fast-food restaurants. Before you know it, the winding streets and frenetic energy of San Francisco seem miles away—you've entered, not the Twilight Zone, but *suburbia.* But life does not end here, it only seems that way. The South Bay has its own interesting, amusing, or just plain weird attractions that San Francisco snobs thoroughly underrate (or don't know about). The cities that stretch south from San Francisco to San Jose lie on what locals refer to as the **Peninsula,** a finger of land wedged between the San Francisco Bay on the east and the Pacific Ocean on the west; a number of cities, including Palo Alto—home to acclaimed Stanford University—make for easy day trips from San Francisco.

The best-kept secret of the South Bay is Highway 1 and the secluded **San Mateo County Coast**—more than 75 miles of winding shoreline and gently undulating hills that seem a world away from the overdeveloped inland communities. Along the highway are long, sandy beaches, frequently devoid of any life aside from the local sea lions, surfers, and gulls; small towns just beginning to awaken to their potential as tourist destinations; and redwood groves filled with great hiking trails. The only bummer here is the weather: Though hilly inland areas like La Honda and Pescadero are nearly always cool to warm in spring and fall, and hot (but not oppressively so) in summer, the beaches more often than not are windswept and chilly—better suited for a brisk walk than an afternoon of sunbathing. The quickest way to reach the northern end of the San Mateo County Coast from San Francisco is to follow I–280 south to Highway 1; it'll only take 10–15 minutes to reach Pacifica from downtown. Public transportation is sketchy.

Palo Alto

Palo Alto, about 30 miles south of San Francisco, is mostly known as the location of Stanford University; it's certainly worth the drive just to check out the beautiful 8,200-acre campus.

However, contrary to popular Bay Area opinion, the town of Palo Alto itself has some cultural attractions that are worth a look, as well as a cute, if overpriced, downtown area. Off U.S. 101, **University Avenue,** between Middlefield Road and High Street, is Palo Alto's main drag; west of El Camino Real it metamorphoses into **Palm Drive,** Stanford's entrance and main thoroughfare. University Avenue travels through Palo Alto's oldest and wealthiest neighborhood—keep your eyes peeled for the grand mansions. In the downtown area, University Avenue and its side streets are loaded with restaurants, cafés, galleries, boutiques, and bookstores. All are disappointingly upscale for a student shopping district, but at least the streets are punctuated by pleasant little plazas with benches and plants.

As any Stanford student will lament, Palo Alto is seriously hurting in the nightlife department. The local dive bar can be found across the street at the excellent **Antonio's Nut House** (321 California Ave., at Birch St., tel. 415/321–2550), where you can get Guinness on tap ($3), free peanuts from the gorilla cage, and drinks until 2 AM nightly—a rarity around here.

When you're looking for that *other* buzz, head across the street to **Printer's Inc.** (310 California Ave., tel. 415/327–6500) and peruse the extensive 'zine selection (about 900 titles) while tossing back an espresso or three. On the other side of town, about a mile north of campus, **Café Borrone** (1010 El Camino Real, near Ravenswood Ave. in Menlo Park, tel. 415/327–0830), coupled with **Kepler's Books** (tel. 415/324–4321) next door, happily fuses caffeine and literature once again, attracting a yuppie college crowd that tends to sprawl out onto the brick patio. Dixieland jazz bands often play on weekend nights.

The huge, sprawling campus itself is best explored by bike, and the biking is even better in the foothills west of the university. For rentals, try **Campus Bike Shop** (551 Salvatierra St., on campus, tel. 415/325–2945), which can get you rolling on a mountain bike for $20 or a three-speed for $10 a day. Either kind of bike requires a hefty cash, check, or credit card deposit.

STANFORD UNIVERSITY Sometimes called the Ivy League university of the West Coast, Stanford opened its doors to scholars in October 1891. Its co-founder, railroad mogul Leland Stanford, also served as governor and U.S. senator for California. Busy guy. Nicknamed "The Farm" because the land was once a stud farm (that's certainly no longer the case), Stanford consists of look-alike, mustard-colored buildings that combine Romanesque squatness with the ranchy feel of a Spanish mission, giving the campus an austere and refined flavor. Some of its more disenchanted students, however, refer to the university as an oversized Taco Bell.

From downtown, enter campus along the aptly named Palm Drive, which will take you to the **quad,** the heart of campus and a popular hangout. You can pick up free maps or take a guided walking tour from the **information office** (tel. 415/723–2560) in Memorial Hall. The quad is dominated by the sprightly, Romanesque **Memorial Church,** best known for its Venetian mosaics. Near the entrance to the quad, the grassy **Memorial Court** has a couple of Auguste Rodin statues—dedicated to Stanford men who died for their country—that depict some 14th-century English martyrs, *The Burghers of Calais,* "at the moment of painful departure from their families and other citizens." A New Guinean **sculpture garden,** installed in 1995, can be found near the intersection of Lomita Drive and St. Theresa Street. Just to the south of the quad, the 280-foot **Hoover Tower** (tel. 415/723–2053) thrusts mightily into the sky, home of the ultra-conservative Hoover Institution for the Study of War, Revolution, and Peace. To get the classic view of campus and parts of Palo Alto, pay $2 to climb to the tower's observation deck, which offers an excellent 360° vista.

Like many colleges these days, Stanford prides itself on tolerance and diversity, but in 1994 a group of students vandalized a campus gay-pride statue, drawing the ire of the Bay Area's sizable gay community. The statue, located on the west side of the main quad, has since been restored.

Rodin Sculpture Garden. For now, this is as close as you'll get to **Stanford's Museum of Art,** seriously damaged in the 1989 Loma Prieta earthquake and closed until at least June 1997. The 20 or so works by French sculptor Auguste Rodin (1840–1917) are clustered in a small area to the left of the museum. Most pieces depict nudes in various stages of introspection, ecstasy, or anguish. Check out the particularly intense *Gates of Hell;* the giant iron doors are the scene of lots of wild action. The sculpture garden is open all hours, drawing late-night adventurers out to frolic with the lifelike figures. Descriptive tours are given at 2 PM Wednesday and on weekends; call for details. *Museum Way and Lomita Dr., tel. 415/723–3469. From Palm Dr., turn right on Museum Way, 1 block past Campus Dr.*

STANFORD LINEAR ACCELERATOR Even if you're only vaguely interested in science, make the trek up Sand Hill Road (west from campus toward I–280) to see this masterpiece of modern ingenuity. The 2-mile-long atom smasher is truly amazing—thousands of house-size machines, dials, diodes, and scientists who get excited when you mention n-orbits and electrons. Reserve space in advance for the free two-hour tour, held twice a week, which includes a slide show and lecture (days and times vary); it's geared toward lay people and is extremely interesting. *2575 Sand Hill Rd., Menlo Park, tel. 415/926–2204. From I–280, exit east at Sand Hill Rd.*

BARBIE HALL OF FAME "Barbie mimics society; whatever we've done, she's done," says Evelyn Burkhalter, founder of the Barbie Hall of Fame. She's put together the largest collection of Barbie dolls on public display in the world, with 16,000 of the plastic bombshells in residence. Evelyn says that Barbie has changed constantly and considerably over the years, and indeed, just about every fashion and lifestyle trend of the past few decades can be seen in these halls. Don't miss the infamous "talking-math Barbie," who says "math is *so hard*"—Mattel took a lot of heat from feminists for that one. *433 Waverly St., at University Ave. in Palo Alto, tel. 415/326–5841. Admission: $4. Open Tues.–Fri. 1:30–4:30, Sat. 10 AM–noon and 1:30–4:30.*

NEAR PALO ALTO

NASA AMES RESEARCH CENTER For a true technological trip, visit this 140-acre research center, devoted to the design of all types of flying machines, which is located at Moffett Field in Mountain View (about five miles southeast of Palo Alto). The **NASA Visitor's Center Museum** (open weekdays 8–4:30) showcases aviation and space-flight paraphernalia, but the research facility itself is normally closed to the general public. The real score is to call two weeks ahead and sign up for one of the two or three escorted tours of the main plant they offer each week (days and times vary). Depending on what's available that day for snooping, the two-hour free tour may take you around flight simulators, design centers, retired research crafts, or construction hangars. *Tel. 415/604–6274. From U.S. 101, exit at Moffett Field, left on Moffett Blvd. at the main gate, and head toward the space shuttle.*

Dying to Get to Colma

If you're driving south on I–280 to Palo Alto, you'll pass the small city of Colma, a modern-day necropolis filled with cemeteries and macabre graveyard art. In 1914, San Francisco's mayor ordered most city cemeteries to relocate their occupants to Colma, since the city needed the land for its more active residents. Since then, no new cemeteries have been created within San Francisco's city limits. The Colma Town Hall (1198 El Camino Real, at Serramonte Blvd., tel. 415/997–8300) offers a self-guided tour of the city's cemeteries ($2.50), from the prestigious Cypress Lawn to the eerie Pet's Rest, littered with flea collars and dog toys. Look for the graves of Dodge City's Wyatt Earp and a local baseball legend, former San Francisco Seals' manager Lefty O'Doul. Colma has more dead than living residents, the only such city in the US, although some might disparagingly claim this to be true of other South Bay towns.

San Jose

People are too hard on San Jose. True, Northern California's largest city is marked by the same mini-mall sprawl you'll find all over America. Emphatically middle-class, San Jose is the sort of charmless suburbia everyone loves to hate. Despite all this, San Jose has an oddly comfortable and cosmopolitan feel. Encircled by mountain ranges, buffered by city parks and gardens, San Jose is home to museums, symphonies, and wineries as well as industrial parks, computer companies, and corporate headquarters.

The new billion-dollar **downtown** is a good place to start exploring. Hop on the **Light Rail** (tel. 408/321–2300) that connects San Jose State University on one end with the Center for Performing Arts on the other (fare is $1.10); its numerous stops should give you a good overview of the city center, which is architecturally interesting in its—generally successful—attempt to meld existing Old West themes with modern styles and materials (note the traditional small-town clock tower built from marble and stainless steel). Cruising the heart of downtown, around the intersection of Market and San Carlos streets, there are a number of pedestrian plazas and a host of museums, including **The Tech** (145 W. San Carlos St., across from Convention Center, tel. 408/279–7150), a hands-on technology museum that definitely inspires admiration for the wizardry of the computer age; the $6 admission price is well worth it. **Plaza Park** (S. Market St., in front of Fairmont Hotel) is a pleasant grassy strip that runs for two blocks, complete with benches and a fountain you can play in (the water shoots straight up out of grates in the ground).

The student population of San Jose State has gradually encouraged the growth of a trendier side of downtown that has become known as **SoFA** (South of First Street)—a small section of downtown roughly between East Carlos and West Reed streets. Make a beeline here if you find yourself in San Jose after dark; the rest of the city is infested with heavy metal discos and tedious sports bars. At **Café Matisse** (311 First St., at San Carlos St., tel. 408/298–7788), open daily until midnight, you can join the youngish but hip crowd, sit back in one of the overstuffed chairs, nurse a latte ($2.50), and watch the people coming out of the tattoo parlor across the street.

The **Rosicrucian Egyptian Museum and Planetarium** houses one of the most impressive collections of Egyptian, Assyrian, and Babylonian artifacts west of the Nile. Truly fascinating are the animal and human mummies, the underground tomb, and the decorative wall reliefs. The planetarium shows here also hold their own; call 408/947–3634 for show times and ticket prices. *1342 Naglee Ave., at Park Ave., tel. 408/947–3636. Get off I–880 at Alameda East exit, turn right at Naglee Ave. Admission: $6, $4 under 18. Open daily 9–5, last entry 4:35 PM.*

NEAR SAN JOSE

GARBAGE MUSEUM Californians generate more garbage per capita than any other group of people in the world, and this museum gives you some dramatic ways to feel guilty about it. The massive 100-foot "Wall of Garbage" exhibit represents merely one second's worth of what the country is continually throwing out. At least there's the Recycling Hall, where a huge magnet separates steel and iron from a mountain of tin cans. *1601 Dixon Landing Rd., Milpitas, tel. 408/432–1234. Take Dixon Landing exit off I–880, 5 mi north of San Jose; the recyclery is visible from freeway. Admission free. Open weekdays 7:30–5.*

GREAT AMERICA If you've got the urge to spin around until you feel nauseated, eat gooey food, and buy monstrous pairs of sunglasses, head to this Crayola-colored amusement park loaded with excellent roller coasters and hokey gift shops. It's owned by the Paramount/Viacom megacorporation, so you get movie-theme attractions like the **Days of Thunder** racing simulator and the amazing **Top Gun Jet Coaster.** Popular favorites include the double-looped **Demon,** the occasionally drenching water ride called **Logger's Run,** and the stand-up **Vortex** coaster, built a few years ago for a whopping $5 million.

To shave a few bucks off the price, call the number listed below and ask about any current discount schemes (usually by bringing a Coke can or a token from some fast-food restaurant).

Another tip: They don't let people bring food in (so you'll be forced to buy their pricey, greasy eats), but you can get around the rule by bringing your own chow, leaving it in a locker near the front gate, and eating in the picnic area outside. *Great America Pkwy., Santa Clara, tel. 408/998–1800. Take Great America Pkwy. exit off U.S 101, about 10 mi north of San Jose. Admission: $26. Open spring and fall weekends; summer, daily 10–9 (Sat. until 11 PM).*

The San Mateo County Coast

PACIFICA AND MONTARA

Pacifica and Montara—about 20 minutes south of San Francisco along Highway 1—mark the northern end of the spectacular, underpopulated San Mateo County Coast. Two particularly sleepy seaside towns on a coastline known for its lethargy, Pacifica and Montara are great for a quick escape from urban chaos. The "historic" section of Pacifica, located on the northernmost outskirts of town, is full of unpretentious, bungalow-style homes that once served as weekend retreats for wealthy San Franciscans but today house a majority of the town's locals. Pacifica's small commercial district, to the south, is an eclectic combination of old mom-and-pop stores and upscale specialty shops, the latter suggesting that the town is growing a little weary of its backwater authenticity and wants to start attracting some of San Francisco's yuppie weekend tourists. Linking past and present are the recently renovated paved boardwalk and old fishing pier. Come here to smell the saltwater, feed the pigeons, and watch local fishermen ply their trade; the pier also affords brilliant views of San Francisco and Marin County.

Pacifica's star attraction is its dark sand beaches. About two miles south of old Pacifica is **Rockaway Beach,** consisting of two large dollops of sand on either end of a gorgeous cove—just large enough for half a dozen sunbathers and a handful of surfers and fishermen. Immediately south of Rockaway, you'll come to the more popular **Pacifica State Beach,** a longer stretch of sand favored by surfers and a fair number of local sun worshipers. Pacifica is also home to some fine hiking trails (*see* Chapter 8).

Just a few miles farther removed from San Francisco, Montara is pretty much all beach—its commercial district is virtually nonexistent. **Montara State Beach,** on the north end of town, two miles south of Devil's Slide (*see box, below*), is a wide, picturesque stretch of sand, less crowded than Pacifica's beaches. It's a good place to catch some rays, play Frisbee, have a picnic, or take long, contemplative walks. Half a mile farther north, **Gray Whale Cove State Beach** (tel. 415/728–5336) is an American anomaly: a government-supported clothing-optional beach. Entrance to the spectacular, secluded cove is $5 (or you can pay $175 for an annual pass). Keep your voyeuristic tendencies in check—cameras are strictly forbidden. Immediately south of the Montara city limits in Moss Beach, the rich tide pools of the **James V. Fitzgerald Marine Reserve** (tel. 415/728–3584) stretch along the coast for 4 miles. Go at low tide (call ahead to find out when) to check out abalone, barnacles, kelp, shells, and maybe an octopus or two; but remember, this is a reserve, so look, but don't touch. To reach the reserve from the Point Montara Lighthouse Hostel (*see* Chapter 7), where you can obtain a tidal timetable, take Highway 1 south to California Avenue and turn right. The beaches and reserve are open from dawn to dusk.

During Prohibition, the Moss Beach Distillery (Beach Way and Ocean Blvd., tel. 415/728–5595) served as a speakeasy roadhouse for politicians and silent film stars who came from San Francisco to drink bootlegged whiskey while enjoying the romantic ocean view over the cliffs.

For a meal in Pacifica, head straight to Francisco Boulevard, paralleling Highway 1 to the west. Here you'll find **Pacifica Thai Cuisine** (1966 Francisco Blvd., tel. 415/355–1678)—which features traditional specialties like chicken curry in coconut milk ($6)—and the oddly named **Pacifica Harry** (1780 Francisco Blvd., tel. 415/738–8300), an upscale Chinese restaurant with enticing entrées like cashew-nut shrimp ($8). Both restaurants offer vegetarian options. In Montara, **A Coastal Affair** (Hwy. 1, at 8th St., tel. 415/728–5229), ⅓-mile north of the Point Montara Lighthouse Hostel (*see* Chapter 7), is a combination craft gallery and café with excellent espresso ($1.75–$2.75) and freshly made sandwiches (about $4). Half a mile south of the hostel in Moss Beach, **El Gran Amigo** (2448 Hwy. 1, at Virginia Ave., tel. 415/728–3815) serves up a wide variety of authentic Mexican specialties including enchiladas ($5) and nachos ($2.50). Across the street, **Coastside Market** (501 Virginia Ave., tel. 415/728–3142) is an amply stocked spot to buy picnic supplies. The area also features abundant seafood restaurants, but most are pretty generic.

HALF MOON BAY

Famous for growing Halloween pumpkins, Christmas trees, and flowers, Half Moon Bay—28 miles south of San Francisco—is the closest thing to a major town along the San Mateo County Coast. With its seaside/rural/small-town feel, natural beauty, and wealth of activities (well, compared to the other dinky villages around here), it's the most inviting of the coastal communities. The "revitalized" downtown area centers around **Main Street,** which parallels Highway 1; the cozy street is cluttered with craft stores, produce markets, gardens, cafés, and straightforward burger joints. If lolling on the beach is more your speed, follow Kelly Avenue west from Highway 1 to the popular **Half Moon Bay State Beach,** actually a series of beaches covering more than two miles. To avoid the $5 parking fee, walk from downtown. It will probably get unpleasantly cold near the water before too long, a perfect excuse to trek 2 miles inland along Highway 92 and sample—free of charge—the local wines at **Obester Winery** (12341 San Mateo Rd., tel. 415/726–9463), open daily 10–5.

Half Moon Bay hosts literally dozens of annual festivals, any one of which you could plan a visit around. The largest and most popular one is the **Art and Pumpkin Festival,** held the weekend after Columbus Day. The high-spirited fall celebration includes live music, local foods, crafts, vendors, a children's parade, and outrageous pie-eating and pumpkin-carving contests. Also popular is the aptly named **Coastal Flower Market,** which takes place on the third Saturday of each month in May through September. Other yearly events include the riotous **Human Race** every May, in which entrants use every wacky scheme they can devise to carry other contestants along the course; the **Brew Ha-Ha** beer and sausage tasting festival each spring; and a daring **California Coast Air Show** that takes place at Half Moon Bay's tiny airport in the fall. For more information on any of these festivals, contact the **Half Moon Bay Chamber of Commerce** (520 Kelly Ave., at Main St., tel. 415/726–8380 or 415/726–5202).

For a meal, Half Moon Bay offers everything from reasonably priced health food markets to way-outta-range seafood restaurants. The best of the former is **Healing Moon Natural Foods Market** (523 Main St., tel. 415/726–7881); if you're not looking for groceries, serve yourself a cup of soup and eat it on the peaceful outdoor patio. Across the street, colorful **McCoffee** (522 Main St., tel. 415/726–6241), serves sandwiches, salads, and milk shakes, each for less than $4. On the northern end of downtown, **Sushi Main Street** (315 Main St., tel. 415/726–6336) is a trendy local favorite. Squeeze yourself into the tiny sushi bar and order

The Devil's Work

Devil's Slide, a breathtaking stretch of Highway 1 between Pacifica and Montara, is surrounded by a familiar California problem—a mountain that is determined to fall into the sea. 1995's torrential downpours exacerbated the damage from continuing erosion, closing the road for more than six months. Despite temporary repairs and reinforcements, the California Department of Transportation is searching for a long-term solution, such as building a bypass or tunnel; both of these plans draw the ire of Bay Area environmentalists, which in turn draws the ire of coastal residents who commute to the city to earn their daily bread. Ah, California. Call 800/427–ROAD for the latest.

up a cup of hot sake ($2) with sushi ($2–3). Their sushi combos (about $10) offer such creations as the Nothin's Raw Special (octopus, grilled eel, prawns, mussels, and scallops—a veritable seafood overdose). Despite its chain-restaurant exterior, **3 Amigos** (200 N. Cabrillo Hwy., on Hwy. 1 at Kelly Ave., tel. 415/726–6080) offers tasty, cheap Mexican food (veggie burritos $3) and every Mexican beer under the sun ($2.25) daily until midnight. You'll find reasonably priced seafood (a rarity in this area) at the **Flying Fish Grill** (99 San Mateo Rd., at Main St., tel. 415/712–1125), open Tues.–Sun. 11–8. Chow down on clam chowder ($3) and a variety of deep-fried and grilled fresh fish ($7–10).

SAN GREGORIO TO AÑO NUEVO

The desolate stretch of coastline south of Half Moon Bay is nearly deserted year-round, and for good reason. The beaches here are cold; the choice of affordable food and lodging is limited; and the number of worthwhile "sights," depending on your criteria, can be almost negligible. But the very fact that the area is so empty means that, with the exception of Año Nuevo State Reserve during the elephant seals' mating season, there's almost nothing you can do here that will require advance planning. Day-trippers seeking sand, sea, and forest in quiet simplicity are more likely to find it here than in the more touristed Half Moon Bay. The rich tide pools at Pescadero State Beach, the cliff-hugging Pigeon Point Lighthouse Hostel, and the sky-high trees lining Highway 84 through La Honda all make this chunk of coastline extremely worthwhile for people seeking serious solitude on short notice.

SAN GREGORIO Although not much of a destination in itself, San Gregorio is a worthwhile stop if you're traveling up or down the coast between Santa Cruz and Half Moon Bay. The drive in from the coast to this hitching post of a town, at the junction of Highways 1 and 84, is half the fun, even if you don't come by the spectacular coast road. **Highway 84,** the east–west road running to San Gregorio from I–280, (also known as La Honda Road) is for the strong of stomach only; but if you can take it, the highway is so thick with redwoods you'll barely believe it's daytime. Best of all, the road spits you out at the isolated **San Gregorio State Beach,** where you can lie back and soak up some rays, or, more likely, throw on a sweater and battle the wind as the fog comes rolling in. If you get too cold, the bluff north of the parking lot is a good place for a brisk, blood-warming walk.

If you're in the area, don't miss the **San Gregorio General Store** (tel. 415/726–0565; open daily 9–6, Fri. until 7), a mile east of Highway 1 on Highway 84. This eclectic, Old West-style store, which has served the ranching and farming community since 1889, sells everything from used books and stuffed animals to cast-iron pots and antiques—it also doubles as the town saloon and community center. You might even catch some Bulgarian bluegrass or Irish R&B if you show up on the right weekend night.

LA HONDA If you're getting tired of relentlessly magnificent coastal scenery, you should either seek psychiatric help or head inland to the densely forested community of La Honda, 11 miles east of Highway 1. About the size of a postage stamp, La Honda seems almost lost in the shadow of countless giant redwoods on Highway 84 (*see* San Gregorio, *above*). The town consists of **Pioneer Market** (La Honda Center, tel. 415/747–9982), where you can stock up on camping supplies and sandwiches ($3.50); the **Clear Water Café** (8725 La Honda Rd., tel. 415/742–9600), offering barbecued chicken sandwiches ($4.50) and espresso drinks (about $2), open daily until 8; a post office; and **Apple Jack's Tavern** (La Honda Rd., tel. 415/747–0331). The last is a scruffy bar that should absolutely not be missed, no matter what time of day you're passing through town. Open weekdays noon–2 AM and weekends 10 AM–2 AM, Apple Jack's is today's version of an Old West saloon: The men drink their whiskey straight-up, the women are loud and boisterous, and a brawl seems ready to erupt any minute. You'll feel equally comfortable pulling up on a Harley Davidson or on a horse.

Even more than Apple Jack's, though, it's the old-growth redwoods surrounding La Honda that will make your visit here a mind-blowing experience. If you don't have time to head north to California's redwood country, La Honda is a surprisingly good substitute. Four—that's right, four—state and county parks ring this tiny town, and their forested hills provide excellent terrain for hiking, biking, and being inspired by the ancient giants (for details, *see* Chapter 8).

Take Highway 84 about a mile west of La Honda, make a left on Alpine Road, and 4½ miles later you'll come to the parking lot of **Pescadero Creek County Park** (for info call Memorial County Park, tel. 415/879–0238), a secluded expanse of fir- and pine-covered hills crisscrossed by a series of gentle streams. From the parking lot, follow the **Tarwater Trail Loop** in either direction for a moderate hike of about 2 miles, which will take you from a ridge with ocean views down through the scrub and into the redwoods. Don't blame Pacific Gas & Electric Co. for the crude oil bubbling in Tarwater Creek—it's natural. If you haven't had your fill of towering redwoods, Douglas fir, and pine trees, drive a bit farther along Alpine Road and you'll reach the turnoff for **Portola State Park** (Portola State Park Rd., tel. 415/948–9098), 2,400 acres of even more remote and scenic forest—the only drawback is the $5 parking fee. Just past the entrance to the park, the visitor center sells wood ($3) and trail maps ($1). For info on hikes here, *see* Chapter 8. And if night comes and you still can't tear yourself away, check it out: You can camp here (*see* South Bay, in Chapter 7).

Two more woodsy parks lie on Pescadero Road, which meets up with Alpine Road a mile south of Highway 84. The first is **Sam McDonald County Park** (for info call Memorial County Park, tel. 415/879–0238), a small, almost deserted redwood forest good for short hikes and complete solitude. Thankfully, there's no charge for day use of the park. A bit farther along Pescadero Road, you'll come to **Memorial County Park** (tel. 415/879–0238), the most developed of the four parks, whose attributes include a fresh-water swimming hole, picnic areas, fire roads popular with mountain bikers, and a number of short and medium-length hiking trails through the redwoods (for details on hiking and biking, *see* Chapter 8). To avoid the $4 parking fee at Memorial, park on the side of the road just outside the entrance.

PESCADERO Over 100 years ago, all of the wooden buildings in the small fishing village of Pescadero were painted white, with paint that washed up on shore when the clipper ship *Carrier Pigeon* crashed into the rocks off Pigeon Point, a few miles south of town. Today, the bakery, general store, bank, local post office, and other shops that populate Pescadero still retain their whitewashed uniformity, giving this town, in the flatlands a mile inland from the coast on Pescadero Road, a calming, subdued ambience.

After you've rambled around the three blocks that make up Pescadero's commercial district, head straight to **Duarte's Tavern** (202 Stage Rd., at Pescadero Rd., tel. 415/879–0464), open 7 AM–9 PM daily, a combination bar and restaurant that's been run by four generations of Duartes since 1894. The homey restaurant serves everything from peanut butter and jelly sandwiches ($3) to lamb chops ($14), but it's most famous for its cream of artichoke soup, made with local produce, ($4), fresh seafood plates ($6–$20), and homemade pies ($3).

On the coast just west of town, you'll find **Pescadero State Beach,** a long, sandy expanse with vibrant tidal pools, perfect for checking out the Pacific's aquatic denizens. Immediately north of the beach, the **Pescadero Marsh Reserve** (tel. 415/879–2170) is a protected area favored by ornithologists. Free guided walks leave from the parking lot just south of Pescadero Creek on Saturdays at 10:30 AM and Sundays at 1 PM year-round. If you prefer to hike or bike in the

The Merry Pranksters

In the early 1960s La Honda was home to one of the hippie era's most renowned groups of psychedelic crazies, the Merry Pranksters. Led by the multitalented bohemian Ken Kesey, author of One Flew Over the Cuckoo's Nest, the Merry Pranksters spent several years on a La Honda farm exploring "states of non-ordinary reality," i.e., dropping acid, eating mushrooms, and smoking dope. When La Honda became too limiting, they outfitted an old school bus with psychedelic Day-Glo paintings, and filming and recording equipment, and set off to travel across the country, a journey made famous by Tom Wolfe in his popular chronicle The Electric Kool-Aid Acid Test.

hills, **Butano State Park** (tel. 415/879–0173), five miles south of Pescadero on Cloverdale Road, has 20 miles of trails on 2,700 acres (for hiking and biking info, *see* Chapter 8). You can reach the park from Gazos Creek Road, off Highway 1 near Año Nuevo State Reserve (*see below*), or take Pescadero Road a couple miles east from town and head south on Cloverdale; there's a $5 parking fee.

ANO NUEVO STATE RESERVE Named by explorer Sebastian Viscaino on New Year's Day, 1603, the Punta del Año Nuevo is one of the few places in the world where you can safely view live elephant seals close up and personal. Not only that, if you're here between December and March, you get to watch them do the wild thing. During mating season, you'll need to make reservations up to eight weeks in advance through MISTIX (tel. 800/444–PARK), and you can only visit the reserve on one of the 2½-hour guided walks ($4, plus a $4 parking fee). If you're lucky, you may catch sight of migrating gray whales at the same time. Sea lions, sea otters, and harbor seals have also been known to make appearances, mostly off the coast and on Año Nuevo Island, inhabited only by seals and birds.

Since drag queen Divine kicked the bucket some years ago, this may be your only chance to watch overfed, under-exercised, 200-pound-plus honking balls of blubber perform their mating rituals. Don't miss it.

Though not as thrilling as the fighting and preening of mating season, the elephant seals come ashore from April through September to shed their old, furry brown skin for a sleek, new one; the yearlings stick around until November, gaining strength for the upcoming months spent entirely in the water. At these times, you can gain access to the reserve by obtaining a free permit from the visitor center (tel. 415/879–2025), open Apr.–Sept. 8–6, Oct. and Nov. 8–4. To avoid the $4 parking fee, continue about ¼ mile south past the main reserve entrance and park on the west side of Highway 1 (where you'll also find an alternate trail to the reserve). The path to the elephant seals' beach from the main parking lot is 1½ miles long; and if you come in spring, you'll be treated to the sight of thousands of colorful wildflowers along the trail. The reserve, about 40 miles south of San Francisco, can be reached on SamTrans Bus 96C (*see* Getting In, Out, and Around, in Chapter 1). Wheelchair access to the viewing areas is available with one day's advance notice.

SHOPPING 3

By Cynthia Leung

S

Spending money is too easy in the Bay Area. As if the vacuum effect that rent and food have on your wallet isn't enough, San Francisco's stores will coax you into spending your last penny on some treasure, be it a low-rider bicycle from the Mission, an extinct vinyl recording from the Haight, or leather chaps from SoMa. If you want to look even half as cool as most young people here, you've got your work cut out for you. But with a little effort and patience, you'll come across some real finds at decent prices.

Never mind the overpriced, sophisticated emporia of downtown's Union Square: San Francisco has a lot to offer the budget shopper. Infamous **Haight Street**—home to the trés hip in fashion, furniture, and music—is a good place to start, but prices include an "atmosphere and attitude" tax that makes the **Mission district**'s overflowing warehouses even more appealing. Here you'll find everything from piles of antiques to rare fashion finds. **Chinatown** has tons of cheap electronic goods and silk items; **North Beach** has unique (and often expensive) specialty stores which may still reek of pasta-chomping tourists; and the **South of Market** area has bargain warehouses that stock slightly flawed, brand-name threads at damaged prices.

The East Bay suffers less from "ambience sickness." With the exception of a few small areas like **Piedmont Avenue** and **Rockridge** (College Ave., btw Alcatraz Ave. and Broadway), you won't find much in Oakland unless you dig discount emporiums. Additionally, most Oakland stores are open 9–5, while the rest of the Bay Area seems to operate on a more worker-friendly 11–7 schedule. Instead, follow your nose to Berkeley's incense- and patchouli-scented **Telegraph Avenue,** which is all student, all the time. The exception to the rule is on weekends, when even San Franciscans roam the Avenue to check out stands selling tie-dyes, cheap silver rings, and hair-weaving services. Sandwiched between the sweatshirt and T-shirt shops that shove the Cal logo down your throat are some *fierce* bookstores, music shops, and clothing stores.

Suburbia does have one advantage over the cosmopolitan parts of the Bay Area: space. If outlet malls are your gig, the peninsula is your paradise. Worth checking out are the **Metro 280 Center** (Colby Blvd., at I–280 in Colma) and **Marina Square** (Marina Blvd., at I–880 in San Leandro). On the other hand, if you (inexplicably) pine for overpriced, touristy boutiques, head north across the Golden Gate Bridge to Sausalito. You'll be back pretty darn quick.

New Clothes

SAN FRANCISCO

You'll find everything from Armani suits to Afghani rugs in the city. The huge department stores housed in the **San Francisco Shopping Centre** (865 Market St., btw 4th and 5th Sts.), may make you tired of shopping before you've even found the right floor, but deals can be found in some of the smaller stores, like **Cignal** (Third Floor, tel. 415/979–0209), where both men and women can find low-priced (compared to Union Square) suits and separates. There's also the **Embarcadero Center** (Clay and Battery Sts., btw Drumm and Sacramento Sts.), an 8-block complex of chichi shops customized for Financial District customers rushing around on their lunch breaks. In general, the farther you go from downtown, the better deal you'll find.

Mega-department stores like Macy's, Nordstrom, Emporium-Capwell, and Nieman-Marcus are perfect for the shopper with the patience of Buddha and the bank account of Trump.

Behind the Post Office. Before X-Large came to the Haight, there was Behind the Post Office. Stocked with the latest and greatest hip-hop gear, including smart-ass T-shirts, skate-girl dresses, and baggy pants for when you're feeling phat, this tiny shop specializes in lesser-known local labels. On weekends local DJs spin tunes, and this is a great place to pick up info on underground jazz and hip-hop scenes. *1504 Haight St., at Ashbury St., tel. 415/861–2507.*

Betsey Johnson. Postmodern designer-goddess Betsey Johnson brings you her outrageous women's fashions in a campy art-deco and neon-lit environment. The often silly clothes aren't cheap, but their limited appeal leads to regular ½-off sales. *2031 Fillmore St., btw Pine and California Sts., tel. 415/567–2726. Other location: 160 Geary St., btw Stockton and Grant Sts., tel. 415/398–2516.*

Esprit Factory Outlet. You, too, can look like a fresh-scrubbed young American, and now at substantial savings! For best results, head for the back. *499 Illinois St., at 16th St., tel. 415/957–2550.*

Joshua Simon. This Noe Valley store stocks an eclectic selection of women's garments—from flowing pants and romantic-looking dresses to unusually woven vests and painted clothing. Some items are imported from Indonesia; others are fashioned by local designers. *3915 24th St., btw Sanchez and Noe Sts., tel. 415/821–1068.*

Na Na. Part of a national chain that has stores in New York and Los Angeles, Na Na sells trendy shoes and clothes to hip men and women. The store carries a number of local labels—and even the big-name lines aren't carried in bulk, so you won't look like everyone and their mother at the next party. *2276 Market St., near Noe St., tel. 415/861–NANA.*

Rolo. All three branches of this boutique, especially popular among gay and lesbian club-goers, carry some really groovy threads for those who like to see and be seen. The store on Market is heavy on conservative wear for men; the Howard Street store features a flashier women's selection; and the Mill Valley branch emphasizes casual clothes for women. *1301 Howard St., at 9th St., tel. 415/861–1999. Other locations: 2351 Market St., near Castro St. in S.F., tel. 415/431–4545; 438 Miller Ave., Mill Valley, tel. 415/383–4000.*

Shoe Biz. Don't let the humdrum name stop you from finding a deal on some European-style shoes. The friendly staff will set you up with sneakers, Docs, or anything else your feet desire. The last-size sale corner has tons of high-quality shoes at big discounts. *1446 Haight St., at Masonic Ave., tel. 415/864–0990.*

EAST BAY

Although you can find almost anything in San Francisco, the East Bay, with its masses of students, holds its own. Come to Telegraph Avenue and around to find street vendors, collegiate threads, and lower prices for comparable styles.

Deep Threads. Hip-hop fans, rejoice: Deep Threads has all the baggy jeans, baseball caps, beanies, and parkas you could possibly want. They also carry decks, trucks, and wheels, if you're in the market for a new rig. This is a good source for info on the Oakland hip-hop scene. *5243 College Ave., at Broadway in Oakland, tel. 510/653–4790.*

Futura. A strange mix of folks flock to Futura to check out the store's eclectic blend of new and used clothes. There's a good selection of men's gas-station shirts, vintage jackets, and corduroy jeans. Women can find baby tees, pricey dresses, and baggy pants. *2360 Telegraph Ave., near Durant Ave. in Berkeley, tel. 510/843–3037.*

New West. You're tired of flares and polyester, and your platforms have given you one too many sprained ankles. Guys and gals, head to New West to spruce up your wardrobe with big-name seconds and samples at markdown prices. *2967 College Ave., at Ashby Ave. in Berkeley, tel. 510/849–0701. S.F. location: 426 Brannan St., btw 3rd and 4th Sts., tel. 415/882–4929.*

Urban Outfitters. This place—sort of a left-of-center, pay-to-look-poor Gap—is actually part of a chain, though it feels one-of-a-kind with its unusual assortment of casual urban wear, jewelry, shoes, and apartment furnishings. Accessories are cheap and sometimes unique, but a T-shirt could run you $30. *2590 Bancroft Way, at Bowditch St. in Berkeley, tel. 510/486–1300. S.F. location: 80 Powell St., btw Ellis and Market Sts., tel. 415/989–1515.*

X-Large. X-Large brings cool clothes, phat hip-hop beats, and a comfortable couch to Telegraph Avenue. It's part of a chain fronted by Beastie Boy Mike D, and Sonic Youth bassist Kim Gordon has taken the time to design some of the threads for you hip-hop Bettys—so you *know* they're cool. *2422 Telegraph Ave., Berkeley, tel. 510/849–9242. S.F. location: 1415 Haight St., tel. 415/626–9573.*

Secondhand Clothing

SAN FRANCISCO

Naturally, the Mission and the Haight abound with vintage clothing, secondhand duds, and thrift shops. The big name stores—Wasteland and Buffalo Exchange—are always dependable for flannel, a polyester shirt, or a basic black dress, but you'll find better hunting and gathering (at cheaper prices) in the city's smaller shops: To start with, try Mission and Valencia streets between 15th and 18th streets. If you want to browse Haight Street, start at Fillmore Street and go all the way up to Stanyan Street, concentrating on the Upper Haight (from Masonic to Stanyan). Thrift-store sophisticates looking for a silk Chanel suit or a 1930s beaded satin gown will want to head off the beaten path to Divisadero Street (btw Pine and Bush Sts.) and Fillmore Street (btw Bush and Sacramento Sts.) where they'll find ritzy vintage shops and high-end secondhand stores that carry designer brands tossed aside by Pacific Heights society mavens.

AAardvark's Odd Ark. AAardvark's keeps the thrifty crowd coming back with a wide selection of used clothing. It's a good source for men's basics, cotton dress shirts, and vintage Levi's. *1501 Haight St., at Ashbury St., tel. 415/621–3141.*

American Rag Compagnie. This store mixes old and new, and precious little is cheap. But the dreck has been filtered out, the clothes are in good shape, and everything is sanitized for your protection. They arguably have the best selection of black vintage dresses in San Francisco, plus racks of stylish suits and hip, retro-looking jackets classy enough for the day job. *1305 Van Ness Ave., btw Sutter and Bush Sts., tel. 415/474–5214.*

Buffalo Exchange. This thrift store doesn't try to be cutting-edge, but the selection is consistent and pretty cheap. The store mixes vintage with contemporary clothes—keep this in mind if you want to sell that Gap stuff you got for your birthday. *1555 Haight St., btw Ashbury and Clayton Sts., tel. 415/431–7733. Other locations: 1800 Polk St., near Washington St. in S.F., tel. 415/346–5726; 2512 Telegraph Ave., Berkeley, tel. 510/644–9202; 3333 Lake Shore Ave., Oakland, tel. 510/452–4464.*

Clothes Contact. This is a true thrift shop, where shirts are between $3 and $4, dresses cost $5, and Levi's run $10. It's an especially good place to come if you have a weakness for funky old dresses or are in dire need of a suit and a Hawaiian print tie. *473 Valencia St., near 16th St., tel. 415/621–3212.*

Construction Zone. Hey, boys! Do as the signs urge and DRESS UP YOUR MAN in an occupational uniform or otherwise enticing costume. You and your construction worker, military man, or cowboy will be all set to hang out with the boys at the YMCA. *2352 Market St., near Castro St., tel. 415/255–8585.*

Crossroads Trading Co. This secondhand clothing store has three locations in the Bay Area, each with a small, carefully selected, and relatively cheap stock. The Fillmore store tends to be rife with early '80s wear, while the other two stores are better for jeans, unusual dresses, and classic vintage. *2231 Market St., btw Sanchez and Noe Sts., tel. 415/626–8989. Other locations: 1901 Fillmore St., at Bush St., S.F., tel. 415/775–8885; 5636 College Ave., near Keith St., Berkeley, tel. 510/420–1952.*

Departures From the Past. This immaculate vintage shop has formal attire and costumes for both sexes, as well as casual wear from eras past. Each item is handpicked by the owner, and prices are slightly higher than you'll find elsewhere. They'll rent any item in the store for half the price, including penguin suits, which go for about $30–$55 per night. *2028 Fillmore St., btw California and Pine Sts., tel. 415/885–3377.*

Thrift Town. A large, traditional thrift store and occasional repository of decades-old designer clothing and accessories, Thrift Town is a good source for everything from silver sandals to used cribs. *2101 Mission St., at 17th St., tel. 415/861–1132.*

Wasteland. One of the more popular secondhand stores in San Francisco, Wasteland brings you the trendy and outrageous at reasonable prices—including a groovy selection of bell-bottoms and other fashion items you hoped to never see again. It's also a good source for vintage costume jewelry, gowns, and suits. *1660 Haight St., btw Belvedere and Clayton Sts., tel. 415/863–3150.*

A Barter Society

When the stretch from paycheck to paycheck seems longer than usual, clean out your closets, bookshelves, and CD racks, and head to one of the Bay Area's secondhand stores, where you can get cash or trade for the stuff you don't want anymore. Clothing stores pay a percentage of what they can sell the item for, which is determined by the buyers—the dragons at the gate, so to speak—based on style, age, and condition. Wasteland, Buffalo Exchange, Futura, and Crossroads all give about 40% in cash or 60% in trade. Pay attention to the season when you sell: If it's summer, you're going to have a hard time unloading your fake fur.

Music stores subscribe to the chaos theory of buying, and set no definite equations, since what comes in is so varied. Expect anywhere from $1 to $6 in trade or cash for a basic domestic CD, and anywhere from 5¢ to $5 for records and cassettes. Buyers include Reckless, Recycled Records, Streetlight, and Rough Trade. Book stores are even less forgiving. Prices vary based on a book's condition and reputation: If a book didn't sell well the first time around, chances are good you'll get a fat rejection at the counter. San Franciscans in the know head east to Berkeley to sell books—specifically to Moe's, Shakespeare's, and Half-Price Books.

Worn Out West. This Castro district store provides secondhand western wear and leather goods to budget-conscious cowboys manqué. *582 Castro St., near 18th St., tel. 415/431–6020.*

EAST BAY

The East Bay has a great variety of thrift stores, especially along Telegraph Avenue near the U.C. campus in Berkeley and on College Avenue in Rockridge. The farther you stray from the stores with velvet in the windows, the more likely you are to find a real steal, like a $5 pair of Levi's that some collector would pay $50 for.

Madame Butterfly. In one corner you've got your '50s- and '60s-style dresses, pillbox hats, gloves, and overwhelming amounts of rhinestone jewelry; in another, you'll find a small rack of men's retro suits and ties. Either side will make you dig deep into your pockets. *5474 College Ave., Oakland, tel. 510/653–1525.*

Mars Mercantile. Mars is the most reliable vintage clothing store on Telegraph, with selectively chosen and well-organized merchandise. The prices aren't rock-bottom cheap, but they're reasonable. Besides racks of vintage dresses, acrylic men's shirts, fake fur, and genuine leather, the store boasts the flashiest window displays in Berkeley. *2398 Telegraph Ave., at Channing Way, Berkeley, tel. 510/843–6711.*

Rockridge Rags. Browse through the orderly racks of secondhand clothing and you'll find lots of stuff to wear when you're doing temp work downtown, including the occasional Anne Klein suit or Polo chinos. *5711 College Ave., Oakland, tel. 510/655–2289.*

Slash. With its huge stock of cheap Levi's ($15), overalls ($20), and corduroys of all colors, Slash feels like somebody's messy closet. Owners Carla Bell and Ocean Edgars are always happy to help you dig through the piles on the floor—which is half the fun anyway—to find the perfect pair of 5-0-whatevers. *2840 College Ave., at Russell St., Oakland, tel. 510/841–7803.*

Books

SAN FRANCISCO

Looking for a good book to take to bed, to act as a prop when you're lounging in a café, or to read on that 12-hour flight? This city has more than 200 bookstores—new and used, tiny and huge, nonprofit and corporate—for every language, political bent, or cultural interest. Don't forget to support smaller, local bookstores: You'll find them peppered throughout the city, but concentrated in the Mission and the Haight. Every bookstore has its own personality and loyal following; it's up to you to sniff around and find one to suit your literary fantasies.

Acorn Books. Desperate customers in search of antiquarian, out-of-print, or used books know the friendly staff at Acorn would hunt a book down to the ends of the earth—although the well-stocked store probably already has it somewhere on its gigantic shelves. *740 Polk St., btw Eddy and Ellis Sts., tel. 415/563–1736.*

Bound Together Book Collective. Here you'll find anarchist literature—mostly new—from all over the world, as well as nifty stickers declaring you vehemently anti-establishment. Don't tell the FBI. *1369 Haight St., near Masonic St., tel. 415/431–8355.*

City Lights, the legendary home of the Beat Generation, was once busted on obscenity charges for selling Allen Ginsberg's "Howl."

City Lights. For some, a trip to San Francisco is not complete without an evening spent browsing the stacks at City Lights, surely the city's most famous bookstore. Owned by poet Lawrence Ferlinghetti, City Lights is *the* source for Beat literature, much of it published under the store's own imprint. Opened in 1955, this beautiful bookshop has a fantastic upstairs poetry room and a "little press" alcove filled with local journals and 'zines. All books are new. *261 Columbus Ave., at Broadway, tel. 415/362–8193.*

A Different Light. You'll find a large selection of new lesbian, transgender, and gay-oriented literature here, as well as queerzines (*see* Media, in Chapter 1), T-shirts, and stickers. Regular book signings and readings attract the local gay community. *489 Castro St., near 18th St., tel. 415/431–0891.*

Eastwind Books and Arts, Inc. Stocking new books on China, Asia, and Asian America, Eastwind has both a Chinese- and English-language store. *Chinese-language bookstore: 1435A Stockton St., tel. 415/772–5877. English-language bookstore/art gallery: 633 Vallejo St., tel. 415/772–5899.*

European Book Company. Come here for European magazines and newspapers, as well as foreign-language dictionaries and travel guides. *925 Larkin St., near Geary St., tel. 415/474–0626.*

Green Apple Books. Not for those who require order and neatness, this ramshackle Richmond district store jumbles together the new, the used, and the rare in a space reminiscent of Grandma's attic. One of the city's better bookstores, Green Apple is also known for its knowledgeable and friendly staff. *506 Clement St., btw 6th and 7th Aves., tel. 415/387–2272.*

Marcus Books. Specializing in books "by and about African Americans," Marcus Books is a longtime community resource for all-new titles on history, religion, fiction, art, and more. There's a great selection of children's and young adult literature; recent readings by Sister Souljah, Maya Angelou, and Rosa Parks exemplify an impressive weekly reading series. *1712 Fillmore St., btw Post and Sutter Sts., tel. 415/346–4222. Other location: 3900 Martin Luther King Jr. Way, Oakland, tel. 510/652–2344.*

Modern Times. Leftists can choose from lots of new titles with a politically progressive, multicultural bent; oft-browsed sections include cultural theory, gay/lesbian issues, Spanish-language books, art, and current affairs. Modern Times is collectively run, carries underground papers and 'zines, and hosts regular readings and forums, often with a—you guessed it—political focus. *888 Valencia St., btw 19th and 20th Sts., tel. 415/282–9246.*

Old Wives' Tales. And young career women's tales, and middle-aged divorced mothers' tales, and some pimply, troubled adolescent girls' tales, too. Specializing in women's issues and women authors, this is a good resource for feminists of all shapes and sizes. Especially notable is the "Women's Voices" project: weekly readings, performances, and forums put on by the friendly female staff. *1009 Valencia St., btw 21st and 22nd Sts., tel. 415/821–4675.*

San Francisco Mystery Bookstore. This Noe Valley shop stocks everything imaginable for the armchair gumshoe in your life. New and used books, both in and out of print, abound; they also stock a few gay and lesbian mysteries. *746 Diamond St., at 24th St., tel. 415/282–7444. Closed Mon. and Tues.*

Sierra Club Bookstore. Along with a wide range of shiny-new titles on all aspects of environmentalism—including political tomes, nature poetry, and practical guides for hiking and camping—you'll find topo maps and kids' books. Call before stopping by; at the end of 1995 the store was planning to move. *730 Polk St., btw Eddy and Ellis Sts., tel. 415/923–5600. Other location: 6014 College Ave., Berkeley, tel. 510/658–7470.*

Small Press Traffic. At press time, Small Press was still searching for a new room of its own, but struggling writers can stop by Lodestar Books in the Castro to check out at least part of Small Press's collection of small press and self-published titles. Call (tel. 415/281–9338) or write (2215R Market St., S.F. 94114) for more information on Small Press's literary events and workshops. *Lodestar Books: 313 Noe St., at Market St., tel. 415/864–3746.*

Would-be writers take note: Small Press Traffic is the ultimate place to peruse, ponder, and peddle obscure poetry.

William Stout Architectural Books. This store stocks an international, professional collection of architecture and design books and periodicals. Even nonindustry types should admire the store's collection of out-of-print books. *804 Montgomery St., btw Jackson and Pacific Sts., tel. 415/391–6757.*

EAST BAY

The East Bay intelligentsia doesn't have to trek to San Francisco to look for quality new and used books. With a huge university in its midst and more pretentious intellectuals per square mile than anywhere outside the Académie Française, you'll find enough bookstores here to keep you occupied for a year. Telegraph Avenue has the highest concentration of tried-and-true general bookstores, though some fine shops lie farther from campus.

Black Oak Books. Locals, professors, and local professors frequent this friendly, well-stocked, new and used bookstore in North Berkeley. Boasting an impressive collection of both rare books and cheap paperback fiction, Black Oak also sells a beautiful collection of broadsides (quotations from literary works, artfully printed on heavy decorative paper)—an excellent gift for the serious bookworm. *1491 Shattuck Ave., Berkeley, tel. 510/486–0698.*

Cody's. Here's a Berkeley institution if there ever was one. Take a break from Telegraph Avenue and wander among the stacks upon stacks of shiny new volumes, covering every imaginable genre—from poetry and philosophy to self-defense and women's studies. Cody's also has an impressive newsstand, a cheery kids' substore, and free gift wrapping. Regular readings by famous and almost-famous authors are popular social events. *2454 Telegraph Ave., at Haste St., Berkeley, tel. 510/845–7852.*

De Lauer's Super Newsstand. De Lauer's isn't kidding. Open 24 hours daily, they carry maps, foreign language and domestic newspapers, and an overwhelming number of magazines—from the *Columbia Journalism Review* to *Beauty Pageant* magazine. *1310 Broadway Ave., at 14th St., Oakland, tel. 510/451–6157.*

Check out the wall at De Lauer's labeled YOUR HOMETOWN PAPER *when you're feeling homesick.*

Gaia Books. The East Bay's home for books on spirituality, ecology, holistic health, and sexuality, Gaia occupies a bright, airy space that's perfect for its regular readings and lectures. *1400 Shattuck Ave., at Rose St., Berkeley, tel. 510/548–4172.*

Mama Bears. In this bookstore/café you'll find new and used books on feminist political theory and lesbian issues, plus fiction by women writers and kids' books—but no PMS jokes. The coffeehouse doubles as a space for live readings and workshops. *6536 Telegraph Ave., at 66th St., Oakland, tel. 510/428–9684.*

Moe's. Moe's is one of Berkeley's most successful bookstores, thanks to the efforts of the gruff, cigar-chomping owner, Moe Moskowitz. Browse his five floors of new, used, and antique books, with a strong emphasis on the used and antique part. Moe's is a good first stop when you're trying to sell. *2476 Telegraph Ave., near Haste St., Berkeley, tel. 510/849–2087.*

Shambhala. Specializing in Eastern religions (and Western slants on Eastern religions), Shambhala also stocks new and used books on alternative medicine, the "new" sciences, and mysticism, yet remains free of a New-Agey stigma. *2482 Telegraph Ave., near Haste St., Berkeley, tel. 510/848–8443.*

University Press Books. Titles from over 100 university presses represent the absolute latest in intellectual thought. Buy a hot treatise on cultural theory and read it at the Musical Offering café next door—make sure everyone can see the title as you read. *2430 Bancroft Way, near Telegraph Ave., Berkeley, tel. 510/548–0585.*

Walden Pond. Pay a visit here, and a trip to the chain Walden-*Books* becomes unnecessary. Frequent discounts on both the new and used selections, as well as a comfortable upstairs reading room, foster a loyal clientele. The friendly, funny family that owns and operates the shop orders stock based on customer requests. Nice. *3316 Grand Ave., near Grand Lake Theater, Oakland, tel. 510/832–4438.*

On Friday and Saturday nights, Bay Area bookstores become somewhat of a pickup joint for earnest intellectuals.

Records, Tapes, and CDs

San Francisco may be the center of the Bay Area's *live* music scene, but when you're ready to blow a few hundred greenbacks on tunes, you can't do much better than the music shops on Berkeley's Telegraph Avenue. Within 5 blocks of the U.C. campus sit no fewer than four enormous record stores—a music lover's paradise. East Bay stores do more buying from the public, increasing the diversity of what's available: Even the discriminating collector should find the jazz, grunge, indie, hip-hop, or New Age 7" she's been looking for.

The quality of vinyl available at Bay Area music stores may have you begging Dad for his old turntable.

SAN FRANCISCO

Groove Merchant. Groove Merchant's owners run the highly recommended Luv 'n Haight and Ubiquity labels, both of which put the spotlight on the local acid jazz scene. The store has plenty of great finds for the collector, DJ, or serious amateur. *687 Haight St., btw Pierce and Steiner Sts., tel. 415/252–5766.*

Prince Neville's Reggae Run-Ins. Jah, mon, this is a reggae wonderland, with records, tapes, videos, T-shirts, jewelry, and other paraphernalia in red, gold, black, and green. *505 Divisadero St., btw Fell and Hayes Sts., tel. 415/922–2442.*

Reckless Records. A good source for used cassettes and CDs, Reckless also carries new music, T-shirts, posters, and video games. They specialize in independent and corporate rock, hip-hop, and soul. *1401 Haight St., at Masonic St., tel. 415/431–3434.*

Ritmo Latino. This colorful, Carnaval-esque store in the heart of the Mission sells an enormous variety of Latin music: ranchero, mariachi, salsa, Tex-Mex, merengue, norteño, and more. Best of all, the store has listening stations where you can check out any of the store's CDs before laying down hard-earned cash. *2401 Mission St., at 20th St., tel. 415/824–8556.*

Star Classics. The Blockbuster Video of classical music, Star Classics stocks only new classical CDs and cassettes. The adjoining Star Classics Recital Hall hosts vocal and musical performances every Friday and Sunday. *425 Hayes St., at Gough St., tel. 415/552–9622.*

Streetlight Records. Because they buy and sell for great prices to a diverse clientele, the selection of records, tapes, and CDs is usually offbeat and always fresh. *3979 24th St., btw Noe and Sanchez Sts., tel. 415/282–3550. Other location: 2350 Market St., near Castro St., tel. 415/282–8000.*

For Middle Eastern music, try Samiramis Imports (2990 Mission St. tel. 415/824–6555).

Tower Records. The branch on Columbus Avenue and Bay Street, near Fisherman's Wharf, has an excellent selection of international music, specially designed to calm pangs of overseas homesickness. Otherwise, this chain emporium offers a wide spectrum of new rock and pop, as well as jazz, hip-hop, classical, and show-tune music. Tower occasionally surprises with some offbeat selections, and hosts a number of in-store signings, giveaways, and performances by big-name artists. Call for the location nearest you. *Columbus Ave. and Bay St., tel. 415/885–0500.*

EAST BAY

Amoeba. Amoeba employees claim their store has more used CDs than any other in the country. They definitely have the widest and best selection of used CDs and new/used 7" records in the Bay Area, including well-rounded jazz, international, indie, import, and rock sections. The experienced, music-loving staff will show you the newest artists, dig out their rarest records, and cut you a fair deal for your used records, CDs, and tapes. *2455 Telegraph Ave., at Haste St., Berkeley, tel. 510/549–1125.*

Groove Yard. Music lovers fawn over this in-the-middle-of-nowhere store, which mixes mostly used jazz and soul records with a fair number of Latin and Brazilian discs. They also carry a little acid jazz, a little funk, and a bit of blues. The owner greets almost everyone who comes in the store by name—from DJs to dealers to students looking for more than Harry Connick Jr. Groove Yard happily gives trade or cash for high quality LPs and CDs. *4770 Telegraph Ave., at 48th St., Oakland, tel. 510/655–8400.*

Mod Lang. A single from your favorite long-haired British band is released overseas. Four days later you'll find it at Mod Lang, where shipments of ambient, indie, and psychedelic '60s music come in every week and sell at lower prices than on Telegraph. *2136 University Ave., near Shattuck Ave., Berkeley, tel. 510/486–1880.*

Rasputin's. If you can't find it at Amoeba, head to this glass coliseum filled with a gigantic selection of new and used CDs, records, and tapes. The indie, house/techno/ambient, and rock sections are your best bets here. The store regularly hosts live performances; otherwise, entertain yourself by further provoking the already rude staff. *2401 Telegraph Ave., at Channing Ave., Berkeley, tel. 510/848–9005.*

Reid's. Preacher putting you to sleep? A visit to Reid's will reaffirm your faith in gospel—they stock CDs, cassettes, robes, the works. *3101 Sacramento St., at Prince St., Berkeley, tel. 510/843–7282.*

Tower Records. Tower sells only new and mostly mainstream records, tapes, and CDs. Still, because it's a huge corporation, you can sometimes find better deals here on blank tapes and Top 40 bestsellers. If you love classical, check out **Tower Classical** (2585 Telegraph Ave., tel. 510/849–2500), a few blocks away. *2510 Durant Ave., at Telegraph Ave., Berkeley, tel. 510/841–0101.*

Household Furnishings

The Bay Area might be a nightmare when it comes to finding a place to live, but it's a dream when it comes to furnishing your pad. Garage, sidewalk, estate, and yard sales abound; check the *Bay Guardian, SF Weekly,* or *San Francisco Chronicle,* and watch for fliers on telephone poles, especially on summer weekends. The Mission district's thrift stores also overflow with cheap stuff. Try dependable **Community Thrift** (623 Valencia St., tel. 415/861–4910) or **Thrift Town** (*see* Secondhand Clothing, *above*) for the largest selections at the best prices. In the East Bay, Berkeley has nearly perfected the art of furnishing student apartments on the cheap. You'll find moderately priced furniture basics on San Pablo Avenue near University Avenue; University itself is lined with futon shops; and north of University, Fourth Street is slowly accumulating upscale furniture outlet stores (a good place to window shop for decorating ideas). Nearby, venerable **Whole Earth Access** (29907 7th St., at Ashby Ave., tel. 510/845–3000) is a convenient one-stop shop with moderate prices.

SAN FRANCISCO

Cookin': Recycled Gourmet Appurtenances. Here are used fondue makers, espresso pots, cookie cutters, Jell-O molds, pots, pans, and everything else you can't afford new. *339 Divisadero St., btw Oak and Page Sts., tel. 415/861–1854.*

Revolution at 33⅓

In San Francisco you can buy records and foment revolution at the same time. Epicenter (475 Valencia St., at 16th St., tel. 415/431–2725), an anarchist-oriented community center, has a huge selection of new and used punk rock albums, as well as pool tables, bulletin boards, and a library with tons of independent 'zines. It's an awesome resource for the new radical in town. Come by weekdays 3–8, Saturday noon–8, or Sunday noon–7.

Hocus Pocus. This is probably the worst place to be during an earthquake. Oak chairs and out-of-commission clocks are stacked literally to the ceiling in this groovy Mission district shop, where you can pick up everything from cheap dressers to overpriced antique jewelry. *900 Valencia St., at 20th St., tel. 415/824–2901.*

Jim's Used Furniture. Looking like it's been around for decades, Jim's rewards those willing to venture off the well-shopped part of Valencia Street with a neat-o chair for $10 or a worn coffee table for $5. *1499 Valencia St., at 26th St., tel. 415/285–2049.*

EAST BAY

Crate and Barrel Outlet. The only outlet store in the state for Crate and Barrel's popular wooden furniture, kitchenware, and decorative items, most of the stock consists of irregular or discontinued items, but everything is functional and priced about 30%–50% lower than at their regular stores. *1785 4th St., near Hearst St., Berkeley, tel. 510/528–5500.*

Urban Ore. Need a door, a chandelier, a toilet bowl, or some other household amenity you didn't even know you wanted until you saw it here? Head to this outdoor treasure trove (or junkyard, depending on the day) and leave raving about your incredible find. *7th St. at Gilman St., Berkeley, tel. 510/559–4450.*

Flea Markets

Noe Valley, particularly Church Street between 19th and 27th streets, is garage-sale paradise. So, too, are Dolores and Guerrero streets between 16th and 24th.

Flea markets are overwhelming anywhere, and in the Bay Area they can approach the size of small towns—entire fairgrounds, parking lots, or football fields, all full of good deals on antique furniture, clothes, toys, books, bikes . . . anything remotely old, quirky, or dusty. For more complete listings, pick up a copy of the free *Classified Flea Market,* available at most newsstands and convenience stores. If you're a real hound, either set the alarm clock and get there before the professionals move in, or go late in the day when sellers would rather lower prices than reload the damn truck.

One Person's Garbage . . .

The cheapest furniture of all comes from the street. Scavenging is best on the first and last days of every month, when people move out of their apartments and leave their sofas and wood furniture to the winds of fate. Even better, however, are the legendary Neighborhood Cleanups, when residents of a particular neighborhood are allowed to leave furniture, appliances, and any other hefty pieces of so-called junk on the street; in the morning, the city hauls it away for free. Most folks will put their stuff out around 8 or 9 PM; get at it early, before the secondhand-furniture salespeople sweep everything into their big trucks. Russian Hill, Pacific Heights, and the Marina generally have the most tony goods. For specific San Francisco Neighborhood Cleanup dates, call Sunset Scavenger (tel. 415/330–1355). In Berkeley, where Neighborhood Cleanup happens only once a year in each neighborhood, call Berkeley Refuse (tel. 510/644–8856). A better deal in the East Bay, though, comes every May when year-round residents "dumpster shop" for the stuff departing U.C. students can't fit in the U-Haul. Before you start your search, remember that free don't always mean tasteful; the lower your standards and the better your sense of humor, the more luck you'll have.

Ashby BART Flea Market. This is the most popular place to buy stuff on sunny Saturdays and Sundays. Although it's small compared to flea markets in the South Bay and Marin County, the mix of goods is very Berkeley. Used furniture vendors sell basic wood cabinets, old ottomans, funky desks, and love seats; clothing vendors always have a good vintage coat they're willing to lower the price on; and there's a sprinkling of manly-man tools, blenders, African-American jewelry, and secondhand (or thirdhand) books for cheap, as well as fresh produce from local farmers. *Ashby BART Station, 1937 Ashby Ave., Berkeley, tel. 510/644–0744.*

De Anza College Flea Market. At perhaps the friendliest flea market in the Bay Area, vendors congregate the first Saturday of every month in this community college parking lot and sell everything from vintage clothing to lawn flamingos. Grandfathers come for the houseplants and antiques, collegiate types come to sell the clothes off their backs, and kids come for the cheap toys. *21250 Stevens Creek Blvd., at Stelling Rd., Cupertino, tel. 408/864–8414.*

Marin City Flea Market. If you can wade through the mountains of stuff here you might find a real bargain, but don't hold your breath. It's strictly for true flea-market fanatics, who show up in the hope of unearthing obscure treasures. Drag your butt out of bed early if you have your heart set on finding a true treasure. *147 Donahue Rd., U.S. 101 at Sausalito/Marin City exit, tel. 415/332–1441.*

San Jose Flea Market. One of the world's largest, this market to end all markets houses some 2,600 vendors over a 120-acre area, selling everything from furniture to car parts to clothes to farm-fresh produce. *12000 Berryessa Rd., tel. 408/453–1110. 13th St. exit from U.S. 101. Open Wed.–Sun. dawn–dusk.*

Specialty Items

The Bay Area attracts weird specialty goods the way a black hole attracts . . . well, you get the idea. Maybe it's because San Francisco and Berkeley harbor such an abundance of special-interest groups and bizarre individuals; maybe it's because people come here to "create" a lifestyle for themselves and need the proper accessories. In the city, the Castro abounds with places that complement almost any kind of queer lifestyle; the Haight offers lots of head shops and tie-dye boutiques for the neo-hippie crowd; and both the Mission and the Haight provide *botanicas* and other "magic" shops for those who want to flirt with the occult. If you have no lifestyle, try Macy's downtown. Head to Berkeley if you're looking for political consumerism, "herbal" products, or the street-fair atmosphere of Telegraph Avenue.

SAN FRANCISCO

ART AND PHOTOGRAPHY **Adolph Gasser.** Your best source for photography and video equipment, Gasser has the largest inventory of such items in Northern California. *181 2nd St., btw Howard and Mission Sts., tel. 415/495–3852. Other location: 5733 Geary Blvd., at 22nd Ave., tel. 415/751–0145.*

Lifestyles for Sale

Can't stand to pay $20 for a beach-glass ashtray at Z Gallerie, or $30 for a pair of candle holders at Urban Outfitters? Join the too-cool-to-be-suckered club and head to one of the original "lifestyle" stores—your neighborhood Salvation Army, Goodwill, or St. Vincent de Paul—where you can flick around a fiver and get more than attitude back. The Salvation Army is best for $5 lamps and $10 desks; St. Vincent de Paul is dependable for $15–$50 sofas, chairs, desks, and ancient televisions and stereos; and Goodwill is awash in 20¢ ashtrays and "I Luv U Grandma" mugs. Now you know. And knowing is half the battle.

Art Rock Gallery. Put Hole or Green Day on your wall for $10 and up. Handmade silkscreened posters run $15–$20. *1153 Mission St., btw 7th and 8th Sts., tel. 415/255–7390.*

CHARITABLE CAUSES **Planet Weavers Treasure Store.** Politically correct products, especially ones related to environmental concerns, abound in this UNICEF-run store. They've got a colorful selection of drums, maps, toys, textiles, candles, and eco-conscious games for kids. A portion of the proceeds goes to the U.N. children's fund. *1573 Haight St., btw Ashbury and Clayton Sts., tel. 415/864–4415.*

Under One Roof. They share a roof with the NAMES project and sell goods gathered from 62 AIDS organizations. You'll find all kinds of gifts, including radical queer T-shirts, household goods, and cards. *2362B Market St., btw Noe and Castro Sts., tel. 415/252–9430.*

BODY DECORATIONS **Body Manipulations.** The staff is ultra-professional and courteous, and they want what's best for your body—if your belly button is unfit for piercing, they'll say so. *254 Fillmore St., at Haight St., tel. 415/621–0408.*

Everlasting. This is a thrice-sterilized, squeaky-clean hole in the wall with a good reputation and an artistic staff who thoughtfully advertise tattooing possibilities all over their own bodies. *1939 McAllister St., btw Lyon St. and Central Ave., tel. 415/928–6244.*

Gauntlet. The only reminders of its hardcore S&M past are a few scary black leather and metal displays in the lobby. Gauntlet has been piercing safely since 1975. The well-informed staff can answer any questions you have, as well as provide tips on caring for your pierce. *2377 Market St., at Castro St., tel. 415/ 431–3133.*

Nomad. The employees are versed in tribal mythologies, and piercings lean toward wood and ivory, though they're educated in the ways of the implant-grade, surgical-steel spike as well. Piercings take place among lush plants and soothing African rhythms. *1881 Hayes St., btw Ashbury St. and Masonic Ave., tel. 415/563–7771.*

Primal Urge. If you feel the need to tattoo an ancient Sumerian hieroglyph from the post-Mesolithic period on your bum, Primal Urge will accommodate, provided you have an ID proving you're over 18. Appointments are necessary if your interests are much more complicated than a heart or a daisy. *2703 Geary Blvd., at Masonic, tel. 415/474–3442. Closed Mon.–Tues.*

BODY PRODUCTS **The Body Shop.** This international corporation brought natural health and beauty aids—and a modicum of environmental and political consciousness—to America's shopping malls. They sell reasonably priced soaps, lotions, essential oils, and other fun stuff, and provide informational pamphlets on their business practices (buying ingredients from tribes in the Amazon rain forest, for example). *865 Market St., San Francisco Shopping Centre, tel. 415/281–3760. Other locations: 16 California St., at Drumm St., tel. 415/397–7455; 2106 Chestnut St., at Steiner St., tel. 415/202–0112; 506 Castro St., btw 18th and 19th Sts., tel. 415/431–8860.*

New York Cosmetics & Fragrances. Come here for name-brand cosmetics and perfumes at a discount. *318 Brannan St., btw 2nd and 3rd Sts., tel. 415/543–3880.*

GAMES AND TOYS **FAO Schwarz Fifth Avenue.** Remember when Tom Hanks performed "Chopsticks" in the movie *Big* by jumping around on an enormous keyboard? He was in FAO Schwarz, home to some of the most lavish, elaborate toys you never knew you needed. To feel especially starry-eyed (or nauseated, depending on your tastes), come near holiday time, when Mummy and Daddy are buying Junior a mini Mercedes and kids are whining and drooling in every corner. *48 Stockton St., at O'Farrell St., tel. 415/394–8700.*

Gamescape. They've got sci-fi and war board games, playing cards, gambling paraphernalia (for recreational use only, of course), tarot cards, and lots more for those long, boring winter nights. *333 Divisadero St., btw Page and Oak Sts., tel. 415/621–4263.*

HATS AND JEWELRY **African Outlet.** Reasonably priced African textiles, shell jewelry, hats, and other accessories line the walls here. *524 Octavia St., btw Hayes and Grove Sts., tel. 415/ 864–3576.*

Gallery of Jewels. Gallery of Jewels stocks rhinestone, glass, silver, and metal jewelry crafted by local artisans. The styles are eclectic, the prices high—but it's not Tiffany's nor is it cheap-o-rama junk. *1400 Haight St., at Masonic Ave., tel. 415/255–1180.*

Nancy's Originals. Here you'll find hats for the urban dweller: porkpie, Bogart-type, and a bunch of caps reminiscent of the Jackson Five. *1429 Haight St., near Ashbury St., tel. 415/861–3910.*

Zeitgeist. Remember when watches were built to last? So do the fully apprenticed owners of Zeitgeist, who repair and restore clocks, jewelry, and any watch worth salvaging. They also sell beautiful vintage wristwatches and pocket watches from the likes of Grüen and Bulova. *437B Hayes St., at Gough St., tel. 415/864–0185.*

PAPER, CARDS, AND STATIONERY **Does Your Mother Know . . .** This queer card shop features coming-out cards, same-sex love cards, and *fabulous* gay humor cards. *4079 18th St., near Castro St., tel. 415/ 864–3160.*

Kozo Bookbinding. Beautiful Japanese stationery, blank books, wall hangings, and other frivolities cost a pretty penny here. *531 Castro St., btw 18th and 19th Sts., tel. 415/621–0869.*

SEX ACCESSORIES **Good Vibrations.** This cooperatively owned, feminist sex shop in the Mission stocks a dazzling selection of vibrators (there's even an antique vibrator museum), other sex toys, videos, and literature on all topics sexual. If you think all sex shops are sleazy, you haven't been here—the store is designed to make women feel comfortable (though men are welcome). *1210 Valencia St., at 23rd St., tel. 415/974–8980. Other location: 2504 San Pablo Ave., at Dwight Way, Berkeley, tel. 510/841–8987.*

Image Leather. They'll accommodate all your intimate leather needs with a wide variety of nipple rings, harnesses, whips, collars, and boots. The adventurous will enjoy the store's "Dungeon Room." *2199 Market St., btw Noe and Church Sts., tel. 415/621–7551.*

SKATEBOARDS AND MOTORCYCLES **Deluxe.** Kick back with a regular posse of skaters and watch skate videos in a relatively upscale environment. Street wear and decks ($40–$45) abound, and the store features work (including display mannequins) by local skater/artist Kevin Ancell. *1831 Market St., btw Guerrero and Octavia Sts., tel. 415/626–5588.*

Wanna skate? Cruise over to Harrison Street (btw 16th and 20th Sts.) and the warehouses that function as makeshift skate playgrounds.

Dudley Perkins Harley-Davidson. This is the oldest Harley-Davidson dealership in the world. Check out the vintage Harleys for sale and on exhibit, and start saving your pennies. *66 Page St., btw Franklin and Gough Sts., tel. 415/703–9494.*

MISCELLANEOUS **Bob Mandell's Costume Shop, Inc.** Ball gowns, fake hands, clown ruffles, vampire teeth, capes, and other miscellany await you—for the holidays or for every day. *1135 Mission St., btw 7th and 8th Sts., tel. 415/863–7755.*

Guitar Solo. You probably can't afford a 1968 Ramirez or one of the upper-end steel-string guitars sold here, but it's still fun to dream. Their stock is expansive, but if they don't have that obscure piece of music you're searching for, they'll order it. *1411 Clement St., btw 15th and 16th Aves., tel. 415/386–0395.*

Lady Luck Candle Shop. The proprietor of this tiny shop is so convincing that even the most bitter cynic will feel compelled to buy a hope candle. The devotional candles, love potions, and wide selection of incense will thrill your favorite mystic. *311 Valencia St., btw 14th and 15th Sts., tel. 415/621–0358.*

Naked Eye Video. This is definitely not Blockbuster. Come here for offbeat and hard-to-find titles (to rent or buy), and to peruse the racks of obscure, foreign, and alternative-lifestyle 'zines. *533 Haight St., btw Fillmore and Steiner Sts., tel. 415/864–2985.*

Yahoo Herb'an Ecology. Yahoo promotes urban ecology through the sale of compost materials (like worm boxes and organic seeds), and their fund-raising benefits include hip-hop shows and poetry readings. Call before stopping by as the staff takes regular siestas. *968 Valencia St., btw 20th and 21st Sts., tel. 415/282–9676.*

EAST BAY

Annapurna. A "trip" to Berkeley is incomplete without a visit to the city's infamous head shop to pick up some incense, specialty cigarettes, hookahs, or a decorative pipe (for tobacco, of course). *2416 Telegraph Ave., near Haste St., Berkeley, tel. 510/841-6187.*

Blue Buddha Tattoo. A basic tattoo parlor, the Blue Buddha's location across from Ashby BART is prime. Tattoos run the gamut from basic flesh art to elaborate designs, and prices are lower than other Berkeley parlors nearby. *1959 Ashby Ave., Berkeley, tel. 510/549-9860.*

Body Time. The oldest body shop in the Bay Area makes a huge variety of natural skin- and hair-care goods for men and women. They also carry loofahs, sponges, brushes, even tea pots. The woman-owned and -run business manufactures its products locally. *2509 Telegraph Ave., at Dwight Way, Berkeley, tel. 510/548-3686. Other locations: 2911 College Ave., at Ashby Ave., Berkeley, tel. 510/845-2101; 1942 Shattuck Ave., Berkeley, tel. 510/841-5818; 5521 College Ave., Oakland, tel. 510/547-4116.*

Games of Berkeley. This toy store is for the kid in all of us, whether that inner child requires board games, puzzles, cards, or small plastic thingies that hang off pencils. *2010 Shattuck Ave., near University Ave., Berkeley, tel. 510/540-7822.*

Lhasa Karnak. An excellent source for herbs and herbal information, Lhasa Karnak's staff is knowledgeable and friendly. Take advantage now—before the FDA regulates or outlaws herbs. *2513 Telegraph Ave., at Dwight Way, Berkeley, tel. 510/548-0380. Other location: 1938 Shattuck Ave., Berkeley, tel. 510/548-0372.*

Movie Image. This is the place for film noir in Berkeley. Most titles are for rent only, but a few new and used videos are sold. The friendly staff will happily order titles they don't carry. *64 Shattuck Sq., Berkeley, tel. 510/649-0296.*

FOOD 4

By Alice Chang and Kelly Green, with Sharron Wood

The Bay Area is blessed with enough restaurants to satisfy a staggering variety of tastes—from seafood to tofu to the exotic beyond. Waves of Asian and Mexican immigrants have made San Francisco a flavorful and festive hotbed of cheap taquerías, backstreet Chinese holes-in-the wall, gracious Thai and Vietnamese establishments, reasonably priced sushi houses, and Korean and Mongolian barbecue joints. Oakland is known for southern-style eats and its less-touristy version of Chinatown. Berkeley's Gourmet Ghetto is the undisputed epicenter of American nouvelle cuisine. Even Marin County and the suburban South Bay host dining spots to boast of—if only for their waterfront views.

California cuisine won world renown for its commitment to the idea that fresh, home-cultivated ingredients (no matter how expensive) are vital to the success of a dish, and that portions are to be savored, not shoveled in. If it weren't for Berkeley chef Alice Waters, who in 1971 opened the now legendary **Chez Panisse** (1517 Shattuck Ave., Berkeley, tel. 510/548–5525), you might—horror of horrors—never have heard of sun-dried tomatoes, free-range chicken, goat cheese, or arugula. But not all of us have $65 to drop for one of Chez Panisse's five- to six-course meals, and that's okay. A huge, messy burrito or a bounteous bowl of fresh Chinese noodles can be yours for less than $5. Or you can spend a few more bucks and get your quota of food and entertainment all in the same place at one of San Francisco's newly hip supper clubs (*see box* on supper clubs, in Chapter 6).

It's rumored that if every one of the city's residents were to go out to dinner at the same time, there would be enough seats for all of them.

While searching out the perfect place to feed your head, you may notice that a surprising (if not suspicious) number of the Bay Area's more than 4,000 restaurants have received favorable reviews, which they dutifully display in their windows, usually conspicuously close to their menus. Such reports should be read with wary eyes: Always check the dates of reviews, because writers frequently update their impressions, and restaurants regularly change hands and chefs. One reliable reviewer is Jim Wood, who writes for the daily ***Examiner.*** Dan Leone of the city's free weekly the ***Bay Guardian*** is another who can be trusted for his wit and taste. In fact, the *Guardian* has extensive food reviews and is one of the best sources for new Bay Area budget restaurants.

San Francisco

Each of San Francisco's neighborhoods offers its own eating agenda: Head to North Beach for Italian food, the Mission for Mexican food, and Chinatown and Japantown for—you guessed it.

If you're after more exotic flavors, some excellent Burmese, Indonesian, Cambodian, and Afghan restaurants have recently taken the city by storm. Also look for a slew of superb new Greek and Mediterranean dining spots, most serving up heaping, inexpensive platters of food with unique spices that provide a refreshing change from traditional American fare—though you'll find plenty of that here, too.

CASTRO DISTRICT

The Castro district teems with cutesy, slightly pricey restaurants, many with outdoor patios to optimize your people-watching pleasure. Mimosas and espressos flow freely on weekend mornings, and the crowd is always jovial and loud. Brunch seems to be the Castro's most popular meal. Follow the sunglass-wearing masses to the two hottest brunch spots, **Café Flore** (*see* Chapter 5) and the **Patio Café** (*see below*), and brace yourself for a long afternoon of Bloody Marys. Ranking a close third, **Pasqua** (4094 18th St., tel. 415/626–6263) stays packed with toned, tanned locals who come for the excellent scones ($1.50) and coffee and stay for the GQ-style social scene. Pasqua is great on a warm day, when patrons spill onto the benches outside on **Castro Street.** The after-hours eating scene is just as lively—you don't have to look too far for a 24-hour diner or late-night pizza joint.

➢ **UNDER $5 • Amazing Grace.** This cafeteria-style, no-nonsense vegetarian restaurant offers an inventive and tasty array of dishes that changes daily. An order of Moroccan vegetables with couscous, or tofu loaf with a cashew and mushroom sauce, will run you $4.25. The soups and curry dishes are also amazing. *216 Church St., at Market St., tel. 415/626–6411. Open Mon.–Sat. 11–10. Wheelchair access. No credit cards.*

Hot 'n' Hunky. This pink, perky little restaurant with a preponderance of Marilyn Monroe posters on the walls is a Castro institution for thick, juicy burgers. With names like the Macho Man (three patties; $4.25), I Wanna Hold Your Ham (burger with ham and Swiss; $4), and Ms. Piggy (burger with cheddar and bacon; $4), ordering your food is half the fun. *4039 18th St., near Castro St., tel. 415/621–6365. Open Sun.–Thurs. 11 AM–midnight, Fri.–Sat. 11 AM–1 AM. No credit cards.*

Marcello's. These guys conjure up some of the best pizza in San Francisco, and it's right across the street from the Castro Theatre (*see* Movie Houses, in Chapter 6)—very convenient when it's almost show time. They sell by the slice ($1.75–$2.50) or the pie ($7.50–$18.50), and you can always find unusual ready-made combo slices like ham and pineapple or spinach with black olives and feta. They're open late on weekends, and they deliver for free. *420 Castro St., near Market St., tel. 415/863–3900. Open Sun.–Thurs. 11 AM–1 AM, Fri.–Sat. 11 AM–2 AM. Wheelchair access. No credit cards.*

➢ **UNDER $10 • Bagdad Café.** Hogging an entire street corner to itself (no small feat in the packed Castro), this 24-hour restaurant is as famous for its expansive street-level windows—in an area where people-watching is a high art—as its home-style breakfasts. Two eggs with home fries cost $4.25; sandwiches run $5–$6. Dinner fare is mainly of the middle-American variety (meat, meat, and more meat), but there is a small vegetarian menu. *2295 Market St., at 16th St., tel. 415/621–4434. Open daily 24 hrs. Wheelchair access. No credit cards.*

Josie's Cabaret and Juice Joint. By night it's a well-known performance venue; by day it's an easygoing neighborhood hangout with a 100% vegetarian menu of fresh organic juices, salads, sandwiches, and breakfast items. Vegetarian entrées of any kind won't cost much more than $5; pastas are $6.50; and you can get a small salad, or a soup, or a fruit smoothie for less than $3. Come on a sunny day and eat outside on the pretty back patio. *3583 16th St., at Market St., tel. 415/861–7933. Open daily 9–8. No credit cards.*

La Méditerranée. This small, personable restaurant on the edge of the Castro district serves great Middle Eastern and Greek food, including dolmas, salads, hummus, baba ghanoush, and levant sandwiches (appetizers cost $4–$5; entrées go for $6–$10). If you can't decide, get the Middle Eastern combination plate—two meaty phyllo pastries, a levant sandwich, luleh kabob, and salad for $7. Dessert lovers shouldn't miss the *datil* ($3.50), a dense roll made of dates, phyllo dough, nuts, and cream that is most decadent. *288 Noe St., at Market St., tel. 415/431–7210. Open Sun. and Tues.–Thurs. 11–10, Fri.–Sat. 11–11. Other locations: 2210 Fillmore St., at Sacramento St., tel. 415/921–2956; 2936 College Ave., Berkeley, tel. 510/540–7773.*

No-Name (Nippon) Sushi. Everybody calls it No-Name Sushi, even though the proprietors did eventually put up a tiny cardboard sign in the window officially dubbing it "Nippon." This small wood-paneled restaurant on Church Street almost always has a line out the door because it serves huge sushi combos at deliciously low prices—try $6–$10 on for size. No alcohol is served. *314 Church St., at 15th St., no phone. Open Mon.–Sat. noon–10. No credit cards.*

Orphan Andy's. If you're looking for inexpensive American grub late at night, head to this Castro hangout adorned with red vinyl booths, a lunch counter, and a jukebox. Bring a date and pretend you're Joanie and Chachi (or, more likely, Richie and Fonzie) in a secluded back booth. Burgers cost $5, and omelets run $4–$6. *3991 17th St., at Market and Castro Sts., tel. 415/864–9795. Open daily 24 hrs. Wheelchair access. No credit cards.*

Patio Café. The Castro's premiere brunch spot operates out of an enormous converted greenhouse complete with fake parrots perched among the foliage. Enough Bloody Marys ($3) are consumed here to conk out a small army. Eggs with home fries go for $4–$5, and sinful cheese blintzes with cherry sauce are $7. You can also chow down on sandwiches, burgers, and pastas (all $7). *531 Castro St., btw 18th and 19th Sts., tel. 415/621–4640. Open daily 8–4 and 4:30–10.*

Sparky's. This 24-hour diner has a menu that reminds one of Denny's but—for what it's worth—serves a *much* trendier clientele. To grab your quotient of hip for the night, arrive at 3 AM in Doc Martens and join the throngs of hungry clubbers who come for burgers ($6), pizzas (small, $8–$14), and breakfast (bulging omelets $6–$7). If you're feeling lazy, they'll deliver. *242 Church St., near Market St., tel. 415/626-8666. Open daily 24 hrs.*

Thailand Restaurant. The climb up steep stairs to this second-story Thai restaurant is definitely worth the effort. Located directly across the street from the landmark Castro Theatre (*see* Movie Houses, in Chapter 6), this dainty spot serves up a mean plate of *pad Thai* (fried noodles with shrimp and tofu; $6) and an excellent *pad kao pod* (sautéed chicken with garlic and baby corn; $6). Even if you're not an appetizer person, the *goong gra bawg* (shrimp in crispy batter; $6) is a must. *488A Castro St., btw Market and 18th Sts., tel. 415/863–6868. Open Mon.–Thurs. 11–10, Fri.–Sat. 11–10:30.*

➢ **UNDER $15** • **Anchor Oyster Bar.** Small, bright, and clean, the Anchor draws a crowd that likes reasonably priced oysters ($7 for six) and innovative pasta and seafood dishes, such as linguine with scallops, shrimp, and asparagus in a white wine sauce ($14), as well as an awesome clam chowder ($3). *579 Castro St., btw 18th and 19th Sts., tel. 415/431–3990. Open weekdays 11:30–10, Sat. noon–10, Sun. 4:30–9:30.*

CHINATOWN

Finding something to eat in Chinatown is a cinch. Finding something *good* to eat—well, that's a little trickier. Steer clear of the glaringly tourist-oriented places (where you have to ask for chopsticks and the patrons are all carrying shopping bags of souvenirs) and instead wander through the heart of Chinatown—**Washington, Clay,** and **Sacramento streets** between Mason and Kearny streets—until you find a restaurant that has the four elements that spell success: small, spare, cheap, and packed with locals.

Dim sum, or Chinese finger food, is to Chinatown as bagels are to New York. Traditionally, the dim sum is wheeled around on carts and you choose your meal on the spot. You may not want to ask what's inside your pot stickers (dumplings), though.

➢ **UNDER $5** • **Kowloon.** One of the few all-vegetarian restaurants in Chinatown, Kowloon packs in tree huggers and true Buddhists with its excellent selection of vegetarian dim sum. A pot sticker or a dense mushroom cake sells for only about 60¢. If you get impatient eating your meal one item at a time, choose from a huge number of rice dishes (brown rice optional) for $3–$6, topped with such exotica as vegetarian duck gizzards and vegetarian pork tripe. *909 Grant Ave., near Washington St., tel. 415/362–9888. Open daily 9–9. Wheelhair access. No credit cards.*

Lucky Creation. This small restaurant in the heart of Chinatown serves fantastic meatless fare. From the green sign to the green tables and menus, this place declares loud and clear its aim to please the vegetarian palate—and it's cheap. Mixed veggies over rice go for $3.75, and braised eggplant in a clay pot will run you $4. *854 Washington St., near Stockton St., tel. 415/989–0818. Open Thurs.–Tues. 11–9:30. No credit cards.*

➢ **UNDER $10 • Chef Jia's.** Next door to the ever-popular House of Nanking (*see below*), Chef Jia's manages to survive, indeed thrive, thanks to its top-notch Hunan and Mandarin cuisine. It's noisy and crowded, and the decor leaves a lot to be desired, but the onion cakes ($2) and the spicy yams in garlic sauce ($4) are both to die for. Best of all, you'll be halfway through your mouthwatering chicken breast with yams ($4.50) before the Nanking diehards even reach the front door. *925 Kearny St., btw Jackson and Columbus Sts., tel. 415/398–1626. Open daily 11–10. No credit cards.*

House of Nanking. This Chinatown hole-in-the-wall typically overflows with locals and tourists alike, all clamoring for excellent Shanghai home cooking at righteously low prices. Decor is nonexistent, you may be crammed into tiny tables with total strangers, and the no-nonsense waiters keep you on your toes—all of which only add to the Nanking experience. Ask for the delicious shrimp cakes in peanut sauce ($4)—they're not on the menu—or try the chicken Nanking ($5), a version of General Tso's chicken. Beware if you're claustrophobic. *919 Kearny St., btw Jackson and Columbus Sts., tel. 415/421–1429. Open weekdays 11–10, Sat. noon–10, Sun. 4–10. No credit cards.*

R&G Lounge. You wouldn't call this place lively—in fact, it's a bit sterile and depressing—but the R&G Lounge serves super-fresh seafood dishes, such as a tasty oyster clay pot ($7.50). Another nice dish, mushrooms with bok choy ($11), features delicate greens. Go for lunch ($4–$6) and watch the staff prepare egg rolls ($4) in the dining room. *631B Kearny St., btw Sacramento and Clay Sts., tel. 415/982–7877. Open daily 11–9:30.*

➢ **UNDER $20 • Empress of China.** If you can stomach the cheesy photographs of the owner with various stars and politicos—and the somewhat imperial prices—you'll find much to recommend this place. Stunning views of Coit Tower, elegant Han Dynasty decor, and *damn* good food go far to dispel any lingering doubts you may have about being here. Entrées will set you back anywhere from $10 to $38, so stay away from delicacies like abalone ($37.50!) and stick to the basics, like Phoenix and Dragon chicken (chicken and prawns with ginger and mushrooms; $14.50), to spare yourself the indignity of walking penniless past a grinning George Bush on your way out. *838 Grant Ave., btw Clay and Washington Sts., tel. 415/434–1345. Open Mon.–Sat. 11:30–3 and 5–11, Sun. 12:30–11. Wheelchair access.*

CIVIC CENTER

For a bite on your way to—or a cuppa joe after—the opera, walk along **Hayes** or **Grove streets** between Franklin and Laguna. This area is a good example of gentrification in progress, with trendy cafés and restaurants sprouting up beside dingy storefronts. **Spuntino** (524 Van Ness Ave., at McAllister St., tel. 415/861–7772) is perfect if you're headed to the movie theaters on Van Ness Avenue. Salads are about $5 and *panini* (Italian sandwiches) go for $8.

➢ **UNDER $5 • Main Squeeze.** If you are overcome by the degradation on display around the Civic Center, duck over to this space-age juice bar on Polk Street, innovatively designed with industrial materials molded into postmodern pieces of fruit. They specialize in juices ($2.75–$3.75) and have a decent breakfast and lunch menu that's 100% vegetarian and includes some vegan dishes. Focaccia sandwiches ($4–$5) and soups ($2.50) cater to the health-conscious crowd. *1515 Polk St., at California St., tel. 415/567–1515. Open Mon.–Sat. 8–6, Sun. 9–7.*

Tommy's Joynt. This lively cafeteria-style hofbrau and bar is a longtime San Francisco fixture. Specialties include buffalo stew ($6) and bean-and-beer soup ($2.50). Tommy's also serves inexpensive carved-meat sandwiches ($3.50) and dinner platters, as well as a vast selection of obscure beers from around the world ($2.50–$3). *1101 Geary St., at Van Ness Ave., tel. 415/775–4216. Open daily 11 AM–2 AM. Wheelchair access. No credit cards.*

➢ **UNDER $10 • Ananda Fuara.** Escape from grimy Market Street into this soothing vegetarian restaurant with sky-blue walls. Servers sway by the tables in flowing saris, bringing sandwiches ($5) and entrées like curry with rice and chutney ($8). The massive Brahma burrito ($5) will fill you up for the rest of the day. *1298 Market St., at 9th St., tel. 415/621–1994. Open Mon.–Sat. 8–8 (Wed. until 3). Wheelchair access. No credit cards.*

Grubstake. Housed in a converted railroad car in Polk Gulch, this late-night eatery serves decent breakfasts ($5) and thick, messy burgers ($5–$6). Ask for the delicious homemade quince jelly to spread atop your toast. *1525 Pine St., btw Polk St. and Van Ness Ave., tel. 415/673–8268. Open weekdays 5 PM–4 AM, weekends 10 AM–4 AM. No credit cards.*

Moishe's Pippic. This Chicago-style Jewish deli near the Civic Center will satisfy the corned-beef pangs of relocated, alienated East Coasters. They've got it all: kosher salami, hot dogs, corned beef, chopped liver, pastrami, tongue, bagels and lox, matzo ball soup, Polish sausage, knishes . . .a big wet Bronx cheer to obsessively healthy California cuisine. Hot dogs start at $2.50, sandwiches at $5. *425A Hayes St., at Gough St., tel. 415/431–2440. Open weekdays 8–4, Sat. 9:30–4. No credit cards.*

Food Snob for a Day

There's a tier of restaurants in San Francisco that is normally out of reach for the mere mortals among us—except for maybe one glorious day a month: payday. In the euphoric 24 hours before the rent and credit-card demons start crowding your conscience, you can be the richest, hippest, swankiest person you can imagine. So, call a friend, put on your finest duds, and splurge like hell at one of the city's toniest restaurants, where you'll pay $40 and up per person. Critics and locals argue endlessly about which is the best restaurant in San Francisco, taking into consideration criteria like attentiveness of service, chicness of ambience, and artistic presentation. Among those vying for the top title are:

- ***Aqua. Seafood with a French accent. 252 California St., btw Battery and Front Sts., tel. 415/956–9662.***
- ***Elka. Artfully presented seafood with French and Japanese influences. 1625 Post St., at Laguna St., tel. 415/922–7788.***
- ***Flying Saucer. Unusual and diverse American fare, beautifully presented in an elegant and quirky atmosphere. Its Mission district location discourages the pretentiousness of downtown. 1000 Guerrero St., at 22nd St., tel. 415/641–0055.***
- ***Postrio. California cuisine with Asian and Mediterranean influences. 545 Post St., btw Taylor and Mason Sts., tel. 415/776–7825.***
- ***Restaurant LuLu. Rustic cuisine from the French and Italian rivieras. You have your choice of three ways to dine: LuLu Bis's fixed price dinners; Restaurant LuLu's full menu; or Café LuLu's less ritzy—and cheaper—selections. 816 Folsom St., btw 4th and 5th Sts., tel. 415/495–5775.***
- ***Stars. Inventive California cuisine. Nearby, at 500 Van Ness, Stars Café isn't as good as the mother restaurant, but it's not as expensive either. 150 Redwood Alley, off Van Ness Ave., tel. 415/861–7827.***

Racha Café. In a city filled to the rim with Thai restaurants, this is an exceptional choice for both the food and the service. Try the spicy mint chicken (around $6) or the vegetables with peanut sauce ($5.50). *771 Ellis St., at Polk St., tel. 415/885–0725. Open daily 11–9:30. Wheelchair access.*

Vicolo. Popular with the symphony crowd, this pizzeria serves up gourmet slices and pies in a hard-to-find Civic Center alleyway. Choose from basic varieties (cheese, pepperoni, sausage, veggie, and low-fat) or several more exciting seasonal selections. Prices are high, but the cornmeal crust makes a slice more filling than it appears. A piece of, say, wild mushroom pizza ($3.50), plus a Caesar salad ($5) shared with a friend, may well suffice. *201 Ivy St., btw Franklin and Gough Sts. and Hayes and Grove Sts., tel. 415/863–2382. Open Mon.–Sat. 11:30–11, Sun. noon–10. Other location: 473 University Ave., Palo Alto, tel. 415/324–4877.*

➢ **UNDER $15** • **Golden Turtle.** Here you can consume some of San Francisco's best Vietnamese food in high style, among carved-wood pieces that look like they belong in an Asian art collection. The barbecued quail is excellent ($5), and a number of vegetarian dishes, such as spicy lemongrass vegetable curry ($9), round out the menu. *2211 Van Ness Ave., btw Broadway and Vallejo St., tel. 415/441–4419. Open Tues.–Sun. 11–3 and 5–11.*

Phnom Penh. With its lace curtains and dainty table settings, this Civic Center restaurant looks ready for an elaborate tea party. Despite the rawness of the neighborhood, expect friendly service and excellent Cambodian food, including lots of spicy grilled-meat dishes ($8.50) and coconut-milk curries ($7–$8) that you can order with chicken, prawns, or halibut. Lunch runs about $6. *631 Larkin St., near Eddy St., tel. 415/775–5979. Open weekdays 11–3 and 5–9, weekends 5–9.*

Politicians can open their mouths wider than the tiny Swan Oyster Depot, which consists of nothing more than a lunch counter, a few stools, and some of the best damn seafood in town.

Swan Oyster Depot. The genial staff welcomes you with open arms and will promptly set you up with a bowl of clam chowder, thick sourdough bread, and an Anchor Steam beer for a fiver. Don't be surprised if you find yourself ordering a half-dozen oysters and a cracked Dungeness crab. Such gluttony could cost upwards of $20, but if the mood is right, you just won't care. *1517 Polk St., btw California and Sacramento Sts., tel. 415/673–1101. Open Mon.–Sat. 8–5:30. No credit cards.*

➢ **UNDER $20** • **California Culinary Academy.** How'd you like to eat someone's homework assignment? You can at the Culinary Academy, where fledgling chefs prepare their lessons under the watchful eyes of skilled instructors. The results vary, but even the worst is never all that bad. The academy offers two restaurants: At the more formal **Careme** (lunch $10–$15, dinner $13–$19), you can watch student chefs at work; the **Grill** offers basic grill food for lunch ($4–$9) and buffet dinners ($10–$12) weeknights only. *625 Polk St., at Turk St., tel. 415/771–3500. Open weekdays noon–1:30 and 6–8:30.*

Miss Pearl's Jam House. Miss Pearl's live reggae and calypso music (Thurs.–Sat. nights) and Soul-Food Sunday gospel performances attract a young, lively crowd. You'll have to traipse through a scuzzy neighborhood to get here, but once you arrive, you can eat poolside (weekends

Meals on Wheels

Why settle for the old standbys—Chinese and pizza—when you want your food delivered? For a $6-per-stop fee, two save-the-day services will bring you hot meals from a slew of San Francisco restaurants. Waiters on Wheels (tel. 415/252–1470) and Dine-One-One (tel. 415/771–DINE) will deliver anything from burgers to Italian to Greek and Mediterranean. To weigh your options, pick up their free delivery guides at street-corner boxes or newspaper stands around town, or call and they'll mail you one.

only; the pool belongs to the attached Phoenix Hotel) or in the Jamaican-style dining room. In addition to Caribbean entrées ($12–$18), the restaurant serves inventive appetizers like corn and manchego cheese *arepas* (corn fritters) with smoked tomato salad ($5). The Jamaican-style jerk chicken ($11) is famous in these parts. *601 Eddy St., at Larkin St., tel. 415/775–5267. Open Wed.–Thurs. 6 PM–10 PM, Fri.–Sat. 6 PM–11 PM, Sun. 11–2:30 and 5:30–10.*

Zuni Café. Watch yuppies and artsy types with trust funds sneer at each other over oysters ($1.50 each) at this crowded, sleek café on Market Street. Zuni offers friendly service and slick food for those times when you're in a what-the-hell frame of mind. It's most fun to come for appetizers and drinks. Try the Caesar salad ($8)—regulars swear it's the best they've ever had. Another popular item is roasted chicken for two ($28) with Tuscan bread and salad. *1658 Market St., btw Haight and Page Sts., tel. 415/552–2522. Open Tues.–Sat. 7:30 AM–midnight, Sun. 7:30 AM–11 PM.*

DOWNTOWN

Downtown abounds with old, classic restaurants that evoke San Francisco's golden years, and lunch counters still feature blue plate specials and chocolate malts. **Lori's Diner** (336 Mason St., at Geary St., tel. 415/392–8646), earnestly nostalgic for the '50s, is one of a few diners in the area that's open 24 hours. In recent years, however, haunts catering to a high-rolling Financial District clientele have flourished; you'll also run into the occasional health-food joint. The **International Food Fair** (24 Ellis St., at Market St.) probably contains the highest concentration of cheap food in all of downtown: Persian, Greek, Burmese, Korean, Mexican, Japanese, Chinese, and American fast-food stands rub shoulders, offering $3–$5 lunch specials. The **Bush and Kearny Food Center** (cnr Bush and Kearny Sts.) is a good place to look for Chinese, Mexican, and Thai dishes for less than $5.

➢ **UNDER $5** • **Specialty's.** These four tiny take-out stands bake 14 kinds of bread, including potato-cheese and carrot-curry, with which they will make any of 40—count 'em, 40—fresh sandwiches (most around $3–$7). They also sell soup ($2–$3) and insanely rich sweets. If you don't feel like eating on the sidewalk, take your lunch over to the rooftop garden at Crocker Galleria (cnr Kearny and Post Sts.) and relax. *312 Kearny St., btw Bush and Pine Sts.; 22 Battery St., at Market St.; 150 Spear St., btw Mission and Howard Sts.; 1 Post St., at Market St. Tel. 415/896–BAKE for daily specials, 415/512–9550 for phone orders. Open weekdays 6–6. No credit cards.*

➢ **UNDER $10** • **101 Restaurant.** In the downtrodden Tenderloin, this highly respected restaurant serves up tasty *chao tom* (shrimp and sugarcane; $8), *ga xao lang* (coconut chicken and lemongrass; $5.25), and other Vietnamese favorites. At lunch they have a great $4.75

How to Eat for Free, Get Sloshed, and Network at the Same Time

Happy hour, the working-stiff perk that provides free hors d'oeuvres to anyone who buys a drink, is of course practiced in San Francisco. You can nosh on some pretty wonderful food, including pizza, chicken wings, nachos, egg rolls, and fried calamari. Some of the happiest hours in town happen at the Cadillac Bar (1 Holland Ct., off Howard St. btw 4th and 5th Sts., tel. 415/543–8226; weekdays 4–6:30); the London Wine Bar (415 Sansome St., btw Sacramento Ave. and Clay St.; weekdays 5–7); ¡WA-HA-KA! (1489 Folsom St., at 11th St., tel. 415/861–1410; weekdays 5–7); and Bull's Texas Café (25 Van Ness Ave., at Market St., tel. 415/864–4288; weekdays 4:30–6:30). There's enough free food to keep you sated till breakfast. Drinks range from $2 to $6—which may not be enough to keep your name out of some Rolodexes you'd rather not be in.

special that includes soup, an imperial roll, and your choice of barbecued beef, chicken, or pork. *101 Eddy St., at Mason St., tel. 415/928–4490. Open Mon.–Sat. 11–9.*

Clown Alley. This splashy burger joint is popular with the Financial District's lunchtime crowd and late-night North Beach revelers in need of a red-meat fix. These tasty burgers ($4–$5) are no joke, and big fries and shakes round out the fun. *42 Columbus Ave., at Jackson St., tel. 415/421–2540. Open Mon.–Thurs. 7 AM–1 AM, Fri.–Sat. 7 AM–2 AM, Sun. 9 AM–7 PM. No credit cards. Other location: 2499 Lombard St., at Divisadero St., tel. 415/931–5890.*

The Fruit Gallery. Come here for healthy food in a bright, clean space that features changing art exhibitions. The quality of the art varies, but the food remains steadfastly wholesome and reasonably priced. Breakfast ($2–$6) includes egg dishes and a variety of granolas. For lunch try a veggie burger with a side salad ($6.25), grilled chicken (about $6), or healthful soups and salads. *301 Kearny St., at Bush St., tel. 415/362–2216. Open Mon.–Thurs. 7–3 and 5–9, Fri. 7–3.*

Tu Lan. Located in a really seedy part of downtown, this place rewards adventurous diners with terrific Vietnamese food. The expansive menu (entrées $3.75–$6.25) includes plenty of choices for vegetarians. Sit at the packed counter and watch the kitchen staff prepare your food, including addictive imperial rolls ($4) and chicken with five herbs ($5). *8 6th St., at Market St., tel. 415/626–0927. Open Mon.–Sat. 11–9. No credit cards.*

➢ **UNDER $15** • **Café Bastille.** Stop by for neat little French appetizers, like onion soup, pâté, or baked goat cheese on eggplant ($3–$5), in a happening, Frenchy atmosphere. For a more substantial meal, try a sandwich ($5–$7), crêpe dinner ($7.25), or real meat-and-potatoes fare ($7–$10). Filled with quasi-hip Financial District workers and bohemians with a few bucks to blow, the café gets pretty fun and friendly, especially Wednesday through Saturday when there's live jazz. *22 Belden Pl., btw Pine and Bush Sts. and Kearny and Montgomery Sts., tel. 415/986–5673. Open Mon.–Thurs. 11–10, Fri. 11–11, Sat. 11 AM–2 AM.*

Café Claude. Live jazz accompanies your meal most nights at this youthful but bourgeois French bistro in the Financial District. With a more relaxed atmosphere than Café Bastille (*see above*), this is a great place to while away a lazy afternoon. The menu includes two types of salad ($2.50–$7); soup ($4); and hot and cold sandwiches and entrées ($8–$10). *7 Claude Ln., off Bush St. btw Grant and Kearny Sts., tel. 415/392–3515. Open Mon. 8 AM–9 PM, Tues. and Wed. 8 AM–9:30 PM, Thurs. 8 AM–10 PM, Fri. and Sat. 8 AM–10:30 PM.*

The food at Café Claude is so good, the atmosphere so nearly authentic, that you may dare a French phrase or two.

Il Fornaio. This posh but sterile restaurant serves authentic Italian cuisine at surprisingly reasonable prices. The pizza is baked the old-fashioned way—in a brick, wood-burning oven—and the pastas are usually terrific, especially the angel-hair pasta with fresh tomatoes and basil ($10). A spin-off, the Il Fornaio Bakery (2298 Union St., tel. 415/563–0746), serves pizza by the slice ($3.75) and mouthwatering loaves of Italian bread ($3–$4). *1265 Battery St., at Greenwich St., tel. 415/986–0100. Open Mon.–Thurs. 7 AM–10:30 AM and 11:30AM–11 PM, Fri. 7 AM–10:30 AM and 11:30 AM–midnight, Sat. 9 AM–midnight, Sun. 9 AM–11 PM. Other location: 520 Cowper St., near University Ave. in Palo Alto, tel. 415/853–3888.*

Sol y Luna. Smack in the heart of downtown, this upscale Spanish restaurant serves excellent *tapas* (appetizers), including *gambas al ajillo* (prawns sautéed with garlic and olive oil; $5.50) and *berenjena* (grilled eggplant in roasted tomato sauce; $3.75). Make a meal of them, or splurge on the *paella marinera* (Spanish rice topped with prawns, scallops, clams, mussels, cod, and vegetables; $13). Wednesday through Saturday after 10 PM you can dance away your dinner to live Latin music. *475 Sacramento St., btw Battery and Sansome Sts., tel. 415/296–8696. Open weekdays 11:30–2:30 and 5:30–10, Sat. 5:30–10.*

Yank Sing. With a location in the Financial District and one South of Market, Yank Sing is a great place to feast on dim sum (small dumplings that you choose from passing carts and pay for by the plate) in a tasteful, modern setting. A meal should cost about $10–$15, but watch out: Let your appetite run away with you and next thing you know your pants are unbuttoned, your head is nodding, stacks of plates are sliding off the table, and the waiter is handing you a bill the size of Beijing. *427 Battery St., at Clay St., tel. 415/362–1640. Open weekdays 11–3, weekends 10–4. Other location: 49 Stevenson Pl., btw 1st and 2nd Sts., tel. 415/495–4510. Open weekdays 11–3.*

FISHERMAN'S WHARF

Steer clear of the mediocre, high-priced seafood restaurants that compete for tourist bucks all along the wharf. The best dining experience you could have here would involve a loaf of sourdough, some shrimp or perhaps a crab, a bottle of wine, a seat on the pier, and a tantalizing dining partner. The corner of **Jefferson** and **Taylor streets** is jam-packed with street stands that hawk all sorts of seafood goodies, including shrimp, prawn, or crab cups ($2.50) and thick clam chowder in a bread bowl ($3.50).

➢ **UNDER $10** • **Buena Vista Café.** This brass-and-wood bar, just down the road from Fisherman's Wharf at the Hyde Street cable-car turnaround, serves burgers and sandwiches ($4–$7.50) as well as Irish coffee, which they insist they introduced to America. Though the tourists are sometimes packed in elbow to elbow, the café manages to retain its dignity. *2765 Hyde St., tel. 415/474–5044. Open weekdays 9 AM–2 AM, weekends 8 AM–2 AM. No credit cards.*

Eagle Café. Lifted whole from its former location two blocks away and dropped onto the upper story of Pier 39, this bar/restaurant is authentically rustic, unlike the rest of this area. Windows and patio tables offer a view of the waterfront and Alcatraz. It's a good place to eat a bowl of clam chowder ($4) or a burger ($5) and plan your escape from Fisherman's Wharf. After lunch, the Eagle becomes a bar only. *Upper level, Pier 39, tel. 415/433–3689. Kitchen open Mon.–Sat. 7:30 AM–2:30 PM, Sun. 7:30 AM–3 PM. Wheelchair access. No credit cards.*

HAIGHT-ASHBURY AND WESTERN ADDITION

The Haight is renowned for its breakfast spots, including the **Pork Store Café,** the **Crescent City Café,** and **Kate's Kitchen** (*see below*). These places are full of the youth of today—in case you can't tell, they're the ones smoking, wearing black, looking ragged, and sucking up coffee like it's the primal life force. For dinner the Haight offers a few trendy hot spots and a preponderance of pizza joints, which cheaply provide the necessary carbohydrates to propel you to the next bar.

➢ **UNDER $10** • **Crescent City Café.** Every so often, we at the *Berkeley Guides* find a restaurant that we like so much, we don't want to review it. The situation is especially grave in the case of this New Orleans–style café, which has just six small tables and maybe a dozen counter seats. Whatever you do, please do not come for brunch on weekends, which is when you'll find our editors gorging themselves on Andouille hash ($5.75) and hefty plates of pork chops and eggs ($6). Another bad deal is the Thursday night barbecued-rib special ($8). Do us a favor and order your po-boy catfish sandwich ($6) to go. *1418 Haight St., at Masonic St., tel. 415/863–1374. Open daily 8–4 and 5–10.*

Kan Zaman. Patrons pack into this trendy Mediterranean restaurant to sit on big floor pillows, listen to hypnotic Middle Eastern music, and indulge in hummus ($3), baba ghanoush ($3), and spinach pies ($3.25). If you need that final push to reach a dreamlike state, fork over $7 for a huge hookah (a traditional water pipe) with your choice of flavored tobacco—the apple is especially good. On Friday, Saturday, and Sunday nights the Fat Chance Belly Dancers do their seductive thing. *1793 Haight St., at Shrader St., tel. 415/751–9656. Open Mon. 5 PM–midnight, Tues.–Fri. noon–midnight, weekends noon–2 AM. No credit cards.*

Kate's Kitchen. Get to this popular breakfast spot early, especially on weekends, unless you want to wait forever for a table. The wholesome food, though, is worth the wait. Chummy servers bring you specials like buttermilk-cornmeal pancakes ($4 short, $6 tall) or hush puppies with honey butter ($1.75 for six). If you're looking for lunch fare, try the Smiling Cow (steamed vegetables on brown rice with soy sauce and salsa; $5.50). *471 Haight St., btw Fillmore and Webster Sts., tel. 415/626–3984. Open Tues.–Fri. 8 AM–2:45 PM, weekends 9–3:45.*

Massawa. If you've never had Ethiopian food before and you (1) like to eat with your hands, (2) relish unusual spices, or (3) are one of those ignoramuses who is guilty of making dumb jokes about Ethiopian cuisine, then you must come here. You get a dinner platter filled with tender lamb or beef ($8–$10), usually with side portions of lentils, greens, or yellow split-pea paste. (They have all-vegetarian dishes as well.) All plates come with *injera,* a flat, spongy bread used instead of silverware to scoop up food. *1538 Haight St., btw Ashbury and Clayton Sts., tel. 415/621–4129. Open Tues.–Sun. noon–10.*

Pork Store Café. This Haight Street joint is a great place to eat away your hangover. Mounds of grits ($1 for a side order), big fluffy omelets ($4.25–$5.50), and plate-size pancakes (a chocolate short stack is $4) are all slapped together on the same griddle. The café serves lunch, too—try the pork chops and apple sauce ($6.75) when you need a little comfort food. While you're waiting in line (with a cup of complimentary coffee), check out the collection of posters from Haight-Ashbury street fairs past—they're almost as entertaining as the stream of locals strutting by. *1451 Haight St., btw Ashbury St. and Masonic Ave., tel. 415/864–6981. Open Mon.–Fri. 7 AM–3:30 PM, Sun. 8 AM–4 PM. Other location: 372 5th St., at Harrison St., tel. 415/495–3669.*

Spaghetti Western. The pierced-and-tattooed set eats breakfast and then hangs around all day at this chaotic lower-Haight spot. Gorge yourself on the Spuds O'Rama ($4.55), a huge, quivering mound of home-fried potatoes topped with cheese and sour cream, or the thick sourdough French toast ($4.75). *576 Haight St., near Steiner St., tel. 415/864–8461. Open weekdays 7 AM–3:30 PM, weekends 8 AM–4 PM.*

Squat and Gobble Café. This sprawling café-turned-breakfast-spot serves up home-style breakfasts to lower-Haight types who come armed with the Sunday paper, a pack of Marlboro reds, and nothing to do all day. Try the massive lower-Haight omelet, with fresh veggies, pesto, and cheese ($5), or any number of inventive crepes, including the Zorba the Greek, with feta, olives, artichokes, spinach, and cheddar ($6). They also have a decent selection of salads and sandwiches. If you're the type who needs a pot of coffee before you can focus, be aware that refills are not free. *237 Fillmore St., btw Haight and Waller Sts., tel. 415/487–0551. Open daily 8 AM–10 PM. No credit cards.*

Ya, Halla! This new Middle Eastern restaurant on lower Haight hasn't yet attracted the attention it should, possibly because it's on a particularly grimy stretch of Haight Street. The lack of crowds creates a peaceful little enclave, replete with soothing Middle Eastern music, where you'll find some of the freshest, most delicious falafel and hearty main dishes ($6–$8) around. Beware the addictive Super falafel ($4), with hummus, mulabal, and tabouleh in a burrito-style wrap. *494 Haight St., at Fillmore St., tel. 415/522–1509. Open daily 11–11. Wheelchair access.*

➢ **UNDER $15 • Cha Cha Cha.** You'll enjoy the skillfully prepared tapas and the pseudo-Catholic icons on the walls, but you'll wait all night for a table. The heyday of this Caribbean joint has lasted a little too long, as evidenced by the wanna-be-hip crowd it now draws. Entrées range from $10 to $13, but it's de rigueur to stick to tapas like fried plantains with black beans and sour cream ($5.25) or shrimp sautéed in Cajun spices ($6.75). Wash it all down with plenty of sangria (which can help you pass your possibly two-hour wait in a painless haze). To avoid the crowds, come for a late lunch. *1801 Haight St., at Shrader St., tel. 415/386–7670. Open Mon.–Thurs. 11:30–3 and 5–11, Fri. 11:30–3 and 5–11:30, Sat. 11:30–4 and 5–11:30, Sun. 11:30–4 and 5–11. No credit cards.*

If you don't feel like sitting at one of Ganges's tables, you can remove your shoes and park yourself on cushions in the back room, though after a couple of Taj Mahal beers, getting up may pose something of a challenge.

Ganges. Those who think vegetarian food is dull and tasteless should come to this small Indian restaurant. The delicious, extra-spicy Surti cuisine, which contains no meat, no fish, and only homemade cheeses, can fill you up for about $10; but if you order the "number one" package (raita, papadum, chapati, chutney, appetizer, rice, vegetable, curry, and dessert), you'll have a feast for under $15. À la carte curry dishes like *chana masala* (a garbanzo-bean delicacy) and stuffed zucchini cost $6. Friday and Saturday nights you'll dine to live sitar and tabla music. *775 Frederick St., btw Stanyan and Arguello Sts., tel. 415/661–7290. Open Tues.–Sat. 5–10.*

Thep Phanom. This small, daintily decorated lower-Haight Thai establishment finally seems to be nearing the end of its trendy phase when hour-plus waits were common. It can be a relaxing place to grab a savory bowl of *tom kha gai* (coconut chicken soup; $7). Critics also rave about the duck dishes and curries, but expect to pay a bit more than you normally do for Thai entrées ($8–$10 instead of the standard $6–$7)—the price of inventiveness and fame. *400 Waller St., at Fillmore St., tel. 415/431–2526. Open daily 5:30–10:30.*

JAPANTOWN

In the **Japan Center** (1737 Post St., btw Geary and Fillmore Sts.), the veritable heart of Japantown, a bunch of decent restaurants—spanning a wide range of price categories—display their edibles via shiny photos or shellacked plastic miniatures. If nothing piques your interest, explore the surrounding streets for older, more divey places that occasionally turn out to be gems. The cheapest option of all is to visit the Japanese market **Maruwa** (open Mon.–Sat. 10–7, Sun. 10–6), on the corner of Post and Webster streets. Along with fruits and vegetables and all manner of Japanese products, the delicatessen offers sushi, rice and noodle dishes, and individual cuts of meat. When you're done eating, go blow the rest of your money on a cheesy action movie at the multiscreen Kabuki 8 (*see* Movie Houses, in Chapter 6), in the same complex.

➢ **UNDER $10** • **Isobune.** Patrons at this touristy but fun sushi restaurant pack in around a large table, elbow to elbow, and fish their sushi off little boats that bob about in the water in front of them. Kimono-clad chefs deftly mold the sushi and replenish the boats' cargoes as fast as they are emptied. Prices range from $1.20 for two pieces of mackerel or fried bean cake to $2.50 for two pieces of salmon roe or red clam. It may not be the best sushi you'll ever eat, but it's good enough for the price. *Japan Center, 1737 Post St., tel. 415/563–1030. Open daily 11:30–10. Wheelchair access.*

Mifune. A steady stream of Asian and American patrons slurp up cheap, tasty *udon* and *soba* noodles and *donburi* (rice) dishes in the simple Mifune dining room. The noodles, which come with various meats and vegetables, cost anywhere from $3.50 for a plain broth to $8.50 for one with jumbo shrimp. *Japan Center, 1737 Post St., tel. 415/922–0337. Open daily 11–9:30. Wheelchair access.*

➢ **UNDER $15** • **Now and Zen.** This "enlightened vegetarian restaurant" a half-block from the Japan Center began three years ago as a wholesale vegan bakery. So, of course, the highlight here is the cakes and pastries that contain no eggs, milk, or sugar. Also offered at this friendly little café is a full range of delicious vegetarian meals with a Japanese twist. For dinner try the *vermicelli japonais* (pasta with oyster, shiitake, and enoki mushrooms in a soy, sake, Japanese basil, and seaweed sauce; $10). *1826 Buchanan St., tel. 415/922–9696. Open Mon.–Thurs. 11–4 and 5–9, Fri.–Sat. 11–10, Sun. 10–3 and 5–9:30. Wheelchair access.*

Sanppo. Japanese restaurants, like Japan, have a reputation for costliness. But Sanppo, a longtime Japantown fixture, offers familiar specialties at prices that won't break the bank, including vegetable tempura for $7.50, salmon teriyaki for $8.25, and three six piece avocado sushi rolls for $6.25. *1702 Post St., at Buchanan St., tel. 415/346–3486. Open Tues.–Sat. 11:45–10, Sun. 3–10.*

MARINA DISTRICT

A few blocks inland from Fisherman's Wharf, lots of upscale restaurants—from grills to sushi spots to California-cuisine eateries—line **Chestnut** and **Union streets.** It's a nice place to take your honey for dinner when she passes the bar exam.

➢ **UNDER $10** • **Hahn's Hibachi.** This tiny restaurant, little more than a take-out counter, dishes up healthy portions of delicious Korean-barbecued chicken, beef, or pork with rice and kimchi for about $6. Vegetarians will pay even less ($4) for a bowl of vegetable *udon* (noodle soup). So many people order takeout that there's rarely a wait for the five or so tables. *3318 Steiner St., btw Chestnut and Lombard Sts., tel. 415/931–6284. Open Mon.–Sat. 11:30–10. Other location: 1710 Polk St., at Clay St., tel. 415/776–1095. No credit cards.*

➢ **UNDER $15** • **Doidge's Kitchen.** If someone asks you to "do breakfast" in the Marina, this is likely where you'll end up. Curtains shelter upscale Doidge's patrons from the street life outside. Expensive and delicious California-cuisine breakfasts run the gamut from a chutney omelet with sour cream ($7.50) to French toast with strawberries and bananas ($8.50). Reserve in advance. *2217 Union St., at Fillmore St., tel. 415/921–2149. Open weekdays 8 AM–1:45 PM, weekends 8 AM–2:45 PM. No credit cards.*

➢ **UNDER $25** • **Greens.** On your birthday, or if you want a treat after a long day of museums and cultural enrichment, head here. This place will make you entirely reevaluate your notion of vegetarian dining. No Kraft macaroni and cheese or carrot sticks here—Greens serves state-of-the-art meals in a beautifully spacious, gallerylike setting with a romantic view of the Golden Gate Bridge. Soups, salads, and bread by the Tassajara Bakery are all highly recommended, but be prepared for small portions and haughty waiters. Sunday brunch is probably the best deal; full dinners cost around $20. *Fort Mason, Bldg. A, tel. 415/771–6222. Open Tues.–Fri. 11:30–1:45 and 5:30–9:30, weekends 11:30–2:15 and 6–9:15.*

MISSION DISTRICT

Here you can wander from taquería to café to bookstore to taquería again in a salsa-and-cerveza-induced state of bliss. To add to the zillions of Mexican and Central American spots that already crowd the neighborhood, a smattering of trendy new restaurants has sprouted up on **16th Street** between Valencia and Guerrero. What other two-block area do you know that offers eight different types of cuisine for no more than $10 per person? The Mission's restaurants are accessible from either the 16th St./Mission or the 24th St./Mission BART stations.

➢ **UNDER $5** • **Cancun Taquería.** In the midst of Mission Street's mayhem sits this *típico* taquería, which serves one of the best veggie burritos ($3) around, chock full of beans, rice, and thick avocado slices. The tasty *cebollitas* (grilled green onions; $1.50) are also a big hit. *2288 Mission St., btw 18th and 19th Sts., tel. 415/252–9560. Open weekdays 10 AM–12:30 AM, weekends 10 AM–1:30 AM. No credit cards.*

Casa Sanchez. With a colorful outdoor patio that's great for sunny days and warm nights, Casa Sanchez is a good choice for a favorite taquería. Fiercely loyal patrons come back again and again for the homemade tortillas, chips, and salsa. Hefty combo platters ($4–$5) will fill you to the bursting point. *2778 24th St., btw York and Hampshire Sts., tel. 415/282–2400. Open weekdays 8–7, Sat. 8–6. No credit cards.*

El Farolito. Stagger in here for a burrito ($2.50–$3.50) as late as 3 AM (4 AM on Sat.). The grimy, cafeteria-style atmosphere is depressing, but after a couple of drinks in the wee hours of the morning, you probably won't even notice. *2777 Mission St., at 24th St., tel. 415/824–7877. No credit cards.*

El Toro. This lively corner taquería provides a wealth of choice: black or pinto beans, refried or whole, and no less than ten kinds of meat for your burrito ($3–$5), including *lengua* (tongue) and *cabeza* (brain). You'll have plenty of time to study the menu, since the line often snakes out the door. It's a good place for gringos: The burritos are a little on the bland side. *598 Valencia St., at 17th St., tel. 415/431–3351. Open daily 11–10. No credit cards.*

El Trébol. What El Trébol lacks in decor it quickly makes up for with incredibly cheap Central American fare and an animated, Spanish-speaking clientele. Specialties include *salpicón* (chopped beef), *chancho con yuca* (fried pork with cassava), and *pollo encebollado* (chicken with onions). Most entrées come with beans, rice, and tortillas, and all cost under $4. *3324 24th St., at Mission St., tel. 415/285–6298. Open weekdays noon–9, Sat. noon–8. Wheelchair access.*

La Cumbre. Large, colorful Mexican paintings line the walls, and the requisite Virgin Mary statue guards the front door of this bustling taquería. The burritos with *carne asada* (marinated beef; $2.50–$5) are so good they can bring a vegetarian back to the herd, so to speak. Dinner platters ($7) with meat, beans, and rice will fuel you through the night and most of the next day. *515 Valencia St., at 16th St., tel. 415/863–8205. Open Mon.–Sat. 11–10, Sun. noon–9. Wheelchair access. No credit cards.*

New Dawn. This slacker hangout dishes out hangover breakfasts loaded with cholesterol, fat, starch, and everything else you need to ensure you remain immobilized for the rest of the day. Try the huge portion of veggie home fries, an assortment of vegetables topped with a load of potatoes ($5.50), or go the familiar route with a basic two-egg breakfast ($3.50). *3174 16th St., btw Valencia and Guerrero Sts., no phone. Open Mon. and Tues. 8:30–2:30, Wed.–Fri. 8:30–8:30, weekends 8:30 AM–9:30 PM. No credit cards.*

New Dawn is decorated with the most bizarre collection of kitsch you've ever seen, including a life-size Jesus wearing sunglasses.

Pancho Villa. This always-packed taquería is a step above the myriad others, with a full range of dinner plates including garlic prawns ($7) in addition to your basic burrito ($4). The eclectic, ever-changing artwork is always fun to peruse. *3071 16th St., btw Mission and Valencia Sts., tel. 415/864–8840. Open daily 10 AM–midnight. Wheelchair access. No credit cards.*

➢ **UNDER $10 • Boogaloos.** Recently opened by the owners of Spaghetti Western (*see* Haight-Ashbury and Western Addition, *above*), Boogaloos has quickly become a popular breakfast spot for carefully disheveled, late-to-rise young locals. Choose a sidewalk table for people watching, or sit indoors and enjoy the colorful walls decorated with shards of pottery and abstract art. One of the better breakfast dishes is the polenta and eggs with salsa, black beans, and sour cream ($5.25). Wash it down with a mimosa if you're feeling frisky. *3296 Valencia St., at 22nd St., 415/824-3211. Open weekdays 8–4, weekends 9–4. Wheelchair access. No credit cards.*

Esperpento. Tapas and sangria have lately become very popular as a reasonably priced and festive dinner. When this tapas joint opened in the Mission in 1992, it skyrocketed to instant popularity, as lines out the door on weekends will attest. Brightly lit and decorated with all sorts of surreal, Daliesque touches, it serves delicacies like garlic shrimp ($6.50), red pepper salad ($4), and *tortilla de patatas* (potato and onion pancake; $4.75), as well as huge *paella* (stew) dinners ($26 for two). Come with a bunch of friends to celebrate something, like the end of the day. *3295 22nd St., btw Valencia and Mission Sts., tel. 415/282–8867. Open daily 11 AM–3 PM and Mon.–Sat. 5 PM–10 PM. No credit cards.*

Nicaragua. The fried plantain and cheese dinners ($4–$6) are, in the words of one Nicaraguan, an "explosion of flavors." The restaurant is a classic dive, with plastic tablecloths, cheesy pictures of Nicaragua on the walls, and a jukebox that plays Mexican and Central American music. The area is seedy, so be careful at night. *3015 Mission St., near César Chavez (Army) St., tel. 415/826–3672. Open Thurs.–Tues. 11–9:45. No credit cards.*

Panchita's. You could walk down 16th Street a hundred times without noticing this basic but excellent El Salvadoran restaurant. If your idea of charming includes home cooking, mismatched silverware, and a jukebox loaded with mariachi tunes, plan on eating many meals here. For breakfast there's *huevos rancheros* (eggs with tortillas, salsa, and guacamole; $4.75), for dinner *camarones al ajillo* (garlic shrimp; $9) and *plantanos con crema* (fried bananas with refried beans and cream; $4.75). The best deal is the king-size super burrito ($4). *3091 16th St., at Valencia St., tel. 415/431–4232. Open Sun.–Thurs. 9 AM–11 PM, Fri.–Sat. 9 AM–2 AM.*

Ti Couz. A youngish crowd lines up outside the door, waiting to get a taste of the succulent, piping-hot crêpes whipped up at this Mission joint, styled after Breton crêperies in western France. You'll want one of the light pancakes for dinner *and* dessert, no doubt. A main course, with savory fillings like spinach, mushrooms, and ricotta, will run you $3–$5, while a sweet crêpe will set you back $2–$5. Warm and friendly, Ti Couz is perfect for dinner on a long summer evening or lunch on a rainy afternoon. *3108 16th St., at Valencia St., tel. 415/252–7373. Open weekdays 11–11, Sat. 10 AM–11 PM, Sun. 10–10.*

➢ **UNDER $15 • La Rondalla.** A strolling mariachi band follows iron-haired waitresses serving up decent, reasonably priced Mexican dinners in a room decorated with Christmas ornaments year-round. If that isn't enough of a draw, it's open until 3 AM—plenty of time to drink margaritas ($10.50 a pitcher) and shout yourself hoarse over the live music. The enchilada, taco, and chili relleno combination goes for $8.50. *901 Valencia St., at 20th St., tel. 415/647–7474. Open Tues.–Sun. 11 AM–3 AM. Wheelchair access. No credit cards.*

Scenic India. This small restaurant serves up excellent *saag paneer* (spinach with homemade cheese; $7), shrimp *tandoori* (baked in a clay oven; $13), and other traditional Indian specialties. Delicious breads ($2 each) help keep the curries and other spicy sauces from a-wastin' in the bottom of your bowl. Think of the slow service as a bonus, not a drawback—just that much more time to knock back your fill of Taj Mahal beer. If the portions were a little bigger and the prices a little lower, Scenic India would be perfect. *532 Valencia St., btw 16th and 17th Sts., tel. 415/621–7226. Open Mon. 5–10, Tues.–Sun. 11–3 and 5–10.*

Timo's. The menu at this dimly lit, cozy restaurant features a huge selection of Spanish- and Mediterranean-style tapas ($7–$10), including delicate salads; roasted potatoes with garlic mayonnaise; grilled prawns; quail; and salt-cod potato cake with mint salsa. Come with friends and order a slew of different tapas, along with some Sangre de Toro wine. *842 Valencia St., at 19th St., tel. 415/647–0558. Open Sun.–Wed. 5–10:30, Thurs.–Sat. 5–11:30.*

Zante Pizza and Indian Cuisine. You may ask, "Pizza and Indian food? What?" Trust us, it works. A large selection of Indian curries ($5–$7) and tandoori dishes ($6–$12) sit proudly alongside greasy and satisfying slabs of pepperoni pizza. To fully understand this unlikely union, try the delicious Indian pizza (small, $12), topped with ginger, eggplant, lamb, garlic, green onion, chicken, prawns, spinach, and cauliflower. Enjoy your food—and the velour wall hangings—in the spacious dining room, or have your dinner delivered right to your door. *3489 Mission St., at Cortland St., tel. 415/821–3949. Open daily 11:30–10:30.*

NOE VALLEY

Just up the hill from the frenetic Mission district, Noe Valley is a placid oasis awash in young couples with baby strollers. It's a lazy Sunday-brunch type of place, and Noe's cafés and restaurants rally to meet this pressing need. The two most popular spots, neither of them cheap, are **Café Sanchez** (*see below*) and **Chloe's Café** (1399 Church St., at 26th St., 415/648–4116).

➢ **UNDER $5** • **Tom Peasant Pies.** Tom serves only one thing—pies. Not big, meaty pies, but butter-and-cholesterol-free, fresh-outta-the-oven pies, at $2.50 a pop. One fits neatly into the palm of your hand, and two will easily satisfy your hunger. Start with shrimp or potato-rosemary and finish with chocolate-raspberry. The "atmosphere" consists of a few bar stools lined against the front window, so plan to get your pies to go. *4108 24th St., at Castro St., tel. 415/642–1316. Open daily 9:30–7. Wheelchair access. No credit cards.*

➢ **UNDER $10** • **Café Sanchez.** At this small café, owned and sometimes gruffly run by two women, young families politely vie with local hipsters for outdoor tables. Gourmet omelets ($5–$7) are served with fresh-baked muffins and enough home fries to let you skip lunch. Large, rich espresso drinks ($2) that come in bowls instead of mugs should help you fight off the inevitable food coma. Later in the day, pick out hefty sandwiches like roasted eggplant and fontina ($6.25) on warm focaccia. *3998 César Chavez (Army) St., at Sanchez St., tel. 415/641–5683. Open Tues.–Fri. 7:30 AM–9:30 PM, Sat. 8 AM–9:30 PM, Sun. 8–8. Wheelchair access.*

➢ **UNDER $20** • **Firefly.** Somehow both elegant and friendly, Firefly captures the small-town charm of Noe Valley while serving a fresh and innovative menu that has made it the darling of San Francisco food critics—readers of the *Bay Guardian* voted it best new restaurant of 1995. The vegetarian-friendly menus revolve around different cuisines and change biweekly. Entrées ($12–$17) might be Basque or Mediterranean and always taste homemade. Reservations are a must. *4288 24th St., at Diamond St., tel. 415/821–7652. Open daily 5:30–10. Wheelchair access.*

NORTH BEACH

This old-time Italian neighborhood is about strong coffee, fresh pasta, spicy sausages, and the highest concentration of restaurants (and lowest concentration of parking) in the city. **Columbus Avenue** and **Grant Avenue** north of Columbus are lined with reliable, reasonably priced Italian restaurants from which you can pick and choose. If you overindulge, go directly to the nearby Church of Saints Peter and Paul at Washington Square Park to atone for your gastronomic sin.

➢ **UNDER $5** • **San Francisco Art Institute Café.** Usually the only way you can eat with a view like this is by dressing up, subjecting yourself to a rude wait staff, and dishing out beaucoup cash at the top-floor restaurant of a downtown skyscraper. Not here! A couple of steep blocks up Russian Hill from North Beach, this café inside an art school provides all of the view and none of the pretentiousness of those *other* places. On top of that, you get great food cheap: Superlative garden burgers, regular burgers, and sandwiches all run about $4. *800 Chestnut St., 1½ blocks uphill (west) from Columbus Ave., tel. 415/749–4567. Open winter, weekdays 9–9, Sat. 9–4; summer, Mon.–Sat. 9 AM–2 PM. No credit cards.*

Nose rings and tattoos are de rigueur at the Art Institute Café, and a sign at the counter promises PSEUDO-BOHEMIANS WELCOME.

➢ **UNDER $10** • **Bocce Café.** Most dishes are $6–$8 at this high-ceilinged restaurant hidden away from the craziness of North Beach. For your money you'll get a fresh Caesar or chicken salad, or a large individual pizza, or a choice of five types of pasta with about 15 sauces (including mussels, feta, olive, and tomato or risotto with wild mushrooms), or an oven dish like lasagna. On warm Friday and Saturday evenings you can eat in the garden to the strains of live jazz. *478 Green St., at Grant Ave., tel. 415/981–2044. Open Mon.–Thurs. 11:30–11, Fri.–Sat. 11:30–11:30.*

Hunan. This old North Beach favorite put the "hot" in hot-and-sour chicken ($7). Come for painfully spicy but delicious MSG-free Chinese food. The space resembles a big warehouse, perfect for when you and 20 of your closest friends want to get obnoxious. *924 Sansome St., near Broadway, tel. 415/956–7727. Open daily 11:30–9:30. Other locations: 674 Sacramento St., near Kearny St., tel. 415/788–2234; 1016 Bryant St., btw 8th and 9th Sts., tel. 415/861–5808.*

Il Pollaio. This small Italian kitchen overlooking Columbus Avenue serves grilled chicken, and lots of it, in a homey, casual atmosphere. You can get a terrific half chicken with salad, bread, and wine for less than $10; without the wine it's around $7. *555 Columbus Ave., btw Union and Green Sts., tel. 415/362–7727. Open Mon.–Sat. 11:30–9. Wheelchair access.*

L'Osteria del Forno. In this small North Beach café, the ambience is Italian with a capital "I", right down to the crockery. Salads, antipasti, and sandwiches ($3–$5) feature Mediterranean touches like red peppers, imported cheese, and Greek olives. The pizza has won a few kudos, too. You can get it by the slice ($2–$4) or by the pie (small, $10–$17). *519 Columbus Ave., at Green St., tel. 415/982–1124. Open Mon. 11:30–9, Wed.–Thurs. 11:30–11, Fri.–Sat. 11:30–10:30, Sun. 1–10. Wheelchair access. No credit cards.*

Mario's Bohemian Cigar Store and Café. With about 10 tables and a big polished-wood bar, this old-time Italian café has been feeding 'em strong espresso, a glass of Chianti, or a beer for the last 50 years. You can also get a fine sandwich (meatball, roasted eggplant, Italian sausage, and chicken, among others) on homemade focaccia ($5–$6). The windows overlook Washington Square Park and the Church of Saints Peter and Paul, in case you didn't already feel like you were in Italy. *566 Columbus Ave., at Union St., tel. 415/362–0536. Open Mon.–Sat. 10 AM–midnight, Sun. 10 AM–11 PM. No credit cards.*

North Beach Pizza. Everyone swears this spot serves the best pizza in North Beach. From a bustling kitchen come messy, heaping pizzas like Verdi's special, with spinach, pesto, onions, and feta cheese (medium, $15). The only drag is that they don't sell by the slice. *1499 Grant Ave., at Union St., tel. 415/433–2444. Open Sun.–Thurs. 11 AM–1 AM, Fri.–Sat. 11 AM–3 AM. Wheelchair access. No credit cards. Other locations: 1310 Union St., at Vallejo St., tel. 415/433–2444; 800 Stanyan St., at Beulah St., tel. 415/751–2300; 4789 Mission St., btw Persia and Russia Sts., tel. 415/586–1400; 3054 Taraval St., at 41st Ave., tel. 415/242–9100.*

➢ **UNDER $15** • **Capp's Corner.** Capp's doesn't have the best food in North Beach, but it's always a party. Come to this crowded yet comfortable Italian restaurant for lunch during the week when former boxing manager Joe Capp himself, sporting fedora and trench coat, seats the customers. A complete five-course dinner ($11.50–$13.50), served family style, includes minestrone soup, salad, pasta, and an entrée, plus the mandatory dish of spumoni ice cream. After the meal you can catch Beach Blanket Babylon (*see* Theater, in Chapter 6) next door. *1600 Powell St., at Green St., tel. 415/989–2589. Open weekdays 11:30–2:30 and 4:30–midnight, weekends 4:30–midnight.*

The Gold Spike. It first opened as a candy store back in 1927 (conveniently manufacturing bathtub gin on the side), but for over 50 years now this cluttered, unpretentious restaurant has served up reasonably priced Italian fare to loyal regulars and gawking tourists. Once you get over the baffling array of trinkets on display, sit back and enjoy entrées like eggplant or chicken parmigiana, sautéed calamari (around $10), and basic pasta dishes ($7–$9). *527 Columbus Ave., btw Union and Green Sts., tel. 415/986–9747. Open Mon.–Tues. and Thurs.–Fri. 5–10, weekends 5–10:30.*

Helmand. This North Beach spot serves Afghan food and presents a perfect opportunity for budget eaters to experience a new cuisine in an elegant setting. Lamb, chicken, and vegetarian entrées run $10–$15, and once you see how lovely and well-presented everything is, you'll agree it's one of the best eating-out deals in San Francisco. *430 Broadway, btw Kearny and Montgomery Sts., tel. 415/362–0641. Open Sun.–Thurs. 6 PM–10 PM, Fri.–Sat. 6–11.*

➢ **UNDER $20** • **Buca Giovanni.** This sedate, rustic, bricked-lined cave at the bottom of a short stairway features solid northern Italian food in an area sadly lacking it. Dishes like rabbit with prosciutto, mushrooms, and Italian liqueur ($16) seem to come straight out of a rural Italian farmhouse. The *salsa rossa,* a sun-dried tomato, anchovy, and caper spread that comes with your bread, is incredible. *800 Greenwich St., at Mason St., tel. 415/776–7766. Open Tues.–Sat. 5:30–10:30.*

RICHMOND AND SUNSET DISTRICTS

From the way San Franciscans talk, you'd think the Richmond and Sunset districts were in another county. Fact is, these districts (flanking Golden Gate Park) are only a few minutes away from the Haight and Japantown by car or just three to four more stops on the MUNI. For a little extra effort you get good, cheap food and the opportunity to brag about exploring the city to your friends. In the Richmond district, Vietnamese, Chinese, Thai, and Japanese places line **Clement Street** between Arguello Boulevard and 9th Avenue and between 20th and 25th avenues, where you'll also find produce markets brimming with items strange to a Western eye. On the other side of the park, in the Sunset, **Irving Street** between 5th and 25th avenues yields numerous Chinese and Thai restaurants. You'll also find excellent Mediterranean delis where you can purchase take-out tubs of hummus, falafel, and tabouleh.

➢ **UNDER $10** • **Empress Garden.** Although the Sunset teems with Chinese restaurants, this tastefully decorated establishment has muscled its way to the top. Every night of the week, Asian locals pack in around the party-size tables. Chicken dishes run about $5, but the house specialty, minced or deep-fried squab ($8–$10), is worth the splurge. An inlaid fish tank filled with live, kicking crabs (poor fellas) attests to the food's freshness. *1386 9th Ave., btw Irving and Judah Sts., tel. 415/731–2388. Open daily 11:30–9:30.*

Shangri-La. This all-vegetarian Chinese restaurant in the Sunset offers a delicious array of dishes, including bean-curd balls with garlic sauce ($4.75), vegetarian chicken with black-bean sauce ($5.25), and golden-brown gluten with sweet-and-sour sauce ($4.75). Although the faux-wood walls and inadequate lighting may be a turnoff, the food definitely makes up for the blah decor. *2026 Irving St., btw 21st and 22nd Aves., tel. 415/731–2548. Open daily 11:30–9:30.*

➢ **UNDER $15** • **Angkor Wat.** This Cambodian restaurant has won its fair share of awards, but it's not immediately apparent why. The moral: Put aside your high expectations and simply enjoy the decent food and elegant surroundings, not to mention Cambodian dance performances on Friday and Saturday nights. Appetizers like papaya salad and chicken satay cost about $4; entrées, including a great barbecued pork, run $9–$14. *4217 Geary Blvd., at 6th Ave., tel. 415/221–7887. Open Sun.–Thurs. 5–10, Fri.–Sat. 5–10:30. Wheelchair access.*

Khan Toke Thai House. This attractive, dimly lit Richmond district restaurant serves Thai cuisine that always seems to be winning some prize in a "Best of the Bay Area" contest. As a bonus, they make you take off your shoes and sit on the floor to eat. Most dishes cost $5–$10. *5937 Geary Blvd., at 24th Ave., tel. 415/668–6654. Open daily 5–11. Wheelchair access.*

If you're feeling erudite, choose from a special section of Khan Toke's menu called "Thai Curries Mentioned in Thai Literature."

SOUTH OF MARKET

The SoMa warehouse wasteland yields surprisingly good restaurants on the unlikeliest, grimiest corners. Wander along **Folsom Street** between 7th and 12th streets, or along **11th** and **9th streets** between Howard and Harrison streets, and you'll have the SoMa eating scene in the palm of your hand. Oddly, there are few late-night eating spots to satiate clubbers' cravings. Besides **Hamburger Mary's** (*see below*), you can try **20 Tank Brewery** (*see* Bars, in Chapter 6), which serves sandwiches, nachos, and other munchies ($4–$6) until 1 AM and beer until 1:30. **Pizza Love** (1245 Folsom St., btw 8th and 9th Sts., tel. 415/225–LOVE) has cheap pizza slices ($1.75, toppings 25¢ each) until midnight Sunday–Wednesday, 2 AM Thursday, and 4 AM Friday and Saturday. The decor is ugly, but at 4 AM who cares?

➢ **UNDER $10** • **Hamburger Mary's.** The messy hamburgers ($5–$8) and the cluttered decor go together wonderfully. Come by at 1 AM to hang out with SoMa clubbers in various states of drunkenness and undress. Vegetarians can feast on the tofu burger ($6) or the Meatless Meaty, a hot sandwich of mushrooms, cream cheese, and olives. *1582 Folsom St., at 12th St., tel. 415/626–5767. Open Tues.–Thurs. 11:30 AM–1 AM, Fri.–Sat. 10 AM–2 AM, Sun. 10 AM–1 AM. Wheelchair access.*

Manora's Thai Cuisine. The location on Folsom is trendier than most Thai restaurants in the city, and big crowds wait at the bar before being seated. The Mission branch is smaller and quieter. At both, the fresh, attractive dishes are worth the wait. Garlic quail is $8, and spicy Japanese eggplant with prawns, chicken, and pork goes for $7. *1600 Folsom St., at 12th St., tel. 415/861–6224. Open weekdays 11:30–2:30 and 5:30–10:30, Sat. 5:30–10:30, Sun. 5–10. Wheelchair access. Other location: 3226 Mission St., at 29th St., tel. 415/550–0856.*

¡WA-HA-KA! This Mexican eatery specializes in California-style burritos and is popular with large (and often drunken) groups. Grab a ¡WA-HA-KA! burrito or an order of Baja rolls (Mexican sushi) before you head off to the nearby clubs; either one runs $4.50 à la carte or $6 with rice, beans, and salad. The margarita cantina opens at 5; a WA-HA-Karita can be yours for $3. *1489 Folsom St., at 11th St., tel. 415/861–1410. Open Mon.–Wed. 11:30–10, Thurs. 11:30–11, Fri. 11:30 AM–1 AM, Sat. 11 AM–1 AM, Sun. 5 PM–10 PM. Wheelchair access. No credit cards. Other location: 2141 Polk St., btw Broadway and Vallejo St., tel. 415/775–1055.*

➢ **UNDER $15** • **Acorn.** Come on a warm day and station yourself on the back patio of this flowery, romantic café—a surprising find in industrial SoMa. The inventive, changing menu will do you right for lunch or weekend brunch; dinner, at $20 and up, is a little steep. Lunch entrées might include a potato-cheddar frittata with ratatouille ($7) or garlic-roasted artichoke with marinated clams and mussels ($10.50). For the nutritionally correct, they use organic produce whenever possible. *1256 Folsom St., btw 8th and 9th Sts., tel. 415/863–2469. Open for lunch Tues.–Fri. 11–5, for dinner Wed.–Sat. 6–10, for brunch weekends 10:30–3.*

South Park Café. Pretend you're Hemingway, Gertrude Stein, or Henry Miller in glorious Parisian exile while you gnaw on *boudin noir* (blood sausage; $10) and *frites* (french fries; $1.75) and watch the world go by. This French bistro opens at 8 AM with fresh croissants and coffee and stays open for country-cooked lunches ($5–$10) and dinners ($6–$15). *108 South Park Ave., btw 2nd and 3rd and Bryant and Brannan Sts., tel. 415/495–7275. Open for coffee weekdays 8 AM–10 PM, for meals weekdays 11:30–2:30 and 6–10, Sat. 6 PM–10 PM.*

East Bay

With all of San Francisco's diverse dining choices, why eat anywhere else? Well, believe it or not, the East Bay outdoes San Francisco in some types of cuisine. This is the best place to find an Ethiopian meal, or to pick up a barbecued-rib dinner. Oakland's Chinatown rivals San Francisco's in authenticity, and Berkeley offers a classier breakfast scene than the Haight for about the same price.

BERKELEY

California cuisine, that designer fuel for the yuppie generation, got its start in Berkeley, and locals take their food very seriously. The area around **Shattuck Avenue** at Vine Street has become known as the Gourmet Ghetto and is home to a number of high-quality restaurants, including the famed **Chez Panisse** (*see* chapter introduction, *above*). On **Telegraph Avenue** between Dwight Way and the U.C. campus, you'll find the city's cheapest restaurants serving fast food with a Berkeley twist (heaping green salads and gourmet sandwiches are far more common than burgers). West of campus, along **University Avenue,** there's a string of mostly Asian and Indian restaurants. Both **College Avenue** (running south from campus into Oakland) and **Solano Avenue** (just north of Berkeley in Albany) are lined with cafés, sandwich shops, and upscale restaurants that cater to the neighborhood's students, professors, and granolafied yuppies.

Great Licks

Slurp it, lick it, let it melt all over your face and hands. Along with Ghirardelli (see Fisherman's Wharf, in Chapter 2), the spots listed below should take care of all your ice cream needs.

- ***Ben & Jerry's. This rich, politically correct ice cream is available right on the corner of Haight and Ashbury streets; in North Beach on Columbus Avenue (btw Union and Green Sts.); and at a stand on Pier 39. Cherry Garcia and Wavy Gravy are the flavors of choice on Haight Street, naturally. 1480 Haight St., tel. 415/249–4685.***
- ***Mitchell's Ice Cream. This popular, family-owned shop in the Mission features a variety of weird and delicious homemade ice creams, in addition to traditional flavors for the vanilla-ice-cream types. If you're a daredevil there's always avocado and yam flavors. 688 San Jose St., at 29th St., tel. 415/648–2300.***
- ***St. Francis Soda Fountain and Candy Store. They make their own ice cream, syrups, and candy at this old-fashioned soda shop in the Mission. Order a phosphate, an egg cream, or a chocolate malt and wax nostalgic. 2801 24th St., at York St., tel. 415/826–4200.***
- ***Swensen's. Climb to the top of Russian Hill and you'll find the original Swensen's ice cream parlor. You might need a chocolate double dip if not a respirator to get going again. 1999 Hyde St., at Union St., tel. 415/775–6818.***
- ***Toy Boat. Come here for a scoop and marvel for hours at the hundreds of old and new toys lining the walls. 401 Clement St., at 5th St., tel. 415/751–7505.***

➢ **UNDER $5** • Telegraph Avenue near the Berkeley campus is full of places that cater to students' thin pocketbooks. Several food carts park along Bancroft Avenue where Telegraph ends and sell everything from bagels and smoothies to Japanese food, burritos, and stuffed potatoes. For the cheapest Chinese food in Berkeley, head to **Chinese Express** (2488 Channing Way, at Telegraph Ave., tel. 510/845–3766) where each entrée from the 20-dish buffet goes for $1. For pizza with an "eat-it-or-screw-you" attitude, stop by **Blondie's** (2340 Telegraph Ave., near Durant Ave., tel. 510/548–1129), popular with street freaks and bleary-eyed students in need of a pepperoni fix at 1AM (2 AM Fridays and Saturdays). The jaded, underpaid employees provide constant entertainment, the stand-up counter is always packed, and your basic, greasy, and filling slice costs $2. **Bongo Burger** (2505 Dwight Way, at Telegraph Ave., tel. 510/540–9147) serves some of the cheapest meals in town—two eggs, home fries and toast; a Polish dog; or a falafel sandwich cost about $2 each. Bongo Burger also has a location just north of campus (1839 Euclid Ave., tel. 510/540–9573). A few blocks south of campus at Dwight Way, **Ann's Soup Kitchen and Restaurant** (2498 Telegraph Ave., tel. 510/548–8885) dishes out exceptionally cheap breakfasts, homemade soups, and sandwiches ($1.75–$4).

If you have ID to prove it, Blondie's will hand you a free slice of pizza on your birthday.

Café Intermezzo. This Berkeley institution, with a harried, occasionally rude staff, indisputably serves the biggest and best salads around. The veggie delight ($4.80) is a family-size mound of greens topped with kidney and garbanzo beans, hard-boiled egg, sprouts, avocado, and croutons. Salads are served with your choice of homemade dressings and include a bookend-size slab of fresh-from-the-oven, honey-wheat bread. Or try one of the humongous sandwiches on inch-thick slices of the same delicious bread ($4). *2442 Telegraph Ave., at Haste St., tel. 510/849–4592. Open daily 7:30 AM–11 PM. Wheelchair access.*

Cheese Board Pizza Collective. If you can get to this makeshift pizza café during their ridiculously short open hours, you will experience one of Berkeley's true delights. An offshoot of the nearby Cheese Board collective (*see* Specialty Markets and Delicatessens, *below*), this tiny kitchen offers just one kind of vegetarian pizza each day, made with toppings like eggplant, red peppers, pesto, feta or goat cheese, and cilantro (pies $14, slices $1.75). *1512 Shattuck Ave., at Cedar St., tel. 510/549–3055. 8 blocks north of Berkeley BART. Open Tues.–Thurs. 11:30–2, Mon. and Fri. 4:30–around 6:30, Sat. noon–2. Wheelchair access.*

Crêpes-A-Go-Go. The owner of this small café on busy University Avenue used to sell crêpes on the streets of Paris. Now, bless him, he's settled in Berkeley, offering sweet and savory crêpes

Little Bit of Buddha in Every Bite

Sundays between 10 and 2, families set up food stands, tables, and folding chairs in the courtyard behind the Thai Buddhist Temple and Cultural Center in Berkeley and serve up homemade Thai specialties. In fair or foul weather, exchange your money for tokens and choose among a heaping plate of pad Thai; a spicy soup of noodles, meatballs, and beef; or various seafood curries ($3 each). The freshly sliced mango over sticky rice with coconut cream ($3) is heavenly. Side dishes, including neat packages of glutinous rice filled with taro root, banana, or coconut and wrapped in banana leaves, are $1. Be brave and taste one of the artistic but hard-to-identify desserts ($1.50) stacked next to Thai iced tea, iced coffee, and logan drink (75¢ each). This brunch is popular among Thai families and anthropologist types; proceeds benefit the temple. On your way out, check the information board for listings of Thai language and yoga classes. 1911 Russell St., btw Martin Luther King Jr. Way and Otis St., tel. 510/540–9734. 1 block west of Ashby BART.

like Nutella and banana ($3.25) or spinach, green onions, and cheeses ($3.50). One is filling, two will leave you staggering out the door. *2125 University Ave., at Shattuck Ave., tel. 510/841–7722. 2 blocks north of Berkeley BART. Open daily 9 AM–10 PM. No credit cards.*

Juice Bar Collective. Smack in the middle of the Gourmet Ghetto, the Juice Bar offers fresh and organic sandwiches as well as hot dishes like spinach lasagna ($3–$4). But their focus, as the name suggests, is conjuring up fruit smoothies like the Sunset ($3.25), made with bananas, orange juice, and yogurt. *2114 Vine St., tel. 510/548–8473. Open Mon.–Sat. 10–4:30. Wheelchair access.*

➢ **UNDER $10 • Berkeley Thai House.** The interior of this restaurant near the Berkeley campus is about as boring as it gets, but the peaceful flower-lined patio, set off from the street by tall bushes, is a wonderful escape from the Telegraph Avenue crowds. Locals and students in the know come to wolf down pad Thai ($4.25) and other reasonably priced lunch specials ($5–$6). For dinner, try the *mus-s-mun* (beef with red curry, peanuts, potatoes, carrots, and coconut milk; $6). *2511 Channing Way, at Telegraph Ave., tel. 510/843–7352. Open Mon.–Thurs. 11–9:30, Fri.–Sat. 11–10, Sun. 2–9:30.*

Bette's Oceanview Diner. In the midst of the home-decoration stores on 4th Street near I–80, this bright, crowded, '50s-style diner offers yummy breakfasts and lunches from the grill ($5–$8). Bette's takes a more upscale approach than the usual diner. Grilled American cheese and white bread? Try jack and cheddar on sourdough ($4.75). If you're not up for a half-hour wait on weekends, Bette's To Go next door offers take-out salads ($2–$4 for ½ pint) and sandwiches ($3.50–$4.50). *1807A 4th St., near University Ave., tel. 510/644–3230. Open Mon.–Thurs. 6:30 AM–2:30 PM, Fri.–Sun. 6:30 AM–4 PM. Wheelchair access.*

Blue Nile. This is one of Berkeley's best Ethiopian eateries, serving everything from thick split-pea stew and pepper-cooked beef to *tej* (honey wine) and freshly blended fruit shakes. The food is served family style, and you use *injera* bread instead of silverware to scoop it up. As with most restaurants along Telegraph Avenue, the Blue Nile attracts lots of U.C. students and faculty for lunch ($5) and dinner ($6–$8). *2525 Telegraph Ave., btw Dwight Way and Parker St., tel. 510/540–6777. Open Mon.–Sat. 11–10. Wheelchair access.*

Brick Hut Café. This mom-and-mom café, a collective owned and operated by women, is one of the best breakfast joints around. It's also a hot lesbian pickup spot on an increasingly womanish stretch of San Pablo Avenue. The pesto eggs ($5.50) are a house favorite, and for lunch the Hut serves salads, burgers, and sandwiches. The high ceilings, exposed-brick walls, polished wooden floors, and friendly wait staff create an atmosphere conducive to postmeal lingering. *2512 San Pablo Ave., at Dwight Way, tel. 510/486–1124. Open Mon., Thurs., Fri. 7–3, Sat., 8 AM–10 PM, Sun. 8 AM–3 PM.*

Café Panini. A popular lunch destination for downtown office workers, this open-air café, hidden away from Shattuck Avenue in sunny and quiet Trumpetvine Court, serves sandwiches with a Mediterranean flair. The menu, consisting of a half-dozen inventive selections, changes daily; a typical choice is vegetarian eggplant Romanesco with white cheddar, tomatoes, greens, and red onions ($5.50). *2115 Allston Way, tel. 510/849–0405. Enter from Shattuck Ave., at Trumpetvine Court, btw Center St. and Allston Way. Open weekdays 7:30–4, Sat. 10–4.*

Cha Am. This airy restaurant—one of Berkeley's best Thai spots—feels removed from Shattuck Avenue, even though its greenhouselike window seats overlook the street. Try the magical *domka gai* (chicken and coconut soup; $6) or the mixed seafood plate with chili, garlic, and vegetables ($8.75). *1543 Shattuck Ave., at Cedar St., tel. 510/848–9664. 7 blocks north of Berkeley BART. Open Mon.–Thurs. 11:30–4 and 5–9:30, Fri. 11:30–4 and 5–10, Sat. noon–4 and 5–10, Sun. 5–9:30.*

Chester's Café. Looking out over the bay from Chester's sunny upstairs deck is one of the best ways to start a lazy weekend morning. The friendly staff will do you up with mug after mug of hot coffee and a brunch with all the fixings. Weekend specials include eggs Juneau (poached eggs and smoked salmon on an English muffin topped with Hollandaise sauce; $7.50). If you wake up on the lunch side of brunch, console yourself with warm chicken salad with sautéed red, yellow, and green bell peppers ($7). *1508B Walnut Ave., at Vine St., tel. 510/849–9995. Open Mon.–Sat. 8 AM–9 PM, Sun. 8–5.*

Homemade Café. You'll have a hard time deciding what to order from the extensive menu, and you'll probably have to wait for a table (at least on weekends), so grab a cup of coffee and a menu, park yourself on the sidewalk, and start deliberating. The whole-wheat buttermilk waffle made with cinnamon and nutmeg ($3) seems like one of the less indulgent items until you start adding pecans (75¢) and homemade blueberry sauce ($1.50). Also popular are the *matzoh brei* (matzo with scrambled eggs and cheese; $5.50) and the famous Home-Fry Heaven (home fries with cheese, salsa, sour cream, and guacamole or pesto; $4.75). *2454 Sacramento St., at Dwight Way, tel. 510/845–1940. Open weekdays 7 AM–2 PM, weekends 8–3.*

Juan's Place. This traditional Mexican restaurant has the feel of an old cantina, complete with piñatas, mirrored beer ads, and cheesy portraits of matadors. Juan's dishes out large portions of standard fare, including tacos, burritos, and tamales. The crab enchilada with red sauce and cheese ($7 for two) overflows with tender crabmeat. Try a wine margarita ($2.50 a glass, $10 a pitcher) from the adjoining bar. Juan's is stuck on the fringes of Berkeley, surrounded by steel factories and warehouses. *941 Carleton St., at 9th St., tel. 510/845–6904. 2 blocks west of San Pablo Ave. Open weekdays 11–10, weekends 2–10.*

Kabana. This Pakistani restaurant has a wonderful mango *lassi* (sweetened yogurt shake; $2.50) to help you handle the spicy food. Vegetarians should try the *tinda* (summer squash with herbs and spices, served with rice or spicy flat bread; $5.50). The massive tropical wall mural and friendly wait staff brighten the sparse atmosphere. You'll also find plenty of parking (a rarity in Berkeley). *1106 University Ave., at San Pablo Ave., tel. 510/845–3355. Open Tues.–Sun. 11–9:30. Wheelchair access. No credit cards.*

Rick and Ann's. Join East Bay yuppies in bicycle shorts (babies and dogs in tow) as you wait for the best breakfast in town—and in Berkeley, that's really saying something. Try the Down South ($7.25), a combo of two cornmeal pancakes, two spicy turkey sausages, and two fluffy scrambled eggs with cheese. The special omelets and scrambles are also delicious, as is the French toast, made with *challah* (egg bread). *2922 Domingo St., near Ashby St., tel. 510/649–8538. Across from Claremont Resort. Open daily 8–2:30 and 5:30–9:30.*

Saul's. In the midst of the Gourmet Ghetto, this is the closest thing to a New York deli in the East Bay. Shelves of Manischewitz products line the entryway, and a glass deli counter displays bowls of chopped liver, sauerkraut, and whole smoked fish. Sandwiches ($5–$8) are stuffed with pastrami, corned beef, brisket, or tongue. Jewish specialties include knishes ($3), potato latkes with sour cream and applesauce ($6 for three), and matzo-ball soup ($3.50). Saul's gets noisy and crowded during peak hours; avoid the lunch-hour wait by getting your food to go. *1475 Shattuck Ave., at Vine St., tel. 510/848–3354. 8 blocks north of Berkeley BART. Open daily 8–9:30.*

➢ **UNDER $15** • **Pasand Madras Cuisine.** If you feel like going for the gusto at this southern Indian restaurant, get a complete *thali* dinner, including lentil curry, lentil vegetable soup, spicy tamarind soup, yogurt with vegetables, a selection of Indian flat breads, rice pilaf, sweet mango chutney, and a dessert surprise. The boneless ginger chicken masala curry ($8 à la carte, $10.50 thali) is a winner, as are the vegetable curries ($5.50–$9.50)—though even the ones labeled "spicy" are pretty tame. A raised seating area offers views of cross-legged sitar and tabla players who play into a musical frenzy during dinner. A downstairs lounge features live jazz nightly and salsa dancing Thursdays. *2286 Shattuck Ave., at Bancroft Way, tel. 510/549–2559. 2 blocks south of Berkeley BART. Open Sun.–Thurs. 11–10:30, Fri. and Sat. 11–11. Wheelchair access.*

Stuff yourself silly for $6 at Pasand's all-you-can-eat lunch buffet (11 AM–2:30 PM).

➢ **UNDER $20** • **Sushi Ko.** The decor at this Berkeley restaurant is spartan, and the food is exceptional. Check out the special rolls listed on a board by the sushi bar. The spider roll, filled with soft-shell crab, fish eggs, cucumber, and lettuce ($7), is a good bet, as is the spicy tuna handroll ($3.50). In addition to delicate and flavorful sushi, Sushi Ko has unusual cooked dishes like grilled calamari with ginger sauce ($5.50). *64 Shattuck Sq., near University Ave.,* *tel. 510/845–6601. 1 block north of Berkeley BART. Open Mon.–Sat.. 11:30–2 and 5:30–9:30 (Fri.–Sat. until 10), Sun. 5:30–9.*

Venezia. This restaurant goes to great lengths to evoke the atmosphere of a Venetian piazza. The walls are painted to look like Italian shops and houses and have protruding wrought-iron balconies and flower boxes. There's even a clothesline strung overhead, complete with drying boxers. Luckily, the food measures up to the decor. Start with the *insalata di pollo* (salad with smoked chicken, pistachios, grapefruit, and scallions; $5.50) and check the board for daily pasta and fresh fish specials, like grilled salmon with olive-fennel relish ($13). *1799 University Ave., at Grant St., tel. 510/849–4681. Reservations advised. Open Mon.–Thurs. 11:30–2:30 and 5:30–10, Fri. 11:30–2:30 and 5–10, Sat. 5–10, Sun. 5–9:30. Wheelchair access.*

➢ **UNDER $30 • Chez Panisse Café.** The world-famous Chez Panisse restaurant may be out of reach, but the café upstairs serves many of the same dishes for half the price, and there's less silverware to contend with. You can make same-day lunch reservations, but for dinner you'll just have to suffer—go early and expect to wait an hour or more for a table. Among the starters, Heidi's garden salad with goat cheese ($8) is exquisite, as are the pizzas ($13.50–$15); the prosciutto, garlic, and goat cheese calzone makes a great appetizer to share or a main dish for one. The café feels like an upscale living room, and patrons sport everything from jeans to suits and evening wear. *1517 Shattuck Ave., at Cedar St., tel. 510/548–5049. 7 blocks north of Berkeley BART. Open Mon.–Thurs. 11:30–3 and 5-10:30, Fri.–Sat. 11:30–4 and 5–11:30.*

OAKLAND

From southern-style barbecue shacks to El Salvadoran holes-in-the-wall, Oakland is loaded with cheap and colorful eateries. Because the city's population is so diverse, you can find just about every type of cuisine imaginable—explore this area with eager taste buds and an open mind. Oakland's **Chinatown** is a less touristy version of its counterpart across the bay. Bounded by 7th, 10th, Broadway, and Alice streets downtown, Chinatown offers increasing numbers of Southeast Asian restaurants and markets, as well as the older and more established Chinese ones. The **Fruitvale** district, encompassing the neighborhoods around the Fruitvale BART station, has dozens of cheap Mexican and Central American restaurants. It is safest, however, to restrict your visits here to main streets and daylight hours. If you don't feel like having an

Late Night Bites in the East Bay

After 2 AM, it's harder than you might think to find something besides Denny's in the East Bay. Keep in mind that these tried-and-true spots are known for the hours they keep and not necessarily for their cuisine.

- ***Jack London Inn Coffee Shop. Across the street from the Oakland waterfront, this friendly locals' diner is lost in a '70s time warp. 444 Embarcadero West, at 1st St., tel. 510/763–9764.***
- ***J.J.'s Diner. The hefty eggs-bacon-toast special ($6.25) will leave you wallowing in a cholesterol haze. 315 27th St., at Broadway, Oakland, tel. 510/893–7480.***
- ***Neutron Bakery. Conveniently located one block from the Berkeley BART station, you can play pinball and munch on donuts if you miss the last train out. 2124 Center St., at Shattuck, Ave., tel. 510/540–7431.***

adventure along with your meal, two long avenues in Oakland offer a wide selection of familiar delis, burger joints, and gringo burrito shops: From downtown Oakland, Bus 59 or 59A will take you to **Piedmont Avenue;** for **College Avenue,** take BART to Rockridge.

➢ **UNDER $5** • **Taquería Morelia.** Come to this Oakland joint for one of the best quesadillas ($2) around, a fried flour or corn tortilla oozing cheese and sprinkled with chopped tomatoes and cilantro. Locals of all ages flow between the restaurant and adjacent dive bar, Talk of the Town, carrying cheap beer and plastic baskets of tacos and burritos ($2.50–$4 each). *4481 E. 14th St., near High St., tel. 510/535–6030. About 7 blocks southeast of Fruitvale BART. Open Mon.–Wed. 10–10, Thurs. and Sun. 10–11, Fri.–Sat. 10–midnight.*

➢ **UNDER $10** • **Asmara Restaurant.** Colorful baskets and rugs suspended from the ceiling cheer up the interior of this East African restaurant in North Oakland. Sample three of the excellent entrées in the combination platter, either meat ($5.50 lunch, $8 dinner) or vegetarian ($5.50 lunch, $7.50 dinner). The red lentil stew is the most flavorful of the vegetarian dishes. Those who like lamb should try *ye-beg alicha,* made with curry and spices ($4.75 lunch, $7.50 dinner). In keeping with Ethiopian tradition, food is served family style with injera bread and a notable lack of utensils—use your fingers. *5020 Telegraph Ave., near 51st St., tel. 510/547–5100. Open Mon., Wed.–Fri. 11–11, weekends noon–11. Wheelchair access.*

True carnivores should head to El Taco Zamorano, a silver truck parked in Oakland at the corner of East 14th and High streets, where the delicious burritos ($2), tacos ($1), and tortas are filled with beef head, beef tongue, and pork skins.

Barney's Gourmet Hamburger. This Rockridge joint specializes in gourmet burgers, like the Parisian, served on a baguette with bleu cheese ($5). The prices are reasonable and the portions enormous. They even cater to those trying to avoid red meat—you can order your burger with grilled chicken instead. Round off your meal with an order of fries and a chocolate malt. *5819 College Ave., near Chabot Ave., tel. 510/601–0444. Open Mon.–Thurs. 11–9:30, Fri.–Sat. 11–10, Sun. 11–9:30. Other locations: 4162 Piedmont Ave., Oakland, tel. 510/655–7180; 1591 Solano Ave., Albany, tel. 510/526–8185; 4138 24th St., at Castro St., San Francisco, tel. 415/282–7770.*

Flint's. Regarded by some as the best barbecue shack in the world, Flint's caters to large appetites during the wee hours. Choose from pork or beef ribs, links, or chicken (around $7) piled high on a paper plate, crowned with a couple slices of all-American white bread (to soak up the grease) and potato salad. Sandwiches are around $5. You'll be getting your food to go, as there are no seats here. Keep your wits about you on San Pablo Avenue, especially after dark. *3114 San Pablo Ave., at 31st St., tel. 510/658–9912. Open daily 11 AM–midnight.*

Lois the Pie Queen. Despite the name, most people come to this Oakland eatery for breakfast, not dessert. A family-run diner (vinyl swivel chairs, checkered tablecloths, and root-beer floats) that's gone California chic (pink walls and espresso drinks), Lois's offers all the breakfast favorites as well as excellent burgers and fries. Two eggs with homemade biscuits and grits is $4, as is the tuna melt. Don't forget the pies that made Lois a monarch; a slice of sweet potato or lemon ice-box goes for $2.50–$3. *851 60th St., 1 block west of Martin Luther King Jr. Way, tel. 510/658–5616. Open weekdays 8 AM–2 PM, Sat. 7–3, Sun. 7–4.*

Los Cocos. Fruitvale's best (and only) El Salvadoran restaurant is famous for its fried bananas ($4.50) and *pupusas* (stuffed tortillas; $3 for two). It may not look like much from the outside (or the inside, for that matter), but the food is excellent and cheap. The friendly family of cooks chatting in the small open kitchen brings life to the sparse yellow room. *1449 Fruitvale Ave., at 14th St., tel. 510/536–3079. Open Tues.–Sun. 10–10. Wheelchair access.*

Lucy's Creole Kitchen. A sunny, friendly diner with some of the best southern seafood west of the Mississippi River Delta. Daily hot lunch specials like jambalaya ($6) or smothered short ribs ($7.50) attract crowds from the neighborhood, as does straight-up southern fare like black-eyed peas, cabbage, and greens ($1.25 each) cooked with smoked turkey. And let's not forget the spicy crab burger ($4.50) and catfish with fries, coleslaw, or potato salad ($6.25).

1601 San Pablo Ave., at 16th St., tel. 510/763–6706. 7 blocks SW of 19th St. BART. Open Mon.–Thurs. 7:30–5. Wheelchair access. No credit cards.

Mama's Royal Cafe. Although you can get lunch here after 11:30, the restaurant's real raison d'être is breakfast (served until closing). Huge omelets ($6–$9), which come with home-style potatoes, fruit, and a muffin, are available in no fewer than 31 flavors. The seasonal fresh-fruit crêpes ($6.50) and the popular eggs Benedict ($8.25) could send you into a coma. Eat in a room covered with old-fashioned aprons or one that displays vintage radios. *4012 Broadway, at 40th St., tel. 510/547–7600. Open weekdays 7 AM–3 PM, weekends 8–3. No credit cards.*

Mexicali Rose. Come here with a bunch of friends late at night when you need to make lots of noise and gorge yourselves on Mexican food. The massive portions are served on sizzling hot platters (not plates, *platters*). The bilingual menu is heavy on the meat dishes, though nonstrict vegetarians will not be disappointed. The *nopales* (cactus) with eggs, rice, beans, and tortillas ($8) is a delicious—though acquired—taste. Two people could easily split the Mexicali Rose combo ($9.55): taco, stuffed chile, green enchilada, guacamole salad, rice, beans, and a drink (phew!). Right across from the Oakland jail, Mexicali's regular clientele sometimes includes both recently released jailbirds and their arresting officers. *701 Clay St., at 7th St., tel. 510/451–2450. 6 blocks SW of 12th St. BART. Open daily 10 AM–3:30 AM.*

Nan Yang. Although it's in Oakland's Chinatown, Nan Yang serves authentic Burmese cuisine. The atmosphere is less than intimate but the service is fast and cordial. Stick with the Burmese specialties rather than the supplementary Chinese dishes. Especially tasty are the curry chicken noodle soup ($5.50), the ginger salad ($4.75), and the curry shrimp ($6.50). They also serve vegetarian entrées. *301 8th St., at Harrison St., tel. 510/465–6924. Open Tues.–Thurs. 11–9, Fri.–Sat. 11–9:30, Sun. noon–9. Wheelchair access. Other location: 6048 College Ave., at Claremont Ave., Rockridge, tel. 510/655–3298.*

Phó' Lâm Viên. This Vietnamese restaurant in Oakland's Chinatown is worth a trip for those with a sense of culinary adventure. Ignore the piped-in Muzak and focus on pork with fish sauce, spicy lemongrass gluten, and all sorts of other dishes you never knew existed ($5–$7). The beverages are no less exotic—you can quench your thirst with a tall glass of pennywort juice ($1) or a concoction made from seaweed, barley, dried logan, lotus seed, and apples ($1.50). *930 Webster St., btw 10th and 11th Sts., tel. 510/763–1484. Open Sun.–Mon., Wed.–Thurs. 11–11, Fri.–Sat. 11 AM–midnight.*

Starlite Restaurant II. Smack in the middle of Chinatown, the Starlite boasts a daunting 17-page menu. Most of the Vietnamese and Chinese entrées, including *phó-bo* (a vat of soup with rice noodles, veggies, and your choice of meat), run $4–$6 and all are amply sized. Top off your meal with *café suã da hay nóng* ($1.60), a brew-it-yourself dark French coffee mixed with condensed milk and poured over ice. *820 Franklin St., near 9th St., tel. 510/444–1142. Open daily 9–9, weekends until 10.*

Tin's Teahouse. On the edge of Oakland's Chinatown, Tin's serves great dim sum for about $5 per person. Feast on shark's-fin dumplings, chicken buns, stuffed bell peppers, and taro triangles. One house specialty is steamed rice-noodle crepes with shrimp, beef, or pork. *701 Webster St., at 7th St., tel. 510/832–7661. Open Mon., Wed.–Fri. 9–3, weekends 8:30–8:30.*

Zachary's Chicago Pizza Inc. When stuffed Chicago pizza is what you seek, visit Zachary's, the acknowledged master. People rave about the spinach and mushroom special (medium, $16.50). But whatever toppings you choose to fill your pizza, they'll come surrounded by a wall of chewy crust and topped with a layer of mozzarella and stewed tomatoes. The line may snake around the corner, but it's definitely worth the wait. Zachary's doesn't take reservations, but you can place your order so the pizza will be ready when your table is. At lunch, grab a thin slice for $1.75–$2. *5801 College Ave., near Rockridge BART, tel. 510/655–6385. Other location: 1853 Solano Ave., Berkeley, tel. 510/525–5950. Both open Sun.–Thurs. 11–10, Fri.–Sat. 11–10:30. Both wheelchair accessible.*

➢ **UNDER $15** • **Le Cheval.** After you've passed the scary laughing Buddhas at the door to this downtown Vietnamese restaurant, warm up with the popular firepot soup (medium $6), which mixes prawns, calamari, clams, fish balls, and fresh vegetables. Vegetarians will appreciate dishes like sautéed eggplant and tofu ($6.50). Follow it all up with a cup of *café phin* ($2.25), a sweet but strong coffee prepared iced or hot with condensed milk. *1007 Clay St., at 10th St., tel. 510/763–8495. Open Mon.–Sat. 11–9:30, Sun. 5–9:30. Wheelchair access.*

➢ **UNDER $30 • Bay Wolf.** As you enter this elegant restaurant, you might think you are visiting someone's beautiful home. Inside you're treated to friendly service and excellent food that mixes Provençal, northern Italian, and California influences. The menu, with entrées in the $13–$17 range, changes every two weeks and includes such tasty creations as grilled duck with ginger-peach chutney and smoked trout salad with arugula, pickled beets, and dill crème fraîche. When it's warm enough, you can dine on the outdoor patio. *3853 Piedmont Ave., btw 40th St. and MacArthur Blvd., tel. 510/655–6004. Open weekdays 11:30–2 and 6–9, weekends 5:30–10.*

Kincaid's Bayhouse. On the waterfront at Jack London Square, this spiffy restaurant spit-roasts, sear-grills, and hardwood-broils steaks and seafood. Savor the renowned crab cakes ($17, $8 as an appetizer) or the coconut-beer prawns ($15, $7 as an appetizer). Even if you can't afford a meal here, you can hang out at the bar during happy hour (weekdays 4:30–6:30) and watch sailboats breeze into the harbor. *1 Franklin St., in Jack London Sq., tel. 510/835–8600. Open Mon.–Thurs. 11:15–10, Fri. 11:15–10:30, Sat. 11:30–10:30, Sun. 10:30–9. Wheelchair access.*

Marin County

In this land of the rich and established, it's hardly surprising that most restaurants cater to older folks with plenty of cash to spare. You'll have to look hard for budget eats, and don't expect anything too exciting—Marin is no hotbed of ethnic diversity. Your best bet is to pack a picnic and dine in the open, far from the din of well-heeled civilization. For Marin County picnic supplies, and for restaurants on the Marin County Coast, including Stinson Beach, Bolinas, and Point Reyes, *see* Marin County, in Chapter 2.

SAUSALITO

Restaurants and cafés line **Bridgeway,** Sausalito's main street, but they're generally overpriced and touristy. Expect to pay at least $15–$20 for seafood on the waterfront. If you head one block inland to **Caledonia Street,** you'll find much better bargains without the tourist brouhaha. Your cheapest bet is to picnic at one of the grassy areas between Bridgeway and the bay.

➢ **UNDER $10 • Hamburgers.** If you're lucky enough to see a few locals in Sausalito, it'll be in the line outside this hole-in-the-wall. As the name suggests, all they do here are a few variations on the hamburger ($4–$5) and fries ($1.50) theme. Most people take their food to one of the benches in the park rather than eat in the steamy restaurant. If neither option appeals, head to Paterson's Bar next door, where they'll serve you the same burger for about a buck more. *737 Bridgeway, tel. 415/332–9471. Open daily 11–5.*

Lighthouse Coffee Shop. Open at the crack of dawn seven days a week, the Lighthouse has surprisingly cheap breakfasts and lunches, generally priced under $6. They specialize in hearty Danish food: Try Danish meatballs with potato salad ($7) or the Copenhagen burger ($8) with horseradish, pickles, capers, onion, and egg yolk. This is a popular, no-frills sort of place. *1311 Bridgeway, tel. 415/331–3034. Open weekdays 6:30 AM–3 PM, weekends 7–3.*

➢ **UNDER $15 • Arawan.** It ain't much to look at, but once you eat at unpretentious Arawan, you'll see why loyal Thai-food devotees patronize the place regularly. Though the lunch specials are standard (pad Thai is $6), they pull out all the stops at dinner when a chef with poetic leanings serves up savory entrées ($8.50–$11) like Spicy Angel of the Sea (fried calamari with chili garlic sauce) and Shrimp Lost in the Woods (shrimp with snow peas, bamboo shoots, and black mushrooms in oyster sauce). *47 Caledonia St., 1 block inland from Bridgeway, tel. 415/332–0882. Open weekdays 11:30–3 and 4:30–10, weekends 4:30–10.*

TIBURON

In general, Tiburon's restaurants—found mostly on **Main Street**—are more notable for their views than for their food. Most offer decks hanging out over the bay, but you'll pay for the privilege of gazing at the San Francisco skyline or Angel Island. If you're really short on money, pack a picnic, take a ferry over from San Francisco (*see* Getting In, Out, and Around, in Chapter 1), and eat on the grass at the tip of the peninsula.

➢ **UNDER $10 • Conditori Sweden House Café.** This Tiburon café serves up fresh and unusual breakfasts and lunch on a peaceful wooden deck jutting out over the water. Regulars order the Swedish pancakes with lingonberries and sour cream ($6.25). Also check out the granola with yogurt ($5.50) or fresh seasonal fruit ($6.75). For lunch your options are mainly salads ($6–$8.25) and open-faced sandwiches ($6–$8.25). Ordering one of the decadent pastries ($3) for dessert is practically a moral imperative. *35 Main St., tel. 415/435–9767. Open for coffee weekdays 7:30–6, weekends 8–7; kitchen open weekdays 8–3, weekends 8–4.*

➢ **UNDER $15 • Sam's Anchor Café.** One of the less expensive waterfront restaurants, Sam's attracts a lot of Marin County locals, who cram onto the deck and sip Famous Ramos gin fizzes ($4.50) and Bloody Marys. Even on wet and windy days, diehards eat big brunches (served on weekends until 2 PM) or dinner on the deck. Hearty breakfast dishes are $7–$9; if you're feeling adventurous, try the Hangtown Fry omelet ($7.50) with oysters, bacon, scallions, and cheese. Fresh seafood dishes are $8–$16, burgers $7–$9, sandwiches $7 and up. *27 Main St., tel. 415/435–4527. Open Mon.–Thurs. 11–10:30, Fri. 11–11, Sat. 10 AM–11 PM, Sun. 9:30 AM–10:30 PM. Wheelchair access.*

➢ **UNDER $20 • Guaymas.** It's not cheap, but this restaurant next to the Tiburon ferry landing serves some of the best, most innovative Mexican food in the Bay Area. If you're on a tight budget, fill up on the fresh corn tortillas and three salsas brought to your table before you order, and stick to the appetizers ($4–$9). As well as the usual quesadillas, look for *chalupas* (tortilla pockets with chicken breast, cheese, and jalapeños; $4.75), and *cazuelitas* (potato and corn tortillas with baked zucchini and cheese; $4). If you want to go all out, tack on a main course ($9–$18)—there are heaps of seafood options. The outside deck is heated, but in this case the colorful interior is as attractive as the view. *5 Main St., tel. 415/435–6300. Open Mon.–Sat. 11:30–10:30, Sun. 10:30–10. Wheelchair access.*

Order a Guaymas margarita ($4.50) to find out what the drink is supposed to taste like.

MILL VALLEY

You'll pass through Mill Valley on your way to Muir Woods, Mt. Tamalpais, Stinson Beach, or Point Reyes. If you're eager to push on through to the coast, grab a quick slice of thin pizza ($2–$3)—served by a guy who actually speaks Italian—at **Stefano's Pizza** (8 E. Blithedale Ave., at Throckmorton Ave., tel. 415/383–9666).

➢ **UNDER $10 • Jennie Low's.** While Marin may not be a hotbed of international cuisine, Jennie Low's is a respectable Chinese option. The fairly standard menu features entrées like spicy eggplant ($6.50) and Hunan prawns ($9); if you're in a sampling mood, the *pu pu* platter ($10.50 for two) is a collection of chicken, beef, prawns, and other goodies that you heat over your own little hibachi. *38 Miller Ave., at Sunnyside Ave., tel. 415/388–8868. Open Mon.–Sat. 11:30–3 and 4:30–9:30, Sun. 4:30–9:30.*

Mama's Royal Café. If you're anxious to get an early start on the day, this funky café serves unbeatable huevos rancheros ($6) and omelets ($5–$7.50). It's full of thrift-store artifacts and psychedelic murals and has outdoor seating. At lunch and dinner Mama's features the Caspar Whineburger ($6), a burger with jack cheese and green chilies. They have promised to reinstate live acoustic music in the evenings now that Mill Valley has relaxed its (idiotic) law against live music—call for details. *393 Miller Ave., at Locust Ave., tel. 415/388–3261. Open Mon. 7:30 AM–2:30 PM, Tues.–Fri. 7:30 AM–10 PM, Sat. 8:30 AM–10 PM, Sun. 8:30 AM–3 PM.*

SAN RAFAEL

Compared to most of Marin County, San Rafael has a down-to-earth restaurant scene with lots of cafés, Mexican joints, and other ethnic eateries lining **4th Street** downtown.

➢ **UNDER $10** • **Royal Thai.** You'd hardly expect to find great Thai food in a leafy courtyard called the French Quarter in San Rafael, but people all over the Bay Area rave about this great restaurant, started by a couple who defected from the kitchen at San Francisco's popular Khan Toke Thai House (*see above*). The friendly staff serves up no-frills seafood and curry dishes for less than $10 in a restored Victorian house. *610 3rd St., btw Hetherton and Irwin Sts., tel. 415/485–1074. Open weekdays 11–2:30 and 5–10, weekends 5–10. Other location: 951 Clement St., San Francisco, tel. 415/386–1795.*

San Rafael Station Café. This breakfast and lunch spot has a real neighborhood feel—pictures of people's pooches line the mirror behind the counter, and locals hang out on weekends reading the paper and ingesting phenomenal amounts of cholesterol. Omelets of every persuasion run $5–$8. Sandwiches are $3.50–$7.50. *1013 B St., btw 4th and 5th Sts., tel. 415/456–0191. Open weekdays 6:30–3, weekends 8–3. Wheelchair access.*

➢ **UNDER $15** • **Mayflower Inne.** Few people would mistake the British pub grub here for haute cuisine. Still, their fish and chips ($7.50) and hearty sandwiches ($6) are some of the best lunch deals in town. And if you're sick of delicate California cuisine, you'll appreciate dinners like the huge ploughman's platter ($10) or bangers 'n' mash ($11). A chummy local crowd congregates around the bar all day long, breaking out into badly sung folk tunes on Friday and Saturday nights. An adjacent specialty store is piled high with British food items. *1533 4th St., tel. 415/456–1011. From U.S. 101 north, take Central San Rafael exit to 4th St. and turn left. Kitchen open weekdays 11:30–3 and 5–9, Sat. 5–9, Sun. 5–10. Wheelchair access.*

South Bay

Most restaurants on the suburbanized peninsula south of San Francisco are predictably bland. You'll find a cluster of semi-intriguing restaurants around Palo Alto and the Stanford campus, but they're not as cheap as the eats in most student areas. You might do better to head out to the coast—the food's certainly no more exciting, but it's bound to taste better when you're gazing out at the roaring Pacific. For coastal restaurants, *see* South Bay, in Chapter 2.

PALO ALTO

University Avenue, which runs west from U.S. 101 into the Stanford University campus, is one long food court with cutesy, yuppified restaurants everywhere you look. You'll pay just enough more than usual for your burrito, your burger, or your beer to make it annoying. If you really want to eat cheaply, head to **El Camino Real,** home to both fast-food chains and a number of local takeouts. At **Mr. Chau** (3781 El Camino Real, at Curtner Ave., tel. 415/856–8938), open daily until 10, $3 goes a long way for buffet-style Chinese food. Another alternative is casual California Avenue, east of Stanford, where you'll find café/bookstore **Printer's Inc.** (310 California Ave., at Birch St., tel. 415/327–6500) serving sandwiches and salads for less than $8.

➢ **UNDER $10** • **Jing Jing.** This popular Chinese restaurant near the Stanford campus is the place to come for spicy food. Though it's now slightly overshadowed by the new southwestern-style bar next door, you're sure to run into students and professors, and the large tables are the loci of many a departmental lunch. Most dishes are in the $5–$10 range, with $4–$5 lunch specials (11:30–2). Expect a wait. *443 Emerson St., off University Ave., tel. 415/328–6885. Open daily. 11:30–2 and 4:30–9:30 (Fri. and Sat. until 10).*

Mango Café. The Mango just settled into a new, splashier location, but the food remains the same: authentic Caribbean dishes like hot curried goat with vegetables ($9) and jerked joints ($5.50), a spicy chicken dish. Fruit-juice smoothies ($3), served in glasses the size of fishbowls, come in a wide range of exotic flavors. They also cater to vegetarians. *435 Hamilton*

Ave., at Fulton Ave., tel. 415/325–3229. From U.S. 101, take University Ave. exit west (toward Stanford), left on Fulton Ave. Open Mon.–Sat. 11–3 and 6–10. Wheelchair access. No credit cards.

Miyake Sushi. Despite the din of saké-drinking college students and waiters yelling greetings to customers across the restaurant, you get surprisingly good sushi at a truly reasonable price—about $1–$2 per piece. For just a bit more you can order specialties like the Tarzana roll (yellowtail, wild carrots, sprouts, and flying fish roe; $4). They also have a small menu of filling teriyaki and tempura dinners ($7–$12). There's almost always a wait, so consider squeezing in at the sushi bar. *261 University Ave., btw Bryant and Ramona Sts., tel. 415/323–9449. Open daily 11:30–10. Wheelchair access.*

Oasis Beer Garden. This grubby but immensely popular college hangout near the Palo Alto–Menlo Park border serves tasty burgers and sandwiches ($4–$7). You can play pinball, watch sports on TV, or soak up sun at one of the outdoor tables. *241 El Camino Real, tel. 415/326–8896. Just north of Stanford campus, at Cambridge St. Kitchen open daily 11 AM–1:30 AM.*

➢ **UNDER $15** • **Sushi Ya.** The regular clientele, a mix of students and office workers, will more than vouch for the sushi and sashimi here. This inconspicuous restaurant near Stanford's campus does a good business in all the staples, from yellowtail and tuna rolls ($3.50 each) to *kaiso* (seaweed) salad ($6). The soft-shell crab ($6.50) is especially good. There are a few tables, but most patrons prefer to sit at the bar and chat with the owner while he skillfully prepares the food. *380 University Ave., btw Waverly and Florence Sts., tel. 415/322–0330. From U.S. 101, take University Ave. exit west. Open weekdays 11:30–2 and 5:30–9:30, Sat. 5–9:30. Wheelchair access.*

SAN JOSE

The Bay Area's biggest city has it's fair share of good eats, but it's too far from San Francisco to make a special trip. **Chez Sovan** (*see below*) is the only exception. If you find yourself in San Jose—perhaps at the Garbage Museum (see Chapter 2)—and need a good, cheap meal, try **Taco Al Pastor** (400 Bascom Ave., at San Carlos St., tel. 408/275–1619), which has been serving excellent Mexican food for more than 15 years.

Chez Sovan. Every weekend, carloads of Bay Area residents make the 45-minute trek to San Jose for Chez Sovan's incredible Cambodian cuisine. The owners have just opened a second Chez Sovan just south of San Jose in Campbell (2425 S. Bascom Ave., Campbell, tel. 408/371–7711), and now the original location serves lunch only. The food—including a selection of ginger-cooked meats and vegetables, coconut and leek soups, and other traditional Cambodian specials—at both locations is well worth the journey; most dishes start at $5. *923 Oakland Rd., I block north of Hedding, where 13th St. becomes Oakland Rd., tel. 408/287–7619. Open weekdays 11–3.*

Specialty Markets and Delicatessens

SAN FRANCISCO

Grocery shopping in San Francisco need not be a mundane chore. Not only is there an outlet for every imaginable cuisine, ethnicity, and dietary restriction, but time spent searching for the ideal ingredients can yield greater rewards: a date, perhaps. In one easy step you can check out a potential love interest *and* make sure they're not committing any food faux pas. Stores whose windows can be counted on to steam up on occasion include the **Safeway** in the Marina district, where yuppies size up each other's sportswear and fret about the onset of love handles; the **Safeway** on Market and Church streets, for all types of gay men; the **Harvest Ranch Market** (*see below*), for the young health- and fashion-conscious gay and lesbian set; and the **Mission's Rainbow Grocery** (*see below*), for lesbians and politically radical types of all persuasions. You may leave the house with a list reading "lettuce, toilet paper, marshmallow cream" and come home with a whole lot more.

If all you want is cheap and unusual food items, don't restrict yourself to the big stores. Head instead to San Francisco's neighborhood markets. In the Mission you'll find bodegas stacked with piñatas, fresh tortillas, and myriad varieties of dried chilies. The Asian markets on Clement Street in the Richmond district will cheaply accommodate your every produce need; the delis in North Beach will load you down with extra-virgin olive oil and fresh mozzarella; and the Middle Eastern delis on Irving Street in the Sunset district pack pints of hummus and tabouleh. Once you see all the city has to offer, you'll never go back to Safeway again—unless you're lonely.

Harvest Ranch Market. This always-busy market in the heart of the Castro is packed with organic produce, organic bulk foods (including 10 varieties of cereal), and tons of canned goods—most sans fat and preservatives. They also offer an organic salad bar and the ever-popular Tassajara bread. The outside benches are popular munching (and flirting) spots on the weekends. *2285 Market St., near Noe St., tel. 415/626–0805. Open Sun.–Thurs. 9 AM–11 PM, Fri.–Sat. 9 AM–midnight.*

House of Bagels. Besides serving 15 kinds of fresh, chewy bagels with four different flavors of cream cheeses, this friendly neighborhood deli in the inner Richmond district also has an entire *wall* of fresh-baked breads, both baguettes and loaves. You can get a basic garlic bagel with veggie cream cheese for $2.10; bags of a dozen day-olds cost only $2. Official daily open hours are 6–5:30, but if your need is acute, knock politely on the window any time after 5:15 AM. *5030 Geary Blvd., btw 15th and 16th Aves., tel. 415/752–6000.*

Just Desserts. Since 1974, this excellent bakery has captured the hearts and stomachs of the Bay Area with its decadent desserts—and they've got a mile-long list of awards to prove it. Following the motto "No mixes, no preservatives, no freezing, no compromise," Just Desserts produces sweet treats to die for: lemon tarts; carrot, chocolate fudge, and sour cream cakes; cheesecakes; and buttermilk raisin scones ($1.25–$3.50 a pop). Since hooking up with Tassajara Bakery (*see below*), they also offer first-rate breads and baguettes. Look for six branches throughout the Bay Area; the main location on Church Street in San Francisco has a beautiful outdoor courtyard. *248 Church St., at Market St., tel. 415/626–5774. Open Mon.–Thurs. 7 AM–11 PM, Fri. 7 AM–midnight, Sat. 8 AM–midnight, Sun. 8 AM–11 PM.*

Molinari Delicatessen and **Lucca Ravioli Delicatessen.** Although these two establishments lie worlds apart from each other (Molinari is in the heart of North Beach, Lucca in the Mission district), they have similar selections, prices, and jovial Italian service. At both you can get reasonably priced homemade pastas, cheeses, vino, bread, and a wide variety of specialty items. Enormous sandwiches, dripping with fresh mozzarella and a trillion slices of salami, make both places popular lunchtime spots. *Molinari: 373 Columbus Ave., at Vallejo St., tel. 415/421–2337. Lucca: 1100 Valencia St., at 22nd St., tel. 415/647–5581. Molinari open Mon.–Fri. 8–6, Sat. 7:30–5:30; Lucca open Mon.–Sat. 9–6.*

Rainbow Grocery. This cooperatively owned-and-run grocery store on the edge of the Mission district stocks organic produce, oils, honey, syrup, grains, pastas, herbs, spices, and other stuff in bulk. They've got just about every food item a vegetarian could dream of, and the prices aren't bad for organic food. The attached general store is your source for vitamins, herbal supplements, health books, and natural soaps. They also provide a bulletin board and a card file if you're looking for a room or a ride or a dog or a cause. *1899 Mission St., at 15th St., tel. 415/863–0620. Open Mon.–Sat. 9–8:30, Sun. 10–8:30.*

Real Foods. This delicatessen on the upscale stretch of Polk Street sells all sorts of prepared food items (salads, casseroles, noodle dishes, desserts) to folks who have sauntered down from Russian Hill to see what the peasants are up to. If you've got a little extra cash to blow on a gourmet picnic, you're in the right place; if not, you can always enjoy a coffee and a cookie while those around you spend the big bucks. Real Foods also has a grocery store and deli in Cole Valley, near the Haight. *2164 Polk St., at Vallejo St., tel. 415/775–2805. Open daily 8–8. Other location: 1023 Stanyan St., at Carl St., tel. 415/564–1117. Open weekdays 7 AM–8 PM, weekends 9–8.*

Tassajara Bakery. The bakery that began in a kitchen at the Tassajara Zen Center in Marin County doesn't advertise itself as the purveyor of nirvana through taste; that's something you have to discover on your own. In addition to many unusual varieties of freshly baked bread, Tassajara sells healthy, hearty soups, excellent vegetarian sandwiches, focaccia bread drizzled with herbs and garlic, and other food items in a tranquil location a few blocks south of Haight Street. Bring a newspaper and while away the afternoon. They've recently merged with the outstanding local chain Just Desserts (*see above*). *1000 Cole St., at Parnassus St., tel. 415/664–8947. Open Mon.–Sat. 7 AM–10 PM, Sun. 8 AM–10 PM.*

Your Black Muslim Bakery. Specializing in "good-for-you" baked goods, this bakery, with two outlets in San Francisco and six in the East Bay, is a haven for vegans and the health conscious. Most items contain no sugar, salt, milk, or eggs. The natural sweet rolls ($3), honey and carrot pies ($10), and honey chocolate chip cookies ($3 for five) are excellent. They also sell vegetarian sandwiches and luscious tofu burgers ($4–$5), as well as all-natural beverages ($2–$3). On the cultural tip, the bakeries carry books on black history and display posters promoting African-American community events. *609 Cole St., at Haight St., tel. 415/387–6384. Open Mon.–Sat. 10–8. Other S.F. location: 160 Eddy St., btw Mason and Taylor Sts., tel. 415/929–7082. Main bakery in Oakland: 5832 San Pablo Ave., btw Stanford Ave. and 59th St., tel. 510/658–7080.*

EAST BAY

Berkeley is enamored of European-style specialty markets, but even these come with a Berkeley twist (i.e., heavy on organic and pesticide-free produce, light on butcher shops). **The Cheese Board** (1504 Shattuck Ave., btw Cedar and Vine Sts., tel. 510/549–3183) is one of a few successful collectives remaining in Berkeley and features an incredible selection of

Farmers' Markets

One of the best ways to get organic produce cheaply is to go to local farmers' markets, which usually take place once or twice a week. The farmers' market at San Francisco's United Nations Plaza happens Wednesday and Sunday 8 AM–5 PM and is chock full of fruits, vegetables, breads, honey, jellies, and salsas. Another market bustles at the Ferry Building, at the downtown end of Market Street, Saturdays from 9 AM to 1 PM. And at 100 Alemany Boulevard, at Crescent Avenue (tel. 415/647–9423) in Bernal Heights just south of the Mission, residents do some serious produce shopping Saturday 6–5.

Every Friday from 8 to 2 you can buy from East Bay farmers and bakers at the Old Oakland Certified Farmers' Market (Broadway and 9th St., tel. 510/452–FARM). Oakland's other farmers' market takes place at Jack London Square (Broadway and Embarcadero, tel. 510/798–7061) Sundays 10–2. You can also stock up on farm-fresh products at one of Berkeley's farmers' markets, sponsored by the Ecology Center (tel. 510/548–2220). They happen every Saturday 10–2 on Center Street at Martin Luther King Jr. Way; Sunday 11–3 on Haste Street at Telegraph Avenue (May through November); and Tuesday from 2 until dusk on Derby Street at Martin Luther King Jr. Way.

In Marin, the Downtown San Rafael Farmers' Market (tel. 415/457–2266), which takes place every summer Thursday from 6 PM to 9 PM on 4th Street, is more like a weekly block party than a simple produce sale. Locals come to buy handicrafts, listen to live music, and let the kids take pony rides. For more information on Marin's 10-plus farmers' markets, call 415/456–3276.

cheeses and freshly baked breads. Stop by in the morning for a scone or a sourdough cheese roll ($1.50). The staff likes nothing better than to explain the subtle variations in cheeses to you, and they'll give you free samples as they help you choose.

Farther south, **Berkeley Bowl Marketplace** (2777 Shattuck Ave., at Stuart St., tel. 510/843–6929) represents alternative and cooperative grocery shopping at its best. The organic produce selection is endless, the bulk grains come cheap, and the seafood department features the freshest fish in Berkeley at reasonable prices. The attached **café** (tel. 510/845–5168) serves up wonderful grub for breakfast and lunch Monday–Saturday. In Emeryville, a branch of the chain **Trader Joe's** (5796 Christie Ave., at Powell St., tel. 510/658–8091) sells inexpensive wine and beer and lots of affordable gourmet food. A decent bottle of wine will set you back only about four bucks. **Seabreeze Market** (598 University Ave., tel. 510/486–8119) offers fresh shellfish, fruits, and vegetables. They also serve sandwiches, but get yours to go because the market sits right next to an I–80 on-ramp. Fortunately, you're not far from the Berkeley Marina.

For bagels, try the ever-popular **Noah's Bagels** (3170 College Ave., tel. 510/654–0944; 2344 Telegraph Ave., tel. 510/849–9951; 1883 Solano Ave., tel. 510/525–4447), a New York–style shop famous for its flavored cream-cheese schmears. A bagel with your choice of schmear (except lox) and a cup of java is $2. Noah's also has two San Francisco branches (742 Irving St., at 9th St., tel. 415/566–2761; 2075 Chestnut St., btw Steiner and Fillmore Sts., tel. 415/775–2910).

Berkeley is full of specialty bread outlets offering fresh-baked loaves—such as seeded baguettes or potato rosemary bread—still warm from the oven. If you can't make it down to their retail outlets, both **Semifreddi's** (372 Colusa Ave., Kensington, tel. 510/596–9935) and **Acme** (1601 San Pablo Ave., Berkeley, tel. 510/524–1327; 2730 9th St., Berkeley, tel. 510/843–2978) supply many Bay Area markets with fresh bread daily. Or visit **Il Fornaio** (2059 Mountain Blvd., Oakland, tel. 510/339–3108), a slick European-café chain with branches in Oakland, San Francisco, and Marin. If you can deal with the atmosphere, you'll be rewarded with interesting (but expensive) breads.

In downtown Oakland you'll find a huge variety of ethnic markets, especially in Chinatown, which is full of Chinese and Southeast Asian groceries. On the other side of Broadway, **Mi Rancho Tortilla Factory** (464 7th St., at Broadway, tel. 510/451–2393) sells ready-made tacos (95¢) and burritos ($2.50–$4) as well as the fixings for making your own. **Housewives Marketplace** (9th and Clay Sts., tel. 510/444–4396) is a warehouse full of specialty stands with a southern flair. You'll find a small grocery store, a deli, a butcher, a fish and seafood counter, a sausage shop, and dry goods such as beans, roasted peanuts, and mix for Cajun jambalaya. Locals come here for fresh produce and smoked meats, such as ham hocks. A few stands offer fast-food items like Louisiana burgers with jalapeño cheese ($3.50). **G. B. Ratto & Company** (821 Washington St., btw 8th and 9th Sts., tel. 510/832–6503) is your source for delicacies like buffalo-milk mozzarella and many varieties of olive oil. They also prepare sandwiches (about $4) and have everything you need for a gourmet picnic.

Reference Listings

BY CUISINE

AMERICAN

UNDER $5
Ann's Soup Kitchen and Restaurant (Berkeley)
Café Intermezzo (Berkeley)
Main Squeeze (Civic Center)
New Dawn (Mission)
San Francisco Art Institute Café (North Beach)
Specialty's (Downtown)
Tom Peasant Pies (Noe Valley)
Tommy's Joynt (Civic Center)

UNDER $10
Bagdad Café (Castro)
Bette's Oceanview Diner (Berkeley)
Boogaloos (Mission)
Brick Hut Café (Berkeley)
Buena Vista Café (Fisherman's Wharf)
Café Sanchez (Noe Valley)
Chester's Café (Berkeley)
Chloe's Café (Noe Valley)
Crescent City Café (Haight-Ashbury)
Eagle Café (Fisherman's Wharf)
Flint's (Oakland)
The Fruit Gallery (Downtown)
Homemade Café (Berkeley)
Hungry Joe's (Noe Valley)
Kate's Kitchen (Haight-Ashbury)
Lois the Pie Queen (Oakland)
Lori's Diner (Downtown)
Lucy's Creole Kitchen (Oakland)
Mama's Royal Café (Oakland, Mill Valley)
Moishe's Pippic (Civic Center)
Orphan Andy's (Castro)
Pasqua (Castro)
Patio Café (Castro)
Pork Store Café (Haight-Ashbury)
Rick and Ann's (Berkeley)
San Rafael Station Café (San Rafael)
Saul's (Berkeley)
Spaghetti Western (Haight-Ashbury)
Sparky's (Castro)
Squat and Gobble Café (Haight-Ashbury)

UNDER $15
Sam's Anchor Café (Tiburon)

UNDER $20
California Culinary Academy (Civic Center)

BURGERS

UNDER $5
Hot 'n' Hunky (Castro)

UNDER $10
Barney's Gourmet Hamburger (Berkeley)
Clown Alley (Downtown)
Grubstake (Civic Center)
Hamburger Mary's (SoMa)
Hamburgers (Sausalito)
Oasis Beer Garden (Palo Alto)

CALIFORNIAN

UNDER $5
Cheese Board Pizza Collective (Berkeley)
Juice Bar Collective (Berkeley)

UNDER $15
Acorn (SoMa)
Doidge's Kitchen (Marina)

UNDER $20
Firefly (Noe Valley)
Zuni Café (Civic Center)

UNDER $25
Greens (Marina)

UNDER $30
Bay Wolf (Oakland)
Chez Panisse Café (Berkeley)

CHINESE

UNDER $5
Chinese Express (Berkeley)
Kowloon (Chinatown)
Lucky Creation (Chinatown)
Mr. Chau (Palo Alto)

UNDER $10
Chef Jia's (Chinatown)
Empress Garden (Richmond/Sunset)
Jennie Low's (Mill Valley)
Jing Jing (Palo Alto)
House of Nanking (Chinatown)
Hunan (North Beach)
R&G Lounge (Chinatown)
Shangri-La (Richmond/Sunset)
Tin's Teahouse (Oakland)

UNDER $15
Yank Sing (Downtown)

UNDER $20
Empress of China (Chinatown)

ETHIOPIAN

UNDER $10
Asmara (Oakland)
Blue Nile (Berkeley)
Massawa (Haight-Ashbury)

FRENCH

UNDER $10
Crêpes-A-Go-Go (Berkeley)
Ti Couz (Mission)

UNDER $15
Café Bastille (Downtown)
Café Claude (Downtown)
South Park Café (SoMa)

UNDER $30
Bay Wolf (Oakland)

INDIAN

UNDER $10
Ananda Fuara (Civic Center)

UNDER $15
Ganges (Haight-Ashbury)
Pasand Madras Cuisine (Berkeley)

Scenic India (Mission)
Zante Pizza and Indian Cuisine (Mission)

ITALIAN

UNDER $10
Bocce Café (North Beach)
Caffe Europa (North Beach)
Café Panini (Berkeley)
Il Pollaio (North Beach)
L'Osteria del Forno (North Beach)
Mario's Bohemian Cigar Store and Café (North Beach)
Spuntino (Civic Center)

UNDER $15
Capp's Corner (North Beach)
The Gold Spike (North Beach)
Il Fornaio (Downtown)

UNDER $20
Buca Giovanni (North Beach)
Venezia (Berkeley)

JAPANESE

UNDER $10
Isobune (Japantown)
Mifune (Japantown)
Miyake Sushi (Palo Alto)
No-Name (Nippon) Sushi (Castro)

UNDER $15
Now and Zen (Japantown)
Sanppo (Japantown)
Sushi Ya (Palo Alto)

UNDER $20
Sushi Ko (Berkeley)

MEDITERRANEAN AND MIDDLE EASTERN

UNDER $5
Bongo Burger (Berkeley)

UNDER $10
Kan Zaman (Haight-Ashbury)
La Méditerranée (Castro)
Ya, Halla!

MEXICAN AND CENTRAL AMERICAN

UNDER $5
Cancun Taquería (Mission)
Casa Sanchez (Mission)
El Farolito (Mission)
El Taco Zamorano (Oakland)
El Toro (Mission)
El Trébol (Mission)
La Cumbre (Mission)
Pancho Villa (Mission)
Taquería Morelia (Oakland)

UNDER $10
Gaucho's Café (Oakland)
Juan's Place (Berkeley)
Los Cocos (Oakland)
Mexicali Rose (Oakland)
Nicaragua (Mission)
Panchita's (Mission)
WA-HA-KA! (SoMa)

UNDER $15
La Rondalla (Mission)

UNDER $20
Guaymas (Tiburon)

PIZZA

UNDER $5
Blondie's (Berkeley)
Cheese Board Pizza Collective (Berkeley)
Marcello's (Castro)
Pizza Love (South of Market)
Stefano's Pizza (Mill Valley)

UNDER $10
North Beach Pizza (North Beach)
Vicolo (Civic Center)
Zachary's Chicago Pizza Inc. (Berkeley)

SEAFOOD

UNDER $10
R & G Lounge (Chinatown)

UNDER $15
Anchor Oyster Bar (Castro)
Lucy's Creole Kitchen (Oakland)
Sam's Anchor Café (Tiburon)
Swan Oyster Depot (Civic Center)

UNDER $30
Kincaid's Bayhouse (Oakland)

SPANISH AND CARIBBEAN

UNDER $10
Esperpento (Mission)
Mango Café (Palo Alto)

UNDER $15
Cha Cha Cha (Haight-Ashbury)
Sol y Luna (Downtown)
Timo's (Mission)

UNDER $20
Miss Pearl's Jam House (Civic Center)

THAI

UNDER $5
Thai Buddhist Temple (Berkeley)

UNDER $10
Berkeley Thai House (Berkeley)
Cha Am (Berkeley)
Manora's Thai Cuisine (SoMa)
Racha Café (Civic Center)
Royal Thai (San Rafael)
Thailand Restaurant (Castro)

UNDER $15
Arawan (Sausalito)
Khan Toke Thai House (Richmond/Sunset)
Thep Phanom (Haight-Ashbury)

VIETNAMESE AND CAMBODIAN

UNDER $10
101 Restaurant (Downtown)
Angkor Palace (Marina)
Phó' Lâm Viên (Oakland)
Starlite Restaurant II (Oakland)
Tu Lan (Downtown)

UNDER $15
Angkor Wat (Richmond/Sunset)
Golden Turtle (Civic Center)

Le Cheval (Oakland)
Phnom Penh (Civic Center)

OTHER

UNDER $10
Conditori Sweden House (Swedish; Tiburon)
Hahn's Hibachi (Korean; Marina)
Kabana (Pakistani; Berkeley)
Lighthouse Coffee Shop (Danish; Sausalito)
Nan Yang (Burmese; Oakland)

UNDER $15
Helmand (Afghan; North Beach)
Mayflower Inne (British; San Rafael)

SPECIAL FEATURES

BREAKFAST/BRUNCH

UNDER $5
Ann's Soup Kitchen and Restaurant (Berkeley)
New Dawn (Mission)
Thai Buddhist Temple (Berkeley)

UNDER $10
Bette's Oceanview Diner (Berkeley)
Boogaloos (Mission)
Brick Hut Café (Berkeley)
Café Sanchez (Noe Valley)
Chester's Café (Berkeley)
Chloe's Café (Noe Valley)
Conditori Sweden House (Tiburon)
Crescent City Café (Haight-Ashbury)
The Fruit Gallery (Downtown)
Homemade Café (Berkeley)
Hungry Joe's (Noe Valley)
Kate's Kitchen (Haight-Ashbury)
Lighthouse Coffee Shop (Sausalito)
Lois the Pie Queen (Oakland)
Mama's Royal Café (Oakland, Mill Valley)
Pasqua (Castro)
Patio Café (Castro)
Pork Store Café (Haight-Ashbury)
Rick and Ann's (Berkeley)
San Rafael Station Café (San Rafael)
Spaghetti Western (Haight-Ashbury)
Squat and Gobble Café (Haight-Ashbury)

UNDER $15
Acorn (South of Market)
Doidge's Kitchen (Marina)
Sam's Anchor Café (Tiburon)

DINNER AND ENTERTAINMENT

UNDER $10
Bocce Café (North Beach)
Kan Zaman (Haight-Ashbury)

UNDER $15
Angkor Wat (Richmond/Sunset)
Café Bastille (Downtown)
Café Claude (Downtown)
Ganges (Haight-Ashbury)
La Rondalla (Mission)
Pasand Madras Cuisine (Berkeley)
Sol y Luna (Downtown)

UNDER $20
Miss Pearl's Jam House (Civic Center)

LATE-NIGHT EATS (AFTER 1 AM)

UNDER $5
Blondie's (Berkeley)
Cancun Taquería (Mission)
Dave's Coffee Shop (Oakland)
El Farolito (Mission)
Hot 'n' Hunky (Castro)
Marcello's (Castro)
Neutron Bakery (Berkeley)
Pizza Love (SoMa)
Tommy's Joynt (Civic Center)

UNDER $10
20 Tank Brewery (SoMa)
Bagdad Café (Castro)
Buena Vista Café (Fisherman's Wharf)
Clown Alley (Downtown)
Grubstake (Civic Center)
Hamburger Mary's (SoMa)
Jack London Inn Coffee Shop (Oakland)
J.J.'s Diner (Oakland)
Kan Zaman (Haight-Ashbury)
Lori's Diner (Downtown)
Mexicali Rose (Oakland)
North Beach Pizza (North Beach)
Oasis Beer Garden (Palo Alto)
Orphan Andy's (Castro)
Panchita's (Mission)
Sparky's (Castro)

UNDER $15
Café Bastille (Downtown)
La Rondalla (Mission)

OUTDOOR EATING

UNDER $5
Casa Sanchez (Mission)
Juice Bar Collective (Berkeley)
Thai Buddhist Temple (Berkeley)

UNDER $10
Berkeley Thai House (Berkeley)
Bocce Café (North Beach)
Boogaloos (Mission)
Café Panini (Berkeley)
Café Sanchez (Noe Valley)
Chester's Café (Berkeley)
Conditori Sweden House Café (Tiburon)
Gaucho's Café (Oakland)
Josie's Cabaret and Juice Joint (Castro)
Oasis Beer Garden (Palo Alto)

UNDER $15
Acorn (SoMa)
Café Bastille (Downtown)
Café Claude (Downtown)
Sam's Anchor Café (Tiburon)

UNDER $20
Guaymas (Tiburon)
Miss Pearl's Jam House (Civic Center)

UNDER $30
Bay Wolf (Oakland)

VEGETARIAN

UNDER $5
Amazing Grace (Castro)
Cheese Board Pizza Collective (Berkeley)
Juice Bar Collective (Berkeley)
Kowloon (Chinatown)
Lucky Creation (Chinatown)
Main Squeeze (Civic Center)

UNDER $10
Ananda Fuara (Civic Center)
Josie's Cabaret and Juice Joint (Castro)
Shangri-La (Richmond/ Sunset)

UNDER $15
Ganges (Haight-Ashbury)
Now and Zen (Japantown)

UNDER $25
Greens (Marina)

CAFÉ CULTURE 5

By Alice Chang

These days, you can find espresso in the strangest of places—Iowa, movie theaters, even 24-hour convenience stores—but a few cafés in Berkeley and San Francisco can boast of having had the same java-obsessed customers for more than 30 years. The rest of the world is finally realizing what participants of Bay Area coffee culture have known all along: Four shots of espresso is the best legal high around. San Francisco's cafés can be as crowded on Friday nights as the local bars. And meeting for coffee isn't just something to do when you're bored; it's a cherished way of life.

Bay Area cafés come in every style imaginable. You can drink your morning espresso in a small establishment with sofas and classical music, have your noon latte in a postmodern warehouse space with a bunch of people in Armani suits, and sip your evening cappuccino in a place where English is a rarity and the jukebox plays opera. If you like to hang out with students, politicos, or New Age prophets, head to Berkeley. Otherwise, your scene—be it a stylish, older crowd (North Beach), black leather and body piercings (either the Haight or the Castro, depending on sexual orientation), or something else entirely—can be found somewhere in San Francisco. In an effort to be true to the "culture" part of café culture, many Bay Area cafés do a lot more than crank out coffee. Local artists are invited to display their works, Bay Area bands ply their trade, and open-mike poetry readings (*see box, below*) can be found every night of the week.

SAN FRANCISCO

San Francisco is a city of people who believe strongly in the connection between coffee and the arts. Early converts to the café-as-muse philosophy include renegades Jack Kerouac and Allen Ginsberg, who held all manner of performances at the still-pumping Caffè Trieste in North Beach. With its European-style park and tiny streets, North Beach is still a popular place to grab a demitasse on a rainy day, especially if you have someone to hold hands with under the table. Postmodern hipsters, however, would be more comfortable South of Market, in the Haight, and especially in the Mission. The new hotbed for experimental art in San Francisco, the Mission has recently sprouted all manner of java dens for bohemians new and old, who write poems, novels, letters, and laundry lists as they soak up the atmosphere.

Proper café etiquette includes busing your own table and tipping the counterperson.

CASTRO DISTRICT **Café Flore.** The Castro's premier gay hangout, Flore is a hotbed of activity day and night, drawing pseudo-artists, political activists, and trendy boys. If you can't find a place at one of the outside tables, strike a pose and loiter until someone makes room for you—sharing tables is de rigueur. Expect noise, commotion, and, in the midst of it all, an incredibly attractive someone sipping chamomile tea and looking furtively your way. Preferred reading material: Jean Genet (just pretend to read). *2298 Market St., at Noe St., tel. 415/621–8579. Open daily 7:30 AM–11:30 PM (Fri.–Sat. until midnight).*

Cup a Joe. This funky place with maroon walls has all the ingredients of a successful café: a mean cuppa joe ($1.10 for an espresso), tasty pastries (75¢ after 5:30 PM), and an art-student clientele. The café hosts spoken-word performances Tuesday nights at 8 PM and sponsors events like an evening of readings by disabled poets. Preferred reading material: the *Bay Times,* Armistead Maupin's *Tales of the City. 3801 17th St., at Sanchez St., tel. 415/252–0536. Open weekdays 7 AM–10 PM, weekends 8 AM–10 PM.*

Café Flore is also known as Café Bore, Café Floorshow, Café Hairdo, Café Hairdon't, Café Hairspray, and Café le Pretense.

Jumpin' Java. Make a night of it here and sit down with a good read, a powerful cup of coffee ($1.25 for a large), and a spinach-and-cheddar quiche ($3.25). Hell, come here every night. Rarely does one find such a centrally located café (steps away from Market Street) with zero pretension, no grating music, and no squealing groups of work buddies. Students, gays, and young couples (dressed in black or college sweatshirts) make up the crowd. Preferred reading material: anything by Rita Mae Brown. *139 Noe St., btw Henry and 14th Sts., tel. 415/431–5282. Open daily 7 AM–10 PM.*

CIVIC CENTER **Mad Magda's Russian Tea Room and Café.** The deep-blue ceiling is dotted with yellow stars, the walls sprout onion domes, the peaceful garden is scattered with statues, and on Wednesday afternoons a tarot and tea-leaf reader waits to tell you all ($13, Wed. 1–5). Sandwiches ($3–$6) come with provocative names, like the Khrushchev (ham, Swiss, and herb mayo) or the Fabergé (eggplant, mozzarella, and basil). A word of caution: Some have complained about the service and cleanliness level. Preferred reading material: *Alice in Wonderland. 579 Hayes St., near Octavia St., tel. 415/864–7654. Open Mon.–Tues. 9–9, Wed.–Sat. 9–midnight, Sun. 10–7.*

Momi Toby's Revolution Café. A Sunday-morning hangout for Hayes Valley locals, Momi Toby's encourages artistic expression by providing a piano, sketchbook, crayons, and markers. Prefer to read quietly? You'll find a small shelf of quality literature next to the counter. Momi Toby's also serves appealing snacks like tuna bagels ($3) and veggie or chicken burritos ($3), as well as beer and wine. Preferred reading material: *Norton Anthology of World Masterpieces. 528 Laguna St., at Fell St., tel. 415/626–1508. Open weekdays 7:30 AM–9:30 PM, weekends 8:30 AM–9:30 PM.*

DOWNTOWN **Paninoteca Palio d'Asti.** This very modern Italian café attracts suits, Italophiles, and espresso junkies with its powerful coffee ($1.20 for a single espresso) and damn good lunch items. You'll find an extensive array of *panini* (Italian sandwiches on focaccia bread). Try the San Pietro (prosciutto and pungent Italian cheese, $6.75) or the San Secondo (fresh mozzarella, roasted peppers, and Gorgonzola, $5.25). On sunny days, you can sit outside on nearby Commercial Alley. Preferred reading material: conservative Italian newspapers (in Italian), the *Washington Post. 505 Montgomery St., near Sacramento St., tel. 415/362–6900. Open weekdays 7–4.*

In January 1995, San Francisco banned smoking in all cafés, though a liquor license provides a convenient loophole.

Yakety Yak. A worthy respite from the bustling downtown traffic, this mellow coffeehouse—with brightly colored walls that contrast rebelliously with the gray surroundings—really *wants* to be in Noe Valley. Hopeful artists from the nearby Academy of Arts find their caffeine fixes and a huge selection of fresh pastries here. Yakety Yak has an S.F. Net hookup (*see box below*) and open-mike poetry readings Wednesdays 7–9. Preferred reading material: *Cups: A Café Journal, S.F. Bay Guardian. 679 Sutter St., at Taylor St., tel. 415/885–6908. Open Mon.–Sat. 7 AM–10 PM, Sun. 8 AM–10 PM.*

HAIGHT-ASHBURY AND WESTERN ADDITION **The Crêpery Café.** This fetching sidewalk café where Cole Valley locals, UCSF medical students, and Haight Street hipsters while away sunny days serves an extensive menu of crêpes. Favorite fillings include strawberries and cream or hot brandied bananas ($4.50) or, for dinner, chicken and vegetables or beef stroganoff (with salad for $7.25). Preferred reading material: *Gray's Anatomy. 86 Carl St., at Cole St., tel. 415/566–4433. Open Mon.–Sat. 8 AM–10 PM, Sun. 8 AM–9 PM.*

The Horseshoe. Here you'll find more disaffected youths with tattoos, piercings, and time on their hands than perhaps anywhere else in the city. Come for a strong cuppa joe and enjoy a shouted conversation over the blasting music, or peruse the millions of flyers on the walls seeking band members or advertising artistic events. You might even leave toying with the idea of just a small tattoo. Preferred reading material: *Modern Primitives, Guitar* magazine. *566 Haight St., near Steiner St., tel. 415/626–8852. Open daily 7:30 AM–1 AM.*

Jammin' Java. This sunny café that serves great, strong coffee ($1.25–$2), light food (quiche is $3.50), and lackluster desserts is a welcome respite from Haight Street's frenzy. The indoor and outdoor tables are populated day and night, and an interesting variety of music plays in the background. Open-mike poetry happens Wednesdays at 8 PM. Preferred reading material: *Harper's. 701 Cole St., at Waller St., tel. 415/668–5282. Open daily 7 AM–11 PM. Other location: 398 Judah St., at 9th Ave., tel. 415/566–JAVA.*

MISSION DISTRICT **Café Istanbul.** The Syrian owner of this unique café serves authentic and delicious Middle Eastern food ($2–$5) and beverages ($1–$3) in a dark, tapestried setting. Definitely a contrast to your average café, Istanbul boasts an exotic pillowed platform area

Choosing Your Poison

If the only two choices you know for coffee are "black" or "with cream," you're going to be overwhelmed by Bay Area coffeehouses. Practically every café here offers drinks with names spanning four different languages. This handy little cheat sheet will help you order like a sophisticate.

- ***ESPRESSO is made via a process that pumps steam, instead of water, through finely ground coffee. It comes in a tiny cup, and should be drunk quickly before it turns bitter.***
- ***CAPPUCCINO—espresso topped with thick milk foam and a sprinkling of chocolate or cinnamon on top—was named for the colors of Capuchin monks' robes.***
- ***CAFFÈ LATTE is espresso with a lot of steamed milk and a little foam, usually served in a tall pint glass.***
- ***Order CAFÉ AU LAIT and you'll get French roast coffee with steamed milk.***
- ***KAFFE MIT SCHLAG (also known as espresso con panna) is espresso with whipped cream.***
- ***ESPRESSO MACCHIATO is espresso with just a tiny bit of milk foam.***
- ***CAFFÈ MOCHA is hot chocolate and whipped cream fortified with espresso.***
- ***BORGIA is espresso with Italian syrup as sweetener (hazelnut is a favorite).***
- ***A DEPTH CHARGE is regular coffee with a shot of espresso.***
- ***A WHY BOTHER is a double-decaf latte with nonfat soy milk; a CUPPA JOE is simple diner coffee.***

and intricately scrolled, gold-colored trays that function as tabletops. Take off your shoes and hunker down with a pot of mint tea and delicately flavored *dolmas* (grape leaves), or baklava and cardamom-spiked Turkish coffee. A wide variety of Middle Eastern music completes the ambience, along with belly dancing on Wednesday nights. There's a $1 cover charge, and reservations are advised. Preferred reading material: anything by Rumi. *525 Valencia St., btw 16th and 17th Sts., tel. 415/863–8854. Open daily 11–11.*

La Bohème. Right across the street from the BART station, this Mission district institution has supplied locals with hearty breakfasts (fruit and granola, poached eggs, bagels) for years. Day and night, a steady stream of jazz or Stevie Wonder flows from the stereo while a multiracial, all-ages clientele gathers around large, antique-looking tables. Preferred reading material: anything by Pablo Neruda (*en español, por supuesto*). *3318 24th St., at Mission St., tel. 415/285–4122. Open weekdays 5 AM–11 PM, weekends 7 AM–11 PM.*

Mission Grounds. Tucked between a bookshop, a record store, and the popular Kilowatt club (*see* Live Music, in Chapter 6), this café is a good spot to meet with friends before a night on the town. You can be a window display at one of two elevated tables or relax at one of the big wooden tables in back. They serve crêpes ($2–$6) and omelets ($4) all day. *3170 16th St., at Guerrero St., tel. 415/621–1539. Open daily 7 AM–10 PM.*

Red Dora's Bearded Lady. A self-proclaimed "dyke café (everybody welcome)," this small coffeehouse is a visible expression of San Francisco's young, energetic queer culture. It's decorated with votive candles and mismatched furniture and blasts a variety of contemporary music, and there's a lovely garden in back. Dora's serves the usual café eats, plus a tasty breakfast burrito ($4) and a tofu burger ($4.50). Spoken-word and musical performances often take place Fridays and Saturdays at 8 PM after the café closes, but call ahead to confirm. Preferred reading material: *On Our Backs* (for arousal), *Off Our Backs* (for edification). *485 14th St., at Guerrero St., tel. 415/626–2805. Open weekdays 7–7, weekends 9–7.*

NORTH BEACH **Caffè Greco.** An international crowd fills this attractive café, whose windows overlook Columbus Avenue. Rich Italian espresso ($1.40 a cup) accompanies bad Italian pop music in a bustling atmosphere, and you'll find a colorful selection of desserts—regulars worship the decadent tiramisù ($4). Preferred reading material: *Sunday New York Times*. *423 Columbus Ave., btw Vallejo and Stockton Sts., tel. 415/397–6261. Open daily 7 AM–midnight (Sat.–Sun. until 1 AM).*

Greco uses Illy Caffè, reputed to be the strongest espresso in existence.

Caffè Trieste. This is the legendary home of the Beat generation; it was here that Kerouac and his gang oozed cool from

Plug In, Tune In, Drink Up

If you're yearning to jump on the Internet bandwagon, or if face-to-face interaction just isn't your thing, try San Francisco Net, a computer network that connects several cafés in the Bay Area. As you drink your latte, you can dive into cyberspace and exchange messages with people at other cafés hooked up to the system. Here's how it works: You put in your quarter (yes, it costs money), log on with a nickname of your liking, and chat away, feeding the computer more money every so often. Who knows—maybe you'll find your future mate. But then again, you might just meet a bunch of technoids who have nothing better to do. S.F. Net can be found in more than 13 San Francisco cafés, including Brainwash (1122 Folsom St., at Langton St., tel. 415/861–3663), the two Jammin' Java locations (see above), and Muddy Waters (521 Valencia St., at 16th St., tel. 415/863–8006). You can also log on at home if you have a modem. The remote access number is 415/824–8747.

every pore. The café doesn't seem to have changed a bit: It's as smoky as ever, with '50s decor and an opera-spouting jukebox. The delicious coffee drinks are $1–$3. Saturday afternoons at 1:30, the owner's family serenades guests with old Italian tunes and opera. Preferred reading material: *The Beat Reader. 601 Vallejo St., at Grant Ave., tel. 415/392–6739. Open daily 6:30 AM–11:30 PM (Fri.–Sat. until midnight).*

Gathering Caffè. Jazz aficionados should not miss this spot, where there's no cover charge for the nightly live music—you'll just pay an extra 50¢ for your coffee drink. The small marble tables and black-and-white checkered floor evoke a tiny jazz bar in Florence, not a San Francisco café 3 blocks from the "Girls! Girls! Girls!" of Broadway. Preferred reading material: Nat Shapiro's *The Jazz Makers. 1326 Grant Ave., at Green St., tel. 415/433–4247. Open daily 11 AM–11:30 PM (Fri.–Sat. until midnight).*

North End Café. The young and the restless of North Beach congregate here over massive bowl-sized cups of coffee. While you can easily sit and read a book undisturbed, the urge to gaze at the beautiful people may overpower you. The coffee is strong—one cup could render you giddy, two will leave you babbling incessantly. Preferred reading material: *Details* magazine. *1402 Grant Ave., at Green St., tel. 415/956–3350. Open Mon.–Thurs. 7 AM–11 PM, Fri. 7 AM–1 AM, Sat. 10 AM–1 AM, Sun. 10 AM–11 PM.*

SOUTH OF MARKET **Café Natoma.** This lunch-hour café names its sandwiches after SoMa streets and alleys, such as the Natoma Street Original (smoked ham, $4) and the Yerba Buena (veggie, $4). A shot of espresso is 95¢. Because the café is directly behind the Museum of Modern Art, office workers and museum-goers vie for tables. Preferred reading material: *Fortune* magazine. *145 Natoma St., at 3rd St., tel. 415/495–3289. Open weekdays 7 AM–4:30 PM.*

Caffè Centro. This café draws multimedia types, film production people, and the occasional bike messenger in search of a light lunch and midday caffeine fix. The sidewalk tables look out on South Park, formerly a low-rent spot that's becoming quickly gentrified—the pretension level is often overwhelming. Preferred reading material: *Mac World. 102 South Park Ave., btw 2nd and 3rd and Bryant and Brannan Sts., tel. 415/882–1500. Open weekdays 8 AM–7:30 PM, Sat. 9 AM–5 PM.*

Free Verse

Like their Beat predecessors, bohemians today enjoy airing their ghastly, turbid secrets to strangers at coffeehouses. That's what open-mike poetry is all about—occasionally fabulous, more often incomprehensible, sometimes offensive or silly, but always San Francisco. If you can wow these audiences with your poetry, you've got it made. Poets run the gamut from pros who never falter to novices with shaky voices and trembling hands. Some audiences ignore the whole thing, engrossed in conversation or a chess game, while others voice their encouragement or disapproval. The smaller cafés tend to draw a more attentive audience.

Jammin' Java (see above) offers poetry, plus some music and performance art, at 8 PM on Wednesdays; Red Dora's (see above) features poetry, comedy, and music at 8 PM Fridays and Saturdays; The Blue Monkey (see below) has mostly poetry, with some music and storytelling, at 7:30 PM on Tuesdays; Café International (508 Haight St., at Fillmore St., tel. 415/552–7390) offers readings—often with an ethnic bent—at 9 PM on Fridays; Brainwash (1122 Folsom St., at Langton St., tel. 415/861–3663) features poetry and other readings at 8 PM on Saturdays.

Mr. Ralph's. Stroll down Natoma, off Second Street, and you'll find a tiny, bright-green brick building that houses this funky little coffeehouse. Unwind with the mellow, artsy-professional crowd after a few hours of cultural overload at the new MOMA. Preferred reading selection: *Candide. 90 Natoma St., btw 1st and 2nd Sts., tel. 415/243–9330. Open Mon.–Wed. 7–7, Thurs.–Fri. 7 AM–9 PM, Sat. 8:30–2:30.*

OUTLYING NEIGHBORHOODS So you've ventured beyond the parts of the city where espresso bars run two to a block. Shame on you. Luckily, there are places in almost every neighborhood to get your caffeine fix—like the times when you're visiting your aunt, expanding your horizons, getting a part for your car, going to the dentist, or enjoying the sunset.

Blue Danube. A homey Richmond district café with ceiling fans and changing art exhibits, the Danube is a great place to dig into the books you just bought down the street at Green Apple (*see* Books, in Chapter 3). The café serves breakfast and sandwiches for about $5, as well as beer and wine, so you could conceivably spend all day here. It's full of college students, resident youth with time on their hands, and thirtysomethings who still remember how to laze away the weekend. Preferred reading material: *Sassy* magazine, *SF Weekly. 306 Clement St., btw 4th and 5th Aves., tel. 415/221–9041. Open Mon.–Thurs. 7 AM–11:30 PM, Fri.–Sat. 7 AM–12:30 AM, Sun. 7 AM–10:30 PM.*

The Blue Monkey. A quiet, small café with a gorgeous mural on the wall and open-mike nights (*see box, above*), the Blue Monkey lies just a block off Fillmore Street, right where the neighborhood is transformed from the Fillmore of expensive boutiques and restaurants to the Fillmore of liquor stores and housing projects. Preferred reading material: anything by Amiri Baraka. *1777 Steiner St., btw Sutter and Post Sts., tel. 415/929–7117. Open Mon.–Fri. 7–6 (Tues. until 10 PM), Sat. 7:30–4, Sun. 8–3.*

Farley's. Besides the classic features of a good café—strong coffee, local art displays, lots of sidewalk tables—this Potrero Hill coffeehouse has a magazine rack with more than 20 titles, a stack of games, and loads of journals. Try one of the homemade pastry creations ($1), or bring your own munchies—the management doesn't mind. Farley's loses a few points in the friendliness category, though, since the young Pot Hill locals sometimes give strangers a cold shoulder. Preferred reading material: whatever you want. *1315 18th St., btw Texas and Missouri Sts., tel. 415/648–1545. Open weekdays 7 AM–10 PM, weekends 8 AM–10 PM.*

Java Beach. What do surfers at Ocean Beach do when the waves are blown out? They go to Java Beach, the only decent café in the Outer Sunset. Here you'll enjoy a good selection of coffee drinks and tea while lounging on the cushy couches or perusing the small library in back. Weekly live music includes traditional Irish folk. Preferred reading material: Bill Morris's *Stoked. 1396 La Playa St., at Judah St., tel. 415/665–JAVA. Open weekdays 6 AM–11 PM, weekends 7 AM–11 PM.*

Finding Your Fix in the Dark

It's 10 PM and the latte you had after dinner is wearing off. You're on the second page of a 20-page paper due at 8 AM, or have some other task that simply must be completed. You need a caffeine fix, and how! What do you do? Where do you go? Your first option is to head to North Beach, where most coffeehouses go until midnight on weekdays, 1 AM on weekends. Java joints Greco, Trieste, Puccini, and the North End have more of a study-hall ambience than the Gathering (see above), where the live jazz might prove distracting. Can't get to North Beach? Try the Horseshoe in the Lower Haight (see above), which stays open—and belligerent—until 1 AM nightly. Café Flore in the Castro (see above) keeps the espresso machine on until midnight Fridays and Saturdays, but don't expect to get much done.

Tart to Tart. The only problem with this large, lively café in the Inner Sunset (near UCSF medical school) is the military-style seating—the long, hard tables are not at all conducive to intimate conversation. Otherwise, this place whips up a mean cup of coffee and plenty of excellent desserts ($2–$4), salads ($4), and entrées. Preferred reading material: *Parenting* magazine. *641 Irving St., btw 7th and 8th Aves., tel. 415/753–0643. Open weekdays 7:30 AM–11 PM, Sat. 8:30 AM–midnight, Sun. 8:30 AM–11 PM.*

BERKELEY

Without its cafés, the People's Republic of Berkeley would collapse. Students would have nowhere to be seen while "studying"; skate punks would have nowhere to hang while cutting class; artists and poets would have no place to share their angst. Luckily, within a square mile of the U.C. campus no less than 50 cafés peacefully coexist. Smokers, however, should take note: In 1994, Berkeley banned smoking in all indoor *and* outdoor cafés.

Café Fanny. Opened by Chez Panisse maven Alice Waters and named for her daughter Fanny, the shady, trellised patio at this west Berkeley café draws weekend crowds of young mothers and gourmet yuppies. The food is not exactly cheap, and the portions are small: If you're on a tight budget, get a bowl-sized latte ($2) and homemade granola ($4), or try the buckwheat crêpes ($4.75), available with a variety of fillings. On your way home, stop next door at Acme Bread for a fresh-baked baguette. Preferred reading material: Marcel Pagnol's *Fanny. 1603 San Pablo Ave., at Cedar St., tel. 510/524–5447. Open weekdays 7–3, Sat. 8–4, Sun. 9–3.*

Caffè Mediterraneum. Featured in the film *The Graduate*, the Med has nurtured countless bursts of inspiration and the occasional failed revolution. These days, it's one of the few places where lifelong Berkeleyans and open-minded students converge for conversation over a shot of caffeine (most students stick closer to campus). Besides espresso drinks and desserts, the

Folger's? No Way.

If the novelty of the café scene ever wears off, you might be faced with making your own coffee. Do you buy a can of tasteless ground beans at the supermarket? Nah. Just visit one of the Bay Area's purveyors of by-the-pound gourmet coffees. But be prepared to face a million choices: Sumatra or house blend? Ground or whole? It'll make your head spin, and java ignorance can brand you an outsider quicker than having an accent can. Here's a crash course in the fine art of roasting and buying.

Coffee bean flavor is related to country of origin: Beans from the Americas have a tangy, bright flavor; Arabian and African beans have a sweeter, fruity taste; and beans from the Pacific Rim taste nuttier due to lower acidity. Fresh beans have shiny, oily coatings and uniform color. Once purchased, your precious jewels should be stored in the freezer, and when you do brew, try reusable stainless steel filters for a purer, and more eco-conscious, pot.

Now, where to buy? Peet's Coffee & Tea sells 33 kinds of coffee and is the undisputed java champion. The original Peet's opened in the '60s in Berkeley (2124 Vine St., at Walnut St., tel. 510/841–0564); the newest location (there are 13 total) is in San Francisco (2257 Market St., at Noe St., tel. 415/626–6416). If it's big business, and not caffeine, that gives you the jitters, try Uncommon Grounds in Berkeley (2813 7th St., btw Hines and Greyson Sts., tel. 510/644–4451), which sells beans retail and wholesale.

Med's small kitchen (open daily 7–3) serves omelets, sandwiches, burgers, and pasta at reasonable prices. The café—but not the second-floor rest room—is wheelchair accessible. Preferred reading material: Jack Kerouac's *On the Road,* Paulo Freire's *Pedagogy of the Oppressed. 2475 Telegraph Ave., btw Haste St. and Dwight Way, tel. 510/549–1128. Open daily 7 AM–midnight.*

Caffè Strada. There's little indoor seating, but the sprawling outdoor patio attracts a good mix of architecture students, frat and sorority types, and visiting foreigners. It's a social spot, so don't expect to get much work done. Instead, bring a newspaper, relax in the sun, and eavesdrop while you sip your latte ($1.50) and munch on your pastry ($1–$2). Preferred reading material: *San Francisco Chronicle. 2300 College Ave., at Bancroft Way, tel. 510/843–5282. Open daily 7 AM–11:30 PM.*

Carraras Café and Gallery. Emeryville—midway between Berkeley and Oakland and home to a small collection of converted warehouses and artists' lofts—is experiencing a cultural renaissance of sorts, as is evident in its burgeoning café scene. Carraras, the best of the lot, is housed in a one-story brick warehouse whose high walls provide ample space for paintings by local artists. The café caters to young artsy types more than to students, but it's a good place for anyone who wants to enjoy an Anchor Steam beer ($2.50) after a long day. The food's not cheap (sandwiches are $6–$7), but the desserts are worth the price: The selection changes daily and features delicacies like the raspberry Linzertorte ($3.50). Preferred reading material: *The Spirit of Community and the Reinvention of American Society. 1290 Powell St., at Hollis St., tel. 510/547–6763. From I–80, take Powell St. exit north 3 blocks. Open Mon. 7 AM–11 PM, Tues.–Fri. 7 AM–midnight, Sat. 9 AM–midnight. Wheelchair access.*

The Musical Offering. With its airy interior and constant stream of classical music, this café caters to a tweedy and mature crowd. Coffees, sandwiches, vegetarian fare, and soups are sold in front, classical CDs and cassettes in back. The smoked-trout salad will set you back $6; a latte is $1.50. Shopper's hint: Buy a CD or tape on the composer's birthday and receive a 20% discount. Preferred reading material: the *Brandenberg Concertos. 2430 Bancroft Way, near Telegraph Ave., tel. 510/849–0211. Café open daily 8–8, music store open daily 10–9.*

Nefeli Caffè. This quality coffeehouse north of the U.C. campus is popular with students and professors for its innovative, reasonably priced menu. The impressive selection of Italian-style panini includes an unusually delectable sandwich with eggplant, roasted peppers, feta, and Kalamata olive spread ($4.25). Nefeli also has a variety of wine and beer, as well as sangria ($2.75), and you shouldn't leave without sampling the house specialty, caffè freddo (espresso, sugar, and Sambuca, $2.50). Poetry readings take place Monday nights, followed by open-mike performances. Preferred reading material: anything by Nikos Kazantzakis. *1854 Euclid Ave., at Hearst St., tel. 510/841–6374. Open Mon.–Thurs. 7 AM–10 PM, Fri. 7 AM–midnight, Sat. 8 AM–midnight, Sun. 8 AM–10 PM.*

Red Café. This gem of a café-bar, one of a few as yet undiscovered by students, fills with an older, artsy, postgrad crowd. The red-brick walls, exposed beam ceiling, and massive skylight (that actually opens) create a warm, welcoming ambience. The full kitchen serves carefully prepared, mostly vegetarian sandwiches, salads, and pastas ($3–$6), and the café has a fine selection of beers. The coffee is smooth, the service is super-friendly, and you'll find occasional live jazz on the weekends. Preferred reading material: the want ads. *1941A University Ave., at Grant St., tel. 510/843–8607. Open weekdays 7 AM–midnight, weekends 9 AM–midnight. Wheelchair access.*

AFTER DARK 6

By Ray Klinke, with Baty Landis

The sun has edged its way into the ocean, leaving you to face that all-consuming question: What am I going to do tonight? Well, the Bay Area's got a lot of answers. If you don't find your scene in one of the area's 10,000 bars, you can go see an old movie in a funky theater, check out a live show at a local club, head to a performance space to watch some unbridled genius, or dance all night long at an underground party.

Local bars range from the seedy to the snooty, and it's not hard to find booze and fine entertainment under the same roof. Check *SF Weekly* or the *Bay Guardian* (both available at newsstands and cafés citywide), or flyers posted in the hipper parts of town—the Mission, the Haight, and South of Market—for details. The weeklies are prime resources for info on dance clubs that travel from spot to spot, but you should also drop by clothing and record stores, which often have the lowdown on music and clubs. Both the free weekly *Bay Times* and the magazine *On-Q* are good places to look for gay and lesbian listings.

If your interests involve hard-core clubbing, tattooed rockers, or the gay scene and all of its subscenes, you're best off in the city. Otherwise, the East Bay has plenty of bars and a handful of good places to hear live music. Come to Oakland to sample world-class blues and jazz, or to Berkeley if you just can't get enough of inebriated college students. Flip through the free weekly *East Bay Express* for a complete events calendar, including films, lectures, readings, and music.

While both Marin County and the South Bay can be entertaining during daylight hours, when the sun sets these areas become very, very quiet. Still, if you missed the last bus for the city, you should be able to ferret out a local bar and maybe some live music in Marin; even the South Bay offers a few diversions near the Stanford campus. For nightlife in Marin and the South Bay, *see* Chapter 2.

Bars

SAN FRANCISCO

In San Francisco, choosing a place to drink is no easy matter. Maybe you're looking for Doc Martens and grunge rock, maybe black leather and chaps. Or you might be more comfortable around football posters and college sweatshirts, or even cowboy hats and pickup trucks. In any case, San Francisco caters to tastes both subtle and flamboyant, and you shouldn't have any trouble finding a new favorite bar. Keep in mind that this city of hills, fog, and one-way streets is particularly treacherous for those who drink and drive; instead, take the bus or call a cab.

CASTRO DISTRICT This safe, very gay quarter of San Francisco plays host to some of the wildest festivals in the city. You're far more likely to kindle a romance here if you're enamored of the same sex, but open-minded straight folks frequent a few of the less intense pickup bars after an evening at the grand old Castro Theater (*see* Movie Houses, *below*) or one of the area's fine restaurants.

The Café. This large, lively bar with mirrored walls and neon lights caters mainly to lesbians, although gay men also frequent the place. If there's no room on the dance floor, you can hang out on the balcony and watch the Castro strut by. *2367 Market St., near Castro St., tel. 415/861–3846.*

The Detour. Minimally decorated with a chain-link fence and pool table, this bar caters to a youngish leather-queen-wanna-be crowd sporting goatees. Even with no dance floor, the urgent techno-house music causes the level of sexual frustration in the room to skyrocket. If you forget the address, listen for the music, since the black-on-black sign is impossible to see at night. *2348 Market St., btw Castro and Noe Sts., tel. 415/861–6053.*

Beers are $1 on Friday and Saturday nights at the Detour.

Midnight Sun. Three video screens help alleviate the need for conversation in this crowded, colorful bar that shows a mix of weird TV shows and current music videos. *4067 18th St., near Castro St., tel. 415/861–4186. Wheelchair access.*

The Orbit Room. Besides having a groovy name, the Orbit has a smart-looking, high-ceilinged drinking area where you can enjoy a cocktail or espresso with a mostly straight crowd that doesn't mind the artsy, slightly uncomfortable bar stools. The subdued lighting, stucco walls, and innovative design scheme make you feel like you're on display at some swank art gallery. *1900 Market St., at Laguna St., tel. 415/252–9525.*

The Phoenix. This is a good place for shy types to pick up a sexy new lover boy. Admission is free, and it's the only gay bar on Castro Street with a dance floor. *482 Castro St., btw 17th and 18th Sts., tel. 415/552–6827.*

Twin Peaks. David Lynch has nothing to do with this casual, lounge-like gay bar; in fact, the Peaks has been around for more than 15 years, and proudly claims to have been the first gay bar in the city with clear—as in, not tinted—floor-to-ceiling windows. Twin Peaks enjoys its high visibility on the corner of Market and Castro; on weekends expect big crowds of both newcomers and an older, established clientele. *401 Castro St., at Market St., tel. 415/864–9470.*

CHINATOWN By day a maelstrom of gaudy souvenir shops, pungent markets, and overcrowded sidewalks, Chinatown transforms into a quiet, genuine neighborhood at night. Step into one of the local bars for a reminder of whose part of town this is.

Li Po's. By 1 AM the coveted back booths in this oddly mystical bar are filled with boisterous escapees from the North Beach scene, who are almost daring—and drunk—enough to join in the occasional karaoke. After last call, stop into Sam Wo's around the corner for some downright cheap chow mein. *916 Grant St., btw Jackson and Washington Sts., tel. 415/982–0072.*

Mr. Bing's. This horseshoe-shaped spot on the edge of Chinatown draws a heterogeneous mix of drinkers who line the narrow V-shaped bar and, when given the chance, gladly share their latest misadventures. There's also the ubiquitous video–poker machines and a jukebox that plays scratchy Sinatra tunes. *201 Columbus Ave., at Pacific St., tel. 415/362–1545.*

DOWNTOWN AND CIVIC CENTER The downtown area isn't the greatest place to be after sundown, unless you enjoy getting heckled by streetwalkers in microminis or witnessing shady business transactions. Nevertheless, there are a few bars worth braving if you have door-to-door transportation.

Edinburgh Castle. This diamond in the rough was established before the Tenderloin earned its reputation for squalor. A British pub with a beautiful bar, it's a great place to play darts, eat greasy fish 'n' chips, sip pints of Guinness or Bass, and make friends with thick-accented U.K. types. *950 Geary St., btw Polk and Larkin Sts., tel. 415/885–4074.*

Motherlode. This Tenderloin landmark is the city's most popular transvestite haven, although there's no "dress" code posted at the door. The area is often dangerous and the crowd occasionally seedy, but the flamboyant patrons provide an energetic, entertaining night of thrills. Come for the free drag shows on Friday and Saturday nights—but please refrain from gawking. *1002 Post St., at Larkin St., tel. 415/928–6006.*

Place Pigalle. The vibes are hip and European at this sleek, low-key, French-owned wine bar and gallery space. Stop in for a glass of wine after work and stay for the evening; there's live jazz Thursday through Saturday nights, and occasional spoken-word performances during the week. *520 Hayes St., btw Octavia and Laguna Sts., tel. 415/552–2671. Cover: up to $3. Wheelchair access.*

QT. At the "Quick Trick" you can cozy up to hustlers and drag queens in an unassuming atmosphere. There's live music Friday and Saturday nights, and free male strip shows, both professional and amateur, on Sundays and Tuesdays. Legend has it that the owner gave Anita Baker her start. *1312 Polk St., btw Bush and Pine Sts., tel. 415/885–1114.*

HAIGHT AND THE WESTERN ADDITION Ah, Haight-Ashbury—over 25 years of hipness. This neighborhood might overdo it at times, and the crowd is always close on the heels of the latest trend, but there are a variety of spots where you can toss down a few. The Upper Haight is still host to vacant-looking hippies mourning Jerry and their dogs, as well as lots of cocktail-quaffing tourists who've just spent the day buying pricey but "hip" togs. When you want a watering hole that's slightly rougher around the edges, head downhill to the lower Haight.

The Deluxe. Come on the weekend to this slick, retro bar on the upper Haight, order a martini, and take a look around: You'll get the uncanny feeling that the year is 1945. Patrons enjoy donning their finest '40s duds (hairdos and shoes included) and acting *very* cool. There will usually be a crooner, with backup swing band, or at least owner Jay Johnson doing Sinatra his way. Denim-wearers are welcome. *1511 Haight St., btw Ashbury and Clayton Sts., tel. 415/552–6949. Cover: $3–$5 weekends.*

The Gold Cane. With very little in the way of atmosphere or trendiness, and the cheapest drinks ($2.25 well) on the street, this is a good place to pound a few cold ones in the upper Haight before heading out to hear some music. *1569 Haight St., btw Ashbury and Clayton Sts., tel. 415/626–1112.*

Rack 'Em

Intimidated shooting stick in front of an unsympathetic bar crowd? Tired of waiting half an hour for a table, only to scratch the eight ball on your first shot? Pay a visit to one of San Francisco's pool halls, where, for an hourly fee, you can practice that bank shot or hustle your friends without interruption. Serious players should head to one of the 37 tables at Hollywood Billiards (61 Golden Gate Ave., near Market St., tel. 415/252–9643). Mondays, students play for up to five hours for $5; Wednesdays, women can play up to three hours for free. Hollywood is open 24 hours and has a full bar, but the downside is that it's not in the best neighborhood. At South Beach Billiards (270 Brannan St., near 2nd St., tel. 415/495–5939)—a sleek SoMa pool hall open until 2 AM nightly—tables are $12 an hour, and there are weekly beer specials. With only five tables, the pool room at Park Bowl (1851 Haight St., btw Shrader and Stanyan Sts., tel. 415/752–2366) occasionally fills up, but the dirt-cheap tables ($5.50 an hour for two people) are worth the wait, and it's a casual place to spend a rainy afternoon with some friends and a cue ball.

Mad Dog in the Fog. This British-style pub in the heart of the lower Haight is frequented by people who don't mind communicating in screams over loud grunge music and cold, frothy beer. You can also play darts here, and during the day you might get lucky and enjoy a moment of peace on the back patio. In the mornings, they serve up greasy breakfasts, including Thatcher's Thick Head (English bacon and tomato on English muffin with scrambled eggs, $3.50). *530 Haight St., btw Fillmore and Steiner Sts., tel. 415/626–7279.*

Midtown. Watch lower Haight Street have a beer. The clientele is young, tattooed, perpetually smoking, and good at pool. Arrive early on weekends to snag the lone table, as the crowd can be fierce in the standing room. *582 Haight St., btw Fillmore and Steiner Sts., tel. 415/558–8019.*

Murio's Trophy Room. Murio's, in the upper Haight, is often overcrowded with bikers and Haight Street slackers, but it can be fun and low-key on weekdays. When the conversation lags, there's a pool table, jukebox, and TV. *1811 Haight St., btw Shrader and Stanyan Sts., tel. 415/752–2971.*

The Noc Noc. Step inside this lower Haight institution and you'll find yourself in a postmodern cave complete with chunky Flintstones-style furniture and a very eclectic music repertoire. Expect a healthy variety of beers, a couple kinds of wine, and sake—but no hard liquor. Visiting Europeans leave little room at the bar for folks from the neighborhood. *557 Haight St., btw Fillmore and Steiner Sts., tel. 415/861–5811.*

The Toronado. A narrow, dark dive in the lower Haight with lots of folks in leather, the Toronado features one of the widest selections of microbrews in the city. The jukebox blares a refreshing mix of kitschy country and western in addition to the standard grunge anthems. *547 Haight St., btw Fillmore and Steiner Sts., tel. 415/863–2276.*

MARINA DISTRICT The nightlife in this affluent, homogenous section of lower Pacific Heights is typified by the bevy of bars in the "Triangle," the intersection of Fillmore and Greenwich streets, which attract hordes of sporty professionals (i.e., postcollege frat boys) eager to drink and practice the art of the pickup.

Pierce Street Annex Drinking Establishment. Packed with aspiring yuppies and those who claim allegiance to a fraternity or sorority, this festive bar has a dance floor, pool tables, and nightly drink specials. Mondays are karaoke nights and Wednesdays feature live reggae. *3138 Fillmore St., near Greenwich St., tel. 415/567–1400.*

MISSION DISTRICT Lately, the Mission has been sprouting hip bars, cafés, restaurants, and clubs faster than a Chia pet sprouts alfalfa, attracting a young bohemian crowd with a predilection for thrift stores. The neighborhood, however, has long had a shady reputation. The poorly lit side streets are the diciest, but even on more heavily trafficked streets like Valencia and Mission, late-night bar-hoppers should take care.

The city's best margaritas are mixed at Puerto Alegre (546 Valencia St., near 16th St., tel. 415/626–2922), about a block from the Elbo Room. Order a strawberry and munch on some tortilla chips to get fueled up for the evening ahead.

The Albion. Come here for a young crowd, a fine pool table, and loud grunge rock, all served up in the glow of pink neon lights. *3139 16th St., btw Valencia and Guerrero Sts., tel. 415/552–8558.*

The Elbo Room. This stylish Mission watering hole becomes unmanageably popular as the night progresses. Upstairs, live jazz and hip-hop acts, as well as occasional DJs, attract the crowds. Plus, the drinks are cheap enough ($2–$3) to keep you around until closing. *647 Valencia St., near 17th St., tel. 415/552–7788.*

The 500 Club. Here's a little slice of Americana—complete with a huge neon sign and two cramped pool tables—that rarely reaches maximum capacity. Everyone here has checked their attitude at the door and succumbed to the lure of cheap American beer. *500 Guerrero St., at 17th St., tel. 415/861–2500.*

The Lone Palm. There's something about this place that's reminiscent of a David Lynch film. The neon palm out front? The surreal comments your waitress makes? The funny facial tics of the guy at the counter? Hard to say, but they combine to make this quiet bar a dark, retro, and generally weird place to have a cocktail. *3394 22nd St., near Guerrero St., tel. 415/648–0109.*

The Rite Spot. The piano in the corner, candlelit tables, and understated decor all lend a sense of timelessness to this outer Mission bar that's a favorite among locals. *2099 Folsom St., at 17th St., tel. 415/552–6066.*

The Uptown. Sit at the long oak bar and get rowdy with friendly barflies, grab a game of pool with neighborhood hipsters, or stand outside watching hookers and drug dealers do their thing. Several well-worn couches in back make you feel right at home. *200 Capp St., at 17th St., tel. 415/861–8231.*

Zeitgeist. This is the original no-frills biker bar—albeit a bit trendier and friendlier—for every kind of biker. In the afternoons, it fills with bike messengers relating the day's near encounters with the Big Grille in the Sky; by night the BMW motorbike crowd clogs the outdoor deck, waiting its turn at the lone pool table. *199 Valencia St., at Duboce Ave., tel. 415/255–7505.*

NOB HILL AND RUSSIAN HILL This area caters to an upscale, often touristy crowd. There are a few bars that the city's more conservative youth swear by, but Nob and Russian hills are dominated by four- and five-star hotels, and don't offer much to dive-bar aficionados.

Johnny Love's. Young urban professionals let their hair down and dance on the tables at this Russian Hill lounge, much touted by the press as *the* singles bar for postcollege types who have managed to find a steady job. In other words, it's the most upscale meat market in town. *1500 Broadway, at Polk St., tel. 415/931–8021.*

The Tonga Room. This Tiki kitsch-o-rama bar is custom-made for tourists who wish it was still 1955, but you'll secretly love the bamboo-and-palm-leaf decor as much as they do. The waiters wear muumuus; a simulated rainstorm regularly occurs in the simulated lagoon; and, best of all, your potent drink comes with fruit, umbrellas, and all sorts of paraphernalia. Of course, you'll pay handsomely for all this—even during happy hour (5–7 PM), drinks will set you back $2.50–$4.50. *Fairmont Hotel, California and Mason Sts., tel. 415/772–5278. Enter on California St., btw Mason and Powell Sts.; turn down the first hall on the right. Wheelchair access.*

Every 30 minutes or so, a small hurricane blows through the Tonga Room, and at 8 PM most nights a soft-rock band performs from a thatched hut in the middle of a lagoon.

Top of the Mark. Breathtaking views of the city compensate for the expensive drinks and snooty clientele at San Francisco's classic, old-time cocktail lounge. Certain locals consider this *the* place to be seen in heels and pearls or a suit. Arrive before 8 PM to avoid the $2–$4 cover. *1 Nob Hill, at top of Mark Hopkins Hotel, tel. 415/392–3434. Cnr of California and Mason Sts.*

NORTH BEACH North Beach is famous for its Italian restaurants, cafés, and tiny cobblestone alleys. While it does have a small red-light district on Broadway, the generally civil crowd,

Moe's Tavern

Now that The Simpsons airs on Sunday nights, you may not feel so lame when you stay home to watch it. But you'll have a lot more fun getting your Homer fix at the Rat and Raven (4054 24th St., near Church St., tel. 415/550–9145), where every Sunday you can enjoy a loud and clear episode of The Simpsons, plenty of beer (though no Flaming Moes), and a crowd of folks who know what you mean when you say, "It's funny, because it's true." Arrive by 7 PM to get a seat. If you can't make it all the way to Noe Valley, watch Marge and Homer at the Zeitgeist (199 Valencia St., at Duboce Ave., tel. 415/255–7505), or at the Toronado (547 Haight St., btw Fillmore and Steiner Sts., tel. 415/863–2276).

which usually includes a number of out-of-towners, is more attracted to the bars and cafés that line Columbus Avenue and Grant Avenue.

Savoy-Tivoli. This North Beach institution caters to an amorous set recuperating from a hard day in the Financial District. The large, covered front patio opens when the weather's nice, making the Savoy prime territory to drink wine, watch the world go by, and generally feel like you're in Italy. *1434 Grant Ave., btw Union and Green Sts., tel. 415/362–7023.*

Specs'. Its given name is Specs' Twelve Adler Museum Café, but this classic North Beach hangout for the perennially half-sloshed is popularly known as Specs'. It's a jovial, divey, no-attitude sort of place where, if the conversation sucks, you can gaze for hours at the quirky memorabilia papering the walls. *12 Saroyan Pl., tel. 415/421–4112. Off Columbus Ave., next to Tosca (see below), btw Broadway and Pacific Sts.*

Tosca. This classic vintage establishment in North Beach is renowned for its liqueur-laced coffee drinks, its beautiful old espresso machine, its opera-only jukebox, and its celebrity patrons (Francis Ford Coppola and Mikhail Baryshnikov occasionally pop in). *242 Columbus Ave., near Broadway, tel. 415/391–1244. Wheelchair access.*

Vesuvio. A bohemian hangout during the Beat era, Vesuvio has somehow managed to avoid having the life stamped out of it by tourist boots. Have a glass of red and peruse the copy of *Howl* you just bought next door at City Lights, or listen for words of wisdom from the crowd of wizened regulars. Check out the "Booth for Lady Psychiatrists" upstairs. *255 Columbus Ave., near Broadway, tel. 415/362–3370.*

If you prefer cocktails with your sunrise, head to Vesuvio (see above), the Motherlode (see above), or the Peaks (1316 Castro St., near 24th St., tel. 415/826–0100), all of which open at 6 AM for your drinking pleasure.

SOUTH OF MARKET A roughshod area of warehouses, outlet stores, and a few upscale spots, South of Market has few bars but lots of dance clubs. However, there are several gems you should go out of your way to check out—come early and sip a few before the sweaty crowds invade.

20 Tank Brewery. Catch a few pints (brewed on the premises) before heading across the street to DNA or Slim's, or skip the clubs and just catch the pints. Located in a beautiful old warehouse, 20 Tank generally avoids that common brewery pitfall of resembling a big frat party by attracting a reasonably diverse mix of patrons. They also serve hearty appetizers and sandwiches. *316 11th St., near Folsom St., tel. 415/255–9455. Wheelchair access.*

Hotel Utah. All manner of local rock, jazz, and acoustic sounds reverberate off the woody interior of this casual SoMa bar. If you don't want to hang in the tiny music room, take a seat at the long mahogany bar (shipped from Belgium during the Civil War) and avail yourself of the fine assortment of beer and liquor. The friendly crowd ranges from lawyers to bikers to dogs (yes, dogs); the wood floor occasionally creaks; and a fine view of a U.S. 101 off-ramp is yours through the front windows. *500 4th St., at Bryant St., tel. 415/421–8308. Wheelchair access.*

Julie's Supper Club. Past music greats (captured in black-and-white photos) gaze down at professionals and preprofessionals nibbling interesting appetizers and sipping cocktails. The art-deco interior and innovative munchies, including calamari and quesadillas ($4–$6), make this a good place for an after-work or preclub cocktail. *1123 Folsom St., near 7th St., tel. 415/861–0707.*

EAST BAY

BERKELEY Berkeley doesn't offer high-concept bars, but you'll find plenty of casual places to have a beer. The bars along Telegraph Avenue can't help but appeal to student tastes and budgets. To peer more deeply into Berkeley's psyche, head to one of the watering holes scattered along San Pablo Avenue, which tend to be seedier, but more genuine. Even here, though, it's hard to completely escape the collegiate contingent.

The Albatross. This no-nonsense, no-attitude pub attracts both students and working folk. The cheap beer (starting at $1.25) tastes even better with free popcorn, and there's a cozy fireplace and a whole row of dart boards. *1822 San Pablo Ave., btw Hearst Ave. and Delaware St., tel. 510/849–4714. From Berkeley BART, Bus 51 west to San Pablo Ave., walk 1½ blocks north.*

Le Bateau Ivre. Neither the elegant bar nor the adjoining upscale restaurant is cheap, but both are beautifully decorated in a French château style. There's a fireplace in the back room and a candle on every table—perfect for a romantic bottle of wine with your significant other. Cheese and fruit plates are $7, and a decadent slice of cheesecake goes for $3.50. Le Bateau Ivre also serves one of the creamiest pints of Guinness west of Dublin. Dress ranges from formal to blue jeans. *2629 Telegraph Ave., at Carleton St., tel. 510/849–1100. 6 blocks south of U.C. campus.*

Bison Brewing Company. Berkeley's most colorful crowd—all fully pierced and tattooed—call Bison home when they want to drink, but any beer enthusiast will want to try the homemade stout, ale, and cider. Live bands, ranging from blues to Irish folk, entertain Thursday through Saturday ($1–$2 cover charge). Happy hour (weekdays 4–6) features $1.75 pints and attracts huge crowds. *2598 Telegraph Ave., at Parker St., tel. 510/841–7734. 5 blocks south of U.C. campus. Wheelchair access.*

Brennan's. The bar is woefully nondescript, but the potent drinks make it worth the trip. Try the Irish coffee ($2.75) or a white Russian ($3.25), guaranteed to put a spark in your step. Popular with heavy drinkers, this is as far from student Berkeley as you can get. *720 University Ave., near I–80, tel. 510/841–0960. From Berkeley BART, Bus 51 west to 4th St. Wheelchair access.*

Café Bistro. The low lighting and European feel make this place popular with the beret-and-spectacles set. Nightly live jazz accompanies your intelligent conversation and glass of brandy. *2271 Shattuck Ave., at Durant Ave., tel. 510/848–3081. 4 blocks south of Berkeley BART.*

The Ivy Room. The pool table costs only two quarters, Patsy Cline rules the jukebox, and Bud is $2 a bottle. Come on down and join the bar rats. *860 San Pablo Ave., near Solano Ave., tel. 510/524–9220. From Berkeley BART, Bus 43 west to Solano Ave.*

Jupiter. This spacious wine-and-beer bar across from Berkeley BART is popular with a more down-to-earth crowd. It's got 20 microbrews on tap, a terraced patio, and live music Thursday–Saturday (no cover), all of which conspire to make this a great place to relax with friends. Get a beer at the bar, and try to make a game out of finding an empty table. *2181 Shattuck Ave., near Center St., tel. 510/843–8277.*

Leona's. Although it sits about seven steps away from the U.C. campus, this little lounge upstairs from the famous blues club Larry Blake's manages not to feel too obnoxiously collegiate. Come after school or work for a plate of free hors d'oeuvres and a stiff drink ($2.50–$3). *2367 Telegraph Ave., btw Durant Ave. and Channing Way, tel. 510/848–0886.*

The Pub. This cozy gathering spot is great for cheap pints and thick coffee, a place where the regulars patiently put up with a smirking collegiate crowd. Its overstuffed sofas, oak tables, and pipe-tobacco aroma go nicely with that novel you're reading or writing. If you forgot your book, borrow one of theirs. The Pub teems with students on weekend nights, but during the week things are generally quiet. *1492 Solano Ave., tel. 510/525–1900. From Berkeley BART, Bus 43 north to Santa Fe Ave.*

Spats. The inventive drink selection rivals anyone's anywhere: Choose from concoctions like the Nutty Buddy (Frangelico, cream, and crème de cacao; $4.25) or the Scorpion (rums, fruit juices, brandy, almond flavor, and two straws; $8.75). Then settle into a cushy old Victorian sofa in the parlor-like bar, and let yourself slip into romantic reminiscences. *1974 Shattuck Ave., tel. 510/841–7225. 2 blocks north of Berkeley BART.*

Triple Rock Brewery. At this popular microbrewery, the 1950s reign supreme, with goofy posters and nostalgic knickknacks lining the walls. On weekend nights, look for grad students talking shop, frat and sorority types pounding homemade ale (it comes in light, red, or dark), and office workers unwinding after a stressful day. The crowd is loud and raucous in a collegiate sort of way, but folks are friendly. During the day munch on excellent pub food (nachos, grilled sandwiches, and the like) on the outdoor patio. *1920 Shattuck Ave., at Hearst Ave., tel. 510/843–2739. 3 blocks north of Berkeley BART. Wheelchair access.*

OAKLAND Did your last evening in San Francisco end in a conversation about Wim Wenders? The merits of Treasury bills versus mutual funds? Heidegger and the Who of Dasein? Don't despair—head to Oakland, where the bars are cheaper, more sincere, and generally rougher around the edges.

The Alley. This is the only bar in Oakland where you can sit at a piano and sing along with your drunken compadres. It's been in business since the late 1940s and has the clientele and bar staff to prove it. It's dark, musty, and unassuming—a great place to hang out with low-key locals. Live piano music usually begins at 9 PM; drinks are $3–$5. *3325 Grand Ave., 3 blocks east of Lake Merritt, tel. 510/444–8505. From 19th St. BART, Bus 12 east to Santa Clara Ave.*

At the Alley, sit next to the piano and don't be shy about singing your favorite Barry Manilow or Sinatra song. It's like karaoke, but without the subtitles or cheesy video.

George and Walt's. G&W's is a stylish, somewhat sterile place filled with smoke, pool tables, and sports-laden conversation. On weekend nights you should probably steer clear unless you like bumping into crowds of U.C. Berkeley students. *5445 College Ave., tel. 510/653–7441. 1 block north of McNally's (see below).*

The Kingfish. No-nonsense drinking and camaraderie are the norm at this lively, cellar-like sports bar. Order yourself an ice-cold beer and bide your time: It'll be only a matter of minutes before someone starts talking about the A's. Drinks start at $2. *5227 Claremont Ave., tel. 510/655–7373. From MacArthur BART, Bus 40 north to Claremont Ave.*

McNally's Irish Pub. This place has the smell, feel, and whiskeys of a real Dublin pub. Grab a pint of Guinness, Bass, or Harp and warm yourself by the stone fireplace, or groove to the jukebox while playing bumper-pool in back. *5352 College Ave., tel. 510/654–9463. 4 blocks south of Rockridge BART.*

Oliveto. Although it's more restaurant than bar, Oliveto is a fine choice for solid pints and fine California-Italian appetizers. The soothing interior, done in salmon-colored pseudo-adobe with wrought-iron furnishings, will make you forget your hectic day. The clientele includes yuppie commuters fresh off BART and kids on furlough from the nearby art school. *5655 College Ave., tel. 510/547–5356. Across from Rockridge BART.*

Pacific Coast Brewing Company. In Old Oakland, this brew pub serves four homebrews and has 16 other beers on tap. It's popular with the thirtysomething crowd and a bit yuppie, but the beers are top drawer. Drinks are around $3. *906 Washington St., near 10th St., tel. 510/836–2739. From 12th St. BART, 3 blocks SW on Broadway, 1 block west to Washington St.*

Stork Club. The country–western flavor and Christmas lights decorating this downtown dive make it a great watering hole, especially at 6 AM. Recently, the Stork has been booking some decent local bands and has started to attract a hipper crowd. *380 12th St., tel. 510/444–6174. 1½ blocks east of Broadway.*

Clubs

Bay Area residents, like many city dwellers, often take their nightlife more seriously than their jobs. As a result, it can be hard for the uninitiated to break the ice with the club-going crowd and plug in to the underground scene. Your best bet is to check smaller, alternative retail and record shops for flyers. Many spaces host different clubs on different nights of the week; check the *Guardian* or *SF Weekly* for complete listings of the Bay Area's rotating club nights, and always call ahead—the hot spots change as quickly as fashion trends. *Klub* magazine, available at ravewear shops, lists clubs in San Francisco, as well as in New York and Los Angeles.

SAN FRANCISCO

Those with itchy feet in San Francisco definitely have options: Spaces large and small play music for every age, style, and level of rhythmic ability. There's a huge variety of quite casual and even reasonably priced dance venues, as well as some that ooze pretension. Dance purists can even find spaces that allow no alcohol or smoking. On the other end of the spectrum are the raves (*see box, below*)—still going strong in warehouses and fields—where substance abuse is by no means limited to alcohol and smoking. For current listings of gay and lesbian discos (as well as the latest gossip), flip through the free monthly *Odyssey,* available in cafés and bookstores around the Castro district.

STRAIGHT **Bahia Cabana.** A multigenerational, international crowd gets its samba fix at this colorful downtown supper club with mural-covered walls. Wednesdays it's reggae; other nights feature Afro-Brazilian music and shows by local dance troupes. *1600 Market St., at Franklin St., tel. 415/282–4020 or 415/861–4202. Cover: $5–$10.*

Barefoot Boogie. Neither a drop of alcohol nor a puff of smoke invades this Mission district dance studio, but the moves people execute in various states of undress belie your expectation of a nice, straight dance party. The event takes place at the Third Wave Dance Studio twice a week (Sun. and Wed. 7:30–10:30), and the music ranges from classical to deep house to samba to hip-hop. People often bring their own drums and other rhythm machines. *3316 24th St., at Mission St., tel. 415/282–4020. Cover: $6.*

Cat's Grill and Alley Club. The back room of this mostly after-hours club in SoMa features everything from jazz to ambient house to industrial. A standard selection of grill food is served from 6 PM–11 PM at the small eatery in front. *1190 Folsom St., near 8th St., tel. 415/431–3332. Cover: $5.*

Cesar's Latin Palace. Cesar's Latin All-Stars play salsa most nights, with occasional guest artists from all over Latin America. Early on you'll find older folks and even families here; later it's mostly young, well-dressed Latinos. Open Fridays and Saturdays only, the club keeps going until 5 AM. *3140 Mission St., near César Chavez (Army) St., tel. 415/648–6611. Cover: about $8.*

Deco. If there weren't three floors of funk, hip-hop, and dance hall grooves pulsating through this downtown club, it might be mistaken for a good neighborhood bar with an impressive selection of beer. The multicultural crowd isn't afraid to break a sweat on the floor, but many come just to kick back in dimly lit corners downstairs. *510 Larkin St., btw Turk and Eddy Sts., tel. 415/441–4007. Cover: $2–$5.*

DNA Lounge. This is a dependable choice for late-night dancing (until 4 AM nightly) and eclectic acts that range from bands to tattoo/piercing shows. You can hear a diverse range of live sounds (from accordion to industrial) early in the evening, but it's the leather-jacket SoMa

Rave Culture

Though the hype surrounding this techno-shamanic dance trend has passed, you can still find rave enthusiasts who dance ecstatically—and sometimes nonstop—to thumping techno-house music. The drug of choice is MDMA (a.k.a., Ecstasy), which creates a state of general bliss and a sense of being at peace with the world—all for the low price of about $20. These days, reliable rave tips can be obtained through the Buzzline (415/568–1338) or by flipping through Urb magazine. Otherwise, start talking to people, or look for flyers in ravewear shops like House Wares (1322 Haight St., tel. 415/252–1440) or Behind the Post Office (1504 Haight St., tel. 415/861–2507). The average rave cover charge, minus drinks and illegal substances, is $8–$15.

crowd that dances until the wee hours of the morning. *375 11th St., at Harrison St., tel. 415/626–1409. Cover: $5.*

Nickie's BBQ. Red-vinyl booths and Christmas lights decorate this racially mixed lower Haight hole-in-the-wall that's admirably cheap and entirely lacking in pretension. Everything from '70s funk, soul, and hip-hop to reggae, Latin, and world beat booms through the speakers every night except Monday. *460 Haight St., btw Webster and Fillmore Sts., tel. 415/621–6508. Cover: $3–$5.*

MIXED **The Box.** This Thursdays-only SoMa club plays hard-core hip-hop, funk, and house, and you'll find little attitude here because everybody's sweating on the dance floor. For an extra treat, go-go platforms mounted on the walls showcase dancers who gyrate their breathtaking bodies at full throttle. The city's most accomplished DJs—including Page Hodel, S.F.'s most famous queer DJ—and club dance troupes appear here. While the club is lesbian-run, the multicultural crowd includes straights, too. *715 Harrison St., btw 3rd and 4th Sts., tel. 415/972–8087. Cover: $6. Wheelchair access.*

DV8. Occupying four floors, this SoMa institution hosts an eclectic variety of clubs almost every night of the week, ranging from the gothic "House of Usher" to the pulsating sounds of "Lift." All different types come for the deep grooves and good vibes. Call for up-to-date listings. *540 Howard St., btw 1st and 2nd Sts; tel. 415/957–1730. Cover: $5–$10.*

El Río. This casual neighborhood hangout in the Mission attracts multiethnic nubos (new bohemians), lesbians, gay men, pool players, and regular folks. Get loose Wednesdays at the '70s dance party (no cover), come Fridays for international dance music at "Club nZinga," or stop by Sundays for salsa. The neighborhood isn't the best; women especially should avoid walking alone on Mission Street at night. *3158 Mission St., near César Chavez (Army) St., tel. 415/282–3325. Cover: up to $5.*

The Sound Factory. The latest, largest disco to roll into town is designed after New York and L.A. clubs. A maze of rooms in this SoMa space hosts a variety of acts and sounds, but deep house is the music of choice among the young rave crowd. Call for upcoming clubs and events. *525 Harrison St., at 1st St., tel. 415/543–1300. Cover: $5–$10.*

1015 Club. This SoMa spot hosts various clubs on a nightly basis. Fridays, "Dakota" (tel. 415/431–1200) captures the history of disco in three rooms: deep funk and tribal beats in the basement, '70s disco in the Gold Room, and high house in the main dance pit. Dress up for this one. Saturdays, "Release" (415/337–7457) keeps you going with '70s funk and disco, high house, and acid jazz. Call for a complete listing of club nights. *1015 Folsom St., btw 6th and 7th Sts., tel. 415/431–0700. Cover: about $10.*

Trocadero Transfer. Wednesdays only, Trocadero hosts the somewhat tame "Bondage A Go-Go," where tongue-tied beginners of both sexes can engage in a little light bondage, get whipped by a professional-looking dominatrix, or, more often, gape at the pros. It's a sort of light intro to real underground S&M culture. Women can get free drinks if they handcuff themselves to the bar. Other nights, this SoMa club features industrial dancing and live hard-core music. The Trocadero is all-ages when the music is live, and 18-and-over for "Bondage A Go-Go." *520 4th St., btw Bryant and Brannan Sts., tel. 415/995–4600. Cover: $5.*

GAY AND LESBIAN **Club Townsend.** This SoMa dance mecca hosts "Pleasuredome," San Francisco's most popular gay and lesbian club, on Sunday nights. The crowd is mostly male, but "Club Universe" on Saturdays is less gender-specific. Both are flashy and groovy; don't bother showing up if you can't take the loud, deep sounds of house music. *177 Townsend St., btw 2nd and 3rd Sts., tel. 415/974–6020. Cover: $7–$10.*

Covered Wagon. Black light illuminates the Western decor on the walls, as well as the lint on your shirt, at this dark SoMa bar. The CW hosts several clubs, including "Faster Pussycat" (Wednesdays) and Muffdive (Sundays), both catering—surprise—to women-loving women. CW-as-watering-hole is a good bet, too, with its clientele of underemployed musicians and bike messengers. *917 Folsom St., btw 5th and 6th Sts., tel. 415/974–1585. Cover: $3–$5.*

The EndUp. Venues change as fickle hipsters try to keep up with trends, but the EndUp always has a sweaty crowd gettin' down. The bar features a pool table, a patio with an elevated deck, and a waterfall, all surrealistically situated almost underneath U.S. 101 in SoMa. Come at 6 AM Sundays for the immensely popular "Sunday Tea Dance": $3 for all the dancing you can handle until 2 AM Monday—nice way to start the work week. Call the information line for details. *401 6th St., at Harrison St., tel. 415/487–6277. Cover: $7–$10.*

Esta Noche. Tucked away in the Mission, Esta Noche plays a good mix of Latin, house music, and '70s disco. The crowd consists mostly of young Latinos and the men who love them. European-American patrons are respectfully requested to refrain from doing the cha-cha. *3079 16th St., btw Mission and Valencia Sts., tel. 415/861–5757. Cover: generally $4.*

The Stud. This SoMa club is a San Francisco legend and a good watering hole any night of the week. Dress up or come as you are, and have fun flirting with innocent out-of-towners. Thursdays, the Stud hosts "Junk," a thrash-dance club for lesbians; Wednesdays it's "Oldies" and a beer bust; and Sundays it's "80something," a new-wave dance party. *399 9th St., at Harrison St., tel. 415/863–6623. Cover: up to $6.*

EAST BAY

The dance scene is much sparser here than in San Francisco—generally, the feel is less flash and flesh and more like a house party where everyone's dancing. You can check the *East Bay Express* under "Dance Clubs" for a thorough listing, but you're likely to discover that East Bay clubbers make the drive to the city when they want serious after-hours dancing.

Blake's. This few-nights-a-week scene, basically a DJ in the basement playing for U.C. students and Oakland natives, is as hip as Berkeley gets. A very sweaty basement that's ruled by funk, soul, hip-hop, and rare groove sounds, Blake's might not be the pinnacle of cool, but it should serve your dance needs just fine. *2367 Telegraph Ave., near Durant Ave., Berkeley, tel. 510/848–0886. Cover: about $3.*

The Caribee Dance Center. Occasional live music and Sunday dance classes (3–6 PM, $7) are supplemented five nights a week (Wed.–Sun.) with dancing to reggae, salsa, and African music. Drinks cost $2–$5. *1408 Webster St., Oakland, tel. 510/835–4006. From 12th St. BART, 2 blocks east on 14th St. Cover: $5–$10.*

White Horse Inn. Get down under a gleaming disco ball at this easygoing place on the Oakland–Berkeley border. Most patrons are gay or lesbian, but other fun-seekers are welcome as long as they behave themselves. A DJ is in the house Thursday–Saturday after 9 PM, and the bar's open daily 3 PM–2 AM. *6551 Telegraph Ave., at 66th St., Oakland, tel. 510/652–3820. From MacArthur BART, Bus 40 south on Telegraph to 66th St.*

"Tripping" the Light Fantastic

Lacking the Fred Astaire touch? Stumbling over two left feet? Take heart: Cheap or free help can be found at some of San Francisco's dance clubs, where a sympathetic soul will impart some basic moves to make stepping out more enjoyable, if not less embarrassing. Local dance companies (see Dance, below) sometimes offer affordable lessons as well. At Café du Nord (see Live Music, below), swing lessons can be had for a $3 cover Sundays 8–9 PM, when the jazz venue is still mostly empty. If you want salsa to be your thing, head to 330 Ritch Street (330 Ritch St., off Townsend St. btw 3rd and 4th Sts., tel. 415/522–9558) on Tuesdays for free lessons from 8 to 9 PM. Barring the above, a coy glance and a polite inquiry might enlist the company of a willing, and hopefully capable, partner.

Live Music

SAN FRANCISCO

Because of its propensity to draw people willing to be outlandish for art's sake, San Francisco—while not at the forefront of any new musical revolution—has an eclectic and extensive music scene. Bars and clubs feature live music on any given night of the week, usually for a modest cover. Sometimes you can see hugely talented bands for free in parks, music stores, bars, cultural centers, and the occasional alley; in such venues, your money will go a long way (Bud in a brown paper bag is cheap). For a price, you can also see lots of national and international acts, as befits a world-class metropolis. Your best bets for up-to-the-minute music listings are *SF Weekly* and the *Bay Guardian.*

The **Great American Music Hall** (859 O'Farrell St., btw Polk and Larkin Sts., tel. 415/885–0750), a gorgeous old theater that serves as a midsize concert venue, books an innovative blend of rock and world music. Tickets cost $8–$15. Bands on the verge of MTV stardom often play at the **Warfield** (982 Market St., btw 5th and 6th Sts., tel. 415/775–7722) or at the historic, recently reopened **Fillmore** (1805 Geary Blvd., at Fillmore St., tel. 415/346–6000), where tickets run $15–$25.

ROCK **Bottom of the Hill.** This neighborhood space at the bottom of Potrero Hill showcases a huge variety of local bands. Come here for a few nights and you'll acquire a comprehensive sense of the local music scene. On Sunday afternoons the all-you-can-eat barbecue ($3) draws mammoth crowds. *1233 17th St., at Texas St., tel. 415/626–4455.*

Club Chameleon. This cheap, cramped space in the Mission is a haven for indie bands and local, experimental music. When your eardrums start to hurt, head downstairs for Ping-Pong and video games. *853 Valencia St., btw 19th and 20th Sts., tel. 415/821–1891. Cover: $2–$5.*

Kilowatt. On Thursdays, Saturdays, and Sundays, this Mission district bar hosts local, alternative rock bands for an audience seeking minimum attitude and maximum noise. *3160 16th St., btw Guerrero and Valencia Sts., tel. 415/861–2595. Cover: $3–$7.*

Nightbreak. Park your Harley and head inside this trendoid club in the upper Haight for cheap beer and straightahead rock. Come on Sundays at 4 PM for cheap sushi and free live music. *1821 Haight St., btw Shrader and Stanyan Sts., tel. 415/221–9008. Cover: up to $5.*

Paradise Lounge. The quality of music varies widely (to put it kindly) at this hip SoMa cocktail lounge, but with three stages to choose from and a constant flow of people, it's a reliable weekend destination. Upstairs you can play a game of pool, listen to low-key music, or participate in a poetry reading. *1501 Folsom St., at 11th St., tel. 415/861–6906. Cover: $3–$5.*

The Purple Onion. Indulge in $2 pints of Pabst Blue Ribbon, kick back in one of the oversized red vinyl booths, and enjoy garage-style punk and surf music at this underground North Beach lounge. The Onion is open Fridays and Saturdays only. *140 Columbus Ave., btw Pacific Ave. and Jackson St., tel. 415/398–8415. Cover: $3–$5.*

JAZZ Don't fret if you missed the Summer of Love, because San Francisco is once again spearheading something wonderful: a rash of local bands who have taken it upon themselves to stretch the boundaries between funk, hip-hop, and jazz. Venues like the Elbo Room (*see below*), Café du Nord (*see below*), and Club 181 (*see box, below*) devote much space to these new acts: Look for the Broun Fellinis (freestyle jazz with a funky bass line), Alphabet Soup (upbeat, reggae-influenced jazz with *two* rappers), Midnight Voices (jazz-influenced hip-hop), and the Charlie Hunter Trio (more straight-ahead jazz).

The Ace Café. The atmosphere at this SoMa club tends to be cool and sedate, but the quality of the local jazz acts that play here Thursdays and Saturdays warrants attention, and might even put a stop to that intimate conversation you're having. *1539 Folsom St., btw 10th and 11th Sts., tel. 415/621–4752. Cover: $4–$6.*

Café du Nord. The specialty at this often overcrowded Castro-area club is jazz you can afford. The $3–$5 cover charge gets you some *fine* local bands, pool tables, and the chance to stare at young, natty San Franciscans reliving the Jazz Age. *2170 Market St., btw Church and Sanchez Sts., tel. 415/861–5016.*

CoCo Club. A variety of acts come through this small restaurant and performance space South of Market—everything from acoustic rock to avant-garde jazz and blues. It's a good place for a date or casual dinner. *139 8th St., btw Mission and Howard Sts., tel. 415/626–7668. Cover: $3–$5. Entrance to bar on Minna St.*

Noe Valley Ministry. An adventurous booking policy draws some serious talent—from experimental jazz and blues artists to world music acts—into this no-smoking/occasional-drinking church in Noe Valley that moonlights as a performance space. *1021 Sanchez St., near 24th St., tel. 415/282–2317. Cover: $8–$15.*

The message is in the music at St. John's African Orthodox Church (351 Divisadero St., near Oak St., tel. 415/621–4054), where services consist of a rousing two hours of jazz-great John Coltrane's sounds of salvation. All are welcome at both the Sunday (11:45 AM) and Wednesday (6 PM) services.

Pearl's. At this yup-scale jazz joint in North Beach, the surroundings are so comfy, the lights so low, that you fall asleep. Luckily, the music is eye-opening, at least if mainstream, traditional jazz is your thing. And if you stick around late, after the tourists' and middle-aged patrons' bedtimes, you might catch some smoking improvisational jams. *256 Columbus Ave., at Broadway, tel. 415/291–8255. No cover; 2-drink minimum.*

Up and Down Club. Sleek deco digs and live jazz make this SoMa spot the lounge of choice for those who like to pretend San Francisco is New York City. Upstairs you'll find a DJ laying down tracks, but little room to dance. *1151 Folsom St., btw 7th and 8th Sts., tel. 415/626–2388. Closed Tuesdays. Cover: $5; free Wed.*

Upstairs at the Elbo Room. Upstairs at this popular Mission bar you'll find the city's best local hip-hop and jazz bands along with a jovial, young crowd busting a move on the tiny dance floor. *647 Valencia St., near 17th St., tel. 415/552–7788. Cover: $3–$5.*

BLUES While Oakland's blues scene is more renowned, San Francisco's devoted blues followers are pros at supporting local acts and making the most out of what their city has to offer. Several venues, most notably **Slim's** (*see below*) and the **Great American Music Hall** (*see above*), are often stops for traveling blues legends.

The Blue Lamp. This friendly, downtown bar books a variety of blues, jazz, folk, and rock bands nightly, and attracts an equally diverse mix of patrons. Arrive early to stake your spot near the fireplace. *561 Geary St., btw Taylor and Jones Sts., tel. 415/885–1464. Cover: up to $5.*

Grant and Green Blues Club. This dark, smoky bar hosts some raucous blues shows, a welcome change in North Beach, where too many folks sit stiffly in coffeehouses discussing obscure litcrits over bottles of wine. *1731 Grant Ave., at Green St., tel. 415/693–9565. Cover: $2–$5.*

Jacks. Thursdays, Fridays, and Saturdays, Jacks serves up a wide variety of beers and some smokin' jams in a casual, down-home atmosphere. John Lee Hooker has been known to stop by on occasion. As befits a blues club with any class, this lower Fillmore club is *not* located in the best of San Francisco's neighborhoods. *1601 Fillmore St., at Geary Blvd., tel. 415/567–3227. Cover: $5.*

Slim's. This club, owned by Boz Scaggs, features all types of American roots music. A wide variety of blues and jazz acts play here, not to mention the punkers, funkers, and gospel singers who also make occasional appearances. It's personable and fun for all ages (21 and over, that is). *333 11th St., btw Folsom and Harrison Sts., tel. 415/621–3330. Cover: $7–$12.*

EAST BAY

The East Bay music scene is fickle and fly-by-night. Some evenings you won't be able to choose which of several raging scenes to grace with your presence, while other nights it'll seem like you live in the sticks. Berkeley is better known for its student bars and cafés than for its music venues, with only a few real exceptions, such as Blake's (for blues and jazz) and 924 Gilman Street (for straight-edge punk). Though folk, jazz, and world music are prevalent in the East Bay, it's the soulful blues that lure people into the depths of Oakland, home of the West Coast blues.

ROCK **924 Gilman Street.** This all-ages, alcohol-free cooperative features local hard-core garage bands and occasional big-name acts. The music is generally loud and aggressive, the crowd young, sweaty, tattooed, and not afraid to throw themselves around. Most shows cost $5, but you have to buy a $2 membership (valid for one year) to get in the first time. *924 Gilman St., at 8th St., Berkeley, tel. 510/525–9926. From Berkeley BART, Bus 9 north to 8th St.*

The pop-punk band Green Day got its start at 924 Gilman. Now that the band has gone multiplatinum and gets corporate radio play, it only gets sneers from the demanding Gilman Street crowd.

The Berkeley Square. Once the hippest venue in Berkeley for alternative music, both local and national, this 18-and-over club still occasionally attracts some big names. However, its golden years have passed; nowadays, the Square caters to the young and fashionable (i.e., East Bay high-school kids). Call for current schedule. *1333 University Ave., Berkeley, tel. 510/841–6555. From Berkeley BART, Bus 51 west. Cover: $5–$6.*

Merchant's Lunch. Lace up your Doc Martens on Friday and Saturday nights and head to this downtown Oakland club for loud alternative rock. *401 2nd St., at Franklin St. in Oakland, tel. 510/465–8032. Cover: $3–$5.*

JAZZ Jazz greats come through Oakland on a regular basis, making appearances at established venues and putting on special shows. **Koncepts Cultural Gallery** (tel. 510/763–0682), still lacking a room of its own, hosts a fall series at various venues that includes "Jazz in Tongues" and "Word Songs," two evocative forums that blend poetry and music.

Supper Clubs Redux

Recently making a grand reappearance on San Francisco's nightlife scene, supper clubs are an old, savory concept combining live music, classy duds, and fancy food. In the classic vein, the plush, swank Club 181 (181 Eddy St., tel. 415/673–8181) books funky bands—the Mod Squad is a current favorite—for your listening pleasure while you dine on seafood risotto ($13) or cozy up to the elegant, curved bar. A similar crowd is drawn to 330 Ritch Street (330 Ritch St., off Townsend St. btw 3rd and 4th Sts., tel. 415/522–9558), which alternates between jazz and salsa; international tapas (appetizers) are less than $8, and dinner is served until 3:30 AM Fridays and Saturdays. At the apex of sophistication, Julie Ring's Heart and Soul (1695 Polk St., tel. 415/673–7100) attracts classier, professional types and features a pianist 5:30–8:30 PM and jazz thereafter. Pretension does not run rampant here, though you may want to dress up a bit to fit in with the darkly hued interior and snazzy bar. A younger crowd comes out on Fridays and Saturdays to dine and dance at Miss Pearl's Jam House (601 Eddy St., tel. 415/775–5267), unabashedly Caribbean in its menu, music, and decor.

Other supper clubs worth checking out include: 11 (374 11th St., tel. 415/431–3337) for Italian cuisine, jazz, and a good-looking crowd; and Coconut Grove (1415 Van Ness Ave., tel. 415/776–1616), the most upscale joint in town—Tom Jones was featured on opening night. All are worth a visit when you want more with your meal than a mariachi band.

Kimball's East. In Emeryville, a small community tucked between Berkeley and Oakland, look for this excellent jazz and supper club, which books well-known jazz musicians Wednesday through Sunday. Downstairs, **Kimball's Carnival** draws big names in Latin jazz and Caribbean music, with an audience of mostly older professionals. *5800 Shellmound St., tel. 510/658–2555, Emeryville. From MacArthur BART, Bus 6 or 57 west on 40th St. to Pacific Park Plaza. Cover: $10–$25.*

While it's more "background" than "spotlight" jazz, the music at the Bistro (see Bars, above) is always good and always free.

Yoshi's. Yoshi's is a historic club and restaurant, serving up sushi and jazz in sophisticated style. The clientele knows its music, and past acts have included Cecil Taylor, Anthony Braxton, and Ornette Coleman. Visit while you can—Yoshi's is considering closing its doors, and may or may not relocate to Jack London Square. *6030 Claremont Ave., Oakland, tel. 510/652–9200. From Rockridge BART, walk 3 blocks north on College Ave., left on Claremont Ave. Cover: $5–$30.*

BLUES In the years following World War II, Oakland gave birth to the gritty, hurts-so-bad-I'm-gonna-die music known as the West Coast blues. Even after 50 years, it still flourishes in clubs and bars all over town. Dedicated to the preservation of blues, jazz, and gospel, the **Bay Area Blues Society** (tel. 510/836–2227) sponsors shows and festivals year-round, and is a wellspring of information about West Coast blues.

Blake's. This restaurant and jazz joint opened in the late 1940s, and since then it's become a Berkeley institution. The upstairs dining room serves decent food to a yuppie crowd, but the cramped basement downstairs—a no-frills bar with a sawdust-covered floor—occasionally hosts some of the best blues acts in the area, plus the occasional alternative rock band. *2367 Telegraph Ave., near Durant Ave., Berkeley, tel. 510/848–0886. 1 block from U.C. campus. Cover: $5 and up.*

Oakland's blues scene is rough around the edges, but that only adds to its smoky, sweaty, raspy charm.

Eli's Mile High Club. The reputed birthplace of West Coast blues remains a consistently good bet, continuing to highlight promising local acts plus more renowned performers. It's a small club with a pool table, soul food, and music Thursday–Sunday. The kitchen opens around 6:30 PM and music starts by 9. *3629 Martin Luther King Jr. Way, Oakland, tel. 510/655–6661. From Berkeley, Bus 15 south on Martin Luther King Jr. Way. Cover: $3–$8.*

The Fifth Amendment. High-quality blues and jazz acts play to a largely African-American crowd of professionals, students, and neighborhood old-timers. Dress up a bit for some absolutely searing music. *3255 Lakeshore Ave., Oakland, tel. 510/832–3242. From MacArthur BART, Bus 57 to cnr Lakeshore Ave. and Lake Park Way. Cover: $5–$10.*

FOLK **The Freight and Salvage.** At this low-key coffeehouse you'll find Berkeley's thriving (and aging) folk-music community enjoying a wide variety of entertainment—everything from world-class accordionists to spoken-word performers to lefty singer/songwriters. *1111 Addison St., near San Pablo Ave. in Berkeley, tel. 510/548–1761. From Berkeley BART, Bus 51 west to San Pablo Ave., 1 block south to Addison St. Cover: $7–$13. Wheelchair access.*

The Starry Plough. This popular Irish pub near the Berkeley–Oakland border offers an eclectic mix of folk music and not-too-extreme rock bands, usually for about $5. Join the older, politically left crowd for a pint or two of Guinness, Bass, or Anchor Steam and a game of darts. *3101 Shattuck Ave., at Prince St., Berkeley, tel. 510/841–2082. From Ashby Bart, walk 1 block east on Prince St. Cover: up to $6. Wheelchair access.*

Join both the pros and the amateurs at the Starry Plough on Monday nights at 7 PM for free Irish dance lessons.

WORLD MUSIC **Ashkenaz.** There's a different live beat here every night, from African to Cajun to Bulgarian folk. You can take dance lessons first or just come and wing it. You won't find any brain-dead ravers here, only a devoted group of older locals and students out to broaden their cultural horizons. Light vegetarian fare ($2.50–$3) is served starting at 8 PM. *1317 San Pablo Ave., Berkeley, tel. 510/525–5054. From Berkeley BART, Bus 9 west to San Pablo Ave. Cover: $5–$8. Wheelchair access.*

La Peña. This Latin American cultural center offers a wide selection of live music, political lectures, performance pieces, and films on Central and South American issues. Many shows are benefits, so covers often masquerade as "donations" ranging from $5 to $15. *3105 Shattuck Ave., Berkeley, tel. 510/849–2568. Next to Starry Plough (see above). Wheelchair access.*

Movie Houses

Somehow, even with the scope of nightlife available, going to the movies remains a consistently popular source of entertainment in the Bay Area, where you can find everything from the latest Quentin Tarantino sensation to the celluloid masterpiece of an unknown film student. You can also catch lots of limited screenings at the independent theaters scattered around, or take advantage of the numerous film festivals that occur each year (*see below*). And, if you keep an eye out for matinees and sneak in your own Junior Mints, seeing a flick won't cost you a small fortune.

SAN FRANCISCO

For new releases, everyone goes to the **Kabuki 8** (1881 Post St., at Fillmore St., tel. 415/931–9800), even though some of the octoplex's screens are pretty tiny and seating is limited. Tickets run $7, but you get a $2 discount with student ID. Take advantage of the validated parking in Japan Center, since some of the streets here aren't too safe for your car. The *Bay Guardian* and *SF Weekly* have complete listings and reviews for both first-run theaters and rep houses.

During spring and summer, five big film festivals roll through town, starting in March with the 14-year-old **San Francisco Asian-American Film Festival** (tel. 415/863–0814). In April look for the **San Francisco International Film Festival** (tel. 415/931–3456), which features quality films from all over the world. During the last two weeks in June, the much-loved **International Lesbian and Gay Film Festival** (tel. 415/703–8650) coincides with gay pride week and is the largest such event in the world. The **Jewish Film Festival** (tel. 510/548–0556) breezes into town—one week at the Castro Theatre in San Francisco and one week at the U.C. Theater in Berkeley—the end of July and beginning of August. Finally, September brings the increasingly popular **Festival Cine Latino** (tel. 415/553–8135).

If all this inspires you to make your own movies, a great resource is **Artists' Television Access** (992 Valencia St., at 21st St., tel. 415/824–3890), a nonprofit media-arts center in the Mission founded in 1986 to perpetuate knowledge about television, video, and film. You can rent editing facilities at reasonable rates—or take workshops on production and editing—then show your homemade video to other artists and get feedback. Their screenings of offbeat films provide a night of cheap entertainment at $3–$5.

The Casting Couch Micro Theatre. Come to this deluxe 46-person screening room for an intimate and unique viewing experience. Sink into one of the sofas and let the wait staff bring you cookies while you check out not-so-recent releases and older, hidden gems. *950 Battery St., btw Green and Vallejo Sts., tel. 415/986–7001. Admission: $8.50.*

Castro Theatre. The most beautiful place to see a film in San Francisco, the Castro shows a wide selection of rare, foreign, and unusual films that play anywhere from a night to a week or two. However, the specialties here are camp, classics of all genres, and new releases of interest to lesbian and gay viewers. And the man who rises out of the floor playing the Wurlitzer organ is guaranteed to make you giggle for the sheer kitschiness of it all. *429 Castro St., btw Market and 18th Sts., tel. 415/621–6120.*

The Red Vic. Films at this co-op range from the artsy to the cultish to the rare, and you can order herbal tea or coffee to accompany your popcorn with yeast. *1727 Haight St., btw Cole and Shrader Sts., tel. 415/668–3994.*

The Roxie. Movie snobs—unite! This theater in the Mission shows political, cult, and otherwise bent films. The audience can get raucous, probably because they're blowing off steam after carrying the weight of the world on their shoulders all day long. *3117 16th St., at Valencia St., tel. 415/863–1087.*

EAST BAY

Of the several big cinema complexes that show first-run releases in the East Bay, the **Grand Lake Theatre** (3200 Grand Ave., tel. 510/452–3556) is by far the most stylish. Built in 1926, this ornate movie house just east of Oakland's Lake Merritt has been (regrettably) divided into four midsize theaters—slightly diminishing its grandeur. Discriminating film enthusiasts head to Berkeley, which has two theaters specializing in the rare, the old, and the avant-garde. The **U.C. Theater** (2036 University Ave., tel. 510/843–6267), in operation since 1917, shows foreign films and classics; double features are juxtaposed with great creativity, and billings change daily. The theater is cavernous, the seats lumpy, and the popcorn refreshingly cheap. In case you've never seen a performance of *The Rocky Horror Picture Show,* it plays here at midnight Saturdays.

The **Pacific Film Archive,** in the U.C. Berkeley Art Museum (2621 Durant Ave., tel. 510/642–1124), caters to hard-core film enthusiasts with its impressive collection of rare titles. Films change nightly and often center around a certain theme—past offerings have included film portrayals of people with disabilities and an evening of Clint Eastwood films. Filmmakers often show up to discuss their work before the show. Admission costs about $7, $5 for PFA members. No food or drinks are allowed.

Theater

The strength of the Bay Area's theater scene lies firmly in the modern, the multicultural, and the experimental. Recent NEA cuts have hit hard here—the underground scene is reeling but still on its feet. Local troupes to search out include the **Sick and Twisted Players** (tel. 415/861–8972), a mostly gay group that specializes in campy, staged interpretations of films. Also keep an eye on **A Traveling Jewish Theater** (2860 Mariposa St., tel. 415/399–1809); they received a large NEA grant in 1995 and are growing nicely into their new Project Artaud space. If your tastes are less experimental, **ACT** (American Contemporary Theater, tel. 415/749–2228) and the Berkeley Repertory Theater (*see below*) are both large operations that generally present quality productions. The truly mainstream, Broadway-type shows usually appear at the downtown **Curran Theater** (445 Geary St., tel. 415/474–3800).

In addition to housing Theater Artaud, the Noh Space, and A Traveling Jewish Theater, Project Artaud serves as an artists' "loft space": By qualifying as professional actors, painters, or musicians, artists can get bargain long-term leases and rents on live/work studios. It's basically a huge dorm, only filled with intriguing people.

Sometimes, however, "theater" sounds too involved and you just want a night of cabaret. The productions at **Josie's Cabaret & Juice Joint** (3583 16th St., near Market St., tel. 415/861–7933), an established gay cultural center, lean toward campy cabaret and riotous stand-up, though you'll see the occasional serious piece as well. At **Climate Theater** (252

When Style is Paramount

An art-deco landmark in downtown Oakland, the Paramount Theatre is a beautifully restored motion picture palace that now houses both the Oakland Symphony and the Oakland Ballet (see below). Classic and silent films are featured on intermittent Friday evenings, complete with pre-show organ music and old newsreel clips. Live rock or jazz performances are also sometimes held at this stately venue. Tours of the theater are available the first and third Saturday of the month at 10 AM for $21. 2025 Broadway, near 19th St., tel. 510/465–6400. Wheelchair access.

9th St., tel. 415/626–9196), you can catch small ensembles and solo performers doing original work. Tickets at both venues cost around $10.

SAN FRANCISCO

Beach Blanket Babylon. This treasure trove of San Francisco lore has been selling out most nights for the past three decades. While it's slightly tired, the revue still entertains with talented musicians, polished performers, impeccable timing, extra-large headgear, and a zesty, zany script that changes to incorporate topical references and characters. Get tickets well in advance, say "Ouch!," and be comforted that a significant chunk of your $18–$43 goes to local charities. The under-21 set can attend Sunday matinee performances only. *Club Fugazi, 678 Green St., tel. 415/421–4222.*

Brava Studio Theater. Brava! For Women in the Arts is the official name of this resident theater company, a stronghold of women's work. The mostly experimental programming includes a spring series of works-in-progress by local playwrights and performance artists. Tickets run $10–$15. *2180 Bryant St., tel. 415/487–5401.*

Exit Theater. One of the best venues downtown is this café-theater, where small but imaginative productions focus on drama, sometimes drawing in video, music, or other media. The subject matter can get pretty raunchy—one recent performance was titled "Jesus on the Rag"—but the shows are well done, especially for the price of $5–$10. *156 Eddy St., at Mason St., tel. 415/673–3847.*

Lorraine Hansberry Theatre. A consistently high-quality place for African-American theater, the Lorraine Hansberry performs experimental, musical, and classical works by African Americans and other writers of color. The work of talented young playwrights is often premiered at the theater. The 1996 playbill includes a new play about Huey Newton and the Black Panthers—*Servant of the People,* by local playwright Robert Alexander—and the world premier of Ifa Bayeza's *Homer G and the Rhapsodies,* a hip-hop transposition of Homer's *The Iliad* set in modern-day Detroit. Tickets cost $18–$22, with same-day, half-price seats available for students. *620 Sutter St., tel. 415/474–8800.*

Magic Theater. The Magic is San Francisco's standby for the modern and mildly experimental. Sam Shepherd wrote a lot of his plays for this venue in the late '70s and early '80s; the theater continues to premiere innovative American works, and Sam himself returns from time to time. Tickets for performances run $15–$35. *Fort Mason Center, Bldg. D, tel. 415/441–8822.*

The Marsh—one of San Francisco's best experimental theaters—uses the slogan, "a breeding ground for new performance." Get it?

The Marsh. This is one of the best venues around for experimental solo performance. The Marsh hosts primarily new, local works, and has been a springboard to greater fame. Though the shows are not consistently excellent, they are almost always intriguing. The 99 house seats include a cozy corner of sofas. Tickets cost $8–$15. *1062 Valencia St., near 22nd St., tel. 415/826–5750.*

San Francisco Mime Troupe. This agitprop ensemble puts on scathing political comedies and musicals—free! They appear in Golden Gate Park and other Bay Area parks between July 4 and Labor Day. Bring a picnic and spend a terrifically entertaining sunny afternoon. *Tel. 415/285–1717.*

Theatre Rhinoceros. The only strictly gay and lesbian theater company in San Francisco stages consistently reliable dramas and comedies in its tiny Mission district hall. Ticket prices are $12–$18, with $2 off for students. Stagings for 1996 include a drag-king musical called *Hillbillies on the Moon,* by Leigh Crow (a.k.a. Elvis Herselvis) and Kelly Kittell. *2926 16th St., tel. 415/861–5079.*

Theater of Yugen/Noh Space. The mission of this theater is to bring the Japanese aesthetic to Western audiences. Of the four East/West fusion works staged each year, three are primarily in English and deal with Japanese stories or themes, while the fourth is *kyogen,* traditional

Japanese comedy, performed in Japanese on a simple, black-draped stage. Tickets cost $8–$15, with small discounts for students. *2840 Mariposa St., at Alabama St., tel. 415/621–0507.*

EAST BAY

Berkeley Repertory Theater. Berkeley is currently cultivating an arts movement downtown, with the Berkeley Repertory Theater as its keystone. The company, which is about to expand, is Berkeley's main venue, staging performances every night except Mondays; they also have some matinees in the smaller theater. The works are rarely experimental, but they are meticulously produced and well worth the $22–$35 ticket price—and only half of that if you can score student rush tickets a half hour before the show. In March 1996, the Berkeley Rep will stage *Slavs,* a new play by Tony Kushner (of *Angels in America* fame). *2025 Addison St., tel. 510/845–4700.*

The "Noh Space" is more than a meaningless bad pun: it's a bad pun based on "noh," the 600-year-old tradition of Japanese tragedy.

Black Repertory Group. Founded in 1965, this Oakland company continues to be committed to the production of works by black authors and the celebration of black culture in the United States. Biggies like Langston Hughes and James Weldon Johnson are most frequently represented, in haphazard but heartfelt musical and dramatic productions. The $10 admission ($8 students) is worthwhile if you don't get hung up on missed cues and warbling singers. If you do, consider the $5 Saturday matinee. Sometimes the most interesting works are the one-act plays shown for $3 on Sundays. *3201 Adeline St., tel. 510/652–2120.*

Multimedia

As technology increasingly affects theater, video, dance, and music, it also becomes a link—a point of fusion—for different types of creative expression. The following venues are most committed to exploring the evolving relationship among performance media.

Center for the Arts at Yerba Buena Gardens. The bright yellow and red of this modern theater's lobby give way to the more metallic luster of the interior space. Though recent budget problems have threatened the center's ambitious mission, it currently draws top dancers, musicians, and dramatists and sometimes combines them in large-scale ways. The theater itself has superb acoustics and is absolutely souped-up technologically. Despite the 750 seats it feels like an intimate space. Tickets start at around $10. *700 Howard St., at 3rd St., tel. 415/978–2787.*

Cramped Quarters

San Francisco artists have a wonderful habit of gathering together groups of friends and devising tiny performance venues of their own. We can't guarantee the longevity of any of the following, but we can promise intimate, intriguing shows, often for under $5. These spaces can also provide an entry into other facets of San Francisco's alternative arts culture. Luna Sea (2926 16th St., 415/863–2989) is a women's group upstairs from Theatre Rhinoceros in the Mission; they sponsor readings, music, and other events, often as benefits. In the Western Addition, 848 Community Space (848 Divisadero St., tel. 415/387–9410) specializes in screwy productions in a variety of media—sometimes all at once. Z Space (940 Howard St., tel. 415/543–9505), formed by Zuni Café's wait staff (see Civic Center, in Chapter 4), often hosts readings of new plays by local writers in its SoMa locale.

George Coates Performance Works. Technological wizard George Coates has brought his prowess to the theater, where he mixes the latest computer technology with the stage. Performances, held under the soaring vaulted ceiling of a former church, involve music, video, and motion and use only a scrim to create "virtual" sets. The effect—with your polarized glasses (provided)—is phenomenal, a real challenge to the meaning and substance of live performance. A left-leaning political moral usually accompanies all this wizardry. Tickets cost $25–$35. *110 McAllister St., at Leavenworth St., tel. 415/863–8520.*

Intersection for the Arts. The stark, stone-walled space in the Mission seats 65 for solo and group musical performances, poetry readings, workshops, and lectures. The gallery space upstairs features intriguing sound and/or visual installations. The 30-year-old Intersection is San Francisco's oldest alternative art space; shows here are not only experimental but also consistently good. Ticket prices vary widely but are usually around $10–$20, a couple dollars less for students. *446 Valencia St., btw 15th and 16th Sts., tel. 415/626–2787. Free nighttime parking at 670 Valencia.*

In March 1995, Intersection for the Arts witnessed a historical moment by hosting the largest known didgeridoo jam session ever assembled in the United States: 17 of the Aborigine, bamboo trumpets wailing together in a single piece.

New Langton Arts. This far-reaching organization has been around for a couple decades, providing local artists with both grants to complete their work and an audience to appreciate it. New Langton's work is similar to that of Theater Artaud, but on a smaller scale. Upstairs is a bright, continually changing gallery; downstairs is a 75-seat, well-equipped multimedia theater. *1246 Folsom St., tel. 415/626–5416.*

Theater Artaud. Artaud boasts one of the most interesting performance halls in town: a cavernous warehouse space that you enter from behind the scaffolding of 300 seats. The space yields eerie echoes that, because of the experimental nature of what goes on here, generally add to the effect. The local and traveling shows—often dance, drama, and music all at once—are excellent and provide insight into the experimental scene both in San Francisco and internationally. Tickets run $10–$20 and are cheaper weeknights. The neighborhood is sketchy, but the experience is worth it. *450 Florida St., btw 17th and Mariposa Sts., tel. 415/621–7797.*

Classical Music

SAN FRANCISCO

San Francisco Symphony. The big news here is Michael Tilson Thomas, the vibrant new conductor who's already shaken things up after 10 years of Herbert Blomstedt's steady but less than daring leadership. Tilson Thomas made a name for himself with the London Symphony Orchestra and is bringing new and needed energy to the San Francisco's biggest symphony. Promising 1996 programs include Milhaud's *La Création du Monde,* Berlioz's *Symphonie Fantastique,* and Stravinsky's *Canticum sacrum* and *Symphony of Psalms.* The Lego-inspired interior of Davies Symphony Hall is surreal at first glance, but the odd interior architecture creates good acoustics for even the cheapest balcony seats ($22). The best deal, though, are the $9 center terrace seats: A limited number are available in advance but sell out quickly; 40 more go on sale two hours before the show. The seats hover directly over the orchestra, yielding an off-balance sound but a fantastic, face-on view of the conductor and an intimate look at the musicians' work. *Davies Symphony Hall, 201 Van Ness Ave., at Grove St., tel. 415/864–6000.*

San Francisco Opera. The local opera company puts on quality performances, often hurling huge amounts of money into one truly knockout production each season (usually a work by Wagner). The resident chorus and soloists are quite good, and the opera usually manages to lure a few real-life opera stars each year. Unfortunately, astronomical ticket prices force serious consideration before running after one's favorite prima donna; tickets start at more than $20, and for acceptable seats you'll pay closer to $50. Student rush tickets go on sale two hours before curtain and cost $20, and there's almost always something left. The shows are good, but very few of them are worth the advance ticket prices. The War Memorial Opera House (301 Van Ness Ave.) is closed for renovations until 1997; until then the company will stage its operas at the Bill Graham Memorial Civic Auditorium (cnr Grove and Polk Sts.) and at the Orpheum Theater (1192 Market St., near 8th St.). *Box office: 199 Grove St., at Van Ness Ave., tel. 415/864–3330.*

Herbst Theater. World-class soloists and occasional groups play at the elegant Herbst, located in the Veterans Building downtown, usually drawing $20 and up per seat. Though the theater is plush, the acoustics are mediocre. *401 Van Ness Ave., tel. 415/392–4400.*

San Francisco Conservatory. The city's major music school has something going on almost nightly, whether it's performed by students (generally free), faculty ($6–$10), or the Conservatory Orchestra ($6–$10). Quality is unpredictable, but with the school's fine reputation, odds are you'll see something worthwhile. *1201 Ortega St., tel. 415/759–3477.*

San Francisco Contemporary Music Players. The biggest-name contemporary company in the area sadly hosts only six performances a year. Concerts cost $14 ($6 students), and generally feature a few brand-new works, some "oldies" like Steve Reich, and works by foreign composers. Performances take place, and tickets can be purchased, at Center for the Arts. *700 Howard St., at 3rd St., tel. 415/978–ARTS or 415/252–6235 for programming info.*

In 1996, the San Francisco Opera will present the West Coast premiere of Harvey Milk, a contemporary opera based on the life and death of the San Francisco supervisor who was the first openly gay person elected to U.S. public office. He was shot and killed at City Hall in 1978 by ex-Supervisor Dan White.

EAST BAY

While the East Bay puts on fewer major productions, you can easily find an inexpensive, peaceful venue for a concert. For chamber music, jazz, or world music in a beautiful, intimate set-

Classics on the Cheap

If you're not sure you like this fine-arts stuff enough to pay big money, the following options will introduce you to highbrow culture without saturating your credit card.

If you want to pay nothing at all, hope for blue skies. On summer Sundays, the Stern Grove Midsummer Music Festival (tel. 415/252–6252) brings the symphony and ballet to Stern Grove in San Francisco for 2 PM performances. During spring, summer, and the Christmas season, the Brown Bag Opera series (415/565–6434) pitches divas against traffic noise for your listening pleasure: Performances are held at 12:15 at 1 Bush Street and 50 Post Street, among other Bay Area locations. You can also find free, or nearly free, concerts at local universities: U.C. Berkeley's free Wednesday Noon Concerts (tel. 510/642–4864 or 510/642–2678) showcase talented professors and students; Oakland's Mills College (see below) is well known for its sometimes-free contemporary music program; and the San Francisco Conservatory hosts free performances, which generally (see above) keep to the straight and narrow.

If you're willing to spend a little, try TIX Bay Area (251 Stockton St., btw Post and Geary Sts., tel. 415/433–7827), a same-day, half-price ticket booth on Union Square. Otherwise, most venues provide discounts for students with ID, and larger venues often offer student rush tickets.

ting, try the **Maybeck Recital Hall** (1537 Euclid Ave., Berkeley, tel. 510/848–3228), designed by revered Berkeley architect Bernard Maybeck. Also in Berkeley, the **New Giorgi Gallery** (2911 Claremont Ave., tel. 510/843–9930) holds small weekend performances by local artists for $10 ($8 students); Thursday nights bring poetry readings or more experimental performances for $5.

Berkeley Opera. For a company that began only 16 years ago as a mom-and-pop venture (the ex-professor who started it just wanted to *sing*), the Berkeley Opera is doing pretty well. The company stages four operas each season in small venues, like the Maybeck-designed Hillside Club (2286 Cedar St.) in north Berkeley, to crowds of 200 or so. Talented singers help the quarters feel intimate, rather than cramped. The leads often come from the San Francisco Opera Chorus—younger singers looking for a break—and a few have reportedly gone on to the Met. Tickets sound pricey at $25 (students $20), but for opera-lovers who have experienced only large houses, this is a pleasant change. Tickets can be purchased by phone or at the opera venue. *Tel. 510/841–1903.*

Berkeley Symphony Orchestra. By an unbelievable stroke of luck, the Berkeley Symphony Orchestra has managed to hang onto Kent Nagano, a world-famous conductor who spends part of the year with Berkeley, part with the renowned Lyon Opera in France. His inspired performances—at venues throughout town—cost $16–$30 and are well worth it. *Tel. 510/841–2800.*

Mills College. One of the hottest places around for contemporary composition and performance, Mills College hosts an extensive season of classical and experimental concerts. The wonderfully colorful hall is out of the way in the Oakland hills; if you're lucky enough to be coming by car, call ahead for directions. Some shows are free; some run $5–$10. *5000 MacArthur Blvd., Oakland, tel. 510/430–2296. From Coliseum BART, Bus 56 west.*

Dance

The world's very best dance troupes pass through the Bay Area, many of them stopping at **Zellerbach Hall** (U.C. Berkeley campus, tel. 510/642–9988) or at the **Palace of Fine Arts** (3301 Lyon St., San Francisco, tel. 415/563–6504). The Bay Area's strength, as usual, lies in the more progressive and experimental companies. One Oakland-based troupe to watch for is the **Dance Brigade** (tel. 510/652–0752), a casually feminist, very cool troupe that subverts classics; look for shows like *Revolutionary Nutcracker Sweetie.* Also in Oakland, look for **Dimensions Dance Theater** (1428 Alice St., tel. 510/465–3363), a young, vibrant company that plays with African influences. Check the *Bay Guardian* for schedules and consistent recommendations from dance critic Rita Felciano.

Cal Performances (tel. 510/642–9988), a first-class series of dance, theater, and music performances, takes place in Zellerbach Hall, on the Berkeley campus.

SAN FRANCISCO

San Francisco Ballet. Somehow this company has managed to build a reputation as one of the premier ballets in the country, raising questions about our national standards. The productions are minimum-standard and mainstream, the performances competent but generally uninspired. The $10 ticket price is better spent on smaller, more progressive groups. While the War Memorial Opera House is closed for renovations, the ballet will bounce between the Center for the Arts (700 Howard St.), the Palace of Fine Arts (3301 Lyon St.), and Zellerbach Hall (U.C. Berkeley campus). *Box office (1996 only): 455 Franklin St., at Grove St., 415/703–9400.*

Asian-American Dance Collective. This studio and its fantastically energetic resident dance company, Unbound Spirit, meld modern and traditional Asian movements into unique dance forms, performing the fascinating results both in-house and at theaters throughout town ($15, $8 students). At least one show each year features the work of an independent Asian-American choreographer. *223 Mississippi St., at Mariposa St., tel. 415/552–8980.*

Footwork Studio. Want to experience the cutting edge in the dance world? Try this local company's weekend shows. The small, informal space is packed to capacity most nights with avid audiences enjoying the vibrant creativity of the Joe Goode performance group. The first Thursday of each run is free for students; otherwise, students get a couple dollars off the usual $5–$12 admission. Footwork also offers beginner and intermediate dance classes ($9 per class). *3221 22nd St., at Mission St., tel. 415/824–5044.*

Third Wave Dance House. The spirit of Third Wave is African-driven. Performances, which cost $10–$15, are often experimental and almost always feature live percussionists. Wednesday and Sunday evenings bring "Barefoot Boogie" jams ($6) at 7:30 PM. Dance classes for all abilities, at $10 a pop, delve into Haitian, hip-hop, and West African dance traditions, among others. *3316 24th St., at Mission St., tel. 415/282–4020.*

EAST BAY

Oakland Ballet. Thirty years in the business hasn't spoiled this company. By staying flexible, it's avoided the trap of mediocrity that constantly threatens San Francisco's ballet, symphony, and opera. This a classical troupe, but company productions often explore the outer boundaries of classicism. Seasons often feature successful revivals from the early 1900s as well as new works set to contemporary music. Performances are held in the grand old Paramount Theater downtown (*see box, above*); tickets run $12–$34. *Oakland Ballet box office: 1428 Broadway, tel. 510/452–9288.*

WHERE TO SLEEP 7

By Danna Harman, with Alice Chang and Sharron Wood

San Francisco offers the best selection of lodging in the Bay Area. You'll find some truly unusual bed-and-breakfasts here; even the cheap hotels have a little bit of character. For those who are looking for gorgeous open space surprisingly close to the city, Marin County's hostels and campgrounds offer a night at a woodsy hostel or beach campsite for less than $10. But the best-kept secret in the Bay Area is the San Mateo County Coast—its hostels and campgrounds are as beautifully situated as those in Marin, but are much less populated. Other options are less attractive—grimy motels in the East Bay, astronomically priced bed-and-breakfasts in Marin County, or chain hotels in the South Bay that cater to business travelers.

San Francisco

San Francisco's neighborhoods are each quite distinctive—the sanitized hipness of North Beach and Russian Hill, home of MTV's *The Real World;* the grunge-meets-hippie fusion in the Haight; the gay culture of the Castro; and the city's Latino and bohemian hangout, the Mission district. Visitors can sample the city's distinct flavors in specialty hotels, some of which you probably wouldn't take your grandmother to. Only in San Francisco will you find a leather-and-Levi's gay B&B, an art B&B complete with easels and plenty of light, or an inn whose nightly accommodations include "The Summer of Love Room" and "The Japanese Tea Garden Room."

For an expensive city, San Francisco has a surprisingly large assortment of reasonably priced accommodations. For a great no-frills deal, stay in one of the city's nine hostels, where a bed will only set you back about $12, or in one of the residential hotels that populate downtown and North Beach. For a little bit more ($30–$50 a night), many small downtown hotels offer charming "European-style" rooms (i.e., the toilet's down the hall). And while there are no campgrounds within the city limits, free—and beautiful—sites are available just north of the Golden Gate Bridge in the Marin Headlands (*see* Sausalito, *below*).

If you don't reserve one to two weeks in advance in summer, you may be exiled to the strip of generic motels along Lombard Street in the Marina District. These motels are about a 20-minute bus ride from downtown (on Bus 76), but are quite close to Fisherman's Wharf, the Marina Green, and the Golden Gate Bridge. On Lombard, you'll pay $50–$70 for a double—stay here only as a last resort. Sixth Street in the South of Market area has its share of similar "last resort" places, but the neighborhood can be unsafe; if you do want to stay in SoMa, try one of the hostels. The places listed below will put you up for a night, a week, or (in some cases) a month. If you just can't bear to leave, we've included some tips on how to find a long-term home.

HOTELS AND MOTELS

Directions below are given from the downtown BART/MUNI stations along Market Street. To reach the stations from San Francisco International Airport, take SamTrans (*see* Getting In, Out, and Around, in Chapter 1): The 7F is an express bus that has luggage limits, while the 7B is a local bus that allows heavy bags. Either one will drop you off on Mission Street, 1 block south of Market; just ask the driver for the stop nearest your station.

THE CASTRO Not surprisingly, the most prominent gay neighborhood in the United States offers a wide variety of accommodations tailored to gay and lesbian travelers. Although the ones nearest Castro Street are pricey, the hotels on upper Market are more affordable. In June, reserve way, way, way in advance as thousands of visitors arrive in the area for the San Francisco Lesbian, Gay, Bisexual, Transgender Pride Celebration, San Francisco Pride for short (formerly known as the Gay and Lesbian Freedom Day Parade). For a map of Castro lodging, *see* Haight, Castro, and Mission Lodging map, *below.*

➢ **UNDER $55 • Twin Peaks.** Despite being newly redone in pastels, the generic motel decor is still nondescript, though firm beds and clean bathrooms more than compensate. Doubles are just $38 ($45 with private bath); weekly rates are $135–$170, depending on room size. You should be able to get a room any time, though they recommend calling first. *2160 Market St., btw Church and Sanchez Sts., tel. 415/621–9467. MUNI K, L, or M Streetcar to Church St., walk 1 block SW on Market St. 60 rooms.*

➢ **UNDER $85 • 24 Henry.** This charming B&B has six doubles (two with bath) and caters to a mostly gay and lesbian clientele. The rooms are colorful and cozy, the showers are big enough for two, and a complimentary breakfast is served in the Victorian-style parlor. Rian and Walter, the proprietors, are happy to help point you in the right direction—whether toward a restaurant or the gym. Singles are $55–$95 per night, doubles $75–$95. *24 Henry St., btw 14th and 15th Sts., tel. 415/864–5686 or 800/900–5686. MUNI J Streetcar to 16th and Church Sts., walk 3 blocks west to Noe St., 3 blocks north to Henry St. Reservations advised.*

➢ **UNDER $100 • The Black Stallion.** The city's only leather-and-Levi's B&B provides gay men—as well as a few lesbians and adventurous straight couples—with an immaculate, comfortable home base three blocks south of Harvey Milk Plaza. The Black Stallion has nine rooms, each with a variety of original artwork and sculptures, as well as gorgeous woodwork and one working fireplace. None has a private bathroom, though. Room rates ($85–$110, depending on the season and room size) include a hearty breakfast and unlimited use of the kitchen and sun deck. *635 Castro St., at 19th St., tel. 415/863–0131. MUNI K, L, or M Streetcar to Castro St., walk south 2 blocks on Castro St. Reservations a must in summer.*

CHINATOWN Chinatown is noisy, with recent immigrants crowded onto narrow sidewalks filled with meat and produce markets that open right onto the sidewalk. This is tourist central, bounded on one side by North Beach and on the other by the Financial District and Union Square. But Chinatown is almost as quiet at night as it is bustling during the day, and can provide a peaceful place to lay your head after an evening out on the town. For a map of Chinatown hotels, *see* Downtown San Francisco Lodging map, *below.*

➢ **UNDER $40 • Hotel Astoria.** This hotel near the Chinatown Gates is a real bargain—if you're prepared to share a bathroom. Pleasantly decorated singles with TVs cost $31 a night, doubles with two twin beds are $36. For a double with a private bath, expect to pay $51 and up. Although the rooms are decent and clean, the best thing about this place is its location, in a relatively safe neighborhood a few blocks from Union Square and North Beach, inches from Chinatown. Europhiles will be glad to know that the Goethe Institute is next door and that a café and an international newsstand specializing in French publications are right across the street—but you didn't come to Chinatown to sip espresso with Europeans, did you? *510 Bush St., at Grant Ave., tel. 415/434–8889. From Montgomery St. BART/MUNI, walk 2 blocks west on Post St., 2 blocks north on Grant Ave. 80 rooms. Credit card required for reservations.*

➢ **UNDER $65 • Grant Plaza.** Near the Chinatown Gate, this large, characterless hotel offers a bargain comparable to hostel rates for groups of four—two double beds for $74. You also get some luxuries that AYH doesn't provide, including private baths, color TVs, and phones.

If you're not traveling in a posse, expect to pay $42 for one person, $55 for two. The small but immaculate rooms are popular with families and older travelers. *465 Grant Ave., btw Bush and Pine Sts., tel. 415/434–3883 or 800/472–6899. From Montgomery St. BART/MUNI, walk 2 blocks west on Post St., 2½ blocks north on Grant Ave. 72 rooms.*

CIVIC CENTER The area around the Civic Center should be a great place to stay. Davies Symphony Hall, the Opera House, and a host of theaters are all within easy walking distance, and many of the city's public transport lines converge here. Sadly, the Civic Center can also be quite dangerous, especially at night, due to an active drug scene. After dark, solo travelers—especially women—should avoid the triangle formed by Market, Larkin, and Geary streets. For a map of Civic Center hotels, *see* Downtown San Francisco Lodging map, *below.*

➢ **UNDER $40** • **Aida Hotel.** Tourists from all over the world sleep at this centrally located hotel on Market Street, one block from Civic Center BART. Doubles with TV and phone cost $37; rooms with a private bath cost $8 more. The generic motel decor wouldn't satisfy a true diva, but at least the rooms are new and clean. And since there are 174 rooms, you can probably get something at the last minute, even during high season. *1087 Market St., at 7th St., tel. 415/863–4141. From Civic Center BART/MUNI, walk 1 block NE on Market St. Breakfast included, luggage storage available.*

➢ **UNDER $55** • **Albergo Verona.** In a neighborhood that's central but dicey, this beautifully renovated turn-of-the-century hotel is a safe haven that attracts all sorts of international tourists. Rooms, some with private bath, are a good deal at $40–$50 for a double. Ask about weekly rates. They also have 14 dorm spaces in two-, four-, and six-person rooms, which rent for $17 per person; all rates include morning coffee and doughnuts. *317 Leavenworth St., at Eddy St., tel. 415/771–4242 or 800/422–3646. From Powell St. BART/MUNI, walk 4 blocks west on Eddy St. 67 rooms.*

➢ **UNDER $100** • **Phoenix Hotel.** Nestled among the strip bars and streetwalkers of the Tenderloin district, this lively hotel has a strong reputation among young hipsters. A whole host of bands have stayed here, including the Red Hot Chili Peppers, NRBQ, Simple Minds, and Living Colour; original work by Bay Area artists spices up the alternately tropical and Southwestern design scheme. The Phoenix is joined at the hip, as it were, to the lively Miss Pearl's Jam House (*see box* on supper clubs, in Chapter 6). In high season, you'll pay $89 for a single or double, but rates go down as much as $20 in winter. If you seek a quiet night, request a room away from Miss Pearl's. Or ask at the front desk for earplugs (where you'll also find complimentary condoms and dental floss). *601 Larkin St., at Eddy St., tel. 415/776–1380. From Powell St. BART/MUNI, Bus 31 west on Eddy St. 44 rooms.*

A special legal exemption was obtained for the Phoenix's swirling black-tile pool bottom, since an obscure state law requires pool bottoms to be a certain shade of blue.

Zen and the Art of Sleeping

If you have an honest interest in enlightenment and aren't just looking for a cheap place to crash, the San Francisco Zen Center, between the Civic Center and the lower Haight, has a few rooms for visitors. For $30–$40 (single) or $40–$50 (double with shared bath) you get a spotless, nicely furnished room overlooking a courtyard, plus a hearty breakfast. This working temple also offers a guest-student program ($10 a night), during which monks-in-training adhere to the center's meditation, work, and meal schedule for one to six weeks. Reserve in advance, especially during summer. 300 Page St., at Laguna St., tel. 415/863–3136. From Market St. downtown, take Bus 7 or 71 west to Page and Laguna Sts.

Downtown San Francisco Lodging

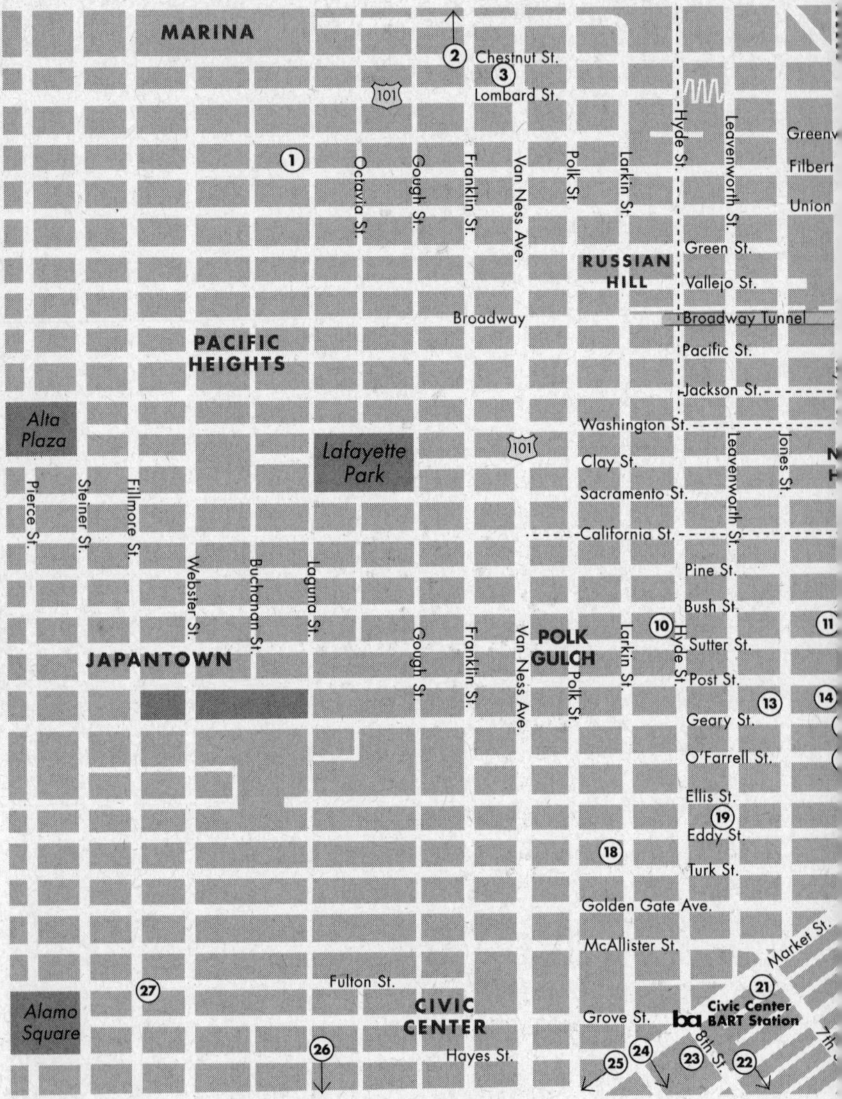

Adelaide Inn, **14**
Aida Hotel, **21**
Albergo Verno, **19**
Alexander Inn, **17**
Amsterdam, **11**
Art Center Bed and Breakfast, **1**
AYH Hostel at Union Square, **16**
Brady Acres, **13**
Cornell, **12**
David's Hotel, **15**
Europa Hotel, **5**
European Guest House, **24**
Ft. Mason International Hostel, **2**
Globetrotter's Inn, **20**
Grand Central Hostel, **25**
Grant Plaza, **8**
Green Tortoise Guest House, **6**
Hotel Astoria, **9**
Hyde Plaza Hotel, **10**
Interclub Globe Hostel, **23**
Pacific Tradewinds, **7**
Phoenix Hotel, **18**
Rodeway Inn, **3**
San Francisco International Student Center, **22**
San Francisco Zen Center, **26**
San Remo Hotel, **4**
Sappho's, **27**

Downtown San Francisco Lodging

DOWNTOWN Downtown San Francisco is the city's financial center, a collage of fog-shrouded buildings, old architecture, and snazzy restaurants. The area is also packed with high-priced corporate hotels; you'll need to check side streets for more reasonable rates. Sleeping downtown offers the advantage of easy access to North Beach, Fisherman's Wharf, Chinatown, and Union Square. But the neighborhood is deserted and not always safe at night, so be alert.

➢ **UNDER $40** • **Alexander Inn.** Two blocks west of Union Square, the Alexander is an upscale version of a European-style hotel, with deferential employees, sunny rooms, real wood furniture, and an international clientele. Most rooms have private baths, color TVs, and coffee makers. If you're willing to share a bath, you pay a super-low $35 per night (singles and doubles with private bath cost $72). Reserve at least one week in advance. *415 O'Farrell St., at Taylor St., tel. 415/928–6800 or 800/843–8709. From Powell St. BART/MUNI, walk 2 blocks west on Eddy St., 2 blocks north on Taylor St. 76 rooms, most with bath.*

Hyde Plaza Hotel. In limbo between three radically different neighborhoods—Van Ness Avenue, the Tenderloin, and Nob Hill—this European-style hotel offers basic furnishings in 50 spacious, clean rooms, most with shared bath. Nightly rates run anywhere from $30 per double to $45 for a room sleeping four; the weekly rate for a double is about $150. The beautiful old building has an adjoining restaurant. *835 Hyde St., near Sutter St., tel. 415/885–2987. From Montgomery St. BART/MUNI, walk west 10 blocks on Sutter St. or Bus 2, 3, or 4 west to Hyde St. Cable TV, laundry, luggage storage.*

➢ **UNDER $55** • **Adelaide Inn.** The comfortable Adelaide, on a short dead-end street just minutes from Union Square, is popular with Europeans. The decor will remind you of a kitschy Swiss chalet—the kind of place where, if they had a mantelpiece, you'd expect to see a cuckoo clock. Rates include a continental breakfast; some kitchen facilities are also available. Singles run $32–$38, doubles $42–$48, depending on room size and availability. All have shared baths. *5 Isadora Duncan Ln., near Taylor St., tel. 415/441–2261. From Montgomery St. BART/MUNI, Bus 38 NW to Geary and Taylor Sts., walk ¾ block north on Taylor St., and turn left. 18 rooms. Reserve in summer.*

➢ **UNDER $65** • **Brady Acres.** Come to this small, comfortable hotel near the Theater District if you're sick of being on the road and want the comforts of home. Each room includes a kitchenette with microwave, toaster, coffee maker, and a mini-fridge filled with chocolates and jam; the bathrooms feature apricot and papaya shampoos; and the beds are covered with colorful quilts. Your phone comes with an answering machine and each room has a TV and a radio/cassette player. Singles are $50–$60, doubles $60–$75; ask the friendly management about weekly specials. Reservations are advised in summer. *649 Jones St., btw Post and Geary Sts., tel. 415/929–8033 or 800/627–2396. From Montgomery St. BART/MUNI, Bus 38 west to Geary and Jones Sts. 25 rooms. Laundry.*

➢ **UNDER $85** • **Amsterdam.** For a Victorian bed-and-breakfast two blocks from Nob Hill, this is a sweet bargain—$69 for two people, $60 for one. The recently renovated rooms have cable TV and private baths. When the temperature drops to a windy 50°F at night and you just can't face going out, the reading room is a nice alternative. And when the sun shines, your complimentary breakfast is served on the outdoor patio. *749 Taylor St., btw Sutter and Bush Sts., tel. 415/673–3277 or 800/637–3444. From Montgomery St. BART/MUNI, Bus 2, 3, or 4 west on Sutter St. 34 rooms.*

Cornell. This small, French country-style hotel on Nob Hill offers beautifully decorated doubles (a bit heavy on flowers and lace) for $80–$90 per night. The French owners also operate a small restaurant in the cellar with a $14 fixed-price menu, stained glass, and groovy medieval accoutrements on the walls. *715 Bush St., btw Powell and Mason Sts., tel. 415/421–3154. From Powell St. BART/MUNI, walk 5½ blocks north on Powell St., left on Bush St. 55 rooms, most with bath, all no-smoking.*

➢ **UNDER $100** • **David's Hotel.** Serving up kishkes on Theater Row for more than 40 years, David's delicatessen is the main act at this joint hotel/restaurant (everything on the menu, from the kreplach to the chocolate decadence cake, is fantastic). Stay at the hotel and you get breakfast at the deli for free and a 15% discount on lunch and dinner. In the ultimate compliment, the hotel is popular among visitors from the New York area. The spotless rooms cost $69 (single) or $89 (double). David's provides free airport transportation and free parking for guests who stay for two or more nights. Two floors of the hotel are reserved for nonsmokers. *480 Geary St., at Taylor St., tel. 415/771–1600 or 800/524–1888. From Powell St. BART/MUNI, walk 2½ blocks north on Powell St., 2 blocks west on Geary St. 50 rooms. Cable TV. Wheelchair access.*

HAIGHT AND WESTERN ADDITION Rock bands (the Dead, Janis Joplin), poets (Allen Ginsberg), psycho cults (the Manson Family), and runaway hippie children have settled in the Haight at various times; it remains a fun, eclectic neighborhood. Staying here will give you a great introduction to how the post-college set lives in San Francisco; it also puts you close to other fine neighborhoods like the Castro and the Mission district. **Lower Haight Street** (especially between Laguna and Pierce) can be dicey at night, but the upper Haight seems more seedy than it actually is. The Western Addition, on the other hand, was genuinely seedy a few years ago, but is undergoing something of a revival as artists and musicians discover its (relatively) cheap rents. Nevertheless, caution is advised at night.

The Haight has strict zoning codes limiting hotel construction. Only a few hotels have survived the bureaucratic red tape; those that have are able to charge exorbitant rates, since there's a high demand and short supply—remember Chapter One of your economics book?

➢ **UNDER $55 • Metro Hotel.** The first thing you'll notice about the Metro is its neon sign, which lights up Divisadero, a major street in the Western Addition. This is a good middle-range option; the whole place was recently redone and the rooms are large and comfortable. Ask for a room in the back, away from the street noise. Singles and doubles go for $45 (add $10 for a third person). If you're lucky, you might run into a rock band scheduled to play at a nearby club. *319 Divisadero St., btw Oak and Page Sts., tel. 415/861–5364. From Market St. downtown, Bus 7 or 71 west to Divisadero and Haight Sts.; walk north 1½ blocks on Divisadero. 23 rooms, all with private bath. Cable TV. Reservations advised in summer.*

➢ **UNDER $85 • Stanyan Park Hotel.** So your bell-bottoms reek of stale incense, you've been humming Grateful Dead songs for days, and you can't bear to look at anything tie-dyed ever again. This hotel on the eastern edge of Golden Gate Park offers a respite from the Haight's hectic pace—Victorian furniture, brass fixtures, and intelligent conversation. The immaculate but unspectacular rooms cost $83 per day and the staff is friendly. Breakfast is included. *750 Stanyan St., btw Waller and Beulah Sts., tel. 415/751–1000. From Market St. downtown, Bus 71 west to Haight and Stanyan Sts., walk 2 blocks south on Stanyan St. 36 rooms. Reservations advised. Wheelchair access.*

➢ **UNDER $100 • The Red Victorian.** At the Red Vic, an immensely popular Haight Street landmark, each room is decorated according to a particular theme. Come here if you want to spend the night in The Japanese Tea Garden Room ($96); The Summer of Love Room ($86),

My Sister's Place

Traveling through the city, new in town, or in transition from one home to another? Sappho's (859 Fulton St., near Fillmore St., tel. 415/775–3243) provides single women with a safe and affordable temporary home for the night, week, or month. This seven-bedroom Victorian house in the Western Addition offers a bed in a two- or three-woman room for $20 per night (monthly rates are available October–April). For this, you get access to employment and housing resources and use of a shared kitchen, outdoor barbecue pit, and meditation garden. If you're lucky, you may end up sharing quarters with an all-girl punk band or with lesbian film directors in town for the San Francisco Lesbian and Gay Film Festival. Smoking is not allowed in any of the rooms.

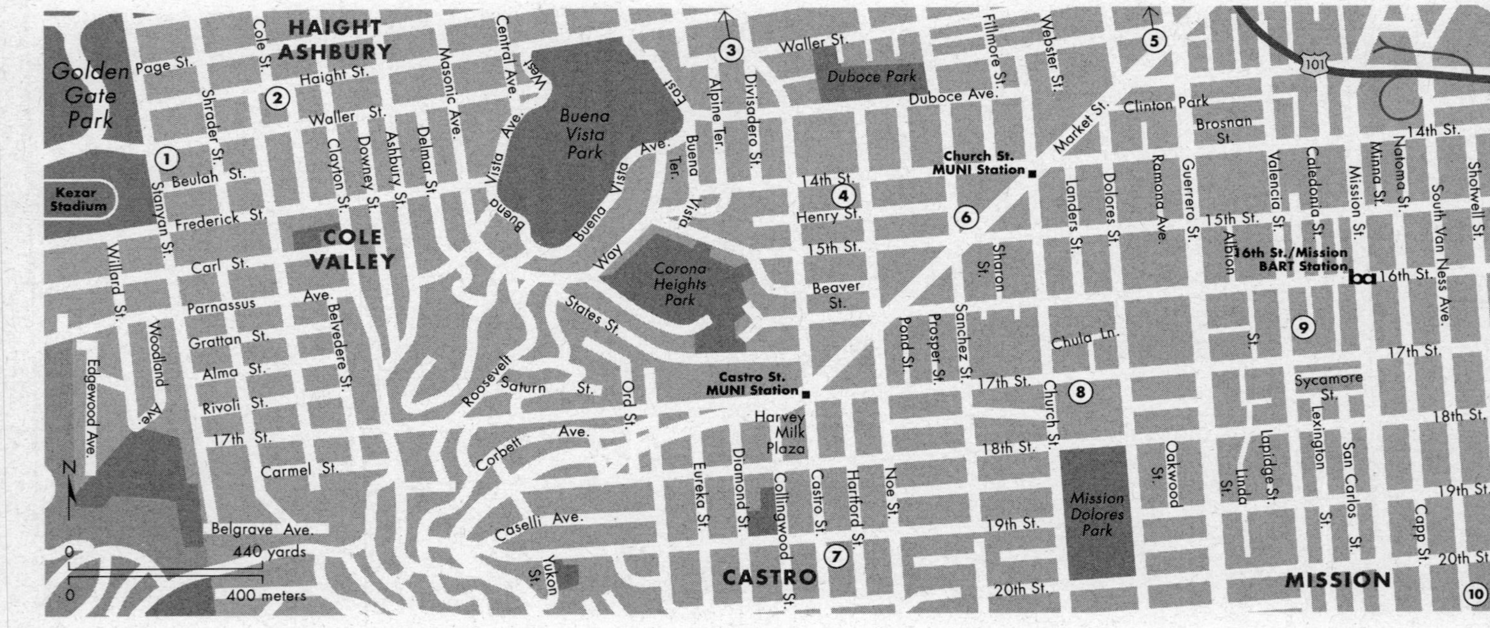

24 Henry, **4**
Black Stallion, **7**
Curtis Hotel, **9**
Dolores Park Inn, **8**
Inn San Francisco, **10**
Metro Hotel, **3**
Red Victorian, **2**
San Francisco Zen Center, **5**
Stanyan Park Hotel, **1**
Twin Peaks, **6**

Haight, Castro, and Mission Lodging

complete with a tie-dye canopy and authentic '60s concert posters; or The Skylight Room ($86), painted in deep jewel tones and featuring a skylighted ceiling. Some rooms are more gimmicky than others, but it's clear from the moment you walk in that the proprietors and the employees of the Red Vic have taken great care with every aspect of the place. *1665 Haight St., btw Belvedere and Cole Sts., tel. 415/864–1978. From Market St. downtown, Bus 7 or 71 west to Haight and Cole Sts. 18 rooms, most with shared bath. Reservations advised in summer.*

THE MARINA The Marina district is a quiet, safe residential neighborhood popular with young folks climbing the corporate ladder. It's a long walk from North Beach, Chinatown, and downtown, but the views of the bay and the Golden Gate Bridge from the nearby waterfront are tremendous. Union and Fillmore streets offer a good selection of yuppified restaurants and singles bars. Unfortunately, most of the cheap lodging in this area lies along busy **Lombard Street,** not the part of Lombard with the world's crookedest street, but rather a major thoroughfare leading to the Golden Gate Bridge. The **Rodeway Inn** (1450 Lombard St., at Van Ness Ave., tel. 415/673–0691) isn't too bad—in a last resort kind of way—with clean singles for $55, doubles $65. For a map of Marina hotels, *see* Downtown San Francisco Lodging map, *above.*

➢ **UNDER $100** • **Art Center Bed and Breakfast.** The owners like to call this place a country inn with a city built around it; when you see it you'll understand why. Staying here is like visiting your country uncle, if you have one that paints. The inn, near the Presidio and the yuppie bars of Union Street, is filled with paintings and art-related knickknacks. If you like to take brush to canvas yourself, the proprietors will be glad to set up an easel for you; there's a garden in back where you can go for inspiration. Two studios and a pair of two-room suites ($85–$95 per day) have double beds, TV and radio, microwave ovens, hot plates, and refrigerators. A three-room apartment with the same amenities runs $125 for two people. *1902 Filbert St., at Laguna St., tel. 415/567–1526. From Embarcadero BART/MUNI, Bus 41 NW to Laguna St., walk 1 block north, turn left. Reserve 2 weeks in advance in summer.*

MISSION DISTRICT This lively, colorful neighborhood is not only home to the city's Mexican and Central American communities, but also to a sizable population of lesbians, riot grrrls, and young, politically radical types. It's not the safest part of San Francisco, but intellectually it's an exciting place to be. For a map of Mission district hotels, *see* Haight, Castro, and Mission Lodging map, *above.*

➢ **UNDER $40** • **Curtis Hotel.** The Mission has its share of shady characters, but the owner of this residential hotel works hard to keep the riffraff out. If you get too wild, the owner will throw you back out on the street. The rules include a ban on loud noises after 9 PM, no alcohol, and no parties. Still, if you can hold your reveling tendencies in check, a sweet deal awaits: A clean single with shared bath is just $85 a week (they have no doubles). Talk to the manager about shorter stays. Guests must pay in advance (checks are not accepted) and flash a picture ID. *559 Valencia St., near 16th St., tel. 415/621–9337. From Mission/16th St. BART, walk 1 block west on 16th St., turn left on Valencia St. 60 rooms, none with bath. Key deposit ($2).*

➢ **UNDER $100** • **Dolores Park Inn.** This lovely B&B—actually a Victorian home built in 1874—is quiet, restful, and almost entirely furnished with antiques. It's located on a sedate street between the Mission and the Castro, one block south of Mission Dolores. Single rooms are $60, doubles $90–$165. All guests have access to the garden and parlor. The price includes a full breakfast. *3641 17th St., near Dolores St., tel. 415/621–0482. From any BART/MUNI station downtown, MUNI J Streetcar to 16th and Church, walk 1 block south on Church St. to 17th St., turn left. 5 rooms, 1 with private bath. No-smoking, two-night minimum stay.*

Come to North Beach if you want to be near many of the city's best restaurants, bars, and cafés; another, ahem, attraction is the group of tacky strip joints along Broadway.

NORTH BEACH North Beach—where Italian immigrants and Beat poets have converged on narrow sidewalks—is a uniquely San Francisco experience and a great place to stay. The neighborhood is near downtown, Chinatown, and Fisherman's Wharf. Unfortunately, this is also where most the tourists congregate, so hotel rates are correspondingly high. You'll have to search hard for something affordable. An appealing option is the **Green Tortoise Guest House** (*see* Hostels, *below*). For a map of North Beach hotels, *see* Downtown San Francisco Lodging, *above.*

➢ **UNDER $40** • **Europa Hotel.** Located next door to an establishment boasting "totally, completely, entirely nude girls," the Europa tries to be the last bastion of morality in this sinful city. The sign at the counter prohibits visitors after 6 PM, illegal drugs, weapons, pets, alcohol, and loud noise. The security entrance (guests are buzzed in) makes the hotel fairly safe, though it looks divey and some strange characters were spied wandering the incense-scented halls. If you don't mind street noise, ask for a room with a view of Broadway and Columbus to alleviate the hotel's musty barrenness. Better yet, pay $30 for a double, shower in the ugly but functional shared bathroom, and spend your time and savings on good coffee at a chic Italian café down the street. *310 Columbus Ave., at Broadway, tel. 415/391–5779. From Montgomery St. BART/MUNI, Bus 15 north from Kearny St. to Columbus Ave. and Broadway. 76 rooms, none with bath.*

➢ **UNDER $65** • **San Remo Hotel.** A short walk from both Fisherman's Wharf and North Beach, the San Remo is an incredible bargain in a pricey area: $55–$65 for a double with shared bath. The hotel boasts helpful management, beautiful redwood furnishings, stained-glass windows, and quiet, spotless rooms. *2237 Mason St., btw Francisco and Chestnut Sts., tel. 415/776–8688. From Montgomery St. BART/MUNI, Bus 15, north Chestnut St., walk 1 block west to Mason St. 64 rooms. Laundry. Reservations advised in summer.*

HOSTELS

Hostels affiliated with American Youth Hostels (AYH), the American branch of Hostelling International (HI), offer a certain welcome predictability, but private hostels are often cheaper and filled with a more eclectic crowd. Perhaps due to the dearth of other budget accommodations in the area, the hostels are extremely popular; you should make reservations before you arrive in San Francisco. In a pinch, you could also try **Albergo Verona** (*see* Civic Center, *above*), which charges $17 for one of 14 dorm spaces.

AYH Hostel at Union Square. This huge hostel one block from Union Square sleeps more than 220 people in rooms with one to four beds ($14 for members, $17 for nonmembers). The inte-

Romantic Rendezvous

After an evening at the symphony (or show at the Fillmore Auditorium), and after the last bottle of wine (or whiskey) is empty, the nearest cookie-cutter motel just won't do. Luckily, the San Remo Hotel (see North Beach, below) has a penthouse room for $85 that will help put both of you in the mood. Up on the roof, you're removed from the prying eyes of the world—all the better to enjoy the sweeping views of the bay and Marina. Others may prefer soaking in a private hot tub at the sumptuous Inn San Francisco (943 S. Van Ness Ave., near 21st St., tel. 415/641–0188), in the Mission district. The price, $195, may deter all but the most infatuated, but the inn also has smaller rooms with shared bath ($75) that are furnished with antiques, crystal, stained glass, and Oriental rugs. Other perks include breakfast, a peaceful garden with gazebo and hot tub, and complimentary sherry. Larger rooms also have extras that include a sun deck, fireplace, or claw-foot bathtub. A third amorous option is the women-only House O' Chicks (tel. 415/861–9849), with an atmosphere that is artsy, homey, and very sex- and gay-positive. Each of the three rooms ($75) has a custom-made mattress, a TV, and a stereo with CDs; all guests share a bath and the video library, which includes lesbian erotica. Located near the Castro, the proprietors prefer to speak with potential guests before accepting reservations.

rior is bright and pleasant; the hostel includes such amenities as a TV room, smoking room, library, and kitchen (with microwaves, toasters, and refrigerators). Bulletin boards offer info on San Francisco nightlife and other attractions. About 40% of the rooms are set aside for reservations, which must be made at least 48 hours in advance ($14 deposit). You can stay a maximum of six days in high season, 14 days otherwise. *312 Mason St., btw O'Farrell and Geary Sts., tel. 415/788–5604. From Powell St. BART/MUNI, walk 1½ blocks north on Powell St., 1 block west on O'Farrell St., turn right. No curfew, no lockout. Reception open daily 24 hrs. Wheelchair access.*

European Guest House. A good choice for those who want to take advantage of the nightlife south of Market, this mid-size hostel offers decent, if unspectacular, lodging in one 15-bed room ($10 per person), four-person dorms ($12 per person), or rooms sleeping two ($14 per person). It's got a sun roof, a common room, and a cozy kitchen. *761 Minna St., tel. 415/861–6634. Near Mission St. btw 8th and 9th Sts. From Civic Center BART/MUNI, walk 2 blocks south on 8th St., turn right on Minna. No curfew, no lockout. Reception open daily 24 hrs. Deposit ($5), laundry. Reservations advised in summer.*

Ft. Mason International Hostel. This AYH hostel, perched high above the waterfront, will dazzle you with its views of the bay and the Golden Gate Bridge. The rules are tedious and complex, however, so listen up. It's almost impossible to stay here unless you reserve in advance. Reservations (by phone or in person) must be made at least 24 hours ahead with a credit card, or by sending the cost of your first night's stay at least two weeks prior to your arrival, with the names and genders of the people in your party and the dates you intend to stay. Get here *really* early if you don't have a reservation. Beds are $13–$14 a night for both members and nonmembers. During the summer, you can stay a maximum of 14 nights. You're required to perform a chore each day and smoking is not allowed. Whew. *Ft. Mason, Bldg. 240, Box A, San Francisco, CA 94123, tel. 415/771–7277. From Transbay Terminal, Bus 42 to Van Ness Ave. and Bay St., turn right on Bay St., and follow signs. 150 beds. No curfew, lockout 11 AM–3 PM. Reception open daily 7–2 and 3–midnight. Bike and luggage storage, common room, free linens, kitchen, laundry.*

Globetrotter's Inn. The lack of restrictions (curfew, chores, et cetera) and small size (it sleeps only 39 people) are among the strengths of this independent hostel on the edge of the down-and-out Tenderloin district. It's not as new or as sunny as some of the others, but the staff has done its best, putting artwork on the walls and creating a comfortable common space with a TV, plants, and a 24-hour kitchen. A space in a double or in a four- or six-person dorm costs $12; singles are $24. Many young Europeans stay here while looking for a more permanent situation and the bulletin board lists job openings on a regular basis. *225 Ellis St., btw Mason and Taylor Sts., tel. 415/346–5786. From Powell St. BART/MUNI, walk ½ block north on Powell St., 1½ blocks west on Ellis St. No curfew, no lockout. Reception open daily 8–1 and 5–9. Key deposit ($5), laundry.*

Grand Central Hostel. This former flophouse, in a central but seedy location, has been transformed into a snazzy hostel. Dorm space costs $12 per night ($75 per week in winter); singles run $20 per night, doubles $30. Other perks include an exercise room, unlimited free coffee, complimentary breakfast, all kinds of social events, free linens, a pool table, a jukebox, table tennis, and TV rooms. All visitors, even Americans traveling within the United States, must show a passport and travel documents to stay here. *1412 Market St., at 10th and Fell Sts., tel. 415/703–9988. From Van Ness MUNI, walk 1 block NE on Market St. 122 rooms. No curfew, no lockout. Reception open daily 24 hrs. 21-day maximum stay.*

Green Tortoise Guest House. From the popular people who have brought you budget bus travel for the past 20 years comes one of the best hostels in San Francisco. Green Tortoise is located in the middle of hip North Beach, just blocks from downtown and Chinatown. Cool Euro-backpackers inhabit most of the rooms, which are clean, spacious, and rarely vacant—call ahead. There's no curfew or lockout, and the managers are friendly and laid-back. A single bunk costs $13 per night, a private double is $32. *494 Broadway, btw Montgomery and Kearny Sts., tel. 415/834–1000. Five blocks north of TransAmerica Pyramid. From Montgomery St. BART/MUNI, Bus 15 or 9X north. 40 rooms. No curfew, no lockout. Reception open daily 24 hrs. Complimentary breakfast, common rooms, kitchen, laundry, sauna.*

Interclub Globe Hostel. Intended for international travelers (but passport-carrying Americans are not turned away), this SoMa hostel has few rules and a warm, relaxed atmosphere—not to mention a pool table and a sun deck that has a grand view of the city. With more than 100 beds, guests sleep four to a room and each room has a bathroom; two floors are reserved for nonsmokers. A bed is $15 per night in summer, $12 all other times. At the adjoining canteen, you can get dinner for less than $5. *10 Hallam Pl., near Folsom St. btw 7th and 8th Sts., tel. 415/431–0540. From Civic Center BART/MUNI, walk 3 blocks south on 8th St., turn left on Folsom St. No curfew. Reception open daily 24 hrs. Laundry.*

The bar next door to the Interclub Globe Hostel hosts weekly $1 beer nights for guests of the hostel.

Pacific Tradewinds. The antithesis of an institutional hostel, this homey place in Chinatown has only four rooms (with a total of 32 beds), plus a friendly common space and kitchen. There's no official lockout (although they like people to be gone during the afternoon) and if you want to come in after midnight, the proprietors will give you a key ($10 deposit). They'll also let you know about cheap restaurants and other attractions in the area. Beds are usually $14 per night, but the price fluctuates, so call ahead. If you stay seven nights, you pay for only six; in summer, they ask that you pay for the week in advance. *680 Sacramento St., near Kearny St., tel. 415/433–7970. From Montgomery St. BART/MUNI, walk 1 block west on Post St., then take Bus 15 north on Kearny St. Reception open daily 8 AM–midnight.*

San Francisco International Student Center. Small, homey, and right in the middle of hip SoMa, the student center has 16 rooms with three to five beds in each. It has a small kitchen, a sunny rooftop, a common room, and an owner who doesn't believe in television. Beds cost $13 a night, $84 a week. The center rents rooms to students only; Americans must present a passport and travel documents. *1188 Folsom St., near 8th St., tel. 415/255–8800. From Civic Center BART/MUNI, walk 3 blocks south on 8th St. to Folsom. No curfew, no lockout. Reception open 9 AM–11 PM.*

LONGER STAYS

So you think you want to stay awhile? Monthly rents in San Francisco range from $250 for a closet in an eight-bedroom house to $350–$450 for an average room to $500–$850 for studios and one-bedroom apartments. Still want to stay? If so, there are several ways to find a semi-affordable place to live in the city. If you need a whole apartment or house, investigate the classified ads in the ***San Francisco Chronicle*** or the ***San Francisco Examiner.*** Buy the Sunday papers on Saturday night to get a jump start on your search. Another option is to visit a rental agency with private listings. For example, **Community Rentals** (470 Castro St., tel. 415/552–8868) provides listings of vacant apartments, flats, and houses all over San Francisco. You tell them what you're looking for (price range, neighborhood, type of housing) and they give you listings, each with about a quarter-page of info. Their fee is $75 for two months, $50 of which is refundable if you don't find a place through them. **Metro Rents** (2021 Fillmore St., tel. 415/563-7368) charges $65 for 40 days, refunds $40 if you don't find a place, and has good info for neighborhoods between the Fillmore and the Marina. Look in the Yellow Pages for other agencies and keep in mind that a service is likely to have more listings in the neighborhoods adjacent to it.

In order to find their soul (room)mate, industrious folks with a room for rent will often stick up a flyer in a café or laundromat with 10 to 15 adjectives strung together: "Bass-playing, cat-owning vegetarian household seeks gay, guitar-playing, no-smoking, spiritual roommate for jam sessions and hearty soup . . . "

One of the cheapest ways to find an apartment is simply by walking around. Look up, and you'll see countless FOR RENT signs in windows, with a few details about the apartment and a phone number to call. The best strategy is to settle on a neighborhood that you like and walk the streets, jotting down the phone numbers and addresses of places for rent, then calling to set up appointments to see them.

If you're looking for a sublet, or a room in someone else's apartment, you have all kinds of options. Struggling artists and other poor folks often take their chances with the bulletin boards that appear in just about every café in the city. Another free way to find roommates is at **Rainbow Grocery** (*see* Specialty Markets and Delicatessens, in Chapter 4). A set of file boxes at the store contains listings, both sublet and long-term, for your dream San Francisco roommate—a cynical leftist with a futon and two standoffish cats. Those who can spend a little bit of money to find a home often have good luck with a roommate referral agency. For a fee of $25–$50, these agencies will give you access to computer databases of places with vacant rooms. The listings, which include as much as a page of information, are tailored to your price range, personality, room requirements, food preferences, music tastes, neuroses, and whatever else you and your potential housemates want to declare about your inner selves. Most agencies let you view the listings for as long as it takes to find a good living situation. **Community Rentals** (*see above*) has information on shares in the Castro, Noe Valley, and the Haight. Other agencies include **The Original S.F. Roommate Referral Service** (610A Cole St., at Haight St., tel. 415/558–9191), which charges $34 for four months of service, and the **Roommate Network** (3129 Fillmore St., near Filbert St., tel. 415/441–2309), which charges "working professionals" $50 for an indefinite period of time. Many people also find roommates through the classified ads under "Shared Housing" in the ***Bay Guardian*** and ***S.F. Weekly,*** San Francisco's largest free weekly newspapers.

East Bay

BERKELEY

Lodging in Berkeley is often either shabby or downright expensive—sometimes both. If that isn't enough, it's also often hard to come by: In mid-May, when thousands of graduating Berkeley students don their caps and gowns, reservations for nearly all motels and hotels become *absolutely* essential, since most of the nicer places sell out four to five months in advance. To add insult to injury, all Berkeley lodgings add 12% tax to the prices listed below.

Most of the city's motels are on **University Avenue,** west of campus, and most of these motels are not recommended. Your life isn't necessarily in danger here, but expect a general air of seediness (i.e., velvet curtains, the reek of cheap perfume . . .). Unless you're researching a documentary on the lives of sex workers, it's best to stick to the campus end of University Avenue; the farther west you go, the shoddier the surroundings become. To reach all of the motels in the vicinity from Berkeley BART, walk 2 blocks north to University Avenue and head west, or take Bus 51.

Berkeley has no youth hostels, but the **YMCA** (2001 Allston Way, tel. 510/848–6800)—open to both men and women—is cheap and within easy reach of Berkeley's sights. Its 80 dorm-style singles cost $25 per night ($27 if you stay only one night) and are available on a first-come, first-served basis. After 14 days, you're eligible to stay longer, at around $100 per week. Bathrooms are shared.

➢ **UNDER $55** • **Campus Motel.** This place is located right on noisy University Avenue, but it *is* close to campus (6 blocks west) and the rooms are neat and clean. Some rooms allow smoking, some don't, and all have cable TV and coffee makers. Singles are $45, doubles $50. *1619 University Ave., btw McGee Ave. and California St., tel. 510/841–3844. 23 rooms.*

Travel Inn. This pink motel is cheap, clean, far enough from the street to escape traffic noise, and has plenty of parking. The rooms are decorated with eclectic furnishings and the management is friendly. Singles cost $40, doubles $47. *1461 University Ave., btw Sacramento and Acton Sts., tel. 510/848–3840. 3 blocks south of North Berkeley BART. 42 rooms.*

➢ **UNDER $85** • **Travelodge.** If you're not concerned about price or atmosphere, you can always settle for the generic blue-and-white Travelodge, 3 blocks from campus, where basic, very clean doubles start at $76. *1820 University Ave., near Grant St., tel. 510/843–4262. 30 rooms.*

UNIVERSITY HOUSING **University Summer Visitor Housing** (tel. 510/642–4444) offers summer dorm accommodations on the Berkeley campus for $38–$48 per night. Rooms are nothing to write home about (bed, desk, chair, phone). Linen, soap (maybe write home about the generosity of the university), and parking are available for an additional $3 per day. There are many young people around and the dorms are a very safe place to stay.

LONGER STAYS Every fall, thousands of Berkeley students scramble to find a place to live. Those that hit the jackpot are rewarded with a cheap apartment or room close to campus and are too wise to give it up come summer vacation. Their solution is to sublet the space (at about two-thirds the normal rent). Look for sublets in the campus newspaper ***The Daily Californian,*** the ***East Bay Express,*** or the ***East Bay Guardian,*** all of which are available for free in most cafés

Pampering Mom and Dad

Going crazy trying to tidy up your room before the folks come into town? Forget the cleaning frenzy, leave the ashtrays in view, and book Mom and Pop into one of Berkeley's posh hotels. The popular, wheelchair-accessible Durant Hotel (2600 Durant Ave., tel. 510/845–8981) is the closest to both campus and the dorms; the $99 charge for a double includes breakfast. The lobby is quite elegant and the beds are big and comfy, though the dull earth-tone decor is a downer.

The froufrou set will be delighted with Gramma's Rose Garden Inn (2740 Telegraph Ave., at Ward St., tel. 510/549–2145). As you open the little gates from grimy Telegraph Avenue, you enter a wonderland of chintz, flower beds, and cute stone paths. Doubles in the main house are $85–$95; the surrounding cottages offer more spacious, higher-priced rooms ($125–$145). Prices include a complimentary breakfast and wine and cheese in the evenings. The inn is wheelchair accessible.

The Berkeley City Club (2315 Durant Ave., tel. 510/848–7800) was designed by famed Northern California architect Julia Morgan; its gorgeous high ceilings and Moorish/Gothic touches have made it a historical landmark. The sparsely furnished rooms are a letdown, but many boast bay views and all are wheelchair accessible. The club offers a fitness center and a swimming pool where you can swim your laps to the beat of piped-in Mozart or Beethoven. Doubles run $85, breakfast and parking included.

Doubles at the French Hotel (1538 Shattuck Ave., btw Cedar and Vine Sts., tel. 510/548–9930), North Berkeley's little Euro inn, cost $85 (one room is only $68) and the location is prime. All rooms have a minuscule but sunny patio; most include a complimentary breakfast. Connected to the hotel is a hugely popular café, packed with yuppies sipping espresso. The surrounding neighborhood, nicknamed the "Gourmet Ghetto," has some of America's finest restaurants, including Chez Panisse, as well as excellent bookstores.

If you really want luxury, head uphill to the Claremont Resort, Spa, and Tennis Club (Ashby and Domingo Aves., tel. 510/843–3000), a striking all-white palace in the Oakland–Berkeley Hills that has been a favorite destination of the wealthy since the 1920s. The prices will stun you as much as the building: Bay-view doubles go for $205 and doubles with a hillside view for a paltry $185 (ask about special weekend deals). Ouch. As a guest, though, you can use the heated pools, saunas, whirlpools, and tennis courts. The resort's rooms are wheelchair accessible.

around Bancroft Way and Telegraph Avenue. A number of cafés, including **Café Milano** (2522 Bancroft Way, near Telegraph Ave.), have large bulletin boards that boast a glorious mess of flyers and scraps of paper with apartment listings. **Sproul Plaza,** on the Berkeley campus, is another bulletin-board resource.

Those who have access to a valid Berkeley student ID can browse the community rental listings at the **Housing and Dining Services** office (2401 Bowditch St., tel. 510/642–3106). Another route is to look in the Yellow Pages for a rental agency. Popular ones include **Berkeley Connection** (2840 College Ave., tel. 510/845–7821), which charges $50 for one month (the second month is free if nothing comes up), and **Homefinders** (2158 University Ave., tel. 510/549–6450), which charges $55 for 30 days (the second month is free, or ask for a $30 refund if you find something elsewhere). These companies will give you a long list of properties for rent in the area; for short-term housing, however, you're better off looking on your own.

Another option is staying in the student-owned and -operated co-ops. Inquire and make all reservations at the **University Students' Cooperative Association** (2424 Ridge Rd., tel. 510/848–1936). The co-ops are open to students from any college; for $700–$1,200 you can stay all summer (from mid-May–mid-Aug.). Ask about the all-vegetarian **Lothlorien** (2405 and 2415 Prospect St.) southeast of campus, where you can frolic in the Jacuzzi, or the women-only **Sherman Hall** (2250 Prospect St.), one of the cleanest and best-maintained co-ops. Also worth looking into are **Rochdale Village** (2424 Haste St.) and the **Northside Co-op** (2526 and 2540 Le Conte Ave.), both of which are part co-op and part apartment complex. If you're not a student, you may be able to bend the rules a little by wandering into one of the larger co-ops, like grimy **Cloyne Court** (2600 Ridge Rd., tel. 510/549–6300). Show desperation, share whatever you have on you, and you may be offered someone's floor space for a while.

Berkeley's **fraternities** also rent rooms in the summer, as do some of the sororities (women can comfortably stay in the frats, too). The price is stylin': generally you can stay the whole summer for about $500. Most fraternities are southeast of campus, on and around Piedmont Avenue and Channing Way. You can try calling, but generally no one answers the house phone; you're better off just scouting the neighborhood on foot. Head east up Bancroft, turn right at Piedmont, and start your hunting. Fraternities often advertise by hanging a big sign on their house. When something catches your eye, knock on the door and ask for the house manager. Scope out the bathrooms and kitchens—one glance should tell you if the place is livable. The list of frats that rent rooms changes each summer, so stop by **102 Sproul Hall** (Sproul Plaza, at Bancroft and Telegraph Aves., tel. 510/642–5171) for a complete list of addresses and phone numbers.

Berkeley's fraternities offer cheap summer lodging, if you can stand dirt, loud music, a plain room (just a bed and a desk), and the constant company of frat guys.

OAKLAND

For travelers concerned about price and safety, Oakland's budget lodging scene isn't a pretty sight. Hotels are either geared toward executives with expense accounts or they're in the middle of grimy, scary neighborhoods. And, sad to say, Oakland has no youth hostels. Of course, if you're desperate, there are faceless chain motels in downtown Oakland and near the airport with rooms for $50–$75 per night.

Along **West MacArthur Boulevard,** near MacArthur BART in North Oakland, there are a number of motels that are used for illicit, after-hours business transactions. Women should not stay here alone. If you have your heart set on staying on West MacArthur, east of Telegraph Avenue you'll find a few reasonably priced motels in semi-safe surroundings. Check out the **Imperial Inn** (490 W. MacArthur Blvd., at Telegraph Ave., tel. 510/653–4225), where mediocre singles cost $30, doubles $35.

➢ **UNDER $40** • **Avondale Residence Hotel.** On a residential street, not far from downtown Oakland, the Avondale offers singles only at an unbeatable price: $20–$30 for a room with private bath. The manager is extremely gracious, but the neighborhood can get a bit noisy at night. You should also be careful here, even though the neighborhood is safer than some other parts of Oakland. *540 28th St., tel. 510/832–9769. From MacArthur BART, Bus 40 or walk 7 blocks south on Telegraph Ave., then turn right.*

➢ **UNDER $55** • **Civic Center Lodge.** One of the few centrally located and cheap hotels in Oakland, this basic, no-frills hotel is located right next to a highway but within easy reach of the waterfront, Lake Merritt, and downtown bars and restaurants. Singles cost $38 per night, doubles $48. *50 6th St., tel. 510/444–4139. From Lake Merritt BART, walk 3 blocks down Oak St. to 6th St., turn left. 32 rooms.*

CAMPING **Anthony Chabot Regional Park.** Camp at one of 75 sites east of downtown in the Oakland hills. Tent sites, in a pleasant wooded area, are $13 per night, RV hookups are $18; you also have to pay a $5 reservation charge. The campground has showers and is about a mile from Lake Chabot; a 9-mile trail meanders around the lake (*see* Hiking, in Chapter 8). You need your own wheels to get here. *Tel. 510/562–CAMP. From I–80, I–580 east to Redwood Road exit, turn left, follow Redwood Road 4½ mi to park gate (it's another 2½ mi to campground).*

Marin County

Across the Golden Gate Bridge from San Francisco, Marin County is the home of scenic views, quaint B&Bs, and hot-tubbing former hippies who no longer believe that owning property is a form of theft. Unfortunately, hotel accommodations here aren't cheap. The best budget bet is one of the area's many campgrounds. If you've got cash to spare, though, the **Bed and Breakfast Exchange of Marin** (contact Suellen Lamorte, tel. 415/485–1971) books brief or extended stays in private homes and bed-and-breakfasts; expect to pay $55–$150 per night. She can also set two people up in a houseboat for about $150 per night, though the deal gets better when four to six people pay about $225 for a whole boat.

ALONG U.S. 101

SAUSALITO While tourists crowd Sausalito's streets during the day, all but the richest have to find somewhere else to spend the night. Luckily, an excellent hostel and free camping are only a 10-minute drive away.

➢ **UNDER $85** • **Alta Mira Continental Hotel.** This Spanish-style hotel in the Sausalito hills offers amazing views of the bay, but you'll pay dearly for them. Doubles without views start at $70; rooms with a view are $115–$170. If you stay in one of the cheaper rooms, have a drink on the terrace and enjoy the view of the bay. The stately rooms are tastefully decorated with antiques and all come with a TV and telephone. *125 Bulkley Ave., tel. 415/332–1350. From U.S. 101, Sausalito exit and follow signs to Bridgeway, turn right at Princess Ave. (the 9th stoplight), continue 3 blocks. 28 rooms. Reservations advised.*

➢ **HOSTEL** • **Golden Gate AYH-Hostel.** Built in 1907, this beautiful, friendly hostel is located in the Marin Headlands in historic Ft. Barry. There's a communal kitchen, laundry room, tennis court, Ping-Pong table, pool table, and a common room with a fireplace. Beds cost $10 per night and are often available at the last minute, but it's best to call at least one week in advance. A recently opened second building has "family rooms" that sleep up to four, so couples may get their own room on slow nights. Membership is not required. Getting to the hostel by public transportation is a bit difficult, but well worth the effort. If you're coming from San Francisco, catch Golden Gate Transit Bus 10 or 50 from the Transbay Terminal and ask to be let off at the bottom of the Alexander Avenue off-ramp. From here, it's a stiff 4-mile hike to the hostel. On Sundays only, MUNI Bus 76 goes from the Transbay Terminal all the way up to the Marin Headlands Visitor Center, one block from the hostel. *Ft. Barry, Bldg. 941, tel. 415/331–2777. From U.S. 101, Alexander Ave. exit, cross under freeway, make first right after* MARIN HEADLANDS *sign. After 1 mi, turn right on McCullough Rd., left on Bunker Rd., follow signs to visitor center (hostel is just up hill). 101 beds. No curfew, lockout 9:30–3:30. Reception open daily 7:30 AM–9:30 PM. Key deposit ($10).*

➢ **CAMPING** • **Marin Headlands.** Four free tent camping areas are available in the headlands, which are part of the Golden Gate National Recreational Area and is only a few miles north of San Francisco. **Hawkcamp** is the most primitive; to enter requires a 3½-mile hike. Fires are not allowed here. Campers can drive right up to **Bicentennial,** the only campground with piped-in water. Backcountry permits are required; to reserve a site, call between 9:30 and noon no more than 90 days in advance. *Tel. 415/331–1540. Picnic tables, pit toilets. Some wheelchair access.*

TIBURON AND ANGEL ISLAND Not surprisingly, yuppie-infested Tiburon has no inexpensive lodging. If you don't want to head to the Golden Gate Hostel a few miles south (*see above*), consider a ferry trip to Angel Island for a night of camping.

➢ **CAMPING** • **Angel Island State Park.** Get away from it all without losing sight of good old San Francisco. Nine showerless environmental campsites ($9) are scattered around the island. Sites 3 and 4, with views of the Golden Gate Bridge, are the most popular; Sites 1 and 2, surrounded by pine trees and with a view of the East Bay, offer more privacy and shelter from the wind. Wherever you camp, prepare for a 2-mile hike into the park. Reserve a few weeks ahead for a weekend stay; on weekdays, you can almost always get a site on the same day. For directions, *see* Tiburon and Angel Island, in Chapter 2. *Tel. 415/435–1915 (info) or 800/444–PARK (reservations). Barbecue grills, drinking water, pit toilets.*

MILL VALLEY Staying in Mill Valley offers easy access to Muir Woods, Mt. Tamalpais, and Highway 1. But as long as you're this close, why not push on through to Mt. Tam's more scenic Steep Ravine cabins and campsites (*see below*)?

➢ **UNDER $85** • **HoJo Inn.** Actually one freeway exit south of Mill Valley, Corte Madera's branch of the Howard Johnson motel-and-coffee-shop chain provides clean, comfortable rooms and efficient service. A tiny rose garden and colorful flower pots lend a bit of character. Most of the year, rooms that sleep two cost $59 on weekdays, while rooms with two double beds cost $69 (add $10 on weekends). However, be prepared for prices to change according to season, day of the week, or phase of the moon. Rooms come with TV, telephone, a small refrigerator, and occasionally a microwave. *1595 Casa Buena Dr., Corte Madera, tel. 415/924–3570. Off U.S. 101 at Paradise/Tamalpais exit. 18 rooms.*

SAN RAFAEL San Rafael is Marin's most down-to-earth town and boasts the county's best nightlife, shops, and cafés. While the hotels here could hardly be called budget, they're at least more affordable than the options in the surrounding area.

➢ **UNDER $55** • **San Rafael Inn.** The decor of this generic pink motel won't be featured on your postcards home, but the owners are friendly, the rooms are clean, and a pool and Jacuzzi lie right across the parking lot from the rooms. Singles are $48, doubles $48–$54, and all come with telephones and TV (some have a mini-fridge). Tack on about $5 on weekends and other busy periods. Request a room toward the back to avoid freeway noise. *865 E. Francisco Blvd., tel. 415/454–9470. From U.S. 101, Francisco Blvd. exit, left on Bellum Blvd., left on E. Francisco Blvd. 32 rooms. Wheelchair access.*

Panama Hotel. It's not uncommon for locals to use this hotel to escape the real world. The very private rooms are individually decorated, some with canopy queen beds and some with claw-foot tubs. All but one comes with TV, and some of the higher-priced ones offer kitchenettes and patios. The hotel's restaurant has a mouth-watering menu (lunch costs around $10, dinner $15–$20) and a beautiful outdoor area draped with wisteria. The owner is terrific, the setting is perfect, the location is convenient, and—most amazing—the prices are reasonable. Rooms without bath start at $45; those with bath are $70–$110. *4 Bayview St., tel. 415/457–3993. From U.S. 101 north, Central San Rafael exit, left on 3rd St., left on B St., go 4 blocks to where B St. becomes Bayview St. 15 rooms, 9 with bath. Reservations advised.*

➢ **UNDER $100** • **425 Mission.** This wood-shingled cottage offers homey rooms furnished with antiques, rosewood and wicker furniture, and the occasional claw-foot tub. The downstairs living room is a comfortable place to watch the news, listen to music, or read a book. You can also hang out on the deck when the weather is nice. Rooms cost $85 on weekdays and $95 on weekends, including a gourmet breakfast and use of a hot tub in the backyard. If you stay awhile, the innkeeper will do your laundry for free, just like Mom. The location is also convenient; it's an easy walk from Old San Rafael. *425 Mission Ave., tel. 415/453–1365. From*

U.S. 101, Central San Rafael exit, go 5 blocks to Mission Ave., turn right. 4 rooms, 2 with bath. Reservations advised.

➢ **CAMPING • China Camp State Park.** The trappings of civilization fade as you enter the 1,600-acre China Camp State Park, 4 miles northeast of San Rafael. Here you can pitch your tent at one of 30 walk-in campsites near San Pablo Bay. The sites aren't far from the parking lot, or from each other, but they're well sheltered by oak trees. And you get hot water to boot. Sites are $14 per night ($12 off-season), and parking costs an additional $3. Call MISTIX (tel. 800/444–PARK) to reserve. *Tel. 415/456–0766. N. San Pedro Rd. exit east from U.S. 101 and follow signs. Fire pits, flush toilets, showers.*

COASTAL HIGHWAY 1

MT. TAMALPAIS The Pantoll campsites (*see below*), near the Mt. Tamalpais Ranger Station and many trailheads, are perfect for hard-core hikers who want to make tracks up and down the mountain. On the other hand, the Steep Ravine cabins, perched along the rocky coast, are perfect for solitude seekers who want to get away from it all (including roads and flush toilets).

➢ **CAMPING • Pantoll.** Fifteen campsites, relatively close together but well sheltered by trees, are about a 100-yard walk from the parking lot of the Pantoll Ranger Station in Mt. Tamalpais State Park and cost only $14 per night. A 16th site ($3 per person) is reserved for those without a car. All sites are available on a first-come, first-served basis. *Tel. 415/388–2070. From Hwy. 1, follow signs to Mt. Tamalpais State Park, then Panoramic Hwy. to Pantoll Ranger Station. Drinking water, flush toilets.*

Steep Ravine Campground and Cabins. Off Highway 1 in Mt. Tamalpais State Park, Steep Ravine has six walk-in campsites for $9 per night. Cabins with two double beds and two small bunk beds, as well as an indoor wood stove and outdoor barbecue, cost $30 per night. If you can deal with a pit toilet, this place is absolutely unbeatable—just you and a few other guests with a view of the dramatic coastline as far as the eye can see. Unfortunately, Steep Ravine is not an unknown gem, so cabins are fully booked well in advance, except in winter. *Tel. 800/444–PARK for reservations. From U.S. 101, Stinson Beach/Hwy. 1 exit and follow Hwy. 1 until you see signs.*

STINSON BEACH Stinson Beach is full of B&Bs that are quaint in every detail except price. Expect to pay upwards of $90 a night. The only semi-cheap option is the **Stinson Beach Motel** (3416 Hwy. 1, tel. 415/868–1712), which has inviting doubles set around a shady garden for $50–$80, all with private bath.

POINT REYES In addition to its excellent hostel, **Point Reyes National Seashore** has four free campgrounds, open to backpackers only, in isolated wilderness areas. You may have to hike in as far as 6 miles to reach one, but if you could drive there, it wouldn't be nature anymore, would it?

➢ **HOSTEL • Point Reyes AYH-Hostel.** Eight miles west of the Point Reyes Visitor Center, the hostel is popular with both foreign travelers and local college kids. It makes a great base camp for excursions onto the peninsula; there are hundreds of hiking trails nearby. The two common rooms have wood-burning stoves and plentiful reading material. Dorm beds cost $10 per night for members, $12 for nonmembers. Reservations are advised; if you want them to hold a bed, call and use your Visa or MasterCard or mail them a check. *Box 247, Point Reyes Station, CA 94956, tel. 415/663–8811. From Hwy. 1, head left (west) in Olema on Bear Valley Rd. 1 block beyond stop sign; 1½ mi farther, left at LIGHTHOUSE/BEACHES/HOSTEL sign, turn left after 6 mi at Crossroads Rd. 44 beds. Curfew 10 PM, lockout 9:30–4:30. Reception open daily 7:30–9:30 and 4:30–9:30. Kitchen, linen rental, on-site parking.*

➢ **CAMPING •** To reserve a campsite up to one month in advance in Point Reyes, call the **Point Reyes Visitor Information Center** (tel. 415/663–1092) weekdays between 9 and noon. Trails to the campgrounds leave from the visitor center, which is on the entrance road (turn left off Hwy. 1 just past Olema). All sites have picnic tables and pit toilets, but none has running water or allow fires, so bring plenty of supplies, a camp stove, and warm clothing.

Coast Camp is a 3-mile hike from the youth hostel parking lot (*see above*) or a 9-mile trek from the visitor center, but you'll sleep within a stone's throw of the ocean at any of the 15 sites. People tend to avoid **Glenn Camp** because it's 5 miles from the nearest road, but it's located in a quiet valley surrounded by trees, perfect for those who want to get away from civilization. The 16 sites at **Sky Camp** are the most popular. You'd have to walk a steep 2½-mile trail from the visitor center to get here, but the ranger can direct you to a pullout up the road that's a gentler 1-mile hike away. The campground is perched on a small mountain ridge with an outstanding view of the peninsula and seashore. For the true misanthrope, **Wildcat Camp,** a stiff 6½ miles from the nearest road, has 12 sites scattered in a dense thicket. Privacy is never a problem.

Samuel P. Taylor State Park. Six miles east of Point Reyes on Sir Francis Drake Boulevard, 60 campsites are available for $14 per night (hike/bike sites cost $3 per person). They feature—blessing of all blessings—hot showers, at 50¢ for five minutes. Reservations can be made through MISTIX (tel. 800/444–PARK); during summer, even weekdays get booked up. Think about taking the hike up to Barnaby Peak (four or five hours round-trip). It's a beautiful campground and redwood grove, not as overrun as Muir Woods. Golden Gate Transit Bus 65 stops at the park on weekends and holidays (*see* Getting In, Out, and Around, in Chapter 1). *Tel. 415/488–9897. From U.S. 101, go about 15 mi west on Sir Francis Drake Blvd.*

South Bay

The area along U.S. 101 feels like many other parts of the United States; strip malls, fast food, and chain motels abound. You'll find the latter at just about every freeway off-ramp, and double rooms invariably cost $50–$70 per night. For a cheap weekend getaway, the San Mateo County Coast has two excellent hostels and several secluded campgrounds. For longer stays, consult Santa Clara County's free weekly newspaper, *Metro.* It's available in cafés, bookstores, and sidewalk vending machines and lists summer sublets and long-term rentals. College bulletin boards are also promising places to look for apartments, especially the one in Tressider Student Union at Stanford University in Palo Alto.

PALO ALTO

While Palo Alto isn't exactly a mecca of budget accommodations, it's probably the most happening place to stay in the South Bay. A healthy number of pricey restaurants, bars, and cafés cater to Stanford University students. Most of Palo Alto's budget motels are located along **El Camino Real.**

➢ **UNDER $55 • Coronet Motel.** Traffic on El Camino Real makes it noisy, but the Coronet wins points for location and value. It's only a few blocks from Stanford University, and Stanford Shopping Center is a short drive away. Doubles are $40 and the rooms—some with kitchenettes—are comfortable, if not exactly modern. *2455 El Camino Real, btw California Ave. and Page Mill Rd., tel. 415/326–1081. From U.S. 101, Embarcadero Rd. exit west, turn left on El Camino Real. 21 rooms.*

Stanford Arms Motel. This blue-and-white, rustic-looking motel is less generic than most others in its price range and it's conveniently located near the Stanford campus and the Stanford Shopping Center. The rooms are clean, if tired-looking; singles cost $42, doubles $44 ($10 extra for rooms with kitchenette). *115 El Camino Real, at Harvard St., Menlo Park, tel. 415/325–1428. From U.S. 101, Embarcadero Rd. exit west, turn left on El Camino Real. 14 rooms.*

➢ **UNDER $100 • Cowper Inn.** This Victorian B&B is the perfect place for your parents to stay when they're in town. The spacious rooms are filled with antiques, yet they retain a fresh and airy feeling. Doubles start at $60 with shared bath, $100 with private bath. Breakfast is included, and all rooms have phones and cable TV. Mom and Dad can sip sherry and munch on almonds in the parlor before taking you to an expensive dinner to tell you how proud of you they are. *705 Cowper St., tel. 415/327–4475. From U.S. 101, University Ave. west 2–3 mi, turn left on Cowper St., and go 2 blocks. 14 rooms, 12 with bath. Reservations advised.*

HOSTELS **Hidden Villa Hostel.** This is an actual working farm—complete with animals and organic gardens. Set in a 1,500-acre canyon in the Los Altos Hills between Palo Alto and San Jose, the hostel offers easy access to hiking trails and peaceful dirt roads. Large, rustic dorm-style cabins dot the canyon, each with communal bathroom facilities. HI members pay $10 per night, nonmembers $13. Bring your own food. Unfortunately, public transportation doesn't come anywhere near here. *26870 Moody Rd., Los Altos, tel. 415/949–8648. From San Francisco, I–280 south past Palo Alto to El Monte/Moody Rd. exit, turn right on El Monte Ave., left on Moody Rd. at stop sign, and go 1.7 mi. Reception open daily 8–9:30 and 4:30–9:30. Closed June–Aug.*

Sanborn Park Hostel. This is one of the most attractive hostels in California, perfectly situated for avid hikers and easily reached by public transportation. The main cottage, a wooden cabin that dates from 1908, is surrounded by the dense 300-acre redwood forest of Sanborn Park, which is also home to a nearby nature museum. Hostelers stay in a large hall and have access to a rec room, a volleyball court, a grill, laundry facilities, and the standard HI kitchen—all for $7.50 per night for members and $9.50 for nonmembers. It's a busy place, but they try to find room for anyone who shows up. You need to bring your own food; the only restaurants and grocery stores are 4 miles away in downtown Saratoga. *15808 Sanborn Rd., Saratoga, tel. 408/741–0166. I–280 south to Saratoga/Sunnyvale exit, turn right, go 5½ mi to Hwy. 9, turn right (toward Big Basin), go 2½ mi, turn left at SANBORN SKYLINE COUNTY PARK sign, go 1 mi, and turn right. Or, Santa Clara County Transit Bus 54 from Sunnyvale CalTrain station, get off at Saratoga post office, and call hostel for a ride. Curfew 11 PM, lockout 9–5. Reception open daily 5 PM–11 PM. Sheet rental 50¢. Wheelchair access.*

SAN MATEO COUNTY COAST

The desolate coastline south of San Francisco has some of the area's most striking scenery. **Half Moon Bay,** the largest and most centrally located town, is not the best choice for accommodations, since all of its offerings are quite expensive. Instead, head for one of two gorgeous hostels, either of which may be the best lodging deal in the Bay Area.

PACIFICA AND MONTARA This area features a number of generic budget motels that are virtually indistinguishable from each other. The hostels are far more memorable.

➢ **UNDER $55** • **Marine View Motel.** With roomy doubles ($42) that include enough carpeted floor space for at least six, this run-down but acceptably clean motel is the best bet in Pacifica. It's an easy walk to the beach and the old town, but the noise from Highway 1 is slightly annoying. *2040 Francisco Blvd., Pacifica, tel. 415/355–9042. 14 rooms. If manager is out, inquire in Room 7. Wheelchair access.*

➢ **HOSTEL** • **Point Montara Lighthouse AYH-Hostel.** This functioning lighthouse and its adjoining hostel are perched on a cliff ½ mile south of Montara State Beach. As if that weren't enough, it has incredible views of the coastline and access to a beach and tide pools. Inside, there's a fireplace in the comfortable living room, a communal kitchen, a dining area, and an outdoor redwood hot tub ($5 per person for one hour, two-person minimum). Beds go for $11 per night ($14 for nonmembers), and everyone must do a small chore. The range of guests is greater than at most hostels; expect to see anyone from San Franciscans on a weekend holiday to German travelers on a cross-country trek, with a few 50- and 60-year-olds scattered among the twentysomethings. Reservations can be made anywhere from three days to six months in advance and are advised for summer weekends. *Hwy. 1, at 16th St., Montara, tel. 415/728–7177. From Daly City BART, SamTrans Bus 1L or 1C southbound and ask driver to let you off at 14th St. 45 beds. Curfew 11 PM, lockout 9:30–4:30. Reception open daily 7:50–9:30 and 4:30–9:30. Laundry. Deposit of first night's fees required for reservation.*

HALF MOON BAY If you can afford it, the **Old Thyme Inn** (779 Main St., tel. 415/726–1616), dating from 1899, is the nicest bed-and-breakfast in town. Each of its seven rooms is named for and decorated with a different herb, and each has an old-fashioned claw-foot bathtub. Some rooms also have a whirlpool or a fireplace. Rates range from $85 to $160 per night and include a hearty breakfast. The **San Benito House** (356 Main St., tel. 415/726–3425), built at the turn of the century, has 12 rooms with a beautiful garden backyard and a pricey restaurant overlooking Main Street. Rates are $60–$95 per night. If all else fails, a 20-room **Ramada Inn** (3020 Hwy. 1, tel. 415/726–9700 or 800/2–RAMADA) on the north end of town has doubles starting at $72 weekdays, $98 weekends, including breakfast.

➢ **UNDER $65** • **Cameron's Inn.** This tiny hotel on the southern outskirts of town has three clean, simple doubles that feel distinctly European. Big beds and fine-art prints lend some style to the rooms, all of which share a common bath. You'll hear big-rigs downshifting on the highway as you drift off, but at $50 on weekdays and $60 on weekends, it's about as cheap as you'll find anywhere in the area. *1410 S. Cabrillo Hwy. (Hwy. 1), tel. 415/726–5705.*

Unless you camp, there is virtually no lodging in Half Moon Bay for under $50. There are four hotels that cost $200 a night, though.

➢ **CAMPING** • **Half Moon Bay State Beach.** Because of its proximity to downtown, this place attracts teenage partiers and weekend-warrior types, especially during summer. Though you'll fall asleep to the sound of waves and arise to the smell of the sea, it's hardly the great outdoors. Located at the base of a small sand dune, the 55 characterless sites cost $14 per night; all sites are doled out on a first-come, first-served basis. *95 Kelly Ave., Half Moon Bay, tel. 415/726–8820. Kelly Ave. west from Hwy. 1. Cold showers, fire pits, flush toilets, food lockers, picnic tables.*

LA HONDA There are four excellent choices for staying in La Honda. Three of the area's parks have campgrounds and one has a hostel that caters to backpackers. The **Hiker's Hut** in Sam McDonald County Park ($10 per night per person, $8 for Sierra Club members) has sleeping space for 14 (bring a sleeping bag). The Scandinavian A-frame cabin sits atop a ridge—a fairly steep 1½-mile hike from the parking lot. From the deck, you can see the ocean on a clear day. Pit toilets and kitchen facilities are available. Reservations (which require a 50% check deposit) must be made well in advance, especially during summer weekends, when the hostel fills up two months ahead. Reserve through the Loma Prieta chapter of the Sierra Club (3921 E. Bayshore Rd., Palo Alto, CA 94303, tel. 415/390–8411). For info on Sam McDonald State Park, including directions, *see* South Bay, in Chapter 2.

➢ **CAMPING** • If you want to pitch a tent, the most developed sites are in **Portola State Park** and **Memorial County Park,** while **Pescadero Creek County Park** has more primitive, secluded hike-in campgrounds. Memorial is a thick old-growth forest that offers 135 quiet sites ($12), all with picnic tables, fire pits, and hot showers. Although popular with car campers on summer weekends, the campground is sparsely visited at other times. Sites are allotted on a first-come, first-served basis. In Portola State Park, the 53 "family" and seven hike-in campsites ($14) see little light in their cool berth beneath the redwoods. The family sites have running water, showers, fire pits, and picnic tables. Reserve through MISTIX (tel. 800/444–PARK). For a spot at one of Pescadero Creek's 15 hike-in sites ($7), located in dense second-growth forest along the river, contact the rangers at Portola State Park (tel. 415/948–9098). For directions to these parks and info on exploring them, *see* South Bay, in Chapter 2.

PESCADERO This pristine town overlooks miles of unblemished coastline; an enchanting hostel and peaceful campgrounds are situated among the redwoods.

➢ **HOSTEL** • **Pigeon Point Lighthouse Youth Hostel.** Perched on a small bluff 5 miles south of Pescadero State Beach are four bungalow-style dorms, including an outdoor, bluff-side hot tub ($3 per person per half-hour). Free tours of the historic lighthouse on the grounds are also available. One night in any of the 54 comfortable beds costs $10 ($13 for nonmembers); another $10 secures a private room for two people. All guests must do a chore each day of their stay. The maximum stay is three nights. Bummer. *Pigeon Point Rd. and Hwy. 1, tel. 415/879–0633. From Daly City BART, SamTrans Bus 96C. Curfew 11 PM, lockout 9:30–4:30. Reception open daily 7:30–9:30 and 4:30–9:30. Reservations advised. Wheelchair access.*

➢ **CAMPING** • Surprisingly few visitors venture to the 27 campsites ($14) and 18 hike-in sites ($7) in quiet **Butano State Park** (tel. 415/879–2040). The drive-in sites have fire rings, picnic tables, and food lockers. Reservations can be made through MISTIX (tel. 800/444–PARK) up to eight weeks in advance, but are usually not necessary. None of the sites has showers, but, hey, welcome to the great outdoors. For directions to Butano and more info on the park, *see* South Bay, in Chapter 8.

OUTDOOR ACTIVITIES 8

By Emily Hastings

One young Berkeley resident gets up before dawn to windsurf for several hours before going to work. Another local, with a degree in economics, is content to keep his job as a bicycle mechanic because it allows him a daily mountain-biking jaunt through the forest. Then there's the 40-year-old attorney who leaves work in time to grab a longboard and catch some evening waves. It's no surprise—many people choose to live in the Bay Area precisely because it's so easy to drive 15 minutes from the city and enjoy some of the most spectacular natural attractions this country has to offer. The cool, moist woodlands of Marin County are prime territory for hikers, bikers, horseback riders, and bird watchers. The afternoon breezes make San Francisco Bay ideal for windsurfing. And when the summer winds die down, you can put away your sail and dust off the surfboard for the winter waves. With so many sporting options and such a moderate climate, it's hard for Bay Area residents to think of excuses to stay inside.

In fact, so many locals head for the mountains and the coast that it's sometimes hard to distinguish those places from the city you're trying to leave behind. Outdoor enthusiasts are often outraged to find that their "secret" spot is more congested than the freeway at rush hour. Mountain bikers lock horns with hikers, and hikers with equestrians; novice surfers get in the way of expert surfers; and ultimate Frisbee players fight soccer players for field space. It's the price of convenience. If you're trying to escape humanity as well as exhaust fumes and urban neurosis, you'll need to drive a little farther than 15 minutes.

To escape weekend crowds, avoid Marin County and Point Reyes. The South Bay is undiscovered in comparison to its northern neighbors, and the farther you go from the city, the more likely you are to find true solitude among the redwoods. The parks in the East Bay hills don't get the harsh wind and dense fog of the coast, though they're not nearly as lush. If you just want to let off some steam after work, the concentration of young people in San Francisco and Berkeley makes it easy to find a pickup game of basketball, volleyball, soccer, or ultimate Frisbee at a nearby park or rec center. With some persistence and one of those "no fear" attitudes, you'll find something to tickle your athletic fancy.

A great place to start exploring the outdoors is actually *indoors,* at **Outdoors Unlimited** (OU), a co-op fueled by funds from U.C. San Francisco and the community. Volunteers here teach clinics on everything from fly fishing to CPR, organize backpacking and cycling outings, and even lead moonlight kayak trips. While UCSF students have priority in signing up for some of the activities (which are unbelievably cheap, and sometimes even free), the general public is welcome. OU is also a great resource for information on specialized co-ops and networks, and they offer a variety of rentals. To receive their quarterly newsletter, send one stamped (55¢), self-addressed envelope to Outdoors Unlimited, Box 0234A, University of California, San Francisco

94143. *Office: cnr 3rd and Parnassus Aves., beneath UCSF library, tel. 415/476–2078. Open Mon., Tues., Fri. 11:30–1:30 and 5–7, Wed. and Thurs. 11:30–1:30 and 4–6.*

Berkeley's **Cal Adventures**—similar in scope to OU—reserves the best deals for U.C. students, but it's also a great resource for the East Bay community, with a wide variety of affordable outings and lessons in such sports as sailing, kayaking, and windsurfing. Located on the U.C. campus, Cal Adventures rents equipment at low prices. Call for a brochure. *Recreational Sports Facility, 2301 Bancroft Way, tel. 510/642–4000 or 510/643–8029. Open Mon.–Thurs. 10–6, Fri. 10–7.*

Another East Bay resource for competition as well as recreation is the **Cal Sport Club Program.** Individual clubs include boxing, fencing, ultimate Frisbee, and cycling. Membership eligibility varies from club to club—call ahead and check it out. *Recreational Sports Facility, 2301 Bancroft Way, Suite 4420, on the U.C. Berkeley campus, tel. 510/643–8024.*

The best places to stock up on pamphlets, books, and maps are the **Sierra Club Bookstore,** in San Francisco (730 Polk St., tel. 415/923–5600) and Oakland (6014 College Ave., tel. 510/658–7470), and **REI** (1338 San Pablo Ave., tel. 510/527–4140) in Berkeley.

League Sports and Pickup Games

For city folk, pickup games and organized sports leagues are a great way to get the blood moving without having to go far to do it. You can join pickup games on just about every court and field in the Bay Area, though skill levels vary from place to place. Weekends draw the largest crowds, but warm weekdays and long evenings generally guarantee activity. Get in touch with your local community center, park department, or YMCA to get involved with activities in your neighborhood.

For women's sports info try "The Women's Sports Page," published in Berkeley (P.O. Box 5187, Berkeley 94705, tel. 510/655–6750), or call the Women's Sports Connection in San Francisco (tel. 415/241–8879).

The **San Francisco Urban Professionals Athletic League** offers two indoor basketball leagues and four indoor volleyball leagues, including one co-ed and one gay/lesbian league. The end of each season is marked with barbecues and a competitive all-star game. For more information contact Clyde Harrison at 415/431–6339. The **Bay Area Outreach and Recreation Program** (830 Bancroft Way, Berkeley, tel. 510/849–4663) sponsors athletics for people with physical disabilities, including motorized- and manual-chair basketball and soccer.

BASKETBALL Pickup games are almost universally male, and competition levels vary dramatically. In other words, peruse the courts in your neighborhood before you lace up those high-tops. To find out about men's leagues in the city, call Gilbert Rocha at the **Mission Recreation Center** (2450 Harrison St., at 21st St., tel. 415/695–5012) or Marty Arenas at the **Eureka Valley Recreation Center** (100 Collingwood St., 1 block from 18th St., tel. 415/554–9528). For information on women's leagues, contact Jim Jackson at the **San Francisco Recreation and Park Department** (tel. 415/753–7027).

In the East Bay, the **City of Berkeley Recreation Department** (2180 Milvia St., at Center St. in City Hall, tel. 510/644–6530) offers men's and women's leagues January–March. The **Oakland Recreation Department** (1520 Lakeside Dr., at 14th St., tel. 510/238–3494) also offers winter and spring leagues for men and spring leagues for women.

➢ **WHERE TO PLAY** • The following San Francisco courts usually get going weekday afternoons while it's still light out and weekend mornings between 8 and 11. **Grattan Playground** (Alma and Stanyan Sts.), near Golden Gate Park, sees a mixed group weekday afternoons around 3 or 3:30; weekends bring a bigger crowd and a higher level of play to the courts. In the Marina, the popular **Moscone Recreation Center** (Chestnut and Laguna Sts.) has courts with night-lighting and unforgiving double rims. Weekends tend to be a zoo. The skill level varies at the **Chinese Playground** (Broadway and Larkin St.), but it's among the city's few lit courts, and people are almost always here in the evenings. Games at the **Potrero Hill Recreation Center** (Arkansas and 22nd Sts.) get pretty competitive, especially Monday and Thursday nights. Fights of the white-men-can't-jump variety are not rare on these well-lit courts. Four-on-four games get going early on the weekends at the small courts at Noe Valley's **James Lick Middle School** (Clipper and Castro Sts.). The small courts in the Panhandle of Golden Gate Park, between Oak and Fell streets, are going all the time and play is very competitive.

In North Berkeley, the short court at **Live Oak Park** (Shattuck Ave. and Berryman St.) hosts weekend three-on-three games, but the wait can be unbearable. A more intimidating game goes on at **Ohlone Park** (Hearst St., near California St.). In South Berkeley, the court at **People's Park** (Haste St., btw Telegraph Ave. and Bowditch St.) is always hopping, though the skill level swings wildly. If you really want to get serious, you'll find competitive players on the courts at the **Recreational Sports Facility** on the U.C. Berkeley campus (2301 Bancroft Way, tel. 510/643–8038).

SOCCER Those who thought there was no life after A.Y.S.O. will be happy to know that Bay Area soccer leagues were kicking long before the World Cup brought the sport to this country's attention. The **Golden Gate Women's Soccer League** has four divisions in the East Bay, Marin County, and San Francisco. To join either the fall or spring season, contact Ashley Young (tel. 510/658–8337). In the highly competitive men's **San Francisco Football Soccer League,** the players are a truly international crew. The season runs September–May, with six divisions playing all over the city on Sundays. Sunset Soccer Supply (*see below*) has a list of coaches' phone numbers and game locations; try-outs are required. The high-caliber **Latin American Soccer League** (tel. 510/732–6804), with half as many divisions, fills in the summer gap for men's soccer. Co-ed leagues keep you dribbling year-round: Contact the **San Francisco Co-Ed Recreational Soccer League** (tel. 415/330–8900) for more information.

Sunset Soccer Supply can hook you up with a new pair of cleats or help men interested in the San Francisco League find a team that has openings. The staff is up on the soccer scene and the shop carries the best supplies in the city. While you're here, pick up a free copy of the *Soccer America Yellow Pages* for a listing of leagues, clubs, and some tournaments. *3214 Irving St., near 33rd Ave., San Francisco, tel. 415/753–2666. Open Mon. and Wed. 11–6, Fri. 11–7, Sat. 10–6, Sun. 11–5.*

➢ **WHERE TO PLAY** • Sunday mornings year-round, a crowd gathers at Golden Gate Park's **Polo Field** (Middle Dr. W near Martin Luther King Jr. Dr.) for an impromptu game of soccer. The almost exclusively male players represent a range of skill levels. League teams square off at **Beach Chalet,** also at the western edge of the park. You'll find women's teams there on Saturdays and men's on Sundays. Wednesdays after work, postcollege players kick around at the **Marina Green** (Marina Blvd. and Fillmore St.). There are no lights here, so long summer days see more games than winter.

While San Francisco's got it going on with league teams, Berkeley's the winner when it comes to pickup games. The field at the top of Berkeley's **Clark Kerr Campus,** a.k.a. **Dwight/Derby** (off Dwight Way, east of Warring St.), has co-ed pickup games weekday evenings, women (usually) Tuesday or Thursday evenings, and mostly men on weekend mornings. A good place to come if you're looking for fun rather than competition, the scene here quiets down some when the university is not in session. Down the hill, **Willard Park** (Derby St., btw Hillegass Ave. and Regent St.) usually has Friday-afternoon pickup games from 2 or 3 until 6. Look for a friendly co-ed game (i.e., varied ages and skill levels) Tuesday, Thursday, and Friday noon to 1 at **San Pablo Field** (btw Mabel, Russell, Park, and Ward Sts.). On the more serious side, AstroTurf pickup games take place weekdays at 5 and weekends at 4 at **Kleeberger Field** (Piedmont Ave. at Stadium Rim Way). It's mostly a male thang (ages 25–50), and testosterone levels run high.

ULTIMATE FRISBEE The rules of ultimate are much like those of football, except that ultimate is a noncontact sport with no referees, and players call their own fouls. The best way to get the scoop on leagues, club teams, and tournaments is to go to the pickup games at the parks listed below. Or call the **Ultimate Players Association** (tel. 800/UPA–4384) or the **Cal Sport Club Program** (*see* chapter introduction, *above*).

➢ **WHERE TO PLAY** • **Sharon Meadow,** off Kezar Drive in Golden Gate Park, sometimes sees co-ed pickup games of up to 40 people. Frisbee fanatics gather here every Tuesday and Thursday evening while it's still light out, and late mornings every weekend. **Julius Kahn Play-**

ground (W. Pacific Ave., btw Spruce and Locust Sts.), near the southeast corner of the Presidio, hosts pickup games Wednesday evenings and Saturday mornings. In Berkeley, pickup ultimate follows soccer at 6 on Fridays in **Willard Park** (*see* Soccer, *above*). One of the most popular places to play in the East Bay, though, is **Oakland Tech High School** (4351 Broadway, at 43rd St.).

VOLLEYBALL The **Central YMCA** (220 Golden Gate Ave., at Leavenworth St., tel. 415/885–0460) and the Richmond district's **S.F. Volleyball Association** (tel. 415/931–6385) have co-ed leagues nearly year-round; the former hosts open play between seasons for $3 a night. To join a women's volleyball league in San Francisco, contact Jim Jackson at the **San Francisco Recreation and Park Department** (tel. 415/753–7027), which sponsors several leagues for different skill levels; the season runs from October to mid-December.

The **City of Berkeley Recreation Department** (tel. 510/644–6530) organizes a co-ed league with several seasons for advanced and recreational players. **City Beach Sports and Recreation Center** (4701 Doyle St., at 47th St., tel. 510/428–1221) in Emeryville offers some serious choices: five levels of play in men, women's, and co-ed leagues, made up of teams of two, four, five, or six people. They have three hard courts and two sand, all indoors.

➢ **WHERE TO PLAY** • On weekends in San Francisco, people set up their own nets at the **Marina Green** (Marina Blvd. and Fillmore St.) and nearby at the **Moscone Recreation Center** (Chestnut and Laguna Sts.). At both locations you'll usually find high-skill two-on-two games. Also intimidating are the six-on-six weekend games at several spots along John F. Kennedy Drive in **Golden Gate Park.** You can rent nets for $11 for the weekend at **Outdoors Unlimited** (*see* chapter introduction, *above*).

The S.F. Recreation and Park Department hosts open play 7–9 on Monday nights at **Kezar Pavillion** (Stanyan and Waller Sts.). In summer, the Pro-Am Basketball League has Monday games there, so the schedule switches to Tuesdays. These games generally attract a 20- to 30-year-old crowd. Admission is $2.

Every other summer (during even-numbered years) the S.F. Recreation and Park Department and **Club One** (2 Embarcadero, tel. 415/788–1010) sponsor **Embarcadero Beach Sand Volleyball.** Starting at the end of May, the smell of sunscreen permeates the Financial District as corporate types loosen their ties and outside hitters drag themselves downtown to **Justin Herman Plaza** for free open-play weekdays and some weekends until the beginning of August. For info call the Embarcadero Center (tel. 415/772–0500).

In the East Bay, **People's Park** (*see* Basketball, *above*) has two outdoor sand courts, but you may have to fight for your right to play. Tuesday night, pickup games take place at the asphalt court in **Live Oak Park** (*see* Basketball, *above*). People also set up on the grass in **Ohlone Park** (Hearst Ave., btw. Sacramento Ave. and Milvia St.) and goof around Saturday morning. For $5, summers only, you can take part in open play in Emeryville at **City Beach** (*see above*). Games take place Mondays, Tuesdays, Thursdays, and Fridays 11–2 and 5–11, and Saturdays 10–6.

Hiking

The Bay Area is filled with an impressive array of hiking spots close to home where you can get away from car horns and concrete for the afternoon, work up a sweat, and marvel at giant trees, deep canyons, and the gloomy ocean. And if you hit the trail with **Golden Gate Hikers,** you may even score a date along the way. Sponsored by Hostelling International, this hiking club is filled with singles ages 25–50. You don't have to be an HI member to hike—just bring a buck for each event and a few dollars to cover transportation costs. Participants usually meet on Sundays at 9:30 AM at 2209 Van Ness Avenue (near Broadway) for day hikes; also look for a number of overnights throughout the season. For a free quarterly hiking schedule, write to 55 Vandewater St. #11, San Francisco 94133, or call the **Hikers' Hotline** (tel. 415/550–6321).

At **Outdoors Unlimited** (*see* chapter introduction, *above*), in true co-op spirit, all of the hiking trips are free—you only pay transportation costs. You don't need to be a member to participate; just sign up on the trip sheet posted at the OU office (cnr 3rd and Parnassus Aves., beneath

UCSF library) up to 11 days prior to the trip. The **Sierra Club** also sponsors hikes all over the Bay Area. They're free, though a donation may be requested, and carpoolers are expected to share gas, parking, and bridge tolls. Pick up a schedule at the Sierra Club Bookstore (*see* chapter introduction, *above*) or send a check for $4.50 (payable to the Sierra Club) to Chapter Schedule, 5237 College Ave., Oakland 94618.

SAN FRANCISCO Even if you don't have the time or the means to leave the city entirely, you can still escape the concrete jungle (at least for a little while). The **Coastal Trail** follows 9 miles of San Francisco's shoreline, from the cliffs near Golden Gate Bridge over dirt roads, onto residential sidewalks, around craggy headlands, and along the beach all the way down to Fort Funston.

Begin at the **Golden Gate Bridge** toll plaza parking lot. Walk west underneath the toll plaza, turn left onto Merchant Road, and continue west to find the trailhead. After about 10 minutes you get your first hint of why this hike is not to be missed: The view takes in 200-foot cliffs, the Golden Gate Bridge, and the Marin Headlands all at once. The trail then heads inland; when the path ends on Lincoln Blvd., take the dirt road to the right that leads to **Baker Beach.** Enjoy the sandy dunes and salty air as you forge ahead in a westerly direction; cross the parking lot and head into the forest (keep to the right every time the trail forks). About five minutes later, the trail spits you out onto **El Camino Del Mar,** which travels through the extravagant **Seacliff** neighborhood. The dirt trail begins again on the right just where the houses end. The next 1.7 miles of the trail, passing through **Lands End,** takes you past San Francisco's wildest little corner, full of rocky cliffs, grassy fields, crashing surf, and magnificent views. Wise hikers will heed the warning signs and stay off the unstable cliffs, though a quick peek over the edge won't hurt (look for seals diving among the rocks). The dirt trail ends in a parking lot overlooking the **Sutro Baths;** head downhill past the aptly named **Cliff House** to **Ocean Beach.** From here to **Fort Funston** (4.7 mi south) you'll pass **Golden Gate Park** and the **San Francisco Zoo** on your left. If you make it all the way to Fort Funston, you'll find picnicking areas with great views of the ocean and local hang gliders practicing their craft. Once you hit Ocean Beach, you can catch a bus back to downtown at almost any cross-street. For a map of the Coastal Trail, call or visit the **Golden Gate National Recreation Area Visitor Center.** *West end of Point Lobos Ave. at the Great Highway, under the Cliff House, tel. 415/556–8642. Open daily 10–4:30.*

For a less strenuous and time-consuming urban stroll, try the **Golden Gate Prominade.** Starting from the same parking lot as the Coastal Trail, head east down the stairs that lead to **Fort Point National Historic Site** (*also see box* Chilling by the Ocean, in Chapter 2). From here follow the 3.5-mile, mostly asphalt path, which traces the bay from Fort Point to the **Hyde Street Pier.** The popular jogging route takes you by the windsurfers at Crissy Field, around the yacht harbor, past Marina Green, and over the hill of Fort Mason to Aquatic Park near Fisherman's Wharf.

➢ **THE PRESIDIO** • For another intimate encounter with the native flora and fauna of San Francisco, try the Presidio (*also see* Neighborhoods, in Chapter 2). The Presidio is nearly impossible to get lost in—a boon or a bust, depending on the mood of the moment. Check out the 2-mile **Ecology Trail** that starts at the southeasternmost corner (Presidio Blvd. and Pacific Ave.) of the Presidio. The trail travels through cool, springy forest beds and provides an intimate introduction to some of San Francisco's most distinctive plant life, including the endangered, pink-flowered *Presidio clarkia* or the small, white-flowered *Marin duarte* flax. You can get more information on the Ecology Trail or the guided tours offered by the National Park Service at the **Presidio Visitor Information Center.** *Montgomery St., Bldg. 102, tel. 415/556–0865. Open daily 10–5.*

EAST BAY If you really want to escape the city, a trip to any one of the 50 parks in the **East Bay Regional Park District** (tel. 510/562–PARK) should do the trick. The district spans two counties, includes more than 75,000 acres of parkland, and provides a varied terrain of dark redwood forests, blustery hills with ocean views, warm grassy fields, lakes . . . everything a nature lover could want. At any one of six visitor centers you can get free maps, and for a well-spent dollar you can own the "Regional Parks" brochure; it includes information on all the parks and attractions, including the 31-mile **Skyline Trail** that connects the six East Bay Regional Parks running through the Berkeley–Oakland hills. From the north trailhead in **Wildcat Canyon Park,** the trail snakes south through **Tilden Regional Park** (*see below*); **Sibley Vol-**

canic National Reserve, with its volcanic dikes and lava flows; **Huckleberry Botanic Regional Reserve,** known for its endangered and rare plant life such as the pallid manzanita, which only grows two places in the world; **Redwood Regional Park** (*see below*); finally reaching the southern trail terminus at **Anthony Chabot Regional Park.** It's tempting but nearly impossible to traverse this trail in one attempt, but since the only available camping is at Anthony Chabot (*see* The East Bay, in Chapter 7), you have no other choice. Parking and admission to all East Bay parks is free unless otherwise noted.

➢ **TILDEN REGIONAL PARK** • When Berkeleyans want to commune with nature, they head to Tilden Park in the Berkeley Hills. Tilden contains two of the highest points in the East Bay—**Volmer Peak** (1,913 feet) to the south and **Wildcat Peak** (1,250 feet) to the north. The hike to Wildcat Peak from **Inspiration Point** is just a moderate sweat-breaker. In fact, the trail, called **Nimitz Way,** is 4½ miles of wheelchair-accessible road. The hike should take a good two hours, during which you'll have plenty of time to absorb the view of the bay and of the San Pablo and Briones Reservoirs. Nimitz Way is a better bet than most of Tilden's poorly maintained dirt trails, on which poison oak and brambles run rampant. To reach Inspiration Point by car from University Avenue, turn left on Oxford Street, right on Rose Street, and left on Spruce Street. Follow Spruce to the top of the hill, then turn right on Wildcat Canyon Road; the Inspiration Point parking lot is on your left after about 15 minutes.

You can disentangle yourself from the overgrown trails by heading to the more open and grassy central part of Tilden Park. Starting at Lake Anza, head northeast on the **Lake Anza Trail,** which encircles the lake. When you reach the far northeast corner of the lake, look for the **Wildcat Gorge Trail** on your left. The initial steep descent past a century-old springhouse is no indication of things to come: The trail tunnels through a wide, rocky gorge but eventually rises to 80 feet above the creek that carved it. Continue for a half-mile until the trail forks. To the right, the **Curran Trail** rises sharply for .7 miles to Inspiration Point. Otherwise, the Wildcat Gorge Trail, one of the nicest in Tilden, continues on through groves of California bay laurels. About .3 miles up the trail on your right, you'll pass a hill with a practically vertical path upward (this isn't on the official Tilden map). At the top of the hill you'll have a 360° view of the park. Return to the Wildcat Gorge Trail and backtrack to Lake Anza for an easy to moderate 1½-hour hike.

A moderate 3-mile (round-trip), 800-foot climb through woods and fields to the top of Wildcat Peak begins at the Environmental Education Center: Head east on **Laurel Canyon Trail,** cross the fire road, continue uphill, and turn left onto the **Wildcat Peak Trail.** A turnoff to the right leads all the way to the top, where you can look out over Oakland, San Francisco, and Marin. Head back down the way you came, turn right onto Wildcat Peak Trail, and go left on the **Sylvan Trail,** which leads back to the nature center.

To reach Tilden Park, take University Avenue east from I–80 to Oxford Street; go left on Oxford, right on Rose, and left on Spruce to the top of the hill. Cross Grizzly Peak Boulevard, make an immediate left on Canon Drive, and follow the signs. For maps or if you have questions, stop by the **Environmental Education Center** at the north end of the park (tel. 510/525–2233).

➢ **WILDCAT CANYON REGIONAL PARK** • During summer and fall, Wildcat Canyon is the dried-up fire hazard adjoining Tilden to the north. In winter, the 2,500-acre park is as green as a golf course, and in spring it erupts with wildflowers. You'll share the grassy hills and stunning views of San Pablo Bay with grazing cattle; don't forget to close the gates that block them from many of the canyon trails. The best trail loop is a moderate 4-mile hike: From the **Wildcat Creek Trail**—which starts at the EEC in Tilden Park and is different from Wildcat *Peak* Trail—head up 1½ miles through the tall grass on the **Mezue Trail** for an excellent view; then turn right and continue ¾ mile along the paved **Nimitz Way.** Turning right onto the **Havey Canyon Trail** will return you to the Wildcat Creek Trail on a winding 1½-mile path (avoid this trail when it's wet, or you'll spend more time on your butt than your feet). Wildcat Canyon adjoins Tilden to the north, and it is often hard to tell where one park ends and the next begins. The main entrance to Wildcat Canyon is on Park Avenue at the north end of the canyon; parking is readily available and you'll also find a park office (tel. 510/236–1262). To get here, take I–80 to the Solano/Amador exit. Turn right on McBryde Street and follow signs to the park office from the first stop sign.

➢ **REDWOOD REGIONAL PARK** • While the tourist hordes head to Muir Woods to see California redwoods, you can slip away to Redwood Regional Park in the Oakland Hills south of Tilden, Sibley, and Huckleberry parks. The park's original redwoods were mowed down at the start of the California gold rush, so the trees you'll see are youngsters—not even 100 years old. But unlike Muir Woods, where the trails sport guard rails and a few too many tourists, Redwood offers an environment rough enough to let you know you're outdoors and not at the mall. The trick to enjoying the park is to avoid the dusty perimeter trails by staying at the bottom of the canyon under the moist redwood canopy.

Connecting the northern and southern entrances are two main trails, the **East Ridge Trail** and the **West Ridge Trail.** Both, along with the **Stream Trail,** start at the Skyline Gate parking lot. The West Ridge Trail is the main thoroughfare through the park, and too much time on its broad path may get you flattened by a speed-crazed mountain biker. Luckily, other trails are more secluded. From the Skyline Gate entrance, take the 3-mile (one way) **Stream Trail,** which, after a steep (and often hot and dry) descent to the valley floor, meanders through the redwoods. If you'd rather have shade and the company of redwood groves on your way down, follow the West Ridge Trail a little further to the strenuous **French Trail.** To return to the Skyline Gate entrance from the valley floor, simply pick any trail heading up and to the right; you'll soon connect with the West Ridge Trail, which will lead you back to the park entrance. You'll find free trail maps at the Skyline Gate entrance. *Tel. 510/ 635–0135, ext. 2578. From I–580, take Hwy. 24 east to Hwy. 13 south. Exit north on Joaquin Miller Rd., turn left on Skyline Blvd.; Skyline Gate entrance is about 4 mi further on the right.*

Hike the nature trail at Huckleberry Botanical Preserve in early spring and you might spy the first blossoms of the season; since the park is outside the fog belt, the plants bloom one to two months ahead of others in the vicinity. To reach Huckleberry, follow the directions for Redwood Regional Park.

➢ **ANTHONY CHABOT REGIONAL PARK** • South of Redwood Regional Park, Anthony Chabot covers almost 5,000 acres. Much of the northern section of the park was once covered with eucalyptus trees, but during the intense storms of the past few winters, many of the groves were destroyed. Some hiking trails may be closed for replanting; up-to-date maps are available at the Marina entrance, and if you stay near Lake Chabot you shouldn't have any trouble. The walk around the lake's perimeter, about 7.5 miles, is mostly flat, so if you're looking for a work-out you should head elsewhere. The real reason to take this walk is for a close-up view of the wildflowers and waterfowl that abound in this habitat. To get really close, rent a rowboat ($8 an hr, $23 a day), or a canoe or pedal boat (both $9 an hr, $25 a day). *Tel. 510/635–0135 ext. 2570 for camping and hiking info; tel. 510/582–2198 for lake info. From I–580 east, exit Fairmont Dr. east, which merges with Lake Chabot Rd.; then follow signs. Parking: $3; park along road for free.*

Thinking on Your Feet

If you can read a map while running at breakneck speed, dodging tree limbs, and leaping over fallen logs, you've got what it takes to go orienteering. You'll find people to join you in your crazy quests at the Bay Area Orienteering Club. Three or four times a month they plot a new route through the Bay Area or around Lake Tahoe and leave you to find your way along the marked path as fast as your feet can carry you, armed with a compass, a topographic map, and a suicidal drive. You can race against the clock for a personal challenge or forget about time altogether and stop for a picnic. There are a variety of skill levels, and club members say it's a great opportunity to build self-esteem and survival skills. Events are $6–$10 for nonmembers; $12 will earn you membership and a spot on the mailing list. For more information call 408/255–8018.

MARIN COUNTY A short drive north from San Francisco over the Golden Gate Bridge deposits you in Marin County, chock full of the kind of hiking most people will travel hours for—trails through virgin redwoods, over grassy mountain fields, and past dramatic surf. Many of Marin's best hiking spots, including Muir Woods, Mt. Tamalpais, and Point Reyes National Seashore, lie along Highway 1, which winds up the coast.

➢ **MARIN HEADLANDS** • The Marin Headlands are home to rolling hills covered with coyote bush, low-lying grasses, precipitous bluffs, oak and bay trees, and tons of hardy wildflowers. Often covered with fog and plagued by a steady wind, the headlands are still a popular weekend escape for urbanites. A good place to start your visit is at the **visitor center** (tel. 415/331–1540), open daily 9:30–4:30, where you can get maps ($1.50) and trail suggestions from the staff. Cross the Golden Gate Bridge on U.S. 101, take the first exit (Alexander Ave.), turn left under the freeway, then turn right before the entrance to U.S. 101 south and follow the signs to the visitor center. Most trails start here and parking is free.

For a leisurely stroll, take a spin around the perimeter of the **Rodeo Lagoon.** With all the opportunities to stop and look at the waterfowl, the 1½-mile tour may take longer than you think. For a better view and a more strenuous hike, charge north up the **Coastal Trail.** From the visitor center parking lot, head up the closed-off road (*not* the left stairway). Persevere for about 2 miles, turn right onto the **Wolf Ridge Trail,** and head up the grassy hill (alias Wolf Ridge) for 1.6 miles to the top. When you're ready to stop gazing at the Tennessee Valley, continue for .7 miles down the verdant leeward side of the hill until it hooks up with the **Miwok Trail,** which you follow south. The trail wanders above the edge of the grassy Gerbode Valley, where you may spot a black-tailed deer or bobcat basking in the chaparral. In about 2 miles you'll be back at the visitor center.

The **Tennessee Valley Trail,** at the end of Tennessee Valley Road (from U.S. 101 north, take the Hwy. 1 exit west and make the first left), is a broad path that meanders next to a small creek and through grassy fields for an easy 2 miles. In no time you'll be on black, sandy **Tennessee Beach,** in the company of many families. Here you can see the namesake of the valley—the shipwreck of the SS *Tennessee* (only at *very* low tide, though, so don't strain your eyes). If you're in the mood for a more strenuous hike, follow the Tennessee Valley Trail 1.3 miles from the parking lot and veer right onto the **Coastal Trail.** You may start to regret your decision when the going gets tough after ¾ mile; the trail wildly snakes above the secluded **Pirates Cove** for 2.2 miles, with stunning views of the jagged coast, and eventually leads you down to **Muir Beach** in the next .8 miles. Before you head back, relax a while at the **Pelican Inn** (*see* Muir Beach, in Chapter 2). On your return, see the less dramatic side of the Tennessee Valley by turning left off the Coastal Trail at **Coyote Ridge Trail** after .8 miles. Here, keep your eyes peeled for deer, bobcats, hawks, and great horned owls. Continue for 1½ miles and take the **Fox Trail** back to the Tennessee Valley Trail. You complete the 8-mile round trip with a short walk north, back to the parking lot.

➢ **ANGEL ISLAND** • Almost all 750 acres of this island in San Francisco Bay, accessible by ferry, are covered with forest or sweeping grasses. **Perimeter Road,** which encircles the island, is wheelchair accessible, though steep in some places. Hiking trails lead in from Perimeter Road. On the **Sunset Trail,** immediately southeast of the park headquarters, 2 miles

Whistle While You Walk

A few mountain lions were spotted on Mt. Tam in 1995, brought out of hiding by the end of the drought. Though catching a glimpse of one is rare, if you do have a close encounter, don't act like prey. Don't run or turn your back; wave your arms slowly above your head, speak in a loud voice, and don't crouch down or bend over. Back away slowly to give the lion a chance to escape. If you are attacked, fight back. In remote areas, whistling or singing as you hike will warn a lion of your presence.

of ascending switchbacks afford stunning views of San Francisco to the west. As you circle the 781-foot summit, **Mt. Caroline Livermore,** you'll reach a crossroads; take a left up the paved road to the top for a 360° view of the Bay Area. After you backtrack to the crossroads, return to the ferry via the **North Ridge Trail** to view the eastern side of the island. The entire loop, Angel Island's most difficult hike, takes 2½–3 hours. For information on how to reach the island, *see* Tiburon and Angel Island, in Chapter 2. For recorded information, call 415/435–1915; dial 415/435–5390 to speak to a ranger.

➢ **MUIR WOODS** • You'll share the awesome sight of ancient, towering redwoods (the oldest has been around more than 1,200 years) with hordes of tourists who clog the paved paths on the valley floor. An estimated two million sightseers shuffle past the redwoods annually, but luckily, less than 10% venture forth onto the network of hiking trails that start here. You can make a quick escape by following any of the trails that head up from the valley floor. The $1 brochure for sale at the park entrance and in the gift shop gives great explanations of flora and fauna and a complete trail map.

One way to avoid the crowds at Muir Woods is to come on a rainy day—yes, that's right, a rainy day. The forest's canopy is so dense that it keeps out much of the rain, and the dripping ferns and moss give the illusion that you've ventured into a rain forest.

For an easy 2-mile hike that will get you away from the crowds and give you a view of the redwoods, head to the fourth bridge from the park entrance and take the **Hillside Trail** to your left. For a more spectacular view and workout, head up the **Ben Johnson Trail,** starting from the same spot. You'll climb up through the forest for 2 miles (the last ½-mi is quite steep) until you reach the top of a hill with a wonderful view of several canyons and the Pacific. You can either head east on the **Dipsea Trail** to complete a 4½-mile hike, or, if you're still full of energy, follow it 2 miles west down a steep gulch to **Stinson Beach.** The full hike is one of the best around, and it's more than 9 miles, so you'll be damn pleased with yourself when you're done. If you're here on a weekend or holiday, you can cut down the hike back by hopping on Golden Gate Transit Bus 63 (*also see* Getting In, Out, and Around, in Chapter 1) at the Stinson Beach park entrance. For $1.25 it'll transport you to Mountain Home Inn, where you can pick up the **Panoramic/Ocean View Trail,** which leads 2 miles downhill to the parking lot. *Tel. 415/388–2596. From U.S. 101, follow signs from Stinson Beach/Highway 1 exit.*

➢ **MT. TAMALPAIS** • On a clear day you can spot the Sierra Nevada from the top of Marin's highest mountain, Mt. Tamalpais ("Mt. Tam" to the natives). Of all Mt. Tam's well-worn trails, the trip to the top is the most popular. If you want to sweat a lot and hike more than 3 miles on your journey to the summit, park at the Bootjack Day-Use Area (5 miles from Panoramic Highway, *see below*) and head north on the **Bootjack Trail.** At the Mountain Theater, turn right onto Ridgecrest Boulevard, following the well-marked paths to the summit. Or conserve your energy and drive up most of the way. If you park at the free East Peak parking lot, you need only mosey an easy .7-mile on a paved road to the top for a spectacular view.

In the annual 7-mile Dipsea Race, usually held the second Sunday in June, runners take off from Mill Valley and sprint over Mt. Tamalpais before collapsing on Stinson Beach at the finish line. The race originated in 1905 and is now limited to 1,500 manic runners.

The 2-mile **Steep Ravine Trail** follows a redwood-lined creek down to the ocean. The trail begins at the west end of the parking lot at **Pantoll Ranger Station** (tel. 415/388–2070); the trail map ($1) for sale here is an excellent investment. Along the trail, look for waterfalls, especially in springtime. It's all downhill to **Stinson Beach;** take the 1½-mile **Dipsea Trail,** or stick to the trail that leads to **Rocky Point** and the **Steep Ravine Environmental Camp** (1 mi south of Stinson Beach on Hwy. 1), where you can get a close look at teeming marine life such as seals, sea lions, star fish, and beach crabs. To get to the Pantoll Ranger Station from U.S. 101, take the Stinson Beach/Highway 1 exit, turn left at the first traffic light onto Highway 1, and right again onto Panoramic Highway. Parking at the station is $5, but you can park for free at the pull-outs along the road.

➢ **BOLINAS** • Serious hikers should consider the 45-mile **Coast Trail,** which stretches from the Palo Marin trailhead in Bolinas (*see* Marin County, in Chapter 2) into the middle of the

Point Reyes National Seashore. The trailhead is at the end of Mesa Road, just past the bird observatory. For a healthy day hike, follow the trail to **Bass Lake** (5½ mi round-trip) or **Pelican Lake** (7 mi round-trip). Either way, you'll walk through eucalyptus groves and untamed wetlands and along the edge of the cliffs that overlook the Pacific Ocean. Camping along the trail is allowed only within the boundaries of the national seashore and only in designated campgrounds; permits are required.

➢ **POINT REYES** • Even though it's not that far from the city, Point Reyes seems a world away. Gazing out at the rest of Marin County from here, you might get the feeling that you're on a separate island, which is almost true, except that the Tomales Valley joins the little peninsula to the mainland. The San Andreas fault runs right through the valley, putting Point Reyes on a different tectonic plate than the rest of the continent. Within the peninsula, the geography varies greatly; in just a few miles you can see meadows, forests, peaks with panoramic vistas, craggy cliffs overlooking the ocean, and isolated coves. The area erupts with wildflowers from mid-February through July; and though winter sees a lot of rain, that's when the rivers and ponds teem with life and the whales migrate south. Point Reyes feels so far removed that you may not want to go home; fortunately, there are plenty of places to camp here (*see* Marin County, in Chapter 7).

The best place to gear up for hiking is the **Bear Valley Visitor Center** (tel. 415/663–1092), where you can get a trail map and talk to the rangers. To get here, take Bear Valley Road off Route 1 just west of the village of Olema. For a hike along a narrow peninsula, with the Pacific crashing on one side of you and Tomales Bay gently lapping the other side, head out to **Tomales Point,** the northernmost spot in the park. From the visitor center, take Bear Valley Road, go left at the stop sign on Sir Francis Drake Boulevard, and bear right at Pierce Point Road, which ends at the Historic Pierce Point Ranch. The **Tomales Point Trail** picks up here and heads right through the Tule Elk Range; keep your eyes peeled for the graceful animals. Three miles down the road, the official trail ends and the sandy footpaths to the cliffs (1½ mi) begin.

For a steep, strenuous hike, head to the highest point in the park, Mt. Wittenberg (1,407 feet). The **Mt. Wittenberg Trail** begins .2 miles from the Bear Valley Trailhead, at the south end of the parking lot by the visitor center. The trail rises 1,250 feet in elevation; the final push follows an unmaintained offshoot up to the peak, where you'll be rewarded with a panorama of land and sea. To get down, head back to the Mt. Wittenberg Trail, hang a right, then take the **Horse Trail** to the Bear Valley Trail, where another right completes your 6-mile loop.

SOUTH BAY The gently rolling hills that shelter the San Mateo County Coast from the outside world provide excellent opportunities for hiking. Not only that, but you'll actually feel like you're heading into the country as you pass the small towns and farms south of San Francisco. Less popular than the hiking spots in Marin County, the South Bay's parks offer solitude—and you won't have to compete with mountain bikers for trail space since bikes are allowed only on fire trails and paved roads. The inland town of **La Honda** on Highway 84 (*see* San Mateo County Coast, in Chapter 2) is a good place to stop for picnic supplies before you head into one of the nearby state or county parks.

➢ **PACIFICA** • The hiking at **Sweeney Ridge** is mediocre, but its proximity to the city and its amazing view of the coastline make it a worthwhile getaway. The 1,047-acre park, which separates San Bruno from Pacifica, was added to the Golden Gate National Recreation Area in 1984. To reach the peak, hike 2 miles up a moderate grade through coastal scrub and grasslands that bloom with wildflowers in spring; the trailhead is at the end of Sneath Lane. A monument to the Spanish captain, Gaspar de Portola, who supposedly discovered San Francisco Bay from this point in 1769, stands atop the peak. Most people are content to contemplate the view from here, but if you want to keep going you can hike the **Baquiano Trail** about 2 more miles down to Pacifica. Since the ridge is so close to the coast, you'll definitely encounter some wind, and you may have to combat zero visibility on foggy summer afternoons. To get here, take I–280 or Skyline Boulevard (Hwy. 35) to the Sneath Lane exit in San Bruno. Follow Sneath Lane west for 10 minutes all the way to the Sweeney Ridge Gate. For information on ranger-led hikes, call 415/556–8371.

San Pedro Valley County Park has several mellow hiking trails that take you through shady woods and meadows exploding with wildflowers. In winter and spring, the ½-mile **Brooks Falls**

Overlook Trail offers great views of a three-tiered, 275-foot waterfall. The even shorter **Plaskon Nature Trail,** which gives you the opportunity to get up close and personal with a variety of plant species and wildlife, is wheelchair accessible. For more trail tips or a detailed guide to the nature trail, stop by the **visitor center** (600 Oddstad Blvd., tel. 415/355–8289). To reach the park, take Highway 1 into Pacifica and turn east on Linda Mar Boulevard. When it deadends, make a right onto Oddstad Boulevard; the entrance is 50 yards up on the left.

➢ **LA HONDA** • Near tiny La Honda, 11 miles east of Highway 1 along Highway 84, lies scenic **Portola State Park.** Stop by the **visitor center** (tel. 415/948–9098) at the entrance for a trail map (75¢) and info on guided nature walks and other activities. For a moderately difficult 4½-mile hike through redwood groves, catch the steep **Coyote Ridge Trail** just north of the visitor center, follow it to Upper Escape Road, where you'll turn left; hang a left again onto the **Slate Creek Trail,** shoot downhill on the steep **Summit Trail,** and follow the service road back to the visitor center. All told, the hike lasts two to three hours. To reach Portola, take I–280 to Highway 84 west to Skyline Boulevard (Hwy. 35). Go south 7 miles, then turn west on Alpine Road. Parking is $5.

➢ **BUTANO STATE PARK** • This little-known state park in the Santa Cruz Mountains occupies a small canyon with diverse flora and fauna. Even when its campsites are full, you can still find solitude in Butano. Definitely invest in the 50¢ map available at the entrance station. In addition to marking the trails, it has information on the park's wildlife communities.

A great hike, one that will introduce you to the park's beautiful terrain, starts at the **Año Nuevo Trail** to the right of the entrance station. This trail is so dense with lush growth that the narrow path is constantly under the threat of being overgrown: Watch out here for stinging nettles and poison oak. The first ½-mile—a steep ascent—is punctuated with benches; at the second bench you'll find the **Año Overlook**—on a clear day, you can see south to Año Nuevo Island. Continuing on, you'll run into **Olmo Fire Road.** Turn left and left again on **Goat Hill Trail** for a 2-mile walk through the quiet forests. When the trail hits the main road, follow it to the right for the highlight of the hike: **Little Butano Creek Trail,** where the trail meanders along Little Butano Creek, crisscrossed by fallen redwoods. You will also see waxy (and slimy) yellow banana slugs and California newts with their bright orange stomachs. At the end of the trail you can turn right onto the main road, right onto **Mill Ox Trail,** then left onto **Jackson Flat Trail,** which takes you through forests and fields of wildflowers while the creek rushes along far below. Jackson Flat will deposit you back at the entrance station for a total hike of about 7 miles.

For a gentler introduction to Butano, check out one of the ranger-led, 1½-hour nature walks, which happen every Saturday and Sunday at 2 and leave from the park entrance. To get to Butano, take Highway 1 about 15 miles south of Half Moon Bay to Pescadero; turn left on Pescadero Road, right on Cloverdale Road, and go about 5 miles to the park entrance. It costs $5 to park within the grounds, but you can usually ditch your car for free at the turnoff just south of the Cloverdale Road entrance.

Biking

An incredible human-powered movement takes place in the Bay Area every month. Hundreds of recreational riders, cycling-rights activists, bike messengers, and businesspeople on their daily commute gather in downtown San Francisco and take off on a 1½-hour ride through the city. The group, called **Critical Mass,** is responding to the predominance of cars in the city by encouraging bicycles as an alternative means of transport. They meet around 5:30 PM on the last Friday of each month at Justin Herman Plaza to tie up traffic, piss off motorists, aggravate police officers, and generally have a good ol' time. The route is decided on the spot and varies each time but usually ends at Dolores Park. The East Bay's Critical Mass gathers at the same time on the second to last Friday of the month at the downtown Berkeley BART. The East Bay group tends to be smaller and more politically active, as demonstrated by their pro-cycling chanting, antidriving pamphlets, and occasional obstruction of I–80. Police on bikes sometimes escort the San Francisco and East Bay groups in an effort to prevent problems and direct traffic.

If you want to rub spokes with other cyclists on a *planned* recreational ride, check out the calendar of events in the free monthly *Northern California Bicyclist*, available at bike shops. The **Sierra Club** (*see* Hiking, *above*) organizes group rides on terrains that range from farmland to challenging hills. You need at least a 10-speed bike for all but the most level routes, and you

Roll, Roll, Roll Your Boat

Bay Area sea kayakers tackle waters both calm and rough. Beginners will get acquainted early on with Richardson Bay, between Tiburon and Sausalito in Marin County. With its calm waters, stunning scenery, and bird-watching opportunities, Richardson is a hot spot for novices, and it makes a good launching point for an intermediate-level trip to Angel Island or an advanced trip through the rough and dangerous currents under the Golden Gate Bridge. For even calmer waters, head farther north to Bolinas Lagoon, a protected estuary where you'll paddle past egret nesting sites and see more birds than you ever imagined. Drake's Estuary, another bird-infested spot, is a beautiful bay on the Point Reyes peninsula with calm waters for beginners. The placid waters of Tomales Bay, off the coast of Point Reyes National Seashore in Marin County, claim a resident flock of white pelicans as well as jellyfish and starfish. Beginners and intermediates will feel comfortable in the western part of the bay, which offers stunning views of coves and beaches on shore.

To get in touch with the Bay Area kayak scene, contact Penny Wells of the 400-member Bay Area Sea Kayakers Co-op (tel. 415/457–6094). For $25 a year, you'll receive a newsletter and info about their frequent trips throughout the Bay Area. Also check the quarterly bulletin published by Outdoors Unlimited (see chapter introduction, above) for listings of free kayak and canoe workshops and volunteer-led trips. OU's day trips and moonlight paddles are the cheapest around—some are free, and for others you pay $50. Berkeley's Cal Adventures (see chapter introduction, above) also offers sea-kayaking day trips, instruction, and rentals.

Canoes and kayaks are all they do at California Canoe and Kayak (409 Water St., Jack London Sq., Oakland, tel. 510/893–7833 or 800/366–9804), and they're damn good at it. This retail and rental store offers the widest range of classes and trips, including testosterone-free lessons and outings for women only. Two-day introductory classes run about $150 and outings cost $80–$500, depending on destination and length of the trip. Sea Trek (Schoonmaker Point Marina, Sausalito, tel. 415/488–1000 or 415/332–4465) also has classes and rentals, and they offer special kayak trips with naturalist guides. Sea Trek rents equipment for about $7–8 an hour, and a seven-hour introductory class costs about $80. Outings include a $40 sunset or full moon paddle and a $110 full-day trip to Angel Island. If you're looking to buy equipment, take a free spin during Sea Trek's "Demo Days" before you close your bank account. Like California Canoe and Kayak, they offer free testing of canoes and kayaks on a designated day each month from early spring through early fall.

must show up with a helmet. Pick up their activities schedule for a list of planned rides. The **Bicycling Group** co-op organizes rides about once a month, with an emphasis on social as well as physical activity; check out the bulletin board at **Outdoors Unlimited** (*see* chapter introduction, *above*) for specifics.

Northern Californians have the dubious distinction of having reinvented the wheel. Legend has it that mad scientists in Fairfax (some say Mill Valley) created the monster that became the mountain bike from the parts of racing ten-speeds and sturdy beach cruisers. But the mountain bike ultimately owes its existence to the invention of a reinforced tire rim that can withstand the punishment of riding over rocks and bumps. The notoriously hilly Bay Area provides some of the nation's best testing ground for your climbing machine. Unfortunately, there's intense competition for this prime real estate: Many hikers see bikers as a threat to their safety and to the land. The controversy has grown into a fight for control of state parkland, and bikers seem to be losing the battle. Bikes have been banned from most single-track trails in the Bay Area, leaving only fire roads for pedaling.

EQUIPMENT AND RENTAL

Mountain-bike technology is constantly being improved, and the innovations show in the price tag. Top-of-the-line bikes can easily sell for more than $500. Look for used bikes on bike-shop bulletin boards and in free magazines geared toward cyclists (pick them up in bike stores). Of course, the cheapest option is rental. In San Francisco, **Park Cyclery** (1865 Haight St., at Stanyan St., tel. 415/751–RENT) rents mountain bikes for $5 an hour or $30 a day. If you're renting in the East Bay, you are a lucky dog because you can hook up with the friendly, intelligent folks at **Missing Link Bicycle Co-op** (1988 Shattuck Ave., Berkeley, tel. 510/843–7471), who will rent you a mountain bike for $20 a day and then load you up with a veritable cornucopia of biking info. Across the bay in Marin, **Wheel Escapes** (30 Liberty Ship Way, No. 210, Sausalito, tel. 415/332–0218) rents modest mountain bikes for $5 an hour or $21 a day. Higher-performance bikes cost $8 an hour or $35 a day.

WHERE TO BIKE

SAN FRANCISCO San Francisco can be a tough city to ride in: You've got cars, jaywalking pedestrians, those damn streetcar tracks, one-way streets, and thigh-straining hills. But you also have an incredible variety of scenery within a relatively small area and less smog than in most big cities. If you plan on doing a lot of riding in the city, take a look at the *San Francisco Biking/Walking Guide,* a $3 map that shows street grades and bike-friendly routes. It's available at bike shops and outdoor-oriented bookstores.

Changing the angle of your body in relation to the bike makes going up and down hills less strenuous. For uphill riding, raise the bike seat about 1.5" above crotch level so your legs can extend fully; for downhill lower your seat.

The following 21-mile ride takes you through Golden Gate Park, into the Presidio, across the Golden Gate Bridge, and along the coast. Start at the west end of Golden Gate Park, where **Jonn F. Kennedy Drive** hits the Great Highway. Follow J.F.K. Drive along a slight incline to the east end of the park, turn left on **Conservatory Road,** left again on **Arguello Boulevard,** exit the park, and head through residential neighborhoods and onto the curvy, downhill roads of the **Presidio.** Hang a right on Moraga Avenue, then take another right onto **Presidio Boulevard** for a quick tour of the historic former military base. Make a hard left onto **Lincoln Boulevard** almost immediately; it leads to the windy view area/toll plaza of the Golden Gate Bridge, where signs tell you how to cross according to the time and day of the week. When you return, follow Lincoln Boulevard west; it turns into **El Camino del Mar** and runs through the beautiful, grand **Seacliff** neighborhood. At the Palace of Legion of Honor, the road veers right and becomes **Legion of Honor Drive** before dumping you back onto **Clement Street.** Turn right on Clement, and when it dead-ends take **Point Lobos Avenue** past the **Cliff House** back to the Great Highway, where you can either collapse on the beach for some well-earned rest, continue down the coast, or head back into Golden Gate Park.

EAST BAY To escape the asphalt obstacle course of Berkeley's streets, take this strenuous 7-mile loop along the ridge of the Berkeley Hills and into Tilden Park. From the intersection of **Grizzly Peak Boulevard** and **Spruce Street** in North Berkeley, head south up Grizzly Peak Boulevard. This is the hardest part of the ride; the winding, steep street at times has only a narrow shoulder, and the trip can get hairy. Not far beyond the two lookouts, make a left on **South Park Drive,** which takes you down through Tilden Park and past several picnic grounds. The street dead-ends at **Wildcat Canyon Road;** go left and ride over rolling hills past Lake Anza, back to the intersection with Grizzly Peak Boulevard. Taking this loop in the opposite direction involves potentially dangerous sharp curves and limited visibility. Spruce Street is the main access road to Grizzly Peak Boulevard north of town; **Tunnel Road,** which goes up into the hills past the Caldecott Tunnel, is the main access road to the south.

➢ **TILDEN/WILDCAT REGIONAL PARKS** • Named after Major Charles Lee Tilden, first president of the park-district board, Tilden Park contains 2,078 acres of eucalyptus trees and rolling hills, filled with hikers, picnickers, and families. Wildcat Regional Park, directly northwest of Tilden, is nowhere near as developed or crowded. Poison oak is common in both parks. As in most Bay Area parks, mountain bikes are limited to the fire trails.

A beautiful, moderately strenuous 13⅓-mile loop through both parks begins just west of the Inspiration Point parking lot (*see* Hiking, *above*). Head down the rocky **Meadows Canyon Trail** that starts to the left of the paved Nimitz Trail; when you come to **Loop Road** hang a left, which will lead you to the **Environmental Education Center.** On the west side of the EEC, pick up **Wildcat Creek Trail,** and 6 miles further head right on the **Belgum Trail** for a steep and often muddy ascent of just less than a mile. Make another right onto the **San Pablo Ridge Trail,** a steep uphill grade that affords spectacular views of the bay. From here, you can pick up the paved **Nimitz Way Trail,** which leads back to Inspiration Point. For a shorter ride that avoids the most challenging stretch of the Belgum Trail, turn right off Wildcat Creek Trail onto **Conlon Trail.** To reach Tilden Park rangers, call 510/562–7275.

➢ **REDWOOD REGIONAL PARK** • More than a hundred years ago, sailors entering San Francisco Bay used the giant redwood trees growing on the hills east of Oakland as a landmark from the water. Unfortunately, most of those trees are now furniture. Only a few virgin redwoods remain in Redwood Regional Park, but the second-growth forest is still impressive. The 9-mile bike loop through the redwood forest is moderately difficult, with some strenuous areas. From Redwood Gate, follow the road past the picnic areas to the trailhead. **Canyon Trail** begins with a steep climb (which gets nice and muddy in the rainy season). After ½ mile, bear left on the **East Ridge Trail** for a gentle 3⅓-mile ascent up to the **West Ridge Trail.** The road levels out for a bit, but the downhill stretch has plenty of danger zones, so watch your speed. After about 5 miles, the West Ridge Trail becomes the **Bridle Trail,** which runs into the Fern Dell Picnic Area. From here, turn right and take the **Stream Trail** all the way back.

To get to Redwood Gate, take I–580 east toward Hayward and exit at 35th Avenue/MacArthur Boulevard. Take 35th Avenue, which becomes Redwood Road, east past Skyline Boulevard. The park entrance is about 2 miles farther down the road. Parking inside costs $3 on weekends, but you can park along the road for free. To talk to a ranger, call 510/635–0135, ext. 2578.

➢ **ANTHONY CHABOT REGIONAL PARK** • This is one of the few East Bay parks with a campground (*see* Chapter 7), and the blue waters of Lake Chabot are a refreshing sight after a long haul. Not refreshing, however, is the "No Swimming Allowed" rule. Bikers enjoy making the hilly 14-mile loop around Chabot Park because it affords all sorts of terrain. From the parking area at the marina, take the **East Shore Trail.** Cross the bridge, turn right on **Live Oak Trail** for a steep, rutted ascent of just under a mile that will deter any 10-speeder and even a few mountain bikers. Then turn right on **Towhee Trail** to the **Red Tail Trail.** Follow Red Tail—where you will be serenaded by the sounds of gunshots from the local rifle range—until you meet the **Grass Valley Trail,** which may inspire you to stop and talk with the nearby cows just for a chance to rest. Follow the **Brandon Trail**—a U-turn after the gate at the end of Grass Valley Trail—to the **Goldenrod Trail;** if you make it this far your reward is a drinking fountain for cows and humans to share. Nope, you're not *even* done. Next is the **Bass Cove Trail,** another rain-rutted trail that ends up on the **West Shore Trail,** which takes you back to the lake.

For driving directions to Lake Chabot, *see* Hiking, *above.* For biking and camping info, call 510/635–0135, ext. 2570; for lake info dial 510/582–2198.

MARIN COUNTY Ironically, the birthplace of the mountain bike is now a battleground where bikers are squaring off with hikers who want to keep the two-wheelers off the trails. Marin County has been particularly zealous about curtailing the use of mountain bikes. Trails that haven't been closed have a 15 mph speed limit (5 mph around turns), and rangers aren't shy about giving out hefty tickets ($180–$200) for violations. Some cyclists deliberately don't carry identification and give false names when rangers stop them. Other bikers have formed organizations to encourage better relations among everyone who wants to enjoy the wilderness. The **Bicycle Trails Council of Marin** (tel. 415/456–7512) maintains contact with park administrators and performs acts of community service, like leading bike trips for underprivileged urban kids and helping to maintain trails.

➢ **MARIN HEADLANDS** • The Marin Headlands, part of the **Golden Gate National Recreation Area,** are so close to San Francisco that most people leave the car at home and just bike across the Golden Gate Bridge. The headlands are often foggy in summer and are always windy, so dress in layers. The trails, which start almost immediately on the north side of the bridge, are sure to be crowded on rare sunny weekends. If you're driving from the city, cross the Golden Gate Bridge and take the first exit (Alexander Avenue). Pass under the freeway, turn right before the entrance to U.S. 101 south, and follow the signs to the **visitor center** (tel. 415/331–1540). You can park there and pick up a map of legal trails daily 9:30–4:30. Rangers sometimes lead mountain-biking tours; call for details.

A popular series of fire trails offers a great panorama of the Golden Gate and the Pacific. The 11½-mile loop described below is moderate, with some pretty steep sections. Take the **Miwok Trail** (from the parking area near the visitor center) to the **Bobcat Trail,** and continue 3½ miles uphill to the **Marincello Trail.** This gravelly downhill run drops you on **Tennessee Valley Road,** which leads to the beach. To return, go back up Tennessee Valley Road and pick up **Old Springs Trail,** which picks up on the road leading into Miwok Stables. Once you get back to the Miwok Trail, hang a right and head back down to the trailhead.

➢ **MT. TAMALPAIS STATE PARK** • Mt. Tam's rangers take trail restrictions very seriously—some spend their whole day hunting for mountain bikers who are speeding or riding illegal trails. You should definitely get a map ($1) from the **Pantoll Ranger Station** (tel. 415/388–2070) to see which trails are legal. For directions to the station, *see* Hiking, *above.*

The following bike ride takes you up to Mt. Tam's East Peak, for an exhilarating view from the top. Though you're climbing a mountain, the gradual gain in elevation makes this a relatively easy ride. If you continue past the East Peak, you're in for an all-day journey. From the ranger station, take the **Old Stage Road** uphill ½ mile to the West Point Inn, where you can grab a glass of lemonade. From the inn, go left on **Old Railroad Grade,** which runs for 2 miles almost to the top of Mt. Tam. It's one of the most popular rides on the mountain and gets quite crowded on weekends, so go carefully, especially on the way down.

From the top, you can either head back the way you came or turn your ride into a 20-mile loop (total) that takes you back down Mt. Tam and halfway up again. If you've got the stamina, go down **East Ridgecrest Drive** and pick up the **Lagunitas–Rock Springs Trail,** which begins on the other side of the dirt parking lot. After a short climb, the trail descends to Lake Lagunitas, where you should turn right and go around the lake. Turn right again on **Lakeview,** and eventually you'll meet **Eldridge Grade,** where you start another ascent. Go left at **Indian** and enjoy a steep and bumpy downhill ride. Turn right on **Blithedale Ridge** (past the Hoo Koo E Koo Trail), and take either of two spurs that drop down to the right toward the **Old Railroad Grade.** When you hit West Point Inn—now are you ready for that lemonade?—go left on **Old Stage Road** and head back to the ranger station.

➢ **POINT REYES** • Most of the pristine trails in Point Reyes National Seashore are closed to bikers, but a few open paths and the park's paved roads make for scenic riding. A trail map from the **Bear Valley Visitor Center** (*see* Hiking, *above*), off Bear Valley Road from Highway 1, should set you straight. For an easy, beautiful ride, take the **Bear Valley Trail** from the south end of the parking lot. About 3 miles into the ride, you'll reach a rack where you can lock your bike while you hike .8 miles out to the coast.

If you're up for something more serious, a strenuous 13-mile ride leaves from Five Brooks, a well-marked parking area off Highway 1 about 3 miles south of Olema. Pick up the **Olema Valley Trail,** which leads to the **Randall Trail** (on the left); cross Highway 1, ascend to Bolinas Ridge, and go right on the **Bolinas Ridge Trail.** About 1⅓ miles down the road, pick up the **McCurdy Trail,** cross Highway 1 again, and take the Olema Valley Trail all the way back.

SOUTH BAY Most parks in the South Bay are completely closed to mountain bikers; fire roads and paved roads are the only options you have, but the relative lack of crowds can still make the South Bay an appealing destination.

Some of the best mountain-biking in the area is to be found in **Pescadero Creek County Park,** near the town of La Honda. You can access the trails from nearby San Mateo County Memorial Park (9500 Pescadero Rd., Loma Mar, 415/879–0212): From Memorial's visitor center, take Pescadero Road back toward La Honda, turn right on Wurr Road, cross the bridge, and you'll come to the well-maintained, dirt and gravel **Old Haul Road,** where you can ride to your heart's content.

In **Butano State Park** (*see* Hiking, *above*), you can ride on any of the fire roads, though mountain bikes are forbidden on trails. Your best bet is to park at the entrance gate near the corner of Cloverdale and Canyon roads, about a mile north of the main park entrance, and ride the **Butano Fire Road.** If you're in good shape you can take it all the way to the **Olmo Fire Road,** which leads back to the park's main road, and pedal back to your car.

Surfing

If you want to take on the waves in the city, you're gonna earn your keep. The closest surf is brutal, paddling out can be exasperating, and the water is cold enough to remind men that they have nipples, too. Surfers looking for forgiving conditions head south toward Santa Cruz. Anywhere you go in the Bay Area, though, swells are best during fall and winter, when storms far out at sea send ripples across the Pacific. Call **Wise Surfboards** (tel. 415/ 665–WISE) for a recorded message on conditions in the city. For conditions at Stinson Beach call **Livewater** surf shop (*see below*); for Santa Cruz conditions call **O'Neil Surf Shop** (*see below*); and for Pacifica conditions call **Nor-Cal** surf shop (*see below*).

Local surfers are territorial about their waves. They can be more hostile than the ocean when you violate surf etiquette, the unwritten law that the first person riding the wave has ownership. Novices should avoid practicing at popular, crowded spots like Rockaway Beach (*see below*), where there's competition for waves. In addition, the current around San Francisco claims lives every year. Beginners are best off heading north to Stinson Beach or south to Santa Cruz.

INSTRUCTION AND EQUIPMENT

If you can't find a friend to teach you, two world-class surfing instructors offer lessons near Santa Cruz. **Richard Schmidt** (tel. 408/423–0928) is a champion whose graceful style inspires his peers to sit back and take notes. The cheapest way to get any of the man's time is to take a surf class through the **Santa Cruz Parks and Recreation Department** (tel. 408/429–3663). A two-day group lesson, two hours daily, costs $63 for nonresidents of Santa Cruz, $55 for residents. Schmidt also offers private instruction, in which he guarantees to have first-time surfers riding their boards. A one-hour private lesson costs $50; equipment is included. **CLUB ED Surf and Windsurf School** (tel. 800/287–7873), run by Ed Guzman, also offers classes in Santa Cruz. Ed owns a concession stand on Cowell Beach, between the Dream Inn and the wharf. He's got boogie boards, windsurfers, kayaks, skim boards, surfboards, and an instructor for every skill level. His one-hour ($45) and two-hour ($75) group lessons start you off on an oversize board, perfect for beginners who don't yet have their balance. If you don't get the hang of it the first time, you can come back for another two-hour lesson for only $35.

In terms of equipment, think like a seal before you hit the water. All year round, locals wear artificial blubber in the form of boots, gloves, and full wet suits, 3/2–4/3 mm thick. The most common mistake newcomers to the area make is buying a board that's too small; a slightly longer, thicker board will help inexperienced surfers catch more waves. Check out the bulletin boards in surf shops to find something secondhand; you should be able to find something for about $200–350. **Wise Surfboards** (3149 Vicente St., San Francisco, tel. 415/665–7745) helps customers re-sell boards without taking a commission.

A frightening number of great white sharks make their home off the coastline stretching from Davenport (near Santa Cruz) to Stinson Beach. Unfortunately, sharks have bad eyesight and mistake slick wet suits for shiny seal fur. Sharks attack a few people annually, but that doesn't keep anyone out of the water. Surfers who have been bitten suggest hitting the shark on the nose to break its grip, then swimming like hell for shore.

To rent a board in the city, go to **Outdoors Unlimited** (*see* chapter introduction, *above*); a weekend surfboard rental costs $8.50 and a 3-mm wet suit $12–$18. **Livewater** (3450 Hwy. 1, Stinson Beach, tel. 415/868–0333) rents buoyant foam boards ($25 a day) for beginners. To the south, knowledgeable local surfers staff **Nor-Cal Surfshop** (5460 Cabrillo Hwy., Pacifica, tel. 415/738–9283), where you can rent a soft board for $10 a day. **O'Neil Surf Shop** (1149 41st Ave., tel. 408/475–2275) in Santa Cruz rents boards for $10 a day and wet suits for $8 a day.

WHERE TO SURF

Surf's up at **Ocean Beach,** west of Golden Gate Park, but you may wish it would go back down. Winter waves here get as big as anywhere in the world (20–25 feet), but only the insane tackle the biggest ones, because the shape of the wave is often poor. Even when the swells are manageable, the current is strong. You don't have to be an expert to surf Ocean Beach, but it's not a place to learn unless you're into self-abuse. Waves are cleaner at **Fort Point,** beneath the Golden Gate Bridge on the southeast side. This overlooked spot is quite convenient for city surfers, but the current and rocks may deter beginners.

If you're just starting out, drive north along Highway 1 to **Stinson Beach.** The shallow beach break is not very demanding, and the waves are neither fast nor big. Stinson is a popular beach for sunbathing, but the water is rarely crowded. **Pacifica State Beach,** also known as **Linda Mar Beach,** is about 45 minutes south of San Francisco along Highway 1. Pacifica breaks best at high tide, with smaller waves for beginners at the southern end of the beach. Just north of the rock promontory, **Rockaway Beach** offers bigger waves, but it's more crowded and competitive. If you're adventurous, check out the underpopulated state beaches between Pacifica and Santa Cruz.

Rebel Wave

Some of the biggest waves in the world can be found at Mavericks in Half Moon Bay. The sight of puny surfers tackling 35- to 40-foot behemoths with little fiberglass boards provides ample reminder of both the awesome power of the Pacific and the equally awesome audacity of human beings. Do not surf here unless you know what you are doing; even then, this reef break can be lethal. A few days before Christmas, 1994, Mavericks claimed the life of Mark Foo, a native Hawaiian and the most famous big-wave surfer in the world. His death—a shocking blow to the surfing world—was caught on video, but remains a mystery. This is one wave you might want to sit out.

Windsurfing

The San Francisco Bay ranks the third-best spot for windsurfing in the United States, after Oregon's Royal Gorge and Maui. Take advantage. Summer is the season to tack across the bay: From April to August, the wind blows west, providing optimal conditions for windsurfing almost anywhere in the Bay Area. Winds are sporadic during the rest of the year, blowing either north or south. During winter, the air can be as cold as the water, and you'll need a wet suit 3/2- or 4/3 - mm thick. Some summer days are warm enough to go bottomless (in regard to wet suits, that is).

INSTRUCTION AND EQUIPMENT

Cal Adventures (*see* chapter introduction, *above*) offers cheap windsurfing lessons. Six hours of instruction on the bay, with an added hour of recreational windsurfing, board included, costs $60 (less if you're a U.C. Berkeley student). After you've completed the course, you can buy a two-month pass for $100 that allows you to use windsurfing equipment during business hours (Mon. morning and all day Wed.–Sun.; closed Thurs. Nov.–Apr. 2).

The conditions on the bay are harsh for a beginning windsurfer, and you should consider learning on a lake. **Spinnaker Sailing** (3160 N. Shoreline Blvd., Mountain View, tel. 415/965–7474) offers beginning and advanced classes on an artificial lake. The two-day beginners' course costs $120. **Windsurf Del Valle** (Lake Del Valle, Livermore, tel. 510/455–4008) has the largest windsurfing school in the country, and is excellent for beginners. The site, on a lake about a half-hour's drive east of Oakland, is the perfect windsurfing location: The water and air temperatures hover in the 80s from April through October. The water is flat, with few waves, and the wind is light. The $95 beginners' course usually lasts two days and earns you the certification necessary for renting equipment at most shops. They guarantee that you will learn the sport and will give you additional days of instruction for free if you need more help.

The **San Francisco School of Windsurfing** (Candlestick Park or Lake Merced, tel. 415/753–3235) specializes in increasing your skill level quickly. Beginners start at Lake Merced, but you soon learn to tackle the more popular bay. The school is renowned for dramatically improving intermediate students' abilities. The owner recommends that you not buy equipment until you've finished the entire course, since your beginning or intermediate board will become obsolete once you've improved. The two-day beginning course costs $95. Rentals cost $15 an hour, including wet suit, booties, and harness; a 10-hour pass is $100.

New windsurfing equipment is expensive—a grand, easy—so you may be forced to nickel and dime yourself with rentals. In addition to their main store, **Berkeley Boardsports** (843 Gilman St., Berkeley, tel. 510/527–7873) has set up shop next to the water at Alameda's Crown Beach and at Larkspur Landing in San Rafael. One hour on a board costs $10, but you can use the board all day for $40, including wet suit. If you're going to buy, it's prudent to look for secondhand equipment. Most windsurfing shops have a bulletin board and free magazines with ads for used gear.

WHERE TO WINDSURF

BEGINNING Alameda's **Crown Beach,** with easy access to shallow waters, offers the best conditions in the East Bay for learning the sport. Forces of nature work to the novice's advantage—the wind is usually light and blows towards the shore, so if you zig when you should have zagged, you won't be lost at sea. For directions to the beach, *see* Cheap Thrills, Oakland, in Chapter 2.

Larkspur Landing, in Marin County, is good for a couple with mixed windsurfing abilities. The light wind close to shore accommodates beginners, while the more advanced windsurfer will be challenged farther out in the bay. Mornings are calmest and best for beginners; the wind picks up in the afternoon. The area is not without its weaknesses—parking your car, for example, is a major hassle. And when the wind is light, it's no fun to access the water: From a rocky shore, you have to paddle out into the bay while keeping a wary eye out for ferries. From U.S. 101, take the San Rafael/Richmond exit east, and continue a quarter-mile past the Larkspur Ferry Terminal.

INTERMEDIATE/ADVANCED The **Berkeley Marina,** at the west end of University Avenue, requires intermediate to advanced skills. Access to the water is problematic, since you must launch off either the dock or the rocks. The windy and choppy conditions are tough on a beginner, but provide lots of wave-jumping opportunities for experienced windsurfers who like to spend time in the air. From I–80, take the University Avenue exit west to the end.

Crissy Field, in San Francisco's Presidio, should challenge advanced windsurfers. Beach access makes getting into the water easy, but with the strong tides and currents, getting out is a task. The current could easily sweep an unprepared windsurfer under the Golden Gate into the Pacific or across the bay to Treasure Island. In addition, boat and ship traffic make the water about as easy to navigate as the freeway at rush hour. If you're up to the challenge, you'll find Crissy Field just southeast of the Golden Gate Bridge.

Smooth Sailing

San Francisco never seems as picturesque as when it's seen from sea level, but it isn't postcard scenery that draws sailors to the bay—it's the remarkably consistent west wind. The San Francisco Bay is one of the most challenging places in the country to sail. Even if you can't scrape up the dough for a yacht, you needn't remain a landlubber. A little charm and a tolerance for grunt work can earn you a job working crew on a boat. Crewing is the cheapest way to learn about sailing, and the water makes the best classroom. Post an ad at your local marina and talk to boaters, and your eagerness will likely win you a sailing invitation. The California sailing magazine "Latitude 38" (look for it in boating stores) is an excellent resource for finding used boats or placing an ad for a crew. They also print a schedule of races every March, just in time for the beginning of the season.

The Berkeley Marina (west end of University Ave.) is a great place to learn about sailing. Cal Sailing Club (tel. 510/287–5905), across from the marina, offers three months of unlimited lessons and equipment use for a membership cost of $45, $40 for U.C. students. You can sail to your heart's content on their 8- to 15-foot (not necessarily well-maintained) boats, but keep in mind that the students of today will be the instructors of tomorrow. To check out the club, take a free sail the first full weekend of each month from 1 to 4 PM—don't forget to wear something warm and waterproof.

Cal Adventures (Recreational Sports Facility, 2301 Bancroft Way, tel. 510/642–4000), on the U.C. Berkeley campus, offers equipment rental if you have the appropriate qualifications and reasonably priced classes if you don't. Also consider Olympic Circle Sailing Club (1 Spinnaker Way, near the Berkeley Marina, tel. 800/223–2984), which has expensive, and highly recommended, courses. If you can't afford a class, show up on a summer Wednesday for the 5:30 sunset sail. The two-hour ride (reservations required) costs $25 per person. Spinnaker Sailing/Rendezvous Charter (Pier 40, South Beach Harbor, San Francisco, tel. 415/543–7333) charters boats and teaches sailing in the city. If you prefer the passenger's seat, they also offer a two-hour sunset sail ($23) on Wednesday, Friday, and Saturday.

At **Candlestick Park** on the Peninsula, not everyone is going to the ball game. Flat water, strong winds, and easy bay access make Candlestick a favorite with windsurfers who want speed. Winds average 19–25 mph, but they can get as high as 55 mph. You have to be an expert to handle the offshore winds, which carry you right out into the bay. If the wind dies, you'll be stranded out there; and if the Coast Guard has to rescue you because of your negligence, you'll pay at least $200. Think twice before windsurfing here on game days: Parking costs about $7 during baseball games and about $10 during football games.

The onshore wind and big chops make **Coyote Point,** south of the San Francisco International Airport, an advanced area. On the inside (close to shore), the wind is moderate, but on the outside (away from shore), it increases and the waves become choppy. The entrance fee for **Coyote Point Park** (tel. 415/ 573–2592) is $4, well worth it for the use of the hot showers. Follow U.S. 101 south past the airport to the Poplar Avenue exit, take Humboldt Street, turn right on Peninsula Avenue, go right across the overpass, and bear left onto Coyote Point Drive.

DAY AND WEEKEND TRIPS

9

By Kelly Green, Kristina Malsberger, and Alan Covington Phulps

Whether you're looking for a day at the beach or a weekend in the mountains, a New Age healing session or an isolated cross-country ski trail, odds are good that you'll find what you want somewhere in the diverse and gorgeous country surrounding San Francisco. Perhaps more than any other major American city, San Francisco is distinguished by its proximity to dramatic natural terrain and interesting small towns. You could easily live here for a decade without exhausting your options for day and weekend trips. North of the city lies California's world-famous **Wine Country;** and to the south, **Santa Cruz** is a gathering point for surfers, New Agers, and neo-hippies. An afternoon's drive east at the right time of year will bring you to that most un-Californian phenomenon, snow, in the mountains surrounding **Lake Tahoe** or in **Yosemite,** California's favorite national park. Tahoe is home to some of the country's best skiing, while Yosemite provides Northern Californians with a place to rock climb, hike, and hang out with the bears and other wildlife of the Sierra Nevada. You can escape to any one of these world-class spots in no more than four hours if you've got access to a car, and with patience and a little pre-trip planning, public transit will get you the hell out of Dodge and into the great wide open as well.

The Wine Country

The Wine Country is only 50 miles northeast of San Francisco, an easy and highly recommended day trip if you have a car. You don't have to be a wine connoisseur to enjoy a visit to this region—even philistines appreciate the rustic beauty of the area and the opportunity to get a free buzz. Many of the wineries will pour you glass after glass of free samples. Choose carefully, though: A number of Napa Valley wineries charge a $2 or $3 tasting fee, which can add up if you're making the rounds. In some places you may have to take a tour or watch a film before you can get to the tasting, but luckily the tours are usually interesting (especially at the smaller wineries).

Most vineyards are concentrated in the Napa and Sonoma valleys, but the Wine Country actually stretches north through Santa Rosa and all the way into Lake and Mendocino counties. Vintners have been making wine here for well over 100 years, but it was only in 1976, when a cabernet sauvignon from Stag's Leap won a blind taste test in Paris, that Californians began boasting and people all over the world began buying. Since then, production has skyrocketed. Twenty-five years ago there were only about 25 wineries; now there are more than 200.

Napa Valley has the greatest number of wineries, but many are expensive and pretentious. Once upon a time, visitors were greeted with open arms—and flowing bottles—by jolly vint-

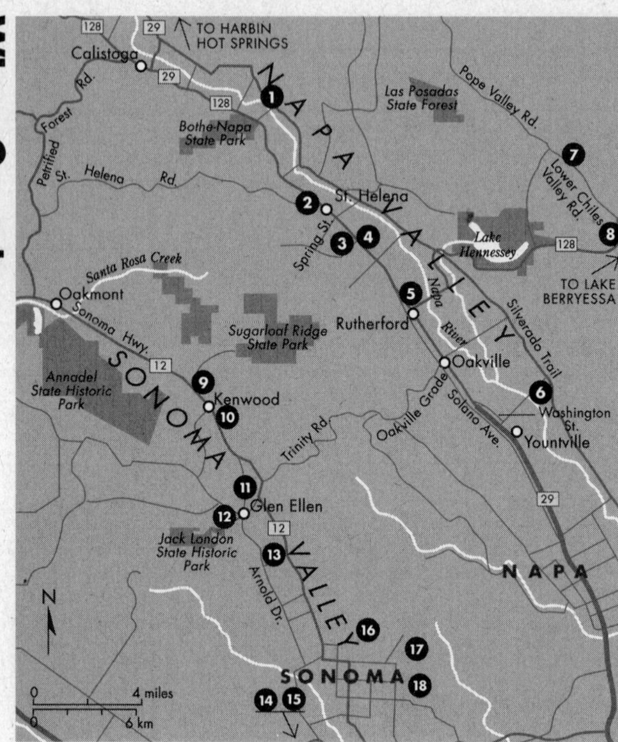

Beaulieu Vineyards, **5**
Benziger, **12**
Beringer Winery, **2**
Buena Vista, **17**
Chateau St. Jean, **9**
Cline Cellars, **15**
Gundlach-Bundschu, **18**
Kunde, **10**
Nichelini, **8**
Prager Port Works, **3**
Ravenswood, **16**
Rustridge, **7**
S. Anderson, **6**
Schug, **14**
Valley of the Moon, **13**
V. Sattui, **4**
Wellington, **11**
Wermuth, **1**

ners thankful for even a trickle of business. These days you'll have to search out the Napa Valley's tiniest wineries to get this kind of reception. A better option is to make a beeline for the Sonoma Valley. While Sonoma has some big, impersonal wineries, it draws fewer tourists and is home to a greater share of rustic, unassuming vineyards. In both counties, the farther you stray from the main drag, the better off you'll be. Remember that it doesn't always work to just drop in at a winery, especially if you want to take a tour. At some of the smaller places, you may need an appointment.

You'll undoubtedly be tempted to buy some of the wine you try, but before stocking up at the winery, check local supermarkets, which may have lower prices.

If you need a break from the wineries, you can luxuriate in the hot springs, mud baths, and mineral baths of Calistoga, loiter in the lovely Spanish mission and old adobes of Sonoma, or browse through the small museums devoted to former residents Jack London and Robert Louis Stevenson, both of whom wrote about the area. Be forewarned, though: An overnight stay in the Wine Country can take a monster-size bite out of your budget. Lodging tends to be even more expensive than in San Francisco, and food is pricey as well. You can survive cheaply by eating at roadside produce stands, drinking free wine, and sleeping in a state park. Otherwise, expect to pay through the nose.

BASICS

VISITOR INFORMATION Before you go (or once you arrive), you may want to call the **Napa Chamber of Commerce** (1556 1st St., Napa, tel. 707/226–7455), open weekdays 9–5, which can help you organize your trip and provide you with more maps than you'll ever need. The **Sonoma Valley Visitors' Bureau** (453 1st St. E, Sonoma, tel. 707/996–1090), open weekdays 9–5 and weekends until 6, gives friendly advice on what to see and do in the "other" valley.

Additionally, most wineries carry the *California's Visitor's Review,* a free weekly that has maps and winery info.

WHEN TO GO The best time to visit is during the autumn harvest season, when you'll see some real action in the wine cellars. In both spring and fall, wildflowers bloom amid the endless rows of manicured vines. Try to avoid the Wine Country in summer, though. The dry, dusty valleys become even drier and dustier, and the crowds can be suffocating—it sometimes feels as if each and every one of the 2.5 million annual visitors is backed up along Highway 29, impatient for another glass of zinfandel.

COMING AND GOING

BY CAR Though traffic can be heavy, especially on weekends and during rush hours (7–9 AM and 4–6 PM), the easiest way to reach the Wine Country is by car. From San Francisco, the best option is to take **U.S. 101** north over the Golden Gate Bridge and connect with **Highway 37** east near Ignacio. From here take **Highway 121** north to **Highway 12** north for Sonoma, or follow Highway 121 as it curves east toward **Highway 29** for Napa. If you're only visiting the Napa Valley or are coming from the East Bay, it's quicker to take **I–80** north and exit to Highway 37 west in Vallejo. Highway 37 joins up with Highway 29 north to Napa. Even when traffic is heavy it shouldn't take more than two hours; on good days you'll be there in an hour.

BY BUS **Golden Gate Transit** (tel. 415/923–2000 or 707/541–2000) provides bus service from San Francisco and Marin County to towns throughout Sonoma County. Bus 90 makes the trek from San Francisco to Sonoma (1½ hrs, $4.50) two or three times a day. **Greyhound** has service from San Francisco's Transbay Terminal (*see* Getting In, Out, and Around, in Chapter 1) once daily to Napa (2½ hrs, $15 one-way) and Middletown (4¼ hrs, $17 one-way), twice daily to Sonoma (3–4 hrs, change in Vallejo or Santa Rosa, $15 one-way). Tickets are usually cheaper if you buy seven days in advance.

GETTING AROUND

Unless you've hit one winery too many, orienting yourself in the Wine Country shouldn't be too difficult: Both the Napa and Sonoma valleys have main north–south arteries (Highways 29 and 12, respectively) that connect towns and vineyards alike. **Highway 29** begins in the medium-size town of Napa and stretches north through Yountville, Oakville, Rutherford, St. Helena, and Calistoga, continuing north to Middletown and Clear Lake. A parallel route, **Silverado Trail,** avoids most of Highway 29's traffic lights and traffic jams, making for a more scenic and speedy ride. In the Sonoma Valley, **Highway 12** runs north from Sonoma's main plaza, zigzagging east and then north through the towns of Glen Ellen and Kenwood before reaching Santa Rosa. East–west crossroads between the two valleys include **Highway 121** from Napa, the scenic **Oakville Grade/Trinity Road** from Oakville, and the **Petrified Forest Trail** from Calistoga.

Quaint and tempting as the **Napa Valley Wine Train** (1275 McKinstry St., Napa, tel. 707/253–2111) may sound, the train is more of a moving restaurant than a means of transportation—no stopping for a taste of the grape. In addition, it's resented by the locals for polluting the valley and bringing too many tourists. If you're still interested, $24 buys you a joyride to St. Helena and back. For that kind of money, rent a car—you can't get drunk, but at least you have the liberty to stop when and where you want. Unscheduled pit stops are equally problematic in one of the rainbow-hued hot air balloons you'll occasionally see floating above the valley; plus, this extravagance costs upwards of $150 per person.

BY CAR When you tour the Wine Country by car, please do everyone a favor and choose a designated driver. In summer, much of the traffic can be avoided by staying off Highway 29 and exploring the less crowded and more scenic **Silverado Trail,** which runs parallel to Highway 29 a mile to the east. Exit Highway 29 at any point between Napa and Calistoga and follow the Silverado Trail signs.

BY BUS It requires creativity to see the Wine Country on public transit, but hey—that's half the fun. In particular, **Sonoma County Transit** (tel. 707/576–7433) connects all cities in

Sonoma County, with buses running weekdays 6 AM–6:30 PM (some until 10 PM), weekends 8–6. Fares are less than $2 to most places (ask for student and disabled discounts), and buses can get you within walking distance of a few wineries. **Napa Valley Transit** (1151 Pearl St., at Main St., tel. 707/255–7631) offers frequent service between Napa and Yountville ($1), St. Helena ($2), and Calistoga ($2) Monday–Saturday.

BY BIKE Biking is perhaps the best way to see the Wine Country. The 50-mile haul from Sonoma to St. Helena may not be too appealing, but within each region the wineries tend to be clumped close together, making them easy to see on two wheels. Cyclists on Highway 29 risk being run over by tipsy drivers, especially on summer weekends—stick to Silverado Trail or Solano Avenue (an access road that parallels Highway 29 from Napa to Yountville). In the town of Sonoma, cyclists can avoid most of the traffic jams and drunk drivers by traveling along Arnold Drive; it splits off from Highway 12 about 4 miles south of town and rejoins the highway just south of Glen Ellen. **Napa Valley Cyclery** (4080 Byway E, at Salvador Ave., tel. 707/255–3380 or 800/707–BIKE), at the northern end of Napa, rents bikes for $6 an hour or $20 a day. Farther north, **St. Helena Cyclery** (1156 Main St., at Spring St., tel. 707/963–7736) charges $7 an hour, $25 a day, or $140 a week. **Sonoma Valley Cyclery** (1061 Broadway, Sonoma, tel. 707/935–3377), on Highway 12, can set you up with a mountain bike for $6 an hour or $28 a day. All these shops offer biking maps and tour suggestions, so squeeze as much info from them as possible before heading out.

One of the best winery routes takes cyclists on an easy ride through Sonoma's fields and vineyards. From Sonoma's downtown plaza, take East Napa Street east, turn left at Sebastiani Winery (4th St. E), then right on Lovall Valley Road. From here follow signs to any of several wineries in the foothills, including **Bartholomew Park** (1000 Vineyard Ln., off Castle Rd., tel. 707/935–9511), **Ravenswood,** and **Buena Vista** (*see* Wineries, *below*). For a longer ride, continue on Lovall Valley Road and turn right on Thornsberry Road, which leads to **Gundlach-Bundschu** winery (*see* Wineries, *below*). After a pit stop at the tasting room, take Denmark Street back toward town. The whole trip is about 7 miles.

Sonoma Valley

Although Napa Valley receives most of the hype, Sonoma Valley is the birthplace of California's wine industry, and it's a better bet for budget travelers. For one thing, almost all of Sonoma's wineries offer free tastings, meaning you can imbibe to your heart's content without spending a dime. In addition, most of the wineries are small, family-owned concerns, more relaxed and less crowded than those in Napa.

The town of **Sonoma** may have recently grown into an upscale bedroom community for San Francisco commuters, but behind the trendy restaurants and chic clothing boutiques lie a small-town sense of humor and a rich California history. It was here that Father José Altimira built the last and northernmost of the California missions, **Mission San Francisco Solano** (1st and Spain Sts., tel. 707/938–1519). The missionaries planted the region's first vines here in 1823 to make sacramental wine. For a $2 fee (also good for entrance to Lachryma Montis and the army barracks) you can see the reconstructed priests' quarters and a collection of 19th-

The Bear Flag Republic

For a short period in 1846, Sonoma belonged not to Mexico, Spain, or the United States, but to the lesser-known Bear Flag Republic—the brainchild of Captain John C. Frémont and a ragtag group of Yankee trappers who decided to resolve tensions between the Mexican government and non-Mexican immigrants by throwing the Mexican commander in prison and creating their own country. The republic was broken up a month later when the U.S. Navy arrived, but the bear remains on the California state flag.

century watercolors by Chris Jorgenson. Just east of the mission lies grassy **Sonoma Plaza,** the largest such plaza in California and the epicenter of Sonoma life. Around the plaza, many adobe buildings remain from the days of Spanish and Mexican rule, including old army barracks and the restored **Toscana Hotel** (20 E. Spain St., tel. 707/938–5889). Friday–Sunday between 1 and 4, kindly gray-haired docents will recount the hotel's colorful past as a general store, library, and home to Italian stone masons. Behind the hotel is Depot Park and the free **Sonoma Depot Museum** (270 1st St. W, tel. 707/938–1762), which chronicles Sonoma Valley history on and off the rails. It's worth a quick peek inside to see a pair of grizzly bear feet worn by Ulysses S. Grant to a San Francisco masquerade ball in the 1860s. Three blocks west of the plaza lie **Sonoma State Historical Park** and **Lachryma Montis** (3rd St. W, off W. Spain St., tel. 707/938–1519), the ornate home of the last Mexican governor, General Vallejo. Admission to the grounds (open daily 10–5) is $2.

The title of Jack London's book "Valley of the Moon" has become an alternate name for the Sonoma Valley. The Native American word "sonoma" actually means "many moons."

In the nearby town of **Glen Ellen,** north of Sonoma off Highway 12, look for **Jack London State Historic Park.** When he tired of drinking and brawling on the Oakland waterfront, London (1876–1916) came here to build his dream home, Wolf House. The house was torched by an arsonist before it was finished, but the impressive stone foundations remain, along with the architects' drawings of what the house would have looked like. From the free Jack London Museum, a shady half-mile walk through the oak trees takes you to the Wolf House ruins and his grave. Poison oak abounds, so stick to the trail. *2400 London Ranch Rd., Glen Ellen, tel. 707/938–5216. From Hwy. 12, take Glen Ellen turnoff and follow signs. Parking: $5. Museum open daily 10–5. Park open daily 9:30–7.*

WHERE TO SLEEP Beds don't come cheap in the Sonoma Valley. If you have a tent, your best bet is to camp. Otherwise you'll probably want to make the half-hour drive north on Highway 12 to Santa Rosa for an affordable room. Even at Sonoma's least expensive motel, **El Pueblo Motel** (896 W. Napa St., on Hwy. 12, tel. 707/996–3651 or 800/900–8844), a clean and generic double will run you a whopping $70 on weekdays, $80 on weekends ($58 daily in winter). At least the motel has a great swimming pool and is close to the central square and several wineries.

Since prices are comparable, consider staying at one of Sonoma's bed-and-breakfasts. **Hollyhock House** (1541 Denmark St., off 8th St. E, tel. 707/938–1809) is an old two-story farmhouse on a quiet country road, with roosters, geese, and a flower garden worthy of Monet. The three doubles cost $80–$90 on summer weekends ($55 in winter), but you can lower the price of the cheapest room to $55–$65 by staying more than one weekend night or coming on a weekday. In Glen Ellen, the **Jack London Lodge** (13740 Arnold Dr., at London Ranch Rd., tel. 707/938–8510) offers comfortable doubles with antique decor for $75; off-season specials can lower rates to $55–$60. The lodge has a pool, a saloon, and a decent restaurant. A small continental breakfast is included on weekends and in summer. Reservations are strongly advised, especially in summer.

➢ **CAMPING • Sugarloaf Ridge State Park.** Only 8 miles north of Sonoma on Highway 12, Sugarloaf has 49 campsites scattered around a large meadow (dry and uninviting in summer). There are 25 miles of trails for hiking, biking, and horseback riding (*see* Outdoor Activities, *below*). If you hike up the trail to your left as you enter the park, you're likely to see deer, especially around sunset when they come out for early evening grazing. Campsites cost $14 ($12 in winter). In summer and on weekends, it's a good idea to reserve ahead through MISTIX (tel. 800/444–PARK). *2605 Adobe Canyon Rd., Kenwood, tel. 707/833–5712. From Sonoma, Hwy. 12 north, right on Adobe Canyon Rd., which dead-ends at park. Day use fee ($5), drinking water, flush toilets.*

FOOD Sonoma is *the* place to get your fill of gourmet-pesto-this and roasted-goat-cheese-that. Fortunately, there are some options for those unable to lay out huge sums of cash: Put together a picnic at the **Sonoma Farmer's Market** Friday 9–noon in Depot Park. An additional market is held in the plaza Tuesday evenings from 4:30 until dusk. Sonoma's best breakfast deal is at the **Feed Store Café and Bakery** (529 1st St. W, off central plaza, tel. 707/938–

2122): From 7 to 11:30 AM you can get a two-egg breakfast, fruity granola, oat bran pancakes, or orange-brandy French toast for under $5. Breakfast at the **Sunnyside Coffee Club and Blues Bar** (140 E. Napa St., near plaza, tel. 707/935–0366) means bittersweet-chocolate banana pancakes with vanilla-bean whipped cream ($6). At lunch (noon–3:30), try the salad with soba noodles ($5). If you're lucky, you'll be treated to live blues as you dine.

No-frills sandwiches ($6–$7) and ice cream are available at the **Old Sonoma Creamery** (400 1st St. E, on plaza, tel. 707/938–2938), open weekdays 9–5 and weekends until 6. For a little extra ($7–$11), dive into delicious pasta dishes (like fettucine with smoked salmon) on the patio at **Pasta Nostra** (139 E. Napa St., tel. 707/938–4166). Or head down the alley east of the plaza to lively **Murphy's Irish Pub** (464 1st St. E, tel. 707/ 935–0660) for homemade lamb stew and vegetables ($6), a pint of stout ($3), and live Irish tunes (summer weekends). For a Mexican-food fix, the roadside **Cocina Cha Cha** (897 W. Napa St., tel. 707/996–1735) is open daily until 9 PM and serves crisp tacos with ground beef for only 99¢. Two people can easily split Cha Cha's enormous burrito grande, filled with the works and topped with a spicy homemade sauce for $6.75.

For an excellent sit-down meal, trek out to the one-street town of Glen Ellen, where you'll find the **Sonoma Mountain Grill** (13690 Arnold Dr., tel. 707/938–2370), open Monday and Wednesday–Friday 11–9, weekends 9–9. The fresh fish special—with a heaping salad, veg-

A Rosé by Any Other Name . . .

In just one tasting session at a Napa or Sonoma winery, you'll be bombarded by as many as six or seven different varieties of wine. Here's a handy cheat sheet:

- ***Cabernet sauvignon: A safe bet for the neophyte, this earthy wine is essentially a higher-class version of the jug wine people drink around the campfire.***
- ***Chardonnay: This dry (not sweet) white wine is usually first in the tasting line. When aged in oak barrels, it picks up a smooth, buttery taste.***
- ***Gewürztraminer: An aromatic white wine that's slightly bubbly and a little spicy. Try one at Chateau St. Jean.***
- ***Merlot: Intrepid tasters should try this fuller, richer red wine. Merlots have a lot of tannins (pigments from grape skins that help preserve all wines and allow reds, in particular, to improve with age). If these wines are too young, their tannic bitterness may leave your lips puckered.***
- ***Muscat: A rich, sweet dessert wine, tasting vaguely of honey. Benziger has a particularly good one.***
- ***Pinot noir: This wine is lighter in tannins (fewer sourpuss expressions) and often picks up rich aromas like vanilla or pepper as it ages.***
- ***Riesling: This sweeter, fruitier wine comes from the Riesling grape, originally from Germany. Those with a nose will be able to pick out a fresh, flowery smell.***
- ***Zinfandel: A low-alcohol, fruity red that's meant to be drunk young. The zinfandel at Ravenswood is well worth a try.***

etables, and rice—is the most expensive thing on the menu ($12–$14), but it's well worth it; with an appetizer, it could feed two.

WINERIES Sonoma Valley is home to some 30 wineries and 6,000 acres of vineyards. It was here that California began its upstart drive to compete with old-world wineries, when Count Agoston Haraszthy planted the first European vines in 1857. You can easily spend a leisurely day driving up Highway 12 through the 17-mile-long valley, stopping to sip a little wine, learn a little history, have a picnic, and laze around in the sun.

Benziger. You're encouraged to roam the beautiful grounds, enjoy the fragrant rose gardens, picnic in any spot you choose, and indulge in many a free taster. Guided tram tours of the grounds are available, though they're not required for tasting. *1883 London Ranch Rd., Glen Ellen, tel. 707/935–3000. From Hwy. 12, take Glen Ellen (Arnold Dr.) turnoff and follow signs for Jack London State Park. Open daily 10–5. Wheelchair access.*

Buena Vista. Count Agoston Haraszthy, the "father of California wine," brought thousands of European grapevine cuttings to the United States in the mid-1800s to start this winery. The guided tour (2 PM) covers his colorful life as well as the history of the vineyard. Free tastings (up to four wines, plus gewürztraminer grape juice) happen in the impressive, ivy-covered main building—definitely try the pinot noir and the Carneros Estate chardonnay. Afterward venture upstairs to see excellent rotating art exhibits and meet the current artist in residence. *18000 Old Winery Rd., Sonoma, tel. 800/926–1266. From plaza, E. Napa St. east, turn left on Old Winery Rd. Open July–Sept., daily 10:30–5; Oct.–June, daily 10:30–4:30.*

Chateau St. Jean. The palatial grounds include a fish pond, a fountain, and an observation tower from which you get a spectacular view of the vineyard and surrounding area. Though tasting is free, the room is crowded, and the staff may be too busy to be very helpful. For a more relaxed time, kick back on the lawn with a picnic and a bottle of their excellent gewürztraminer ($8). *8555 Hwy. 12, Kenwood, tel. 707/833–4134. From Sonoma, Hwy. 12 north past Glen Ellen and look for sign on right. Open daily 10–4:30. Wheelchair access.*

Cline Cellars. You'll pass through grapevines and roses on the way to the tasting room, in an old farmhouse dating from the mid-1800s. At the tasting bar, you can try four of the six wines, as well as homemade mustards, for free. If you've brought your Brie and baguettes, you can picnic on the porch beside one of six ponds fed by neighboring hot springs. *24737 Arnold Dr. (Hwy. 121), Sonoma, tel. 707/935–4310. Btw Hwys. 12 and 37. Open daily 10–6. Wheelchair access.*

Gundlach-Bundschu. Someone at this 137-year-old, family-owned winery has a sense of humor. In the main building (surrounded by trellised wisteria), old photographs of the family and winery sit alongside a picture of Bacchus in shades. Then there are the corks, inscribed: "Leave the kids the land and money—drink the wine yourself." Free tasters of up to five different wines get you in the proper hedonistic mood. *2000 Denmark St., Sonoma, tel. 707/938–5277. From plaza, take E. Napa St. east, turn right on E. 8th St., left on Denmark St. and look for sign on left. Open daily 11–4:30. Wheelchair access.*

Kunde. The folks at Kunde claim it's the friendliest winery in the valley, and they mean it—step into the large tasting room and you'll be greeted by a glass and a smile. Enjoy free tastings in their new airy tasting room or take the half-hour tour through the vast cave cellars. If things are slow, you may even get a tour of the property, including the owner's duck sanctuary and the ruined stone winery where Geena Davis was married. *10155 Hwy. 12, Kenwood, tel. 707/833–5501. From Sonoma, Hwy. 12 north 7 mi; winery is on right, just past Glen Ellen. Open daily 11–5.*

Ravenswood. This small stone winery in the Sonoma foothills has a relaxed, intimate feel. Better yet, the jovial staff doesn't seem to care how many wines you taste. Their motto is *Nulla Vinum Flaccidum* (No Wimpy Wines), and their merlots and zinfandels are definitely worth writing home about. If you didn't bring a picnic to savor on the terrace, try their barbecued chicken or ribs with bread, coleslaw, and potato salad ($6–$7.25), available on summer weekends only. *18701 Gehricke Rd., Sonoma, tel. 707/938–1960. From plaza, Spain St. east,* *turn left on 4th St. E, right onto Lovall Valley Rd., left on Gehricke Rd. Open daily 10–4:30. Wheelchair access.*

Schug. Walter Schug will pour you free tastes of his European-style wines at this mellow, family-run winery. Not many tourists come here, so the family members (who are viticultural experts) have plenty of time to answer questions. They'll give you a tour if you're interested, and you can explore the rooms where the wines are aged and bottled. *602 Bonneau Rd., Sonoma, tel. 707/939–9363. From plaza, Hwy. 12 south, then Hwy. 121 west until it hits Hwy. 116 at stop sign; Bonneau Rd. is straight ahead. Open daily 10–5.*

Valley of the Moon. This intimate winery off the main drag is a breath of fresh air compared to the more crowded vineyards in the upper valley. The staff is friendly and helpful, and in that fine Sonoma Valley tradition, tasting is free. Be sure to sample their port, a brandy-fortified wine that packs a punch. *777 Madrone Rd., Glen Ellen, tel. 707/996–6941. From Sonoma, Hwy. 12 north 6 mi to Madrone Rd. Open Apr.–Oct., daily 10–5; Nov.–Mar., daily 10–4:30. Wheelchair access.*

Wellington. Run by a father-son team, this tiny winery just opened its doors in 1994, and it's still obscure enough to escape the tourist hordes. The tasting room is a down-to-earth affair with a small terrace and a view of the Sonoma Mountains. Tastings of their delicious wines are unlimited—be sure to try the Estate Chardonnay, a combination of fruit and clove flavors that tastes like liquid Christmas. *11600 Dunbar Rd., Glen Ellen, tel. 707/939–0708. From Sonoma, Hwy. 12 north 7 mi, exit left at Dunbar Rd. Open Thurs.–Mon. noon–5. Wheelchair access.*

CHEAP THRILLS Wine isn't the only thing that's free in the Sonoma Valley. If you're pinching pennies, don't miss the free samples at the **Sonoma Cheese Factory** (2 Spain St., Sonoma, tel. 707/996–1931), where the popular Sonoma Jack cheese is made. At the mellower, family-owned **Vella Cheese Company** (315 2nd St. E, Sonoma, tel. 707/938–3232), watch cheese being rolled by hand Monday–Wednesday from noon to 2 PM. Nearby, at Sonoma's central **plaza,** you can throw a Frisbee around, feed the resident ducks, or regress to childhood on the swings and the slide. In summer the **Sonoma Valley Jazz Society** offers free concerts around town. Call 707/996–7423 for schedule info.

Hard-core freeloaders will have a field day at **Viansa** (25200 Arnold Dr., on Hwy. 121, tel. 707/935–4700), a slick, commercial winery equipped with an Italian-style marketplace. Be prepared to fight tooth-and-nail with hungry tourists for free tasters of chocolate sauces, preserves, mustards, oils, and, of course, wine.

OUTDOOR ACTIVITIES Towns like Sonoma and Glen Ellen may be overrun by a wine-sipping, Volvo-driving crowd, but in the rest of the largely rural valley you'll find gentle hills covered with live oak and wildflowers. Spring and autumn, when the weather is cool, are the best times for hiking and mountain biking in area parks. One of the more popular routes, either on foot or two wheels, is the Bald Mountain Trail in **Sugarloaf Ridge State Park** (also *see* Where to Sleep, *above*); you face a steep 3½-mile trek to the summit, but you'll be rewarded by a view that, on a clear day, stretches all the way to the Sierra Nevada. When the summer heat makes the back of your legs stick to the car seat, head to **Morton's Warm Springs** (1651 Warm Springs Rd., off Hwy. 12 in Kenwood, tel. 707/833–5511), a low-key resort full of picnicking families and splashing kids. An entrance fee ($3.75, $5.50 weekends) gets you access to two spring-water pools, a small creek, a grassy picnic area, snack bar, and game room. Morton's is open daily from mid-May through August (weekends only in early May and September).

Napa Valley

While Sonoma is cheaper and more welcoming, it's Napa Valley, about a 20-minute drive east of Sonoma on Highway 121, that lures most visitors to the Wine Country. When the traffic backs up for miles on Highway 29, it's clear that Napa Valley has become one of the Bay Area's biggest tourist attractions north of Fisherman's Wharf. The scenery is still beautiful, the wine (in some cases) still free, the town of **Napa** still lined with attractive Victorian houses and California bungalows, but the Napa Valley is losing some of its old-time charm with each trampling tourist.

The quiet town of **St. Helena,** 16 miles north of Napa on Highway 29, may be fraught with tourists, but the grocery stores and pharmacies (and a no-frills rural appeal) make this a good rest stop on your way up the valley. St. Helena is also home to the **Silverado Museum** (1490 Library Ln., off Adams St., tel. 707/963–3002), which houses a collection of photographs, letters, and manuscripts of former Napa Valley resident Robert Louis Stevenson. The museum is open Tuesday–Sunday noon–4 PM.

Wine may take center stage in the Napa Valley, but a fair share of hedonists come here solely for a peaceful soak in the valley's hot springs and mud baths, most located in or near Calistoga. Though you'd perhaps hesitate to throw yourself in a roadside ditch and roll around in the muck, folks in the Wine Country believe that mud baths and sulfur springs heal all manner of ills. Poverty is not one of them: You'll pay a pretty penny for a day of pampering. On the bright side, you can spend the night at any of several resorts for a decent price, and get free access to mineral pools and Jacuzzis.

WHERE TO SLEEP Although some of the most expensive lodging in the Wine Country is here in the posh Napa Valley, budget travelers can survive by camping or checking into one of Napa's lower-end motels. No matter where you stay, call at least three weeks in advance in summer.

➢ **NAPA** • One of Napa's cheapest options is the **Silverado Motel** (500 Silverado Trail, tel. 707/253–0892), where a tacky but cleanish room is $38 weekdays, $55 weekends ($38 daily in winter). The rooms at the **Napa Motel** (314 Soscol Ave., tel. 707/226–1878) are equally homely and equally cheap ($42 weekdays, $52 weekends). The **Napa Valley Budget Inn** (3380 Solano Ave., off Hwy. 29, tel. 707/257–6111) has clean but spartan doubles starting at $52 ($76 on Friday or Saturday). The swimming pool is perfect after a long day at the wineries, many of which are within biking distance. At the **Wine Valley Lodge** (200 S. Coombs St., tel. 707/224–7911), comfy rooms cost $50 on weekdays, $75 on weekends, and one room is wheelchair accessible. Amenities include a pool and a barbecue in the courtyard.

➢ **CALISTOGA** • Pleasure-seekers planning to hit both the wineries and the hot springs should consider staying in Calistoga. If you want to stay on the main drag, the **Calistoga Inn** (1250 Lincoln Ave., tel. 707/942–4101) has clean, simple bed-and-breakfast rooms with shared baths and full-size beds for $49 ($60 Fri.–Sat.). For $54 (second night $5 off), you can get a cabin for two at the **Triple S Ranch** (4600 Mt. Home Ranch Rd., tel. 707/942–6730). There's no phone or TV, but the complex does include a swimming pool and a pricey steak house. The ranch is north of Calistoga off Highway 128; take Petrified Forest Road west for 2½ miles until you reach Mt. Home Ranch Road. If you can't spend the night without a color TV, try the **Holiday House** (3514 Hwy. 128, tel. 707/942–6174), 3 miles north of Calistoga; watch for the white picket fence. From the outside it looks like you're pulling into a friend's house; the three rooms ($50), though, are strictly Motel 6.

➢ **CAMPING** • Camping is your best budget option in Napa (and the Wine Country in general). Unfortunately, there isn't any public transportation to the campgrounds; unless you have a car, you'll have to hitchhike, walk, or bike back to civilization. If you're getting desperate, head 20 miles east from Rutherford on Highway 128 to Lake Berryessa. The lake is divided into seven campgrounds, including **Pleasure Cove** (tel. 707/966–2172) and **Spanish Flat** (tel. 707/966–7700), for a total of 225 campsites (about $16) near the water. While you get direct access to swimming, fishing, picnicking, and waterskiing facilities, the area around the lake is barren, dusty, and very hot during summer. Reservations are recommended for summer weekends.

Bothe-Napa State Park. This is the Wine Country's most attractive campground, situated in the Napa foothills amid redwoods, madrone, and tan oaks, only 5 miles north of St. Helena and its wineries. The sites are reasonably private, and the park is one of the few with a swimming pool ($3 separate fee), much used on hot summer days. The fee is $14 (half-price disabled camping pass available through MISTIX), and reservations are suggested in summer, especially on weekends. For reservations call MISTIX (tel. 800/444–PARK). *3801 St. Helena Hwy. N, Calistoga, tel. 707/942–4575. From St. Helena, north on Hwy. 29. 48 sites. No cooking facilities, day use fee ($5), drinking water, flush toilets, hot showers. Wheelchair access.*

FOOD If wine tasting is Napa Valley's main attraction, gourmet cuisine runs a close second. The best way to eat well without breaking the bank, however, is to stock up at one of the area's makeshift farmers' markets (*see below*), with bushels of fresh produce at reasonable prices. If you're spending the day in Calistoga, cruise down to the **Calistoga Roastery** (1631 Lincoln Ave., tel. 707/942–5757), open daily 7–6. The bottomless cup of coffee ($1) is a good deal, and the ice cream latte ($2.50) makes a great dessert. For cheap Mexican food, head to the west end of Lincoln Avenue, where it dead-ends at the **Calistoga Drive-In Taquería** (1207 Foothill Blvd., tel. 707/942–0543). A veggie burrito here runs $3.50, and the tortillas and chips are great. The restaurant is wheelchair accessible.

Calistoga Inn. The California cuisine at this casual restaurant is excellent, and for once the portions are fair for the price. Try the grilled lemon-chicken sausage with sauerkraut, roasted potatoes, and coleslaw ($7.25), or cool off in the shady garden with one of their award-winning ales or lagers—only $2 during happy hour (weekdays 4–5:30). *1250 Lincoln Ave., tel. 707/942–4101. Open daily 11:30–3 and 5:30–9:30 (weekends until 10); shorter hrs off-season.*

Chimney Rock Café. This tiny no-frills eatery isn't big on atmosphere (it's located on a golf course, after all), but it serves the cheapest three-egg omelets in the Wine Country (around $4.25). Watch the golfers tee off while you eat. *5320 Silverado Trail, Napa, tel. 707/258–2727. Open daily 6:30–6. Breakfast served until 2 PM.*

The Diner. Several good restaurants line Washington Street in Yountville, but this is the best for the price. You can get huge plates of American or Mexican food for lunch and dinner, or specialty eggs and pancakes for breakfast. Most meals are $7–$10, but portions are generous (consider splitting an appetizer and a main course with a friend). *6476 Washington St., Yountville, tel. 707/944–2626. Open Tues.–Sun. 8–3 and 5:30–9.*

Many wineries provide picnic grounds at no cost. Pull over for a free wine-tasting session, and follow it up with a leisurely lunch in the sun.

Green Valley Café and Trattoria. While it ain't cheap, this St. Helena trattoria is remarkably unpretentious, with tasty pasta entrées like pesto pasta with green beans and potatoes ($9.25) and smoked salmon tortellini ($10.75). Locals come for the $5 sandwiches, unfortunately served at lunch only. All in all it's hearty food for ordinary folks (as far as anyone in the Wine Country might be considered ordinary), in a casual, diner-like atmosphere. *1310 Main St., St. Helena, tel. 707/963–7088. Open Tues.–Sat. 11:30–3 and 5:30–9:30.*

Red Hen Restaurant. Pull into the Red Hen for their popular fajitas ($22 for two people) and margaritas ($5), or one of the hefty side dishes (tamales, burritos, chili rellenos), starting at about $3. Then take a seat on the large outdoor patio and watch people race to the wineries. You, on the other hand, can search for the perfect souvenir at the attached antique store (open 10–5). *5091 St. Helena Hwy. (Hwy. 29), tel. 707/255–8125. 5 mi north of Napa off Oak Knoll Rd. Open weekdays 11–9, weekends 11–10.*

➢ **MARKETS AND DELICATESSENS • Napa Valley Farmers' Market.** This market is held on Tuesdays in Napa and Fridays in St. Helena, with fruits and veggies, cheese, eggs, honey, dressings, cut flowers, baked goods, and countless other edibles. *Napa: West St., btw 1st and Pearl Sts., tel. 707/963–7343. Just west of Cinedome Theatre, which has free parking. Open May–Oct., Tues. 7:30–noon. St. Helena: Old Railroad Depot, tel. 707/963–7343. East on Adams St. off Hwy. 29, left at stop sign, and 1 block up on right. Open May–Oct., Fri. 7:30–11:30 AM.*

Pometta's Deli. This place is famous for its barbecued chicken platters ($7), but you can also get box lunches to go ($9.50–$12.50). Especially good is the vegetarian sandwich (about $4), stuffed with avocado, provolone, zucchini, and jalapeños. The restaurant has indoor and outdoor seating and—wonder of wonders—tournament horseshoe pits (free). *Hwy. 29, at Oakville Grade in Oakville, tel. 707/944–2365. Open daily 9–5.*

WINERIES With literally hundreds of wineries crammed into the 35-mile-long Napa Valley, it's difficult to decide which to visit. Some, like **Sutter Home Winery** (277 Hwy. 29, St. Helena, tel. 707/963–3104), right on the main drag, are packed with drunken revelers, while others, like **Trefethen Vineyards** (1160 Oak Knoll Ave., Napa, tel. 707/255–7700), draw a sedate crowd able to hold forth about a wine's bouquet and tannins. If you're irked by the idea of paying a $3 tasting fee, you'll have to choose wineries carefully.

While wine tasting and mud bathing are both popular Wine Country activities, you won't want to indulge in both on the same day—unless you enjoy the pangs of a fierce headache.

Beaulieu Vineyards. Affectionately known as "BV," Beaulieu has supplied wine to President Eisenhower and Queen Elizabeth, among other notables. Yet this large winery is far from snooty. The staff greets you with a glass of wine at the door of the octagonal tasting room and encourages you to indulge in free samples. If you like dessert wine, be sure to taste their lovely muscat. Free, informative half-hour tours cover the wine-making process and BV's 100-year history. *1960 Hwy. 29, Rutherford, tel. 707/963–2411. Open daily 10–5. Wheelchair access.*

Beringer Winery. Now owned by the controversial Nestlé chocolate corporation, Beringer has an interesting history: It's one of the few wineries to remain in continuous operation throughout the 20th century (since 1876, in fact). A government license to make sacramental wine kept Beringer in business during Prohibition, when most wineries were shut down. The half-hour tour takes you through the winery's 100-year-old caves and beautiful grounds, and concludes with a free tasting (though the finer vintages are only available for a hefty $2–$4 per taste). Be prepared for that impersonal, corporate feel you get at most of the big wineries. While tours and tastings take place year-round, reservations are advised on summer weekends. *2000 Main St. (Hwy. 29), St. Helena, tel. 707/963–7115. Open Nov.–May, daily 9:30–5; Apr.–Oct., daily 9:30–6.*

How to Taste Like a Master

If you want to pass yourself off as a wine aficionado (as opposed to a freeloading swiller), you'll need to know some rules of tasting. First of all, move from light wines to dark, so as not to "clutter your palate," as a vintner might say. Begin by vigorously swirling an ounce of wine in your glass. Put your hand over the glass to hold in the aromas (as well as the wine, if you're new to the swirling business). Raise the glass to your nose and inhale deeply. In young wines, you smell only the grapes (for example, the smell of the pinot noir grape might remind you of black cherries); with aging, the wine becomes more complex, emitting a whole "bouquet" of aromas (in pinot, that can include violets, vanilla, spicy pepper, or even leather). Next, take a sip—you're encouraged to slurp, because air helps you taste the wine. Swish the wine around in your mouth to pick up the more subtle flavors. Before downing the rest of your glass, notice the aftertaste (or "finish"), and then decide what you think. ("It's a cheeky little wine, reminiscent of running naked through verdant pastures.")

If you're seriously interested in viticulture—and not just trying to impress your date—take a course through U.C. Berkeley Extension's Wine Studies department. Offerings include Wines of California and Europe, Country Wines of France, and others. The fees are steep ($125–$150 for a six-week course), but the courses are fun and incredibly informative. Contact U.C. Berkeley Extension (2223 Fulton St., Berkeley 94720, tel. 510/642–4111) for more info.

Nichelini. Napa's oldest family-owned winery (since 1890) lies 11 miles east of Rutherford and is worth every minute of the beautiful drive. Outside, under the shade of walnut trees and next to an old Roman grape press (which looks like a giant garlic press), you can sample several wines for free. Picnic to the strains of traditional Italian music on a hill overlooking the countryside. *Hwy. 128, St. Helena, tel. 707/963–0717 or 800/WE-TASTE. Open May–Oct., weekends 10–6; Nov.–Apr., weekends 10–5.*

In the 1920s, European countries signed a treaty agreeing that only the French could use the name "champagne." Those were Prohibition days in America, and since we were convinced we'd never produce alcohol again, we never signed the treaty. Thus, Americans can still legally make champagne, but many vintners play it safe and use the name "sparkling wine."

Prager Port Works. Owner Jim Prager and the family dog Eno (short for "Enology") know the meaning of hospitality. This rustic winery doesn't even produce enough cases a year to be classified as "small." ("That makes us 'tiny,' " quips Jim.) Tastings run $3, but the fee can be applied toward a bottle of Prager's special port ($35), available only at the winery. The homey garden provides a quiet break from the Highway 29 crowds. *1281 Lewelling Ln., St. Helena, tel. 707/963–PORT or 800/969–PORT. On Hwy. 29, next to Sutter Home. Open daily 10:30–4:30, or whenever the last person leaves. Wheelchair access.*

Rustridge. While you're traipsing through Napa's backwoods, check out this winery, ranch, and B&B ($100 a night). You'll probably be the only visitor indulging in the free tasters, served in a converted barn. Someone might even have to run in from the fields to open the tasting room. You can picnic on the serene grounds of Catacula (Valley of the Oaks), as the native people once called this land. *2910 Lower Chiles Valley Rd., St. Helena, tel. 707/965–2871. From Hwy. 29 north, Hwy. 128 east. Cross Silverado Trail, left at fork (look for Pope Valley sign), first right on Lower Chiles Valley Rd. Open daily 10–5 (winter until 4).*

S. Anderson. Tours are given twice daily, frequently by John Anderson, son of the late Stan (as in "S.") Anderson. He does a wonderful job guiding you through his vineyards and candlelit stone wine caves, modeled after those in the Champagne region of France. The caves hold over 400,000 bottles of sparkling wine, awaiting their "turn" (champagne bottles are turned by hand in a labor-intensive process that removes the yeast). The tour, with tasting, costs $3, but it's more than worth it. Plan for over an hour—John doesn't need much prompting to extend the visit. *1473 Yountville Crossroad, Yountville, tel. 707/944–8642 or 800/4–BUBBLY. From Hwy. 29 in Yountville, take Madison exit and follow signs for Yountville Crossroad. Open daily 10–5; tours at 10:30 and 2:30.*

Not only are smaller wineries more likely to offer free tastings, but the extra attention paid to the product often means better wine. As one vintner explained, "I know every barrel like it was my own child."

Wermuth. Vintner Ralph Wermuth presides over the tiny tasting room and is more entertaining than a barrel of monkeys: He's one part philosopher, one part mad scientist, and one part stand-up comedian. Free tastings of Gamay are accompanied by chocolate chips to "bring out the flavor," while the dry colombard is paired with that gourmet standby, Cheez-Its. Wife and partner Smitty Wermuth designs the winery logos, which depict the old Italian basket presses still used here in the crush. *3942 Silverado Trail, Calistoga, tel. 707/942–5924. From Hwy. 29 north, Hwy. 128 east to Silverado Trail; continue north past Bale Ln. and look for sign on right. Open Tues.–Sun. 11–5.*

HOT SPRINGS The majority of the Napa Valley's mud and mineral baths are located in the offbeat town of Calistoga, at the northern end of the valley. The town's bubbling mineral spring became a spa in 1859, when entrepreneur Sam Brannan slurred together the word California with the name of New York's Saratoga Springs resort; Calistoga has been attracting health seekers ever since. Unfortunately, most visitors are loaded and willing to pay up the wazoo to get their wazoo steam-wrapped. Prices at the Calistoga spas are uniformly steep, varying by only a couple of dollars. Be sure to pick up 10%-off coupons at the **Calistoga Chamber of Commerce** (1458 Lincoln Ave., tel. 707/942–6333), open Monday–Saturday 10–5, Sunday 10–4.

A cheaper option is open-air bathing at rustic retreats like Harbin Hot Springs or White Sulphur Springs (*see below*). You won't get to play human mud pie at the outdoor spas, but you can bathe in natural springs and hike through rolling grounds far from the buzz of urbanity. Not only do these resorts offer many of the same amenities as the Calistoga spas, but you get an affordable room for the night to boot. If you opt for one of the indoor spas, call ahead for a reservation. Most accept walk-ins, but nothing is more stressful than being turned away from the massage you've been aching for.

Golden Haven Hot Springs. A favorite with hetero couples, Golden Haven is the only Calistoga spa to offer private co-ed mud baths (sorry lovebirds, there's still an attendant). The full treatment (mud bath, mineral Jacuzzi, blanket wrap, and 30-minute massage) will run you $64 per person. If you're too relaxed to make it past the front door, you can crash in one of their rooms for $59 ($49 Sept.–June), which includes use of the swimming pool and hot mineral pool. *1713 Lake St., Calistoga, tel. 707/942–6793. From Lincoln Ave. east, left on Stevenson St., right on Lake St. Open daily 9–9.*

Harbin Hot Springs. Forty minutes north of Calistoga, this 1,200-acre community is run by the Heart Consciousness Church, a group that advocates holistic health and spiritual renewal. The retreat, popular with gay men, has three natural mineral pools, varying in temperature from tepid to *very* hot, and a cold, spring-fed "plunge" pool, all open 24 hours. To use the pools, you must pay $5 for a one-month membership or $15 for a year (only one member per group required), plus an additional day-use fee ($12 Mon.–Thurs., $17 Fri.–Sun.). There's also an acclaimed massage school, whose graduates would be happy to show you their stuff ($46 per hour, $60 for 90 minutes). If you bring your own food, you're welcome to use the communal kitchen located above the changing room, though no meat, poultry, or fish is allowed. Otherwise, a vegetarian restaurant serves breakfast (under $8) and dinner ($8–$12). Beds in the ramshackle dorm rooms start at $23 ($35 on weekends), and you have to provide your own sheets or sleeping bag. Private rooms with shared bath are $60 ($90 on weekends). There are campsites along the creek and in nearby meadows, but at $14 per person ($23 Fri.–Sat., $17 Sun.), it's a lot to pay for a night in a tent, especially when the grounds are unkempt and the bathrooms few and far between. Despite the cost, expect a crowd on weekends. *Tel. 707/987–2477 or 800/622–2477 (Northern California only). Hwy. 29 north to Middletown, turn left at junction for Hwy. 175, right on Barnes St.; go 1½ mi to Harbin Springs Rd. and turn left. Rides can be arranged for those taking Greyhound.*

They say "clothing optional," but you're going to feel pretty out of place if you wear anything but a smile into the pools at Harbin Hot Springs. If you have the cash and the curiosity, get "watsu-ed"—an underwater shiatsu massage that's a house specialty.

Lincoln Avenue Spa. With pleasant stone-and-wood massage rooms and a central location, this spa is posh for the price. Their Body Mud Treatment ($38) is the ideal alternative for those squeamish about wallowing in mud someone else has already wallowed in: You get your choice of mud (herbal, sea, or mint) slathered over your body, a relaxing nap on the steam table, and a soothing facial mask. *1339 Lincoln Ave., Calistoga, tel. 707/942–5296. Open daily 9–9.*

Nance's Spa. Of the Calistoga spas, Nance's is one of the cheapest, offering "the works" for $62. You begin by sliding into a tub of hot volcanic mud, then you shower and simmer in a bubbling mineral bath. Next you're swaddled in soft sheets and left to "set" like a human dumpling in preparation for a half-hour massage. The process is supposed to relieve tension and extract toxins from your skin and muscles. Nance's facilities are sex segregated and none too private: The amorous and the modest may opt to go elsewhere. *1614 Lincoln Ave., Calistoga, tel. 707/942–6211. Open weekdays 9–5, weekends 9–7.*

White Sulphur Springs. If you're planning to stay the night in Napa Valley, this St. Helena resort is a bargain. For $65 you get access to 300 acres of land, plenty of hiking and biking trails, a Jacuzzi, a natural mineral bath, even a stand of redwoods; *and* you get a decent room for the night, either in the rustic, dormitory-style carriage house or in the inn, where each room has a half-bath. It's a day and night of decadence for the price of an hour or two at some of Calistoga's spas. An even cheaper option is to stop by during the day and use the facilities for

$15 9 AM–6 PM. If you only want to be there for an hour or two, the management will usually knock down the price—just ask. *3100 White Sulphur Springs Rd., St. Helena, tel. 707/963–8588. From Hwy. 29 north, turn left on Spring St. in St. Helena and go 2.8 mi. Note: Do NOT take Sulphur Springs Rd. from Hwy. 29.*

CHEAP THRILLS If you blow your last buck on a bottle of wine or a mud wrap, you'll still find fun in Napa Valley. In summer, the chamber of commerce sponsors free concerts in downtown Napa's **Veterans Memorial Park** (cnr 3rd and Main Sts.). One of the most popular is the **Napa Valley Jazz Festival,** held annually in mid-July. Sundays from 6–5, junk lovers can rummage among the used furniture, silver jewelry, and Harley-Davidson T-shirts at the **Napa Valley Flea Market** (303 S. Kelly Rd., tel. 707/226–8862), located south of Napa on Highway 29.

For a lesson in maximizing the potential of junk, trek out to **Litto's Hubcap Ranch** in Pope Valley. The Litto legacy began when Emanuelle "Litto" Damonte discovered that several hubcaps had been lost on a turn of the road near his property. Being a kindly fellow, he placed them on the fence for the owners to retrieve. Thirty years and over 2,000 hubcaps later, the metallic splendor of his house and property are a tribute to American folk art. Litto's grandson and family now live in the house and are surprisingly cordial to gawkers. To reach the ranch from Highway 29, take Highway 128 east, cross Silverado Trail, and bear left at the fork. When you reach Pope Valley, turn left on Pope Valley Road—it's a couple miles farther on the right.

OUTDOOR ACTIVITIES If you're determined to beat the heat, it's a half-hour drive from Napa or Rutherford to **Lake Berryessa** (*see* Camping, *above*), where you can rent almost any kind of water vessel—from a Jet Ski to a ski boat—from one of the lake's many resorts. If you're spending the day in Calistoga, pay a visit to **Robert Louis Stevenson State Park** off Highway 29, 9 miles northeast of Calistoga. Here you can hike to the bunkhouse of the Silverado Mine, where the impoverished author honeymooned with his wife, Fanny Osbourne, in the summer of 1880. The stay inspired Stevenson's *The Silverado Squatters.* The park is perched at the top of Mt. St. Helena, which is said to be the model for Spyglass Hill in *Treasure Island.* Its 3,000 acres are largely undeveloped; picnicking is permitted but overnight camping is not.

Skyline Wilderness Park. Perhaps the best way to experience the beauty of the Napa Valley is to get out and hike, preferably on Skyline's 2½-mile Lake Marie Trail, which runs along a shady creek and past overgrown orchards and ruined stone dairies. Swimming in Lake Marie isn't allowed, but you can try your luck fishing for bluegill and bass. *2201 Imola Ave, tel. 707/252–0481. Open Mon.–Thurs. 9–8, Fri.–Sun. 8–8; shorter hrs in winter.*

Lake Tahoe

Straddling the border of California and Nevada on the northern flank of the Sierra Nevada range, Lake Tahoe is one of the West Coast's most popular outdoor playgrounds. During spring and summer, when temperatures hover in the 70s, the lake (about a 3½-hour drive east of San Francisco on I–80) offers boating, fishing, waterskiing, and jet skiing; and the mountains surrounding Tahoe Basin satiate the desires of even the most demanding hikers, bikers, equestrians, and anglers. During the winter season (usually December–April, sometimes extending into May), attention shifts to downhill and cross-country skiing and snowboarding. The West Coast's number-one ski area, Tahoe has earned a worldwide reputation for its "extreme" conditions, provided by the sheer cliffs and steep faces of the Sierra Nevada.

Besides being deep and blue, Lake Tahoe is also damn cold. You can swim in it, but most visitors just dip their feet in and scamper back to shore. On the other hand, a quick dip is said by locals to be the best way to cure a hangover.

Given the array of pleasures, it's no wonder Lake Tahoe draws up to 100,000 tourists at peak periods. On weekends, the traffic on I–80 between the Bay Area and Lake Tahoe has to be seen to be believed. A common way to explore the lake is to drive around its 72-mile perimeter. On an average day the trip takes about three hours, but plan on traffic slowing you down on summer weekends and holidays, and in winter when there's snow on the roads. If the slow driving starts to annoy you, stop

Lake Tahoe

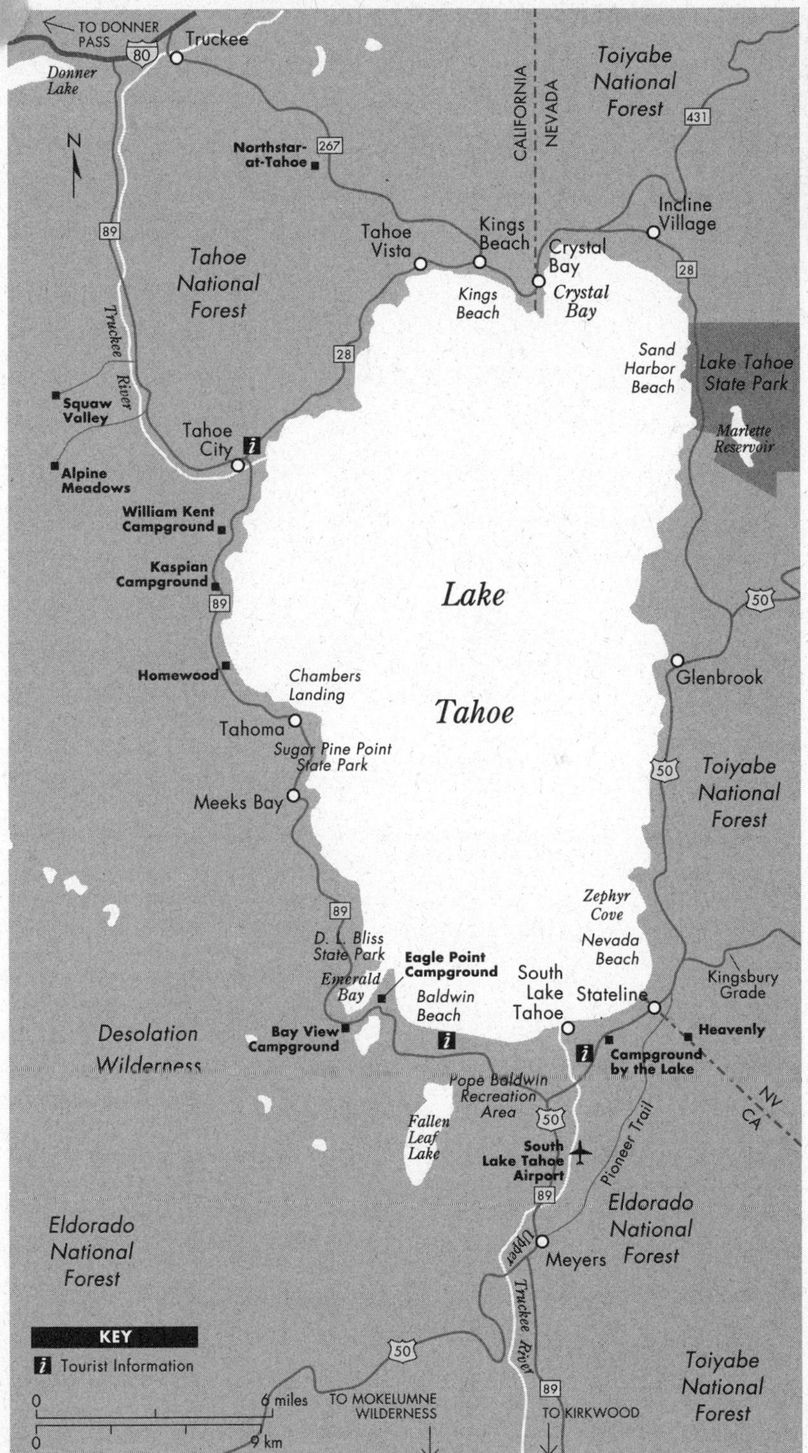

TO DONNER PASS
80
Truckee
Donner Lake
N
267
Northstar-at-Tahoe
Toiyabe National Forest
CALIFORNIA
NEVADA
431
89
Tahoe National Forest
Tahoe Vista
Kings Beach
Crystal Bay
Incline Village
28
Kings Beach
Crystal Bay
Truckee River
28
Sand Harbor Beach
Lake Tahoe State Park
Marlette Reservoir
Squaw Valley
Tahoe City
Alpine Meadows
William Kent Campground
Kaspian Campground
89
Lake
50
Homewood
Glenbrook
Chambers Landing
Tahoe
Tahoma
Sugar Pine Point State Park
50
Toiyabe National Forest
Meeks Bay
Zephyr Cove
89
Nevada Beach
D. L. Bliss State Park
Eagle Point Campground
Emerald Bay
South Lake Tahoe
Kingsbury Grade
Stateline
Baldwin Beach
Heavenly
Desolation Wilderness
Bay View Campground
Campground by the Lake
Pope Baldwin Recreation Area
NV
CA
50
Fallen Leaf Lake
South Lake Tahoe Airport
Pioneer Trail
89
Eldorado National Forest
Eldorado National Forest
Meyers
Upper Truckee River
KEY
Tourist Information
50
Toiyabe National Forest
0
6 miles
0
9 km
TO MOKELUMNE WILDERNESS
89
TO KIRKWOOD

at a few scenic lookouts (especially Emerald Bay on the west shore) and disappear down a hiking path or two.

At regular intervals around the lake is a series of small towns—some charming, some tacky, all dependent on the tourist industry for their survival. Although it's a somewhat subjective division, the lake's locales are usually designated as belonging to either the north shore or the south shore. Thanks largely to the popularity of the ski resort at Squaw Valley, the north shore is the domain of Tahoe's young, energetic set, dedicated to spending as much time as possible exploring the great outdoors and as little time as possible in the restaurants, hotels, and upscale resorts where most of them find employment. The south shore, on the other hand, caters primarily to family vacationers who come to Tahoe to play on the lake in summer, on the ski slopes in the winter, and in the Vegas-style casinos on the Nevada side of the border all year round.

"Tahoe" is a mispronunciation of "Da ow a ga," or "edge of the lake," which is the name the local Washo Indians gave to the area.

The north shore's largest town is **Truckee,** about a 30-minute drive (12 miles) north of the lake, with a modern downtown area to the west and an Old Town (complete with board sidewalks, wood-frame storefronts, and an ancient railroad) to the east. Donner Pass Road connects the two sides of town and serves as the main commercial boulevard. **Tahoe City,** at the lake's northwestern corner, has a small-town warmth lacking in Truckee, and is home to many of Tahoe's younger residents. On the south shore, the city of **South Lake Tahoe** is packed to the gills with restaurants, motels, and rental shops. The pace never flags in summer, and in winter popular ski areas like Heavenly keep the town jumping. Butting up against the east side of South Lake Tahoe is the imaginatively named town of **Stateline,** Nevada, offering a jumble of brightly lit casinos and tacky gift shops. If you venture farther across the state line into the Nevada side of the Lake Tahoe basin, you'll find a few quirky, older casinos, a lot of national forest, and the Ponderosa Ranch, a re-creation of the western town in *Bonanza.*

BASICS

For the lowdown on equipment rental and what to pack for a day on the ski slopes, *see* Skiing, *below.* If you're just looking to load up on tourist brochures, the **North Lake Tahoe Chamber of Commerce** (245 Hwy. 89, Tahoe City, tel. 916/581–6900) lies between the Lucky supermarket and the Bank of America across from the Tahoe City "Y" (a Y-shaped intersection that's impossible to miss). You can also contact the **South Lake Tahoe Chamber of Commerce** (3066 U.S. 50, tel. 916/541–5255) or **Truckee-Donner Visitor Information** (Donner Pass Rd., Truckee, tel. 916/587–2757), at the Truckee Transit Depot in Old Town.

Lake Tahoe Forest Service Visitor Center. In addition to the usual tourist information, the center offers a great location, with beach access and self-guided nature trails. The staff will tell you all you want to know about the lake's natural and human history. This is also the place to pick up campfire and wilderness permits for the Desolation and Mokelumne wilderness areas. Permits are free, but only a limited number are available (*see* Camping, *below*). Depending on funding, they may be closed on certain days of the week—call ahead. *Hwy. 89, btw Emerald Bay and South Lake Tahoe, tel. 916/573–2674. Open summer, daily 8–5:30; closed winter.*

COMING AND GOING

BY CAR Both routes to Lake Tahoe from the Bay Area take 3–3½ hours when road and traffic conditions are at their best. To reach the north shore, follow I–80 east through Sacramento all the way to Truckee. For the south shore, take I–80 to Sacramento and turn onto U.S. 50 east, which leads directly to South Lake Tahoe. You won't be allowed into the mountains without chains if it snows; bring your own or you'll have to pay inflated prices for a set near the CalTrans checkpoint. Even if you brought your own, consider paying the small fee (about $10) to let someone else put them on for you. You will see swarms of jumpsuit-clad people with numbers on their backs at every checkpoint waiting to perform this service.

For recorded info on road conditions, call CalTrans at 800/427–ROAD.

If snow doesn't slow you down, traffic might, especially on Friday and Sunday afternoons, and especially during summer and on holiday weekends. If you must drive to Tahoe on Friday, wait until 7 or 8 PM. Traffic is usually worst on I–80, so consider taking U.S. 50, even if you're headed for the north shore.

BY BUS **Greyhound** (tel. 800/231–2222) runs four buses a day between San Francisco and Truckee (5–6 hrs, $32) and the same number between Truckee and Reno (1 hr, $8). If you're headed to the south shore, Greyhound makes the trip between San Francisco and South Lake Tahoe (5½ hrs, $29) three times a day. Both Amtrak and Greyhound use the **Transit Depot** in the middle of Old Town Truckee (Donner Pass Rd., tel. 916/587–3822), a safe and comfortable place to wait for connections or pick up info at the tourist office. There are a few coin-operated lockers here. In South Lake Tahoe, the Greyhound station (tel. 702/588–4645) is in back of **Harrah's Hotel and Casino,** on U.S. 50 1½ miles south of the South Lake Tahoe "Y."

BY TRAIN **Amtrak** (tel. 800/USA–RAIL) runs two train/bus routes a day between Emeryville and Truckee (transfer in Sacramento, 6 hrs, $49). If you're coming from San Francisco, take the free bus from the CalTrain Station at 4th and Townsend streets to the Emeryville Amtrak Station (5885 Landregan St., at Powell St.). Amtrak also has four trains a week traveling the hour-long route between Truckee and Reno ($12 one way). All trains arrive at the Truckee Transit Depot (*see* Coming and Going by Bus, *above*). Another train/bus combination serves South Lake Tahoe (transfer in Sacramento, 6 hrs, $33).

Although the journey over the mountains can be painfully slow at times, the train ride between the Bay Area and Tahoe, especially the final climb up steep mountain passes, is filled with spectacular scenery.

GETTING AROUND

Once you get there, finding your way around the lake is no sweat. Three intersecting highways form a loop around the lake: **Highway 89** (also known as **Emerald Bay Road**) skirts the western shore of the lake between Tahoe City and South Lake Tahoe; **U.S. 50** (a.k.a. **Lake Tahoe Boulevard**) intersects Highway 89 in South Lake Tahoe and follows the lake's eastern shore; and **Highway 28** (a.k.a. **North Lake Boulevard** or **Lake Shore Boulevard**) runs along the north part of the shore back into Tahoe City. The intersections of Highways 28 and 89 in Tahoe City and Highway 89 and U.S. 50 in South Lake Tahoe are commonly referred to as the **Tahoe City "Y"** and the **South Lake Tahoe "Y,"** respectively.

Tahoe Area Regional Transit (TART, tel. 916/581–6365 or 800/736–6365 outside California) has buses, most equipped with ski and bike racks, that serve the north and west shores of Lake Tahoe, including Squaw Valley. The fare is $1. The **South Tahoe Area Ground Express** (STAGE, tel. 916/573–2080) runs 24 hours within the city limits of South Lake Tahoe; the fare is $1.25.

WHERE TO SLEEP

You face a mind-boggling number of options in choosing a place to stay in the Tahoe area. Hostels, motels, condos, cabins, and campgrounds abound everywhere you look. If you're just passing through for a night or two in summer and want to hang around the lake by day and gamble by night, a motel or campground on the south shore is the cheapest and most convenient alternative. But if you're coming for a week in winter to ski with a group of friends, consider a condo or cabin on the north shore: It's more affordable than you might think. No matter when you come, reserve as far ahead as possible. On holidays and summer weekends everything is completely packed, despite the fact that most places raise their prices indiscriminately at these times.

HOTELS AND MOTELS In general, prices at all but the finest establishments on Lake Tahoe are flexible. Proprietors will charge whatever the traffic will bear, which means prices on weekends and holidays rise substantially. Ask about weekly rates, too; they tend to be cheaper. The quickest way to find a cheap, indoor place to crash for the night is to head to U.S. 50 between South Lake Tahoe and Stateline—cruise the strip and keep your eyes open for the neon. As a last resort, look for cheap deals at the casinos on the Nevada side of both the south and north shores.

➢ **SOUTH SHORE** • **El Nido Motel.** If you're seeking comfort at a reasonable price, the El Nido should end your search. Its excellent amenities include a hot tub and small, modern rooms with TV, VCR, and telephone. Flawlessly clean doubles start at $40 on weekdays, $50 on summer weekends; in the winter prices are about $10 lower. Call for details on winter ski packages. *2215 Lake Tahoe Blvd. (U.S. 50), tel. 916/541–2711. About 3½ mi west of California–Nevada border. 21 rooms.*

Emerald Motel. The rooms are ordinary, but the motel is far enough away from the crowded downtown area to provide a modicum of peace and quiet. Clean doubles with color TV, microwave, and small refrigerator start at $35 on weekdays and $45 on weekends; some rooms also have small kitchenettes, and for about $10 more you can reserve the room with a fireplace. Ask for special rates (negotiable) for stays of four nights or more. *515 Emerald Bay Rd. (Hwy. 89), tel. 916/544–5515. 1 mi north of South Lake Tahoe "Y." 9 rooms.*

Trout Creek Motel. With shag carpet, lumpy beds, and small, dark rooms, this motel in South Lake Tahoe is basically a fleabag. But for just $25 per double on weekdays, who's complaining? At least there's a TV and showers. When the rates jump to $60 or higher during summer and holidays, it's time to look elsewhere. *2650 Lake Tahoe Blvd. (U.S. 50), tel. 916/542–2523. 22 rooms. Wheelchair access.*

➢ **NORTH SHORE** • It's hard to find a budget motel on the north shore, especially in Truckee (though there's no reason to stay in Truckee, anyway). The **Super 8 Lodge** (11506 Deerfield Dr., tel. 916/587–8888 or 800/843–1991), near the Truckee/Squaw Valley exit off I–80, has the best rates in Truckee, but it's far from cheap: Doubles are $68 in winter, $56 in the off-season. For better prices and better location, check out the smaller communities around the lakeshore, like Tahoe Vista or Kings Beach.

North Shore Lodge. While it's not exactly the epitome of class, this plain motel across from Kings Beach charges almost half the price of the motels right on the beach. For about $35 ($45 in winter), you get a double with a small refrigerator, TV, and microwave. In summer you also have use of a heated pool. *8755 North Lake Blvd. (Hwy. 28), tel. 916/546-4833. In Kings Beach, 1 mi west of California–Nevada border. 20 rooms.*

Northwood Pines Motel. Yes, it's shabby and generic. But it's also priced right and centrally located (about 8 miles northeast of Tahoe City), especially if you're in Tahoe to explore the north shore's ski areas. Aging doubles cost $40 on weekdays and $55 on weekends; weekly rates start at $160. *8489 Trout St., tel. 916/546–9829. Take North Lake Blvd. (Hwy. 28) northeast, turn left on Bear St., right on Trout St. 9 rooms.*

River Ranch Lodge. For a great splurge (especially in spring and fall, when prices are lowest), head to the classy River Ranch Lodge, beside the Truckee River between Truckee and Tahoe City. Twenty-one frilly rooms come complete with flower-print curtains and bedspreads, tasteful wallpaper, and wooden furniture. About half have small decks overlooking the river. Doubles start at $50 on spring and fall weekdays ($75 on weekends), $75 on summer weekdays ($100 on weekends), and $90 on winter weekdays ($110 on weekends). Free continental breakfast is included. Several of the noisier rooms above the restaurant go for a slightly lower price, and there's also a "small double"—nice, but not facing the river—for $40–$90, depending on the time of year. *Hwy. 89 and Alpine Meadows Rd., tel. 916/583–4264 or 800/535–9900. 21 rooms.*

Tamarack Lodge Motel. The Tamarack, about a mile north of the lake in Tahoe City, sits in a clearing surrounded by pines and is within walking distance of the beach. Escape the crowds in a clean and comfortable wood-paneled double, starting at $45 weekdays and $50 weekends; another $5 gets a room with a kitchenette. *2311 North Lake Blvd. (Hwy. 28), tel. 916/583–3350. 21 rooms.*

HOSTELS **Doug's Mellow Mountain Retreat.** Billed as "The Perfect Place to Chill Out," this laid-back private hostel resembles a frat house, with team flags on the wall, beds in every square inch of available bedroom space, and drab brown furniture. But Doug's a friendly guy, and he'll let you sit in front of the fireplace and watch movies (he has over 200), use his kitchen, and have barbecues on the deck. He'll even pick you up from the Greyhound station at Harrah's if you call ahead. Doug's house, in a quiet residential neighborhood, is centrally located (about a mile from Heavenly and from the casinos). Beds are only $13, and rooms are co-ed. *3787 Forest St., just west of CA–NV border, tel. 916/544–8065. From South Lake Tahoe, U.S. 50 east, right on Wildwood Rd., left on Forest St. 15 beds in 3 rooms. No curfew, no lockout. Reception hours flexible.*

Squaw Valley Hostel. This privately run hostel, within walking distance of the Squaw Valley ski area, opens only during winter, usually from November 15 to April 15. During the week a dorm bed runs $20; on weekends rates go up to $25. On weekends, when the hostel hosts groups, it's next to impossible to get a room unless you call well in advance and are blessed with good luck. *1900 Squaw Valley Rd., tel. 916/583–7771. From Truckee, Hwy. 89 south, right on Squaw Valley Rd. 100 beds in 9 rooms.*

WEEKEND AND WEEKLY RENTALS If you're planning on spending a weekend or more, consider renting a condo, cabin, or house. It'll cost more than a motel room, but in most places you'll get a kitchen, a color TV, and a fireplace; and it's much easier to sneak six friends past the manager. You may even have access to a pool, a hot tub, a sauna, a weight room, or some combination thereof. Generally located nearer to major ski areas than are motels, rentals allow you to get away from major roads and traffic noise. Prices range dramatically based on location, season (summer is more expensive), and length of stay. As a rule of thumb, the more people in your group and the longer the stay, the more affordable rentals become. At the low end of the scale, you should be able to find a two-to four-person condo for about $75 a night or $425 a week in the off-season, with prices rising roughly 10% in summer.

Literally hundreds of realty and property-management firms in the Lake Tahoe area vie to serve you, so be sure to shop around. If you want help, the **Lake Tahoe Visitors' Authority** (1156 Ski Run Blvd., South Lake Tahoe, tel. 916/544–5050 or 800/AT–TAHOE) will direct you free of charge to a realtor tailored to your needs and price range. On the north shore, the **Tahoe North Visitors' and Convention Bureau** (tel. 916/583–3494 or 800/TAHOE–4U) will put you in touch with local rental agencies or book reservations for $5. **R. RENT** (tel. 916/546–2549) specializes in north-shore budget rentals. If you have the time, you can save a few bucks by arranging a rental directly through a property owner. To find out what's available, check the classified ads in the *Tahoe Daily Tribune* for south-shore listings, or the *Tahoe World*, a north-shore paper that comes out each Thursday.

SEASONAL RENTALS Unless you just won the lottery, the only way to make a seasonal rental affordable is to share a place. If you get together with 10 friends, rent a place for the winter for $4,000 (meaning you pay $400), and stay in it for 10 weekends, you can have yourself a comfortable Tahoe house, often with a hot tub, for the same price as 10 nights in an average motel—not a bad deal.

Be realistic about whether you'll use a seasonal rental enough to get your money's worth—many people fork over several hundred dollars for a place and end up making only one or two trips.

When looking for a seasonal rental, consider location, amenities, what utilities you'll be expected to pay, heating costs, and the snow-clearing situation on nearby roads. Prices and availability of seasonal rentals fluctuate even more dramatically than for weekend or weekly rentals. To use the direct approach, check the *Tahoe Daily Tribune* or *Tahoe World* for listings. Otherwise, contact any of the visitors' bureaus or property-management agencies (*see above*) to start your search.

CAMPING You can hardly drive a half-mile in Lake Tahoe without bumping into a public or private campground, and almost all of them lie in beautiful pine forests. For obvious reasons, all campgrounds close in winter. Free camping in the Tahoe area is restricted, but still available at some lesser-known primitive campgrounds scattered around the lake. If Bay View campground (*see below*) doesn't appeal, check out secluded **Luther Overflow,** on Highway 89 about 10 miles south of South Lake Tahoe, where you can camp anywhere in a number of clearings surrounded by pine and fir trees. There is no running water or toilets, though a number of creeks criss-cross the area. To reach Luther Overflow, follow Highway 89 south from

South Lake Tahoe about 7 miles past the town of Meyers, turn in when you see the BIG MEADOW TRAILHEAD sign, and follow the small dirt road to your right.

On the north shore, dispersed camping is available near Homewood ski resort in **Blackwood Canyon.** From Tahoe City, follow Highway 89 south and look for a sign to BLACKWOOD CANYON on the right. After 2½ miles, veer off to the right on an unmarked dirt road, and you can camp anywhere you please. No permits are necessary here or at Luther Overflow. Ask the Forest Service (*see* Basics, *above*) for directions, maps, and more tips on primitive camping—they're not advertised, for obvious reasons.

➢ **SOUTH SHORE** • The most conveniently located, though certainly not the most picturesque, spot on the south shore is the **Campground by the Lake** (Rufus Allen Blvd., at U.S. 50, tel. 916/542–6096), a spacious campground with 170 sites shaded by young pines. Sites go for $17 and are surprisingly isolated, considering how close you are to downtown South Lake Tahoe (the campground lies between Stateline and the South Lake Tahoe "Y," where U.S. 50 meets the lake). Reservations are necessary only on holiday weekends.

Two inviting campgrounds are just south of Emerald Bay on Highway 89. **Bay View Campground,** on the inland side of Highway 89, has 12 primitive sites amid the pines, with picnic tables and fire pits but no drinking water. A stopping-off point for journeys into Desolation Wilderness, it imposes a two-night limit on stays; but for those two nights you'll sleep for free. If all the sites in Bay View are full, head just up the road to the beautiful **Eagle Point Campground** (Hwy. 89, 1 mi south of Emerald Bay, tel. 916/541–3030 or 800/444–PARK for reservations). Here you'll find 100 well-spaced sites ($14)—all with fire pits, barbecues, drinking water, picnic tables, food lockers, and access to bathrooms and showers—on a hillside covered with brush and pines. Some sites offer incredible views of Emerald Bay.

➢ **NORTH SHORE** • In the north-shore area, **William Kent Campground** (off Hwy. 89, tel. 916/573–2600 or 800/444–PARK for reservations) is a 95-site National Forest campground set well off the highway, 2 miles south of Tahoe City. Like most campgrounds in the Lake Tahoe Basin, William Kent lies in a moderately dense pine forest, and is within walking distance of the lake. Just down the road to the south, the **Kaspian Campground** (tel. 916/544–5994) is specially equipped for wheelchair travelers. For a complete listing of campgrounds, contact the Lake Tahoe Forest Service Visitor Center (*see* Basics, *above*).

FOOD

Though the south shore is more noticeably jam-packed than the north, you'll find hundreds of restaurants all around the lake, serving everything from fast food to lobster dinners. On the south shore, eateries are concentrated along U.S. 50 between South Lake Tahoe and Stateline, Nevada. In Stateline itself, you can get cheap (if generic) food at all-you-can-eat casino buffets. On the north shore, you'll find a heap of restaurants in downtown Truckee (especially on Donner Pass Road) and on Highway 28 in Tahoe City.

For fresh organic produce, bulk foods, and other eco-conscious grocery items, head to **Grass Roots** (2040 Dunlap Dr., at South Lake Tahoe "Y," tel. 916/541–7788) on the south shore. **The Mustard Seed** (7411 North Lake Blvd., Tahoe Vista, tel. 916/546-3525), a small health food shop on the north shore, is another good bet. If you're looking to splurge on local seafood, try **Fresh Ketch Lakeside Restaurant** (2433 Venice Dr. E, in Tahoe Keys Marina in South Lake Tahoe, tel. 916/541–5683) on the south shore, or **Jake's on the Lake** (Boatworks Marina, near Tahoe City "Y," tel. 916/583–0188) on the north shore. A meal at either will run you around $20.

On summer Wednesday evenings, check out the free-for-all drumming on Alpen Sierra's front lawn.

SOUTH SHORE **Alpen Sierra Coffee Co.** With several varieties of organic coffees and teas, a good selection of light breakfast and dessert fare ($1–$3), and a cozy, earthy atmosphere, Alpen Sierra is a good place to grab some quick sustenance before heading to the slopes. Local art adorns the walls, and in summer there's live folk music at night. *822 Emerald Bay Rd. (Rte. 89), tel. 916/541–7449. ⅓ mi NW of South Lake Tahoe "Y." Open daily 6:30 AM–7 PM (until 10 in summer).*

Ernie's Coffee Shop. An unpretentious greasy spoon serving breakfast and lunch only, Ernie's is popular among locals, some of whom keep their personalized coffee mugs hanging on the wall. The coffee is better than average coffee-shop brew, and it's bottomless, to boot. Meals range from the standard two-egg-and-toast breakfast ($4) to more adventurous creations like the tostada omelet ($6.50). *1146 Emerald Bay Rd. (Hwy. 89), South Lake Tahoe, tel. 916/541–2161. ¼ mi south of South Lake Tahoe "Y." Open daily 6 AM–2 PM.*

Los Tres Hombres Cantina. This typical Californianized Mexican restaurant has good, if not highly creative, food. In addition to the standard burritos ($7) and fajitas ($11), Los Tres Hombres—popular with a south-shore crowd in their thirties—offers a couple of specialties, including fish tacos ($8). *765 Emerald Bay Rd. (Hwy. 89), tel. 916/544–1233. ½ mi NW of South Lake Tahoe "Y." Open daily 11:30–10:30.*

Weekdays from 4 to 6 PM is "Fiesta Hour" at Los Tres Hombres, with $1.75 pints of beer, $3 double well drinks, and free chips and salsa.

Sprouts. At South Lake Tahoe's vegetarian paradise, you can feast on great veggie sandwiches ($4–$6), rice and vegetable plates ($4.25–$4.75), tempeh burgers ($4.50), and incredible fruit smoothies ($2.50–$3). They also have a wide selection of microbrewed beers ($2.25–$3.75). The restaurant itself is small and cheery, with a few wooden tables and a small outdoor patio. *3123 Harrison Ave. (U.S. 50), South Lake Tahoe, tel. 916/541–6969. Btw Stateline and South Lake Tahoe "Y," just west of where U.S. 50 meets the lake. Open Mon.–Sat. 8 AM–9 PM, Sun. 8–7. Wheelchair access.*

NORTH SHORE **Bridgetender Tavern and Grill.** Housed in an old wooden cabin with high beam ceilings and trees growing through the roof, the Bridgetender is the north shore's best burgers-and-beer joint. Huge beef patties and tasty veggie burgers, both served with hearty french fries, go for $4 and $6, respectively. During the day you can sit on a patio overlooking the Truckee River; at night patrons come inside to sip beer and shoot pool. *30 Emerald Bay Rd. (Hwy. 89), Tahoe City, tel. 916/583–3342. Next to bridge at Tahoe City "Y." Open daily 11–11.*

China Garden. Truckee's best Chinese restaurant serves up veggie dishes ($6–$6.50), seafood ($7.50–$9), and other Chinese standards in a typical red-carpet-and-lanterns interior. Lunch specials (which come with soup, egg roll, fried rice, and your choice of entrée) run just $4.25–$5.25; dinner specials for two or more start at $8.50. *11361 Deerfield Dr., tel. 916/ 587–7625. In Crossroads Center, off Hwy. 89 just south of I–80. Open Mon.–Thurs. 11–3 and 5–9, Fri. 11–3 and 5–10, Sat. 5–10, Sun. 5–9.*

Coyote's Mexican Grill. Whether you sit on the sun-drenched patio or in the tranquil southwestern dining room, you're bound to like the tasty grub at this woman-owned and -operated, self-service Mexican eatery. Aside from the regular old burritos, tacos, and quesadillas—all under $6—Coyote's also features specialties like tequila-and-lime fajitas ($7.25) and mesquite chicken ($6). Afterward, head to the adjoining Café Luna for a cappuccino and a slice of carrot cake. *521 N. Lake Blvd. (Hwy. 28), Tahoe City, tel. 916/583–6653. ½ mi east of Tahoe City "Y." Open daily 10–10; café open daily 7:30 AM–9 PM.*

The Eggschange. This frilly lakeside cafe, with its shingled walls, gingham curtains, and beautiful view, is the kind of place you'd take your mother to brunch. And if mom's paying, you might want to try one of the pricey but delicious egg dishes ($6–$8); the Neptune ain't a bad choice, with crab, avocado, and poached eggs on an English muffin with hollandaise. If you don't want to spend a day's ration on breakfast, opt for the substantial Mountain Mush (oatmeal with walnuts and raisins; $3.50) or pancakes ($4). And if you have a craving for something that's not on the menu, just tell the chef and he'll try to make it for you. *120 Grove St., off N. Lake Tahoe Blvd., tel. 916/583–2225. Open daily 7 AM–2 PM.*

Truckee River Coffee Company. For the best coffee and desserts on the north shore, head to this homey café furnished with couches, a few small tables, and a piano. Dessert types should try the old-fashioned hot chocolate ($1.75) or the Coffee Nut ($4), made of hazelnut espresso, hazelnut syrup, and vanilla yogurt. *11373 Deerfield Dr., Truckee, tel. 916/587–2583. In Crossroads Center just south of I–80/Hwy. 89 junction. Open daily 7 AM–9 PM (Fri.–Sat. until midnight).*

AFTER DARK

Events on the south shore are covered in *Lake Tahoe Action and Adventures,* a free weekly entertainment magazine put out by the *Tahoe Daily Tribune,* available at most motels. Check the free *North Tahoe/Truckee Week* for nightlife on the north shore.

SOUTH SHORE Considering the number of people on the streets by day, the south shore is surprisingly quiet by night. What limited action there is takes place on the Nevada side of the border in Stateline, where you'll find a number of casinos and the usual array of shows and "revues." Back in California, about 3 miles west of the Nevada border, **Hoss Hogs** (2543 U.S. 50, tel. 916/541–8328) has an unbelievable collection of beer paraphernalia—labels, posters, hats, mirrors, etc.—and live blues and rock on a tiny stage almost every night of the week. On summer nights you can sit out on the patio and listen to live music and play volleyball. **The Brewery at Lake Tahoe** (3542 U.S. 50, tel. 916/544–BREW), 1½ miles west of the California–Nevada border, is one of several microbreweries that have cropped up around the lake in the last few years. Its proximity to Heavenly ski resort makes it a popular place to relax and have a beer after a hard day on the slopes.

In summer the Brewery has live music on the patio. Rumor has it that a flaming-stick juggler even makes an appearance on occasion.

NORTH SHORE Tahoe City is without a doubt the center of the lake's nightlife, whether you're looking for a rowdy bar or a mellow patio to kick back on. Loud, crowded, and filled with hard-drinking youth scoping one another out, **Humpty's** (877 North Lake Blvd., 1 mi NE of Tahoe City "Y," tel. 916/583–4867) features the best live music in the area most nights (cover $2–$7). When Humpty's closes on Tuesdays, the crowds head a few doors down to **Rosie's** (571 North Lake Blvd., tel. 916/583–8504), a large restaurant and bar housed in what was once, no doubt, a beautiful high-ceilinged cabin. At the **Blue Water Brewery** (850 North Lake Blvd., behind Safeway in Tahoe City, tel. 916/581–2583) you can suck down microbrews, munch on some beer chili ($6) or fish-and-chips in beer batter ($7.50), and shoot a game of pool; live bands play Wednesday–Saturday nights.

Catering to a slightly more sedate clientele, the **Naughty Dawg** (255 North Lake Blvd., ¼ mi NE of Tahoe City "Y," tel. 916/581–3294) has the best selection of high-quality beers in town, as well as surprisingly good salads and bar snacks ($3–$7). With a large deck next to the Truckee River and a stylish indoor bar, the **River Ranch Lodge** (*see* Hotels and Motels, *above*) is an excellent place for a quiet drink. During summer this place hosts an outdoor concert series with eclectic bookings ranging from jazz to hard rock (cover $5–$25).

SKIING

Unbelievably sheer faces, narrow chutes, and huge cliffs have attracted a new breed of downhill skier bent on pushing the sport to extremes. But novices shouldn't be intimidated: With over 24 ski resorts, Lake Tahoe offers ample opportunity for beginners and experts alike on downhill (alpine) and cross-country (nordic) slopes. Tahoe, like most ski resorts these days, is also a super-popular venue for snowboarding (*see box, below*).

While the quality of food fluctuates from resort to resort, every mountain restaurant charges extortionate prices for the usual array of burgers, chili, and sandwiches. Plan ahead and pack your own lunch.

WHAT TO PACK The type of gear you'll need depends in large part on the weather: Tahoe's temperatures can dictate several layers of sweaters or shorts and a T-shirt. Don't underestimate the danger of sunburn, even on a cold day (the sun is especially dangerous when it reflects off snow). In addition to skis, poles, and boots, required gear usually includes thermal underwear (preferably polypropylene), thin wool socks, gloves or mittens, a wool hat, sunglasses, goggles, a cotton or polypropylene turtleneck, a cotton or wool sweater, "powder" or "stretch" pants, and either a vinyl shell or a down jacket. Other things to think about, depending on conditions, include sun block, glove and sock liners, a ski mask, waterproof boots, and a visor or baseball cap.

EQUIPMENT RENTAL As a rule of thumb, the closer you get to the ski resorts, the higher the cost of renting a pair of skis or a snowboard. On the other hand, the closer to the mountain you rent equipment, the easier it is to get an adjustment, repair, or replacement in the middle of your vacation. So rent at home only if you know exactly what you want and feel comfortable with the quality of the equipment.

Around Lake Tahoe the same logic applies. You'll save money by renting from any of the hundreds of rental stores crowding the lake's major roads, but if you choose to rent from the higher-priced shops run by the ski resorts, you'll be able to get an adjustment midday. If you choose the former option, the best deal anywhere is the south shore's **Don Cheepo's** (3349 U.S. 50, about ¾ mi west of Heavenly, tel. 916/544–0356), which offers full downhill and cross-country rental packages (skis, boots, and poles) for $10, or the unbelievably low price of $7.60 if you produce a coupon (scattered around local motels and tourist info centers). Snowboards rent for $25, including boots—a very competitive price.

Of north-shore rental outfits, **Porter's** has the lowest rates (full ski packages $10–$14, snowboards $15–$22), good equipment, and three locations, including one in Tahoe City (501 North Lake Blvd., just east of Tahoe City "Y," tel. 916/583–2314) and one in Truckee (in Crossroads Center on Hwy. 89, just south of I–80, tel. 916/587–1500).

THE "BIG FIVE" The "Big Five" ski resorts—**Squaw Valley, Alpine Meadows, Northstar-at-Tahoe, Heavenly Valley,** and **Kirkwood**—all charge in the neighborhood of $40 a day, but if you're

Gambler's Choice

For all the entertainment available out-of-doors in the Lake Tahoe Basin, many visitors spend the majority of their time indoors at the casinos on the Nevada side of the lake. Both the north and south shores offer opportunities to gamble away your last dollars, with very different attitudes and atmosphere on each side of the lake. On the south shore, which has more casinos and more glitz, you'll find the big names, like Harrah's (702/588–6611), Harvey's (702/588–2411), and Caesar's (702/588–3515), all waiting to take your money at blackjack and poker tables, slot machines, keno, and more, while distracting you with free drinks and tacky lounge acts. Here, gambling is usually better on weekdays, when table minimums are lower (blackjack $3 minimum weekdays, $5 weekends) and the tables aren't as jam-packed. The cheapest and most declassé spot on this side—with a McDonald's, even—is Bill's Casino (702/588–2455), with round-the-clock $3 blackjack tables in a lurid, depressing atmosphere (funny how after a few free drinks, you don't seem to notice). And don't forget: Local motels, restaurants, and visitor centers often stock coupons for cheap casino buffets, not to mention free slot machine tokens and other free casino stuff.

The north shore's gambling scene is much more low-key. Of the three casinos in Crystal Bay, only two—the Biltmore (916/831–0660) and the Crystal Bay Club (702/831–0512)—offer anything more than slot machines. However, the atmosphere is much more friendly, the dealers are laid-back, and the players seem to lack the frantic, nerve-racking energy that may drive you insane at south shore casinos. Plus you'll always find a spot at a $2 blackjack table, which is more than you'll pay for the Biltmore's $1.39 breakfast buffet.

careful you can avoid ever paying these prices. For starters, buy multiple-day tickets, which will save you $3–$7 per day. Also scour the local papers, motels, gas stations, and supermarkets for discounts and deals. Otherwise, consider skiing one of the smaller, less expensive resorts (*see* The Best of the Rest, *below*), many of which are quite good, especially if you're a beginning or intermediate skier. Some of the smaller places offer special discounts on midweek skiing.

➢ **SQUAW VALLEY** • A vast resort with over 8,000 acres of open bowls, 2,850 vertical feet, and more than 25 chairlifts, Squaw Valley achieved international fame when it hosted the 1960 Winter Olympics. Today it's unofficially known as the home of "extreme" skiing: The steep faces and 20- to 60-foot cliffs accessible off the **KT-22** and **Granite Chief** lifts provide plenty of challenges. But the beauty of Squaw is that it's truly an all-around ski area—70% of the mountain is suited to beginning and novice skiers, including much of the terrain at the highest elevations, where the views of the lake are best. On weekends Squaw gets quite crowded, and a veritable small town—complete with shops, restaurants, bars, and two recreation centers—has sprung up at the mountain's base to serve visitors.

All-day lift tickets at Squaw are $43, with rental packages starting at $20. First-time skier or snowboarder packages, including equipment and lessons, go for $49. Squaw makes snow along 80 acres at the bottom of the mountain. *Snow report: tel. 916/583–6955. From Truckee, Hwy. 89 south 8 mi, right on Squaw Valley Rd.*

➢ **ALPINE MEADOWS** • Considering that it lies in the physical and figurative shadow of its better-known neighbor, Squaw Valley, the 2,000-acre Alpine Meadows resort has done quite well for itself, thank you. With a high base elevation of 7,000 feet (allowing for a longer season) and 12 lifts servicing over 100 runs, Alpine has built its reputation on the abundant snow and sunshine that grace its two mountains. Over half the runs on the front face and nearly all the runs on the back face of **Scott Peak** earn intermediate designations. But Alpine has also opened a handful of expert runs, notably **Palisades** and **Scott Chute,** two slopes that will make the average skier's hair stand on end for a month.

Most locals agree that Alpine Meadows is the best place for prime spring skiing.

At last look, full-day lift tickets at Alpine were going for $39, with half-day tickets (after 12:30) fetching $26. Rental packages from the ski shop in the main lodge are $19. Alpine Meadows

Mountain Surfing

If you've always wanted to try surfing but feared getting tossed silly by the ocean, spend a day snowboarding. In the past few years the practice of schussing down the mountain with your feet strapped to a board has overtaken Tahoe—and ski areas across the world—like a giant tidal wave. Requiring roughly the same fluidity and balance as surfing and skateboarding, snowboarding has been widely compared to these sports, both physically and culturally. Its devotees initially met with resistance from major ski resorts, but by now most resorts have opened the slopes to boarders. A few, like Alpine Meadows, still say no, to the relief of skiers who criticize the recklessness of this cold-weather subculture.

Snowboards generally rent for $22–$28 a day, including boots, and are available at most ski shops around Tahoe. If it's your first time out, follow these simple rules: Keep your weight back, steer with your rear foot, and maintain that no-pain, no-gain attitude no matter how many times you fall, because you're sure to ache from your feet to your buttocks when the day is over.

is the home of the **Tahoe Handicapped Ski School** (tel. 916/581–4161), the first school in the area to offer ski programs for the mentally and physically challenged. *Snow and weather report: tel. 916/581–8374. Off Hwy. 89, 2 mi south of Squaw Valley.*

➢ **NORTHSTAR-AT-TAHOE** • Northstar-at-Tahoe, the northernmost resort of the "Big Five," has the best views of any north-shore ski area, extensive snow-making capacity, great tree skiing, and two wind-protected bowls that get excellent powder after a snowstorm. The resort certainly tries to be all things to all people, with a split of 25% beginner runs, 50% intermediate runs, and 25% advanced runs. Northstar is farther from the Bay Area than Squaw or Alpine, so it's not as popular. But it's definitely worth coming here for a day, if only for the incredible views of the basin from the top of the 8,610-foot **Mt. Pluto.**

Neck-and-neck with the other large resorts, Northstar charges $39 for an all-day lift ticket, with half-day tickets (after 1 PM) going for $27. Ski rentals run $18 a day, including boots and poles; snowboards are $25. *Snow report: tel. 916/562–1330. Hwy. 267, 7 mi south of Truckee.*

➢ **HEAVENLY** • The only ski resort in Tahoe that straddles the California–Nevada border, the south shore's Heavenly is officially the largest ski area in the United States. That means you'll find over 4,300 acres of skiable terrain, an incredible 3,500-foot vertical drop, and 25 lifts scattered over no less than nine peaks—a ski resort of Vegas-size proportions. And Heavenly's "upside-down" setup, with most of the expert runs toward the bottom of the mountain and many beginner and intermediate runs at the top of the 10,100-foot peak, means that less advanced skiers are afforded a rare opportunity to enjoy the area's best views. For experts, there's the 2,000-acre **Mott Canyon,** a boulder- and tree-filled canyon with steep faces and chutes aplenty. Making Heavenly that much more attractive is its snow-making capacity, the most extensive in Tahoe. Heavenly also has the fastest, most modern chairlifts of Tahoe's ski resorts. Unfortunately its central location means that lines are usually long.

Lift lines are usually shorter at Heavenly's Nevada base, 3 miles up Kingsbury Grade from Lake Tahoe Boulevard.

Heavenly has made a concerted effort to attract beginners with a full-day introductory package for $40, including four hours of instruction, a lift ticket good for novice lifts, and skis. Otherwise, regular tickets cost $40 per full day, $17 per half day (after 1 PM). Ski-package rentals start at $18 a day, snowboards at $25. *Snow report: tel. 916/541–7544. West entrance off Lake Tahoe Boulevard (U.S. 50) in South Lake Tahoe; look for signs. Free shuttle from South Lake Tahoe.*

➢ **KIRKWOOD** • With the highest base elevation of Tahoe's major ski resorts (7,800 ft), Kirkwood boasts the driest snow, which experienced skiers know means the best powder. And despite its relatively small size—10 lifts and 65 runs cover 2,000 acres—laid-back Kirkwood is the favored south-shore destination of advanced skiers, thanks to extreme runs like **Cliff Chute** and **Sisters Chute.** All told, 85% of Kirkwood's runs are designated intermediate or advanced. The resort's secluded location (30 minutes from South Lake Tahoe) is beautiful, but it doesn't afford the spectacular views of the lake you'll find at the other major resorts. The payoff is a ski season that lasts well into late spring.

As with all Tahoe's major resorts, lift tickets at Kirkwood are not discounted on weekdays; whenever you ski you'll pay $35 for a full day, $25 for a half day (9–noon). If you plan on skiing Kirkwood more than three times in the season, buy a Kirkwood Card for $15, good for $5 off every time you ski. Package deals include a "first-time only" special for $40, which buys you a pair of two-hour group lessons, equipment rental, and an all-day lift ticket valid only on designated lifts. *Snow report: tel. 209/258–3000. From South Lake Tahoe, Hwy. 89 south to Hwy. 88 east.*

THE BEST OF THE REST Although Lake Tahoe's "Big Five" offer the best skiing, some of the region's other ski areas are cheaper and less crowded. If you're coming from the Bay Area, you can save 30–45 minutes driving time by skiing at any of the Donner Pass ski resorts—**Soda Springs, Sugar Bowl, Donner Ranch, Boreal,** or **Tahoe Donner.** Of these four, Sugar Bowl, off the Soda Springs/Norden exit of I–80, is the largest and most beautiful. And with 50% of its runs designated advanced, including some of the best tree skiing in Tahoe, Sugar Bowl is especially attractive for experienced skiers. Lift tickets sell for $35, $25 for a half day (after 1 PM). For a snow report, call 916/426–3847. A few miles farther down the road, Donner Ranch, with lift tickets starting at just $10 on weekdays and $20 on weekends, is Tahoe's cheapest ski resort. It's not challenging enough to entice experts, but the five lifts and 360 acres provide plenty of thrills for beginning skiers and snowboarders. If you're planning a trip to Donner, though, try to rent your equipment before you head out of town—ski-rental packages start at $22 and snowboard packages at $30, some of the highest prices around. For a snow report call 916/426–3635.

If you have more than a day for skiing, consider the underrated, 1,260-acre **Homewood.** On a steep peak that rises dramatically from Tahoe's western shore, Homewood offers outstanding views of the lake and a wide variety of terrain, from the bumpy slopes of Exhibition and Double Trouble to long cruises like Miner's Delight. A series of beginner lifts and T-bars provides plenty of room to learn the basics. Lift tickets go for $25 weekdays and $29 on weekends and holidays. Better still, Wednesday is two-for-one day, when you and a friend can ski for $12.50 each. Homewood is on Highway 89, about halfway between Tahoe City and South Lake Tahoe. For snow conditions, call 916/525–2900.

CROSS-COUNTRY SKIING Lake Tahoe is one of the best-known venues in the western United States for cross-country skiing. You'll have no problem finding a trail to suit your abilities at Tahoe's 13 cross-country ski areas, the most famous of which is the north shore's **Royal Gorge** (tel. 916/426–3871), the largest cross-country ski resort in the United States. You can choose from 200 miles of trails running along a ridge above the north fork of the American River; fees are $16.50. From I–80, take the Soda Springs exit south.

Strictly for skiers with at least some experience, **Eagle Mountain** (tel. 916/389–2254), dubbed "one of the area's best-kept secrets" by locals, offers incredible vistas along 45 miles of trails (fee $11). Highlights include the trails on Eagle Mountain itself and the trails on **Cisco Butte,** which overlook Devil's Peak and the Royal Gorge. About an hour west of Truckee, Eagle is the closest to the Bay Area of Lake Tahoe's nordic resorts. Exit I–80 at Yuba Gap and follow signs. Two other cross-country resorts on the north shore, **Northstar-at-Tahoe** (tel. 916/562–1330; fee $14) and **Squaw Creek** (tel. 916/583–6300; fee $10) are right next to downhill ski areas (*see above*), making them great choices for vacation groups with divided loyalties. Of the two, Northstar, with 40 miles of trails, is the more exciting destination.

On the south shore, only **Kirkwood** (*see above;* tel. 209/258–7248) offers both alpine and nordic ski trails, with over 50 miles of cross-country for skiers of all levels ($12). The award for best deal on the south shore, though, goes to **Hope Valley** (tel. 916/694–2266), located in a beautiful valley of the Toiyabe National Forest on the grounds of Sorenson's Resort. It offers 60 miles of trails for all levels—FREE. From South Lake Tahoe, take Highway 89 south to Highway 88 east.

SUMMER ACTIVITIES

Lake Tahoe offers opportunities for just about every fair-weather sport imaginable. If you've done it, thought about doing it, always wanted to do it, or even heard a rumor that someone somewhere does it, chances are you can do whatever "it" is in Tahoe. An abbreviated list would include hiking, biking, fishing, sailing, waterskiing, jet skiing, rock climbing, hot-air ballooning, parasailing, horseback riding, and river rafting. The nearest tourist office (*see* Basics, *above*) can load you down with armfuls of glossy brochures about all these sports. Of course many of the more exotic adventures are pricey, but Tahoe is a great place to splurge.

If you're looking to rent equipment for just about any sport, **Don Cheepo's** (*see* Equipment Rental, *above*) carries everything from waterskis to backpacks and other camping supplies. If you want to buy (or sell) equipment, **The Sport Exchange** (10095 W. River St., tel. 916/582–4510) in Old Town Truckee deals in used skis and fishing gear, as well as backpacking, camping, rock-climbing, and mountaineering equipment.

HIKING Almost every acre in the Lake Tahoe Basin is protected by some national, state, or local agency. **Tahoe National Forest** lies to the northwest, **Eldorado National Forest** to the southwest, and **Toiyabe National Forest** to the northeast and southeast. What this means for visitors is a whole lot of hiking trails, from easy scenic walks to strenuous climbs over mountain passes. The Lake Tahoe Forest Service Visitor Center (*see* Basics, *above*) can provide a complete list of day hikes.

One of the more popular short walks is **Vikingsholm Trail,** a mile-long (one way) paved path leading from the parking lot on the north side of Emerald Bay to the shoreline and the 38-room Vikingsholm Castle, a Scandinavian-style castle built in 1929. From the castle you can walk farther to **Eagle Falls,** the only waterfall that empties into the lake. For something a little more woodsy, try the **Mt. Tallac Trail,** ½ mile north of the Lake Tahoe Forest Service Visitor Center (follow the marked asphalt road opposite Baldwin Beach to the trailhead parking lot). A moderate hike takes you 2 miles through a beautiful pine forest to Cathedral Lake. For a serious day-long trek (with no potable water along the way), continue on the trail another 3 miles as it climbs past a series of boulder fields to the peak of Mt. Tallac, the highest point in the basin at 9,735 feet. At the top you'll find excellent views of the lake and Desolation Wilderness. The trip up and back should take seven to eight hours.

If you're looking to do extensive backcountry camping, you're going to have a hard time choosing where to go. Off the southwest corner of the lake, the 63,473-acre **Desolation Wilderness,** filled with granite peaks, glacial valleys, subalpine forests, and more than 80 lakes, is the most beautiful and popular backcountry destination in the area. South of the lake, **Mokelumne Wilderness,** straddling the border of Eldorado and Stanislaus national forests, has terrain similar to Desolation without the crowds. The region's other protected wilderness areas, **Mt. Rose** to the north and **Granite Chief** to the west, are less popular because they lack the accessibility and breathtaking beauty of Desolation and Mokelumne. Before you enter any wilderness area, either for a day or for an extended visit, it's crucial to pick up a wilderness permit from the Lake Tahoe Forest Service Visitor Center (*see* Basics, *above*)—if you don't you may actually be kicked off the trails.

If you suffer from hay fever, come to Tahoe prepared for battle. In the height of summer, pollen falls through the air like so many snowflakes.

BIKING Lake Tahoe has everything from mellow lakeshore trails to steep fire roads and tricky single-track trails. Several paved, gently sloped paths skirt the lakeshore: Try the 3.4-mile **Pope Baldwin Bike Path** in South Lake Tahoe, at the Pope Baldwin Recreational Center; or the **West Shore Bike Path,** which extends about 10 miles south from Tahoe City to Sugar Pine Point State Park near the town of Tahoma. Also worthwhile are the bike path along the **Truckee River** between Alpine Meadows and Tahoe City, and the **U.S. Forest Service Bike Trail,** an 8½-mile paved path (through pine forest and a rare aspen grove) that starts at Emerald Bay Road just west of the South Lake Tahoe "Y" and ends at the lake.

Expert mountain bikers should definitely check out the famous **Flume Trail,** a 24-mile ride past several lakes and along a ridge with sensational views of Lake Tahoe. Strictly for experienced riders, the trail begins at the parking lot of Lake Tahoe–Nevada State Park, just north of Spooner Junction on the lake's eastern shore (take Highway 28 east from Tahoe City). A map is crucial, and the **"High Sierra Biking Map"** ($6) and its accompanying book ($9) offer a detailed description of the Flume Trail (including a way to cut the ride in half for people with two cars), along with several dozen other excellent rides in the area.

If you like the idea of riding downhill all day, Northstar-at-Tahoe (*see* Skiing, *above*) opens a number of its ski runs for mountain biking June–September. An all-day ticket goes for $15 (bike rental $30, including helmet). Squaw Valley (*see* Skiing, *above*) allows mountain bikers to ride its tram up 2,000 feet, but severely limits the number of ski runs you can come down on. A single tram ride costs $17, unlimited rides $25; bikes rent for $17 per half day, $24 per full day (including helmet).

➢ **BIKE RENTALS** • Dozens of shops around Tahoe rent mountain bikes, generally for $4–$6 an hour or $15–$22 a day. On the south shore there's **Anderson's Bicycle Rental** (Hwy. 89, at 13th St., tel. 916/541–0500), conveniently located a half mile from the U.S. Forest Service Bike Trail. Slightly cheaper is **Don Cheepo's** (*see* Equipment Rental, *above*), near the east end of the Pope Baldwin Bike Path. On the north shore try **Porter's Ski and Sport** (501 North Lake Blvd., tel. 916/583–2314), on Highway 28 just east of the Tahoe City "Y."

BEACHES Dozens of beaches are scattered around the lake's shore, most charging $2–$5 for parking. Two of the best include **Chamber's Landing** near Tahoe City, a favorite of young north shore locals; and **Baldwin Beach,** a gorgeous and usually uncrowded sand beach between South Lake Tahoe and Emerald Bay. **Nevada Beach,** a more populated spot just across the Nevada border in Stateline, offers panoramic views of the lake's mountainous backdrop. **Sand Harbor,** a crescent-shaped beach off Highway 28 on the northeastern shore, is ideal for sunsets.

Despite Tahoe's wide range of outdoor activities, the well-known sport of sitting stagnantly on the beach, drinking a beer, and rising occasionally to take a dip in the lake's cold waters remains a popular pastime.

WATER SPORTS Despite Lake Tahoe's often frigid waters, there's no lack of rental outfits specializing in sailing, waterskiing, jet skiing, motorboating, windsurfing, kayaking, canoeing, sportfishing, and parasailing. Prices fluctuate a bit from shop to shop and according to the time of year, but in general, sailboats go for $30–$35 an hour, $85–$95 a day; Jet Skis run $35–$70 an hour; Windsurfers rent for $10–$15 an hour, $30–$40 a half day; and canoes go for $10–$15 an hour, $30–$40 a half day. Parasailing rides, which usually last about 15 minutes, range from $35 to $50.

Shop around before you plunk down a sizable chunk of change. On the south shore, **South Shore Parasailing and Paradise Watercraft Rentals** (tel. 916/541–6166), with motorboats, canoes, kayaks, and other toys, is one of several shops operating out of **Ski Run Marina,** off U.S. 50 about a half mile west of the California–Nevada border. On the north shore, you'll find rental outfits in the **Sunnyside Marina,** about 2 miles south of Tahoe City on Highway 89.

FISHING Like nearly everything in Tahoe, fishing options are abundant. Obviously, the most convenient spot is (can you guess?) **Lake Tahoe,** stocked occasionally with rainbow trout by the folks at the Fish and Wildlife Service (to find the section of the lake most recently stocked, call 916/355–7040 or 916/351–0832). Also popular is the stretch of the **Truckee River** between Truckee and Tahoe City—just pick a spot and cast your line. To find the latest hot spots, ask around at local sporting-goods stores, many of which sport FISHING INFO HERE signs in their windows. Wherever you fish, licenses ($9 a day, $24 a year) are required by law and available from most sporting-goods shops.

For sportfishing on the lake, contact **Tahoe Sportfishing** (tel. 916/541–5448) in the Ski Run Marina or **Let's Go Fishing** (tel. 916/541–5566) in South Lake Tahoe. Half-day trips generally start at $50–$55, full-day trips at $70–$75.

Yosemite National Park

It's overdeveloped in places, it's crowded, and yes, it's expensive, but there is no other place in the world quite like Yosemite. Glacial cutting and prehistoric activity at the earth's core have formed a land so stunning that even the jaded contend it's not to be missed. Slightly smaller than the state of Rhode Island, Yosemite is packed with waterfalls, sheer granite cliffs, lush forests, and generous expanses of alpine meadows. **Yosemite Valley,** the central and most accessible portion of the park, stretches more than 20 miles from the Wawona Tunnel in the west to Curry Village in the east. The valley's major sites are **Half Dome** and **El Capitan**—two breathtaking but treacherous granite formations—as well as the **Yosemite, Nevada,** and **Vernal falls.**

Because the valley is surrounded by so much hype, it can be hard to step back and let the beauty soak in. Most people never leave its congested confines—complete with tacky lodges and unsightly gift shops—to explore the rest of the park, which is a mistake. And while it's almost impossible to avoid the valley, consider it a departure point for hikes rather than a des-

Yosemite National Park

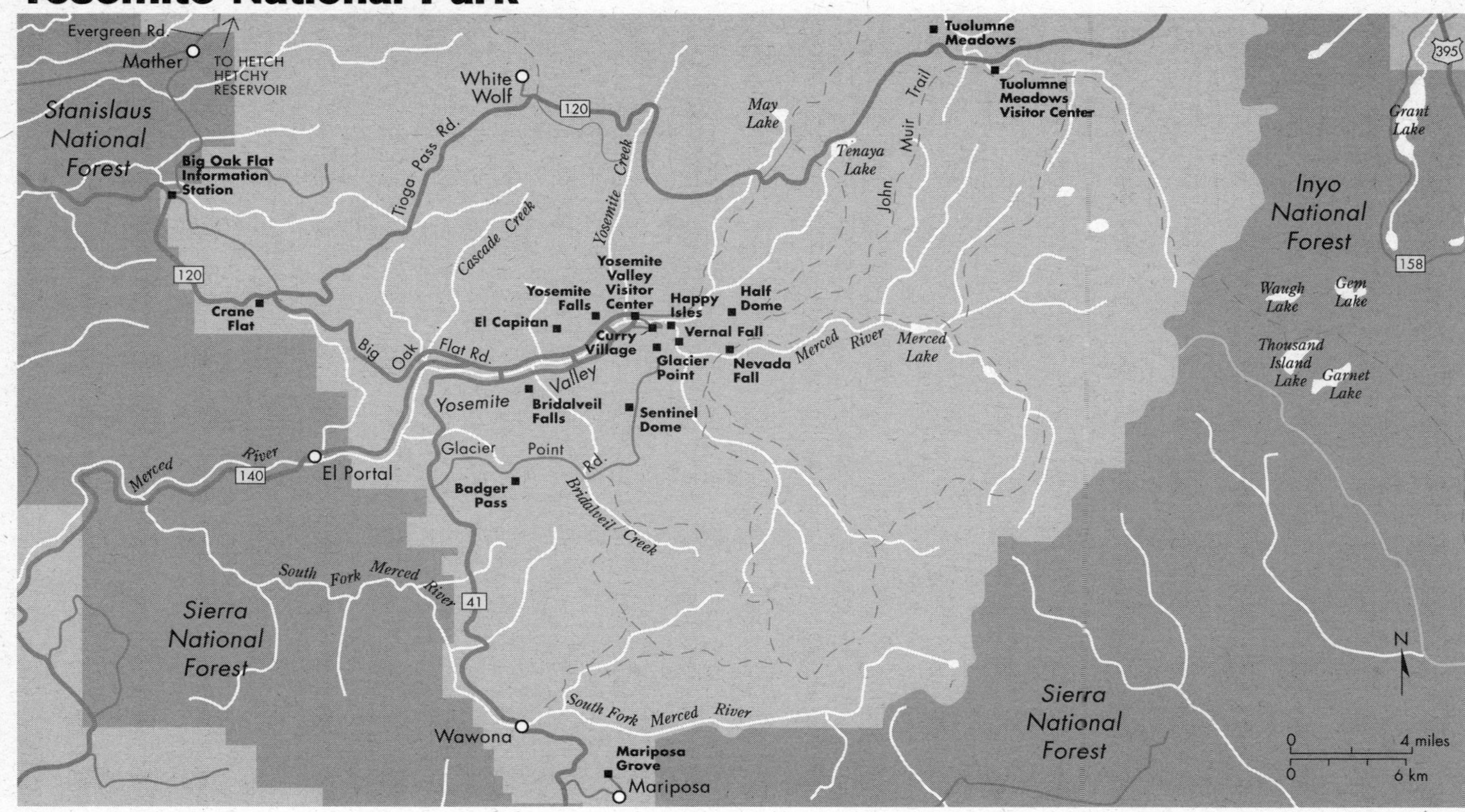

tination in itself. The other side of Yosemite—the undisturbed, forested backcountry with its massive granite formations and plunging waterfalls—is where you'll find the real soul of the park. Among the more spectacular non-valley sights are **Tuolumne Meadows** (pronounced TWA-lo-mee), along Highway 120; the giant sequoias of **Mariposa Grove,** off Highway 41 in the southwest corner of the park; **Glacier Point,** near Badger Pass; and the **Hetch Hetchy Reservoir** (north of Big Oak Flat). These areas are most accessible to backpackers and horseback riders, though numerous turnouts and day-hike areas make them fairly easy to reach from the highway.

To the Ahwahneechee people Yosemite was the sacred belly of the world—the divine embryo where nature's wonders were spewed forth in infinite perfection.

For centuries, Yosemite was inhabited by the Ahwahneechee people, who lived on settlements in the surrounding mountains. Unfortunately the Mariposa Battalion, the first group of whites to enter the area (in 1851), saw Yosemite as a prime hunting and fur-trapping ground. By the late 19th century they had "settled" (i.e., conquered) the Ahwahneechee and established a lucrative lumber business and trading outpost. We have shepherd and naturalist John Muir to thank that Yosemite is today more than a timber company parking lot. By securing the support of some of the nation's most powerful people, Muir played a vital role in the declaration of Yosemite as a national park in 1890, which even then was showing signs of wear and tear.

BASICS

VISITOR INFORMATION Yosemite has two visitor centers, both of which stock maps and brochures and distribute free wilderness permits (required for overnight camping in the backcountry; *see* Longer Hikes, *below*). For current events in Yosemite, check your copy of the *Yosemite Guide,* available at all entrance stations. The **Yosemite Valley Visitor Center** (Shuttle Stops 6 and 9, tel. 209/372–0299) is 6 miles east of the Highway 140 entrance and open daily 8–5 (until 6 in summer). The **Tuolumne Meadows Visitor Center** (tel. 209/372–0263), open daily 9–5 in summer only, is toward the east end of the park, 1 mile east of Tuolumne Meadows on Tioga Pass Road.

It doesn't have much of a tourist desk, but the **Wawona Ranger Station** (tel. 209/372–0563), at the south end of Yosemite on Highway 41, does offer wilderness permits weekdays 8–5. The **Big Oak Flat Information Station** (tel. 209/372–0615), at the Highway 120 west entrance, is open daily 9–5 in summer and Friday–Sunday the rest of the year. If you're not actually in the park, the **Public Information Service** (Box 577, Yosemite National Park 95389, tel. 209/372–0264) is the place to begin your search for info on Yosemite, though getting through on the phone can be a task. Send a self-addressed, stamped envelope for free brochures and maps, or call weekdays between 9 and 5.

Yep, you're in California. Even in Yosemite there are regular meetings of Alcoholics Anonymous, Narcotics Anonymous, and Adult Children of Alcoholics and Dysfunctional Families.

FEES The park fee for one week is $5 per car or $3 per hiker, bicyclist, or bus passenger. You can purchase annual passes for $15 that give you unlimited access to the park.

WHEN TO GO If possible visit during spring or early fall, when crowds are less of a nuisance. Spring (late April–late May) is especially spectacular—the wildflowers are in bloom and the waterfalls are at their peak of sound and fury as snowpack melts in the high country. Of the nearly four million people who visit each year, 70% arrive during summer (June–August), when temperatures reach a high of 85°F and a low of 40°F. During winter (November–March), temperatures drop to a chilly 45°F by day and a downright frigid 15°F by night. You won't be able to explore the park as easily as you can during summer (Tioga Pass and Glacier Point Road usually close by November due to inclement weather), but when dusted with a blanket of snow, Yosemite will definitely sneak its way into your heart.

WHAT TO PACK Rain gear is important year-round. You may never have to battle one of Yosemite's sudden summertime tempests, but unless you want to be stuck sipping hot chocolate in a dreary coffee shop, it pays to be prepared. Water-repellent "shell" pants and a warm jacket with polar-fleece lining are a smart idea, and don't forget wool or wick-dry socks—they'll keep you warm even when it's wet. If you plan to camp in winter—you crazy thing, you—you'll need warm clothing, a sub-zero sleeping bag, and a waterproof (or at least water-resistant) four-season tent. Broken-in hiking boots are a must for exploring the backcountry, and yes, snowshoes or crampons would be a good idea if you want to blaze your own trail. You'll be subject to awful frostbite without your polar-fleece (or wool) hat and gloves.

GENERAL STORES If you're coming into the park from Highway 120, stop first at Oakdale's friendly, well-stocked **Newdeal Market** (888 Hwy. 120, in Oakdale Plaza, tel. 209/847–5919), open daily 7 AM–10 PM. Otherwise you're stuck with the grocery and camping stores in pricey Yosemite Village, 5 miles east of Highway 41 in the middle of the park (at Shuttle Stops 3, 5, and 10). The **Village Sport Shop** (tel. 209/372–1286), open from spring to fall, has fishing and camping gear. Both the **Village Store** (tel. 209/372–1253), open daily 8 AM–10 PM, and the **Wawona Grocery** (Hwy. 41, near south end of park, tel. 209/375–6574), open daily 9–8, stock groceries and basic camping supplies.

Badger Pass Sport Shop (tel. 209/372–8430), open from December to April, has ski clothing and equipment, as well as lotions, waxes, and picnic supplies. It's near Wawona and the Badger Pass ski slopes, off Highway 41 on the south side of the park. In Curry Village, at the far eastern end of Yosemite Valley (Shuttle Stop 14), you'll find a host of stores, including the **Curry Village Mountain Shop** (tel. 209/372–8396), where you can purchase overpriced rock-climbing supplies and topographic maps of Yosemite.

MEDICAL AID The **Yosemite Medical Clinic** in Yosemite Village offers full medical service and 24-hour emergency care. *Btw visitor center and Ahwahnee Hotel, tel. 209/372–4637. Open weekdays 8–5, weekends 9–noon.*

COMING AND GOING

BY CAR You can reach Yosemite on three routes: **Highway 41** from the south, **Highway 140** from Merced in the west, and **Highway 120** from San Francisco. From San Francisco, take I–580 east to I–205 and connect to Highway 120 (4 hrs one way). Highways 41 and 140 terminate in Yosemite Valley, and Highway 120 becomes Tioga Pass Road inside the park. In winter take Highway 140 from the west, since Highway 120 is usually blocked by snow. In spring the eastern portion of Highway 120 (from the valley past Tuolumne Meadows into Inyo National Forest and Lee Vining) is closed.

From late fall to early spring you should carry snow chains. The highways can get treacherous, and the California Highway Patrol often closes the roads to all traffic without snow gear. If you get stuck, you'll have to buy an expensive set of chains ($60) from a gas station (and boy, do they love it when that happens). For current road and weather conditions, call 209/372–0200 or 800/427–ROAD.

BY BUS AND TRAIN There is no direct bus service to Yosemite from San Francisco; all lines stop in either Fresno or Merced, where you have to change coaches. From Merced, a cheap option is **Via Adventures** (tel. 209/384–1315), which runs three buses a day (2½ hrs, $17 one way) from Merced's Greyhound station on 16th and N streets. **Amtrak** (tel. 800/USA–RAIL) offers a thruway service in conjunction with Yosemite Sequoia Tours that takes you from San Francisco to the park and back for $53. The train stops in Emeryville and in Merced, where you board the bus to Yosemite. All buses stop at Yosemite Lodge in the valley. From San Francisco, **Green Tortoise** (tel. 415/956–7500 or 800/867–8647) runs a three-day Yosemite Redwoods Tour out of San Francisco that goes through much of the park and surrounding forest. The tour costs $99, plus $21 for food (for more info on Green Tortoise travel, *see* Getting In, Out, and Around, in Chapter 1).

GETTING AROUND

Curvy **Tioga Pass Road** (a.k.a. **Highway 120**) runs the entire 60-mile east–west length of the park, climbing 8,000 feet in elevation. If you're on a bicycle (*see* Biking, *below*), you may want to limit yourself to the valley, since both Highway 41 and Tioga Pass Road are often narrow and have steep elevation gains.

BY PARK SHUTTLE Free shuttle buses operate throughout the year, though service hours vary according to season. The **East Valley Loop** travels every 20 minutes, year-round, between Curry Village, Yosemite Village, and the Yosemite Lodge (*see* Where to Sleep, *below*). Starting in mid-April, the shuttle operates 7 AM–10 PM; in winter, hours are reduced to 9 AM–10 PM, and some stops receive no service at all. Check the *Yosemite Guide* for a current schedule. During ski season a free shuttle leaves Yosemite Lodge for the **Badger Pass** ski area in the morning and returns in the afternoon. Another shuttle ($9.25 one-way, $17.75 round-trip) runs three times daily from mid-May to early October (weather permitting) between Yosemite Lodge and **Glacier Point** (*see* Scenic Drives and Views, *below*). Stops are well marked; just look for the SHUTTLE BUS signs along the main roads. From July until fall, an early-morning backpackers' shuttle ($3.75) runs once daily between Yosemite Lodge and **Crane Flat.** Call a visitor center for schedules.

WHERE TO SLEEP

Camping is the only real way to "experience" Yosemite. Not only are the hotels completely characterless and packed with tourists, they also charge handsomely for the privilege of four thin walls and a sagging bed. Whichever way you decide to go, reservations are highly—repeat: very, very, very—recommended: Beds and campsites go like hotcakes, especially in summer and fall.

HOTELS AND CABINS Hotel reservations can be made up to 366 days in advance, and believe it or not, most places actually fill up that far ahead. Hotel, lodge, and cabin reservations are all handled through **Yosemite Concessions** (5410 E. Home Ave., Fresno 93727, tel. 209/252–4848). Because Yosemite is so mobbed, you probably won't have a choice when it comes to your hotel accommodations. If you can find a single vacancy, consider yourself lucky.

This said, most people prefer the **Yosemite Lodge** (in Yosemite Valley, 5 mi east of Hwy. 140 entrance, tel. 209/372–1274), which has pleasant cabins with shared bath starting at $53 year-round. Each additional person costs an extra $6. Accommodations in **Curry Village** (east end of Yosemite Valley, tel. 209/372–1233) include canvas tent cabins (starting at $33 in winter, $37 in summer) and simple wood cabins ($53 year-round, $72 with private bath). The fee for extra people in the tent cabins is $5, in the wood cabins $6. Otherwise, look for the shantytown called **Housekeeping Camp** (tel. 209/252–4848) in the valley; here 282 identical cement-and-canvas "tent" units huddle close together, separated only by paper-thin walls. They're not particularly comfortable, but each bare-bones structure houses up to four people for only $39 per night (extra cots are $4 more). The camp is open from mid-March to late October. A grocery store, laundry, bathroom, and showers are nearby.

During summer months, claims a guidebook to Yosemite, "population density in the campgrounds is higher than in Calcutta's most crowded neighborhoods." The only difference, it seems, is that here you have to make a reservation at least eight weeks in advance.

CAMPING Yosemite's developed campgrounds share a number of characteristics: They're all large, flat, near a major road, and shaded by pine trees. Most have picnic tables, fire pits, flush toilets, piped water, and food-storage lockers, but none have direct access to showers (for that, you'll have to head to Housekeeping Camp or Curry Village). All but Tanerac, Yosemite Creek, and Porcupine have wheelchair access. Unfortunately, they're all extremely crowded, especially the ones in the valley. You may get lucky and find an open site during the off-season, but otherwise reservations are a must unless you want to try your luck at one of the walk-in sites. Campground reservations are available up to eight weeks in advance; contact **MISTIX** (tel. 800/365–CAMP) to secure a place. If you're stuck, show up at one of the reservations kiosks (in Curry Village, at the Big Oak Flat Information Station, in Tuolumne Meadows, and in Yosemite Village) between 8 and 10 AM, and put your name on the waiting list in case there's a cancellation.

In Yosemite Valley, **Upper Pines** is the biggest campground, with 238 tent and RV sites ($14) available March–November. It's conveniently located at Shuttle Stop 15, near trailheads to Mirror Lake and Vernal Fall. Misanthropes be warned: This place gets extremely crowded and the RVs pack together like sardines. Across the street at Shuttle Stop 19, **Lower Pines** is open year-round, with 172 tent and RV sites ($14) sandwiched between the Merced River and Storeman Meadow. Expect the same pack of RVs and families you see at Upper Pines. **Upper River Campground,** between Curry Village and Yosemite Valley at Shuttle Stop 2, is the only valley campground reserved for tents only. Open April–October, it's notably quieter than its counterparts. Some of the 124 sites ($14) lie near the Merced River. The nicest views (particularly of the Merced River and Yosemite Falls) can be found across the way at **Lower River Campground** with 126 sites ($14), but the views may not make up for the hordes of screaming brats who overrun the beach.

Outside the valley, look for **Tuolumne Meadows,** an enormous creekside campground perfect for exploring the eastern side of the park. Its 314 sites ($12) lie along Tioga Pass Road (Hwy. 120) and are usually open from July–October, depending on the weather. This campground, in some of the park's most beautiful country, attracts its share of day hikers, but it's still one of the last to fill up. **Hodgdon Meadow,** just past the Highway 120 entrance on the west side of the park, allows you to escape the chaos of the valley and still remain within striking distance (30–40 minutes). It draws nature-loving car campers year-round, except when snow closes the road (sometimes until late spring).

If you can't get a reservation at any of the major campgrounds, there are a few first-come, first-served sites you can try. In particular, check out the valley's only walk-in campground, **Sunnyside,** located about 1 mile west of Yosemite Village on Highway 140. In the '70s, Sunnyside was called Camp 4 and was known to host a particular kind of Bay Area crowd in between Dead shows. Today it's the favorite Yosemite campground of a new kind of subculture: the world's most hard-core rock climbers. Sunnyside has 35 sites ($3 per person) with running water and toilets. For walk-ins outside the valley, try **Tuolumne Meadows** (*see above*), where 25 sites are reserved for backpackers and visitors without vehicles. Tuolumne also reserves half its sites for same-day reservations; check the visitor center (either in the valley or in Tuolumne) for availability. Other walk-ins include **Wawona** (Hwy. 41, at south end of park), with 100 sites ($10); **White Wolf** (Tioga Pass Rd., about 10 mi east of Crane Flat), with 87 sites ($10); **Porcupine Flat** with 52 sites ($6); and **Yosemite Creek** with 75 sites ($6). The latter two are both off Tioga Pass Road east of White Wolf. Keep in mind that all the Tioga Pass Road campgrounds close in winter, usually mid-September or early October to early June. For info on backcountry camping, *see* Longer Hikes, *below.*

FOOD

If you plan on camping, bring as much food as possible. Prices in Yosemite's stores (*see* General Stores, *above*) are considerably higher than in the towns outside the park. A dull variety of American eateries, from fast-food cafeterias to expensive sit-down restaurants, is the only other choice.

The **Yosemite Village** complex, 7 miles east of the Highway 140 entrance, has the largest selection of food in the park. The **Pasta Place** (Shuttle Stop 5, tel. 209/372–8381), open daily 11:30 AM–9 PM, is a cafeteria-style restaurant with basic pasta-with-sauce plates (from $4.60) to choose from. If you have the cash, you might want to stuff yourself with the dinner special ($9–$10): a full pasta plate, caesar salad, bread, and a large drink. Also in Yosemite Village, **Degnana's Deli** (tel. 209/372–8454), open daily 7 AM–9 PM, has sandwiches ($4–$5), salads ($2–$4), and picnic supplies. Next door, **Degnana's Pizza and Ice Cream Parlor** (tel. 209/372–8437), open daily 9–9 in summer and daily 10–7 in winter, is the place to grab a slice of cheese pizza ($1.25).

In **Curry Village** (tel. 209/372–8333), on the west side of the valley near Happy Isles, there's a cafeteria, a small pizzeria, and a burger stand. None is particularly appetizing, but the cafeteria does have cheap burgers, sandwiches, and breakfasts (under $5). It's open 7–10 for breakfast, 11:45–1:30 for lunch, and 5:30–8 for dinner between April and October. Don't go out of your way for the pizzeria's merely tolerable slices ($2).

EXPLORING YOSEMITE

It can take anywhere from a day to the rest of your life to familiarize yourself with Yosemite. Realistically, you'll need at least a few days to venture beyond the crowds. To get a good overview, drive along **Tioga Pass Road** (Highway 120), stopping to take a walk or a hike wherever you're inclined: Scores of trails meander through the park, from relaxing strolls to highly demanding backcountry excursions. If you don't have a car, many trailheads are easily reached by shuttle bus (*see* Getting Around, *above*).

ORIENTATION AND TOURS The **Yosemite Valley Visitor Center** (*see* Basics, *above*) offers a worthwhile slide program on the park's geography and history. The free 20-minute show runs on the hour 10–3:30 Monday–Saturday and noon–3:30 Sunday. Also look for the center's documentaries about John Muir and Ansel Adams, shown in the late afternoon and evenings (call for schedules). Ranger programs like nature walks and storytelling last anywhere from one to three hours and are great ways to learn more about the park.

All kinds of guided bus tours originate in the valley, from two-hour excursions ($14) along the valley floor (every ½ hr daily 9–4) to a day-long grand tour ($40) of Mariposa Grove and Glacier Point (late spring to early fall). For reservations, contact the **Yosemite Lodge Tour Desk** (tel. 209/372–1274) or go to one of the tour booths at Curry Village, the Ahwahnee Hotel, or the Village Store in Yosemite Village.

SHORT HIKES **Yosemite Falls,** also known simply as "The Fall," is the highest waterfall in North America and the fifth highest in the world. It's divided into the upper falls (1,430 ft), the middle cascades (675 ft), and the lower falls (320 ft). From the parking lot, a ⅕-mile, wheelchair-accessible trail leads to the base, and a second 2-mile trail takes you to the lower falls. To reach the top, head to Sunnyside Campground and take the strenuous 3½-mile (one-way) **Yosemite Falls Trail,** which rises over 2,700 feet. The views from the top are breathtaking. If you're not up to the full trek (2–4 hrs round-trip), stop at **Columbia Rock** 1½ miles along the trail. You'll still get a good workout and dizzying vistas of Half Dome and the valley. Get off at Shuttle Stop 7 and follow signs to the trailhead.

The easy and popular 3-mile trail around **Mirror Lake** (Shuttle Stop 17), at the east end of the valley, offers some of the best photo opportunities in Yosemite. Beware of camera-toting tourists here: The trail is the gentlest in the park, so nearly everyone takes it. From the Happy Isles Trailhead (Shuttle Stop 16), the difficult 6-mile trail to **Vernal Fall** (317 ft) and **Nevada Fall** (594 ft) takes two to three hours, but the view from the top is phenomenal. The first half of the trail (aptly named **Mist Trail**) is a great place to soak yourself on a hot day—bring a bathing suit or rain gear, and kiss your hairdo good-bye. A fantastic overnight hike continues past Nevada Fall to Half Dome (*see* Longer Hikes, *below*). If you arrive in Yosemite along Highway 41, your first view of the valley will be at **Bridalveil Falls,** a ragged 620-foot cascade that's often blown as much as 20 feet from side to side by the wind. The Ahwahneechee called it *Pohono* (Puffing Wind). An easy ⅕-mile trail leading to its base starts from the parking lot.

Don't miss Soda Springs—a potable, naturally carbonated spring on an easy half-mile trail in idyllic Tuolumne Meadows. In 1863 William Brewer of the California Geologic Survey called its water "pungent and delightful," though a more recent visitor said, "It tastes like flat seltzer."

Numerous day hikes begin at **Tuolumne Meadows,** including an easy half-mile trail through the meadow to **Soda Springs;** a lovely but arduous (3 hrs, 5 mi round-trip) hike to emerald **Elizabeth Lake** wanders through mountain hemlock and lodgepole pine and across boisterous Unicorn Creek. If you want to camp, you'll need a permit (*see box, below*). These trails are less crowded than those originating in the valley and appeal to a younger crowd.

LONGER HIKES There are hundreds of possible day hikes in Yosemite, but to beat the crowds you'll need to do some serious backpacking in the wilderness, miles away from the stench of civilization. All trails are limited to a certain number of backpackers to prevent overuse, and free wilderness permits are required for overnight stays (*see box, below*). With a permit, you can take any of 70 trails (5–20 miles long) crisscrossing

Yosemite's outback. These often involve strenuous climbs along jagged paths no more than a foot wide, and some trails take upward of a week to complete. Fire rings are interspersed along the way, but you'll need to bring your own tent and provisions, including a water filter or iodine tablets to treat stream water. You can rent special three-pound bear-proof canisters for $3 from any ranger station in the park. Order maps and a pamphlet of hiking suggestions from the **Yosemite Association Bookstore** (Box 230, Yosemite 95389, tel. 209/379–2648). At any of Yosemite's bookstores, you can buy topographic USGS maps ($2.50), but experienced backpackers will recommend Trails Illustrated's waterproof, tearproof topo map ($7.95), available at The Wilderness Center in Yosemite Village.

If you're in top physical condition, take the hike out of Yosemite Valley to **Half Dome.** Follow the trail to Nevada Fall (*see* Short Hikes, *above*), and continue past Little Yosemite Campground to the Half Dome turnoff; then climb and climb and climb until you've risen nearly 5,000 feet. This trip (10–12 hrs, 17 mi round-trip) is not for those with vertigo or weak wills. You can make it an overnighter by camping at **Little Yosemite Campground,** but you'll need a wilderness permit (*see box, below*). You might leave your pack at the campground and climb the last 8½ miles without extra weight. If you want a multi-day trek, turn onto the **John Muir Trail** after the Half Dome turnoff. There are many entrance and exit trails along the way that can shorten the trip, but if you're a pro, you can follow the trail northeast out of the valley and through Tuolumne Meadow, at which point the trail hooks up with the Pacific Crest Trail. Here, truly intrepid hikers have the option of hanging a right and continuing all the way south to Mt. Whitney, for a total of 222 miles.

Hetch Hetchy, one of California's largest reservoirs, has irked conservationists since it was built early in the century. Environmentalists like John Muir fought actively against the damming of the Tuolumne River, which, they argued, would irreparably harm the region's wildlife. But politicians in San Francisco wanted mountain-fresh drinking water. Can you guess who won? Today, despite the massive Hetch Hetchy dam, the area still retains much of its beauty, and it contains the wonderfully isolated, moderately difficult **Rancheria Falls Trail** (13 mi round-trip), which leads to the eponymous lonely falls. You can do this trail in a day. If you have more time (five days) and excellent packing skills, go for the 52-mile **Rancheria Mountain and Bear**

Bucking the System in Yosemite's Backcountry

In the 19th century visitors used to pay for the privilege of hiking the Yosemite Falls Trail, but the days are long gone when only the wealthy could trek through the park. Now, hordes of wilderness enthusiasts crowd the backcountry every year, so many that in 1972 the park had to institute a permit system to limit the number of backpackers on the trails each day. For the uninitiated, here's how the system works:

Half the permits are distributed on a first-come, first-served basis a day in advance at any of the park's six ranger stations. These permits—particularly for popular areas such as the valley and Tuolumne Meadows—go quickly (some in just five minutes), so arrive early the day before your hike with a detailed itinerary, including trails and estimated overnight stopping points. These permits are free, but if you are looking to make reservations, available by mail March 1–May 31, you'll need to pay a reservation fee of $3 and send your dates of arrival and departure, specific trailheads for entry and exit, your main destination in the park, the number in your party, and alternative dates if your first choices aren't available to the Wilderness Office (Box 577, Yosemite 95389, tel. 209/372–0310).

Valley Loop, a strenuous hike that offers a terrific view of the Grand Canyon of Tuolumne River, as well as plenty of secluded camping around Bear Valley Lake. To reach the Rancheria Falls Trailhead, exit the west side of the park on Tioga Pass Road (Highway 120), turn right on Evergreen Road after 1 mile, and continue for 8 miles (you'll see signs).

The area north of Tuolumne River is wild and untrammeled—a good place to get away from it all. The numerous trailheads near **Tuolumne Meadows** are great for backpackers who want to spend at least a few days in the wilderness. Serious hikers should consider the **Tuolumne Grand Canyon Trail** (accessed from either Tuolumne Meadows or Lake Tanaya), a harrowing switchback leading 2 miles down the canyon, 8 miles across, and 2 miles up the far side. The strenuous hike requires at least two full days. Another popular trip out of Tuolumne Meadows from the John Muir Trailhead is an excellent two- to three-day hike (about 30 mi round trip) that leads to **Vogelsang Lake.** Hike up Lyell Fork on the **John Muir Trail** to the **Rafferty Creek Trail,** which becomes steep and difficult. This is a popular trip, so get your permits early (*see box, above*).

SCENIC DRIVES AND VIEWS During summer you can drive up to **Glacier Point** for a spectacular view of the valley and surrounding mountains. The 16-mile road starts at Chinquapin campground (take Hwy. 41 from the south or Hwy. 120 from the west). Better yet, take a shuttle (*see* Getting Around, *above*) to the top and take 4 Mile Trail back down into the valley (3 hrs), bringing you out on South Side Drive. **Tuolumne Meadows,** the largest subalpine meadow in the High Sierra and the site of several backcountry trailheads, is on Tioga Pass Road, 25 miles west of Lee Vining and U.S. 395. This is a gorgeous part of Yosemite, with delicate meadows surrounded by huge granite formations, and it's usually much less crowded than the valley. Tioga Pass Road is closed during winter, and usually opens by late May, but harsh winters can force the road to remain closed even into July.

On the way to Tuolumne (traveling east on Tioga Pass Road), check out the overlook at Olmstead Point—you get a full view of Cloud's Rest (elev. 9,926 ft) and the eastern side of Half Dome.

PARK ACTIVITIES

For those who want to take it easy, the National Park Service rents binoculars ($3) for **birdwatching.** Free 1½-hour **photography walks,** which lead you to prime spots for shooting Yosemite, leave daily around 8:30 AM from the Yosemite Lodge or the Ahwahnee Hotel. In winter, rangers lead free **snowshoe tours;** you can rent snowshoes ($7) from most lodges. **Horseback rides** originate at the stables near Mirror Lake; a four-hour trip to Vernal Fall is $44. In summer, you can take a leisurely 3-mile float (they call it "rafting") down the Merced for $12.50. Sign up at the **rafting** area in Curry Village, open daily 10–4. For more info on all these activities, consult the *Yosemite Guide* or check with the visitor center (tel. 209/372–0299).

BIKING Bikes are not permitted on any hiking trails, but Yosemite Valley has 8 miles of paved bike paths. Try the spectacular trail to Happy Isles and Mirror Lake, off the road to Curry Village; the easy 3-mile loop takes well under an hour unless you stop for a half-mile walk to Mirror Lake. Rent bikes ($5 per hour, $16 a day) from **Curry Village** (tel. 209/372–8333) or **Yosemite Lodge** (tel. 209/372–1274). Serious bikers should consider the 15-mile round-trip from Tuolumne Meadows to Olmstead Point along Tioga Pass Road. The grades are difficult and the roads narrow, but the views are spine chilling.

ROCK CLIMBING Take a look around for two seconds and you'll understand why Yosemite is a mecca for world-class rock climbers. Basic and intermediate lessons ($120 for one person, $85 each for two, $60 each for three to five people) are offered year-round by the **Yosemite Mountaineering School and Guide Service** (tel. 209/372–8344). In summer only, they organize trips from Tuolumne Meadows. Unfortunately you can't rent equipment in the park without enrolling in a class.

SKIING Yosemite's ski season usually lasts from late November or early December to March. Call 209/372–4605 for weather conditions.

➢ **DOWNHILL** • Yosemite has a small ski area, **Badger Pass** (tel. 209/372–8430), that won't pose much of a challenge to accomplished skiers. It's a good place to learn, however, and there are enough relatively uncrowded trails to keep intermediate skiers entertained. It's open daily 9–4:30 in winter. Lift tickets cost $25–$30, depending on the number of lifts open, which in turn depends on snowfall. It usually runs three black-diamond (advanced) lifts and six blue (intermediate) lifts. Ski rentals are $18 a day, snowboards $30 a day. Look for Badger Pass 6 miles east of Highway 41 on Glacier Point Road. For 24-hour snow conditions, call 209/372–1000.

➢ **CROSS-COUNTRY** • Yosemite has 90 miles of cross-country trails through the Badger Pass ski area to Glacier Point. A free shuttle from the valley runs to Badger Pass, departing in the morning and returning in the afternoon. **Glacier Point Road** is a good place to start: Beginners will enjoy the groomed track and advanced skiers will get a workout if they take the whole 21-mile round-trip. The **Cross-Country Ski School** (tel. 209/327-8444) offers two-hour lessons ($18) and four-hour lessons ($40, including rentals). A guided overnight trip—including meals and lodging—is $110 per person. Badger Pass (*see above*) has rentals ($9 half day, $13 full day). The **Tuolumne Grove of Giant Sequoias Trail** (3 mi round trip), which starts at Crane Flat a few miles east of the Big Oak Flat entrance station, has a steep drop, but you get to ski among the largest living things on earth.

Santa Cruz

Originally founded in the late 1800s as a mission town, Santa Cruz has several identities. Old-time residents, many of Italian descent, still look askance at the liberal students and hippies who have been migrating to the town ever since the University of California opened its "alternative, no-stress" branch here in the 1960s. Although the students, hippies, and New Agers might not dominate this spectacular coastal community numerically, the lifestyles of these three overlapping groups have certainly defined Santa Cruz's cultural landscape. From Volkswagen buses to vegan (no meat, no dairy) restaurants, homeopathic healers to drum circles, Grateful Dead T-shirts to long-hairs smoking dope on the streets, you'll see signs of Santa Cruz's liberal attitude wherever you turn.

And though Santa Cruz's reputation as a happy-dappy beach town stretches far and wide, it has its fissure points, including the Loma Prieta fault, which runs through the mountains east of town. Bicycle riders spar with car drivers about bike lanes; small-business owners roll their eyes at the hordes of young people clogging their cafés and panhandling on their sidewalks. Anti-immigration hysteria is taking its toll here too, as migrant farm workers, mostly Mexicans and Mexican-Americans, move to Santa Cruz County in record numbers to work on nearby farmlands. Though they fit snugly into the local economy, these newest pieces of Santa Cruz's puzzle often find themselves made unwelcome by the largely homogeneous (i.e., white) community.

Most of downtown has been rebuilt since 1989's 7.1-magnitude Loma Prieta earthquake, and many say the squeaky-clean new buildings symbolize a sea change toward conservativism. But even if the mall is blander than before, Santa Cruz's sloppy individuality is still very much in place.

Though subject to the conflicts of any sizable California community, Santa Cruz holds on to its idyllic beach-town atmosphere better than many. The carnival-like **boardwalk** is Santa Cruz at its flashiest, drawing legions of hormone-crazed teenagers from Salinas and San Jose every weekend. The boardwalk's most popular attraction is the **Giant Dipper,** one of the oldest wooden roller coasters in the world. The harrowing ride affords you a brief panorama of Monterey Bay before plunging you down toward the beach. If your stomach's not up to such antics, head to Santa Cruz's stunning coast. The rocks off the craggy shore are favored perches for seals, the beaches are thronged by surfers and their retinue, and the hills surrounding the town fade into redwood forests ideal for hiking or musing.

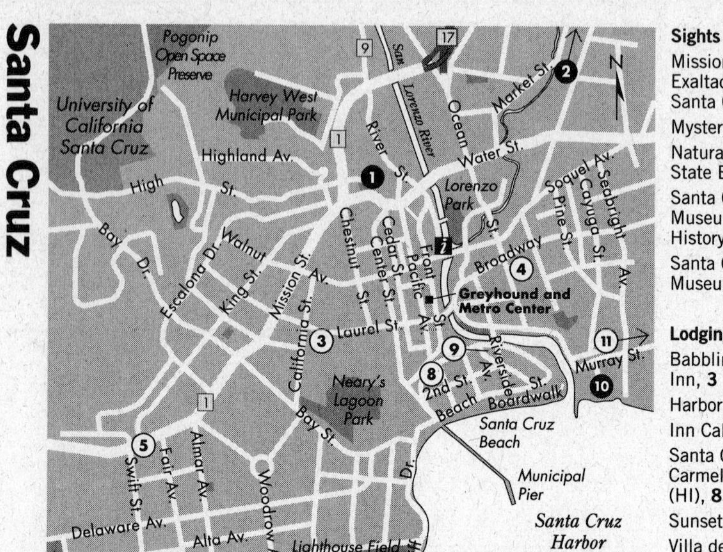

Sights ●

Mission de Exaltaci n de la Santa Cruz, **1**

Mystery Spot, **2**

Natural Bridges State Beach, **6**

Santa Cruz City Museum of Natural History, **10**

Santa Cruz Surfing Museum, **7**

Lodging ○

Babbling Brook Inn, **3**

Harbor Inn, **11**

Inn Cal, **4**

Santa Cruz Carmelita Cottages (HI), **8**

Sunset Inn, **5**

Villa del Mar Motel, **9**

BASICS

Visitor Information Center. A friendly staff has tons of free pamphlets, including the mediocre *California Coast* tourist magazine. They can't help with room reservations, however. Maps will set you back $1.50 each. *701 Front St., tel. 408/425–1234. 2 blocks north of Metro Center. Open Mon.–Sat. 9–5, Sun. 10–4.*

COMING AND GOING

BY CAR The most scenic route from San Francisco, 1½ hours north, is along **Highway 1.** Curvy **Highway 17,** which meets up with I–280, I–880, and U.S. 101, is the faster drive to San Francisco and the East Bay. Avoid Highway 17 on weekend mornings, when the entire Silicon Valley seems to head for the beaches, and at night, when the sharp curves of the road are difficult to see.

BY BUS **Green Tortoise** (tel. 415/956–7500 in California or 800/867–8647), whose touring buses are known for their casual atmosphere, bunk beds, and "soft areas" made of foam pads and cotton pillows, travels from San Francisco to Los Angeles, stopping in Santa Cruz, once a week. Every Friday night at 8 PM, buses from San Francisco (3 hrs, $10) leave from 1st and Natoma streets, behind the Transbay Bus Terminal (*see* Getting In, Out, and Around by Bus, in Chapter 1), arriving in Santa Cruz around 11 PM. Reservations are recommended at least three days in advance, one week ahead in summer.

Greyhound (425 Front St., at Laurel St., tel. 408/423–1800) has direct service between Santa Cruz and San Francisco six times daily (2 hrs, $14). **Highway 17 Express Bus** (tel. 408/425–8600) has hourly service (every 15 min during commute hours) and is the cheapest way to travel between San Jose and Santa Cruz during the week ($2.25). Buses stop in Santa Cruz at the junction of Soquel Drive and Highway 1, and in San Jose at the CalTrain station and at the corner of 3rd Street and San Fernando Avenue, one block from San Jose State University.

BY TRAIN While you can't get to Santa Cruz directly by train, **CalTrain** (tel. 800/660–4287) does offer daily train service between San Francisco and San Jose (1½ hrs, $4.50). Trains run at least once an hour between 8 AM and 3 PM, more frequently during commute hours. From the San Jose CalTrain station (Cahill and W. San Fernando Sts.), take the **Santa Cruz CalTrain Connector** (tel. 408/425–8600) to the Metro Center (*see* Getting Around, *below*) in Santa Cruz. The bus leaves every two hours on weekdays, less often on weekends; it takes an hour and costs $5.

HITCHHIKING Depending on whom you talk to, Santa Cruz is either one of the mellowest or one of the most dangerous places to hitchhike in North America. If you want to give it a go, a good spot to catch a ride north out of town is at the corner of Swift Street and Highway 1 (a.k.a. Mission St.) by the LITTER REMOVAL sign (no kidding). Hitching northeast along Highway 17 toward San Jose or south along Highway 1 is more difficult. Try standing at the Ocean Street on-ramp to Highway 17. A less risky idea is the **UCSC rideboard** at Bay Tree Books (the college bookstore, located in the center of campus). The availability of rides varies with the time of year, and some money to cover the cost of gas is appreciated, if not expected.

GETTING AROUND

Santa Cruz lies on the edge of Monterey Bay and is bisected by the San Lorenzo River. The town is full of crooked and confusing streets, so keep a sharp eye on a map. Highway 1 becomes **Mission Street** when it enters Santa Cruz, and resumes its old identity on the way out of town. **Bay Street** and **High Street** both funnel into UCSC, which is located on a hill 2 miles northeast of downtown, while the boardwalk is on **Beach Street** just west of the river. The boardwalk, the pier, and downtown Santa Cruz (which centers around **Pacific Avenue** and **Front Street**) are all within comfortable walking distance of each other.

BY CAR Except on summer weekends, driving and parking are not difficult in Santa Cruz, even downtown. Free two-hour parking is available along Front and Cedar streets, and on weekends some parking lots are free all day. Possible parking spots include the **Santa Cruz County Building** (701 Ocean St.) and the **River Street Parking Garage** (River St.), which runs shuttles to the beach on weekends (when parking by the boardwalk gets difficult, to say the least).

BY BUS Bus service is efficient and fairly easy to use. The Santa Cruz Metropolitan District Transit (SCMDT), also known as Metro, operates from the **Metro Center** (920 Pacific Ave., at Laurel St.) adjoining the Greyhound Station. Any bus in town will eventually take you to the Metro Center, where you can pick up a copy of "Headways," a free pamphlet that lists all bus routes. The fare is $1, but you can purchase a special all-day pass for $3 on any bus or at the Metro Center. Exact change, in coins or one-dollar bills, is required; change machines are available at the Metro Center. A free shuttle runs between the Metro Center and the boardwalk in summer. *920 Pacific Ave., tel. 408/425–8600 or 408/688–8600. Open daily 7 AM–9 PM. Info booth in lobby open weekdays 8–5.*

BY BIKE Biking is the best way to get around Santa Cruz. Many streets have wide bike lanes, and the weather is quite moderate, especially in spring and summer. Bring wheels from home if you can, since renting can be expensive. The imaginatively named **Bicycle Rental Center** (415 Pacific Ave., at Front St., tel. 408/426–8687), three blocks north of the boardwalk, has a competitive rate of $25 a day.

WHERE TO SLEEP

The price categories below refer to weekday rates, which often multiply as much as three times on weekends. Winter rates are about $10–$30 lower than in summer. The local youth hostel is definitely the best deal around if you can get a room. Camping in the area is great, as evidenced by the fact that campgrounds fill quickly in summer. If all the campgrounds listed below are full, Big Basin Redwoods State Park (*see* Near Santa Cruz, *below*) is 30–45 minutes away. The dorms at U.C. Santa Cruz (*tel. 408/459–2611*) accept guests from the end of June to the beginning of September, but rooms are plain, far from town and the water, and expensive. A single runs $50, $65 with full board; a double is $40 per person, $55 with full board. The dorms are limited to those on "official" business, so you may want to say you're considering enrolling and sign up for a campus tour.

HOTELS AND MOTELS Behind the boardwalk on 2nd Street, 3rd Street, and Riverside Avenue are some fleabag motels that rarely fill up, but you'll find comparably priced places clustered on Mission and Ocean streets that are much more comfortable, and equally convenient if you have a car. In particular, try the **Sunset Inn** (2424 Mission St., tel. 408/423–3471) for clean rooms in a pinch. Weekday rates range from $40 for a double to $85 for a suite that sleeps six. For a decadent treat, stay at one of several good B&Bs. At the downtown **Babbling Brook Inn** (1025 Laurel St., tel. 408/427–2437), rooms with country-French decor are surrounded by manicured gardens and a beautiful waterfall. Rooms come complete with private bath and a fireplace or Jacuzzi. The rates, which include a full breakfast, range from $85 to $165 per night for two.

Santa Cruz is a popular weekend trip for Bay Area residents, so be prepared for exponentially jacked-up weekend rates in motels.

➢ **UNDER $50** • **Harbor Inn.** In a residential neighborhood 10 minutes southeast of town (though not especially close to the water), this inviting inn has large cathedral ceilings and doubles (starting at $45 in summer, $35 in the off-season) with a hodgepodge of old furniture and wooden beds. The antidote to characterless chain motels, the Harbor often fills in summer, so call ahead for reservations. Most rooms have kitchenettes, and larger groups can get a suite ($65–$85, depending on the season). *645 7th Ave., tel. 408/479–9731. From downtown, cross river on Laurel St., right on San Lorenzo Blvd., left on Murray St., left on 7th Ave. Or Bus 65 or 66 to 7th Ave. 19 rooms. Wheelchair access.*

Inn Cal. The clean rooms are decorated à la chain motel, but the inn is only four blocks from the beach. A double goes for $45 during the week in summer, $55 on weekends; prices drop $10 during winter. *370 Ocean St., at Broadway, tel. 408/458–9220. From Metro Center, Bus 68 or 69 to cnr Ocean St. and Soquel Ave. Reservations advised. Wheelchair access.*

Villa del Mar Motel. Its location one block away from the boardwalk and the beach makes the floral decor forgivable. Singles start as low as $38 and doubles at $42, jumping to $60 and $64, respectively, on summer weekends. *321 Riverside Ave., tel. 408/423–9449. From Metro Center, Bus 7 to cnr Beach and Cliff Sts. 23 rooms. Wheelchair access.*

HOSTEL **Santa Cruz Carmelita Cottages (HI).** The cottages are actually a cluster of houses made hosteler-friendly. Located two blocks from the boardwalk on Beach Hill, these new accommodations cost $12 for members and $15 for nonmembers. Private doubles are $30, and "family" rooms (three to five people) cost at least $30–$40, depending on the number of beds. It's just like living in a real house—with a bunch of strangers. Write (Box 1241, Santa Cruz 95061) or call ahead for reservations. *315 Main St., tel. 408/423–8304. From Metro Center, Bus 7 to Main St. 25 beds. Curfew 11 PM, lockout 9–5. Reception open daily 7–9 AM and 5–10 PM. Lockers, sheet rental ($1). Wheelchair access.*

CAMPING **Henry Cowell Redwoods State Park.** Fifteen miles north of Santa Cruz, this 111-site campground is buffered by a redwood forest and a stunning series of cliff faces. Things get a little out of hand during summer, when RVs and screaming teens overrun the place, but otherwise this is a camper's paradise. Reserve through MISTIX (tel. 800/444–PARK). Both tent and RV sites are $16 a night. *101 N. Big Trees Park Rd., Felton, tel. 408/335–4598 or 408/438–2396. From Hwy. 1, Hwy. 9 north; from Metro Center, Bus 30. Drinking water, flush toilets, showers. Closed Dec.–Feb.*

New Brighton State Beach. High above the ocean on a large cliff, this popular campground in Capitola, 5 miles southeast of Santa Cruz, offers an incredible view of the coast from some sites. A steep path leads downhill to the soft beach below. Neither the tent nor RV spaces have much privacy, however. Reservations—available through MISTIX (tel. 800/444–PARK)—are a must between May and September, when the place is filled almost every day. Sites go for $16 in summer, $14 in winter. Follow signs from Highway 1. Otherwise, Bus 71 will take you to the corner of Soquel Ave. and Park Ave., but leaves you with a long walk. *1500 Park Ave., tel. 408/475–4850.*

Sunset State Beach and **Manresa State Beach.** If New Brighton is booked, try these two scruffy beaches, both about 25 minutes south of Santa Cruz. Sunset has 90 campsites, all with fire rings, picnic tables, and hot showers. Spaces, reserved through MISTIX (tel. 800/444–PARK), are $16 in summer, $14 at other times, and go quickly on weekends. On the way to Sunset, you'll pass Manresa, which has 60 walk-in sites with the same facilities, prices, and reservation system as Sunset. Sites are on a hill above the beach or set back in a sparse sprinkling of trees with little privacy. *San Andreas Rd. Sunset: tel. 408/724–1266. Manresa: tel. 408/761–1795. Hwy. 1 south to San Andreas Rd. exit, right at bottom of ramp, right onto San Andreas Rd.*

ROUGHING IT Santa Cruz has a reputation as an easygoing town, but the police nevertheless frown on people sleeping in public places. Lots of homeless people try it anyway, even though the cops periodically patrol the beaches and parks and issue waves of citations. If you're willing to take the risk, try one of the small beaches south of town, along Highway 1. As long as you don't light a campfire or make a lot of noise, you may be left alone.

FOOD

To say that Santa Cruzians are health conscious is a ferocious understatement. Downtown, in the area bordered by Front and Cedar streets in one direction and Laurel and Water streets in the other, reams of cafés, delis, and small restaurants offer health-oriented menus. For fresh produce, much of it organically grown, head to the **farmers' market,** held every Wednesday 2–6 on the corner of Pacific Avenue and Cathcart Street; then trot over to Lorenzo Park (River St., btw Water St. and Soquel Ave.) for a picnic. Also look for the markets and fast-food chains along Mission Street.

➢ **UNDER $5** • For a tasty slice of late-night pizza there's always **Uppercrust Pizza** (2415 Mission St., tel. 408/423–9010), on the west side of town near the Highway 1 turnoff for Natural Bridges State Beach; it's open until 11 PM Sunday–Thursday, 1 AM on Friday, and midnight on Saturday. At less than $2 a slice, Uppercrust is cheaper than **Pizza Amoré** (103 W. Cliff Dr., at Beach St. across from boardwalk, tel. 408/423–2336), open daily noon–10, but the latter's pesto-ricotta slices ($3) are worth a try, and if you want a whole pie they'll deliver free of charge.

For Mexican food, **Tacos Moreno** (1053 Water St., tel. 408/429–6095), a hole-in-the-wall about five minutes east of downtown, sells the cheapest (and some say the best) tacos ($2) and burritos ($3) in town, daily 11–8. For sheer bulk, though, **Taquería Vallarta** (608 Soquel Ave., 1 block east of Ocean St., tel. 408/457–8226) is the place to go. Enormous burritos ($3 vegetarian, $3.50 carnivore) are served up weekdays 10 AM–midnight and weekends 9 AM–midnight.

The Bagelry. This deli warehouse has three locations, one of which is downtown, and specializes in wacky bagel spreads like the homemade Pink Flamingo spread (cream cheese with lox and dill; $2.50) and the Luna spread (pesto, ricotta, and almonds; $2). A plain bagel with cream cheese costs $1.25, but plain bagels are for wimps. If you're short on cash, try the "three-seed slug"—a flat, wide bagel without the hole (55¢). *320A Cedar St., at Laurel St., tel. 408/429–8049. Other locations: 1636 Seabright Ave., tel. 408/425–8550; 4363 Soquel Dr., tel. 408/462–9888. All open weekdays 6:30–5:30, Sat. 7:30–5:30, Sun. 7:30–4.*

Zachary's. The basic breakfast—two eggs, potatoes, and your choice of homemade breads—sells for a reasonable $3.50. If you want something a little more elaborate, the huge stack of pancakes ($3.50) and the family-size omelets ($4 and up) are definitely worth the price. The ultimate breakfast is Mike's Mess ($6): The pile of eggs, bacon, mushrooms, potatoes, cheese, sour cream, tomatoes, and green onions can easily feed two. The eating area is usually crowded, but the outstanding food is worth the wait (except maybe on weekends, when it can take up to an hour to get a table). *819 Pacific Ave., btw Laurel and Maple Sts., tel. 408/427–0646. Open Tues.–Sun. 7–2:30. Wheelchair access.*

➢ **UNDER $10** • **Dolphin Restaurant.** Work your way to the end of Santa Cruz's pier and grab an order of fresh-caught fish-and-chips ($5) from the outside window of the Dolphin. If you'd rather sit, head to the adjoining restaurant, where, in addition to fried fish, there are burgers ($5.50), hearty clam chowder ($4.25 a bowl), and pasta dishes. *End of pier, tel. 408/426–5830. Open summer, Sun.–Thurs. 8 AM–11 PM, Fri. and Sat. 8 AM–midnight; winter hours fluctuate, so call ahead.*

King Chwan. King Chwan has an amazing lunch deal—soup, salad, Chinese entrée, tea, and fortune cookie for $4. A slightly more elaborate combination dinner goes for $6.50. The lighting is bright and the building looks like a large tract house, but for the money you can't complain. Even better, the food isn't half bad. *415 Ocean St., across bridge from Front St., tel. 408/429–5898. Open daily 11:30–10. Wheelchair access.*

Saturn Café. This is a great place to eat, read, and watch the spaced-out locals. If it's warmth you need, try the lentil chili ($3.50). For greens connoisseurs, the Titan salad ($6.25) is big and satisfying—enough for two to share. Better yet, indulge in the locally famous Chocolate Madness ($4.25), a huge conglomeration of chocolate cookies, chocolate ice cream, chocolate mousse, hot fudge, chocolate chips, and whipped cream. *1230 Mission St., near Laurel St., tel. 408/429–8505. Open weekdays 11:30 AM–midnight, weekends noon–midnight. Wheelchair access. No credit cards.*

CAFÉS In a town with more than 15,000 college students, the absence of nighttime diversions for the under-21 set has fueled a serious café scene. And in addition to being a popular hangout spot for college students, cafés are also frequented by locals looking for a lively debate or a place to read a good book.

Caffè Pergolesi. In a big, rambling house downtown graced with a large outside deck, the Perg has all the trappings of a good café—potent house coffee ($1), double-potent espresso drinks ($1–$3), and a large selection of herbal teas (95¢). Try *chai,* a milky Indian spice tea ($2). The small food menu includes veggie lasagna ($5), quiche ($4.50), and sandwiches ($3), as well as the usual bagels ($2) and pastries ($1.50–$2). The crowd is somewhat eclectic, ranging from UCSC students to nouveau-hippies. This is definitely the place to play chess. *418A Cedar St., at Elm St., tel. 408/426–1775. Open daily 8 AM–midnight.*

True to the Santa Cruz health obsession, smoking is forbidden in all indoor cafés.

Herland Book-Café. Although men are allowed at this bookstore/café, Herland was conceived as a safe haven for women. The books, grouped in categories like "Women of the Wild West" or "Women Respond to the Men's Movement," are all female-authored. The café serves coffee (75¢), tea (85¢), espresso drinks ($1.25–$2), and snacks ($1–$3). *902 Center St., at Union St., tel. 408/42–WOMEN. Open Tues.–Sat. 8 AM–10 PM, Sun. and Mon. 10–6.*

Jahva House. Located in a large warehouse, the Jahva House is open, airy, and comfortable. Big oriental rugs are strewn on the floors, and ficus trees stand among the outside tables. The incredibly long coffee bar furnishes zillions of different coffees and teas, including organically grown varieties of both. For something extra special, try a Mexican Mocha ($2.50), a delicious mix of Mexican hot chocolate, espresso, and steamed milk. Excellent banana bread and slices of pie cost about $3. *120 Union St., near Cedar St., tel. 408/459–9876. Open Mon.–Sat. 6 AM–midnight, Sun. 8–8.*

WORTH SEEING

Most of Santa Cruz's sights are downtown, within a walkable area. To explore the jagged coast, though, you'll definitely need a car or one heck of a mountain bike. Downtown, the **Pacific Garden Mall** is the center of the action, strewn with specialty stores, antique shops, restaurants, and cafés, and an easy destination for an afternoon of window-shopping. Two worthwhile bookstores are **Bookshop Santa Cruz** (1520 Pacific Ave., at Locust St., tel. 408/423–0900), a bookstore and café with a humongous selection of books, magazines, and international newspapers; and **Logos** (1117 Pacific Ave., near Lincoln St., tel. 408/427–5100), Santa Cruz's premier used-book and music store. If you're in the mood for a leisurely afternoon walk, the **Mission de Exaltación de la Santa Cruz** (126 High St.), built between 1857 and 1931, has grounds overrun with colorful gardens and fountains. On the beach near downtown lies the

Santa Cruz Beach Boardwalk, a little Coney Island by the Pacific, with amusement-park rides, carnival games, kitschy shops, arcades, cotton candy, and plenty of teenage angst. Admission to the boardwalk is free, but the rides cost—usually \$2 or \$3 a shot. If you do nothing else, ride the Giant Dipper (\$3), a fabulous wooden roller coaster with a spectacular view.

UNIVERSITY OF CALIFORNIA AT SANTA CRUZ Take a quick tour of UCSC, in the thickly forested hills just north of downtown. The info center (tel. 408/459–0111) at the campus entrance is open weekdays 8–5 and has maps and tour schedules. Be sure to investigate the **limestone quarry** near the campus bookstore—it's a nice spot for a picnic—and take a self-guided tour of the organic growing system at the **Farm and Garden Project** (tel. 408/459–4140). If you park along Meder Avenue at the far west end of campus and catch the free shuttle at Bay and High streets, you can avoid the on-campus parking fee. Otherwise take Bus 41 from the Metro Center to the west entrance of campus.

SANTA CRUZ CITY MUSEUM OF NATURAL HISTORY You'll recognize this place by the huge stone statue of a whale out front. The museum is small, but full of information about the Ohlone Native Americans, who originally populated the area, and the seals and sea lions that still do. If you're into honeybees, watch thousands encased under glass doing interesting apiarian things. The museum is on the east side of town, near Pleasure Point—a great place to watch local surfers. *1305 E. Cliff Dr., tel. 408/429–3773. From downtown, walk or drive east on Laurel St., cross river, turn right on San Lorenzo St. (which becomes E. Cliff Dr.). Or Bus 67 from Metro Center. \$2 donation requested. Open Tues.–Fri. 10–5, weekends 1–5.*

SANTA CRUZ SURFING MUSEUM At Lighthouse Point on West Cliff Drive, there's a tiny exhibit on surfing, from its Hawaiian origins to the present, including an explanation of the modern wet suit. The museum is dedicated to the memory of an 18-year-old surfer who drowned in 1965. Also on display is a board bitten by a great white shark in 1987, testimony to the real danger posed by sharks along the coast from Santa Cruz to Pigeon Point. Plop down right outside the lighthouse and watch the surfers on Steamer's Lane, one of the best surf spots in California. Look a little farther out and you'll see Seal Rock, the summertime home of thousands of barking, shiny seals. *Mark Abbott Memorial Lighthouse, W. Cliff Dr., tel. 408/429–3429. Bus 3A or 3B. Admission free. Open Mon., Wed.–Fri. noon–4, weekends noon–5.*

If you want some exercise, the path running parallel to West Cliff Drive from the boardwalk to Natural Bridges State Beach is a great place for a walk, jog, or bike ride. The 2-mile jaunt passes innumerable rocky coves and surfing points, and at least one nude beach.

NATURAL BRIDGES STATE BEACH Two miles west of town, the secluded and spectacular Natural Bridges State Beach is the perfect place to escape the overwhelming sensory stimulation of Santa Cruz. As its name implies, the beach features a series of bridge-like rock formations, as well as excellent tidal pools, picnic tables, barbecue pits, and plenty of soft, warm sand to stretch out on. Also on the grounds of the park is a **monarch butterfly colony,** one of only a few places in the world where you can witness the amazing sight of thousands of brightly colored butterflies mating. The mating season usually lasts from mid-October to February, but call ahead for the latest

Relaxing, Santa Cruz Style

If you're feeling battered by life, Santa Cruz offers the perfect way to enter a state of total relaxation in the form of Kiva, a co-ed, clothing-optional spa favored by locals. For \$10 you can spend as many hours as you like drifting into dreamy tranquility in hot tubs, saunas, and cold dips. The spa is open Sunday–Thursday noon–11 PM, Fridays and Saturdays until midnight; the management reserves Sundays 9–noon for women only and gives women a two-for-one discount Monday through Wednesday. 702 Water St., 1 block east of Market St., tel. 408/429–1142.

(and to make a reservation for guided walks). Park on Delaware Avenue just east of the park entrance to avoid the parking fee. *W. Cliff Dr., tel. 408/423–4609. From boardwalk, follow W. Cliff Dr. until you see signs. Or Bus 3B from Metro Center. Parking $6. Open daily 8 AM–sunset.*

MYSTERY SPOT If you abhor tourist attractions but feel a strange compulsion to "do" at least one, let this be it. This quirky little place lies in the redwoods 3 miles north of Santa Cruz and, in the minds of true believers, is at the center of a mysterious force that makes people taller and compels balls to roll uphill. It's a tacky tourist trap, to be sure, but its gift shop is filled with one-of-a-kind souvenirs and kitschy knickknacks. Your $3 admission also buys you a Mystery Spot bumper sticker. *1953 Branciforte Dr., tel. 408/423–8897. From downtown, east on Water St., left on Market St., go 2½ mi, and follow signs. Open daily 9:30–4:30.*

CHEAP THRILLS

Hiding in the redwoods, **Felton, Ben Lomond,** and **Boulder Creek** are small towns in a grand setting, definitely worth a day trip. All three get a bit crowded on weekends, particularly in summer, but they retain their mountain charm all the same. It will take only 30–45 minutes to travel through all three. At first glance it seems as though these towns haven't changed in 50 years—until you notice the spiritual healers, chiropractors, and eco-conscious grocery stores lining the sidewalks. You won't find much to "do" in any of these towns—Boulder Creek is the most lively of the three, which isn't saying much—but the beautiful drive alone is worth the trip. When you've soaked up enough of the small-town ambiance, pack a picnic and head to Big Basin (*see* Near Santa Cruz, *below*), only 15 minutes farther from Boulder Creek. On weekends, catch Bus 35 from the Metro Center, or drive north along Highway 9.

The oceanside town of **Capitola,** along the coast about 5 miles southeast of Santa Cruz, is popular with locals for its wide, quiet, sandy beach and rickety wooden pier, a welcome change from the sometimes frenetic pace of Santa Cruz. After you're done soaking up the sun, head straight to **Mr. Toot's** (221 Esplanade, tel. 408/475–3679), a café full of old wood tables, comfortable couches, and a deck overlooking the beach. Catch Bus 58 from Santa Cruz's Metro Center, or take Highway 1 south to the Capitola/Park Avenue exit and head toward the Pacific.

For a groovy Santa Cruz experience, go at sunset to **It's Beach,** immediately west of the lighthouse. Almost every day of the year, locals gather here to drum and dance as night falls. Also check out the numerous street performers on **Pacific Avenue** and the area surrounding the boardwalk.

FESTIVALS

The **Cabrillo Music Festival,** usually held during the first week of August, has food, symphonic music, and other live entertainment. Call the Santa Cruz Civic Auditorium Box Office (tel. 408/429–3444) for more info. Tickets cost $6–$25 depending on the performance and seating.

Shakespeare Santa Cruz (tel. 408/459–2121) is served up against a backdrop of beautiful redwoods during a six-week UCSC production of the Bard's works mid-July–August on campus. Tickets start at $15 and peak at $21.

Can you think of 1,001 things to do with fungus? You know, those little mushrooms that cover the forest floor during the rainy season? If you can't, the people at the **Fungus Fair** will be more than happy to assist you. The fair is held every January at the Santa Cruz City Museum of Natural History (*see* Worth Seeing, *above*). Entrance is $4. Call the museum for more info.

AFTER DARK

Much of Santa Cruz's nocturnal activity takes place in the cafés and ends early. Nightlife in the traditional sense is decidedly lacking, and those establishments that do cater to the over-21 crowd check ID stringently. The journal *Good Times* (free at cafés and bookstores) comes out every Thursday with a listing of upcoming events. Look for happy hours and reduced cover charges, usually on Wednesday or Thursday nights.

The Blue Lagoon. This is Santa Cruz's premier gay and bisexual nighttime hangout. There's a $2 cover on weekends, but it's worth it for some of the best DJ dance music in town. *923 Pacific Ave., across from Metro Center, tel. 408/423–7117.*

Boulder Creek Brewing Company. Even though it's 25 minutes north of Santa Cruz, Boulder Creek combines the best beer and the best live music in the area. Try their Ghost Rail Pale Ale ($3) and Redwood Ale ($3); for heartier appetites there's the Mudslide Stout ($2.75), billed "thick as a mudslide, twice as tasty." When live bands play there's usually a cover ($3 and up). Flamenco dancers, Middle Eastern musicians, and blues artists have all performed here. *13040 Hwy. 9, tel. 408/338–7882.*

The Catalyst. It's disparaged by some for its virtual monopoly of the Santa Cruz music scene. Still, The Catalyst attracts a college crowd with local bands nightly and big names on occasion. Covers range from $1 on Thursday nights to $15 for major shows. *1011 Pacific Ave., tel. 408/423–1336.*

Front Street Pub. It's yet another microbrewery in downtown Santa Cruz, but this one has good ciders and its own Lighthouse Amber ($2.50). It tends to be an after-work stop off for those in their twenties and thirties. *516 Front St., at Soquel Ave., tel. 408/429–8838.*

Poet and the Patriot Irish Pub. This is paradise for UCSC students and Santa Cruz's "artsy" crowd, despite the pricey drinks. The pub has lots of smoke in the air (well, lots by Santa Cruz standards), dart boards on the wall, and Irish beer on tap. *320 Cedar St., at Laurel St., tel. 408/426–8620.*

The Red Room. It's a run-down dive that's darkly lit, usually jammed with students, and a true UCSC institution. Don't look for a sign out front; there isn't one. At night the adjacent restaurant becomes a venue for local grunge and punk bands. Some nights you pay a minimal cover. *1003 Cedar St., at Locust St., tel. 408/426–2994.*

In the same building as the Poet and the Patriot Irish Pub, the Kuumbwa Jazz Center (tel. 408/427–2227) hosts jazz and blues shows throughout the year. Call for tickets ($2–$14) and scheduling info.

OUTDOOR ACTIVITIES

HIKING AND MOUNTAIN BIKING The redwood-filled hills surrounding Santa Cruz provide some of Northern California's best hiking and mountain-biking opportunities. Though it's a bit out of town, real enthusiasts should head directly to **Big Basin Redwoods State Park** (*see* Near Santa Cruz, *below*). Closer to town, **Henry Cowell Redwoods State Park** (*see* Camping, *above*) has hundreds of miles of trails, many of which meander through virgin redwood forests. Bikes are allowed on designated fire and service roads, but not on hiking trails. For a beautiful, albeit sometimes crowded, stroll among some of the park's tallest trees, take the Redwood Grove trail; you'll find the trailhead off Highway 9. For more of a workout, head 4 miles uphill to the observation deck for a beautiful view of the valley (walk up Pipeline Road from the nature center and turn left on Ridge Fire Road). To get here from downtown, follow Highway 9 toward Felton.

At the **Forest of Nisene Marks State Park** (Aptos Creek Rd. exit off Hwy. 1, southwest of Santa Cruz, tel. 408/761–3487), you can view the ruins of a Chinese labor camp and hike (2 miles one way) to the epicenter of the 1989 Loma Prieta earthquake; the trailhead is clearly marked from the main parking lot. Nisene Marks is also a favored locale of mountain bikers; the friendly folks at park headquarters will point you toward trails where bikes are allowed. Bike rentals are available back in town (*see* Getting Around, *above*).

SURFING Even though Southern California is reputed to be the state's surfing capital, many locals argue that Santa Cruz has the state's hottest surf spots, the most famous being **Steamer's Lane,** between the boardwalk and the lighthouse. However, beginners would do well to avoid the big breaks, which can be dangerous if you don't know what you're doing. For an easier ride head to Cowell's Beach, between the boardwalk and Steamers' Lane. If you left your board at home, the **Beach 'n' Bikini Surf Shop** (cnr Beach and Front Sts., near boardwalk, tel. 408/427–2355) rents surfboards ($15), body boards ($10), and wet suits ($10) by the day.

Near Santa Cruz

BIG BASIN REDWOODS STATE PARK

One of the flagships of the California State Park system, Big Basin, 23 miles northeast of Santa Cruz off Highway 9, overwhelms you with thousands of acres of gigantic old-growth redwoods, lofty Douglas firs, rushing streams, and flowing waterfalls. All sorts of wildlife call Big Basin home, including black-tailed deer and an occasional fox, bobcat, coyote, or mountain lion. Worthy of at least a day's visit ($5 per car), and more if you groove on the outdoors, this is one park where you must get away from the main roads to fully appreciate nature's splendor. So put on your hiking boots, and go commune with some trees who've been here about 1,500 years longer than you have.

Just past the main entrance you'll come to the **park headquarters** (tel. 408/338–6132), where helpful rangers can give you advice on which trails will best suit your desires and energy level, or simply sell you a map (75¢) and let you go to town. For a relatively easy hike through redwoods, firs, and tan oaks, and past Sempervirens Falls, pick up the **Sequoia Trail** from the south end of the parking lot and follow it to the Skyline-to-Sea Trail, which will take you back to the park headquarters. The 4½-mile walk takes two to three hours.

If you've got a bit more ambition, take the Skyline-to-Sea Trail from the parking lot west to **Berry Creek Falls Trail,** and work your way back to the visitor's center on the **Sunset Trail.** The 10½-mile loop, which affords views of the incredible 75-foot Berry Creek Falls and the Pacific Ocean, takes five to six hours. About a half-mile up the trail, you'll find Silver Falls and Golden Falls, better for private waterfall play than popular Berry Creek Falls. Here you can wade in the pools, run through the falls themselves, or skip across the creek on the redwood logs. Or exert yourself on the strenuous **Howard King Trail,** which takes you up 3 miles of steep, rugged terrain to the Mt. Macabe overlook; relax at the top while you gaze out over the tree-covered mountains, the basin for which the park is named, and the ocean beyond.

The truly fit should tackle the 12½-mile **Skyline-to-Sea Trail**—arguably the most scenic hike in the park—which travels over hill and dale all the way to the coast. This is the park's most popular trek, and those who've done it rave about how satisfying it is to reach the water after gazing at it from such a distance earlier in the trail. Leave a second car at the trail's endpoint at Waddell Beach, and either pay scrupulous attention to a map or accept the possibility of getting semi-lost, since several trailheads converge a few miles into the hike. Mountain biking is only allowed on fire roads in the park and unfortunately there aren't any good loops: Your best bet is to follow North Escape Road a short distance from park headquarters to **Gazos Creek Road,** a 14-mile fire trail that stretches to the coast.

➢ **COMING AND GOING** • To reach Big Basin from Santa Cruz, follow Highway 9 north for 25 miles, then follow the signs for another 9 miles from Boulder Creek. If you're coming from the north on I–280, take Highway 85 south from Cupertino to Highway 9 south, then pick up Highway 236 into the park.

➢ **WHERE TO SLEEP** • All Big Basin's 144 drive-in camping sites have picnic tables, fire pits, food lockers, and access to toilets and showers. Most are spread out under the redwoods with lots of room to breathe, and many are situated on the banks of gentle streams. The sites, which fetch $14 in summer, go quickly on weekends; make reservations through MISTIX (tel. 800/444–PARK) up to eight weeks in advance.

Even more lovely are the primitive sites ($7) at Big Basin's trail camps. Though fires in the trail camps are strictly forbidden due to high fire danger, you'll be compensated by the seclusion and privacy of these sites, most less than 2 miles from a trailhead. Call the park headquarters to reserve a few weeks ahead of time, since these sites are also popular. If you can't tear yourself away from the beauty of the park but didn't bring a tent, rent a tent cabin—essentially a shack with a canvas cover and two cots and a wood stove inside—for about $38 for up to eight people. Call 408/338–4745 for more info.

Index

D

E

F

TELL US WHAT YOU THINK

We're always trying to improve our books and would really appreciate any feedback on how to make them more useful. Thanks for taking a few minutes to fill out this survey. We'd also like to know about your latest find, a new scam, a budget deal, whatever . . . Please print your name and address clearly and send the completed survey to: The Berkeley Guides, 515 Eshelman Hall, U.C. Berkeley, CA 94720.

1. Your name ____

2. Your address ____

________________________________ Zip __________

3. You are: Female Male

4. Your age: under 17 17–22 23–30 31–40 41–55 over 55

5. If you're a student: Name of school __________ City & state __________

6. If you're employed: Occupation ____________________________

7. Your yearly income: under $20,000 $21,000–$30,000 $31,000–$45,000 $46,000–$60,000 $61,000–$100,000 over $100,000

8. Which of the following do you own? (Circle all that apply.)

Computer CD-ROM Drive Modem

9. What speed (bps) is your modem?

2400 4800 9600 14.4 19.2 28.8

10. Which on-line service(s) do you subscribe to apart from commercial services like AOL?

____

11. Do you have access to the World Wide Web? If so, is it through a university or a private service provider? ______________________________

12. If you have a CD-ROM drive or plan to have one, would you purchase a Berkeley Guide CD-ROM? ______________________________

13. Which Berkeley Guide(s) did you buy? ________________________

14. Where did you buy the book and when? City __________ Month/Year ________

15. Why did you choose The Berkeley Guides? (Circle all that apply.)

Budget focus
Outdoor emphasis
Off-the-beaten-track emphasis
Resources for gays and lesbians
Resources for people with disabilities
Resources for women
Design
Attitude
Writing style
Organization
More maps
Accuracy
Price

Other ____

16. How did you hear about The Berkeley Guides? (Circle all that apply.)

Recommended by friend/acquaintance   Bookstore display   TV

Article in magazine/newspaper (which one?) ______________________

Ad in magazine/newspaper (which one?) ______________________

Radio program (which one?) ______________________

Other ______________________

17. Which other guides, if any, have you used before? (Circle all that apply.)

Fodor's	Let's Go	Rough Guides
Frommer's	Birnbaum	Lonely Planet

Other ______________________

18. When did you travel with this book?   Month/Year ______________________

19. Where did you travel? ______________________

20. What was the purpose of your trip?

Vacation	Business	Volunteer
Study abroad	Work	

21. About how much did you spend per day during your trip?

$0–$20	$31–$45	$61–$75	over $100
$21–$30	$46–$60	$76–$100	

22. After you arrived, how did you get around? (Circle all that apply.)

Rental car	Personal car	Plane	Bus
Train	Hiking	Bike	Hitching

23. Which features/sections did you use most? (Circle all that apply.)

Book Basics	City/region Basics	Coming and Going
Hitching	Getting Around	Where to Sleep
Camping	Roughing It	Food
Worth Seeing	Cheap Thrills	Festivals
Shopping	After Dark	Outdoor Activities

24. The information was (circle one):   V = very accurate   U = usually accurate
S = sometimes accurate   R = rarely accurate

Introductions	V U S R	Worth Seeing	V U S R
Basics	V U S R	After Dark	V U S R
Coming and Going	V U S R	Outdoor Activities	V U S R
Where to Sleep	V U S R	Maps	V U S R
Food	V U S R		

25. I would _______ would not _______ buy another Berkeley Guide.

26. Which of the following destinations are you planning to visit in the next five years?

The Americas

Chicago
Washington, D.C.
New Orleans
Los Angeles
Boston
Austin
The Midwest
The South
The Southwest
New England
The Pacific Northwest
Hawaii
Canada
South America

Europe

Spain
Portugal
Greece
Russia
Scandinavia
Berlin
Prague
Rome

Australia/Asia

Australia
New Zealand
Vietnam
Philippines
Indonesia
Thailand
Singapore
Malaysia
Cambodia
India/Nepal

Middle East/Africa

Turkey
Israel
Egypt
Africa